THE ONLY GAME IN TOWN

"Sometimes we sell them, lady, but only to other teams."

THE ONLY GAME IN TOWN

SPORTSWRITING FROM THE NEW YORKER

EDITED BY
DAVID REMNICK

THE MODERN LIBRARY
NEW YORK

Published in the United States by Modern Library,
an imprint of The Random House Publishing Group,
a division of Random House, Inc., New York.

MODERN LIBRARY and the TORCHBEARER Design are registered trademarks
of Random House, Inc.

All of the pieces in this collection were originally
published in *The New Yorker*. The publication date of
each piece is given at the end of the piece.

Originally published in hardcover in the United States by Random House,
an imprint of The Random House Publishing Group,
a division of Random House, Inc., in 2010.

Library of Congress Cataloging-in-Publication Data
The only game in town: sportswriting from the New Yorker/edited
by David Remnick.
p.   cm.
ISBN 978-0-8129-7998-5
1. Sports—United States. 2. Sports stories, American. 3. Sports literature—United
States. I. Remnick, David. II. New Yorker (New York, N.Y.: 1925)
GV704.A57 2010
796'.0973—dc22   2009040009

www.modernlibrary.com

Printed in the United States of America

2 4 6 8 9 7 5 3 1

To Roger Angell

CONTENTS

INTRODUCTION

DAVID REMNICK

Twenty-eight years ago, at *The Washington Post*, adorned with the boiler-room rank of summer intern, I was dispatched to a dim Italian restaurant in the suburbs to interview a writer who was coming through town on a promotional book tour. The book was a collection of baseball pieces called *Late Innings*. The writer was Roger Angell. Like any reader of *The New Yorker*, I felt that I knew him through his work, a jauntily projected self so thoroughly at his ease, so companionable, that you thought of him as just the sort of brilliant friend with whom you'd want to share an afternoon at the stadium. His is a narrative voice thrilled by the simple, daily pleasures of being in the presence of an endlessly fascinating game and its heroic and fallible practitioners. He is erudite yet unpretentious, literate but not arty, with a tone of such buoyancy that to read one of his opening paragraphs is to step into a cool pond on a hot summer's day.

While I was delighted, if nervous, to meet Angell at this dark den of macaroni, I could not quite find him at first, so gloomy was the room. After some frantic searching among the plaster pillars and the Chianti bottles, I found him at last, sitting alone, a dapper mustachioed gent in his early sixties, drumming his fingers on the table and lightly tapping a cordovan penny loafer.

Roger is somewhat forbidding on first meeting. And for good reason. Not only is he a writer of sterling reputation—certainly the best to devote himself so thoroughly to sport—he also has habits that do not immediately suggest a warm invitation. Later, at the magazine, I've noticed, as everyone has, that as he walks the halls, he is like Blazes Boylan, Molly's vital lover in *Ulysses,* who "rattled merry money in his trousers' pocket."

In fact, Angell is hardly cocky. He is friendly, voluble, sensitive, and perhaps never happier than when he is engaged in baseball talk. That day we first met in D.C., he had just got back from a trip to Boston and an evening at Fenway Park. You'd have thought he had just seen the place for the first time. Using sugar packets, toothpicks, and a salt shaker, he undertook a tabletop description of the odd contours of the stadium, the myriad angles of the outfield wall—twenty-two or so, he reckoned: "There's this one spot with such a sharp angle that if the ball gets caught between it it keeps hitting back and forth—*whack, whack, whack.* Fantastic!"

Angell began covering baseball for the magazine in 1962, the same year the Mets took their first wobbly steps. Angell, who came to his rookie season with many years of experience as a fan, got off to a more sure-footed start. No Marvelous Marv Throneberry he. Angell was, and remains, a kind of Burkean idealist—wary of heedless change yet open to surprise and displays of individual genius. As a stylist, he is unpoetic; that is, he does not dip his brush in the lit'ry goo that mars the work of some press-box masters. His sentences have a tensile zing. He is never maudlin—not even about the Brooklyn Dodgers.

The New Yorker is not known foremost for its sports writing. Despite his eminence, Roger's seat in the press box at Yankee Stadium is not reliably better than the sidebar man's from the *Asbury Park Press.* I was once eating lunch in a Las Vegas casino with a few hours to kill before going to cover the Mike Tyson–Evander Holyfield fight. (Tyson saved room at lunch to snack later that night on Holyfield's right ear.) A couple from Houston noticed the dinner-plate-size press credential around my neck and asked what paper I was from. "Not a paper," I said. "I'm from *The New Yorker.*" They were aghast. "We've been reading *The New Yorker* for years," the woman said, "but we never thought the magazine would stoop so low as to cover something so vulgar!" I remind you that she delivered this lecture on vulgarity in a casino. In Las Vegas.

Angell's closest press-box peer at the magazine was A. J. Liebling, whose consuming obsession (when he wasn't seated in front of a mountainous *côte de boeuf*) was the prize ring. Liebling's comic invention was to marry the high tone of his hero, the Regency-era chronicler Pierce Egan, with the homely characters of the ring itself.

It is often said that John Updike's "Hub Fans Bid Kid Adieu"—an account of Ted Williams's last day on the field—is the best baseball piece ever written (or, at least, once you take Angell out of play). It is also the only one he ever wrote for the magazine. Updike accomplished his ode to Williams in a flash—an aberration for the magazine in those days—and, ever since, the piece has held a place in the deadline hall of fame. Similarly, in the unbeatable category, John McPhee, when he was just starting out as a writer, portrayed Bill Bradley at his peak—a serious-minded Princeton undergraduate willing and able to explain in granular detail how an athlete goes about turning constant practice into instinct.

The oldest piece of writing in the collection is Ring Lardner's comic gem from 1930, "Br'er Rabbit Ball." Another piece from the early days of the magazine is an overlooked masterpiece, Alva Johnston's profile of Wilson Mizner, a turn-of-the century playwright and con man, who built a boxing gym in his wife's mansion and then fled the mansion—and his wife, "the forty-million-dollar widow"—for Goldfield, Nevada, where he hung out at the training camps of Joe Gans and Battling Nelson. Some of the more recent entries include Profiles of contemporary icons: Rebecca Mead on Shaquille O'Neal; Henry Louis Gates, Jr., on Michael Jordan; Michael Specter on Lance Armstrong; and David Owen on Tiger Woods, back in the innocent days when golf was the only thing he was famous for. There are also explorations of some of the stranger pursuits in sport: Lillian Ross on Sidney Franklin, easily the greatest matador ever to hail from the Brooklyn area; Nick Paumgarten on his aunt, who gave her life for the love of an early version of extreme skiing; Susan Orlean on Susan Butcher, queen of the Alaskan dog mushers; and Charles Sprawson on Lynne Cox, who has swum from Russia to America and in the slushy seas of the Antarctic.

As usual, I have depended on my colleagues at the magazine for invaluable advice on their own favorites—and on my esteemed colleague Leo Carey for much more than that. Leo not only made numerous and wonderful suggestions; he also edited to consumable, if not bite-size, length the few pieces here that could not be published in full. Our librarians, Jon Michaud and Erin Overbey, dug out the pieces—and many more—from the archives. Pam McCarthy dealt with our friends at Random House. Katherine Stirling and Brenda Phipps did for me what they always do—and with grace. My gratitude to all.

And Roger Angell—well, all that he has done in six decades at *The New Yorker* is set the standard as writer, editor, and colleague. From us to you, Roger: the wave, the cheer, the big standing O.

PART ONE

FROM THE BLEACHERS

"Oh, for goodness' sake, forget it, Beasley. Play another one."

THE WEB OF THE GAME

ROGER ANGELL

An afternoon in mid-May, and we are waiting for the game to begin. We are in shadow, and the sunlit field before us is a thick, springy green—an old diamond, beautifully kept up. The grass continues beyond the low chain-link fence that encloses the outfield, extending itself on the right-field side into a rougher, featureless sward that terminates in a low line of distant trees, still showing a pale, early-summer green. We are almost in the country. Our seats are in the seventh row of the grandstand, on the home side of the diamond, about halfway between third base and home plate. The seats themselves are more comforting to spirit than to body, being a surviving variant example of the pure late-Doric Polo Grounds mode: the backs made of a continuous running row of wood slats, divided off by pairs of narrow cast-iron arms, within which are slatted let-down seats, grown arthritic with rust and countless layers of gray paint. The rows are stacked so closely upon each other (one discovers) that a happening on the field of sufficient interest to warrant a rise or half-rise to one's feet is often made more memorable by a sharp crack to the kneecaps delivered by the backs of the seats just forward; in time, one finds that a dandruff of gray paint flakes from the same source has fallen on one's lap and scorecard. None of this matters, for this view and these stands and this park—it is Yale Field, in New Haven—are renowned for their felicity. The grandstand is a low, penumbrous steel-post shed that holds the infield in a pleasant horseshoe-curved embrace. The back wall of the grandstand, behind the uppermost row of seats, is broken by an arcade of open arches, admitting a soft backlight that silhouettes the upper audience and also discloses an overhead bonework of struts and beams supporting the roof—the pigeonland of all the ballparks of our youth. The game we are waiting for—Yale vs. St. John's University—is a considerable event, for it is part of the National Collegiate Athletic Association's northeast regional tournament, the winner of which will qualify for a berth at the national collegiate championships in Omaha in June, the World Series of college baseball. Another pair of teams, Maine and Central Michigan—the Black Bears and the Chippewas— have just finished their game here, the first of a doubleheader. Maine won it, 10–2, but the ultimate winner will not be picked here for three more days, when the four teams will have completed a difficult double-elimination tournament. Good, hard competition, but the stands at Yale Field are half empty today. Call them half full, because everyone on hand—some twenty-five hundred fans—must know something about the quality of the teams here, or at least enough to qualify either as a partisan or as an expert, which would explain the hum of talk and expectation that runs through the grandstand even while the Yale team, in pinstriped home whites, is still taking infield practice.

I am seated in a little sector of senior New Haven men—Townies rather than Old Elis. One of them a couple of rows in front of me says, "They used to fill this place in the old days, before there was all the baseball on TV."

His neighbor, a small man in a tweed cap, says, "The biggest crowd I ever saw in here—the biggest ever, I bet—was for a high school game. Shelton and Naugatuck, about twenty years ago."

An old gent with a cane, seated just to my left, says, "They filled it up that day the Yankees came here, with Ruth and Gehrig and the rest of them. An exhibition game."

A fan just beyond the old gentleman—a good-looking man in his sixties, with an open, friendly face, a large smile, and a thick stand of gray hair—leans toward my neighbor and says, "When *was* that game, Joe? 1930? 1932?"

"Oh, I can't remember," the old man says. "Somewhere in there. My youngest son was mascot for the Yankees that day, so I could figure it out, I suppose." He is not much interested. His eyes are on the field.

"Say, look at these fellows throw!" he says. "Did you see that outfielder peg in the ball?"

"That was the day Babe Ruth said this was about the best-looking ballpark he'd ever ever seen," the man beyond says. "You remember that."

"I can remember long before this park was built," the old man says. "It was already the Yale ballfield when I got here, but they put in these stands later— Who is this shortstop? He's a hefty-looking bird."

"How many Yale games do you think you've seen, Joe?" the smiling man asks.

"Oh, I couldn't begin to count them. But I haven't seen a Yale team play in— I don't know how long. Not for years. These fellows today, they play in the Cape Cod League in the summers. They let the freshmen play here now, too. They recruit them more, I suppose. They're athletes—you can see that."

The Yale team finishes its warmup ritual, and St. John's—light gray uniforms with scarlet cap bills and scarlet socks—replaces it on the field.

"St. John's has always had a good club," the old man tells me. "Even back when my sons were playing ball, it was a good ball team. But not as good as this one. Oh, my! Did you see this catcher throw down to second? Did you see that! I bet you in all the years I was here I didn't have twenty fellows who could throw."

"Your sons played here?" I ask him. "For Yale?"

"My son Joe was captain in '41," he says. "He was a pitcher. He pitched against my son Steve here one day. Steve was pitching for Colgate, and my other son, Bob—my youngest—was on the same Colgate team. A good little left-handed first baseman."

I am about to ask how that game turned out, but the old man has taken out a small gold pocket watch, with a hunting case, which he snaps open. Three-fourteen. "Can't they get this *started*?" he says impatiently.

I say something admiring about the watch, and he hands it to me carefully. "I've had that watch for sixty-eight years," he says. "I always carried it in my vest pocket, back when we wore vests."

The little watch has a considerable heft to it: a weight of authority. I turn it over and find an inscription on the back. It is in script and a bit worn, but I can still make it out:

PRESENTED TO JOE WOOD
BY HIS FRIEND A. E. SMITH
IN APPRECIATION OF HIS SPLENDID
PITCHING WHICH BROUGHT THE
WORLD'S CHAMPIONSHIP
TO BOSTON IN 1912.

"Who was A. E. Smith, Mr. Wood?" I ask.

"He was a manufacturer."

I know the rest. Joe Wood, the old gentleman on my left, was the baseball coach at Yale for twenty years—from 1923 to 1942. Before that, he was a sometime outfielder for the Cleveland Indians, who batted .366 in 1921. Before *that,* he was a celebrated right-handed pitcher for the Boston Red Sox—Smokey Joe Wood, who won thirty-four games for the Bosox in 1912, when he finished up with a record of 34-5, pitching ten shutouts and sixteen consecutive victories along the way. In the World Series that fall—one of the two or three finest ever played—he won three of the four games he pitched, including the famous finale: the game of Hooper's catch and Snodgrass's muff and Tris Speaker's killing tenth-inning single. Next to Walter Johnson, Smokey Joe Wood was the most famous fastballer of his era. Still is, no doubt, in the minds of the few surviving fans who saw him at his best. He is ninety-one years old.

None of this, I should explain—neither my presence at the game nor my companions in the stands—was an accident. I had been a fervent admirer of Smokey Joe Wood ever since I read his account of his baseball beginnings and his subsequent career in Lawrence Ritter's *The Glory of Their Times,* a cherished, classic volume of oral history of the early days of the pastime. Mr. Wood was in his seventies when that book was published, in 1966, and I was startled and pleased a few weeks ago when I ran across an article by Joan Whaley, in *Baseball Digest,* which informed me that he was still hale and still talking baseball in stimulating fashion. He was living with a married daughter in New Haven, and my first impulse was to jump in my car and drive up to press a call. But something held me back; it did not seem quite right to present myself uninvited at his door, even as a pilgrim. Then Ron Darling and Frank Viola gave me my chance. Darling, who was a junior at Yale this past year, is the best pitcher ever to take the mound for the Blue.

He is better than Johnny Broaca, who went on to pitch for the Yankees and the Indians for five seasons in the mid-1930s; he is better than Frank Quinn, who compiled a 1.57 career earned-run average at Yale in 1946, '47, and '48. (He is also a better all-around ballplayer than George Bush, who played first base and captained the Elis in 1948, and then somehow drifted off into politics instead of baseball.) Darling, a right-handed fastball thrower, won eleven games and lost two as a sophomore, with an earned-run average of 1.31, and this year he was 9-3 and 2.42, with eighty-nine strikeouts in his ninety-three innings of work—the finest college pitcher in the Northeast, according to major-league scouts, with the possible exception of Frank Viola, a junior left-handed curveball ace at St. John's, who was undefeated this year, 9-0, and had a neat earned-run average of 1.00. St. John's, a Catholic university in Queens, is almost a baseball powerhouse—not quite in the same class, perhaps, as such perennial national champions or challengers as Arizona, Arizona State, UCLA, and Southern California, whose teams play Sun Belt schedules of close to sixty games, but good enough to have gone as the Northeast's representative to the national tournament in Omaha in 1980, where Viola defeated the eventual winner, Arizona, in the first round. St. John's, by the way, does not recruit high school stars from faraway states, as do most of these rival college powers; all but one player on this year's thirty-three-man Redmen squad grew up and went to school in New York City or in nearby suburbs. This 1981 St. John's team ran off an awesome 31-2 record, capturing the Eastern College Metro (Greater New York, that is) elimination, while Yale, winning its last nine games in a row, concluded its regular season with a record of 24-12-1, which was good enough to win its first Eastern Intercollegiate League championship since 1956. (That tie in Yale's record was a game against the University of Central Florida, played during the Elis' spring-training tour in March, and was called because of darkness after seven innings, with the score tied at 21–21. Darling did not pitch that day.) The two teams, along with Central Michigan (Mid-America Conference) and Maine (New England Conference), qualified for the tournament at New Haven, and the luck of the draw pitted Yale (and Darling) against St. John's (and Viola) in the second game of the opening doubleheader. Perfect. Darling, by the way, had indicated that he might be willing to turn professional this summer if he were to be picked in an early round of the annual amateur draft conducted by the major leagues in mid-June, and Viola had been talked about as a potential big-leaguer ever since his freshman year, so their matchup suddenly became an obligatory reunion for every front-rank baseball scout east of the Ohio River. (About fifty of them turned up, with their speed-guns and clipboards, and their glowing reports of the game, I learned later, altered the draft priorities of several clubs.)

Perfect, but who would get in touch with Mr. Wood and persuade him to come out to Yale Field with me for the game? Why, Dick Lee would—Dick Lee, *of course.* Richard C. Lee (he was the smiling man sitting just beyond Smokey Joe in our row) is a former Democratic mayor of New Haven, an extremely popular (eight consecutive terms, sixteen years in office), innovative officeholder who, among other things, presided over the widely admired urban renewal of his city during the 1960s and, before that, thought up and pushed through the first Operation Head Start program (for minority-group preschoolers) in the country. Dick Lee knows everybody in New Haven, including Smokey Joe Wood and several friends of mine there, one of whom provided me with his telephone number. I called Lee at his office (he is assistant to the chairman of the Union Trust Company, in New Haven) and proposed our party. "Wonderful!" he cried at once. "You have come to the right man. I'll bring Joe. Count on me!" Even over the telephone, I could see him smiling.

Dick Lee did not play baseball for Yale, but the nature of his partisanship became clear in the very early moments of the Yale–St. John's game. "Yay!" he shouted in a stentorian baritone as Ron Darling set down three St. John's batters in order in the first. "Yay, Ron *baby*!" he boomed out as Darling dismissed three more batters in the second, fanning the last two. "Now *c'mon*, Yale! Let's get something started, gang! Yay!" Lee had told me that he pitched for some lesser-known New Haven teams—the Dixwell Community House sandlot team and the Jewish Home for Children nine (the Utopians), among others—while he was growing up in the ivyless New Hallville neighborhood. Some years later, having passed up college altogether, he went to work for Yale as its public-relations officer. By the time he became mayor, in 1953, the university was his own—another precinct to be worried about and looked after. A born politician, he appears to draw on some inner deepwater reservoir of concern that enables him to preside effortlessly and affectionately over each encounter of his day; he was the host at our game, and at intervals he primed Joe Wood with questions about his baseball past, which he seemed to know almost by heart.

"Yes, that's right, I did play for the Bloomer Girls a few games," Mr. Wood said in response to one such cue. "I was about sixteen, and I was pitching for our town team in Ness City, Kansas. The Bloomer Girls were a barnstorming team, but they used to pick up a few young local fellows on the sly to play along with them if they needed to fill out their lineup. I was one of those. I never wore a wig, though—I wouldn't have done that. I guess I looked young enough to pass for a girl anyway. Bill Stern, the old radio broadcaster, must have used that story about forty times, but he always got it wrong about the wig."

There was a yell around us, and an instantly ensuing groan, as Yale's big freshman catcher, Tony Paterno, leading off the bottom of the second, lined sharply to the St. John's shortstop, who made a fine play on the ball. Joe Wood peered intently out at the field through his thickish horn-rimmed spectacles. He shook his head a little. "You know, I can't hardly follow the damned ball now," he said. "It's better for me if I'm someplace where I can get up high behind the plate. I was up to Fenway Park for two games last year, and they let me sit in the press box there at that beautiful park. I could see it all from there. The groundskeeper has got that field just like a living room."

I asked him if he still rooted for the Red Sox.

"Oh, yes," he said. "All my life. A couple of years ago, when they had that big lead in the middle of the summer, they asked me if I'd come up and throw out the first ball at one of their World Series games or play-off games. But then they dropped out of it, of course. Now it looks like it'll never happen."

He spoke in a quiet, almost measured tone, but there was no tinge of disappointment or self-pity in it. It was the voice of age. He was wearing a blue Windbreaker over a buttoned-up plaid shirt, made formal with a small dark red bow tie. There was a brown straw hat on his bald head. The years had imparted a delicate thinness to the skin on his cheeks and neck, but his face had a determined look to it, with a strong chin and a broad, unsmiling mouth. Watching him, I recalled one of the pictures in *The Glory of Their Times*—a team photograph taken in 1906, in which he is sitting cross-legged down in front of a row of men in baggy baseball pants and lace-up, collared baseball shirts with NESS CITY across the front in block letters. The men are standing in attitudes of cheerful assurance, with their arms folded, and their mushy little baseball gloves are hanging from their belts. Joe Wood, the smallest player in the picture, is wearing a dark warmup shirt, with the sleeves rolled halfway up his forearms, and his striped baseball cap is pushed back a little, revealing a part in the middle of his hair. There is an intent, unsmiling look on his boyish face—the same grave demeanor you can spot in a subsequent photograph, taken in 1912, in which he is standing beside his Red Sox manager, Jake Stahl, and wearing a heavy woollen three-button suit, a stiff collar, a narrow necktie with a stickpin, and a stylish black porkpie hat pulled low over his handsome, famous face: Smokey Joe Wood at twenty-two. (The moniker, by the way, was given him by Paul Shannon, a sportswriter for *The Boston Post;* before that, he was sometimes called Ozone Wood—"ozone" for the air cleaved by the hapless batters who faced him.) The young man in the photographs and the old man beside me at the ballpark had the same broad, sloping shoulders, but there was nothing burly or physically imposing about him then or now.

"What kind of a pitcher were you, Mr. Wood?" I asked him.

"I had a curve and a fastball," he said. "That's all. I didn't even have brains enough to slow up on the batters. The fastball had a hop on it. You had to be *fast* to have that happen to the ball."

I said that I vividly recalled Sandy Koufax's fastball, which sometimes seemed to jump so violently as it crossed the plate that his catcher had to shoot up his mitt to intercept it.

"Mine didn't go up that far. Just enough for them to miss it." He half turned to me as he said this, and gave me a little glance and an infinitesimal smile. A twinkle. "I don't know where my speed came from," he went on. "I wasn't any bigger or stronger-looking then than I am now. I always could throw hard, and once I saw I was able to get batters out, I figured I was crazy enough to play ball for a living. My father was a criminal lawyer in Kansas, and before that out in Ouray, Colorado, where I first played ball, and my brother went to law school and got a degree, but I didn't even graduate from high school. I ate and slept baseball all my life."

The flow of recollection from Joe Wood was perhaps not as smooth and rivery as I have suggested here. For one thing, he spoke slowly and with care—not unlike the way he walked to the grandstand at Yale Field from the parking lot beyond left field, making his way along the grass firmly enough but looking where he was going, too, and helping himself a bit with his cane. Nothing infirm about him, but nothing hurrying or sprightly, either. For another, the game was well in progress by now, and its principals and sudden events kept interrupting our colloquy. Ron Darling, a poised, impressive figure on the mound, alternated his popping fastballs with just enough down-breaking sliders and an occasional curveball to keep the St. John's batters unhappy. Everything was thrown with heat—his strikeout pitch is a Seaver-high fastball—but without any signs of strain or anxiety. He threw over the top, smoothly driving his front (left) shoulder at the batter in picture-book style, and by the third or fourth inning he had imposed his will and his pace on the game. He was rolling. He is a dark-haired, olive-skinned young man (he lives in Millbury, Massachusetts, near Worcester, but he was born in Hawaii; his mother is Chinese Hawaiian by birth) with long, powerful legs, but his pitcherlike proportions tend to conceal, rather than emphasize, his six feet two inches and his 195 pounds. He also swings the bat well enough (.331 this year) to play right field for Yale when he isn't pitching; in our game he was the designated hitter as well as the pitcher for the Elis.

"That's a nice build for a pitcher, isn't it?" Joe Wood murmured during the St. John's fifth. Almost as he spoke, Darling executed a twisting dive to his right to snaffle a hard-hit grounder up the middle by Brian Miller, the St. John's shortstop, and threw him out at first. ("Hey-*hey!*" Dick Lee cried. "Yay, Ronnie!") "*And* he's an athlete out there," Wood added. "The scouts like that, you know. Oh, this fellow's a lot better than Broaca ever was."

Frank Viola, for his part, was as imperturbable as Darling on the mound, if not quite as awesome. A lanky, sharp-shouldered lefty, he threw an assortment of speeds and spins, mostly sinkers and down-darting sliders, that had the Yale batters swinging from their shoe tops and, for the most part, hammering the ball into the dirt. He had the stuff and poise of a veteran relief pitcher, and the St. John's infield—especially Brian Miller and a stubby, ebullient second baseman named Steve Scafa—performed behind him with the swift, almost haughty confidence that imparts an elegance and calm and sense of ease to baseball at its best. It was a scoreless game after five, and a beauty.

"What was the score of that game you beat Walter Johnson in, in your big year?" Dick Lee asked our guest between innings.

We all knew the answer, I think. In September 1912, Walter Johnson came to Fenway Park (it was brand-new that year) with the Senators and pitched against young Joe Wood, who then had a string of thirteen consecutive victories to his credit. That summer, Johnson had established a league record of sixteen straight wins, so the matchup was not merely an overflow, sellout affair but perhaps the most anticipated, most discussed non-championship game in the American League up to that time.

"We won it, 1–0," Joe Wood said quietly, "but it wasn't his fault I beat him that day. If he'd had the team behind him that I did, he'd have set every kind of record in baseball. You have to remember that Walter Johnson played for a second-division team almost all through his career. All those years, and he had to work from the bottom every time he pitched."

"Were you faster than he was?" I asked.

"Oh, I don't think there was ever anybody faster than Walter," he murmured.

"But Johnson said just the opposite!" Dick Lee cried. "He said no one was faster than *you*."

"He was just that kind of fellow, to say something like that," Wood said. "That was just like the man. Walter Johnson was a great big sort of a pitcher, with hands that came clear down to his knees. Why, the way he threw the ball, the only reason anybody ever got even a foul off him was because everybody in the league knew he'd never come inside to a batter. Walter Johnson was a prince of men—a gentleman first, last, and always."

It came to me that this was the first time I had ever heard anybody use the phrase "a prince of men" in a nonsatiric fashion. In any case, the Johnson-Wood argument did not really need settling, then or now. Smokey Joe went on to tie Johnson with sixteen straight victories that season—an American League record, subsequently tied by Lefty Grove and Schoolboy Rowe. (Over in the National League that year, Rube Marquard won *nineteen* straight for the Giants—a single-season mark first set by Tim Keefe of the Giants in 1888 and untouched as yet by anyone else.) Johnson and Wood pretty well divided up the AL mound honors that summer, when Johnson won thirty-two games and lost twelve, posting the best earned-run average (1.39) and the most strike-outs (303), while Wood won the most games and established the best winning percentage with his 34-5 mark (not including his three World Series wins, of course).

These last figures are firmly emplaced in the baseball crannies of my mind, and in the minds of most students of the game, because, it turned out, they represent the autumn of Joe Wood's pitching career as well as its first full flowering. Early in the spring of 1913, he was injured in a fielding play, and he was never near to being the same pitcher again. One of the game's sad speculations over the years has been what Joe Wood's status in the pantheon of great pitchers would be if he had remained sound. I did not need any reminder of his accident, but I had been given one just the same when Dick Lee introduced me to him, shortly before the game. We had stopped to pick up Mr. Wood at his small, red-shuttered white house on Marvel Road, and when he came down the concrete path to join us I got out of Lee's Cadillac to shake the hand that once shook the baseball world.

"Mr. Wood," I said, "this is a great honor."

"Ow—*ow!*" he cried, cringing before me and attempting to extricate his paw.

"Oh, oh . . . I'm *terribly* sorry," I said, appalled. "Is it—is this because of your fall off the roof?" Three years ago, at the age of eighty-eight, he had fallen off a ladder while investigating a leak, and had cracked several ribs.

"Hell, no!" he said indignantly. "This is the arm I threw out in 1913!"

I felt awful. I had touched history—and almost brought it to its knees.

Now, at the game, he told me how it all happened. "I can't remember now if it was on the road or at Fenway Park," he said. "Anyway, it was against Detroit. There was a swinging bunt down the line, and I went to field it and slipped on the wet grass and went down and landed on my hand. I broke it right here." He pointed to a spot just below his wrist, on the back of his freckled, slightly gnarled right hand. "It's what they call a subperiosteal fracture. They put it in a cast, and I had to sit out awhile. Well, this was in 1913, right after we'd won the championship, and every team was out to get us, of course. So as soon as the cast came off, the manager would come up to me every now and then and want to know how soon I was going to get back to pitching. Well, maybe I got back to it too soon and maybe I didn't, but the arm never felt right again. The shoulder went bad. I still went on pitching, but the fastball had lost that hop. I never threw a day after that when I wasn't in pain. Most of the time, I'd pitch and then it would hurt so bad that I wasn't able to raise my hand again for days afterward. So I was about a half-time pitcher after that. You have to understand that in those days if you didn't work you didn't get paid. Now they lay out as long as they need to and get a shot of that cortisone. But we had to play, ready or not. I was a married man, just starting a family, and in order to get my check I had to be in there. So I pitched."

He pitched less, but not much less well. In 1915, he was 15-5 for the Red Sox, with an earned-run average of 1.49, which was the best in the league. But the pain was so persistent that he sat out the entire 1916 season, on his farm, near Shohola, Pennsylvania, hoping that the rest would restore his arm. It did not. He pitched in eight more games after that—all of them for the Cleveland Indians, to whom he was sold in 1917—but he never won again.

"Did you become a different kind of pitcher after you hurt your arm?" I asked. "More off-speed stuff, I mean?"

"No, I still pitched the fastball."

"But all that pain—"

"I tried not to think about that." He gave me the same small smile and bright glance. "I just loved to be out there," he said. "It was as simple as that."

Our afternoon slid by in a distraction of baseball and memory, and I almost felt myself at some dreamlike doubleheader involving the then and the now—the semi-anonymous strong young men waging their close, marvelous game on the sunlit green field before us while bygone players and heroes of baseball history—long gone now, most of them—replayed their vivid, famous innings for me in the words and recollections of my companion. Yale kept putting men aboard against Viola and failing to move them along; Rich Diana, the husky center fielder (he is also an All–Ivy League halfback), whacked a long double to left but then died on second—the sixth stranded Eli base runner in five innings. Darling appeared to be struggling a little, walking two successive batters in the sixth, but he saved himself with a whirling pickoff to second base—a timed play brilliantly completed by his shortstop, Bob Brooke—and then struck out St. John's big first baseman, Karl Komyathy, for the last out. St. John's had yet to manage a hit against him.

In the home half of the sixth, Yale put its lead-off batter aboard with a single but could not bunt him along. Joe Wood was distressed. "I could teach these fellows to bunt in one minute," he said. "Nobody can't hardly bunt anymore. You've got to get your weight more forward than he did, so you're not reaching for the ball. And he should have his right hand higher up on the bat."

The inning ended, and we reversed directions once again. "Ty Cobb was the greatest bat handler you ever saw," Wood said. "He used to go out to the ballpark early in the morning with a pitcher and work on hitting the ball to all fields, over and over. He batted that strange way, with his fists apart, you know, but he could have hit just as well no matter how he held it. He just knew what to do with a bat in hand. And baserunning—why, I saw him get on base and steal second, steal third, and then steal home. *The* best. A lot of fellows in my time shortened up on the bat when they had to—that's what the St. John's boys should try against this good pitcher. Next to Cobb, Shoeless Joe Jackson was the best left-handed hitter I ever saw, and he was always down at the end of the bat until there were two strikes on him. Then he'd shorten up a little, to give himself a better chance."

Dick Lee said, "That's what you've been telling Charlie Polka, isn't it, Joe?"

"Yes, sir, and it's helped him," Wood said. "He's tried it, and now he knows that all you have to do is make contact and the ball will fly a long way."

Both men saw my look of bewilderment, and they laughed together.

"Charlie Polka is a Little League player," Dick Lee explained. "He's about eleven years old."

"He lives right across the street from me," Wood said. "He plays for the 500 Blake team—that's named for a restaurant here in town. I've got him shortened up on the bat, and now he's a hitter. Charlie Polka is a natural."

"Is that how you batted?" I asked.

"Not at first," he said. "But after I went over to Cleveland in 1917 to join my old roommate, Tris Speaker, I started to play the outfield, and I began to take up on the bat, because I knew I'd have to hit a little better if I was going to make the team. I never was any wonder at the plate, but I was good enough to last six more years, playing with Spoke."

Tris Speaker (Wood had called him by his old nickname, Spoke) was the Joe DiMaggio or Willie Mays of the first two decades of this century—the nonpareil center fielder of his day. "He had a beautiful left-handed arm," Joe Wood said. "He always played very shallow in center—you could do that in those days, because of the dead ball. I saw him make a lot of plays to second base from there—pick up what looked like a clean single and fire the ball to second in time to force the base runner coming down from first. Or he could throw the ball behind a runner and pick him off that way. And just as fine a man as he was a ballplayer. He was a southern gentleman—well, he was from Hubbard, Texas. Back in the early days, when we were living together on the beach at Winthrop during the season, out beyond Revere, Spoke would sometimes cook up a mess of fried chicken in the evening. He'd cook, and then I'd do the dishes."

Listening to this, I sensed the web of baseball about me. Tris Speaker had driven in the tying run in the tenth inning of the last game of the 1912 World Series, at Fenway Park, after Fred Merkle and Chief Meyers, of the Giants, had let his easy foul pop fall untouched between them. A moment or two later, Joe Wood had won his third game of the Series and the Red Sox were champions. My father saw that game—he was at Harvard Law School at the time, and got a ticket somehow— and he told me about it many times. He was terrifically excited to be there, but I think my mother must have relished the famous victory even more. She grew up in Boston and was a true Red Sox fan, even though young women didn't go to many games then. My father grew up in Cleveland, so he was an Indians rooter, of course. In 1915, my parents got married and went to live in Cleveland, where my father began to practice law. Tris Speaker was traded to the Indians in 1916— a terrible shock to Red Sox fans—and Joe Wood came out of his brief retirement to join him on the club a year later. My parents' first child, my older sister, was born in Cleveland late in 1916, and the next year my father went off to Europe—off to the war. My mother once told me that in the summer afternoons of 1917 she would often push a baby carriage past League Park, the Indians' home field, out on Linwood Avenue, which was a block or two away from my parents' house. Sometimes there was a game going on, and if she heard a roar of pleasure from the fans inside she would tell herself that probably Tris Speaker had just done something special. She was lonely in Cleveland, she told me, and it made her feel good to know that Tris Speaker was there in the same town with her. "Tris Speaker and I were traded to Cleveland in the same year," she said.

A yell and an explosion of cheering brought me back to Yale Field. We were in the top of the seventh, and the Yale second baseman and captain, Gerry Harrington, had just leaped high to snatch down a burning line drive—the force of it almost knocked him over backward in midair. Then he flipped the ball to second to double off a St. John's base runner and end the inning. "These fellows came to *play!*" Dick Lee said.

Most no-hitters produce at least one such heaven-sent gift somewhere along the line, and I began to believe that Ron Darling, who was still untouched on the mound, might be pitching the game of his young life. I turned to ask Mr. Wood how many no-hitters he recalled—he had seen Mathewson and Marquard and Babe Ruth (Ruth, the pitcher, that is) and Coveleski and the rest of them, after all—but he seemed transfixed by something on the field. "Look at *that*!" he said, in a harsh, disbelieving way. "This Yale coach has his own coaches out there on the lines, by God! They're professionals—not just players, the way I always had it when I was here. The coach has his own coaches . . . I never knew that."

"Did you have special coaches when you were coming up with the Red Sox?" I said, hoping to change his mood. "A pitching coach, I mean, or a batting coach?"

He didn't catch the question, and I repeated it.

"No, no," he said, a little impatiently. "We talked about the other players and the pitchers among ourselves in those days. We players. We didn't need anybody to help us."

He was staring straight ahead at the field. I thought he looked a bit chilly. It was well past five o'clock now, and a skim of clouds had covered the sun.

Dick Lee stole a glance at him, too. "Hey, Joe, doesn't this Darling remind you a little of Carl Hubbell on the mound?" he said in a cheerful, distracting sort of voice. "The way he picks up his front leg, I mean. You remember how Hubbell would go way up on the stretch and then drop his hands down by his ankles before he threw the ball?"

"Hubbell?" Joe Wood said. He shook his head, making an effort. "Well, to me this pitcher's a little like that fellow Eckersley," he said slowly. "The way he moves forward there."

He was right. Ron Darling had exactly the same float and glide that the Red Sox' Dennis Eckersley conveys when he is pitching well.

"How do today's players compare with the men you played with, Mr. Wood?" I asked.

"I'd rather not answer that question," he said. He had taken out his watch again. He studied it and then tucked it away carefully, and then he glanced over at me, perhaps wondering if he had been impolite. "That Pete Rose plays hard," he added. "Him and a few more. I don't *like* Pete Rose, exactly, but he looks like he plays the game the way we did. He'd play for the fun of it if he had to."

He resumed his study of the field, and now and then I saw him stare again at the heavyset Yale third-base coach on our side of the diamond. Scoreless games make for a long day at the ballpark, and Joe Wood's day had probably been longer than ours. More than once, I had seen him struggle to his feet to catch some exciting play or moment on the field, only to have it end before he was quite up. Then he would sit down again, leaning on his cane while he lowered himself. I had more questions for Mr. Wood, but now I tried to put them out of my mind. Earlier in the afternoon, he had remarked that several old Yale players had dropped in at his house before the game to say hello and to talk about the old days. "People come by and see me all the time," he had said. "People I don't even know, from as far away as Colorado. Why, I had a fellow come in all the way from Canada the other day, who just wanted to talk about the old days. They all want that, somehow. It's gone on too long."

It had gone on for him, I realized, for as long as most lifetimes. He had played ball for fourteen years, all told, and people had been asking him to talk about it for nearly sixty years. For him, the last juice and sweetness must have been squeezed out of these ancient games years ago, but he was still expected to respond to our amateur expertise, our insatiable vicariousness. Old men are patronized in much the same fashion as athletes; because we take pride in them, we expect their intimacy in return. I had intruded after all.

We were in the eighth now . . . and then in the ninth. Still no score, and each new batter, each pitch was greeted with clappings and deepening cries of encouragement and anxiety from the stands and the players alike. The close-packed rows hummed with ceaseless, nervous sounds of conversation and speculation—an impatience for the dénouement, and a fear of it, too. All around me in our section I could see the same look of resignation and boredom and pleasure that now showed on my own face, I knew—the look of longtime fans who understand that one can never leave a very long close game, no matter how much inconvenience and exasperation it imposes on us. The difficulty of baseball is imperious.

"Yay! Yay!" Dick Lee cried when Yale left fielder Joe Dufek led off the eighth with a single. "Now come *on*, you guys! I gotta get home for dinner." But the next Yale batter bunted into a force play at second, and the chance was gone. "Well, all right—for *breakfast!*" Lee said, slumping back in his seat.

The two pitchers held us—each as intent and calm and purposeful as the other. Ron Darling, never deviating from the purity of his stylish body-lean and leg-crook and his riding, down-thrusting delivery,

poured fastballs through the diminishing daylight. He looked as fast as
ever now, or faster, and in both the ninth and the tenth he dismissed the
side in order and with four more strikeouts. Viola was dominant in his
own fashion, also setting down the Yale hitters one, two, three in the
ninth and tenth, with a handful of pitches. His rhythm—the constant
variety of speeds and location on his pitches—had the enemy batters
leaning and swaying with his motion, and, as antistrophe, was almost as
exciting to watch as Darling's flair and flame. With two out in the top
of the eleventh, a St. John's batter nudged a soft little roller up the first-
base line—such an easy, waiting, schoolboy sort of chance that the Yale
first baseman, O'Connor, allowed the ball to carom off his mitt: a miserable little butchery, except that the second baseman, seeing his
pitcher sprinting for the bag, now snatched up the ball and flipped it
toward him almost despairingly. Darling took the toss while diving
full-length at the bag and, rolling in the dirt, beat the runner by a hair.

"Oh, my!" said Joe Wood. "Oh, my, oh, my!"

Then in the bottom of the inning Yale suddenly loaded the bases—
a hit, a walk, another walk (Viola was just missing the corners now)—
and we all came to our feet, yelling and pleading. The tilted stands and
the low roof deepened the cheers and sent them rolling across the field.
There were two out, and the Yale batter, Dan Costello, swung at the
first pitch and bounced it gently to short, for a force that ended the
rally. Somehow, I think, we knew that we had seen Yale's last chance.

"I would have taken that pitch," I said, entering the out in my scorecard. "To keep the pressure on him."

"I don't know," Joe Wood said at once. "He's just walked two. You
might get the cripple on the first pitch and then see nothing but hooks.
Hit away."

He was back in the game.

Steve Scafa, leading off the twelfth, got a little piece of Darling's first
pitch on the handle of his bat, and the ball looped softly over the shortstop's head and into left: a hit. The loudspeakers told us that Ron Darling's eleven innings of no-hit pitching had set a new NCAA
tournament record. Everyone at Yale Field stood up—the St. John's
players, too, coming off their bench and out onto the field—and applauded Darling's masterpiece. We were scarcely seated again before
Scafa stole second as the Yale catcher, Paterno, bobbled the pitch.
Scafa, who is blurrily quick, had stolen thirty-five bases during the sea-

son. Now he stole third as well. With one out and runners at the corners (the other St. John's man had reached first on an error), Darling ran the count to three and two and fanned the next batter—his fifteenth strikeout of the game. Two out. Darling sighed and stared in, and then stepped off the mound while the St. John's coach put in a pinch-runner at first—who took off for second on the very next pitch. Paterno fired the ball quickly this time, and Darling, staggering off the mound with his follow-through, did not cut it off. Scafa came ten feet down the third-base line and stopped there, while the pinch-runner suddenly jammed on the brakes, stranding himself between first and second: a play, clearly—an inserted crisis. The Yale second baseman glanced twice at Scafa, freezing him, and then made a little run at the hung-up base runner to his left and threw to first. With that, Scafa instantly broke for the plate. Lured by the vision of the third out just a few feet away from him on the base path, the Yale first baseman hesitated, fractionally and fatally, before he spun and threw home, where Scafa slid past the tag and came up, leaping and clapping, into the arms of his teammates. That was the game. Darling struck out his last man, but a new St. John's pitcher, a right-handed fireballer named Eric Stampfl, walked on and blew the Elis away in their half.

"Well, that's a shame," Joe Wood said, getting up for the last time. It was close to six-thirty, but he looked fine now. "If that man scores before the third out, it counts, you know," he said. "That's why it worked. I never saw a better-played game anyplace—college or big league. That's a swell ballgame."

Several things happened afterward. Neither Yale nor St. John's qualified for the college World Series, it turned out; the University of Maine defeated St. John's in the final game of the playoffs at New Haven (neither Viola nor Darling was sufficiently recovered from his ordeal to pitch again) and made the trip to Omaha, where it, too, was eliminated. Arizona State won the national title. On June 9, Ron Darling was selected by the Texas Rangers at the major-league amateur-player draft in New York. He was the ninth player in the country to be chosen. Frank Viola, the thirty-seventh pick, went to the Minnesota Twins. (The Seattle Mariners, who had the first pick this year, had been ready to take Darling, which would have made him the coveted No. 1 selection in the draft, but the club backed off at the last moment because of Darling's considerable salary demands. As it was, he signed with the Rangers for a hundred-thousand-dollar bonus.) On June 12, the major-league players unanimously struck the twenty-six big-league teams. The strike has brought major-league ball to a halt, and no one can predict when play will resume. Because of this sudden silence, the St. John's–Yale struggle has become the best and most vivid game of the year for me, so far. It may stay that way even after the strike ends. "I think that game will always be on my mind," Ron Darling said after it was over. I feel the same way. I think I will remember it all my life. So will Joe Wood. Somebody will probably tell Ron Darling that Smokey Joe Wood was at the game that afternoon and saw him pitch eleven scoreless no-hit innings against St. John's, and someday—perhaps years from now, when he, too, may possibly be a celebrated major-league strikeout artist—it may occur to him that his heartbreaking 0–1 loss in May 1981 and Walter Johnson's 0–1 loss at Fenway Park in September 1912 are now woven together into the fabric of baseball. Pitch by pitch, inning by inning, Ron Darling had made that happen. He stitched us together.

1981

"All right, all right, try it that way! Go ahead and try it that way!"

AHAB AND NEMESIS

A. J. LIEBLING

Back in 1922, the late Heywood Broun, who is not remembered primarily as a boxing writer, wrote a durable account of a combat between the late Benny Leonard and the late Rocky Kansas for the lightweight championship of the world. Leonard was the greatest practitioner of the era, Kansas just a rough, optimistic fellow. In the early rounds, Kansas messed Leonard about, and Broun was profoundly disturbed. A radical in politics, he was a conservative in the arts, and Kansas made him think of Gertrude Stein, Les Six, and nonrepresentational painting, all of them novelties that irritated him.

"With the opening gong, Rocky Kansas tore into Leonard," he wrote. "He was gauche and inaccurate, but terribly persistent." The classic verities prevailed, however. After a few rounds, during which Broun continued to yearn for a return to a culture with fixed values, he was enabled to record: "The young child of nature who was challenging for the championship dropped his guard, and Leonard hooked a powerful and entirely orthodox blow to the conventional point of the jaw. Down went Rocky Kansas. His past life flashed before him during the nine seconds in which he remained on the floor, and he wished that he had been more faithful as a child in heeding the advice of his boxing teacher. After all, the old masters did know something. There is still a kick in style, and tradition carries a nasty wallop."

I have often thought of Broun's words in the three years since Rocky Marciano, the reigning heavyweight champion, scaled the fistic summits, as they say in *Journal-American*-ese, by beating a sly, powerful quadragenarian colored man named Jersey Joe Walcott. The current Rocky is gauche and inaccurate, but besides being persistent he is a dreadfully severe hitter with either hand. The predominative nature of this asset has been well stated by Pierce Egan, the Edward Gibbon and Sir Thomas Malory of the old London prize ring, who was less preoccupied than Broun with ultimate implications. Writing in 1821 of a "milling cove" named Bill Neat, the Bristol Butcher, Egan said, "He possesses a requisite above all the art that *teaching* can achieve for any boxer; namely, *one hit* from his right hand, given in proper distance, can gain a victory; but three of them are positively enough to dispose of a giant." This is true not only of Marciano's right hand but of his left hand, too—provided he doesn't miss the giant entirely. Egan doubted the advisability of changing Neat's style, and he would have approved of Marciano's. The champion has an apparently unlimited absorptive capacity for percussion (Egan would have called him an "insatiable glutton") and inexhaustible energy ("a prime bottom fighter"). "Shifting," or moving to the side, and "milling in retreat," or moving back, are innovations of the late eighteenth century that Rocky's advisers have carefully kept from his knowledge, lest they spoil his natural prehistoric style. Egan excused these tactics only in boxers of feeble constitution. I imagine Broun would have had a hard time fitting Marciano anywhere into his frame of reference.

Archie Moore, the light-heavyweight champion of the world, who hibernates in San Diego, California, and estivates in Toledo, Ohio, is a Brounian rather than an Eganite in his thinking about style, but he naturally has to do more than think about it. Since the rise of Marciano, Moore, a cerebral and hyperexperienced light-colored pugilist who has been active since 1936, has suffered the pangs of a supreme exponent of *bel canto* who sees himself crowded out of the opera house by a guy who can only shout. As a sequel to a favorable review I wrote of one of his infrequent New York appearances a year ago, when his fee was restricted to a measly five figures, I received a sad little note signed "The most unappreciated fighter in the world, Archie Moore." A fellow who has as much style as Moore tends to overestimate the intellect—he develops the kind of Faustian mind that will throw itself against the problem of perpetual motion, or of how to pick horses first, second, third, *and* fourth in every race. Archie's note made it plain to me that he was honing his harpoon for the White Whale.

When, during some recent peregrinations in Europe, I read newspaper items about Moore's decisioning a large, playful porpoise of a Cuban heavyweight named Nino Valdes and scoop-netting a minnow like Bobo Olson, the middleweight champion, for practice, I thought of him as a lonely Ahab, rehearsing to buck Herman Melville, Pierce Egan, and the betting odds. I did not think that he could bring it off, but I wanted to be there when he tried. What would *Moby-Dick* be if Ahab had succeeded? Just another fish story. The thing that is eternally diverting is the struggle of man against history—or what Albert Camus, who used to be an amateur middleweight, has called the Myth of Sisyphus. (Camus would have been a great man to cover the fight, but none of the syndicates thought of it.) When I heard that the boys had been made for September 20, at the Yankee Stadium, I shortened my stay abroad in order not to miss the Encounter of the Two Heroes, as Egan would have styled the rendezvous.

In London on the night of September 13, a week before the date set for the Encounter, I tried to get my eye in for fight watching by attending a bout at the White City greyhound track between Valdes, who had been imported for the occasion, and the British Empire heavyweight champion, Don Cockell, a fat man whose gift for public suffering has enlisted the sympathy of a sentimental people. Since Valdes had gone fifteen rounds with Moore in Las Vegas the previous May, and Cockell had excruciated for nine rounds before being knocked out by Marciano in San Francisco in the same month, the bout offered a dim opportunity for establishing what racing people call a "line" between Moore and Marciano. I didn't get much of an optical workout, because Valdes disposed of Cockell in three rounds. It was evident that Moore and Marciano had not been fighting the same class of people this season.

This was the only fight I ever attended in a steady rainstorm. It had begun in the middle of the afternoon, and while there was a canopy over the ring, the spectators were as wet as speckled trout. "The weather, it is well known, has no terrors to the admirers of Pugilism and Life," Egan once wrote, and on his old stamping ground this still holds true. As I took my seat in a rock pool that had collected in the hollow of my chair, a South African giant named Ewart Potgieter, whose weight had been announced as twenty-two stone ten, was ignoring the doctrine of apartheid by leaning on a Jamaican colored man who weighed a mere sixteen stone, and by the time I had transposed these statistics to 318 pounds and 224 pounds, respectively, the exhausted Jamaican had acquiesced in resegregation and retired. The giant had not struck a blow, properly speaking, but had shoved downward a number of times, like a man trying to close an overfilled trunk.

The main bout proved an even less grueling contest. Valdes, eager to get out of the chill, struck Cockell more vindictively than is his wont, and after a few gestures invocative of commiseration the fat man settled in one corner of the ring as heavily as suet pudding upon the unaccustomed gastric system. He had received what Egan would have called a "ribber" and a "nobber," and when he arose it was seen that the latter had raised a cut on his forehead. At the end of the third round, his manager withdrew him from competition. It was not an inspiring occasion, but after the armistice eight or nine shivering Cubans appeared in the runway behind the press section and jumped up and down to register emotion and restore circulation. *"Ahora Marciano!"* they yelled. "Now for Marciano!" Instead of being grateful for the distraction, the other spectators took a poor view of it. "Sit down, you chaps!" one of them cried. "We want to see the next do!" They were still parked out there in the rain when I tottered into the Shepherd's Bush underground station and collapsed, sneezing, on a train that eventually disgorged me at Oxford Circus, with just enough time left to buy a revivifying draught before eleven o'clock, when the pubs closed. How the mugs I left behind cured themselves I never knew. They had to do it on Bovril.

Because I had engagements that kept me in England until a few days before the Encounter, I had no opportunity to visit the training camps of the rival American Heroes. I knew all the members of both factions, however, and I could imagine what they were thinking. In the plane on the way home, I tried to envision the rival patterns of ratiocination. I could be sure that Marciano, a kind, quiet, imperturbable fellow, would plan to go after Moore and make him fight continuously until he tired enough to become an accessible target. After that, he would expect concussion to accentuate exhaustion and exhaustion to facilitate concussion, until Moore came away from his consciousness, like everybody else Rocky had ever fought. He would try to remember to minimize damage to himself in the beginning, while there was still snap in Moore's arms, because Moore is a sharp puncher. (Like Bill Neat of old, Marciano hits at his opponent's arms when he cannot hit past them. "In one instance, the arm of Oliver [a Neat adversary] received so paralyzing a shock in stopping the blow that it appeared almost useless," Egan once wrote.) Charlie Goldman, Marciano's hand-chipped tactical adviser, would have instructed him in some rudimentary maneuver to throw Moore's first shots off, I felt sure, but after a few minutes Rocky would forget it, or Archie would figure it out. But there would always be Freddie Brown, the "cut man," in the champion's corner to repair superficial damage. One reason Goldman is a great teacher is that he doesn't try to teach a boxer more than he can learn. What he has taught Rocky in the four years since I first saw him fight is to shorten the arc of most of his blows without losing power thereby, and always to follow one hard blow with another—"for insurance"—delivered with the other hand, instead of recoiling to watch the victim fall. The champion has also gained confidence and presence of mind; he has a good fighting head, which is not the same thing as being a good mechanical practitioner. "A *boxer* requires a *nob* as well as a *statesman* does a HEAD, coolness and calculation being essential to *second* his efforts," Egan wrote, and the old historiographer was never more correct. Rocky is thirty-one, not in the first flush of youth for a boxer, but Moore is only a few days short of thirty-nine, so age promised to be in the champion's favor if he kept pressing.

Moore's strategic problem, I reflected on the plane, offered more choices and, as a corollary, infinitely more chances for error. It was possible, but not probable, that jabbing and defensive skill would carry him through fifteen rounds, even on those old legs, but I knew that the mere notion of such a *gambade* would revolt Moore. He is not what Egan would have called a shy fighter. Besides, would Ahab have been content merely to go the distance with the White Whale? I felt sure that Archie planned to knock the champion out, so that he could sign his next batch of letters "The most appreciated and deeply opulent fighter in the world." I surmised that this project would prove a mistake, like Mr. Churchill's attempt to take Gallipoli in 1915, but it would be the kind of mistake that would look good in his memoirs. The basis of what I rightly anticipated would prove a miscalculation went back to Archie's academic background. As a young fighter of conventional tutelage, he must have heard his preceptors say hundreds of times, "They will all go if you hit them right." If a fighter did not believe that, he would be in the position of a Euclidian without faith in the 180-degree triangle. Moore's strategy, therefore, would be based on working Marciano into a position where he could hit him right. He would not go in and slug with him, because that would be wasteful, distasteful, and injudicious, but he might try to cut him up, in an effort to slow him down so he could hit him right, or else try to hit him right and then cut him up. The puzzle he reserved for me—and Marciano—was the tactic by which he would attempt to attain his strategic objective. In the formation of his views, I believed, Moore would be handicapped, rather than aided, by his active, skeptical mind. One of the odd things about Marciano is that he isn't terribly big. It is hard for a man like Moore, just under six feet tall and weighing about 180 pounds, to imagine that a man approximately the same size can be immeasurably stronger than he is. This is particularly true when, like the light-heavyweight champion, he has spent his whole professional life contending with boxers—some of them considerably bigger—whose strength has proved so near his own that he could move their arms and bodies by cunning pressures. The old classicist would consequently refuse to believe what he was up against.

The light-heavyweight limit is 175 pounds, and Moore can get down to that when he must, in order to defend his title, but in a heavyweight match each Hero is allowed to weigh whatever he pleases. I was back in time to attend the weighing-in ceremonies, held in the lobby of Madison Square Garden at noon on the day set for the Encounter, and learned that Moore weighed 188 and Marciano 188¼—a lack of disparity that figured to encourage the rationalist's illusions. I also learned that, in contrast to Jack Solomons, the London promoter who held the Valdes-Cockell match in the rain, the International Boxing Club, which was promoting the Encounter, had decided to postpone it for twenty-four hours, although the weather was clear. The decision was based on apprehension of Hurricane Ione, which, although apparently veering away from New York, might come around again like a lazy left hook and drop in on the point of the stadium's jaw late in the evening. Nothing like that happened, but the postponement brought the town's theaters and bars another evening of good business from the out-of-town fight trade, such as they always get on the eve of a memorable Encounter. ("Not a bed could be had at any of the villages at an early hour on the preceding evening; and Uxbridge was crowded beyond all former precedent," Egan wrote of the night before Neat beat Oliver.) There was no doubt that the fight had caught the public imagination, ever sensitive to a meeting between Hubris and Nemesis, as the boys on the quarterlies would say, and the bookies were laying 18–5 on Nemesis, according to the boys on the dailies, who always seem to hear. (A friend of mine up from Maryland with a whim and a five-dollar bill couldn't get ten against it in ordinary barroom money anywhere, although he wanted Ahab.)

The enormous—by recent precedent—advance sale of tickets had so elated the IBC that it had decided to replace the usual card of bad preliminary fights with some not worth watching at all, so there was less distraction than usual as we awaited the appearance of the Heroes on the fateful evening. The press seats had been so closely juxtaposed that I could fit in only sidewise between two colleagues—the extra compression having been caused by the injection of a prewar number of movie stars and politicos. The tight quarters were an advantage, in a way, since they facilitated my conversation with Peter Wilson, an English prizering correspondent, who happened to be in the row behind me. I had last seen Mr. Wilson at White City the week before, at a time when the water level had already reached his shredded-Latakia mustache. I had feared that he had drowned at ringside, but when I saw him at the Stadium, he assured me that by buttoning the collar of his mackintosh tightly over his nostrils he had been able to make the garment serve as a diving lung, and so survive. Like all British fight writers when they are relieved of the duty of watching British fighters, he was in a holiday mood, and we chatted happily. There is something about the approach of a good fight that renders the spirit insensitive to annoyance; it is only when the amateur of the Sweet Science has some doubts as to how good the main bout will turn out to be that he is avid for the satisfaction to be had from the preliminaries. This is because after the evening is over, he may have only a good supporting fight to remember. There were no such doubts—even in the minds of the mugs who had paid for their seats—on the evening of September 21.

At about ten-thirty, the champion and his faction entered the ring. It is not customary for the champion to come in first, but Marciano has never been a stickler for protocol. He is a humble, kindly fellow, who even now will approach an acquaintance on the street and say bashfully, "Remember me? I'm Rocky Marciano." The champion doesn't mind waiting five or ten minutes to give anybody a punch in the nose. In any case, once launched from his dressing room under the grandstand, he could not have arrested his progress to the ring, because he had about forty policemen pushing behind him, and three more clearing a path in front of him. Marciano, tucked in behind the third cop like a football ballcarrier behind his interference, had to run or be trampled to death. Wrapped in a heavy blue bathrobe and with a blue monk's cowl pulled over his head, he climbed the steps to the ring with the cumbrous agility of a medieval executioner ascending the scaffold. Under the hood, he seemed to be trying to look serious. He has an intellectual appreciation of the anxieties of a champion, but he has a hard time forgetting how strong he is; while he remembers that, he can't worry as much as he knows a champion should. His attendants—quick, battered little Goldman; Al Weill, the stout, excitable manager, always stricken just before the bell with the suspicion that he may have made a bad match; Al Columbo, the boyhood friend from Brockton, Massachusetts, which is Rocky's hometown—are all as familiar to the crowd as he is.

Ahab's party arrived in the ring a minute or so later, and Charlie Johnston, his manager—a calm sparrowhawk of a man, as old and wise in the game as Weill—went over to watch Goldman put on the champion's gloves. Freddie Brown, the surgical specialist, went to Moore's corner to watch *his* gloves being put on. Moore wore a splendid black silk robe with a gold lamé collar and belt. He sports a full mustache above an imperial, and his hair, sleeked down under pomade when he opens operations, invariably rises during the contest, as it gets water sloshed on it between rounds and the lacquer washes off, until it is standing up like the top of a shaving brush. Seated in his corner in the shadow of his personal trainer, a brown man called Cheerful Norman, who weighs 235 pounds, Moore looked like an old Japanese print I have of a "Shogun Engaged in Strategic Contemplation in the Midst of War." The third member of his group was Bertie Briscoe, a rough, chipper little trainer, whose more usual charge is Sandy Saddler, the featherweight champion—also a Johnston fighter. Mr. Moore's features in repose rather resemble those of Orson Welles, and he was reposing with intensity.

The procession of other fighters and former fighters to be introduced was longer than usual. The full galaxy was on hand, including Jack Dempsey, Gene Tunney, and Joe Louis, the *têtes de cuvée* of former-champion society; ordinary former heavyweight champions, like Max Baer and Jim Braddock, slipped through the ropes practically unnoticed. After all the celebrities had been in and out of the ring, an odd dwarf, advertising something or other—possibly himself—was lifted into the ring by an accomplice and ran across it before he could be shooed out. The referee, a large, craggy, oldish man named Harry

"Good game." "Good game." "Nice game." "Good game."
"I'm in love with you." "Good game." "Nice game."

Kessler, who, unlike some of his better-known colleagues, is not an ex-fighter, called the men to the center of the ring. This was his moment; he had the microphone. "Now Archie and Rocky, I want a nice, clean fight," he said, and I heard a peal of silvery laughter behind me from Mr. Wilson, who had seen both of them fight before. "Protect yourself at all times," Mr. Kessler cautioned them unnecessarily. When the principals shook hands, I could see Mr. Moore's eyebrows rising like storm clouds over the Sea of Azov. His whiskers bristled and his eyes glowed like dark coals as he scrunched his eyebrows down again and enveloped the Whale with the Look, which was intended to dominate his willpower. Mr. Wilson and I were sitting behind Marciano's corner, and as the champion came back to it I observed his expression, to determine what effect the Look had had upon him. More than ever, he resembled a Great Dane who has heard the word *bone*.

A moment later the bell rang and the Heroes came out for the first round. Marciano, training in the sun for weeks, had tanned to a slightly deeper tint than Moore's old ivory, and Moore, at 188, looked, if anything, bigger and more muscular than Marciano; much of the champion's weight is in his legs, and his shoulders slope. Marciano advanced, but Moore didn't go far away. As usual, he stood up nicely, his arms close to his body and his feet not too far apart, ready to go anywhere but not without a reason—the picture of a powerful, decisive intellect unfettered by preconceptions. Marciano, pulling his left arm back from the shoulder, flung a left hook. He missed, but not by enough to discourage him, and then walked in and hooked again. All through the round, he threw those hooks, and some of them grazed Moore's whiskers; one even hit him on the side of the head. Moore didn't try much offensively; he held a couple of times when Marciano worked in close.

Marciano came back to his corner as he always does, unimpassioned. He hadn't expected to catch Moore with those left hooks anyway, I imagine; all he had wanted was to move him around. Moore went to his corner inscrutable. They came out for the second, and Marciano went after him in brisker fashion. In the first round, he had been throwing the left hook, missing with it, and then throwing a right and missing with that, too. In the second, he tried a variation—throwing a right and then pulling a shoulder back to throw the left. It appeared for a moment to have Moore confused, as a matador might be confused by a bull who walked in on his hind legs. Marciano landed a couple of those awkward hooks, but not squarely. He backed Moore over toward the side of the ring farthest from me, and then Moore knocked him down.

Some of the reporters, describing the blow in the morning papers, called it a "sneak punch," which is journalese for one the reporter didn't see but technically means a lead thrown before the other man has warmed up or while he is musing about the gate receipts. This had been no lead, and although I certainly hadn't seen Moore throw the punch, I knew that it had landed inside the arc of Marciano's left hook. ("Marciano missed with the right, trun the left, and Moore stepped inside it," my private eye, a trainer named Whitey Bimstein, said next day, confirming my diagnosis, and the film of the fight bore both of us out.) So Ahab had his harpoon in the Whale. He had hit him right if ever I saw a boxer hit right, with a classic brevity and conciseness. Marciano stayed down for two seconds. I do not know what took place in Mr. Moore's breast when he saw him get up. He may have felt, for the moment, like Don Giovanni when the Commendatore's statue grabbed at him—startled because he thought he had killed the guy already—or like Ahab when he saw the Whale take down Fedallah, harpoons and all. Anyway, he hesitated a couple of seconds, and that was reasonable. A man who took nine to come up after a punch like that would be doing well, and the correct tactic would be to go straight in and finish him. But a fellow who came up on two was so strong he would bear investigation.

After that, Moore did go in, but not in a crazy way. He hit Marciano some good, hard, classic shots, and inevitably Marciano, a trader, hit him a few devastating swipes, which slowed him. When the round ended, the edge of Moore's speed was gone, and he knew that he would have to set a new and completely different trap, with diminished resources. After being knocked down, Marciano had stopped throwing that patterned right-and-left combination; he has a good nob. "He never trun it again in the fight," Whitey said next day, but I differ. He threw it in the fifth, and again Moore hit him a peach of a right inside it, but the steam was gone; this time Ahab couldn't even stagger him. Anyway, there was Moore at the end of the second, dragging his shattered faith in the unities and humanities back to his corner. He had hit a guy right, and the guy hadn't gone. But there is no geezer in Moore, any more than there was in the master of the *Pequod*.

Both came out for the third very gay, as Egan would have said. Marciano had been hit and cut, so he felt acclimated, and Moore was so mad at himself for not having knocked Marciano out that he almost displayed animosity toward him. He may have thought that perhaps he had not hit Marciano *just* right; the true artist is always prone to self-reproach. He would try again. A minute's attention from his squires had raised his spirits and slaked down his hair. At this point, Marciano set about him. He waddled in, hurling his fists with a sublime disregard of probabilities, content to hit an elbow, a biceps, a shoulder, the top of a head—the last supposed to be the least profitable target in the business, since, as every beginner learns, "the head is the hardest part of the human body," and a boxer will only break his hands on it. Many boxers make the systematic presentation of the cranium part of their defensive scheme. The crowd, basically anti-intellectual, screamed encouragement. There was Moore, riding punches, picking them off, slipping them, rolling with them, ducking them, coming gracefully out of his defensive efforts with sharp, patterned blows—and just about holding this parody even on points. His face, emerging at instants from under the storm of arms—his own and Rocky's—looked like that of a swimming walrus. When the round ended, I could see that he was thinking deeply. Marciano came back to his corner at a kind of suppressed dogtrot. He didn't have a worry in the world.

It was in the fourth, though, that I think Sisyphus began to get the idea he couldn't roll back the Rock. Marciano pushed him against the ropes and swung at him for what seemed a full minute without ever landing a punch that a boxer with Moore's background would consider a credit to his workmanship. He kept them coming so fast, though, that Moore tired just getting out of their way. One newspaper account I saw said that at this point Moore "swayed uncertainly," but his motions were about as uncertain as Margot Fonteyn's, or Artur Rubinstein's. He is the most premeditated and best-synchronized swayer in his profession. After the bell rang for the end of the round, the champion hit him a right for good measure—he usually manages to have something on the way all the time—and then pulled back to disclaim any uncouth intention. Moore, no man to be conned, hit him a corker of a punch in return, when he wasn't expecting it. It was a gesture of moral reprobation and also a punch that would give any normal man something to think about between rounds. It was a good thing Moore couldn't see Marciano's face as he came back to his corner, though, because the champion was laughing.

The fifth was a successful round for Moore, and I had him ahead on points that far in the fight. But it took no expert to know where the strength lay. There was even a moment in the round when Moore set himself against the ropes and encouraged Marciano to swing at him, in the hope the champion would swing himself tired. It was a confession that he himself was too tired to do much hitting.

In the sixth, Marciano knocked Moore down twice—once, early in the round, for four seconds, and once, late in the round, for eight seconds, with Moore getting up just before the bell rang. In the seventh, after that near approach to obliteration, the embattled intellect put up its finest stand. Marciano piled out of his corner to finish Moore, and the stylist made him miss so often that it looked, for a fleeting moment, as if the champion were indeed punching himself arm-weary. In fact, Moore began to beat him to the punch. It was Moore's round, certainly, but an old-timer I talked to later averred that one of the body blows Marciano landed in that round was the hardest of the fight.

It was the eighth that ended the competitive phase of the fight. They fought all the way, and in the last third of the round the champion simply overflowed Archie. He knocked him down with a right six seconds before the bell, and I don't think Moore could have got up by ten if the round had lasted that long. The fight by then reminded me of something that Sam Langford, one of the most profound thinkers—and, according to all accounts, one of the greatest doers—of the prize ring, once said to me: "Whatever that other man want to do, don't let him do it." Merely by moving in all the time and punching continually, Marciano achieves the same strategic effect that Langford gained by finesse. It is impossible to think, or to impose your thought, if you have to keep on avoiding punches.

Moore's "game," as old Egan would have called his courage, was beyond reproach. He came out proudly for the ninth, and stood and fought back with all he had, but Marciano slugged him down, and he was counted out with his left arm hooked over the middle rope as he tried to rise. It was a crushing defeat for the higher faculties and a lesson in intellectual humility, but he had made a hell of a fight.

The fight was no sooner over than hundreds of unsavory young yokels with New England accents began a kind of mountain-goat immigration from the bleachers to ringside. They leaped from chair to chair and, after they reached the press section, from typewriter shelf to typewriter shelf and, I hope, from movie star to movie star. "Rocky!" they yelled. "Brockton!" Two of them, as dismal a pair of civic ambassadors as I have seen since I worked on *The Providence Journal & Evening Bulletin,* stood on Wilson's typewriter and yelled "Providence!" After the fighters and the hick delinquents had gone away, I made my way out to Jerome Avenue, where the crowd milled, impenetrable, under the elevated structure. Skirting it as well as I could, I made my way uptown toward 167th Street, the station north of the Stadium.

By boarding a train at 167th Street, you can get a seat before it reaches 161st, which is the Stadium station, and then, if you don't mind people standing on your feet, continue downtown. At least you don't have to fight to get on. If you are not in a great hurry, however (and why should you be at eleven-thirty or twelve on a fight night?), the best plan of all is to walk up to 167th and have a beer in a saloon, or a cup of tea in the 167th Street Cafeteria, and wait until the whole mess clears away. By that time, you may even get a taxi. After this particular fight,

I chose the cafeteria, being in a contemplative rather than a convivial mood. The place is of a genre you would expect to find nearer Carnegie Hall, with blond woodwork, and modern functional furniture imported from Italy—an appropriate background for the evaluation of an aesthetic experience. I got my tea and a smoked-salmon sandwich on a soft onion roll at the counter, and made my way to a table, where I found myself between two young policemen who were talking about why Walt Disney has never attempted a screen version of Kafka's *Metamorphosis*. As I did not feel qualified to join in that one, I got out my copy of the official program of the fights and began to read the high-class feature articles as I munched my sandwich.

One reminded me that I had seen the first boxing show ever held in Yankee Stadium—on May 12, 1923. I had forgotten that it *was* the first show, and even that 1923 was the year the stadium opened. In my true youth, the Yankees used to share the Polo Grounds with the Giants, and I had forgotten that, too, because I never cared much about baseball, although, come to think of it, I used to see the Yankees play occasionally in the 1910s, and should have remembered. I remembered the boxing show itself very well, though. It happened during the spring of my second suspension from college, and I paid five dollars for a high-grandstand seat. The program merely said that it had been "an all-star heavyweight bill promoted by Tex Rickard for the Hearst Milk Fund," but I found that I could still remember every man and every bout on the card. One of the main events was between old Jess Willard, the former heavyweight champion of the world, who had lost the title to Jack Dempsey in 1919, and a young heavyweight named Floyd Johnson. Willard had been coaxed from retirement to make a comeback because there was such a dearth of heavyweight material that Rickard thought he could still get by, but as I remember the old fellow, he couldn't fight a lick. He had a fair left jab and a right uppercut that a fellow had to walk into to get hurt by, and he was big and soft. Johnson was a mauler worse than Rex Layne, and the old man knocked him out. The other main event, *ex aequo*, had Luis Angel Firpo opposing a fellow named Jack McAuliffe II, from Detroit, who had had only fifteen fights and had never beaten anybody, and had a glass jaw. The two winners, of whose identity there was infinitesimal preliminary doubt, were to fight each other for the right to meet the great Jack Dempsey. Firpo was so crude that Marciano would be a Fancy Dan in comparison. He could hit with only one hand—his right—he hadn't the faintest idea of what to do in close, and he never cared much for the business anyway. He knocked McAuliffe out, of course, and then, in a later "elimination" bout, stopped poor old Willard. He subsequently became a legend by going one and a half sensational rounds with Dempsey, in a time that is now represented to us as the golden age of American pugilism.

I reflected with satisfaction that old Ahab Moore could have whipped all four principals on that card within fifteen rounds, and that while Dempsey may have been a great champion, he had less to beat than Marciano. I felt the satisfaction because it proved that the world isn't going backward, if you can just stay young enough to remember what it was really like when you were really young.

1955

HUB FANS BID KID ADIEU

JOHN UPDIKE

Fenway Park, in Boston, is a lyric little bandbox of a ballpark. Everything is painted green and seems in curiously sharp focus, like the inside of an old-fashioned peeping-type Easter egg. It was built in 1912 and rebuilt in 1934, and offers, as do most Boston artifacts, a compromise between Man's Euclidean determinations and Nature's beguiling irregularities. Its right field is one of the deepest in the American League, while its left field is the shortest; the high left-field wall, 315 feet from home plate along the foul line, virtually thrusts its surface at right-handed hitters. On the afternoon of Wednesday, September 28, as I took a seat behind third base, a uniformed groundkeeper was treading the top of this wall, picking batting-practice home runs out of the screen, like a mushroom gatherer seen in Wordsworthian perspective on the verge of a cliff. The day was overcast, chill, and uninspirational. The Boston team was the worst in twenty-seven seasons. A jangling medley of incompetent youth and aging competence, the Red Sox were finishing in seventh place only because the Kansas City Athletics had locked them out of the cellar. They were scheduled to play the Baltimore Orioles, a much nimbler blend of May and December, who had been dumped from pennant contention a week before by the insatiable Yankees. I, and 10,453 others, had shown up primarily because this was the Red Sox' last home game of the season, and therefore the last time in all eternity that their regular left fielder, known to the headlines as TED, KID, SPLINTER, THUMPER, TW, and, most cloyingly, MISTER WONDERFUL, would play in Boston. WHAT WILL WE DO WITHOUT TED? HUB FANS ASK ran the headline on a newspaper being read by a bulb-nosed cigar smoker a few rows away. Williams' retirement had been announced, doubted (he had been threatening retirement for years), confirmed by Tom Yawkey, the Red Sox owner, and at last widely accepted as the sad but probable truth. He was forty-two and had redeemed his abysmal season of 1959 with a—considering his advanced age—fine one. He had been giving away his gloves and bats and had grudgingly consented to a sentimental ceremony today. This was not necessarily his last game; the Red Sox were scheduled to travel to New York and wind up the season with three games there.

I arrived early. The Orioles were hitting fungos on the field. The day before, they had spitefully smothered the Red Sox, 17–4, and neither their faces nor their drab gray visiting-team uniforms seemed very gracious. I wondered who had invited them to the party. Between our heads and the lowering clouds a frenzied organ was thundering through, with an appositeness perhaps accidental, "You *maaaade* me love you, I didn't wanna do it, I didn't wanna do it . . ."

The affair between Boston and Ted Williams has been no mere summer romance; it has been a marriage, composed of spats, mutual disappointments, and, toward the end, a mellowing hoard of shared memories. It falls into three stages, which may be termed Youth, Maturity, and Age; or Thesis, Antithesis, and Synthesis; or Jason, Achilles, and Nestor.

First, there was the by now legendary epoch when the young bridegroom came out of the West, announced "All I want out of life is that when I walk down the street folks will say 'There goes the greatest hitter who ever lived.' " The dowagers of local journalism attempted to give elementary deportment lessons to this child who spake as a god, and to their horror were themselves rebuked. Thus began the long exchange of backbiting, bat flipping, booing, and spitting that has distinguished Williams' public relations. The spitting incidents of 1957 and 1958 and the similar dockside courtesies that Williams has now and then extended to the grandstand should be judged against this background: The left-field stands at Fenway for twenty years have held a large number of customers who have bought their way in primarily for the privilege of showering abuse on Williams. Greatness necessarily attracts debunkers, but in Williams' case the hostility has been systematic and unappeasable. His basic offense against the fans has been to wish that they weren't there. Seeking a perfectionist's vacuum, he has quixotically desired to sever the game from the ground of paid spectatorship and publicity that supports it. Hence his refusal to tip his cap to the crowd or turn the other cheek to newsmen. It has been a costly theory—it has probably cost him, among other evidences of goodwill, two Most Valuable Player awards, which are voted by reporters—but he has held to it from his rookie year on. While his critics, oral and literary, remained beyond the reach of his discipline, the opposing pitchers were accessible, and he spanked them to the tune of .406 in 1941. He slumped to .356 in 1942 and went off to war.

In 1946, Williams returned from three years as a Marine pilot to the second of his baseball avatars, that of Achilles, the hero of incomparable prowess and beauty who nevertheless was to be found sulking in his tent while the Trojans (mostly Yankees) fought through to the ships. Yawkey, a timber and mining maharajah, had surrounded his central jewel with many gems of slightly lesser water, such as Bobby Doerr, Dom DiMaggio, Rudy York, Birdie Tebbetts, and Johnny Pesky. Throughout the late forties, the Red Sox were the best paper team in baseball, yet they had little three-dimensional to show for it, and if this was a tragedy, Williams was Hamlet. A succinct review of the indictment—and a fair sample of appreciative sports-page prose—appeared the very day of Williams' valedictory, in a column by Huck Finnegan in the *Boston American* (no sentimentalist, Huck):

> Williams' career, in contrast [to Babe Ruth's], has been a series of failures except for his averages. He flopped in the only World Series he ever played in (1946) when he batted only .200. He flopped in the playoff game with Cleveland in 1948. He flopped in the final game of the 1949 season with the pennant hinging on the outcome (Yanks 5, Sox 3). He flopped in 1950 when he returned to the lineup after a two-month absence and ruined the morale of a club that seemed pennant-bound under Steve O'Neill. It has always been Williams' records first, the team second, and the Sox non-winning record is proof enough of that.

There are answers to all this, of course. The fatal weakness of the great Sox slugging teams was not-quite-good-enough pitching rather than Williams' failure to hit a home run every time he came to bat. Again, Williams' depressing effect on his teammates has never been proved. Despite ample coaching to the contrary, most insisted that they *liked* him. He has been generous with advice to any player who asked for it. In an increasingly combative baseball atmosphere, he continued to duck beanballs docilely. With umpires he was gracious to a fault. This courtesy itself annoyed his critics, whom there was no pleasing. And against the ten crucial games (the seven World Series games with the St. Louis Cardinals, the 1948 playoff with the Cleveland Indians, and the two-game series with the Yankees at the end of the 1949 season, winning either one of which would have given the Red Sox the pennant) that make up the Achilles' heel of Williams' record, a mass of statistics can be set showing that day in and day out he was no slouch in the clutch. The correspondence columns of the Boston papers now and then suffer a sharp flurry of arithmetic on this score; indeed, for Williams to have distributed all his hits so they did nobody else any good would constitute a feat of placement unparalleled in the annals of selfishness.

Whatever residue of truth remains of the Finnegan charge those of us who love Williams must transmute as best we can, in our own personal crucibles. My personal memories of Williams begin when I was a boy in Pennsylvania, with two last-place teams in Philadelphia to keep me company. For me, "W'ms, lf" was a figment of the box scores who always seemed to be going 3-for-5. He radiated, from afar, the hard blue glow of high purpose. I remember listening over the radio to the All-Star Game of 1946, in which Williams hit two singles and two home runs, the second one off a Rip Sewell "blooper" pitch; it was like hitting a balloon out of the park. I remember watching one of his home runs from the bleachers of Shibe Park; it went over the first baseman's head and rose meticulously along a straight line and was still rising when it cleared the fence. The trajectory seemed qualitatively different from anything anyone else might hit. For me, Williams is the classic ballplayer of the game on a hot August weekday, before a small crowd, when the only thing at stake is the tissue-thin difference between a thing done well and a thing done ill. Baseball is a game of the long season, of relentless and gradual averaging-out. Irrelevance—since the reference point of most individual games is remote and statistical—always threatens its interest, which can be maintained not by the occasional heroics that sportswriters feed upon but by players who always *care;* who care, that is to say, about themselves and their art. Insofar as the clutch hitter is not a sportswriter's myth, he is a vulgarity, like a writer who writes only for money. It may be that, compared to managers' dreams such as Joe DiMaggio and the always helpful Stan Musial, Williams is an icy star. But of all team sports, baseball, with its graceful intermittences of action, its immense and tranquil field sparsely settled with poised men in white, its dispassionate mathematics, seems to me best suited to accommodate, and be ornamented by, a loner. It is an essentially lonely game. No other player visible to my generation has concentrated within himself so much of the sport's poignance, has so assiduously refined his natural skills, has so constantly brought to the plate that intensity of competence that crowds the throat with joy.

By the time I went to college, near Boston, the lesser stars Yawkey had assembled around Williams had faded, and his craftsmanship, his rigorous pride, had become itself a kind of heroism. This brittle and temperamental player developed an unexpected quality of persistence. He was always coming back—back from Korea, back from a broken collarbone, a shattered elbow, a bruised heel, back from drastic bouts of flu and ptomaine poisoning. Hardly a season went by without some enfeebling mishap, yet he always came back, and always looked like himself. The delicate mechanism of timing and power seemed locked, shockproof, in some case outside his body. In addition to injuries, there were a heavily publicized divorce, and the usual storms with the press, and the Williams Shift—the maneuver, custom-built by Lou Boudreau, of the Cleveland Indians, whereby three infielders were concentrated on the right side of the infield, where a left-handed pull hitter like Williams generally hits the ball. Williams could easily have learned to punch singles through the vacancy on his left and fattened his average hugely. This was what Ty Cobb, the Einstein of average, told him to do. But the game had changed since Cobb; Williams believed that his value to the club and to the game was as a slugger, so he went on pulling the ball, trying to blast it through three men, and paid the price of perhaps fifteen points of lifetime average. Like Ruth before him, he bought the occasional home run at the cost of many directed singles—a calculated sacrifice certainly not, in the case of a hitter as average-minded as Williams, entirely selfish.

After a prime so harassed and hobbled, Williams was granted by the relenting fates a golden twilight. He became at the end of his career perhaps the best *old* hitter of the century. The dividing line came between the 1956 and the 1957 seasons. In September of the first year, he and Mickey Mantle were contending for the batting championship. Both were hitting around .350, and there was no one else near them. The season ended with a three-game series between the Yankees and the Sox, and, living in New York then, I went up to the Stadium. Williams was slightly shy of the four hundred at-bats needed to qualify; the fear was expressed that the Yankee pitchers would walk him to protect Mantle. Instead, they pitched to him—a wise decision. He looked terrible at the plate, tired and discouraged and unconvincing. He never looked very good to me in the Stadium. (Last week, in *Life*, Williams, a sportswriter himself now, wrote gloomily of the Stadium, "There's the bigness of it. There are those high stands and all those people smoking—and, of course, the shadows. . . . It takes at least one series to get accustomed to the Stadium and even then you're not sure.") The final outcome in 1956 was Mantle .353, Williams .345.

The next year, I moved from New York to New England, and it made all the difference. For in September 1957, in the same situation, the story was reversed. Mantle finally hit .365; it was the best season of his career. But Williams, though sick and old, had run away from him. A bout of flu had laid him low in September. He emerged from his cave in the Hotel Somerset haggard but irresistible; he hit four successive pinch-hit home runs. "I feel terrible," he confessed, "but every time I take a swing at the ball it goes out of the park." He ended the season with thirty-eight home runs and an average of .388, the highest in either league since his own .406, and, coming from a decrepit man of thirty-nine, an even more supernal figure. With eight or so of the "leg hits" that a younger man would have beaten out, it would have been .400. And the next year, Williams, who in 1949 and 1953 had lost batting championships by decimal whiskers to George Kell and Mickey Vernon, sneaked in behind his teammate Pete Runnels and filched his sixth title, a bargain at .328.

In 1959, it seemed all over. The dinosaur thrashed around in the .200 swamp for the first half of the season, and was even benched ("rested," Manager Mike Higgins tactfully said). Old foes like the late Bill Cunningham began to offer batting tips. Cunningham thought Williams was jiggling his elbows; in truth, Williams' neck was so stiff he could hardly turn his head to look at the pitcher. When he swung, it looked like a Calder mobile with one thread cut; it reminded you that since 1953 Williams' shoulders had been wired together. A solicitous pall settled over the sports pages. In the two decades since Williams had come to Boston, his status had imperceptibly shifted from that of a naughty prodigy to that of a municipal monument. As his shadow in the record books lengthened, the Red Sox teams around him declined, and the entire American League seemed to be losing life and color to the National. The inconsistency of the new superstars—Mantle, Colavito, and Kaline—served to make Williams appear all the more singular. And off the field, his private philanthropy—in particular, his zealous chairmanship of the Jimmy Fund, a charity for children with cancer—gave him a civic presence somewhat like that of Richard Cardinal Cushing. In religion, Williams appears to be a humanist, and a selective one at that, but he and the Cardinal, when their good works intersect and they appear in the public eye together, make a handsome and heartening pair.

Humiliated by his '59 season, Williams determined, once more, to come back. I, as a specimen Williams partisan, was both glad and fearful. All baseball fans believe in miracles; the question is, how *many* do you believe in? He looked like a ghost in spring training. Manager Jurges warned us ahead of time that if Williams didn't come through he would be benched, just like anybody else. As it turned out, it was Jurges who was benched. Williams entered the 1960 season needing eight home runs to have a lifetime total of 500; after one time at bat in Washington, he needed seven. For a stretch, he was hitting a home run every second game that he played. He passed Lou Gehrig's lifetime total, then the number 500, then Mel Ott's total, and finished with 521, thirteen behind Jimmy Foxx, who alone stands between Williams and Babe Ruth's unapproachable 714. The summer was a statistician's picnic. His two-thousandth walk came and went, his eighteen-hundredth run batted in, his sixteenth All-Star Game. At one point, he hit a home run off a pitcher, Don Lee, off whose father, Thornton Lee, he had hit a home run a generation before. The only comparable season for a forty-two-year-old man was Ty Cobb's in 1928. Cobb batted .323 and hit one homer. Williams batted .316 but hit twenty-nine homers.

In sum, though generally conceded to be the greatest hitter of his era, he did not establish himself as "the greatest hitter who ever lived." Cobb, for average, and Ruth, for power, remain supreme. Cobb, Rogers Hornsby, Joe Jackson, and Lefty O'Doul, among players since 1900, have higher lifetime averages than Williams' .344. Unlike Foxx, Gehrig, Hack Wilson, Hank Greenberg, and Ralph Kiner, Williams never came close to matching Babe Ruth's season home-run total of sixty. In the list of major-league batting records, not one is held by Williams. He is second in walks drawn, third in home runs, fifth in lifetime averages, sixth in runs batted in, eighth in runs scored and in total bases, fourteenth in doubles, and thirtieth in hits. But if we allow him merely average seasons for the four-plus seasons he lost to two wars, and add another season for the months he lost to injuries, we get a man who in all the power totals would be second, and not a very distant second, to Ruth. And if we further allow that these years would have been not merely average but prime years, if we allow for all the months when Williams was playing in sub-par condition, if we permit his early and later years in baseball to be some sort of index of what the middle years could have been, if we give him a right-field fence that is not, like Fenway's, one of the most distant in the league, and if—the least excusable "if"—we imagine him condescending to outsmart the Williams Shift, we can defensibly assemble, like a colossus induced from the sizable fragments that do remain, a statistical figure not incommensurate with his grandiose ambition. From the statistics that are on the books, a good case can be made that in the *combination* of power and average Williams is first; nobody else ranks so high in both categories. Finally, there is the witness of the eyes; men whose memories go back to Shoeless Joe Jackson—another unlucky natural—rank him and Williams together as the best-looking hitters they have seen. It was for our last look that ten thousand of us had come.

Two girls, one of them with pert buckteeth and eyes as black as vest buttons, the other with white skin and flesh-colored hair, like an underdeveloped photograph of a redhead, came and sat on my right. On my other side was one of those frowning, chestless young-old men who can frequently be seen, often wearing sailor hats, attending ball games alone. He did not once open his program but instead tapped it, rolled up, on his knee as he gave the game his disconsolate attention. A young lady, with freckles and a depressed, dainty nose that by an optical illusion seemed to thrust her lips forward for a kiss, sauntered down into the box seats and with striking aplomb took a seat right behind the roof of the Oriole dugout. She wore a blue coat with a Northeastern University emblem sewed to it. The girls beside me took it into their heads that this was Williams' daughter. She looked too old to me, and why would she be sitting behind the visitors' dugout? On the other hand, from the way she sat there, staring at the sky and French-inhaling, she clearly was *some*body. Other fans came and eclipsed her from view. The crowd looked less like a weekday ballpark crowd than like the folks you might find in Yellowstone National Park, or emerging from automobiles at the top of scenic Mount Mansfield. There were a lot of competitively well-dressed couples of tourist age, and not a few babes in arms. A row of five seats in front of me was abruptly filled with a woman and four children, the youngest of them two years old, if that. Someday, presumably, he could tell his grandchildren that he saw Williams play. Along with these tots and second-honeymooners, there were Harvard freshmen, giving off that peculiar nervous glow created when a quantity of insouciance is saturated with insecurity; thick-necked Army officers with brass on their shoulders and lead in their voices; pepperings of priests; perfumed bouquets of Roxbury Fabian fans; shiny salesmen from Albany and Fall River; and those gray, hoarse men—taxi drivers, slaughterers, and bartenders—who will continue to click through the turnstiles long after everyone else has deserted to television and tramporamas. Behind me, two young male voices blossomed, cracking a joke about God's five proofs that Thomas Aquinas exists—typical Boston College levity.

The batting cage was trundled away. The Orioles fluttered to the sidelines. Diagonally across the field, by the Red Sox dugout, a cluster of men in overcoats were festering like maggots. I could see a splinter of white uniform, and Williams' head, held at a self-deprecating and evasive tilt. Williams' conversational stance is that of a six-foot-three-inch man under a six-foot ceiling. He moved away to the patter of flash bulbs, and began playing catch with a young Negro outfielder named Willie Tasby. His arm, never very powerful, had grown lax with the years, and his throwing motion was a kind of muscular drawl. To catch the ball, he flicked his glove hand onto his left shoulder (he batted left but threw right, as every schoolboy ought to know) and let the ball plop into it comically. This catch session with Tasby was the only time all afternoon I saw him grin.

A tight little flock of human sparrows who, from the lambent and pampered pink of their faces, could only have been Boston politicians moved toward the plate. The loudspeakers mammothly coughed as someone huffed on the microphone. The ceremonies began. Curt Gowdy, the Red Sox radio and television announcer, who sounds like everybody's brother-in-law, delivered a brief sermon, taking the two words *pride* and *champion* as his text. It began, "Twenty-one years ago, a skinny kid from San Diego, California . . ." and ended, "I don't think we'll ever see another like him." Robert Tibolt, chairman of the board of the Greater Boston Chamber of Commerce, presented Williams with a big Paul Revere silver bowl. Harry Carlson, a member of the sports committee of the Boston Chamber, gave him a plaque, whose inscription he did not read in its entirety, out of deference to Williams' distaste for this sort of fuss. Mayor Collins presented the Jimmy Fund with a thousand-dollar check.

Then the occasion himself stooped to the microphone, and his voice sounded, after the others, very Californian; it seemed to be coming, excellently amplified, from a great distance, adolescently young and as smooth as a butternut. His thanks for the gifts had not died from our ears before he glided, as if helplessly, into "In spite of all the terrible things that have been said about me by the maestros of the keyboard up there . . ." He glanced up at the press rows suspended above home plate. (All the Boston reporters, incidentally, reported the phrase as "knights of the keyboard," but I heard it as "maestros" and prefer it that way.) The crowd tittered, appalled. A frightful vision flashed upon me, of the press gallery pelting Williams with erasers, of Williams clambering up the foul screen to slug journalists, of a riot, of Mayor Collins being crushed. ". . . And they *were* terrible things," Williams insisted, with level melancholy, into the mike. "I'd like to forget them, but I can't." He paused, swallowed his memories, and went on, "I want to say that my years in Boston have been the greatest thing in my life." The crowd, like an immense sail going limp in a change of wind, sighed with relief. Taking all the parts himself, Williams then acted out a vivacious little morality drama in which an imaginary tempter came to him at the beginning of his career and said, "Ted, you can play anywhere you like." Leaping nimbly into the role of his younger self (who in biographical actuality had yearned to be a Yankee), Williams gallantly chose Boston over all the other cities, and told us that Tom Yawkey was the greatest owner in baseball and we were the greatest fans. We applauded ourselves heartily. The umpire came out and dusted the plate. The voice of doom announced over the loudspeakers that after

Williams' retirement his uniform number, 9, would be permanently retired—the first time the Red Sox had so honored a player. We cheered.
The national anthem was played. We cheered. The game began.

Williams was third in the batting order, so he came up in the bottom
of the first inning, and Steve Barber, a young pitcher who was not yet
born when Williams began playing for the Red Sox, offered him
four pitches, at all of which he disdained to swing, since none of them
were within the strike zone. This demonstrated simultaneously that
Williams' eyes were razor-sharp and that Barber's control wasn't.
Shortly, the bases were full, with Williams on second. "Oh, I hope he
gets held up at third! That would be wonderful," the girl beside me
moaned, and, sure enough, the man at bat walked and Williams was
delivered into our foreground. He struck the pose of Donatello's David,
the third-base bag being Goliath's head. Fiddling with his cap, swap-
ping small talk with the Oriole third baseman (who seemed delighted
to have him drop in), swinging his arms with a sort of prancing nervousness, he looked fine—flexible, hard, and not unbecomingly substantial through the middle. The long neck, the small head, the
knickers whose cuffs were worn down near his ankles—all these points,
often observed by caricaturists, were visible in the flesh.
    One of the collegiate voices behind me said, "He looks old, doesn't
he, old; big deep wrinkles in his face . . ."
    "Yeah," the other voice said, "but he looks like an old hawk, doesn't
he?"
    With each pitch, Williams danced down the baseline, waving his
arms and stirring dust, ponderous but menacing, like an attacking
goose. It occurred to about a dozen humorists at once to shout "Steal
home! Go, go!" Williams' speed afoot was never legendary. Lou Clinton, a young Sox outfielder, hit a fairly deep fly to center field. Williams
tagged up and ran home. As he slid across the plate, the ball, thrown
with unusual heft by Jackie Brandt, the Oriole center fielder, hit him on
the back.
    "Boy, he was really loafing, wasn't he?" one of the boys behind me
said.
    "It's cold," the other explained. "He doesn't play well when it's cold.
He likes heat. He's a hedonist."
    The run that Williams scored was the second and last of the inning.

Gus Triandos, of the Orioles, quickly evened the score by plunking a home run over the handy left-field wall. Williams, who had had this wall at his back for twenty years, played the ball flawlessly. He didn't budge. He just stood there, in the center of the little patch of grass that his patient footsteps had worn brown, and, limp with lack of interest, watched the ball pass overhead. It was not a very interesting game. Mike Higgins, the Red Sox manager, with nothing to lose, had restricted his major-league players to the left-field line—along with Williams, Frank Malzone, a first-rate third baseman, played the game—and had peopled the rest of the terrain with unpredictable youngsters fresh, or not so fresh, off the farms. Other than Williams' recurrent appearances at the plate, the *maladresse* of the Sox infield was the sole focus of suspense; the second baseman turned every grounder into a juggling act, while the shortstop did a breathtaking impersonation of an open window. With this sort of assistance, the Orioles wheedled their way into a 4–2 lead. They had early replaced Barber with another young pitcher, Jack Fisher. Fortunately (as it turned out), Fisher is no cutie; he is willing to burn the ball through the strike zone, and inning after inning this tactic punctured Higgins' string of test balloons.

Whenever Williams appeared at the plate—pounding the dirt from his cleats, gouging a pit in the batter's box with his left foot, wringing resin out of the bat handle with his vehement grip, switching the stick at the pitcher with an electric ferocity—it was like having a familiar Leonardo appear in a shuffle of *Saturday Evening Post* covers. This man, you realized—and here, perhaps, was the difference, greater than the difference in gifts—really intended to hit the ball. In the third inning, he hoisted a high fly to deep center. In the fifth, we thought he had it; he smacked the ball hard and high into the heart of his power zone, but the deep right field in Fenway and the heavy air and a casual east wind defeated him. The ball died. Al Pilarcik leaned his back against the big "380" painted on the right-field wall and caught it. On another day, in another park, it would have been gone. (After the game, Williams said, "I didn't think I could hit one any harder than that. The conditions weren't good.")

The afternoon grew so glowering that in the sixth inning the arc lights were turned on—always a wan sight in the daytime, like the burning headlights of a funeral procession. Aided by the gloom, Fisher was slicing through the Sox rookies, and Williams did not come to bat in the seventh. He was second up in the eighth. This was almost certainly his last time to come to the plate in Fenway Park, and instead of merely cheering, as we had at his three previous appearances, we stood, all of us—stood and applauded. Have you ever heard applause in a ball-park? Just applause—no calling, no whistling, just an ocean of hand-claps, minute after minute, burst after burst, crowding and running together in continuous succession like the pushes of surf at the edge of the sand. It was a somber and considered tumult. There was not a boo in it. It seemed to renew itself out of a shifting set of memories as the kid, the Marine, the veteran of feuds and failures and injuries, the friend of children, and the enduring old pro evolved down the bright tunnel of twenty-one summers toward this moment. At last, the um-pire signaled for Fisher to pitch; with the other players, he had been frozen in position. Only Williams had moved during the ovation, switching his bat impatiently, ignoring everything except his cherished task. Fisher wound up, and the applause sank into a hush.

Understand that we were a crowd of rational people. We knew that a home run cannot be produced at will; the right pitch must be perfectly met and luck must ride with the ball. Three innings before, we had seen a brave effort fail. The air was soggy; the season was exhausted. Never-theless, there will always lurk, around a corner in a pocket of our knowledge of the odds, an indefensible hope, and this was one of the times, which you now and then find in sports, when a density of expec-tation hangs in the air and plucks an event out of the future.

Fisher, after his unsettling wait, was wide with the first pitch. He put the second one over, and Williams swung mightily and missed. The crowd grunted, seeing that classic swing, so long and smooth and quick, exposed, naked in its failure. Fisher threw the third time, Williams swung again, and there it was. The ball climbed on a diago-nal line into the vast volume of air over center field. From my angle, be-hind third base, the ball seemed less an object in flight than the tip of a towering, motionless construct, like the Eiffel Tower or the Tappan Zee Bridge. It was in the books while it was still in the sky. Brandt ran back to the deepest corner of the outfield grass; the ball descended beyond his reach and struck in the crotch where the bullpen met the wall, bounced chunkily, and, as far as I could see, vanished.

Like a feather caught in a vortex, Williams ran around the square of bases at the center of our beseeching screaming. He ran as he always ran out home runs—hurriedly, unsmiling, head down, as if our praise were a storm of rain to get out of. He didn't tip his cap. Though we thumped, wept, and chanted "We want Ted" for minutes after he hid in the dugout, he did not come back. Our noise for some seconds passed beyond excitement into a kind of immense open anguish, a wailing, a cry to be saved. But immortality is nontransferable. The papers said that the other players, and even the umpires on the field, begged him to come out and acknowledge us in some way, but he never had and did not now. Gods do not answer letters.

Every true story has an anticlimax. The men on the field refused to disappear, as would have seemed decent, in the smoke of Williams' miracle. Fisher continued to pitch, and escaped further harm. At the end of the inning, Higgins sent Williams out to his left-field position, then instantly replaced him with Carrol Hardy, so we had a long last look at Williams as he ran out there and then back, his uniform jogging, his eyes steadfast on the ground. It was nice, and we were grateful, but it left a funny taste.

One of the scholasticists behind me said, "Let's go. We've seen everything. I don't want to spoil it." This seemed a sound aesthetic decision. Williams' last word had been so exquisitely chosen, such a perfect fusion of expectation, intention, and execution, that already it felt a little unreal in my head, and I wanted to get out before the castle collapsed. But the game, though played by clumsy midgets under the feeble glow of the arc lights, began to tug at my attention, and I loitered in the runway until it was over. Williams' homer had, quite incidentally, made the score 4–3. In the bottom of the ninth inning, with one out, Marlin Coughtry, the second-base juggler, singled. Vic Wertz, pinch-hitting, doubled off the left-field wall, Coughtry advancing to third. Pumpsie Green walked, to load the bases. Willie Tasby hit a double-play ball to the third baseman, but in making the pivot throw Billy Klaus, an ex–Red Sox infielder, reverted to form and threw the ball past the first baseman and into the Red Sox dugout. The Sox won, 5–4. On the car radio as I drove home I heard that Williams had decided not to accompany the team to New York. So he knew how to do even that, the hardest thing. Quit.

1960

THE ONLY GAMES IN TOWN

ANTHONY LANE

According to Pythagoras, there were three types of men, just as there were three types of visitors to the Olympic Games. First and lowest were those who came to sell. Next, halfway up, were the competitors. And last, at the top of the pile, were the people who wanted to watch. The more you look at this ranking, the better it gets. Applied to life, it means a shoo-in for the slacker, the couch potato, and the tremulous voyeur. Applied to the Olympic Games, it makes it simpler for ordinary mortals to gaze upon Michael Phelps—half man, half osprey, with a wingspan three inches greater than his height. "To be honest, I had no idea I was going to go that fast," he said, addressing a press conference as if it were a bunch of traffic cops. The date was August 10, the place was Beijing, and Phelps had just spent a relaxing Sunday morning in the pool, slicing more than a second off his own world record. The event was the men's four-hundred-meter individual medley, in which swimmers are encouraged to prove that, short of dropping depth charges, there is nothing they can't do in the water. Nonetheless, all Phelps did was take a dip, whereas those of us lining the National Aquatics Center were the gods of the Games, the spectators, and that lifted us higher than him. Ask Pythagoras.

The victory was not without its hiccups. Phelps stepped onto the winner's podium, flanked by his compatriot Ryan Lochte, who had taken the bronze. (It's the old Ben Jonson problem: You're a fine playwright, and at any other time you'd be the best, but by lousy luck you happen to overlap with Shakespeare, who takes gold in every medley in town.) It was time for the winner's national anthem, which began with an ominous pop, settled down for a while, gathered itself for the finale, and then stopped. We got the land of the free, but apparently the home of the brave was no longer available. Did someone foreclose? Accidents will happen, but, as a rule, if you're going to screw up the national anthem of another country, especially a major trading partner, try not to do so when the president of that country is in the audience. George W. Bush was indeed in the Aquatics Center, standing at attention, and, even across ten lanes of water, I could tell that I was looking at a con-fused man. Was this insult calculated, and how should he react? The world held its breath. Somewhere nearby was a briefcase with the nu-clear launch codes, possibly held by a man wearing trunks. The crisis passed. The president sat down. The semifinals of the women's hun-dred-meter butterfly got under way. As for the Assistant Button-Pressing Technical Manager for National Anthem Digital Recording Systems (Aquatic Branch), I don't know the poor fellow's name, but his extended family has just been rehoused inside a hydroelectric dam.

The first week of the twenty-ninth Olympiad of the modern era, and the first to be held in China, was always going to be sprinkled with diplomatic tensions. Most were quickly diffused, and many were highly enjoyable. If, during the United States basketball team's casual flatten-ing of their Chinese opponents on Sunday night, you could bear to glance away from LeBron James and up to the stands, there was an ex-quisite awkwardness to be seen in the gestures of Yang Jiechi, the Chi-nese minister of foreign affairs, who was seated next to President Bush. As a matter of etiquette, how excitedly, if at all, should you applaud when your home team scores, given that your honored guest is of the enemy camp? Will the pride of that guest receive a dent? Even when Yao Ming, whose status in China is roughly equivalent to that of Simba at the end of *The Lion King,* opened the scoring in less than a minute, and the whole place went nuts, Yang contented himself with a few soft palm pats, just above his knees, and soon after that went into a perma-nent freeze of geniality.

To be fair, he had had a difficult weekend. On Saturday the ninth, the first full day of the Games, word came through of a stabbing. It turned out that Todd Bachman, the father-in-law of the U.S. men's vol-leyball coach, had been killed, and his wife, Barbara, severely injured, by a Chinese man. Later, an American couple, one of them an employee at the U.S. Embassy, told me how dismayed they were by the way the story spread, in particular by the rolling headline on a news website: "American killed at Olympics." "No, he wasn't," the wife said, and she was right: The couple wore nothing to identify them as Americans, and they were attacked at the Drum Tower, two miles south of the Olympic Green. Still, back home, the connection had been made: China was a danger zone. Among visitors to Beijing, there was a touch of sympathy for the Chinese, who were reminded the hard way, and at the worst time, that you can build a wall against organized threats from without but cannot legislate for the lone wretch with a knife who lurks within. Wang Wei, the executive vice president and secretary general of the Beijing Organizing Committee for the Games, said in response, "We are living in a world where surprises do happen." True enough, although his next phrase seemed to hail from a different world: "We reassure you that nothing like this is going to happen again." It is the imprint of certainty—the implication that fate itself can be bent back into position—that rings oddly in more jaded ears. The American swimmer Larsen Jensen was asked, after taking a bronze in the four-hundred-meter freestyle, if he had been nervous before the race. He said not: "That's what my father taught me. Only worry about the things you can control." The horse sense of Mr. Jensen, Sr., would not pass muster with the authorities in Beijing, where they try to control things until the worry goes away.

That is why the murder was a shock to the Olympic system. We know, in the end, that a sense of security is always false, yet the Beijing authorities had strained every sinew to tell us otherwise—to convince us, and themselves, that we had landed in a safe place. On the principle that every Western visitor is a sucker, to be wooed into believing that the grass is greener inside the fence, they made sure that security measures were not hammered home like rivets but tricked out with homely detail. To leave your hotel in the morning and have your bag and your person searched before you board a bus to the Olympic Green, as if it were a plane, is no hardship; indeed, from a professional point of view, to be felt up and patted down with such eager regularity has given me the first, helpful hint as to what life was like for Jean Harlow. And who would be left unmoved by the fake red velvet, edged in gold, that bedecks the plastic tray on which you are invited to lay your wallet? It was the same at Beijing Airport: The first thing I saw on arrival was a sniffer dog, but instead of some lunging German shepherd, with streaks of Baskerville-style foam along its jaws, there was a beagle. Now, beagles have been sniffing around U.S. airports for years, but this one was chasing a rubber ball. Running behind, at the end of its tether, was the dog's keeper, laughing gaily, and behind him, somewhere in the seven years since Beijing won the Olympic bid, was a committee dedicated solely to canine propaganda. As long as one mutt fancier from the tender-hearted West caught sight of the romping beagle and exclaimed to her husband, "Oh, look at little Snu Pi! See, they don't eat them, they play with them!" the committee's job was done.

The apotheosis of this effort was the opening ceremony at the National Stadium, on the evening of August 8. I arrived well in time for the crash course in audience participation. "The world has given its love and trust to China, and today China will give the world a big warm hug," one of the masters of ceremonies said. While admiring their faultless English, you had to wonder why they had chosen to learn it by watching *Barney's Great Adventure.* How, in less than twenty years, does a place go from mowing down student dissent with tanks to offering unconditional hugs? Was this a front, or had the government realized that the patois of mushy togetherness is now a lingua franca, not least in commercials, and thus well worth acquiring? On every seat was a sack of goodies, and we were duly taught to rattle our drums, wave our Chinese flags, shake our funky light sticks, and finally, at the avian highlight of the ceremony, "imitate the movement of the doves with your hands." Aside from the risk of developing repetitive wing injury, this was all too peaceful for me, and I felt a sudden, heretical yearning for the Paris Olympics of 1900, when the shooting competition used live pigeons. Twenty-one of them were blasted out of the skies by the gold medalist alone, and were presumably last seen heading for the kitchens of the Tour d'Argent. I prayed for something similar on the archery field, when a photographer strayed too close to the targets during the qualifying rounds, but a voice barked from the public-address system—"Please stand down"—and the chance was lost.

In the National Stadium, as the sky darkened and eight o'clock approached, a multitude of figures scuttled forward, each wheeling what appeared to be an outsized laundry basket. For a second, I feared a monstrous pantomime: Would a clown burst forth from every basket, tripping over a pile of sheets? I need not have fretted. They weren't baskets; they were illuminated drums. Cometh the hour, cometh the glowing red drumsticks, the heaving sea of blocks, the Brobdingnagian scroll unspooling before our eyes, and other miracles of visual manipulation. In the course of a long evening, billions of viewers were induced not so much to revise their opinion of China as to realize that its formidable manpower could be harnessed to the cause of astonishment.

China supports a population of 1.3 billion, and the knowledge of that resource was never far away; indeed, the whole evening became an exercise in number crunching, as mass art was constructed from a mass of humanity. One townful of men and women would race on, swarm into a shape, and race off, to be replaced by the next; if, deep below the spectacle, there was an unspoken suggestion that it would be an extremely bad idea to go to war against this nation, it never rose to the surface, although one aerial traveling shot of fireworks exploding in sequence along the street leading up to the stadium, displayed for us on screens inside, was a ringer for bombing-run footage from the Vietnam War.

The obvious precedent for Beijing was the Berlin Olympics, in 1936. Both were showcases for a muscle-flexing nation, although Hitler made an elementary error when he chose not to dress his young National Socialists in lime-green catsuits laced with twinkling fairy lights. By a careful choice of color scheme, China was able to draw the sting from any accusations of militarism, while rarely permitting the result to slide into camp. Whereas the organizers of the Sydney Olympics, in 2000, served up bicycling prawns without a murmur, this was a serious spectacle, and its climax—Li Ning, a former Olympic gymnast and now the owner of a leading sportswear brand, loping through the midnight air, in slow motion, around the inner rim of the stadium—was a pure crystallization of Chinese intent, the entrepreneurial fused with the wondrous. Shares in Li's company soared like the man himself, and that one night reportedly made his life sweeter by thirty million dollars.

Like Berlin's ceremony, Beijing's was entwined with cinema, and with the great expectations that movies leave in our mind's eye. The German Games were filmed by Leni Riefenstahl, and shaped into

Olympia (1938), just as the Nuremberg rallies were commemorated—
and their full meaning revealed—in her 1935 *Triumph of the Will*. The
artistic director of this year's ceremony was Zhang Yimou, recently the
director of *Hero* and *House of Flying Daggers*. His films have been
dreamily beautiful from the start, and, in a sense, to go from *Raise the
Red Lantern*, in 1991, to raising one vast, glowing, earthlike lantern
from the bowels of the National Stadium, with people standing on it at
every angle, like the Little Prince, is not so surprising a progression. But
there was a time, too, when Zhang made trouble for the Chinese authorities, who banned him from accepting a prize at the Cannes Film
Festival in 1994, and when his movies stared hard at the problems of
individual folk. He has softened since then, becoming a dazzling
arranger of hue and motion, and is now the favored son of his home-
land, but we no longer watch his work for the depth of the characters,
any more than we do Riefenstahl's. We watch them both and ask ourselves, what kind of society is it that can afford to make patterns out of
its people? India is hugely populous, too, but a Delhi opening ceremony
would be a more rambunctious affair. Nobody will ever surpass the
mathematical majesty of that night in Beijing, and, in retrospect, that
may be a good thing.

It will be scant consolation, however, to Lord Coe. Formerly Sebas-
tian Coe, part of the shining generation of British middle-distance
runners in the 1980s, he now heads the team that will bring the
Olympics to London in 2012. I tried to pick him out among the VIPs
on that first Friday, but without success. He may have been hiding in

the men's room, calling home to order more lightbulbs. You can imagine the rising panic in his voice: "They had two thousand and eight drummers, all lit up. Yes, two thousand and eight. And what have we got so far? Elton John on a trampoline." I trust that he emerged in time to enjoy the parade of national squads from participating countries, all 204 of them, serenaded by unlikely bands: bagpipes for Monaco, naturally, and a burst of mariachi music for the entrance of the Samoans.

A new academic discipline suggested itself: acoustipolitics, founded on the statistical correlation between the size of a cheer and the current state of relations between any given nation and its host. Thus, the Chinese roar for Pakistan far outstripped its muted reception of India, echoing a preference that harks back to the Cold War. The American team was greeted with an indecipherable blizzard of white noise. The flag bearer for Guam was lauded wholly, and deservedly, for being enormous; most of the female gymnasts could get a good night's sleep inside one of his shoes. A storm of applause even met Vladimir Putin as he rose to wave at his compatriots. He wore the polite smile of a man who knew—as the crowd did not yet know—that he had just dispatched his armored divisions to quell a vexatious neighbor. No doubt he was musing upon the wise words of Ban Ki-moon, the secretary-general of the United Nations, who had opened the proceedings, in a recorded speech, requesting all nations at war to lay down their arms and thus observe "the Olympic Truce." At least it was holding on the stadium field, where more than fifteen thousand bodies mixed and shimmered, girdled by an unbreakable ring of young women in short white tennis skirts, whose smiling never ceased. In less than ten hours, tiny Chinese weight lifters would start picking up lumps of metal as heavy as the man from Guam and holding them over their heads. The Games were under way.

There was much wrangling, ahead of the festivities, over the quality of the air. In all honesty, though, the atmosphere is not that bad: recent analysis uncovered a quantitative ratio of 85 percent nitrogen, 10 percent carbon dioxide, 4 percent oxygen, and 1 percent vichyssoise. On the first day of competition, I watched the cyclists pass through Tiananmen Square, near the start of their road race, and none of them seemed in danger of expiring. Logic suggested that they zip up the east side of the square, since they were heading that way anyhow, but politics demanded that they take the western route, and then hang a right. This allowed them to pass in a pretty blur beneath the portrait of Mao Zedong, who, having overseen the deaths of up to seventy million of his countrymen (and having earned a spot on their banknotes for his pains), was more than happy to survey a handful of fat-free Spaniards in red-and-yellow spandex. I watched the speeding procession in the company of the strapping Goss family, from Amsterdam, all of them rabid fans of volleyball. How did they rate the Dutch chances this year? "We have no volleyball team," Mr. Goss said, with infinite gloom. The Netherlands hadn't qualified. The Gosses would have to make do with the beach equivalent, which is to proper volleyball what Elvis's movies were to Elvis's music.

I hope that the Gosses dropped in to the Aquatics Center, the blue quilted cube at the heart of the Olympic Green, to see four of their compatriots win the women's four-by-one-hundred-meter freestyle relay—their first gold in the event since Berlin, in 1936. Relays, whether in the pool or on the track, are never a disappointment, in part because of the winners' communal delirium: Replays showed Marleen Veldhuis, who swam a storming final leg for the Netherlands, leaping improbably high from the water to punch the air when the official result flashed up. When Olympic swimming dries up for Veldhuis, as it must, she can always get a job at SeaWorld in Orlando, launching herself out of the deep end to take a herring with her front teeth from a nervous guy on a ladder. But relays compel us, too, because they forge a brief, comic link with our own fumbling experience of competition; one of the final track events at the Olympics is the four by four hundred meters, just as it is in high school meets, and when the American sprinters loused up a baton exchange in the men's four by one hundred in Athens, four years ago, I was able to murmur, in bitter fellow-feeling, "I did that, too"—not something that most of us can say to a pole-vaulter or a synchronized diver. The same thing happened with artistic gymnastics on the opening weekend, during the team qualifying rounds; as the Americans flipped and twisted on the central floor (whose surprising bounciness is apparent only when viewed from above), there was an empathetic moan to my left. One of the Italian girls, Francesca Benolli, was up on the balance beam, better known as the Official Olympic Human Life Metaphor. She was standing sideways on it, having a wobble. For a few seconds, she was no longer one of the master race from the Olympic Village, spotless in a silver leotard; she was all of us, gloved and scarved, flapping dumbly on our front paths on an icy morning.

Most people will stay home and watch the events on TV, having no other option, but be warned: What NBC chooses to broadcast is not the Olympic Games. They offer selected clips of selected American athletes, largely in major sports, sometimes hours after the event, whereas, if the bruised Olympic ideal still means anything, it means loosing yourself, for a couple of weeks, from the bonds of your immediate loyalties and tastes. It means watching live sports you didn't know you were interested in, played by countries you've never been to, at three o'clock in the morning—not just watching them, either, but getting into them, deluding yourself that you grasp the rules, offering the fruits of your instant expertise to anyone who will listen ("I think you'll find the second waza-ari counts as ippon"), and, most bewildering of all, losing your heart. If I didn't follow the horrors in Munich, in 1972, it wasn't just because I was too young to understand but because I was occupied with worshipping Lasse Virén, the bearded Finnish policeman who won both the five thousand and the ten thousand meters on the track.

The habit has never left me. To witness four or five events, from ringside, should be sufficient for any sports freak, but, slumping back into my room after midnight, steaming from a walk through hot polluted rain, my soul aquiver with Korean archers and other triumphant minorities, I still found the will to switch on CCTV, the main state-run Chinese channel, and catch the bronze-medal fight in men's lightweight judo. It was a playoff, or heave-off, between Rasul Boqiev, of Tajikistan, and Dirk van Tichelt, of Belgium, and there was no doubt who would score ippon and thereby gain the prize. The Belgian seemed out of gas before he began, pink-browed and gulping for breath, unlike the sterling Boqiev, who looked as if he should be on horseback, surveying the steppe with a falcon on his wrist. At the instant of victory, he raised both hands wide in gratitude to his god, his thumbs strapped and—as is compulsory for judokas, according to *The Complete Book of the Olympics,* by David Wallechinsky—his fingernails trimmed.

The newest edition of Wallechinsky's masterpiece, which he compiled with his nephew Jaime Loucky, may be the most entertaining book ever written. Where else can you read of Martinho de Araujo, the tragic weight lifter from East Timor, who, only eight years ago, having lost his training equipment in the war of independence, "was forced to create a makeshift bar by sticking a pole in buckets of wet cement"? As for Eva Klobukowska, the Polish sprinter who won two medals at Tokyo, in 1964, and became the first athlete to fail a sex test, I wouldn't have believed it were it not for the photograph supplied by Wallechinsky, which confirms that the lady in question resembled Harry Dean Stanton after an evening of rye and Lucky Strikes. Meanwhile, the ever-bristling issue of drugs is put into vivid perspective by Chris Finnegan, the Cassius Clay of Old England. In 1968, he won the middleweight title, fair and square, but failed miserably when it came to the provision of a urine sample. It wasn't that he wouldn't; he just couldn't. "Now, if there's one thing I've never been able to do, it's have a piss while someone's watching me," the eloquent bricklayer explained. "I can never stand at those long urinals you get in gents' bogs, with all the other blokes having a quick squint." Oh, for a new Finnegan, forty years on. It isn't the doping officials I would worry for; it's the Chinese interpreters.

Wallechinsky's guide was with me as I arrived for the water polo. Thanks to him, I was primed to note the fine distinctions between the three kinds of foul that can be committed in the course of a game; after a minute, I laid the book aside, having realized that all three were being committed all the time by everybody. The rules and infringements of this ancient sport are of a solemn complexity, but all are founded on the fundamental desire of one person to treat another as a tea bag. You find your opposite number, grab him (or her), and dunk, regardless of whether the ball is anywhere in the vicinity; neck holding is especially popular, involving, as it does, much frantic splashing on the part of the drowner, and the whole exercise looks weirdly like a lifesaving class, except that the motive is reversed. The sport rode a big wave in 1924, when the American Olympic team in Paris included Johnny Weissmuller—presumably without his chimp, although with water polo it could be hard to tell.

I got to watch America versus China, an appetizer for the basketball encounter later in the day. (America won both.) The water polo took place at the Yingdong Natatorium, which cries out to be modified, once the Games are over, into a global forum for nonsense verse. How can you not love a sport in which, as a hooter signals the start of the game, the public-address system plays the theme from *Jaws,* and the two central attackers sprint-crawl for the ball, which bobs gently in the center of the pool? The halftime entertainment was a moist echo of the opening ceremony: ten young Chinese women in wipe-clean dresses with transparent hems, whacking cylindrical drums filled with running water. It was chaos, in perfect harmony. Four older women had to bustle on afterward with buckets and mops to sponge up the mess. China, in its restless drive for invention, was busy creating needs, like drum-water clearance, that had never existed before, in the confidence that it would always have enough people to meet them. Lord knows what the later stages of the Games will bring, but rest assured: if there are flaming violinists, there will be dedicated musical firefighters standing by with a hose.

Are the Chinese right, however, to douse each conflagration? Olympic history is a merry mixture of sportsmanship and fracas, and the prevailing wish, among aficionados in Beijing, is that the remaining days should pass off peacefully, but not so peacefully that only the boxers get to throw a punch. Croatia and Serbia made a promising start at the Yingdong, with misconduct so unrelenting that three players and a coach were thrown out of the game—shades of Melbourne, in 1956, when the Hungarians, enraged by the Soviet invasion of their country, used water polo as the weapon it was always meant to be. "There was blood in the pool," Donald Hook, an Australian who was there, told me. On August 12, I traveled in similar high hopes to the China Agriculture University Gymnasium, a pleasant spot, where the plan was that Lasha Gogitadze, of Georgia, should bump up against the Russian Nazyr Mankiev in Greco-Roman wrestling, thus prolonging, and perhaps inflaming, a situation that everyone else on the planet was trying to subdue. If all went well, they could aim to smash the record set in 1912, by Russia's Martin Klein and Finland's Alfred Asikainen, whose countries weren't at war but who nonetheless grappled manfully with each other for eleven hours. Regrettably, Gogitadze and Mankiev never came to blows, although I did see Roman Amoyan, a cuboid Armenian who had just won a bronze medal bout, bellow his delight toward an Azerbaijani section of the crowd. That takes nerve.

And thus the attempt to keep politics out of sport, which is as futile as trying to keep the sweat out of sex, began to falter once more. Tempers began to splinter. On the evening of August 11, a cream-colored armored car appeared outside the Main Press Center, half a mile from the National Stadium. In a far from plausible piece of window dressing, it was encircled by a red rope, like Angelina Jolie at a première, and its gun was sheathed in green wrapping. Was that a threat or a subtle joke, on the part of the Chinese military, about the muzzling of a free press? In the same way that President Bush was flummoxed by the buttocks of Misty May-Treanor, as proffered to him during a beach volleyball match, so none of us knew how to treat the armored car. Should we slap it or tap it? In the event, we gave it a quick squint, as Chris Finnegan would say, and walked on by.

2008

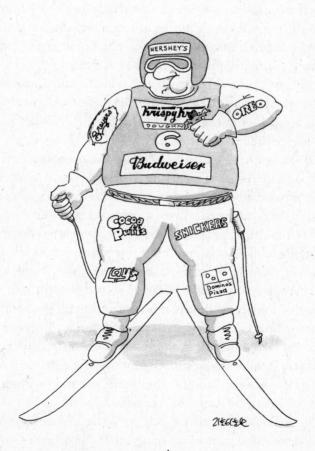

RACE TRACK

BILL BARICH

I am not by nature a compulsive gambler, so it came as a surprise to me when I started playing the horses compulsively. This happened some years ago, during a bleak midwinter season I spent on Long Island. I was visiting my mother, who had cancer. She was a good patient, easy to be around, but the progress of her disease was mean and slow and often difficult to witness. Whenever it overwhelmed me, I left the house and took a walk through the old neighborhood. One afternoon, I passed something I'd never seen before, an Off-Track Betting parlor, and stopped in and made a blind two-dollar bet on a horse named Quiet Little Table, who was running at Aqueduct, and then went home and listened to a broadcast of the race on the radio. Quiet Little Table dropped from contention in the stretch, but the race was still electric, and made my heart pound and my body feel light and untroubled. Even my mother, who had always cautioned her children against gambling, seemed excited; I thought some adrenaline might have seeped into her system and briefly relieved her pain.

The next thing I knew, I was driving to the newsstand every morning to buy a *Daily Racing Form* from a sleepy-eyed Romeo who peppered his otherwise salacious conversation with hot tips. The *Form* is an indispensable publication that gives a compact symbolic history of the horses entered in the day's races at major tracks nearby. Beginners usually find it unwieldy, since it offers more information than anybody could possibly absorb, including a horse's age, sex, color, parentage, birthplace, breeder, owner, trainer, racing record over the past two years, and amount of money won, but most serious gamblers won't make a wager without first studying its contents. At home, I spread the *Form* on the kitchen table and began the perilous exercise known as handicapping, which involves weighing the merits and defects of all the entrants in a given race over and over until the apparent winner emerges. The most telling facts were to be found in the past-performance records. These blocks of statistics, one per horse, showed in copious detail just how well that horse had done in its most recent outings: the fractional times for each of its races; the running line, or exactly where it had been positioned during five different phases—first call, second call, third call, stretch call, and finish—of each race; the caliber of competition it had been facing; its relative speed and preferred distance; and several other factors essential to the handicapping process. I had studied the *Form* before, but never with such intensity; now I bent to the pages like an adept parsing mystical texts. Sometimes they were runic, impossible to decipher, but at other times winners stepped readily forward to speak their names.

When I finished handicapping, I went to the OTB office to fill out my betting slips. I liked to watch people come in and slowly erode the antisepsis of the place, jabbing wet cigar butts into polished ashtrays and dragging muddy boots over clean tile floors. They were intent, blind to their surroundings, and they all looked terrific, at least until the first race had gone off. Optimism put a bloom on every cheek. Anything might happen, could happen, probably *would* happen—that was the notion being entertained at OTB. If you hit the triple, you might walk out the door a millionaire, your pockets crammed with greenbacks. Even the fat man, who was otherwise shrewd, believed this. I met him one afternoon when he squeezed in next to me at the counter. He was so big his trousers had been split at the seam and stretched out by the addition of a panel of unmatching cloth. He had diabetes, he said, and a bum ticker about to burst, and he'd been holed up at his sister's house in Hempstead since Thanksgiving. His own home was in Des Moines, but he couldn't bring himself to go back there. "No OTB in Iowa," he said, and I knew exactly what he meant.

After my mother's funeral, I flew back to Northern California, where I was renting a small house overlooking a river. The river had once been a prime steelhead stream, but now, with the gravel necessary for spawning being excavated, and a dam about to be built, the fish were scarce. But I still anticipated a fresh start, some sort of release.

Early in 1978, I made my escape. I could have chosen a romantic spot—Dubrovnik, Tahiti, or even Florence, where I'd spent many happy hours when I was younger—but I remembered the electricity I'd experienced on Long Island, and decided on a race track: Golden Gate Fields, in Albany, near San Francisco and Oakland. Elegantly situated on Point Fleming, a rocky outcrop that extends into the eastern portion of San Francisco Bay, Golden Gate is a slightly run-down plant featur-

ing indifferent and often curious racing early in the week and more bet-
table affairs toward the weekend. The plant encompasses 225 acres,
with stalls for 1,425 horses, seats for 13,004 human beings, and enough
space over all to cram in a crowd of thirty thousand, although no such
crowd has materialized of late. In 1978, the daily attendance averaged
9,317, down 8 percent from the previous year, while the handle remained firm at about $1,450,000. The average fan wagered $155 every
time through the turnstiles. Two separate racing associations, Pacific
and Tanforan, sponsor meetings at the track. The Pacific meeting usually begins in late January or early February and runs through mid-
April; Tanforan, which is always shorter, ends early in June. Between
them, the associations distribute purses totaling seven million dollars
over ninety-some racing days. The grandstand at Golden Gate, like
grandstands everywhere, is divided into levels connotative of social
class: General Admission, Clubhouse, Turf Club, and the exclusive Directors' Room, a glass-fronted enclosure where the track's directors and
their guests can eat, drink, and wager without plebeian interference. To
the left of the Turf Club and the press box, just beyond the executive offices, there was until quite recently a penthouse apartment reserved for
special friends of the management. Rumor has it that Jimmy Durante
once spent a honeymoon there, but nobody seems to know whether he
won or lost.

In Albany, I had difficulty finding a place to stay. There were a few
motels near the track, but their managers seemed to live in perpetual
fear of guests. One woman spoke to me through a round metal speaker
set into a shield of Plexiglas. Her voice had the absolute timbre of
creaking hinges. "We're all full," she said, but her VACANCY sign was
still blinking when I drove off. At the next motel, I rang the bell five
times, but nobody answered. When I looked through the office window, I saw an old man reclining in a lounger, his paper open to the racing page. Finally, I settled in at the Terrace Motel, in El Cerrito—a
decent place with friendly owners, clean rooms and apartments, three-
legged chairs propped against the walls, and a swimming pool. I never
saw anybody in that pool, not once. The Terrace's population was constantly shifting, except for an Indian who wore his hair in braids and a
few track employees and elderly people who rented apartments, which
were in a building adjacent to the main motel. On warm evenings, just
at twilight, somebody there played songs like "The Impossible Dream"

on a very percussive piano, reminding me of every cocktail lounge I'd ever been in, and the solace of bourbon over ice.

On April 18, the night before the Tanforan meeting began, I sat at my imitation-wood-veneer desk and prepared to handicap the following day's races. I had no system or standard approach, but there were a few things I always took into account before making a tentative selection: *speed*, which could be gauged in general fashion from a horse's recent running times; *class*, which was a function both of breeding and of the level at which a horse had been competing (races were ranked by the size of the purse offered, stakes first, then allowance and handicap, then claiming and maiden); and *condition*, which meant fitness and was expressed by a horse's recent finishes (if they were good or improving, the horse was said to be "on form") and by its showing during the daily exercise period (workout times were given at the bottom of each horse's past-performance record). The trainer and the jockey associated with a horse also affected my decision. Certain trainers were downright inept and never won a race regardless of their stock, and not a few riders at Golden Gate were incapable of handling their mounts.

I also considered post position as a potential factor in the outcome of a race. Before leaving home, I had compiled a post-position survey of races run during the Pacific meeting, which was just ending. I'd done this to see if a horse gained an advantage by breaking from a particular post (the slot a horse is assigned in the starting gate; there are rarely more than twelve horses entered in a race). Moreover, I had wanted to determine whether front-runners—horses who break quickly, take the lead, and try to hold it throughout (going wire to wire)—fared better at Golden Gate than one would expect. The results proved instructive. In races over a mile, called routes, the outside posts, seven through twelve, were as disadvantageous as usual; horses stuck out there had more ground to cover. In races under a mile, called sprints, the survey turned up a surprise. Ordinarily, the best posts in a short race are those closest to the rail, but during the Pacific meet horses starting near the middle of the track, at posts four and five, had won more often than horses inside them. Furthermore, horses breaking from the seven slot had won almost as often as those breaking from the one slot. I discovered as well that front-runners won more than 30 percent of all sprints at Golden Gate. Facts like these can be invaluable when you're trying to choose between two otherwise closely matched Thoroughbreds.

To give me an additional edge, I'd brought along three books on handicapping technique: Tom Ainslie's *Complete Guide to Thoroughbred Racing*, Andrew Beyer's *Picking Winners*, and Steven Davidowitz's *Betting Thoroughbreds*. These books were not typical of the genre; most handicapping tracts are lurid affairs that sucker readers into parting with a few dollars in exchange for an easy-to-follow system guaranteed to produce eight million dollars in just three short weeks. Ainslie, Beyer, and Davidowitz were serious, intelligent men who never underestimated the complexity of the sport. Ainslie was the dean of the company. His book was the most informative about all aspects of racing and is still the best primer around. He favored a balanced approach to making a selection—weighing all the factors, much as I had been doing. Beyer was more dogmatic. As an undergraduate at Harvard, he'd got hooked on racing, and he had since "perfected" a system based on the digital-computer research of Sheldon Kovitz, a fellow student and a doctoral candidate in mathematics. Apparently, Kovitz was too busy feeding numbers into his IBM 360 Model 40 to succeed at handicapping himself, but Beyer saw in his calculations the seed of Something Big, a way to incorporate relativity into speed ratings. Most ratings, like those given in the *Form,* were suspect, because they were derived from nonexistent absolutes. A horse who had earned an 80 on Tuesday was not *exactly* as fast as a horse who had earned an 80 on Wednesday, because the track surface changed every day (or even from moment to moment), and Tuesday's conditions were always different from Wednesday's—faster or slower by critical fractions. Beyer adopted Kovitz's method, improved it, and parlayed the results into a complicated mathematical system. It was the best in the world, he claimed. "Speed figures are the way, the truth, and the light," wrote Beyer. "And my method of speed handicapping is, I believe, without equal." I found Davidowitz's book the most pithy and accessible. He seemed a little tougher than the other men, more hard-nosed, and it showed in his jacket photo. While Ainslie looked like a businessman and Beyer like a computer programmer with a side interest in recreational drugs, Davidowitz looked mean. His face had a demonic cast; an eyebrow was arched in perpetual scrutiny. I liked the knack he had for making direct, incontrovertible statements: *When a three-year-old is assigned actual top weight in a race for horses three years and up, the three-year-old has little or no chance of winning.* Such gems were inlaid throughout the text, always supported by statistics. Davidowitz further endeared himself to me by being quick to point a finger at the criminal element in racing whenever he encountered it. Most turf writers were unwilling to print anything but bland idealizations of the sport.

After skimming through the books, I put all the materials aside and reached into my pocket, as I'd been doing every hour or so since leaving home. Again I counted my money—five hundred dollars in twenty-dollar bills. It looked pitiful stacked on the desk, the smallest stake any would-be gambler ever started with. I felt embarrassed. I thought that the stake was correlated directly with my life: empty wallet, impoverished spirit. Such stupid flashes of guilt often overtook me after midnight. I tried to ignore this one, though, and took a shower and went to bed.

Early the next morning, I went to Golden Gate Fields ready to win. The grandstand was empty and quiet, with the cool feel of a stainless-steel mixing bowl waiting for ingredients. The sun climbed slowly over the eucalyptus trees on Albany Hill—huge blue gums, planted there a century ago to shield the town from the booming of the dynamite factory that had once occupied the point. From the clubhouse railing, I could see the backstretch and the neat rows of wooden barns and the soiled straw piled high at the corners of the rows. The hot-walking machines were turning. They were a recent addition to the track and had made obsolete a job that grooms used to do—walking horses until they'd cooled down after exercising. Each machine consisted of a power pack from which rose a thin shaft with four metal arms at the top forming a horizontal cross. The arms were about six feet long and were about eight feet above the ground. When the power was on, the shaft rotated slowly, and the horses, hitched by their halters to insulated cords dangling from the arms, were forced to circle until their pulse rates dropped and their breathing was not so labored. As they circled, they looked like flywheels turning within the greater geometry of the backstretch, suggesting an intricate timepiece thrown open to bits of biology.

I took the escalator down to the ground floor and toured the vacant paddock. The green wear-forever carpet was worn thin, the railings were chipped and needed paint, and the saddling stalls, green and white, were scarred with half-moons and incised by hooves. I walked over to the infield, crossing the track and then the turf course, which was not nearly as lush and smooth as it had looked from above—weeds and crabgrass gave it a stubbly texture. The par-three course on the in-field green was soon to be closed for lack of patronage, but an OPEN sign hung in the pro-shop window. I heard a harrow going by, and turned to watch it work the track. House sparrows followed behind it, pecking at seeds the harrow had uncovered and hopping around among the horse apples. Nearby, two redwing blackbirds were mating in the caked mud of a drainage ditch. The male's epaulets were scarlet, brilliantly exposed as he drew his lover into a caped embrace.

About eleven-thirty, fans began arriving in steady streams, and as I watched them come in I had the sense of a form evolving, something entirely apart from horses and jockeys. It was modeled on notions of symmetry and coherence. The electronic devices around the track rein-forced the fiction in the warmup patterns they flashed: The infield tote board showed four rows of zeros balanced one on top of another, the smaller totes inside offered odds of five to five at every slot, and the closed-circuit TVs featured tiny dots boxed at perfect intervals within a neatly squared grid. The gift-shop lady displayed her horsehead book-ends in a horseshoe-shaped arc, and the popcorn lady, her striped smock in harmony with the trim of her booth, checked to see that the empty cardboard boxes she would later fill were distributed in evenly matched stacks. The fiction was carefully, if unconsciously, projected, and didn't begin to dissipate until the national anthem had been played and the horses came sauntering up from the barns in single file for the first race. Then order gave way to chaos.

The moment when horses enter the paddock before a race can be a bad one. Statistics that had earlier seemed so definitive are translated peremptorily into flesh, and flesh is heir to miseries—bandaged legs, a limp, a nervous froth bubbling on a filly's neck. Many times, I've heard people groan when they saw what their figures had led them to—some poor creature with downcast eyes. I was fortunate on the opening day of Tanforan. The horse I'd chosen at the Terrace, Southern Gospel, looked good. He was a rangy chestnut gelding with a polish to his coat. He was breaking from the preferential five hole, too, which should have set my mind at ease, but I was feeling anxious. I'd been away from the track for some time, and my responses to its stimuli were heightened, exaggerated. Every flickering movement made an impression on me, and I tried to take each into account. Suddenly, other horses began looking good. Folklore's Lite, who'd earned a high Beyer speed rating, was up on his toes. When I opened the *Form* to compare him with Southern Gospel, I saw instead something I'd missed before—excellent workouts for Top Pass. Was Top Pass ready to make his bid? David-owitz might think so. The more I read, the more confused I became. The *Form* kept bursting open, punctured by discoveries, ruining my cartographic efforts.

Next, I felt the concentrative energy of the bettors around me. They were staring at the paddock just as piercingly as I was, working hard to affect the outcome of the race. It was as though many versions of reality were competing for a chance to obtain. The man next to me was steaming. He wore the intense expression of a monk in his tenth hour of *zazen;* smoke was about to issue from his ears. I stood there paralyzed, unable to make a choice. I was afraid that if I lost my first bet, a downward trend would be irreversibly established. With three minutes to go, I ran to the windows and bet a horse I hadn't even considered before, Spicy Gift, because I had noticed that he'd had some bad luck last time out, which indicated, absolutely, that he was bound, perhaps even *compelled,* to win. When I walked away, I realized I'd just put ten bucks on a twenty-to-one shot. Handicapping overkill, the brain weaving useless webs. Spicy Gift finished somewhere in the middle of the field, beaten by Bargain Hostess, a filly and first-time starter who broke from the outermost post. These factors had eliminated her from contention in my mind; now I saw them for what they were—markers of talent.

But it was too late, I was locked into a loser's mind-set and couldn't shake free of it. All day long, I compounded my mistakes, playing the most improbable nags on the card, hoping to get even, to start over, the slate wiped clean, Hong Kong Flew, Skinny Dink, throwing what little expertise I had out the window, Hey Mister M.A., a toad at fifty-seven to one, *giving* it away, then Queequeg in the eighth race because of Melville and what they'd found taped to the inside of his desk after he died, a scrap of paper on which he'd written *Keep true to the dreams of thy youth,* but Queequeg drowned, too, leaving me adrift, not even a coffin for support, and in the ninth, a broken man, I latched on to the favorite, Crazy Wallet, and watched in disgust as he hobbled home fifth. Down I went, spiralling, down and down, done in but good, sixty dollars fed irretrievably into the belly of the beast and still the breeze did blow.

The whiskey at the Home Stretch bar was soothing, lucid, unstatistical, and I sipped it and stared at the photographs on the back-bar wall: pictures of horses and people, and a large oil painting of Emmett Kelly, the clown, his bumhat wreathed in losing tickets. About seven o'clock, a skinny man in a new denim leisure suit came in, accompanied by a short, silent Mexican who looked as though he'd just eaten a shoe.

"Glad you're alive," the bartender said to the Mexican, grinning sarcastically. "You want more Cutty and Seven, or'd you get enough last night?"

"Give him a beer," the other man said. "He doesn't need any Cutty. He was sick all over the barn this morning. Somebody else had to rub his horses. Isn't that right?"

The Mexican smiled happily and drank his beer.

A slim blond girl, barely out of her teens, was dancing with a man even smaller than the Mexican. He was jockey-size and had the powerful shoulders and arms that jockeys often develop. The blonde drank a beer as she danced, tipping back the bottle and closing her eyes. When the music ended, she came over to the man in the leisure suit, pushed out her chest, and asked to borrow twenty dollars. "I have three tickets I can cash in tomorrow," she said. "I've been holding on to them. As soon as I cash in, I'll pay you back."

"Honey," the man said, not unkindly, "that story has a beard."

She shrugged, looking unruffled, as though she made this pitch on a daily basis and expected a certain percentage of turndowns, and went back to the jockey-size man and asked him for five dollars. When he delivered, she used part of the money to buy a six-pack, then fed the jukebox and started dancing with another man, also very small, and when the music stopped this time, she left with him, wiggling her compact hips.

"You ever see anybody who *needs* money forget to cash in?" the man in the leisure suit asked. "No way. Does not happen. That girl loves jockeys. I think she might be a groupie."

The Home Stretch was often like this—friendly, wistful, and a little ragged at the edges. Grooms, trainers, winners, losers, mailmen, any and all of them were likely to wander in and sit down and order a drink and then tell you their life story, or, at least, the most immediate part of it, how they'd dropped a sawbuck on a sure thing only to see the horse go wide on the turn and wind up in the parking lot. The day bartender, Benny, a cigar-chomping five-by-fiver out of a Joe Palooka comic strip, ran the place with an iron hand and brooked no displays of unnecessary roughness. He yelled as loudly at friends as at enemies. "Whaddaya want? A Bud? Speak up. Can't *hear* you!" Once, I heard somebody say to him, "Benny, like you to meet a friend of mine, he's a nice guy." Benny frowned. "We're *all* nice guys in here," he said. On the wall there was a photo of him and Rocky Marciano. Benny had his head on the Rock's shoulder and he was smiling like a baby. After dark, when the regulars disappeared, the Home Stretch underwent a subtle transformation. Drunken grooms began talking to themselves, and pale outsiders with unauthorized business to effect somewhere in the night sat alone and sipped iced gin, their eyes on the clock.

In the morning, I felt better. Morning is the best, the most optimistic, time at any race track; everything seems possible again. Some mornings when I left the Terrace early, just after six, to watch the horses working out, the dawn light filtering through the fog on the bay echoed the gold I'd seen in painted halos all over Florence. I thought I could feel its healing properties. Out on the freeway, the first commuters were tangling, but from where I stood along the rail I was aware only of the animals. Around me there rose the smells of manure, tobacco, coffee, and new-mown grass, and I found myself agreeing implicitly with Slaughterhouse Red, the gateman who supervised the comings and goings of riders, when he raised his abused face to the sun and said, "Anybody don't like *this* life is daffy!" Red was a former cowboy who had grown up in the old Butchertown section of San Francisco and had earned his keep as a boy by herding cattle from stockyard trains to the slaughterhouses lining the streets. He worked at the track until noon and then, if the weather was good, left for Martinez, where his fishing boat was docked. If the weather was only fair, or if an old buddy was in town, or even if he just had the itch, he stayed around for the afternoon's races. Once in a while, if the itch was bad, he'd drive directly from Golden Gate to Bay Meadows, some thirty-odd miles to the south, so he could catch the quarter-horse races held there at night.

Horses came up from the barns in constant process, differing appreciably in their approach. Some looked half awake, some looked sore, and some looked lazy. Some kicked up their heels because they were feeling good, while others, the rogues in need of stricter handling, bucked and snorted and let it be understood that they were performing under duress. The true race horses were always ready. They took to the track prancing, and when they returned from a gallop they were slick with sweat and their veins protruded in marmoreal splendor. A few of them wanted to keep right on running, and their riders were forced to hold them tight, pulling in on the reins, which put a crook in the animals' necks and gave the horses the look of knights on a chessboard. They were beautiful. Ponies and human beings were interspersed among them, but they provided the movement, the exhilaration. Back at the barns, they were bathed and brushed, then hooked to hot-walkers and set to circling. Everywhere I looked, I saw horses—chestnuts, bays, browns, and blacks—and I felt locked within the clashing perspective of a battle scene painted by Paolo Uccello.

Right from the start, horses move fast. A mare gives birth in something between fifteen and thirty minutes, and during parturition her foal, born with eyes open, begins to pull away, tugging its legs out of the vagina and breaking the umbilical cord. In less than an hour, the foal is standing and looking around, and in two hours it can suckle, walk, vocalize, and show affection for its mother. Before the first day is out, the foal can trot, gallop, protect itself from insects by nipping, kicking, and shaking its tail, play, and even forage. The mare's milk gives the foal antibodies and serves as a purgative. Even the digestive system of horses is geared to acceleration. They process food almost twice as fast as cows and can live on poor-quality graze, because their digestive system rapidly transforms any available protein into amino acids. But they have to eat twice as much, twice as fast, and their teeth are sometimes worn down to the jawbone by the high silica content of grass. In the wild, horses without teeth starve to death. Race horses are fed hay and oats with an occasional taste of mash—a healthy, balanced diet—but their relatives in other parts of the world exist on oddments like grapevines, lawn clippings, compost, bamboo leaves, and dried fish. Whatever they eat passes quickly through them. They defecate from five to twelve times a day and urinate from seven to eleven times. They have a normal body temperature of 100.3 degrees Fahrenheit, which they maintain by shivering and sweating. The panniculus muscle, just beneath their skin, allows them to shake off excess moisture, along with pesky flies, and acts as a thermostatic control.

Horses don't see very well, especially close up. They are often astigmatic, and suffer, too, from color blindness. To them the backstretch—the barn area behind the racing strip, which also functions as a meeting ground and sometimes a home for trainers, jockeys, grooms, and other track habitués—appears as a band of varying shades of gray. They don't register individual items like pails, hoses, or saddles, but they know when their groom is moving, by changes in relative brightness and tone. On the other hand, horses have an excellent sense of hearing. Their ears are concave and can move in any direction, like dish antennae, picking up sounds at a great distance—a mouse scratching five stalls down. When a horse pricks its ears, its nostrils flare simultaneously, so the receptors can work in tandem. Stallions can smell a mare in heat miles away if she's upwind, and even an average animal can locate water or snakes by following its nose.

While I watched the horses come and go, business was booming around me. Jockeys' agents, carrying small notebooks with hand-tooled leather covers, moved from barn to barn booking mounts. If they represented a live rider, a kid who had been winning lately, trainers met them eagerly, and even offered them a cup of coffee, but if they were pushing a loser, their eyes were often sunk in rummy sadness and they were treated like pariahs. "Lemme know if you get something Richie can't handle!" they shouted to Bob Hack, the agent who held Rich Galarsa's book, and Hack steered them on occasion to a needy trainer. Everybody wanted to use Galarsa, because he was live and still had the bug, a five-pound weight allowance granted to apprentice riders—riders who are still in the twelve-month period following their first five wins. Apprentices are called bug boys, because an insectlike asterisk appears next to their names and weights in the program, distinguishing them from journeymen, who receive no allowance.

Trainers had more vital things to do than to mess with importunate jockeys. They had horses to clock, owners to call, grooms to supervise, and orders to place with tack salesmen and feed suppliers, and they had to be ready when the vet arrived to examine sick or damaged stock. Furthermore, they had to waste precious time trying to read the Condition Book, which was about as cleanly written as an IRS pamphlet. The Condition Book set forth the eligibility requirements for future races, and it was updated every ten days. You needed a postgraduate degree to unscramble its sentences:

> Starter Allowance. Purse $9000. For four-year-olds and upward, non-winners of two races at one mile and one-eighth or over in 1978, which have started for a claiming price of $16,000 or less in 1977–78 and since that start have not won a race other than maiden or claiming, or a claiming or starter race exceeding $16,000.

"*Jay-sus!*" the trainers cried, dumping the book into an empty feed bucket. Most of them relied on agents when it came time to enter a horse. "Where do you think I ought to run ole Wind Chime?" they'd ask, and Hack or somebody else would set them straight, presenting the options.

Trainers (they were the first to tell you) had a rough job—even established guys, like Bobby Martin and Bill Mastrangelo. Maybe Mastrangelo seemed relaxed when he walked around the barn singing Jerry Vale ballads at the top of his lungs, but he felt the pressure anyway. He had to feel it, because he had to deal with *owners,* who applied it. Owners were almost always trouble. Sure, they looked classy when you saw them on TV at the Kentucky Derby, rich, polite, soft-spoken, but this image was deceiving. In fact they were part of the incomprehensible freeway universe, and 90 percent of them knew absolutely nothing about horses or racing. Five of the remaining 10 percent *thought* they knew something but didn't, and four of the final 5 percent knew a *little* bit but not enough to make a difference. They'd buy a rickety colt as a tax loss, and when the colt broke his maiden, finally winning his first race after sixteen tries, the jerks thought they owned another Man o' War and ordered the trainer to jump the colt to stakes races, where the competition was much tougher, and then when the colt lost repeatedly, by grotesque margins, they blamed the trainer or fired him or moved the colt to another track and skipped out on the balance of their bill. What could you do, take them to court?

Gary Headley, a trainer, and his groom, Bo Twinn, were having coffee the first time I visited their barn—No. 25, a cobwebby structure situated in nonpreferential territory, among the shops of feed merchants, tack salesmen, and purveyors of riding silks, at least a quarter mile from the track. They sat in lawn chairs, smoking and reading the *Form,* and rested their cups on a round, low-slung table—a salvaged telephone-cable spool. There were doughnuts on the table, and empty almond packs and soda cans. Both men looked tired and dirty after the morning's work. Headley's blue nylon Windbreaker was creased as though he'd slept in it, and his blond hair wandered off in random shocks. Bo hadn't shaved yet, and his face looked weather-beaten and old. It was the sort of face that occurred in hot, dusty places. I'd seen it before, in Depression-era photographs. Over the years, Bo had developed a crusty personality to match his face, and he could be formidably short-tempered on occasion, but he loved horses and they loved him. "If you was smart, you wouldn't have to ask that question," he would say, pursing his lips like a schoolmarm. Headley, who was in his late thirties—younger than Bo—took great pride in employing him. "Best groom on the grounds," he'd say confidentially, hiding his mouth behind a hand, "and the best paid, too." There was no way to substantiate such statements, and, besides, Headley made them all the time.

Headley was a hyperbolic and something of a flake, not the best trainer at Golden Gate but also not the worst. His life so far had been a model of fluctuant behavior. His brother Bruce, a respected trainer on the Southern California circuit, had hired Gary, taught him the trade, and introduced him around, but Gary had never been able to commit himself absolutely to the track, not for any length of time. He'd work for a while, building up his business, then wash out and drift through odd jobs in the real world or (if he had a little money saved) stay in his apartment, behind closed curtains, sipping wine and watching TV. Then he'd decide that training horses really was right for him, and he would go back to work, starting at the bottom, and keep at it for a few years before becoming disillusioned or bored or upset and washing out again. Headley recognized the pattern but seemed incapable of breaking it. This was his major problem. The track, like any subculture, extracts a mean price for ambivalence, and Headley had been paying it too long. His marriage—to a legal secretary, a woman who knew nothing about racing—had recently fallen apart, and the failure bothered him. "First divorce in the family in seven generations," he said, as though reminding himself. These days, almost in compensation, he seemed more dedicated than he had in the past, although the odds were even that he might flip-flop at any minute, disappearing from the backstretch without leaving a forwarding address.

Bo had other problems. He lived in a tack room—a compact space, ten by fifteen feet, ordinarily used for storing saddles, bridles, and the like—and two female cats had adopted his residence as their own and presented him with ten kittens. "I got all kinds of cats," he said, showing me the litter nursing on his bed. The room smelled overpoweringly feline. There was a TV set on the bureau, a few shirts hanging from a rod inside an open closet, and pictures of horses taped to the walls. "The two mama cats, they take turns nursing. I never did see anything like it before. One nurses and then the other. This kitten here's the prettiest." He picked up a long-haired calico by the scruff. "I might even keep her. Don't know what I'll do with them others, though. I got 'em in every possible color. That little guy over there, he's the runt. They push him around. Maybe you'd like a cat for your house?"

Headley took me around his barn, which he shared with Bud Keen, another trainer. Keen kept a goat in his section to help quiet a highstrung filly. When the goat saw us coming, he backed off, making goat noises. Headley had six stalls, and the horses in most of them were hurting in one way or another. "Think this horse is sound?" he asked rhetorically, stopping in front of a bedraggled-looking mare. "She's raced twice in six months, that's how sound she is. I could get a better class of horse, but I don't want the hassle. I used to train a big string at Santa Anita, but the owners drove me nuts. See this?" He pointed to a deep cleft between his eyebrows. "I got this from worrying." Next, he showed me a handsome two-year-old, Urashima Taro, who hadn't raced yet. "I think this colt's a winner," he said. "This colt's my dream horse. I already nominated him for the Del Mar Futurity and the Hollywood Juvenile. It's cheaper to pay the entry fees now than waiting." We continued down the shed row. "See this filly? She was crazy when she came in. I couldn't even touch her. She was wrecked. Her owners are nice people, though. For a change. They gave me plenty of time with her. Now she's rounding into shape. What are those people, Bo? The Sandomirs. What are they? They speak Spanish, but I know they're not Mexicans. The wife speaks English pretty good. I think they might be Panamanian. Are those people Panamanian, Bo?"

"All's I know is they're not Mexicans," Bo said.

"No, they're not Mexicans. I think they might be Panamanians."

"What's the filly's name?" I asked.

"Pichi," Headley said. "Don't ask me what it means."

I never met Gregory Sandomir, a native of Argentina, but his wife, Mary, once explained his involvement in racing quite succinctly. "My husband has the feeling since he's very young," she told me. "He likes the horses very much." Sandomir, who manufactured blue jeans in Los Angeles, had always wanted to own a Thoroughbred, and in the summer of 1976 he began shopping around. He knew some trainers, and they sent him to various breeding farms and ranches to look at the stock for sale, but it took a while before he found what he wanted. At Walnut Wood Farm, in Hemet, California, he fell for an eight-month-old chestnut filly by Dr. Marc R out of Atomic Jay. Sandomir knew little about conformation (the ideal physical structure of a Thoroughbred) or bloodlines (its all-important heritage), but this served him well, because the filly had nothing much to commend her except a distant, minimal relationship to War Admiral, which might have accounted for her willful nature. She was pretty and excitable, and Sandomir, thoroughly smitten, made the purchase and named her Pichi. This had been his nickname for his daughter, who was married now and gone from his house.

As a two-year-old, Pichi was consigned to a Hollywood Park trainer who had no tolerance for her moodiness, and soon she was locked into a battle of wills. She resisted most stringently at the starting gate. She hated the machinery and balked whenever she went near it. Instead of trying to ease her in, comforting her, the trainer apparently used force, which aggravated matters. Horses who have an aversion to the gate can usually be counted on to break poorly in a race, sometimes a half second behind the field, and Pichi followed the rule. In her first race, a five-and-a-half-furlong sprint (eight furlongs equal a mile), she finished eighth by thirteen lengths, and two weeks later, against weaker opponents, she loped home tenth, twelve casual lengths behind the leader. Sandomir became concerned about her condition. She didn't look well. There was no reason, he thought, to extract victory from a horse's hide, so when the meet ended and the action shifted to Del Mar, he arranged for Pichi to be trained by Ross Fenstermaker, who ran her twice at a mile. She improved, breaking better both times, but she was still far from winning a race, or even finishing in the money. Fenstermaker would have stayed with her, but he got an offer to train a string of first-class horses for Fred Hooper, an owner of some prominence. Owners like Hooper tend to demand exclusivity from their trainers in exchange for the privilege of working with quality stock, so Fenstermaker had to get rid of his outlaw. His old friend Gary Headley was just getting back into the game at Golden Gate, and he urged Sandomir to give Headley a try. The competition was much cheaper in the north, and Pichi would have a better chance at breaking her maiden. Fenstermaker gave Headley a single caution: Watch this filly, she's murder in the gate.

Pichi arrived by van in February 1978, toward the end of a long, cold, wet winter that had broken the back of a two-year drought. Rivers were running again, the snowpack was deep around the Sierras, and Pichi, who had spent a few months standing in mud, had an awful-looking pair of hind legs, raw and infected. Headley led her to his barn. He examined his new charge and thought, *Another cripple.* He had plenty of cripples on hand already, representing varying degrees of unsoundness—here a grapefruit-size knee, there a quarter-cracked hoof—and Pichi fit right in. She hadn't raced in half a year and was in miserable shape. Headley found a crescent-shaped scar on her rib cage and figured that somewhere along the line a groom must have hit her with something heavy and broken a rib. But the rib appeared to have mended on its own, although imperfectly. She had other imperfections as well. The tip of her tail was missing, nipped off in a starting-gate accident; she had muscle spasms in her back; and when she ran, her vulva opened abnormally wide and she sucked air into her vagina, which caused a certain amount of discomfort. She also had what Headley called "psychological" problems. She was tense and wouldn't let anybody touch her. Nor would she eat, no matter what was served—oats, hay, some special mixture—and she was mean-tempered and kicked at Bo whenever she could. When she wasn't acting up, she remained aloof, staring at the rear wall of her stall like an infanta trapped in a tower, her regal bearing violated, and she flicked her tail at passersby and pinned her ears at the slightest provocation.

Fortunately, Headley liked working with cripples. They were puzzles to him, engines in need of tinkering, and it gratified him to watch a jockey boot home a horse who only a month before had been sulky and limping, totally unfit. He would have preferred working with good stakes horses, but such animals were not his current lot, and he was realistic enough not to suffer from their absence. He liked Sandomir, because Sandomir didn't push. Some owners demanded that their horses run every ten days regardless of condition, even if it meant injecting an unstable joint with cortisone, but Sandomir was willing to accumulate feed and veterinary bills, which could be staggering, until Pichi felt better. So Headley proceeded slowly. He began by having a vet sew up her vulva, to mitigate the air-sucking problem, and gave her Robaxin, a muscle relaxant, for her back. Then he started her exercise program, walking first, followed by some light galloping. Bo worked on her legs, applying poultices, liniment, and bandages, talking to her in his cranky old flatlands voice. "She's a radical son of a bitch," he would say, mixing genders freely, but he was pleased when at last he could clean her stall without expecting to catch a hoof in the middle of his forehead.

One morning when she seemed particularly calm, Headley decided to school her in the starting gate. He was a little apprehensive, recalling Fenstermaker's warning, but Pichi seemed so placid and yielding he thought she might be ready. A special gate for schooling horses was set up away from the track, back in the shade of some live oaks, and Headley led his pupil to it. But as soon as Pichi approached the gate, she went wild. She attacked the machinery, kicking and rearing, and when it failed to collapse she tried to jump over it. This was precisely as feasible as a cow jumping over the moon. Her exercise rider, with the help of a couple of assistant starters, managed to restrain her and lead her away before she injured herself. Headley was incredulous, but he kept schooling her patiently, with tender supervision, until she went into the gate without resisting and stood there moderately still, waiting to be released.

All gamblers look for signs, and I was given an appropriate one the first week of the Tanforan meeting when a filling from one of my molars popped out. The image of *emptiness* should have been transported to my brain, but it was not, and I kept losing steadily. Naturally, I had alibis, and ample time in which to consider them, but in the end they had no effect on the ledger, which was negative. During one inglorious sixteen-race period, I picked nine consecutive losers. Six of them finished out of the money entirely. Nobody else was doing so poorly, of that I was certain. Scrawny old guys in panama hats and suspenders were cashing in at the fifty-dollar window, and old ladies playing systems based on the sum of their nieces' birthdays divided by the pills in an Anacin bottle were hitting the daily double daily. They jumped, they howled, they clapped their hands and shed joyful tears, and I wanted to bust their kneecaps with a baseball bat.

Losers form strange partnerships; I formed mine with Arnold Walker. Together, we licked our wounds. I thought Arnold resembled a diplomat, in his elegant pin-striped suits and Cesar Romero locks, fog-gray and fragrant as pastilles. The Turf Club matrons loved him. He looked like an envoy sent from a far country for the express purpose of breaking hearts. If all gamblers are innocents, sharing a nostalgic longing for a condition prior to habituation, then Arnold was a superior gambler, by virtue of his superior innocence. He refused steadfastly to learn anything from experience, and even winning thousands of dollars did not satisfy him for long. What he wanted couldn't be found at the track, but there was no telling this to him. He'd spent a lifetime avoiding the truth. He was fifty-three, and thrice married, and his face, tanned to a Boca Raton brown even in April, was entirely free of lines. Arnold liked me, because I was a writer. "Writers are class," he said. He claimed to have seen Ernest Hemingway during the Second World War in the lobby of the Waldorf-Astoria with a gorgeous broad on his arm and a glass of champagne in his hand, and this remained his picture of how writers lived. One night, he insisted on buying me dinner and made me order lobster. Arnold had inherited a chain of drugstores on the peninsula and wanted to show me that money didn't mean a thing to him, but, of course, it did. Over drinks, he confessed to being down three grand for the year. "Down at Del Mar once," he said, cracking a lobster claw, "I had the best day of my life. I hit two exactas big and won thirty-eight hundred dollars. Then I went to a party and picked up a movie star and took her back to the motel." He looked cautiously around before whispering her name. I didn't believe him for a second.

Beyer and his speed figures were the first thing I threw out of my handicapping-support system, not because Beyer was wrong or inaccurate but because using figures went against my grain. I was learning that to win you had to work within the net of your own perceptions. For me, speed had negative connotations. It was too American a preoccupation, too insistently the grammar of motorcyclists and technologists. *Passo a passo si va lontano,* I had heard them say in Florence—step by step, one goes a long way—and this accent on the qualitative aspects of a journey was more to my liking. So I decided to concentrate on factors like class and condition, relegating speed to a secondary position except when it appeared to be the single factor separating one horse from all the others. But even after making this adjustment I lost again the next afternoon. The track, it seemed, was exactly like life, unjust and aleatory. Muggers won handily, thieves tripled their bankrolls, and murderers walked whistling to the parking lot, their blades secured in fat green sheaths.

"You're going to shoot a hundred and fourteen, dear."

I came to think of the trainers as Renaissance princes who ruled the backstretch. Walking the shed rows, I saw that each trainer's barn resembled a principality, embodying a unique blend of laws and mores, an individuated style. Bright-colored placards bearing trainers' names or initials or devices shone in the sun, and it was possible to intuit the flesh of a prince from the sign he displayed. If Eldon Hall's escutcheon showed a white dollar sign on a green background, then it stood to reason that Hall would be tall and lean and southern, wearing an expensive Stetson and specializing in speedy Kentucky-bred two-year-olds. Jake Battles's colors of red and optic blue suggested a feisty, raw-faced character who rode his pony belligerently and wore a monumental turquoise ring. Emery Winebrenner, whose temperament was mercurial, ranging from cheeriness to abject depression, offered a simple but evocative design—the letters EW rendered in sunny yellow against a field as black and sunken as night.

Trainers sometimes had difficulty keeping their principalities intact. Grooms got drunk and vanished, bouts of flu made the rounds and always lingered too long, deadly illnesses like founder shot forth from the clouds to skewer stakes-level performers, and crazy owner-kings were always demanding tribute—a table at the Turf Club or lobsters at Spenger's. Cheap horses were a nuisance. They went easily off form, stopped running the first time they met any opposition, and usually had no heart. The legend of Hirsch Jacobs and his horse Stymie, who was claimed for fifteen hundred and returned almost a million, wasn't really any consolation. A patient trainer might squeeze one win per season from each baling-wire beauty, but the purses offered in low-level events were small indeed and barely covered costs. Pichi, when she deigned to eat, cost as much to feed as Alydar. Trainers charged owners about twenty dollars a day, plus veterinary bills, to stable a horse, but even the stingiest among them had trouble extracting a living wage from dribs and drabs of double sawbucks.

Temptation, then, was everywhere, in every shed row, and certain darkling princes were known to succumb on occasion. By sending a fit horse to post at high odds, they could recoup at the parimutuel windows what they'd lost in feed. There were several time-honored tactics for influencing the outcome of a race. For example, superior workouts might not be listed in the *Form;* clockers made mistakes, especially at dawn. Horses could be worked at private training tracks until they were razor sharp, and trainers were under no obligation to make this information public. Sometimes unwary bug boys were given misleading prerace instructions—told to keep a rail-shy horse on the rail, say. Sometimes a trainer rode a bad jockey for a race or two, then switched to a pro. Sometimes a jockey was told that it might be beneficial to make slight errors in judgment coming into the stretch—to hold the mount in check too long or use him up too soon or go to the whip too late or not go to it at all. They made such mistakes genuinely, and it was almost impossible to separate true from false. There were hundreds of ways to make a horse's past-performance record read like a clinical account of lameness. Masking a horse's true condition was not considered a capital offense, but sudden form reversals artificially induced, those miraculous wake-up victories that resulted in big payoffs, were punishable by law. They occurred nonetheless. A jockey would slap a battery equipped with wire prongs—the device, held in the palm, was called a joint—to his mount's rump at the proper instant and hold on as best he could while the poor electrified beast romped home. New drugs were constantly being developed, drugs for which no equine-testing procedures had yet been devised. These were administered in dark stall corners, and soon thereafter sixty-to-one shots zoomed out of the gate like angels hyped on amphetamines. Those nags ran. They ran once, and once only, before slipping back into nagdom forever, but a hundred bucks selectively invested repaid six thousand big ones at any cashier's window on the grounds. These victories stood out, clearly evident, but stewards were slow to investigate. The unwritten rule around race tracks—not only Golden Gate—seemed to be that you could get away with anything once, but repetition would cost you dear. The penalties for such offenses were supposed to act as deterrents. Princes could be fined or suspended or banished from California, stripped of their licenses and sent packing to distant provinces where the summer county-fair meet was the nonpareil of Thoroughbred racing. Still, there were always a few who were willing to take the risk. Most trainers, though, worked hard and chose to be scrupulous. They'd never have the chance to win a Triple Crown, but their honesty might someday be rewarded with the trainers' championship of Golden Gate Fields. "In so artificial a world," Burckhardt wrote of princes, "only a man of consummate address could hope to succeed; each candidate for distinction was forced to make good his claims by personal merit and show himself worthy of the crown he sought."

I met Bobby Martin, the top trainer at Golden Gate, at his office, a musty tack room furnished with dilapidated armchairs and a vinyl-covered couch that belonged in a bus station. The office felt like Kansas—some inner sanctum on the plains with gas pumps out front and day-old newspapers for sale at the cash register. Martin sat behind a wooden desk and studied a large cardboard chart that listed all thirty-four of his horses and indicated by symbol whether they were scheduled to work (run hard over a specific distance—six furlongs, a mile—usually in preparation for a race), gallop, walk, or rest that morning. I had the impression that the chart wasn't really necessary, that Martin had long since memorized the data but wanted to give them an outward form and make them official. The chart was businesslike, professional, and so was the black phone on the desk, one of the few private lines I ever saw on the backstretch. These accoutrements suited Martin. He was a quietly confident man. He wore a rust-colored ski jacket and blue jeans with a dry cleaner's crease in them. His blondish hair was combed, and he didn't look beaten down, the way many trainers do when they hit forty.

Mike Haversack, a bug boy, sat opposite Martin and stirred the dust with his whip. He had the right face for pumping gas—thin, pale, with that curious race-track hardness creeping in around the mouth. He galloped horses for Martin and sometimes got to ride a maiden. A groom led a big chestnut to the office door, and Haversack stepped out of the office and into the stirrups. The transfer had a surreal quality, especially so early in the morning, but then horses were always showing up in odd places. They filled the available space quite suddenly, and I sometimes had the feeling of being pushed out of frame, like an actor snipped from a key scene. Another rider replaced Haversack on the couch, waiting, in turn, for his mount, and was soon replaced by yet another rider. The men were all dressed just like Martin, in ski jackets and jeans.

Martin bought his first horse, Domingo Kid, when he was nineteen. He paid only seven hundred and fifty dollars, because the horse, who had once run in allowance races, was so broken down and rank that nobody else wanted to deal with him. But Martin was young and ambitious, and gradually conditioned the Kid, and won eleven races with him that first year and twenty-six over all. Martin's name first appeared in the standings at Golden Gate in 1966, when he saddled ten winners in forty-three tries, and he has dominated them ever since.

Young trainers wanted to be like him when they grew up, and old grooms said that Bobby hadn't changed since he was a kid. He was honest and polite, and he treated his horses well and his grooms even better, paying them top dollar and refusing to inflict the usual psychic punishments. Even Tumwater Tom, who started early on his daily quota of Olympia beer, and knew more about horses than most trainers, had stuck with Bobby. There was something of the classic Western hero in Martin's demeanor—the shy, commanding presence of an Alan Ladd. He represented that most estimable race-track quality, *class,* but his soft jawline and slightly lumpy nose would have kept him from ever playing opposite Maureen O'Hara.

There were two main reasons, beyond intelligence and hard work, for Martin's success: his expertise as a conditioner and his mastery of the claiming game. Conditioning a horse properly—getting it into shape and then keeping it fit, on form—is a craft little practiced at cheaper race tracks. Because of financial exigencies and near-terminal shortsightedness—some call it stupidity—trainers often push their horses much too hard in morning workouts, cranking them up for a single race, the cliché Big Effort, and then afterward, when the horses return to the barn feeling tired and sore, have to rest them for a month or two before running them again. This tactic makes no sense, but trainers pursue it zestfully, with oblivious devotion. The real key to conditioning is conservation. Energy expended in a race or a workout has to be restored. So Martin kept close tabs on all his horses, checking their energy levels as he might check the water in batteries, and designed for each of them an exercise program—the chart—that took into account individual strengths and weaknesses. He took the time to *know* his stock, and so he got an optimal performance every race instead of one stellar showing followed by months of eights and nines.

Claiming is a more intricate and cerebral activity—it is called the poker of the backstretch—but, again, success is dependent on knowing your stock. The idea behind claiming races is to create fields of roughly equivalent talent and value. Any horse entered in a claiming race can be claimed, or bought, for a predetermined price, set by the Racing Secretary in the Condition Book. In theory, trainers won't enter a horse worth twenty thousand in a race in which the horse could be claimed by a rival for sixty-five hundred. But, of course, this happens all the time, because trainers, like their constituency, are gamblers. They are *always* looking for an edge. Take, for instance, the hypothetical trainer Profit and his horse Lament, a four-year-old gelding who in the past month finished fourth and second in two $12,500 claiming races. After such good performances, Profit might be expected to enter Lament at a higher level—say, $14,000—to protect him (Lament is clearly worth $12,500), but Profit, a sharper, *drops* the horse in class, and enters him in a race for a price tag of $8,500. This means one of three things: Lament is in bad shape, and Profit wants to get rid of him at a slight loss before his true condition is known; Lament is *not* in bad shape, but Profit wants others to think he is, and hopes to win a race against inferior opponents; Lament is just *beginning* to be in bad shape, getting old, with a kink in his step, and Profit is trying to make him look attractive, a bargain, while in fact he wants the horse to be claimed, having figured that the winner's share of the purse (say, $4,000) plus the claiming price ($8,500) will more than compensate him for the loss. The third tactic is the most difficult to master, predicated, as it is, on keen judgment, and Martin makes better use of it than anybody else at Golden Gate. Of twenty-three head he'd "lost" since January, only three were worth feeding. Sometimes he got stung—this was inevitable—but more often than not his experiences echoed the early one with Domingo Kid. "I do a lot of speculating," Martin said. "You can't get too attached to the horses."

Glen Nolan had made his money operating a drayage company, but he'd diversified into a less predictable enterprise—a hobby for him, really—and now owned Nolan Farms, Inc., a ranch in Pleasanton where he bred horses to race and sell. Around the track, he had a decent reputation. He spent necessary cash without groaning, and his stock was honest and sometimes fairly good. Smart handicappers gave Nolan's starters an edge for condition and maybe talent. He employed a trainer, Steve Gardell, at the farm, and during Golden Gate meetings he always requisitioned a few stalls in which to board horses who would be running regularly. This year, he had three stalls, and they were presided over by Debra Thomas, a princess of the backstretch.

Debra's official title was assistant trainer, but she spent most of her time grooming. The work showed in her body. Her shoulders were broad, her arms were hard and thickly muscled, and her hips were very trim. She had the build of a gymnast, somebody whose specialty was the parallel bars. She wore her blond hair at shoulder length, and her eyes were blue and cool, except when she stepped outside the race-track frame and became a young woman of twenty-two, pretty, a little dreamy, flirtatious, and decidedly feminine. She had three horses in her care: Ali Time, a dumb but honest two-year-old filly; Moonlight Cocktail, a moody four-year-old filly; and Bushel Ruler, a handsome three-year-old gelding who hadn't raced yet. Of them all, she loved only Bushel. She called him Oly, after his dam, Ohlavarc, and thought he'd fixated on her as a mother substitute. When she walked down the shed row in the morning, he'd stick his head out of the stall and whinny and nicker until she gave him some attention. He had personality and a touch of class, and Debra wished she could change his name to something more suitable than Bushel Ruler. Choosing the right name for a horse wasn't easy. The Jockey Club rules state that you are limited to eighteen letters, counting spaces and punctuation, and you can't duplicate names already registered or use those of "famous or notorious people"—no Johnny Rotten, no Richard Nixon—or "trade names, names claimed for advertising purposes, or names with commercial significance." Copyrighted names are permissible five years after their introduction into the culture, and coined and made-up names are permissible if they are accompanied by an explanation. There are also mystical injunctions to consider, like the Arabs' belief that a horse should never be named foolishly or in jest, because it will live up to that name. Debra had once worked for a man who had let her name all his horses, and she said that the best names often came to her at night, in dreams. She was proudest of her choice for a colt by Eskimo Prince: Chill Factor, she'd called him, and it fit perfectly.

On the afternoon I met her, Debra and Steve Gardell were preparing Moonlight Cocktail for the third race, a claimer. Debra said Moony had always been a problem horse. She'd run so poorly the year before, once falling twenty lengths behind when she was favored, that everybody had written her off, but Nolan had shipped her to the veterinary school at the University of California at Davis for a last-chance physical before turning her out. The vets took some X-rays and discovered a painful hoof disease, which they corrected. Now Moony was on the comeback trail. During the Pacific meet, she'd raced twice, but she was only beginning to round into shape. She was no longer crippled, just feisty, and Debra bore the scars. Moony had once kicked her in the leg, and another time the filly had brought her head up quickly, smashing Debra in the nose and barely missing the critical space between her eyes. Every groom and almost every trainer told such tales, but I still found them harrowing. There was really nothing to protect you from the horses except a sort of grace conferred by the animals themselves.

Debra knelt in the straw at the front of the stall and removed packed ice wrapped in towels from Moony's front legs. The ice kept the legs cool and the muscles tight. When the last ice shavings were brushed away, Gardell began wrapping the legs, applying sheets of cotton first, then Ace bandages, wound in a figure eight around the ankle and then wound around the leg almost to the knee and fastened with a strip of adhesive tape. Taped front legs usually indicate that a horse has problems, but Debra said that in this instance the tape was cosmetic, meant to deceive. Moony was making a slight class drop, from eighty-five hundred to seventy-five hundred, and the bandages were supposed to plant a seed of doubt in the minds of other trainers. "She's got a real good chance to win," Debra said. "She was real sharp when she galloped yesterday, and I've been holding her off ever since. She's ready, if she's in the *mood* to run."

Later, I stood by the paddock fence and watched the third-race entries as their grooms walked them around. Flowering bushes along the perimeter of the paddock gave off a soapy smell from white waxen blooms, and I had the impression that the horses had all been recently bathed. Moony looked splendid. She had green yarn laced into her mane, and her dark-brown coat had a fine sheen. Her quarters were tight and had a sculptural intensity, a focussing of power, and as she walked she kept her ears pricked. Debra was also dressed for the occasion, in a Western shirt, a leather belt decorated with blue flowers, and a pair of new jeans. Her hair was brushed, and she wore sunglasses. She held herself very erect, conscious of her posture, and she whispered constantly to Moony as they circled. Their heads seemed confined to a single plane, and they moved forward as a unit. Seeing Debra so brushed up and shiny made me aware of the plight of less presentable grooms. Some of them hated the paddock—its public nature, the way it accentuated their pimples and boils—and though they did their best to clean up and face it squarely, they always looked like recalcitrant children sent off to school. They had too much oil in their hair, bloody shaving nicks on their cheeks, and creases in shirts and blouses that had been badly folded and stored too long in musty bottom drawers. That the world valued beauty, and rewarded it disproportionately, was never so apparent as in the paddock.

I went to the windows, still smelling soap, and bet the selection I'd made the night before. Moonlight Cocktail chose to run, and won by a half length, closing fast and paying $14.20.

Though I hadn't yet learned to distinguish good tips from bad ones, I was learning other things about handicapping at Golden Gate Fields. On hot days, when the track baked to an unyielding consistency the color of piecrust, I looked for front-runners, because their speed seemed to last and they weren't so easily caught from behind. On foggy days, the track was moist and deep, and then I looked for horses who had been running in the Northwest—at Longacres, near Seattle, or Oregon's Portland Meadows—because they were used to heavy strips and often ran better than the *Form* indicated they might. I stopped betting any exacta race in which the favorite went off at less than eight to five, because, for reasons inexplicable to me, these races almost never ran to form. I quit playing the ninth altogether, because it was another exacta—the fourth of the day, a crazy last chance for bettors to win back what they'd lost—and because the Racing Secretary usually carded a long route, a mile and an eighth or a mile and a quarter, and the jockeys often rode in such a controlled and controlling fashion that the outcome was more than a little suspect.

Late in April, Headley gave Pichi her first start of the year, in a maiden race to be run at six furlongs for a purse of six thousand dollars. He engaged Jane Driggers to ride. She looked good in the Sandomirs' colors, yellow and black stripes topped with a black cap. Pichi drew the outermost post, twelve, which wasn't as disadvantageous as it seemed. She lugged in toward the rail, listing always to the left, so she would at least be as far away as possible from that particular problem. Whether it would influence her performance was unclear. Bettors shied from her in great numbers, depositing their money instead on Sailing Flag, who had been bred in Kentucky and had some Fleet Nasrullah blood, and letting Pichi go off at eighty-five to one. Sentiment overtook me, and I put two dollars on her nose.

She behaved well in the gate, much to Headley's relief, and broke well, too, second after the buzzer, but she got into trouble immediately, blocked by other horses, and dropped back into the pack and disappeared. A speedy filly named Hut's Girl took command and, according to the *Form*'s subsequent description, "proved much the best under intermittent urging," winning by eight lengths and leaving Sailing Flag unfurled in the dust. Pichi finished eighth, thirteen lengths behind, but she did make a tiny move in the stretch, expending a minuscule atom of acceleration and gaining a little ground. I saw Headley after the race and expected him to be shattered, his long months of conditioning proved worthless. On the contrary, he seemed pleased, and promised better things from Pichi in the future. "I told you she'd need a race," he said. "You watch her next time out." *Hope,* I thought, that's what you purchase at eighty-five to one.

Before the next race, I fell victim to confusion once again. I was torn between the rational order of things and my intuition and what it proposed. A sensible reading of the *Form* had persuaded me to play Top Delegate, the eight horse, who had been running well against better horses and was dropping down to his proper level, but I kept returning to another horse, Little Shasta, because the name reminded me of Mount Shasta and the fine trout waters around it. Names could be irresistible. I remembered the time my brother and I had rented a boat and tooled across an arm of Shasta Lake and then up into the Pit River, where we camped for the night. We were fresh from Long Island, still unused to the sight of mountains, and our only camping experience was of the backyard pup-tent variety. At dusk, we heard howling in the foothills—a wild, blood-chilling sound that increased after dark. "A killer dog," I said. "You're right," said my brother, and we broke camp immediately and slept in the boat, anchored safely some fifty yards from shore. It had only been a coyote howling, but I didn't realize this until much later, when the call had become familiar. So Little Shasta spoke to me of innocence, of lakes and wildness and pines and the few things in life I'd finally come to know. On the other hand, Top Delegate reminded me of Henry Kissinger, and I was fighting this associational bias all the way to the windows. Suddenly, I was face-to-face with a ruddy-skinned ticket seller in a black cardigan sweater; intuition gave way to reason. "Eight," I said, and then I watched in misery as Little Shasta went wire to wire, winning as decidedly as Pichi had lost.

Every now and then, the structural pattern was broken by instances of pure vision, gifts, and I kept rejecting them. Arnold Walker understood. I bumped into him at the bar at Spenger's. "You're not talking about luck," he said, chewing on a swizzle stick. "That's when you win because the horse in front of your horse falls down and breaks a leg."

"What *am* I talking about?"

"What you're talking about is magic. When your horse is the *only* horse in the race."

The race was for two-year-olds, a five-furlong sprint, and I looked over the stock in the paddock before making my wager. The horses had run only once or twice before, or not at all, and they were still green and had the alert, playful look of the ranch about them. They weren't aware of resistances, opposition, the gradual wearing down of tissue and desire, and some of them had a bafflement in their eyes when they surveyed the grandstand and the people by the paddock fence reading their limbs. I liked to bet two-year-olds, because they were so young and guileless. Older horses, the kind handicappers often call "hard-hitting veterans," were often deceptive before a race, drag-assing around, snuffling, their backs swayed and noses dappling the dust, and more than once I'd lost money when just such an animal rose into himself a hundred yards from the gate, suddenly pumped up on Thoroughbred afflatus, and led the field from wire to wire. Two horses in the present field attracted me—Pass Completion, the favorite, and an outsider, Flight Message. Both looked honest. I was standing in front of a tote board, trying to decide between them, when an old man came up and asked if he could look at my *Form*. He was very polite, with clean pink cheeks, and he smelled of cologne and a dash of clubhouse whiskey; he wore gold-rimmed specs and a traditional senior citizen's shirt, white nylon and short-sleeved, with a sleeveless T-shirt beneath it.

"Haven't read one of these for years," he mumbled, running the spine of his comb under lines of type. "Say, this horse *has* been working well. Raindrop Kid. Raindrop Kid. What're the odds?" he asked, squinting.

"Eighteen to one."

"Eighteen to one? Eighteen to one?" His eyes were gleaming now, and a bit of froth appeared on his lips. "That's an overlay if ever I saw one," he said before vanishing into the six-dollar-combination line.

Around me, people were suddenly moving, prodded into action by the five-minute-warning buzzer, and I was arrested by the swarming colors and shapes, nests of teased hair, lime-green trousers, dark skin. I wondered if the old man knew what he was talking about or was just another trailer-park baron on holiday. It occurred to me that he might be a manifestation, some emissary from the outposts of my consciousness. I looked around. He wasn't there. Time was passing, so I stepped into the flow to play Pass Completion, but when I reached for my money I pulled out something else instead—a small antique medal my brother had given me years ago. I'd used it as a key chain until the hook at the top had broken, and now I carried it for sentimental reasons. It pictured a knickered boy in a golf cap rolling up his sleeves and preparing to flick a marble at other marbles, arranged in a cruciform at the center of a circle. Above the boy's head were the words "United States Marble Shooting Championship Tournament." His feet rested on laurel leaves. There was no illustration on the other side, only text. "Malden Championship Awarded to Emil Lawrence by *The Boston Traveler*," it read. But why had the medal jumped into my hand? The answer, when it struck, seemed obvious—to keep me from putting any cash on Pass Completion. Was the old man hiding behind a pillar somewhere, using his powers of telekinesis? No matter. I knew for certain what I had to do—magic, *magic*—and went dreamily forward and, feeling absolutely certain, bet Raindrop Kid to win.

Sometimes a race unfolds exactly as you've envisioned it, with the horses cleaving to a pattern in your brain, and this seemed to be happening now. Raindrop Kid broke slowly, as I had thought he would, and was seventh after three-sixteenths of a mile, but I expected him to begin moving soon, and he did, on the outside. By the stretch, he was in striking distance. His legs were fully extended, and he moved along in an effortless coltish glide. He trailed My Golly, whom I hadn't even considered, and as he drew up to challenge I waited for the next phase of the pattern to develop, horses hooked and matching stride for stride, and then the final phase, the Kid's slick expenditure of energy he'd held in reserve, his head thrown forward just far enough to nip My Golly at the wire. But it was My Golly who began to accelerate, drawing away, and I watched him pass the finish line and felt the pattern dissolve, soup draining into my shoes.

Then the "Inquiry" sign appeared on the tote board. The stewards were going to review a videotape of the race, because it appeared that Enrique Muñoz, on My Golly, had bumped into Rogelio Gomez and Raindrop Kid in the stretch. The sign had a strange effect on me. It was one turnaround too many, and I felt unpleasantly suspended. I looked away and saw a sparrow trying to pin a moth against the windbreak of the grandstand. The ongoing business of biology made me aware of the sound of my heart and the blood circulating through my body. I took a deep breath, but the air was warm and settled miasmatically in my lungs. Somebody had spilled popcorn down the steps in front of me, and for a while I counted kernels. The waiting was bad, as it always is, and I tried thinking about other things. A sudden explosion of bulbs, brilliant flashes on the tote board, interrupted my cogitation, and then John Gibson, the track announcer, announced in that grand theatrical manner he had, full of hesitations, that after examining the video-tape . . . the stewards . . . had decided . . . to *disqualify* My Golly and award the race to Raindrop Kid. The Kid paid thirty-eight dollars and twenty cents for every two dollars wagered to win, and when I collected my money I could feel the heat in my hands, all through me, and I knew how hot I was going to get.

All week long, I kept winning. It had nothing to do with systems, I was just *in touch*. When I walked through the grandstand, I projected the winner's aura, blue and enticing. Women smiled openly as I passed. I drank good whiskey and ate well. One night, I went to a Japanese restaurant and sat at a table opposite Country Joe McDonald, the singer who had been a fixture at rallies in the sixties. Joe had a new wife with him, and a new baby, who refused to sit still and instead bawled and threw an order of sushi around the room. A chunk of tuna flew past my ear. Even this seemed revelatory, the domestic roundness of a star's life, his interrupted meal, carrying the baby crying into the night, and I knew that someday soon Tuna or Seaweed or Riceball would appear on the menu at Golden Gate and I'd play the horse and win. Things fleshed themselves out before my eyes. I bought two bottles of Sapporo Black at a liquor store and went to sit on the Terrace steps and listen to my upstairs neighbor's piano exercises, the dusky fastnesses of ivory. This tune, I thought, will never end.

1980

PART TWO

IMMORTALS

"Which <u>one</u>? Great heavens, are you <u>mad</u>?"

A SENSE OF WHERE YOU ARE

JOHN McPHEE

The basketball locker room in the gymnasium at Princeton has no blackboard, no water fountain, and, in fact, no lockers. Up on the main floor, things go along in the same vein. Collapsible grandstands pull out of the walls and crowd up to the edge of the court. Jolly alumni sometimes wander in just before a game begins, sit down on the players' bench, and are permitted to stay there. The players themselves are a little slow getting started each year, because if they try to do some practicing on their own during the autumn they find the gymnasium full of graduate students who know their rights and won't move over. When a fellow does get some action, it can be dangerous. The gym is so poorly designed that a scrimmaging player can be knocked down one of two flights of concrete stairs. It hardly seems possible, but at the moment this scandalous milieu includes William Warren Bradley, who is the best amateur basketball player in the United States and among the best players, amateur or professional, in the history of the sport.

Bill Bradley is what college students nowadays call a superstar, and the thing that distinguishes him from other such paragons is not so much that he has happened into the Ivy League as that he is a superstar at all. For one thing, he has overcome the disadvantage of wealth. A great basketball player, almost by definition, is someone who has grown up in a constricted world, not for lack of vision or ambition but for lack of money; his environment has been limited to home, gym, and playground, and it has forced upon him, as a developing basketball player, the discipline of having nothing else to do. Bradley must surely be the only great basketball player who wintered regularly in Palm Beach until he was thirteen years old. His home is in Crystal City, Missouri, a small town on the Mississippi River about thirty miles south of St. Louis, and at Crystal City High School, despite the handicap of those earlier winters, he became one of the highest-scoring players in the records of secondary-school basketball. More than seventy colleges tried to recruit him, nearly all of them offering him scholarships. Instead, Bradley chose a school that offered him no money at all. Scholarships at Princeton are given only where there is financial need, and more than half of Princeton's undergraduates have them, but Bradley is ineligible for one, because his father, the president of a bank, is a man of more than comfortable means.

Bradley says that when he was seventeen he came to realize that life was much longer than a few winters of basketball. He is quite serious in his application to the game, but he has wider interests and, particularly, bigger ambitions. He is a history student, interested in politics, and last July he worked for Governor Scranton in Washington. He was once elected president of the Missouri Association of Student Councils, and he is the sort of boy who, given a little more time, would have been in the forefront of undergraduate political life; as it is, he has been a considerable asset to Princeton quite apart from his feats in the gymnasium, through his work for various campus organizations. In a way that athletes in Ivy League colleges sometimes do not, he fits into the university as a whole. Now his Princeton years are coming to an end, and lately he has been under more recruitment pressure—this time, of course, from the National Basketball Association. In September, however, on the eve of his departure for Tokyo, where, as a member of the United States basketball team, he won a gold medal in the Olympic Games, he filed an application with the American Rhodes Scholarship Committee. Just before Christmas, he was elected a Rhodes Scholar. This has absolutely nonplussed the New York Knickerbockers, who for some time had been suffering delusions of invincibility, postdated to the autumn of 1965, when, they assumed, Bradley would join their team. Two years ago, when the Syracuse Nationals wanted to transfer their franchise and become the Philadelphia '76ers, the Knicks refused to give their approval until they had received a guarantee that they would retain territorial rights to Bradley, whose college is one mile closer to Philadelphia than it is to New York. Bradley says he knows that he will very much miss not being able to play the game at its highest level, but, as things are now, if Bradley plays basketball at all next year, it will be for Oxford.

To many eastern basketball fans, what the Knickerbockers will be missing has not always been as apparent as it is today. Three seasons ago, when Bradley, as a Princeton freshman, broke a free-throw record for the sport of basketball at large, much of the outside world considered it a curious but not necessarily significant achievement. In game after game, he kept sinking foul shots without missing, until at the end of the season he had made fifty-seven straight—one more than the previous all-time high, which had been set by a member of the professional Syracuse Nationals. The following year, as a varsity player, he averaged a little over twenty-seven points per game, and it became clear that he was the best player ever to have been seen in the Ivy League—better than Yale's Tony Lavelli, who was one of the leading scorers in the United States in 1949, or Dartmouth's Rudy LaRusso, who is now a professional with the Los Angeles Lakers. But that still wasn't saying a lot. Basketball players of the highest caliber do not gravitate to the Ivy League, and excellence within its membership has seldom been worth more, nationally, than a polite smile. However, Ivy teams play early-season games outside their league, and at the end of the season the Ivy League champion competes in the tournament of the National Collegiate Athletic Association, which brings together the outstanding teams in the country and eventually establishes the national champion. Gradually, during his sophomore and junior years, Bradley's repeatedly superior performances in these games eradicated all traces of the notion that he was merely a parochial accident and would have been just another player if he had gone to a big basketball school. He has scored as heavily against non-Ivy opponents as he has against Ivy League teams—forty points against Army, thirty-two against Villanova, thirty-three against Davidson, thirty against Wake Forest, thirty-one against Navy, thirty-four against St. Louis, thirty-six against Syracuse, and forty-six in a rout of the University of Texas. Last season, in the Kentucky Invitational Tournament, at the University of Kentucky, Princeton defeated Wisconsin largely because Bradley was busy scoring forty-seven points—a record for the tournament. The size of this feat can be understood if one remembers that Kentucky has won more national championships than any other university and regularly invites the best competition it can find to join in its holiday games.

An average of twenty points in basketball is comparable to baseball's criterion for outstanding pitchers, whose immortality seems to be predicated on their winning twenty games a year. Bradley scored more points last season than any other college basketball player, and his average was 32.3 per game. If Bradley's shooting this season comes near matching his accomplishment of last year, he will become one of the three highest-scoring players in the history of college basketball. Those who have never seen him are likely to assume that he is seven and a half feet tall—the sort of elaborate weed that once all but choked off the game. With an average like his, it would be fair to imagine him spending his forty minutes of action merely stuffing the ball into the net. But the age of the goon is over. Bradley is six feet five inches tall—the third-tallest player on the Princeton team. He is perfectly coordinated, and he is unbelievably accurate at every kind of shot in the basketball repertory. He does much of his scoring from considerable distances, and when he sends the ball toward the basket, the odds are that it is going in, since he has made more than half the shots he has attempted as a college player. With three, or even four, opponents clawing at him, he will rise in the air, hang still for a moment, and release a high parabola jump shot that almost always seems to drop into the basket with an equal margin to the rim on all sides. Against Harvard last February, his ninth long shot from the floor nicked the rim slightly on its way into the net. The first eight had gone cleanly through the center. He had missed none at all. He missed several as the evening continued, but when his coach finally took him out, he had scored fifty-one points. In a game twenty-four hours earlier, he had begun a thirty-nine-point performance by hitting his first four straight. Then he missed a couple. Then he made ten consecutive shots, totally demoralizing Dartmouth.

Bradley is one of the few basketball players who have ever been appreciatively cheered by a disinterested away-from-home crowd while warming up. This curious event occurred last March, just before Princeton eliminated the Virginia Military Institute, the year's Southern Conference champion, from the NCAA championships. The game was played in Philadelphia and was the last of a tripleheader. The people there were worn out, because most of them were emotionally committed to either Villanova or Temple—two local teams that had just been involved in enervating battles with Providence and Connecticut, respectively, scrambling for a chance at the rest of the country. A group of Princeton boys shooting basketballs miscellaneously in preparation for still another game hardly promised to be a high point of the evening, but Bradley, whose routine in the warmup time is a gradual crescendo of activity, is more interesting to watch before a game than most players are in play. In Philadelphia that night, what he did was, for him, anything but unusual. As he does before all games, he began by shooting set shots close to the basket, gradually moving back until he was shooting long sets from twenty feet out, and nearly all of them dropped into the net with an almost mechanical rhythm of accuracy. Then he began a series of expandingly difficult jump shots, and one jumper after another went cleanly through the basket with so few exceptions that the crowd began to murmur. Then he started to perform whirling reverse moves before another cadence of almost steadily accurate jump shots, and the murmur increased. Then he began to sweep hook shots into the air. He moved in a semicircle around the court. First with his right hand, then with his left, he tried seven of these long, graceful shots—the most difficult ones in the orthodoxy of basketball—and ambidextrously made them all. The game had not even begun, but the presumably unimpressible Philadelphians were applauding like an audience at an opera.

Bradley has a few unorthodox shots, too. He dislikes flamboyance, and, unlike some of basketball's greatest stars, has apparently never made a move merely to attract attention. While some players are eccentric in their shooting, his shots, with only occasional exceptions, are straightforward and unexaggerated. Nonetheless, he does make something of a spectacle of himself when he moves in rapidly parallel to the baseline, glides through the air with his back to the basket, looks for a teammate he can pass to, and, finding none, tosses the ball into the basket over one shoulder, like a pinch of salt. Only when the ball is actually dropping through the net does he look around to see what has happened, on the chance that something might have gone wrong, in which case he would have to go for the rebound. That shot has the essential characteristics of a wild accident, which is what many people stubbornly think they have witnessed until they see him do it for the third time in a row. All shots in basketball are supposed to have names—the set, the hook, the lay-up, the jump shot, and so on—and one weekend last July, while Bradley was in Princeton working on his senior thesis and putting in some time in the Princeton gymnasium to keep himself in form for the Olympics, I asked him what he called his over-the-shoulder shot. He said that he had never heard a name for it, but that he had seen Oscar Robertson, of the Cincinnati Royals, and Jerry West, of the Los Angeles Lakers, do it, and had worked it out for himself. He went on to say that it is a much simpler shot than it appears to be, and, to illustrate, he tossed a ball over his shoulder and into the basket while he was talking and looking me in the eye. I retrieved the ball and handed it back to him. "When you have played basketball for a while, you don't need to look at the basket when you are in close like this," he said, throwing it over his shoulder again and right through the hoop. "You develop a sense of where you are."

Bradley is not an innovator. Actually, basketball has had only a few innovators in its history—players like Hank Luisetti, of Stanford, whose introduction in 1936 of the running one-hander did as much to open up the game for scoring as the forward pass did for football; and Joe Fulks, of the old Philadelphia Warriors, whose twisting two-handed heaves, made while he was leaping like a salmon, were the beginnings of the jump shot, which seems to be basketball's ultimate weapon. Most basketball players appropriate fragments of other players' styles, and thus develop their own. This is what Bradley has done, but one of the things that set him apart from nearly everyone else is that the process has been conscious rather than osmotic. His jump shot, for example, has had two principal influences. One is Jerry West, who has one of the best jumpers in basketball. At a summer basketball camp in Missouri some years ago, West told Bradley that he always gives an extra hard bounce to the last dribble before a jump shot, since this seems to catapult him to added height. Bradley has been doing that ever since. Terry Dischinger, of the Detroit Pistons, has told Bradley that he always slams his foot to the floor on the last step before a jump shot, because this stops his momentum and thus prevents drift. Drifting while aloft is the mark of a sloppy jump shot. Bradley's graceful hook shot is a masterpiece of eclecticism. It consists of the high-lifted knee of the Los Angeles Lakers' Darrall Imhoff, the arms of Bill Russell, of the Boston Celtics, who extends his idle hand far under his shooting arm and thus magically stabilizes the shot, and the general corporeal form of Kentucky's Cotton Nash, a rookie this year with the Lakers. Bradley carries his analyses of shots further than merely identifying them with pieces of other people. "There are five parts to the hook shot," he explains to anyone who asks. As he continues, he picks up a ball and stands about eighteen feet from a basket. "Crouch," he says, crouching, and goes on to demonstrate the other moves. "Turn your head to look for the basket, step, kick, follow through with your arms." Once, as he was explaining this to me, the ball curled around the rim and failed to go in.

"What happened then?" I asked him.

"I didn't kick high enough," he said.

"Do you always know exactly why you've missed a shot?"

"Yes," he said, missing another one.

"What happened that time?"

"I was talking to you. I didn't concentrate. The secret of shooting is concentration."

His set shot is borrowed from Ed Macauley, who was a St. Louis University All-American in the late forties and was later a star member of the Boston Celtics and the St. Louis Hawks. Macauley runs the basketball camp Bradley first went to when he was fifteen. In describing the set shot, Bradley is probably quoting a Macauley lecture. "Crouch like Groucho Marx," he says. "Go off your feet a few inches. You shoot with your legs. Your arms merely guide the ball." Bradley says that he has more confidence in his set shot than in any other. However, he seldom uses it, because he seldom has to. A set shot is a long shot, usually a twenty-footer, and Bradley, with his speed and footwork, can almost always take some other kind of shot, closer to the basket. He will take set shots when they are given to him, though. Two seasons ago, Davidson lost to Princeton, using a compact zone defense that ignored the remoter areas of the court. In one brief sequence, Bradley sent up seven set shots, missing only one. The missed one happened to rebound in Bradley's direction, and he leaped up, caught it with one hand, and scored. Even his lay-up shot has an ancestral form; he is full of admiration for "the way Cliff Hagan pops up anywhere within six feet of the basket," and he tries to do the same. Hagan is a former Kentucky star who now plays for the St. Louis Hawks. Because opposing teams always do everything they can to stop Bradley, he gets an unusual number of foul shots. When he was in high school, he used to imitate Bob

Pettit, of the St. Louis Hawks, and Bill Sharman of the Boston Celtics, but now his free throw is more or less his own. With his left foot back about eighteen inches—"wherever it feels comfortable," he says—he shoots with a deep-bending rhythm of knees and arms, one-handed, his left hand acting as a kind of gantry for the ball until the moment of release. What is most interesting, though, is that he concentrates his attention on one of the tiny steel eyelets that are welded under the rim of the basket to hold the net to the hoop—on the center eyelet, of course—before he lets fly. One night, he scored over twenty points on free throws alone; Cornell hacked at him so heavily that he was given twenty-one free throws, and he made all twenty-one, finishing the game with a total of thirty-seven points.

When Bradley, working out alone, practices his set shots, hook shots, and jump shots, he moves systematically from one place to another around the basket, his distance from it being appropriate to the shot, and he does not permit himself to move on until he has made at least ten shots out of thirteen from each location. He applies this standard to every kind of shot, with either hand, from any distance. Many basketball players, including reasonably good ones, could spend five years in a gym and not make ten out of thirteen left-handed hook shots, but that is part of Bradley's daily routine. He talks to himself while he is shooting, usually reminding himself to concentrate but sometimes talking to himself the way every high-school JV basketball player has done since the dim twenties—more or less imitating a radio announcer, and saying, as he gathers himself up for a shot, "It's pandemonium in Dillon Gymnasium. The clock is running out. He's up with a jumper. Swish!" Last summer, the floor of the Princeton gym was being resurfaced, so Bradley had to put in several practice sessions at the Lawrenceville School. His first afternoon at Lawrenceville, he began by shooting fourteen-foot jump shots from the right side. He got off to a bad start, and he kept missing them. Six in a row hit the back rim of the basket and bounced out. He stopped, looking discomfited, and seemed to be making an adjustment in his mind. Then he went up for another jump shot from the same spot and hit it cleanly. Four more shots went in without a miss, and then he paused and said, "You want to know something? That basket is about an inch and a half low." Some weeks later, I went back to Lawrenceville with a steel tape, borrowed a stepladder, and measured the height of the basket. It was nine feet ten and seven-eighths inches above the floor, or one and one-eighth inches too low.

Being a deadly shot with either hand and knowing how to make the moves and fakes that clear away the defense are the primary skills of a basketball player, and any player who can do these things half as well as Bradley can has all the equipment he needs to make a college team. Many high-scoring basketball players, being able to make so obvious and glamorous a contribution to their team in the form of point totals, don't bother to develop the other skills of the game, and leave subordinate matters like defense and playmaking largely to their teammates. Hence, it is usually quite easy to parse a basketball team. Bringing the ball up the floor are playmaking backcourt men—selfless fellows who can usually dribble so adeptly that they can just about freeze the ball by themselves, and who can also throw passes through the eye of a needle and can always be counted on to feed the ball to a star at the right moment. A star is often a point-hungry gunner, whose first instinct when he gets the ball is to fire away, and whose playing creed might be condensed to "When in doubt, shoot." Another, with legs like automobile springs, is part of the group because of an unusual ability to shag rebounds. Still another may not be especially brilliant on offense but has defensive equipment that could not be better if he were carrying a trident and a net. The point-hungry gunner aside, Bradley is all these. He is a truly complete basketball player. He can play in any terrain; in the heavy infighting near the basket, he is master of all the gestures of the big men, and toward the edge of play he shows that he has all the fast-moving skills of the little men, too. With remarkable speed for six feet five, he can steal the ball and break into the clear with it on his own; as a dribbler, he can control the ball better with his left hand than most players can with their right; he can go down court in the middle of a fast break and fire passes to left and right, closing in on the basket, the timing of his passes too quick for the spectator's eye. He plays any position—up front, in the post, in the backcourt. And his playmaking is a basic characteristic of his style. His high-scoring totals are the result of his high percentage of accuracy, not of an impulse to shoot every time he gets the ball. He passes as generously and as deftly as any player in the game. When he is dribbling, he can pass accurately without first catching the ball. He can also manage almost any pass without appearing to cock his arm, or even bring his hand back. He just seems to flick his fingers and the ball is gone. Other Princeton players aren't always quite expecting Bradley's passes when they arrive, for Bradley is usually thinking a little bit ahead of everyone else on the floor. When he was a freshman, he was forever hitting his teammates on the mouth, the temple, or the back of the head with passes as accurate as they were surprising. His teammates have since sharpened their own faculties, and these accidents seldom happen now. "It's rewarding to play with him," one of them says. "If you get open, you'll get the ball." And, with all the defenders in between, it sometimes seems as if the ball has passed like a ray through several walls.

Bradley's play has just one somewhat unsound aspect, and it is the result of his mania for throwing the ball to his teammates. He can't seem to resist throwing a certain number of passes that are based on nothing but theory and hope; in fact, they are referred to by the Princeton coaching staff as Bradley's hope passes. They happen, usually, when something has gone just a bit wrong. Bradley is recovering a loose ball, say, with his back turned to the other Princeton players. Before he turned it, he happened to notice a screen, or pick-off, being set by two of his teammates, its purpose being to cause one defensive man to collide with another and thus free an offensive man to receive a pass and score. Computations whir in Bradley's head. He hasn't time to look, but the screen, as he saw it developing, seemed to be working, so a Princeton man should now be in the clear, running toward the basket with one arm up. He whips the ball over his shoulder to the spot where the man ought to be. Sometimes a hope pass goes flying into the crowd, but most of the time they hit the receiver right in the hand, and a gasp comes from several thousand people. Bradley is sensitive about such dazzling passes, because they look flashy, and an edge comes into his voice as he defends them. "When I was halfway down the court, I saw a man out of the corner of my eye who had on the same color shirt I did," he said recently, explaining how he happened to fire a scoring pass while he was falling out of bounds. "A little later, when I threw the pass, I threw it to the spot where that man should have been if he had kept going and done his job. He was there. Two points."

Since it appears that by nature Bradley is a passer first and a scorer second, he would probably have scored less at a school where he was surrounded by other outstanding players. When he went to Princeton, many coaches mourned his loss not just to themselves but to basketball, but as things have worked out, much of his national prominence has been precipitated by his playing for Princeton, where he has had to come through with points in order to keep his team from losing. He starts slowly, as a rule. During much of the game, if he has a clear shot, fourteen feet from the basket, say, and he sees a teammate with an equally clear shot ten feet from the basket, he sends the ball to the teammate. Bradley apparently does not stop to consider that even though the other fellow is closer to the basket he may be far more likely to miss the shot. This habit exasperates his coaches until they clutch their heads in despair. But Bradley is doing what few people ever have done—he is playing basketball according to the foundation pattern of the game. Therefore, the shot goes to the closer man. Nothing on earth can make him change until Princeton starts to lose. Then he will concentrate a little more on the basket.

Something like this happened in Tokyo last October, when the United States Olympic basketball team came close to being beaten by Yugoslavia. The Yugoslavian team was reasonably good—better than the Soviet team, which lost to the United States in the final—and it heated up during the second half. With two minutes to go, Yugoslavia cut the United States' lead to two points. Bradley was on the bench at the time, and Henry Iba, the Oklahoma State coach, who was coach of the Olympic team, sent him in. During much of the game, he had been threading passes to others, but at that point, he says, he felt that he had to try to do something about the score. Bang, bang, bang—he hit a running one-hander, a seventeen-foot jumper, and a lay-up on a fast break, and the United States won by eight points.

Actually, the United States basketball squad encountered no real competition at the Olympics, despite all sorts of rumbling cumulus beforehand to the effect that some of the other teams, notably Russia's, were made up of men who had been playing together for years and were now possibly good enough to defeat an American Olympic basketball team for the first time. But if the teams that the Americans faced were weaker than advertised, there were nonetheless individual performers of good caliber, and it is a further index to Bradley's completeness as a basketball player that Henry Iba, a defensive specialist as a coach, regularly assigned him to guard the stars of the other nations.

"He didn't show too much tact at defense when he started, but he's a coach's basketball player, and he came along," Iba said after he had returned to Oklahoma. "And I gave him the toughest man in every game." Yugoslavia's best man was a big forward who liked to play in the low post, under the basket. Bradley went into the middle with him, crashing shoulders under the basket, and held him to thirteen points while scoring eighteen himself. Russia's best man was Yuri Korneyev, whose specialty was driving; that is, he liked to get the ball somewhere out on the edge of the action and start for the basket with it like a fullback, blasting everything out of the way until he got close enough to ram in a point-blank shot. With six feet five inches and 240 pounds to drive, Korneyev was what Iba called "a real good driver." Bradley had lost ten pounds because of all the Olympics excitement, and Korneyev outweighed him by forty-five pounds. Korneyev kicked, pushed, shoved, bit, and scratched Bradley. "He was tough to stop," Bradley says. "After all, he was playing for his life." Korneyev got eight points.

Bradley was one of three players who had been picked unanimously for the twelve-man Olympic team. He was the youngest member of the squad and the only undergraduate. Since his trip to Tokyo kept him away from Princeton for the first six weeks of the fall term, he had to spend part of his time reading, and the course he worked on most was Russian History 323. Perhaps because of the perspective this gave him, his attitude toward the Russian basketball team was not what he had expected it to be. With the help of three Australian players who spoke Russian, Bradley got to know several members of the Russian team fairly well, and soon he was feeling terribly sorry for them. They had a leaden attitude almost from the beginning. "All we do is play basketball," one of them told him forlornly. "After we go home, we play in the Soviet championships. Then we play in the Satellite championships. Then we play in the European championships. I would give anything for five days off." Bradley says that the Russian players also told him they were paid eighty-five dollars a month, plus housing. Given the depressed approach of the Russians, Bradley recalls, it was hard to get excited before the Russian-American final. "It was tough to get chills," he says. "I had to imagine we were about to play Yale." The Russians lost, 73–59.

When Bradley talks about basketball, he speaks with authority, explaining himself much as a man of fifty might do in discussing a profession or business. When he talks about other things, he shows himself to be a polite, diffident, hopeful, well-brought-up, extremely amiable, and sometimes naïve but generally discerning young man just emerging from adolescence. He was twenty-one last summer, and he seems neither older nor younger than his age. He is painfully aware of his celebrity. The nature of it and the responsibility that it imposes are constantly on his mind. He remembers people's names, and greets them by name when he sees them again. He seems to want to prove that he finds other people interesting. "The main thing I have to prevent myself from becoming is disillusioned with transitory success," he said recently. "It's dangerous. It's like a heavy rainstorm. It can do damage or it can do good, permitting something to grow." He claims that the most important thing basketball gives him at Princeton is "a real period of relief from the academic load." Because he is the sort of student who does all his academic course work, he doesn't get much sleep; in fact, he has a perilous contempt for sleep, partly because he has been told that professional basketball players get along on almost none of it. He stays up until his work is done, for if he were to retire any earlier he would be betraying the discipline he has placed upon himself. When he has had to, he has set up schedules of study for himself that have kept him reading from 6 A.M. to midnight every day for as long as eight weeks. On his senior thesis, which is due in April (and is about Harry Truman's senatorial campaign in 1940), he has already completed more research than many students will do altogether. One of his most enviable gifts is his ability to regiment his conscious mind. After a game, for example, most college players, if they try to study, see all the action over again between the lines in their books. Bradley can, and often does, go straight to the library and work for hours, postponing his mental replay as long as he cares to. If he feels that it's necessary, he will stay up all night before a basketball game; he did that last winter when he was completing a junior paper, and Princeton barely managed to beat a fairly unspectacular Lafayette team, because Bradley seemed almost unable to lift his arms. Princeton was losing until Bradley, finally growing wakeful, scored eight points in the last two minutes.

Ivy League basketball teams play on Friday and Saturday nights, in order to avoid traveling during the week, yet on Sunday mornings

Bradley gets up and teaches a nine-thirty Sunday-school class at the First Presbyterian Church. During his sophomore and junior years at the university, he met a class of seventh-grade boys every Sunday morning that he was resident in Princeton. If the basketball bus returned to Princeton at 4:30 A.M., as it sometimes did, he would still be at the church by nine-thirty. This year, having missed two months while he was in the Far East, he is working as a spot teacher whenever he is needed. Religion, he feels, is the main source of his strength, and because he realizes that not everybody shares that feeling today, he sometimes refers to "the challenge of being in the minority in the world." He belongs to the Fellowship of Christian Athletes, an organization that was set up eight years ago, by people like Otto Graham, Bob Pettit, Branch Rickey, Bob Feller, Wilma Rudolph, Doak Walker, Rafer Johnson, and Robin Roberts, for the advancement of youth by a mixture of moral and athletic guidance. Bradley has flown all over the United States to speak to FCA groups. One of his topics is a theory of his that conformists and nonconformists both lack moral courage, and another is that "the only way to solve a problem is to go through it rather than around it"—which has struck some listeners as an odd view for a basketball player to have. Nevertheless, Bradley often tells his audiences, "Basketball discipline carries over into your life," continuing, "You've got to face that you're going to lose. Losses are part of every season, and part of life. The question is, can you adjust? It is important that you don't get caught up in your own little defeats." If he seems ministerial, that is because he is. He has a firm sense of what is right, and apparently feels that he has a mission to help others see things as clearly as he does. "I don't try to be overbearing in what I believe, but, given a chance, I will express my beliefs," he says. After the Olympics were over, he stayed in the Far East an extra week to make a series of speeches at universities in Taiwan and Hong Kong.

As a news story once said of Bradley—quite accurately, it seems—he is everything his parents think he is. He approximates what some undergraduates call a straight arrow—a semi-pejorative term for unfortunates who have no talent for vice. Nevertheless, considerable numbers of Princeton undergraduates have told me that Bradley is easily the most widely admired student on the campus and probably the best liked, and that his skill at basketball is not the only way in which he atones for his moral altitude. He has worked for the Campus Fund

Drive, which is a sort of Collegiate Gothic community chest, and for the Orange Key Society, an organization that, among other things, helps freshmen settle down into college life. One effect that Bradley has had on Princeton has been to widen noticeably the undergraduate body's tolerance for people with high ethical standards. "He is a source of inspiration to anyone who comes in contact with him," one of his classmates says. "You look at yourself and you decide to do better."

Bradley has built his life by setting up and going after a series of goals, athletic and academic, which at the moment have culminated in his position on the Olympic basketball team and his Rhodes Scholarship. Of the future beyond Oxford, he says only that he wants to go to law school and later "set a Christian example by implementing my feelings within the structure of the society," adding, "I value my ultimate goals more than playing basketball." I have asked all sorts of people who know Bradley, or know about him, what they think he will be doing when he is forty. A really startling number of them, including teachers, coaches, college boys, and even journalists, give the same answer: "He will be the governor of Missouri." The chief dissent comes from people who look beyond the stepping stone of the Missouri State House and calmly tell you that Bradley is going to be president. Last spring, Leonard Shecter, of the *New York Post,* began a column by saying, "In twenty-five years or so our presidents are going to have to be better than ever. It's nice to know that Bill Bradley will be available." Edward Rapp, Bradley's high school principal, once said, "With the help of his friends, Bill could very well be president of the United States. And without the help of his friends he might make it anyway."

Some of Bradley's classmates, who think he is a slave to his ideals, call him the Martyr, though he is more frequently addressed as Brads, Spin, Star, or Horse. He is also called Hayseed, and teased about his Missouri accent. Additional abuse is piled on him by his five roommates, who kid him by saying that his good grades are really undeserved gifts from a hero-worshipping faculty, and who insistently ask him to tell them how many points he scored in various bygone games, implying that he knows exactly but is feigning modesty when he claims he doesn't. He is a good-looking, dark-haired boy whose habits of dress give him protective coloration on the Princeton campus; like nearly everyone else, he wears khaki trousers and a white shirt. His room is always littered, and he doesn't seem to care when he runs out of things; he has been known to sleep without sheets for as long as five weeks, stretched out on a bare mattress under a hairy bit of blanket. He drives automobiles wildly. When he wastes time, he wastes it hurriedly rather than at leisure. He dates with modest frequency—girls from Smith, Wellesley, Vassar, Randolph-Macon, Manhattanville. Just before leaving his room to go dress for a basketball game, he invariably turns on his hi-fi and listens to "Climb Every Mountain," from *The Sound of Music*. He is introspective, and sometimes takes himself very seriously; it is hard, too, for him to let himself go. His reserve with people he doesn't know well has often caused him to be quite inaccurately described as shy and somber. He has an ambiguous, bemused manner that makes people wonder on occasion whether he is in earnest or just kidding; they eventually decide, as a rule, that half the time he is just kidding.

Bradley calls practically all men "Mister" whose age exceeds his own by more than a couple of years. This includes any NBA players he happens to meet, Princeton trainers, and Mr. Willem Hendrik van Breda Kolff, his coach. Van Breda Kolff was a Princeton basketball star himself, some twenty years ago, and went on to play for the New York Knickerbockers. Before returning to Princeton in 1962, he coached at Lafayette and Hofstra. His teams at the three colleges have won 251 games and lost 96. Naturally, it was a virtually unparalleled stroke of good fortune for van Breda Kolff to walk into his current coaching job in the very year that Bradley became eligible to play for the varsity team, but if the coach was lucky to have the player, the player was also lucky to have the coach. Van Breda Kolff, a cheerful and uncomplicated man, has a sportsman's appreciation of the nuances of the game, and appears to feel that mere winning is far less important than winning with style. He is an Abstract Expressionist of basketball. Other coaches have difficulty scouting his teams, because he does not believe in a set offense. He likes his offense free-form.

Van Breda Kolff simply tells his boys to spread out and keep the ball moving. "Just go fast, stay out of one another's way, pass, move, come off guys, look for one-on-ones, two-on-ones, two-on-twos, three-on-threes. That's about the extent," he says. That is, in fact, about the substance of basketball, which is almost never played as a five-man game anymore but is, rather, a constant search, conducted semi-independently by five players, for smaller combinations that will produce a score. One-on-one is the basic situation of the game—one man, with the ball, trying to score against one defensive player, who is trying to stop him, with nobody else involved. Van Breda Kolff does not think that Bradley is a great one-on-one player. "A one-on-one player is a hungry player," he explains. "Bill is not hungry. At least ninety percent of the time, when he gets the ball, he is looking for a pass." Van Breda Kolff has often tried to force Bradley into being more of a one-on-one player, through gentle persuasion in practice, through restrained pleas during time-outs, and even through open clamor. During one game last year, when Princeton was losing and Bradley was still flicking passes, van Breda Kolff stood up and shouted, "*Will . . . you . . . shoot . . . that . . . ball?*" Bradley, obeying at once, drew his man into the vortex of a reverse pivot, and left him standing six feet behind as he made a soft, short jumper from about ten feet out.

If Bradley were more interested in his own statistics, he could score sixty or seventy-five points, or maybe even a hundred, in some of his games. But this would merely be personal aggrandizement, done at the expense of the relative balance of his own team and causing unnecessary embarrassment to the opposition, for it would only happen against an opponent that was heavily outmatched anyway. Bradley's highest point totals are almost always made when the other team is strong and the situation demands his scoring ability. He has, in fact, all the mechanical faculties a great one-on-one player needs. As van Breda Kolff will point out, for example, Bradley has "a great reverse pivot," and this is an essential characteristic of a one-on-one specialist. A way of getting rid of a defensive man who is playing close, it is a spin of the body, vaguely similar to what a football halfback does when he spins away from a would-be tackler, and almost exactly what a lacrosse player does when he "turns his man." Say that Bradley is dribbling hard toward the basket and the defensive man is all over him. Bradley turns, in order to put his body between his opponent and the ball; he continues his dribbling but shifts the ball from one hand to the other; if his man is still crowding in on him, he keeps on turning until he has made one full revolution and is once more headed toward the basket. This is a reverse pivot. Bradley can execute one in less than a second. The odds are that when he has completed the spin the defensive player will be behind him, for it is the nature of basketball that the odds favor the man with the ball—if he knows how to play them. Bradley doesn't need to complete the full revolution every time. If his man steps away from him in anticipation of a reverse pivot, Bradley can stop dead and make a jump shot. If the man stays close to him but not close enough to be turned, Bradley can send up a hook shot. If the man moves over so that he will be directly in Bradley's path when Bradley comes out of the turn, Bradley can scrap the reverse pivot before he begins it, merely suggesting it with his shoulders and then continuing his original dribble to the basket, making his man look like a pedestrian who has leaped to get out of the way of a speeding car.

The metaphor of basketball is to be found in these compounding alternatives. Every time a basketball player takes a step, an entire new geometry of action is created around him. In ten seconds, with or without the ball, a good player may see perhaps a hundred alternatives and, from them, make half a dozen choices as he goes along. A great player will see even more alternatives and will make more choices, and this multi-radial way of looking at things can carry over into his life. At least, it carries over into Bradley's life. The very word *alternatives* bobs in and out of his speech with noticeable frequency. Before his Rhodes Scholarship came along and eased things, he appeared to be worrying about dozens of alternatives for next year. And he still fills his days with alternatives. He apparently always needs to have eight ways to jump, not because he is excessively prudent but because that is what makes the game interesting.

The reverse pivot, of course, is just one of numerous one-on-one moves that produce a complexity of possibilities. A rocker step, for example, in which a player puts one foot forward and rocks his shoulders forward and backward, can yield a set shot if the defensive man steps back, a successful drive to the basket if the defensive man comes in too close, a jump shot if he tries to compromise. A simple crossover— shifting a dribble from one hand to the other and changing direction— can force the defensive man to overcommit himself, as anyone knows who has ever watched Oscar Robertson use it to break free and score. Van Breda Kolff says that Bradley is "a great mover," and points out that the basis of all these maneuvers is footwork. Bradley has spent hundreds of hours merely rehearsing the choreography of the game— shifting his feet in the same patterns again and again, until they have worn into his motor subconscious. "The average basketball player only likes to play basketball," van Breda Kolff says. "When he's left to himself, all he wants to do is get a two-on-two or a three-on-three going. Bradley practices techniques, making himself learn and improve instead of merely having fun."

Because of Bradley's super-serious approach to basketball, his relationship to van Breda Kolff is in some respects a reversal of the usual relationship between a player and a coach. Writing to van Breda Kolff from Tokyo in his capacity as captain-elect, Bradley advised his coach that they should prepare themselves for "the stern challenge ahead." Van Breda Kolff doesn't vibrate to that sort of tune. "Basketball is a game," he says. "It is not an ordeal. I think Bradley's happiest whenever he can deny himself pleasure." Van Breda Kolff's handling of Bradley

has been, in a way, a remarkable feat of coaching. One man cannot beat five men—at least not consistently—and Princeton loses basketball games. Until this season, moreover, the other material that van Breda Kolff has had at his disposal has been for the most part below even the usual Princeton standard, so the fact that his teams have won two consecutive championships is about as much to his credit as to his star's. Van Breda Kolff says, "I try to play it just as if he were a normal player. I don't want to overlook him, but I don't want to over-look for him, either, if you see what I'm trying to say." Bradley's teammates sometimes depend on him too much, the coach explains, or, in a kind of psychological upheaval, get self-conscious about being on the court with a superstar and, perhaps to prove their independence, bring the ball up the court five or six times without passing it to him. When this happens, van Breda Kolff calls time-out. "Hey, boys," he says. "What have we got an All-American for?" He refers to Bradley's stardom only when he has to, however. In the main, he takes Bradley with a calculated grain of salt. He is interested in Bradley's relative weaknesses rather than in his storied feats, and has helped him gain poise on the court, learn patience, improve his rebounding, and be more aggressive. He refuses on principle to say that Bradley is the best basketball player he has ever coached, and he is also careful not to echo the general feeling that Bradley is the most exemplary youth since Lochinvar, but he will go out of his way to tell about the reaction of referees to Bradley. "The refs watch Bradley like a hawk, but, because he never complains, they feel terrible if they make an error against him," he says. "They just love him because he is such a gentleman. They get upset if they call a bad one on him." I asked van Breda Kolff what he thought Bradley would be doing when he was forty. "I don't know," he said. "I guess he'll be the governor of Missouri."

Many coaches, on the reasonable supposition that Bradley cannot beat their teams alone, concentrate on choking off the four other Princeton players, but Bradley is good enough to rise to such occasions, as he did when he scored forty-six against Texas, making every known shot, including an eighteen-foot running hook. Some coaches, trying a standard method of restricting a star, set up four of their players in either a box-shaped or a diamond-shaped zone defensive formation and put their fifth player on Bradley, man-to-man. Wherever Bradley goes under these circumstances, he has at least two men guarding him, the

man-to-man player and the fellow whose zone he happens to be passing through. This is a dangerous defense, however, because it concedes
an imbalance of forces, and also because Bradley is so experienced at
being guarded by two men at once that he can generally fake them both
out with a single move; also, such overguarding often provides Bradley
with enough free throws to give his team the margin of victory. Most
coaches have played Princeton straight, assigning their best defensive
man to Bradley and letting it go at that. This is what St. Joseph's College did in the opening round of the NCAA Tournament in 1963. St.
Joseph's had a strong, well-balanced team, which had lost only four
games of a twenty-five-game schedule and was heavily favored to rout
Princeton. The St. Joseph's player who was to guard Bradley promised
his teammates that he would hold Bradley below twenty points.
Bradley made twenty points in the first half. He made another twenty
points in the first sixteen minutes of the second half. In the group battles for rebounds, he won time after time. He made nearly 60 percent
of his shots, and he made sixteen out of sixteen from the foul line. The
experienced St. Joseph's man could not handle him, and the whole
team began to go after him in frenzied clusters. He would dribble
through them, disappearing in the ruck and emerging a moment later,
still dribbling, to float up toward the basket and score. If St. Joseph's
forced him over toward the sideline, he would crouch, turn his head to
look for the distant basket, step, kick his leg, and follow through with
his arms, sending a long, high hook shot—all five parts intact—into
the net. When he went up for a jump shot, St. Joseph's players would
knock him off balance, but he would make the shot anyway, crash to
the floor, get up, and sink the dividend foul shot, scoring three points
instead of two on the play. On defense, he guarded St. Joseph's highest-
scoring player, Tom Wynne, and held him to nine points. The defense
was expensive, though. An aggressive defensive player has to take the
risk of committing five personal fouls, after which a player is obliged
by the rules to leave the game. With just under four minutes to go,
and Princeton comfortably ahead by five points, Bradley committed
his fifth foul and left the court. For several minutes, the game was interrupted as the crowd stood and applauded him; the game was being
played in Philadelphia, where hostility toward Princeton is ordinarily
great but where the people know a folk hero when they see one. After
the cheering ended, the blood drained slowly out of Princeton, whose

other players could not hold the lead. Princeton lost by one point. Dr. Jack Ramsey, the St. Joseph's coach, says that Bradley's effort that night was the best game of basketball he has ever seen a college boy play.

Some people, hearing all the stories of Bradley's great moments, go to see him play and are disappointed when he does not do something memorable at least once a minute. Actually, basketball is a hunting game. It lasts for forty minutes, and there are ten men on the court, so the likelihood is that any one player, even a superstar, will actually have the ball in his hands for only four of those minutes, or perhaps a little more. The rest of the time, a player on offense either is standing around recovering his breath or is on the move, foxlike, looking for openings, sizing up chances, attempting to screen off a defensive man—by "coming off guys," as van Breda Kolff puts it—and thus upset the balance of power. The depth of Bradley's game is most discernible when he doesn't have the ball. He goes in and swims around in the vicinity of the basket, back and forth, moving for motion's sake, making plans and abandoning them, and always watching the distant movement of the ball out of the corner of his eye. He stops and studies his man, who is full of alertness, because of the sudden break in the rhythm. The man is trying to watch both Bradley and the ball. Bradley watches the man's head. If it turns too much to the right, he moves quickly to the left. If it turns too much to the left, he goes to the right. If, ignoring the ball, the man focusses his full attention on Bradley, Bradley stands still and looks at the floor. A high-lobbed pass floats in, and just before it arrives Bradley jumps high, takes the ball, turns, and scores. If Princeton has an out-of-bounds play under the basket, Bradley takes a position just inside the baseline, almost touching the teammate who is going to throw the ball into play. The defensive man crowds in to try to stop whatever Bradley is planning. Bradley whirls around the defensive man, blocking him out with one leg, and takes a bounce pass and lays up the score. This works only against naïve opposition, but when it does work it is a marvel to watch. To receive a pass from a backcourt man, Bradley moves away from the basket and toward one side of the court. He gets the ball, gives it up, goes into the center, and hovers there awhile. Nothing happens. He goes back to the corner. He starts toward the backcourt again to receive a pass like the first one. His man, who is eager and has been through this before, moves out toward the backcourt a step ahead of Bradley. This is a defensive error. Bradley isn't going that way; he was only faking. He heads straight for the basket, takes a bounce pass, and scores. This maneuver is known in basketball as going backdoor. Bradley is able to go backdoor successfully and often, because of his practiced footwork. Many players, once their man has made himself vulnerable, rely on surprise alone to complete a back-door play, and that isn't always enough. Bradley's fake looks for all the world like the beginning of a trip to the outside; then, when he goes for the basket, he has all the freedom he needs. When he gets the ball after breaking free, other defensive players naturally leave their own men and try to stop him. In these three-on-two or two-on-one situations, the obvious move is to pass to a teammate who has moved into a position to score. Sometimes, however, no teammate has moved and Bradley sees neither a pass nor a shot, so he veers around and goes back and picks up his own man. "I take him on into the corner for a one-on-one," he says, imagining what he might do. "I move toward the free-throw line on a dribble. If the man is overplaying me to my right, I reverse pivot and go in for a left-handed lay-up. If the man is playing even with me, but off me a few feet, I take a jump shot. If the man is playing me good defense—honest—and he's on me tight, I keep going. I give him a head-and-shoulder fake, keep going all the time, and drive to the bas-ket, or I give him a head-and-shoulder fake and take a jump shot. Those are all the things you need—the fundamentals."

Bradley develops a relationship with his man that is something like the relationship between a yoyoist and his yoyo. "I'm on the side of the floor," he postulates, "and I want to play with my man a little bit, always knowing where the ball is but not immediately concerned with getting it. Basketball is a game of two or three men, and you have to know how to stay out of a play and not clutter it up. I cut to the baseline. My man will follow me. I'll cut up to the high-post position. He'll follow me. I'll cut to the low-post position. He'll follow me. I'll go back out to my side position. He'll follow. I'll fake to the center of the floor and go hard to the baseline, running my man into a pick set at the low-post position. I'm not running him into a pick in order to get free for a shot—I'm doing it simply to irritate him. I come up on the other side of the bas-ket, looking to see if a teammate feels that I'm open. They can't get the ball to me at that instant. Now my man is back with me. I go out to the side. I set a screen for the guard. He sees the situation. He comes toward me. He dribbles hard past me, running his man into my back. I feel the contact. My man switches off me, leaving the pass lane open for a split second. I go hard to the basket and take a bounce pass for a shot. Two points."

Because Bradley's inclination to analyze every gesture in basketball is fairly uncommon, other players look at him as if they think him a little odd when he seeks them out after a game and asks them to show him what they did in making a move that he particularly admired. They tell him that they're not sure what he is talking about, and that even if they could remember, they couldn't possibly explain, so the best offer they can make is to go back to the court, try to set up the situation again, and see what it was that provoked his appreciation. Bradley told me about this almost apologetically, explaining that he had no choice but to be analytical in order to be in the game at all. "I don't have that much natural ability," he said, and went on to tell a doleful tale about how his legs lacked spring, how he was judged among the worst of the Olympic candidates in ability to get high off the floor, and so on, until he had nearly convinced me that he was a motor moron. In actuality, Bradley does have certain natural advantages. He has been six feet five since he was fifteen years old, so he had most of his high school years in which to develop his coordination, and it is now exceptional for a tall man. His hand span, measuring only nine and a half inches, does not give him the wraparound control that basketball players like to have, but, despite relatively unimpressive shoulders and biceps, he is unusually strong, and he can successfully mix with almost anyone in the Greco-Roman battles under the backboards. His most remarkable natural gift, however, is his vision. During a game, Bradley's eyes are always a glaze of panoptic attention, for a basketball player needs to look at everything, focussing on nothing, until the last moment of commitment. Beyond this, it is obviously helpful to a basketball player to be able to see a little more than the next man, and the remark is frequently made about basketball superstars that they have unusual peripheral vision. People used to say that Bob Cousy, the immortal backcourt man of the Boston Celtics, could look due east and enjoy a sunset. Ed Macauley once took a long auto trip with Cousy when they were teammates, and in the course of it Cousy happened to go to sleep sitting up. Macauley swears that Cousy's eyelids, lowered as far as they would go, failed to cover his coleopteran eyes. Bradley's eyes close normally enough, but his astounding passes to teammates have given him, too, a reputation for being able to see out of the back of his head. To discover whether there was anything to all the claims for basketball players' peripheral vision, I asked Bradley to go with me to the office of Dr. Henry Abrams, a Princeton ophthalmologist, who had agreed to measure Bradley's total field. Bradley rested his chin in the middle of a device called a perimeter, and Dr. Abrams began asking when he could see a small white dot as it was slowly brought around from behind him, from above, from below, and from either side. To make sure that Bradley wasn't, in effect, throwing hope passes, Dr. Abrams checked each point three times before plotting it on a chart. There was a chart for each eye, and both charts had irregular circles printed on them, representing the field of vision that a typical perfect eye could be expected to have. Dr. Abrams explained as he worked that these printed circles were logical rather than experimentally established extremes, and that in his experience the circles he had plotted to represent the actual vision fields of his patients had without exception fallen inside the circles printed on the charts. When he finished plotting Bradley's circles, the one for each eye was larger than the printed model and, in fact, ran completely outside it. With both eyes open and looking straight ahead, Bradley sees 195 degrees on the horizontal and about 70 degrees straight down, or about 15 and 5 degrees more, respectively, than what is officially considered perfection. Most surprising, however, is what he can see above him. Focussed horizontally, the typical perfect eye, according to the chart, can see about 47 degrees upward. Bradley can see 70 degrees upward. This no doubt explains why he can stare at the floor while he is waiting for lobbed passes to arrive from above. Dr. Abrams said that he doubted whether a person who tried to expand his peripheral vision through exercises could succeed, but he was fascinated to learn that when Bradley was a young boy he tried to do just that. As he walked down the main street of Crystal City, for example, he would keep his eyes focused straight ahead and try to identify objects in the windows of stores he was passing. For all this, however, Bradley cannot see behind himself. Much of the court and, thus, a good deal of the action are often invisible to a basketball player, so he needs more than good eyesight. He needs to know how to function in the manner of a blind man as well. When, say, four players are massed in the middle of things behind Bradley, and it is inconvenient for him to look around, his hands reach back and his fingers move rapidly from shirt to shirt or hip to hip. He can read the defense as if he were reading Braille.

Bradley's optical endowments notwithstanding, Coach van Breda

Kolff agrees with him that he is "not a great physical player," and goes on to say, "Others can run faster and jump higher. The difference between Bill and other basketball players is self-discipline." The two words that Bradley repeats most often when he talks about basketball are *discipline* and *concentration,* and through the exercise of both he has made himself an infectious example to younger players. "Concentrate!" he keeps shouting to himself when he is practicing on his own. His capacity for self-discipline is so large that it is almost funny. For example, he was a bit shocked when the Olympic basketball staff advised the Olympic basketball players to put in one hour of practice a day during the summer, because he was already putting in two hours a day—often in ninety-five-degree temperatures, with his feet squishing in sneakers that had become so wet that he sometimes skidded and crashed to the floor. His creed, which he picked up from Ed Macauley, is "When you are not practicing, remember, someone somewhere is practicing, and

"Ah, there you are, at last, Mrs. Jennings. Your
horse got back at two-thirty, so we'll only charge you till then."

when you meet him he will win." He also believes that the conquest of pain is essential to any seriously sustained athletic endeavor. In 1963, he dressed for a game against Harvard although he had a painful foot injury. Then, during the pregame warmup, it bothered him so much that he decided to give up, and he started for the bench. He changed his mind on the way, recalling that a doctor had told him that his foot, hurt the night before at Dartmouth, was badly bruised but was not in danger of further damage. If he had sat down, he says, he would have lowered his standards, for he believes that "there has never been a great athlete who did not know what pain is." So he played the game. His heavily taped foot went numb during the first ten minutes, but his other faculties seemed to sharpen in response to the handicap. His faking quickened to make up for his reduced speed, and he scored thirty-two points, missing only five shots during the entire evening.

How Bradley acquired these criteria and became a superstar is not what interests people in basketball. If they think about it at all, they wonder *why* he did it. "Where did this kid get his dedication?" Macauley asks. "Why did he decide to make the sacrifices?" The pattern of his life seems to provide an answer to the question, beginning with the fact that he used the sport as a way to get to know other boys, for he was an only child.

Crystal City, which was once an active river port, now has a population of about four thousand, with a preponderance of Italians, Greeks, French, and Slavs, and a considerable proportion of Negroes. Its principal street, Mississippi Avenue, is paved with red brick and overhung with the limbs of oak and tulip trees. Although the town is fully incorporated, its people see it as a collection of unofficial subdivisions, various neighborhoods being known as Crystal Valley, Crystal Terrace, Crystal Heights, Old Town, Downtown, Crystal Village, and North Crystal. A stranger arriving at night and hearing talk of all these areas might well believe he was in a sprawling megalopolis. In reality, the town has a three-man police force; it has one factory, an enormous one that makes plate glass and that indirectly gave the town its name; and it has one bank president, and one bank president's son.

The Bradleys live on Taylor Avenue, behind picture windows that look out on the Grace Presbyterian Church, across the street, whose ample churchyard forms a kind of town common. Elsewhere in Crystal City, weeds sometimes grow at 45-degree angles out of the clefts where the streets meet the curbstones, and property owners tend to resign themselves to having brown lawns in summer, but in and around the churchyard everything is trim, immaculate, and green. When Warren Bradley, Bill's father, goes to work in the morning, he walks halfway around the churchyard to the Crystal City State Bank, where, according to his wife, he "started out as a penny shiner" in 1921. His father had died in 1910, when he was nine, and he had been able to complete only one year at Crystal City High School before going to work, first as a ticket-seller for the Missouri & Illinois Railroad and later as a yard clerk for the Frisco Line. "The feel of money seemed to appeal to me," he says in explaining his switchover to banking. Sixteen years after joining the bank, he became its president. In the meantime, he compensated for his abbreviated education by reading on his own, and although his son is a Rhodes Scholar, he is still the most incisive and articulate member of the family. He cares about politics with a studious passion and, ignoring the possible effect of his beliefs on his business, is a contentious Republican in a town full of Democrats. He is ordinarily a reserved man, and he has a soft voice, but when something worth reacting to comes along, he reacts, and often bluntly. Four years ago, when his son was under very heavy recruitment pressure from college coaches, Mr. Bradley was disturbed by all the attention his family was getting, because he didn't think that basketball was that important. One day, a man walked into the Crystal City State Bank without an appointment and asked Mr. Bradley's secretary to say that Adolph Rupp had come to call. Rupp, known throughout basketball as the Baron, has for thirty-five years been the coach at the University of Kentucky. He works more meticulously and expensively than any other coach, having movies taken at every practice, which he studies each morning as if he were John Huston going over the daily rushes. He once drove Artur Rubinstein out of his gym because the pianist, preparing for a concert, disturbed the concentration of the Kentucky Wildcats. He has won more than seven hundred games while losing only 145, and he once won three national championships in four years. Rupp still gets indignant when he remembers that Mr. Bradley was too busy to see him immediately. Rupp had to wait an hour and a half.

Thanks to a noteworthy stamina of spirit, Mr. Bradley has overcome the inconveniences of having calcified arthritis of the lower spine, which has made him unable to bend over for nearly twenty-five years. He uses long wooden tweezers to pick up objects from the floor. He was almost forty when he married Susan Crowe, who was a graduate of Central College, in Fayette, Missouri, and was then teaching in a junior high school in St. Louis. She grew up near Herculaneum, a town a few miles up the river from Crystal City, and she played interscholastic basketball for Herculaneum High School—a bit of family history that amuses her son. She is five feet seven, and her husband is six feet one and a half. What Bill Bradley calls the luck of being the son of these parents arises from the marked differences in their personalities. If Mr. Bradley is a contemplative man with "an enlightened disinterest," in his son's words, in regard to athletic pinnacles, Mrs. Bradley is an outgoing and amiably competitive woman of immense dynamism. Her father, a coffee salesman, was a big, rough man who could bend spikes in his hands, could do six things at once, liked to tell jokes all night, and was proud of a mark on his forehead where a stallion had once bit him. Mrs. Bradley, who is full of high spirits herself, spends her life doing things for other people, except when she's on the links at the Joachim Country Club. She says that she couldn't care less who wins and who loses at any game, but she usually wins, and she has been club champion. Edward Rapp, the principal of the Crystal City High School, grew up with Mrs. Bradley and watched with interest as she raised her son. "Susie knew what kind of a son she wanted, and by dint of determination she has him," Rapp says. She herself says, "I wanted a Christian upright citizen, and I thought the best way to begin was by promoting things that would interest a little boy." She always had a busy program planned for him, full of golf lessons, swimming lessons, piano lessons, French lessons, trumpet lessons, dancing lessons, and tennis lessons.

When Bradley went out on his own, he sometimes encountered attitudes that disconcerted him. The churchyard was a favorite site with boys in the town for pickup games of tackle football. Crossing the street with the idea of joining in, he would sometimes hear the other boys say something like "Oh, here comes the banker's son," in a tone that made it clear enough that they did not want him. "This was something that hurt me in a very personal way," he says. "They would not judge me for what I was." In one form or another, the stigma of being the banker's son remained with him for some years, and it made him feel that he had more of a need to prove himself than others did. He gradually became tolerated in the churchyard football games, whereupon he displayed another peculiarity, which no one really minded. All little boys playing tackle do so with the understanding that they are not really themselves but small and temporary incarnations of the greatest playing stars. The other boys in the churchyard would announce their names one by one, all of them claiming to be stalwarts of the University of Missouri or some other Midwestern school. Bradley, for his part, always told them that he was Dick Kazmaier, of Princeton, who in the early fifties won the Heisman Trophy as the outstanding college football player in the United States. Today, Bradley wears on his basketball uniform at Princeton the number 42, which is the number that Kazmaier used in football.

Bradley first played basketball, in the Crystal City YMCA, when he was nine years old. "It was just for something to do," he recalls. When his mother saw that he was interested in the game, she put a basket on the side of the garage so that he could play with his fellow Cub Scouts, to whom she was den mother. Each year, however, the seasonal fever for basketball had just begun to rise when it was time to go to Palm Beach. This was a recurrent frustration, for at the Palm Beach Private School, which he attended, soccer, fencing, and boxing were the major sports. When the school day ended at two, Bradley would hurry out past the limousines that were picking up his classmates, run back to the hotel where his parents stayed, go to his room, and reach under his bed for his basketball—an odd item to take along on a trip to Florida. With a series of tympanic thumps, he would dribble out of the room, across the lobby and the street, and along the sidewalks, under the columnar palms. There was a public schoolyard several blocks away with a basket in it, and he played there every day. Now and then, a few tatterdemalions from West Palm Beach came to the playground, and he befriended them eagerly. "Basketball was a way to get to know guys," he says. But usually he was alone. This, as much as any place, was where the fundamental narcotic of basketball entered his system. He can remember quite vividly how he felt about the game and about himself as he played it, and once, when I asked him about it, he closed his eyes and said, "What attracted me was the sound of the swish, the sound of the dribble, the feel of going up in the air. You don't need eight others, like in baseball. You don't need any brothers or sisters. Just you. I wonder what the guys are doing back home. I'd like to be there, but it's as much fun here, because I'm playing. It's getting dark. I have to go back for dinner. I'll shoot a couple more. Feels good. A couple more."

Toward the end of seventh grade, Bill told his father he wanted to stay in Crystal City in future winters, and his father consented. The Bradley house then became the community center, for Bill had things that the other boys didn't have—television in his bedroom, for example, and a pinball machine in the basement. On the inside of his bedroom door he had a basketball net, and when the weather was bad outdoors he would get down on his knees—he was six feet three when he was in the eighth grade—and play against boys his own age, two at a time. Conditions outside had to be pretty unsavory before that happened, though; he and his friends played around the outdoor basket in gloves, if necessary, and at night, under floodlights. Gradually, Bradley's backyard evolved into a basketball court nearly as good as Princeton's. "Our yard wasn't for the purpose of raising grass," his father recalls. "There was no grass in it at all." This was because they had a macadam surface put over it, flat and smooth, around the steel pole supporting a fan-shaped backboard, whose hoop was exactly ten feet above the ground. There must be at least five million backyard baskets in the United States, yet it is possible to search through a whole community without finding more than half a dozen at the regulation height.

Bradley's high school basketball coach, Arvel Popp (pronounced "Pope"), says that he began cultivating Bradley when the boy was still in grade school. What Popp was mainly cultivating, however, was a football player, because at that time, at least, he was a football coach first and a basketball coach second. Before Bradley reached high school age, Popp told him, "I'm going to make you into the finest end who ever played for the University of Missouri." Bradley therefore incurred double jeopardy when, entering high school, he showed no interest in football. He had to do what he could to dispel gossip that he was chicken, and he had to prove himself as a basketball player to Coach Popp, for Popp was not interested in having boys on his basketball team who didn't play football.

If basketball was going to enable Bradley to make friends, to prove that a banker's son is as good as the next fellow, to prove that he could do without being the greatest-end-ever at Missouri, to prove that he was not chicken, and to live up to his mother's championship standards, and if he was going to have some moments left over to savor his delight in the game, he obviously needed considerable practice, so he borrowed keys to the gym and set a schedule for himself that he adhered to for four full years—in the school year, three and a half hours every day after school, nine to five on Saturday, one-thirty to five on Sunday, and, in the summer, about three hours a day. He put ten pounds of lead slivers in his sneakers, set up chairs as opponents and dribbled in slalom fashion around them, and wore eyeglass frames that had a piece of cardboard taped to them so that he could not see the floor, for a good dribbler never looks at the ball. Aboard the *Queen Elizabeth* on a trip to Europe one summer, he found that the two longitudinal corridors on C Deck, Tourist Class, were each about 450 feet long, making nine hundred feet in all, or ten times the length of a basketball floor. This submarine palaestra became the world's finest training area in two respects. It was not only the longest gym on earth, it was also the narrowest, measuring forty-eight inches across. The width was ideal for the practice of dribbling, since it tended to bunch the opposition, or fellow passengers, who got used to hearing the approaching thump-thump of the basketball, and to seeing what appeared to be a six-foot-five-inch lunatic come bearing down upon them with a device on his face that cut off much of his vision.

Coach Popp, as it turned out, was less inflexible than his reputation suggested. After his varsity basketball team lost its first four games, he decided to put a freshman—Bradley—in his lineup, for the second time ever, and after that the Crystal City Hornets won sixteen out of twenty-one. The older boys on the team resented Bradley's presence a little, and were also suspicious of him, because he would sometimes use the waiting time in the locker room before a game to bring out a textbook and study. They passed to him fairly infrequently in that first year, but, largely as a result of vacuuming rebounds, he averaged twenty points a game. The resentment arose from the natural tendency of high school boys to give a great deal of importance to seniority, and by his third year it was gone. Once an anomaly, he was now a model. One of his teammates of those years, Sam La Presta, has recalled, "Bill did what he did by hard work. Everyone looked up to him. He was sort of inspirational. Basketball was one-millionth of what he had to offer."

At Princeton, Bradley has become such an excellent basketball player that it is necessary to look beyond college basketball to find a standard that will put him in perspective. The standard's name is Oscar Robertson, of the Cincinnati Royals, who is the finest basketball player yet developed. He is five years older than Bradley, and now that Bradley is leaving basketball, the question of who would ultimately have been the better player will not be answered. Robertson, who is known in basketball as the O, stands out among all professionals for the same reason that Bradley stands out among all amateurs. Other players have certain individual skills that are sharper, but Bradley and Robertson are brilliant in every aspect of the game. To make a detailed comparison between Bradley and Robertson as they are now, Robertson is a better rebounder and a better defensive player, notwithstanding the defensive performance that Bradley gave in an exhibition game last fall between the Olympic team and the Royals, when he held Robertson to eleven points. Bradley is as good a passer as Robertson, and they are about even in dribbling, too. Going hard for the basket, Robertson is a better driver. "When I watch Robertson," Bradley says, "I just stand with my mouth wide open. There are so many things he does that I could never do in a hundred years. I could never feel confident, the way he can, that I could shoot jump shots against anybody at all. He's the best basketball player alive." Bradley adds that one of the big differences between his abilities and Robertson's is that the O has better body control and is more deceptive when he moves. Bradley, for his part, has a greater variety of shots than Robertson, and is, in general, a more accurate shooter. As Bradley notes, however, he doesn't have the same jump shot. Bradley is merely outstanding with his jumper. But no one has a jump shot like Robertson's—frozen in the air, with his back arched and his hands behind his head, where the ball is totally protected until he sends it into the basket. Bradley's jump shot is released, more conventionally, from just above his head. The O's jump shot is literally "unstoppable"— the most intoxicating adjective in basketball. If Bradley does enough shooting this year, he may become the second-highest scorer in the records of college basketball, but he will still be nearly five hundred points under the final count that Robertson left behind him at the University of Cincinnati. Robertson and his Royals teammate Jerry Lucas, who played for Ohio State, are the only two basketball players who have been included on the *Sporting News* All-American team, which is picked by the professional scouts, in all three of their college basketball seasons. This year, barring the unforeseen, Bradley will become the third. Among Bradley's Olympic teammates was UCLA's Walt Hazzard, now a Los Angeles Laker, who, like Robertson, is a Negro, and he passed along to Bradley a compliment of unforgettable magnitude. "Where I come from," Hazzard told Bradley, "you are known as the White O."

With all his analyses of its mechanics, Bradley may have broken his game down into its components, but he has reassembled it so seamlessly that all the parts, and also his thousands of hours of practice, are concealed. He is as fluidly graceful as any basketball player I have ever seen. Quite apart from the excitement produced by the scoreboard, a spectator cannot help feeling a considerable elation as he watches Bradley accomplish his fakes and moves and shots. He does it all with a floating economy of motion and a beguiling offhandedness that appeal to the imagination. Many basketball players, outstanding ones included, have a tendency to be rather tastelessly rococo in their style, and Bradley stands out in contrast to them because he adorns nothing that he does. When a game is won beyond doubt, and Bradley leaves the court with three or four minutes to go, the coach of the opposing team has sometimes halted play to walk down to the Princeton bench and shake his hand. The coach doesn't do this just because Bradley has scored thirty-five or forty points but because he has done it so uncompromisingly well.

This season, in the course of a tournament held during the week after Christmas, Bradley took part in a game that followed extraordinarily the pattern of his game against St. Joseph's. Because the stakes were higher, it was a sort of St. Joseph's game to the third power. Whereas St. Joseph's had been the best team in the East, Princeton's opponent this time was Michigan, the team that the Associated Press and the United Press International had rated as the best college team of all. The chance to face Michigan represented to Bradley the supreme test of his capability as a basketball player. As he saw it, any outstanding player naturally hopes to be a member of the country's No. 1 team, but if that never happens, the next-best thing is to be tested against the No. 1 team. And the Michigan situation seemed even more important to him because, tending as he sometimes does to question his own worth, he was uncomfortably conscious that a committee had picked him for the Olympic team, various committees had awarded him his status as an All-American, and, for that matter, committees had elected him a Rhodes Scholar. Michigan, he felt, would provide an exact measurement of him as an athlete. The height of the Michigan players averages six feet five, and nearly every one of them weighs over two hundred pounds. Smoothly experienced, both as individuals and as a coordinated group, they have the appearance, the manner, and the assurance of a professional team. One of them, moreover, is Cazzie Russell, who, like Bradley, was a consensus All-American last year. For a couple of days before the game, the sports pages of the New York newspapers were crammed with headlines, articles, and even cartoons comparing Bradley and Russell, asking which was the better player, and looking toward what one paper called the most momentous individual confrontation in ten years of basketball. One additional factor—something that meant relatively little to Bradley—was that the game was to be played in Madison Square Garden. Bradley had never played in the Garden, but, because he mistrusts metropolitan standards, he refused to concede that the mere location of the coming test meant anything at all. When a reporter asked him how he felt about appearing there, he replied, "It's just like any other place. The baskets are ten feet high."

Bradley now says that he prepared for the Michigan game as he had prepared for no other. He slept for twelve hours, getting up at noon. Then, deliberately, he read the New York newspapers and absorbed the excited prose which might have been announcing a prizefight: FESTIVAL DUEL: BILL BRADLEY VS. CAZZIE RUSSELL . . . CAZZIE—BRADLEY: KEY TEST . . . BRADLEY OR CAZZIE? SHOWDOWN AT HAND . . . BILL BRADLEY OF PRINCETON MEETS CAZZIE RUSSELL OF MICHIGAN TONIGHT AT THE GARDEN!! This exposure to the newspapers had the effect he wanted; he developed chills, signifying a growing stimulation within him. During most of the afternoon, when any other player in his situation would probably have been watching television, shooting pool, or playing Ping-Pong or poker—anything to divert the mind—Bradley sat alone and concentrated on the coming game, on the components of his own play, and on the importance to him and his team of what would occur. As much as anything, he wanted to prove that an Ivy League team could be as good as any other team. Although no newspaper gave

Princeton even the slightest chance of winning, Bradley did not just hope to do well himself—he intended that Princeton should win.

Just before he went onto the court, Bradley scrubbed his hands with soap and water, as he always does before a game, to remove any accumulated skin oil and thus increase the friction between his fingers and the ball. When the game was forty-two seconds old, he hit a jump shot and instantly decided, with a rush of complete assurance of a kind that sometimes comes over an athlete in action, that a victory was not only possible but probable. Michigan played him straight, and he played Michigan into the floor. The performance he delivered had all the depth and variation of theoretical basketball, each move being perfectly executed against able opposition. He stole the ball, he went backdoor, he threw unbelievable passes. He reversed away from the best defenders in the Big Ten. He held his own man to one point. He played in the backcourt, in the post, and in the corners. He made long set shots, and hit jump shots from points so far behind the basket that he had to start them from arm's length in order to clear the backboard. He tried a hook shot on the dead run and hit that, too. Once, he found himself in a corner of the court with two Michigan players, both taller than he, pressing in on him shoulder to shoulder. He parted them with two rapid fakes—a move of the ball and a move of his head—and leaped up between them to sink a twenty-two-foot jumper. The same two players soon cornered him again. The fakes were different the second time, but the result was the same. He took a long stride between them and went up into the air, drifting forward, as they collided behind him, and he hit a clean shot despite the drift. Bradley, playing at the top of his game, drew his teammates up to the best performances they could give, too, and the Princeton team as a whole outplayed Michigan. The game, as it had developed, wasn't going to be just a close and miraculous Princeton victory, it was going to be a rout. But, with Princeton twelve points ahead, Bradley, in the exuberance of sensing victory, made the mistake of playing close defense when he did not need to, and when he was too tired to do it well. He committed his fifth personal foul with four minutes and thirty-seven seconds to go, and had to watch the end of the game from the bench. As he sat down, the twenty thousand spectators stood up and applauded him for some three minutes. It was, as the sportswriters and the Garden management subsequently agreed, the most clamorous ovation ever given a basketball player, amateur or professional, in Madison Square Garden. Bradley's duel with Russell had long since become incidental. Russell scored twenty-seven points and showed his All-American caliber but during the long applause the announcer on the Garden loudspeakers impulsively turned up the volume and said, "Bill Bradley, one of the greatest players ever to play in Madison Square Garden, scored forty-one points." Bradley had ratified his reputation—not through his point total nearly so much as through his total play. After he left the court—joining two of his teammates who had also fouled out—Michigan overran Princeton, and won the game by one basket. Bradley ultimately was given the trophy awarded to the most valuable player in the tournament, but his individual recognition meant next to nothing to him at the time, because of Princeton's defeat. It had become fully apparent, however, that Bradley would be remembered as one of basketball's preeminent stars. And like Hank Luisetti, of Stanford, who never played professional basketball, he will have the almost unique distinction of taking only the name of his college with him into the chronicles of the sport.

1965

EL ÚNICO MATADOR

LILLIAN ROSS

The best bullfighters in the world have come, traditionally, from Spain or Mexico. The old Spanish province of Andalusia has contributed more bulls and more bullfighters to the bull ring than all the rest of Spain. Manolete, probably history's top-ranking matador, who, at the age of thirty, was fatally gored in the summer of 1947, was an Andalusian. Carlos Arruza, who retired last year, at twenty-eight, with a two-million-dollar fortune and the reputation of fighting closer to the bull than any other matador had ever done, was born in Mexico, of Spanish-born parents. Belmonte, an Andalusian, and Joselito, a Spanish gypsy, were the leading figures in what is known in bullfight countries as the Golden Age of Bullfighting, which ended with Belmonte's retirement to breed bulls, in 1921, a year after Joselito's death in the arena. The only Mexican who ranked close to Belmonte and Joselito in their time was Rodolfo Gaona, an Indian, who, in 1925, retired a millionaire with large real-estate interests in Mexico City. Some years ago a Chinese bullfighter named Wong, who wore a natural pigtail, turned up in Mexico as El Torero Chino, and a Peruvian lady bullfighter, Conchita Cintrón, is active today. Only one citizen of the United States has ever been recognized as a full-fledged matador. He is Sidney Franklin, who was born and raised in the Park Slope section of Brooklyn.

Franklin, who is now forty-five, estimates that he has killed two thousand bulls so far. Last winter, in Mexico, he killed thirteen. He is planning to go to Spain this summer to kill as many bulls as he can get contracts to fight, although he is much older than the usual bullfighter is at his peak. "Age has nothing to do with art," he says. "It's all a matter of what's in your mind." He hopes someday to introduce bullfighting to this country, and, if he succeeds, expects it to become more popular than baseball. Ernest Hemingway, who became an authority on bullfighting, as well as on Franklin, while preparing to write *Death in the Afternoon,* maintains that to take to bullfighting a country must have an interest in the breeding of fighting bulls and an interest in death, both of which Hemingway feels are lacking in the United States.

"Death, shmeath, so long as I keep healthy," Franklin says. When aficionados, or bullfight fans, charge that Americans born north of the border are incapable of the passion necessary for bullfighting, Franklin replies passionately that coldness in the presence of danger is the loftiest aspect of his art. "If you've got guts, you can do anything," he says. "Anglo-Saxons can become the greatest bullfighters, the greatest ballet dancers, the greatest anything." When, in 1929, Franklin made his Spanish début, in Seville, the aficionados were impressed by the coldness of his art. "Franklin is neither an improviser nor an accident nor a joker," wrote the bullfight critic for *La Unión,* a Seville newspaper. "He is a born bullfighter, with plenty of ambition, which he has had since birth, and for the bulls he has an ultimate quality—serene valor. Coldness, borrowed from the English, if you please. . . . He parries and holds back with a serene magnificence that grandly masks the danger, and he doesn't lose his head before the fierce onslaughts of the enemy." "Franklin fought as though born in Spain; the others fought as though born in Chicago," another critic observed a year later, in comparing Franklin's manner of dispatching two bulls with the work of the Spanish matadors who appeared on the same bill in a Madrid bull ring. One day early in his career, Franklin killed the two bulls that had been allotted to him, then, taking the place of two other matadors, who had been gored, killed four more. This set off such an emotional chain reaction in the ring that another bullfighter dropped dead of excitement. Today, many aficionados, both Spanish and Mexican, disparage Franklin's artistry. "Manolete made you feel inside like crying, but Franklin does not engrave anything on your soul," a Spanish aficionado of thirty years' standing complained not long ago. "Franklin has no class," another Spaniard has said. "He is to a matador of Spanish blood what a Mexican baseball player is to Ba-bee Ruth." "I am A Number One," Franklin says. "I am the best in the business, bar none."

Franklin was nineteen when he saw his first bullfight. He was in Mexico, having recently run away from home after a quarrel with his father. As he recalls this particular bullfight, he was bored. In Brooklyn, he had belonged, as a charter member, to the *Eagle*'s Aunt Jean's Humane Club and to the old New York *Globe*'s Bedtime Stories Club, which devoted itself to the glorification of Peter Rabbit. "At that time, the life to me of both man and beast was the most precious thing on this planet," he says. "I failed to grasp the point." The following year, he fought his first bull—a twelve-hundred-pound, four-year-old beast with horns a foot and a half long—and was on his way to becoming a professional. In the quarter of a century since then, Franklin has come to feel that the act of dominating and killing a bull is the most important and satisfying act a human being can perform. "It gives me a feeling of sensual well-being," he has said. "It's so deep it catches my breath. It fills me so completely I tingle all over. It's something I want to do morning, noon, and night. It's something food can't give me. It's something rest can't give me. It's something money can't buy." He is certain that bullfighting is the noblest and most rewarding of all pursuits. He often delivers eloquent discourses on his art to men who are more interested in power, money, love, sex, marriage, dollar diplomacy, atomic energy, animal breeding, religion, Marxism, capitalism, or the Marshall Plan. When his listener has been reduced to acquiescence, or at least bewilderment, Franklin will smile tolerantly and give him a pat on the back. "It's all a matter of first things first," he will say. "I was destined to taste the first, and the best, on the list of walks of life." The triumph of man over bull is not just the first walk on Franklin's own list; it is the only one. There are no other walks to clutter him up. "I was destined to shine," he adds. "It was a matter of noblesse oblige."

The expression "noblesse oblige" is one Franklin is fond of using to describe his attitude toward most of his activities in and out of the bull ring, including the giving of advice to people. He is an unbridled advice-giver. He likes to counsel friends, acquaintances, and even strangers to live in a sensible, homespun, conventional, well-tested manner, in line with the principles of saving nine by a stitch in time, of finding life great if one does not weaken, of gathering moss by not rolling, of trying and trying again if success is slow in arriving, and of distinguishing between what is gold and what merely glitters. He is convinced that he thought up all these adages himself. In order to show how seriously he takes them, he often pitches in and helps a friend follow them. He takes credit for having helped at least a half-dozen other bullfighters make hay while the sun shone; for having proved to habitués of saloons and night clubs that there is no place like home; for having taught a number of ladies how to drive automobiles, after telling them emphatically that anything a man can do a woman can do; for having encouraged young lovers to get married, because the longer they waited, the more difficult their adjustment to each other would be; and for having persuaded couples to have babies while they were still young, so that they might be pals with their children while they were growing up. "I was destined to lead," Franklin states. "It was always noblesse oblige with me." Some Americans who have watched Franklin dispose of bulls on hot Sunday afternoons in Spain believe that he is right. "Sidney is part of a race of strange, fated men," says Gerald Murphy, head of Mark Cross and a lover of the arts. Franklin has a special category of advice for himself. "I never let myself get obese or slow," he says. "I make it a point never to imbibe before a fight. I never take more than a snifter, even when socializing with the select of all the professions. I am always able to explain to myself the whys and wherefores. I believe in earning a penny by saving it. By following the straight and narrow path, I became the toast of two continents. My horizon is my own creation."

Franklin, who has never married, is tall—five feet eleven and a half inches—thin, fair-skinned, and bald except for a few wavy bits of sandy-colored hair at the base of his skull. The backs of his hands and the top of his head are spotted with large tan freckles. His eyebrows are heavy and the color of straw. His ears are long. His eyes are brown, narrow, and lacking in depth, and there are a good many lines around them. There is a small scar at the tip of his nose. His build is considered good for bullfighting, because a tall bullfighter can more easily reach over a bull's horns with his sword for the kill. Franklin's only physical handicap is his posterior, which sticks out. "Sidney has no grace because he has a terrific behind," Hemingway says. "I used to make him do special exercises to reduce his behind." When Franklin walks down a street, he seems to dance along on his toes, and he has a harsh, fast way of talking. He sounds like a boxing promoter or a cop, but he has many of the gestures and mannerisms of the Spanish bullfighter. "Americans are taught to speak with their mouths," he likes to say. "We speak with our bodies." When the parade preceding the bullfight comes to a halt, he stands, as do the Mexicans and Spaniards, with the waist pushed forward and the shoulders back. When he becomes angry, he rages, but he can transform himself in a moment into a jolly companion again. In the company of other bullfighters or of aficionados, he glows and bubbles. Last winter, at a hotel in Acapulco, he discovered that the headwaiter, D'Amaso Lopez, had been a matador in Seville between 1905 and 1910. "Ah, Maestro!" cried Franklin, embracing Lopez, who grabbed a tablecloth and started doing *verónicas.* "He is overjoyed to see me," Franklin told his host at dinner. "I'm a kindred spirit." At parties, he likes to replace small talk or other pastimes with parlor bullfighting, using a guest as the bull. (Rita Hayworth is considered by some experts to make his best bull.) Claude Bowers, former United States Ambassador to Spain, used to invite Franklin to his soirées in Madrid. "Sidney loved to perform," an Embassy man who was usually Franklin's onrushing bull has said. "He'd give the most fascinating running commentary as he demonstrated with the cape, and then he'd spend hours answering the silliest questions, as long as they were about bullfighting. He was like a preacher spreading the gospel."

Franklin gets along well with Mexicans and Spaniards. "On the streets of Seville, everybody talks to him," a friend who has seen a good deal of him there says. "He knows all the taxi drivers and lottery vendors, and even the mayor bows to him." Franklin claims that he has made himself over into an entirely Spanish bullfighter. "I know Spain like I know the palm of my hand," he says. "I happen to be much more lucid in Spanish than in English. I even *think* in Spanish." Franklin's lucidity in Spanish has been a help to other Americans. Rex Smith, former chief of the Associated Press bureau in Madrid, occasionally used him as a reporter. During a rebellion in 1932, he commissioned Franklin to look into a riot near his office. "Suddenly, I heard a great hullabaloo outside my window," Smith says in describing the incident. "I looked out, and there was Sidney telling the crowd, in Spanish, where to get off." "Sidney is fabulous on language," Hemingway has said. "He speaks Spanish so grammatically good and so classically perfect and so complete, with all the slang and damn accents and twenty-seven dialects, nobody would believe he is an American. He is as good in Spanish as T. E. Lawrence was in Arabic." Franklin speaks Castilian, *caló* (or gypsy talk), and Andalusian. The favorite conversational medium of bullfighters in Spain is a mixture of *caló* and Andalusian. Instead of saying *"nada"* for "nothing" to other bullfighters, he says *"na', na', na',"* and he says *"leña,"* which is bullfight slang, instead of the classical *"cuerno,"* in talking of an especially large horn of a bull. In conversing with a lisping Spanish duke, Franklin assumes a lisp that is far better than his companion's, and he is equally at home in the earthy language of the cafés frequented by bullfighters. The

Spanish maintain that Franklin never makes a mistake in their tongue. One day, he went sailing in a two-masted schooner. A Spanish companion called a sail yard a *palo*. "You ought to know better than that," Franklin told him, and went on to explain that the sail yard he had spoken of was a *verga*, that *palo* meant mast, and that there were three terms for mast—one used by fishermen, another by yachtsmen, and the third by landlubbers.

When Franklin first went to Mexico, in 1922, he did not know any Spanish. A few years later, while he was training for bullfighting on a ranch north of Mexico City, he started a class in reading and writing for forty illiterate peons, of all ages. After three months, sixteen of Franklin's pupils could read and write. "They idolized me for it," he says. In any restaurant—even a Schrafft's, back home—he follows the Spanish custom of calling a waiter by saying "Psst!" or clapping the hands. His Christmas cards say, "*Feliz Navidad y Próspero Año Nuevo.*" Conversation with bulls being customary during a fight, he speaks to them in Spanish. "*Toma, toro! Toma, toro!*" he says, when urging a bull to charge. "*Ah-ah, toro! Ah-ah-ah, toro!*" he mutters, telling a bull to come closer.

In putting on his coat, Franklin handles it as though it were a bullfighter's cape, and his entire wardrobe is designed to express his idea of a bullfighter's personality. "Sidney always took a long time to dress in the morning," says Hemingway, who often sleeps in his underwear and takes a half minute to put on his trousers and shirt. "I always had to wait for him. I don't like a man who takes a long time to dress in the morning." Most of Franklin's suits were tailored in Seville. "Genuine English stuff—nothing but the best," he tells people. His wardrobe includes a transparent white raincoat, several turtleneck sweaters, some Basque berets, a number of sombreros, and a purple gabardine jacket without lapels. His bullfighting costumes are more elegant and more expensive than those of any other matador in the business. He has three wigs—two parted on the left side, one parted on the right—which are the envy of bald bullfighters who have never been to Hollywood or heard of Max Factor. A bullfighter's looks have a lot to do with his popularity, especially in Mexico, where a bald bullfighter is not esteemed. A Spanish matador named Cayetano Ordóñez, professionally called Niño de la Palma, who was the prototype of Hemingway's young bullfighter in *The Sun Also Rises*, lost a good part of his Mexican public when he lost his hair. In 1927, when he appeared in Mexico City and dedicated one of the bulls he was about to kill to Charles A. Lindbergh, he was young, slender, and graceful, with dark, curly hair. "An Adonis," Franklin says. "Niño had a marvellous figure. All the sexes were wild about him." Eight years later, Niño, who had been fighting in Spain, returned to Mexico heavier and partially bald. The moment he took off his matador's hat in the ring, the ladies in the audience transferred their affections to a slimmer and handsomer matador, and the men turned to the bulls. One day, Franklin showed his wigs to Niño. "Poor Niño was flabbergasted," says a witness. "He put on a wig and stood in front of the mirror for an hour, tears in his eyes. My God, what a scene when Sidney tried to take the wig away from him!" Franklin used to wear his wigs whenever he appeared in public, but lately he has worn them only in the bull ring, at the theater, and when having his picture taken. He says that someday, if the action in the ring gets dull, he is going to hang his wig on the horn of a bull.

In accordance with his belief in noblesse oblige, Franklin feels that he can afford to be generous toward his fellow man. "Sidney doesn't envy his neighbors a thing," says a friend. "He is the extreme of what most men like to think of themselves, so much so that he never thinks about it. He doesn't want things. He thinks he has everything." Although Franklin does not carry noblesse oblige so far as to forgive enemies, he is tolerant of those whose friendship for him has cooled. He has rarely seen Hemingway, whom he had come to know in 1929, since leaving him in Madrid in 1937, in the middle of the civil war. Franklin had been doing odd jobs for Hemingway, then a war correspondent.

"I weighed Ernest in the balance and found him wanting," Franklin remarks. "When he began coloring his dispatches about the war, I felt it was time for me to back out on the deal."

"Obscenity!" says Hemingway in reply.

"Ernest got to the point where I knew his mind better than he did himself. It began to annoy him," Franklin says.

"Obscenity!" says Hemingway.

"I may disagree with Ernest, but I'll always give him the benefit of the doubt, because he is a genius," Franklin says.

"Obscenity obscenity!" says Hemingway.

Franklin is highly critical of most of his confreres, but there are a few he praises when he feels they deserve it. After a bullfight in Mexico

City year ago, a friend commented to him that one of the matadors looked good only because he had been given a good bull to kill—a good bull being one that has perfect vision and is aggressive, high-spirited, and, from a human point of view, brave. Franklin said no—that the bull was a bad bull. "The fellow had the guts to stand there and take it and make a good bull out of a lemon," he said. "You can't understand that, because you have no grasp of noblesse oblige." Because of his own grasp of noblesse oblige, Franklin is determined to go on fighting bulls as long as his legs hold out, and he would like to see Brooklyn continue to be represented in the bull ring after he retires. To this end, he took under his wing for a while a twenty-six-year-old Brooklyn neighbor of his named Julian Faria, nicknamed Chaval, meaning "the Kid." Chaval, whose parents are of English, Spanish, and Portuguese descent and whose face resembles a gentle, sad-eyed calf's, made his début as a matador in Mexico in the fall of 1947, fighting with Franklin in some of the smaller rings. On the posters announcing the fights, Chaval's name appeared in letters an inch high, beneath Franklin's name in letters two inches high, along with the proclamation that Franklin was "El Único Matador Norteamericano."

When Franklin is visiting in New York, he lives with his mother, an unmarried brother, and a sister and her husband in a one-family house on East Twenty-ninth Street in Flatbush. It is a point of noblesse oblige with him to help his neighbors during his visits. "They depend on me," he says. "They're always running in and out when I'm home. It's a regular merry-go-round fixing their stoves and radiators and answering to 'Hey, Sid, the faucet in my house don't work!' I feel duty-bound to lend a helping hand." Some years ago, the Broad Street Hospital invited Franklin to clock the rodeo events at a Madison Square Garden benefit, and he helped it out, too. He turned up in a matador costume of apple-green silk embroidered in gold. "I was obligated to let the audience know who and what I was," he said. During the postwar shortage of men's shirts, a casual New York acquaintance remarked that he needed one. Franklin spent three days looking for what he thought was a proper shirt. "He came back from Fourteenth Street with this goddam pongee silk thing and gave me a bill for fourteen dollars," the beneficiary has since said. "He thought he was doing me a goddam favor."

When Franklin meets Americans in Spain or Mexico, he always volunteers to take them shopping. A lady who with his help bought some silver plates in Madrid several years ago claims that he argued the shopkeeper into letting them go for one-fifth of the original price. "He just reduced the man to pulp," she says.

In his efforts to help his fellow-men, Franklin occasionally offers to make bullfighters out of them. He gave Hemingway's eldest son, John, known as Bumby, who recently returned to the Army with his wartime rank of captain, a cape cut to his size and a small sword, when Bumby was ten, and taught him how to execute passes with the cape. He once thought he had succeeded in making a bullfighter out of Franklin D. Roosevelt, Jr. In 1933, young Roosevelt, then nineteen, visited Spain and told Ambassador Bowers that he'd like to learn something about the country's favorite sport. Franklin was invited to dine at the Embassy. "He hadn't been there more than ten minutes when I found myself agreeing to go off with him on a two-week tour of Spain," Roosevelt recalls. They attended bullfights all over Spain, and after each fight Franklin introduced Roosevelt to the matadors. Then he sent Roosevelt to a friend's ranch to learn bullfighting. "He had a high old time fooling around with calves," Franklin says. "He got a wire from Washington, D.C., saying, 'What your father is doing isn't bad enough, you've got to associate with bullfighters.' He didn't pay any attention to it. I had pulled up the shade for Frankie and the sun was streaming in."

"There are two kinds of people," Franklin repeatedly says. "Those who live for themselves and those who live for others. I'm the kind that likes to serve mankind." He believes that he would have made a wonderful doctor, and he acts as a general practitioner whenever he gets a chance. One afternoon, a bull ripped open one of his ankles. "I took a tea saucer and put some sand in it and mixed it up with tea leaves and manure and applied it to the injured member," Franklin says, with a look of sublime satisfaction. "I was then ready to get right back in the ring, functioning perfectly to a T." Once, when he was working on the ranch in Mexico, a peon accidentally chopped off two of his, the peon's, toes. Franklin claims that he sewed them back on with an ordinary needle and thread. "I put a splint underneath the foot, bandaged it, and told him to stay off it for a few days," he says. "In no time at all, the man was as good as new." In Mexico a few years ago, Franklin stood by as an appendectomy was performed upon his protégé, Chaval, advising

Chaval, who had been given a local anesthetic, not to show any fear or sign of pain, not even to grunt, because other bullfighters would hear about it. Chaval didn't make a sound. "I saw to it that the appendectomy was performed according to Hoyle," Franklin says.

Franklin considers himself an expert on mental as well as physical health. At a bullfight in Mexico City, last winter, he sat next to a British psychiatrist, a mannerly fellow who was attending the Unesco conference. While a dead bull was being dragged out of the ring, Franklin turned to the psychiatrist. "Say, Doc, did you ever go into the immortality of the crab?" he asked. The psychiatrist admitted that he had not, and Franklin said that nobody knew the answer to that one. He then asked the psychiatrist what kind of doctor he was. Mental and physiological, the psychiatrist said.

"I say the brain directs everything in the body," Franklin said. "It's all a matter of what's in your mind."

"You're something of a psychosomaticist," said the psychiatrist.

"Nah, all I say is if you control your brain, your brain controls the whole works," said Franklin.

The psychiatrist asked if the theory applied to bullfighting.

"You've got something there, Doc," said Franklin. "Bullfighting is basic. It's a matter of life and death. People come to see you take long chances. It's life's biggest gambling game. Tragedy and comedy are so close together they're part of each other. It's all a matter of noblesse oblige."

The psychiatrist looked solemn. Another bull came into the ring, and a matador executed a *verónica*. It was not a good one. The matador should hold the cape directly before the bull's face, one hand close to his own body, the other away from his body, stretching the cape, then pull it away from the bull's face in such a manner that when the animal follows it, he passes directly in front of him. This matador held both hands far away from his body, and the bull passed at some distance from him. The crowd whistled and shouted insults. "Look at that, Doc," said Franklin. "There's a guy who doesn't have the faintest grasp of noblesse oblige."

The psychiatrist cleared his throat. The bullfight, he said, might be looked upon as a plastic model of Freud's concept of the mind and its three divisions: the id, the uncivilized brute in man; the ego, a combination of environment, which has tamed the id, and of the id itself; and the super-ego, the conscience, often represented by the father or the mother, who approves or disapproves. He suggested that the id might be represented by the bull, the ego by the bullfighter, and the super-ego by the whistling and hooting crowd. "Many things you do in life," he added, "are a projection, or model, of what is going on in your mind. For instance, you might be fighting bulls because internally you have a conflict between your id and ego, id and super-ego, or ego and super-ego, or possibly a conflict between your combined id and ego and your super-ego. The bullfight, then, might be a good model of your state of mind."

"Nah," said Franklin. "If I had my life to live all over again, I'd do exactly the same thing. Do you grasp my point?"

The psychiatrist thought it over for a while, then said yes, he believed he did.

After the bullfight, Franklin, in saying goodbye to the British psychiatrist, advised him to take care of himself. "If you can't be good, be careful, Doc," he said.

Franklin maintains that he learned a lot about life from Hemingway. "Ernest taught me how to put people into two categories," he says. "One, the good guys, and, two, the bastards. If you're a good guy, anything goes. If not, I don't want to be around you. At first, I used to think, How can this person help me further my career? Now I think, How can this person help me to enjoy life? I've had my pick of the select of all the professions. I've picked those who could help me to enjoy life. It's this never being able to sit down, never knowing what I'll be doing next, that gives me my greatest enjoyment. When I take a trip down a highway anyplace in the world, I can drop in on this one or that one. Not everybody can do that."

One night in Charlottesville, after Franklin D. Roosevelt, Jr., had elected to go to law school in Virginia instead of becoming a bullfighter, he received an unexpected visit. "This guy just knocks on the door and says, 'Remember me?' " Roosevelt has recalled. "It was Sidney. He insisted on spending the rest of the night chewing the fat. He wanted to give me a lot of advice, kind of like an older brother checking up on me." In Paris, some years before that, Sidney dropped in on Roosevelt, then just out of Groton, and asked why he didn't get married. "He told me he knew this Ethel du Pont but was afraid to ask her," Sidney has said. "I got on my high horse and gave him a good talking to. 'Frankie, you're the son of the President, and you can have your choice of any girl in the world,' I told him. I insisted that he ask for Ethel's hand in marriage." Roosevelt says that he doesn't remember ever taking any of Franklin's advice. "After all, I had a father who was pretty good at it," he adds.

The reason he himself has never married, Franklin says, is that he has never found a woman who understood noblesse oblige. "Also, I've been around animal breeding too much, and that has affected my viewpoint," he explains. "Anyway, there's no real love other than a mother's love for her child."

Franklin shows no discrimination in practicing noblesse oblige. "Humanity is humanity," he says. "I serve without fear or favor." A few years ago, he tried singlehanded to prevent a hoof-and-mouth epidemic that had broken out among the cattle in Spain from spreading to other countries. He took it upon himself to deliver lengthy reports to officials in Washington and Mexico City on ships sailing for North America with animals he thought had the disease, and on where the cattle came from, and on the buyers and sellers of infected cattle. "I sent one report by diplomatic pouch from Madrid," he says. "One year later, there was a terrific outbreak of the disease in Mexico, all because those diplomats had been too busy to listen to me." In Washington, a while back, Franklin lunched with several senators, including Barkley, Tydings, Chavez, and Magnuson, ostensibly to tell them how the prevalence of hoof-and-mouth disease in Mexico was affecting the price of beef in this country. An onlooker says that the luncheon topic suddenly became United States domestic and foreign policy, and that Franklin did all the talking. After lunch, the onlooker took Franklin aside and suggested that he might have allowed the senators to get a word in. "What do you mean?" Franklin asked. "How often do senators have the chance to lunch with a bullfighter?"

Franklin's noblesse oblige was extended during the last war to include an offer to the United States government to make himself expendable. The offer was accepted, and he was assigned to some mysterious work in North Africa. "If I had told Sidney to walk barefoot across some high mountains, he would have done it," his superior in the war work recalls. "But it had to be a *big* thing. When you want to get credit for doing something *big* in war, you often get killed. Fortunately, I didn't have anything big for Sidney to do."

Some of Franklin's intimates say that he is one of the small percentage of men to whom friendship really means something. One day, he called at the home of a friend named Grant Mason, in Washington, and was told by Mason's wife that Mason, who had just got out of the Army, was resting for a few months. "Tell Grant to go back to work," said Franklin, and insisted that it would be bad for him to hang around the house all day. "You might say that Sidney is a kind of mother hen," Mrs. Mason has remarked in telling of this. Franklin mothers not only his friends but strangers. When he was in Spain during the Second World War, an American bomber was shot down by German planes over the Bay of Vigo. One injured flier was interned in a hospital at La Coruña, near Vigo. At Christmas time, Franklin, who had heard about the American's internment, spent three days with him. "I didn't want the kid to be alone over the holidays," he explained.

Franklin is always trying to prove that there is nothing man can do with his hands that *he* can't do. "He goes all over your house, getting half a dozen projects started," a New York friend recently recalled. "Then he goes home, and no one around the place knows how to finish them." Once, Franklin decided that a friend who lived in the country needed a doghouse. He went off into the woods, chopped down a tree, and made a rather large doghouse of hewn logs. His friend's dog refused to sleep in it. Another country-dwelling friend says that Franklin is always trying to get him to build a wing on his house, or to put up a garage, or to have a tile floor laid. "He took one look at a rock garden I was breaking my back to build and told me to let it go," the friend says. "He said what I needed was a large circular stone seat, to hold a lot of people. 'But we don't *have* a lot of people coming to our house,' I told him. 'You can never tell when you *will* have,' he said. I built the seat."

Franklin likes to cook, and he has delighted fellow bullfighters in Spain with his dinners. His specialties are lobster and homemade doughnuts. Gerald Murphy, the Mark Cross man, is an admirer of Franklin's cooking. "Sidney is an amazing gourmet, with a remarkably sensuous appreciation of foods," he says. Murphy's wife once let Franklin sample her special hors d'œuvre—slivers of the skin of baked potatoes simmered in butter until brown, a delicacy no guests had ever been able to identify. "Sidney knew immediately what it was," Mrs.

Murphy recalls. Another time, Franklin presented the Murphys with some delectable smoked fish. The Murphys went all over Brooklyn trying to get more of it. "Only Sidney knows where to get that smoked fish, and it's his secret," Mrs. Murphy says. "He knows the people who smoke the fish, and I think he knows the fish."

In general, Franklin says, he likes the life of a bullfighter because of the number of things he can pack into it. "You come into a town, and the moment you arrive, be it by plane, ship, train, or car, everybody is there to receive you," he says. "You barely have time to change your clothes before it's a high old round of banquets and dinners. You don't pay for a thing; others consider it a privilege to pay for you. You're yanked out to go swimming, hunting, fishing, and riding, and if you don't know how to do those things, others consider it a privilege to teach you, to satisfy your every whim and desire. The select of all the professions like to be seen with you." "They're never alone," Hemingway says morosely of bullfighters. "What Ernest has in mind when he says that is that all the sexes throw themselves at you," Franklin explains. "I never went in for that night-owl stuff. I never let myself become detoured. Many of them allow themselves to become so detoured they never get back on the main highway."

Chaval's attitude toward the bullfighter's life is rather different. "I just like to scare girls," he says. "Boy, I bring the bull so close to me, the girls, they scream. Boy, I get a kick out of making girls scream."

Franklin used to lecture Chaval on the significance of noblesse oblige in bullfighting to help the young man stay on the main highway. "I am alive today only because I was in *perfect* condition when I had my accidents in the ring," he sternly told Chaval, who had night-owl inclinations.

"Jeez, Sidney, all you gotta do in the ring is show you're brave," said Chaval. "That's what girls like, when you're brave."

Most bullfighters agree with Chaval, but they state their case with more dignity. A young woman who once met Carlos Arruza at a party in Mexico City complimented him on his bravery in fighting so close to a bull. "You think I am going to be killed, but for you I am courageous in the face of death," Arruza replied gallantly. "This is manliness. I fight to make money, but I like very much to bring the bull to his knees before me." The fearlessness of Manolete is legendary. He specialized in the most difficult and dangerous maneuver in bullfighting—the *pase natural*, which, properly executed, requires the bull to pass perilously close to the body. He had no worthy competitors, but he always tried to outdo himself. "Manolete was a tremendous personality," a Mexican aficionado said recently. "He never smiled." He was gored several times before he received his fatal wound. On more than one occasion, he might have saved himself by moving an inch or two. "Why didn't you move, Manolo?" he was asked after suffering a leg wound one afternoon. "Because I am Manolete," he replied somberly. Lack of fear has been attributed by some people simply to lack of imagination. Franklin disagrees with this theory. "I believe in facing facts," he says. "If you're a superman, you're a superman, and that's all there is to it." Few of the critics who hold to the opinion that Franklin lacks artistry believe that he lacks *valentia*, or bravery. "Nobody ever lives his life all the way up except bullfighters," Franklin says, quoting from "The Sun Also Rises."

In giving advice to Chaval on how to live his life all the way up, Franklin once said, "You've got to be the sun, moon, and stars to yourself, and results will follow as logically as night follows day."

"Jeez, Sidney! I don't get it," Chaval replied. "All I know is I gotta kill the bull or the bull kills me."

"Bullfighting taught me how to be the master of myself," Franklin said. "It taught me how to discard all that was unimportant."

"Jeez, Sidney!" said Chaval.

Franklin began to make history in the bull ring at his Spanish début, on June 9, 1929, in Seville. Aficionados who saw him fight that day wept and shouted, and talked about it for weeks afterward. "On that day, I declared, 'Bullfighting will never again be the same,'" Manuel Mejías, the bullfighting father of five bullfighting sons, has said. "Sidney Franklin introduced a revolutionary style in the bull ring." "Sidney was a glowing Golden Boy," recalls an American lady who was at the fight. "He was absolutely without fear. He was absolutely beautiful."

"I was carried out on the shoulders of the crowd through the gates reserved for royalty," Franklin told Chaval ecstatically not long ago. "The history of the ring was then a hundred and ninety-nine years old. All that time, only four fellows had ever been carried out of the ring on the shoulders of the crowd. I was the fifth. Traffic in the streets of

Seville was wrecked. The next day, they passed a law prohibiting the carrying of bullfighters through the public streets. I was taken out of the ring at seven and deposited at my hotel at twelve-twenty that night. I didn't know what I was doing or what had happened to me. I was so excited I took all my money out of a dresser drawer and threw it to the crowds on the street. The die was cast that day. I was riding on the highest cloud in this or any other world. I felt so far above anything mundane that nothing mattered. I didn't hear anything. I didn't see anything. I looked, but I didn't see. I heard, but nothing registered. I didn't care about food. I didn't care about drink. I was perfectly satisfied to lay my head on the pillow and pass out."

1949

NET WORTH

HENRY LOUIS GATES, JR.

When do you know for sure? Basketball fans still talk about "the shot"—the sixteen-footer that a University of North Carolina freshman named Michael Jordan sank in 1982. With seconds left on the clock, Jordan scored the decisive basket against Georgetown, secured the NCAA crown, and put himself, in his own words, "on the basketball map." David Falk, whom one would be tempted to call the Michael Jordan of sports agents if he weren't Michael Jordan's sports agent, tells about witnessing a similarly prophetic moment in Jordan's career. In 1985, Jordan, a coltish twenty-two, was holding a press conference in Chicago to announce an endorsement deal he'd signed with the Coca-Cola Company. But those were not ordinary times, for New Coke had recently been introduced and a cola Kulturkampf was seething. "Which Coke do you like—New Coke or regular Coke?" a reporter threw at him.

Even now, in the recounting, Falk wants to make sure I get the full picture: an inexperienced young player, the cameras, the microphones, the blazing lights—and his future as a pitchman in the balance. "And Michael instantly responded, 'Coke is Coke. They both taste great.'" As the sportscasters say, nothing but net.

No one could have faulted Jordan had he made a different play—had he plumped for New Coke, and tried to justify the choice without slighting its precursor. "I mean, for me, I would have probably picked one and tried to explain why," Falk says intently. You can tell that the moment is part of his own personal highlights reel: the lights, the cameras, the question, the sudden clutch in his gut, and, finally, Jordan's soaring, effortless dunk. "What a great answer!" Falk exclaims. "He just has amazing instincts." If you're Falk, that's when you know.

Après Coke, le déluge. Edible cake decorations, golf-club covers, shower curtains, pot holders, aprons, rulers, kitchen towels, sleeping bags, canteens, insulated travel mugs, napkins, tablecloths, popcorn tins, foam furniture, first-aid kits, gift wrap, memo pads, book bags, pencil sharpeners, erasers, buttons, key chains, wallet cards, magnets, ring binders, tissue holders, diaries, address books, envelopes, flash-

lights, kites, toothbrush holders, wastebaskets, Sony and Sega play stations, pinball games, soap dishes, walkie-talkies, curtains, acrylic juice
cups, gum, cookies, bandages, and comforters: this isn't a list of all the
commodities that Jordan has endorsed, but it's the beginning of such a
list. The economist Tyler Cowen, who has compiled a far longer list
than this one, has approvingly noted that these endorsements represent
a very simple form of mutualism: "It helps sell their product, and it
makes Michael Jordan more famous."

Two forces contend for the soul of contemporary America, playing
out a sociohistorical version of King Kong versus Godzilla, only with
better special effects. On the one hand, there's the growth of what has
been termed "winner-take-all" markets, visible in every economic and
cultural realm but epitomized by the star system of the NBA. On the
other hand, there's the growth of market micro-segmentation—the
fragmentation of culture into ever narrower niches, from the proliferation of cable channels to the supposed balkanization of the canon. For
at least the past decade, the struggle has been ceaseless, dug-in, brutal.
Corporate behemoths meet and merge; then, buffeted by shareholder
capitalism, spin off divisions like whirling nebulae. Twenty thousand
new consumer products were introduced in this country last year; 90
percent of them will fail. And so the battle continues. A bulletin from
the front: Michael Jordan—the ultimate winner-take-all celebrity—is
gaining the upper hand.

"Forget the endorsements and the swoosh and the dollar sign," Steve
Wulf wrote in *Time* last year. "They just get in the way, like some
beaded curtain that keeps us from truly appreciating what we have"—
to wit, "the greatest athlete in the history of American sports." An up-
lifting sentiment, but you might just as fairly stand it on its head. The
man's grandeur on the court—the dunks, the jump shots, the steals, the
midair acrobatics—has tended to obscure another historic achievement: Michael Jordan has become the greatest corporate pitchman of
all time. As a twentieth-century sports hero, he has plausible competition from Babe Ruth and Muhammad Ali; as an agent of brand equity,
he is without peer.

The first thing you notice when you sit down with Michael Jordan is
how very much like Michael Jordan he is. The resemblance is uncanny,
and not incidental to his success. He's handsome and dark-skinned,

with those three horizontal creases in his forehead which really become visible when he's at the free-throw line, glistening with sweat and glowering at the basket. His baritone is the one you've heard on a thousand commercials. But, more than that, the manner—direct and artless—is familiar. ("He can't really act," Falk was quoted as saying shortly before the Jordan vehicle *Space Jam* had its theatrical release, and it occurs to me only now that Falk was reassuring us, not warning us.) Jordan, who is self-aware without being self-conscious, recognizes that the alchemy of image requires realness, which in turn requires exposure, albeit controlled exposure.

"I know that it's got some coloring to it, and you are only going to see certain portions that they want you to see," Jordan says of his public persona. "But still, when I come in contact with people, I think they see me being a genuine person. And I get along with everybody. I'm a people person, yet I understand the game of corporate America and what they try to project."

We're sitting quietly in his private suite off the second-floor dining room of an establishment called Michael Jordan's Restaurant, on North LaSalle Street, in downtown Chicago. The most noticeable object here is an eleven-by-fourteen-inch photograph of his father, the late James Jordan. Otherwise, the suite is sedate and muted, with cream-colored walls, a couple of tan leather sofas, and a marble dining table. Michael Jordan is across from me, sipping a cup of coffee, nibbling on fruit salad, and occasionally lifting up a piece of flatware, tilting it this way and that.

Jordan was exaggerating when he said he got along with everybody. He minces few words as he speaks about two of his previous coaches at Chicago: Stan Albeck, who he feels was tolerant of mediocrity ("very laid-back—do your job and then go out and party"), and Doug Collins, who was loyal to management but not to his players (" 'Fuck Doug Collins' was the conversation on the court"). Still, when it comes to elements that affect his and his team's performance, you wouldn't expect the most competitive member of the NBA to display an attitude of live-and-let-live. Jordan has been equally acerbic toward teammates who he feels have not pulled their weight. The person who continues to elicit Jordan's special loathing, though, is Jerry Krause, the general manager of the Chicago Bulls and thus Jordan's putative boss.

"I was a piece of meat to him," Jordan says, recounting one of their many disputes. "He felt he could control me, because I had so much value to him. But he didn't realize that I had value to myself: I was independent, and I understood what I was."

Considered even as a piece of meat, Jordan need make no apologies. At six feet six, he weighs almost twenty pounds more than he did when he started his pro career—the result of a strenuous regimen of upper-body weight training. The man is both hulking and suave, and it's easy to see why he has become a totem of black masculinity; he makes Bill Cosby look like Uncle Ben. He's dressed casually today: jeans, a beige T-shirt, and the familiar gold earring, an adornment that seemed faintly daring and piratical when he first adopted it, ten years ago. He does not generally push the limits of the acceptable. He may banter about condoms—he'll never endorse them, he has said, because "they're too small!"—but he seldom edges past PG-13. This is a guy who listens to Toni Braxton and Anita Baker, not to Ice Cube or the Wu-Tang Clan. He has a sense of being at ease with himself—a low center of gravity, so to speak, despite his prowess at the vertical game. Relaxed and polite, he discusses his television advertisements with the same combination of detachment and animation with which he discusses the game.

A Nike spot that Jordan is particularly proud of aired in 1997; in it, he gives a recitation of missed shots and lost games, concluding, "I've failed over and over and over again in my life. And that is why I succeeded." Fade to the Air Jordan logo. "I had to fight the agency about it, because they had wanted to have me work with Oliver Stone on a commercial," he says, making a faint snorting sound, "and Oliver Stone was going to go through that process of trying to figure out why my game is my game. And I said, 'Oliver Stone don't know shit about basketball. Why don't you just show the actual situation? Let the people see exactly what's happened over the twelve years of my career.' The idea is to tell young kids, 'Don't be afraid to fail, because a lot of people have to fail to be successful—these are the many times that I've failed but yet I've been successful.' Let them know that it isn't always good for the people up top. I mean, they have bad things happen to them."

If one of those bad things is being stuck with a general manager like Krause, another, it seems, is being stuck with a team owner like the Chicago real estate developer Jerry Reinsdorf. Jordan tells me about the meeting with Reinsdorf when his Bulls contract for the 1997–98 season—a one-year retainer worth thirty-odd million dollars—was agreed upon: "We shook hands. But one comment stuck with me as we left, and I lost total respect for him when he said it: 'At some point in time, I know I'm going to regret what we just did.'" For the previous eight years, Jordan had been saddled with a contract that had early on failed to keep pace with the escalating NBA marketplace. So the comment wasn't exactly sporting. Now Jordan gives me a meaningful look. "And I'm saying, All these years where you knew I was underpaid and you been making money and your organization's moved from a fifteen-million-dollar business when you bought it to a two-hundred-million-dollar business—all those years have just gone down the drain because you have for once paid me my value. And you regretted that! That hit me so deep inside—that sense of greed, of disrespect for me."

Since this kind of friction is commonplace in the NBA, it's easy to miss how strange the whole situation is. After all, Jordan, considered strictly as an athlete, is the Second Coming, and Reinsdorf, considered strictly as a mogul, is a second-rater. It's as if Pat Robertson were making Jesus punch a time card.

And all this is aside from Jordan's role as culture hero. A Plutarchian progression of biographies have mounted the best-seller list, chronicling the securely working-class childhood in Wilmington, North Carolina (father a foreman at a General Electric plant; mother in customer relations for the United Carolina Bank); the traumatic early failure (as a high school sophomore, he was cut from the varsity team); his taste of greatness as a Tar Heel, under the tutelage of Coach Dean Smith; his debut with the Chicago Bulls and the galvanizing effect he had upon the team and upon the sport in general. Later accounts describe the 1993 murder of his father, and his subsequent decision to leave basketball for minor-league baseball; the jubilation that marked his return to the Bulls in 1995; the ten scoring titles, five MVP titles, and five championships over the past seven seasons. These things have been inscribed on the national memory like the battles of the Revolutionary War. For this is someone who over the past several years has been mentioned in an average of a hundred newspaper and magazine stories a day.

Jordan, for his part, analyzes his celebrity so coolly that he might as well be marking up a playbook with X's and O's. "It could easily be a matter of timing, where society was looking for something positive," he says. "It could easily be a sport that was gradually bursting out into global awareness at a time when I was at the top. And then there's the connections that I've had with corporate America since I started with Coca-Cola and then went to Nike, which has gone totally global." He breaks off. "I really, really can't give you a sufficient answer."

Maybe not, but he's made a good start, as David Stern would agree. David Stern must himself be accounted a factor in Jordan's success: He has been the commissioner of the National Basketball Association for the past fourteen years, and brought a financially troubled and scandal-plagued organization to the land of milk and honey. A shortish man with a head of graying hair, Stern is tough and funny, and a self-professed worrier. (Commending the virtues of institutionalized anxiety, he tells me, "That's why it's good to have a Jewish organization. You worry constantly." True, the NBA has its share of tsuris these days, but it's the kind you get when you've been all too successful: Such troubles we should all have.) The rise of Jordan and the rise of the NBA have been propelled by many of the same trends, and Stern delineates them as well as anyone. "You wind up with a marketing revolution, a television and cable revolution, at a time when our league is also growing in stature," he says. However talented such players as Wilt Chamberlain and Bill Russell were, he points out, the numbers who watched them were minuscule relative to the numbers who watch NBA games today. When Stern started out, there were no regional sports channels; now those channels have fifty-five million subscribers. It's the difference between a vaudeville stage and a modern cineplex.

Then, there's the Jordan factor. "Here was a very handsome, friendly, eminently decent human being," Stern says, "who is the kind of person you'd like to have as a friend, and who just happens to be the most fiercely competitive athlete of his time and the best basketball player perhaps ever." Falk captures that quality in a nice formula: Jordan, he says, is "at once credible and incredible"—a down-to-earth guy who defies gravity on the court.

The guy on the court is the Michael Jordan who, in a game some thought might be his last in Madison Square Garden, drove the baseline, did a one-eighty in midair, then flipped the ball backward over his head and into the basket. During the game, he'd put on his original Air

Jordans—a pair he wore back in 1984—and he played vintage Air Jordan ball. And even when he's acting his age (he now tends toward artful outside fadeaways rather than the banging inside game of his youth), it only underscores his technical mastery. At one point in the second game of the playoffs against the Pacers last week, Jordan nearly lost his footing, then, as he stumbled, launched a high arcing shot to the basket. Nobody who has watched his sheerly kinetic presence on the court has to wonder why every Bulls game since November 20, 1987, has been sold out. Or why a huge bronze statue of him (his hand is as big as this page!) looms near an entrance to Chicago's United Center. Still, athletic preeminence alone doesn't explain why Jordan is a walking brand, and the most recognizable one on the planet.

An inherent feature of what marketers call a "powerbrand," to be sure, is that this very status comes to seem inevitable and natural: We take it for granted that Michael Jordan is Michael Jordan because he's Michael Jordan. And yet neither his athleticism nor his affability suffices to explain his global ubiquity. Nor are conventional theories about celebrity endorsement much help. For decades, research in the subject focused on attributes like "credibility" and "attractiveness," but by the eighties the inadequacies of those models were obvious. In the heyday of *The Cosby Show,* the credible and attractive Bill Cosby did wonders for Coca-Cola and Kodak. Then E. F. Hutton signed him up, with disastrous results. John Houseman triumphed at Smith Barney but bombed at McDonald's. A more sophisticated account—such as one introduced in the late eighties by the anthropologist and marketing theorist Grant McCracken—would register the fact that there were kinds as well as degrees of credibility and attractiveness. Fame wasn't fungible. Different celebrities were repositories of different values and associations: Sigourney Weaver didn't mean the same thing as Loni Anderson. "Celebrities 'own' their meanings because they have created them on the public stage by dint of intense and repeated performance," McCracken declared. Yet meaning still traveled in one direction, from the celebrity to the product, and on to the consumer. "Thus does meaning circulate in the consumer society," McCracken concluded.

Look closer. David Falk, back in the eighties, had intuitively grasped something that was still eluding many business school profs—the way "branding" can be a reciprocal process. Falk had no equity in Nike or McDonald's or Coca-Cola or Chevrolet. He had equity in Michael

Jordan. The corporations wanted Jordan to leverage their brands; Falk would use their brands to leverage Jordan.

"I think that my role in managing Michael's image is one of the most misunderstood aspects of sports marketing," David Falk says. "There is a faction that feels that we have ridden on Michael's coattails as he has taken us along on a joyride through the world of sports marketing for the last thirteen years. There are others who think that I'm Dr. Frankenstein and I cooked up this formula in my laboratory to make Michael the marketing king of the century. And both are really wide of the mark."

David Falk, now forty-seven, is tall and bald (albeit not so tall and bald as his most celebrated client), and, with his Zegna suits and Star-Tac phone, he has become a fixture at the NBA's draft night, where he gets to exercise his skills at coaxing, cosseting, and cudgeling in rapid succession. His position in professional sports is essentially the position that Michael Ovitz once enjoyed in Hollywood, though his style is bristlier and more confrontational. After earning degrees in economics and law, he spent most of his career at the large sports management firm ProServ. He split in 1992 to start his own agency, f.a.m.e., and, unlike Jerry Maguire, he took all his clients with him. Just the other week, Falk sold his company to SFX Broadcasting for an estimated hundred million dollars, though he's promised to stay on as chairman and CEO.

"Protect your assets" is one of Falk's guiding rules, "assets" being the operative word. For what is perhaps the central relationship in Jordan's career has never been a bond of sentiment. To their credit, the two do not pretend otherwise. Jordan speaks of Falk in terms that are businesslike but not brusque—as someone who can be a son of a bitch ("an asshole" is Jordan's precise designation) but his son of a bitch.

Falk's positioning of his client started with an appreciation of how wonderfully American he was. "It was clear when you met him that he grew up in a close-knit family," Falk says. "His parents, James and Deloris, had been very, very close to their children, had great family values—they were disciplined, respectful, pretty much color-blind. And obviously, based on his style of play—and also based upon his tremendous success in the Olympics in Los Angeles in 1984—we felt that he represented something as all-American as apple pie. So the game plan was to get involved with all-American companies, like McDonald's and Coke and Chevrolet. Which we did."

The way Falk recounts the struggle to get Jordan "into the system," you might think he was talking about integrating the lunch counters at Woolworth's. "It took favors and arm-twisting," he says. Even then, the first deals with McDonald's were for local markets, in Chicago and North Carolina; they involved modest sums, and a lot of skepticism about whether a broad-based nonathletic brand could really be boosted by a black athlete—and a team athlete at that.

"In tennis or golf or boxing, the mystique is the individual," Falk says, "whereas, no matter how great Bill Russell or Bob Cousy was, it was the Celtic dynasty—it was always institutional. Michael changed all that. Single-handed. Today, when the NBA markets the teams, it says, Come watch Penny Hardaway and the Orlando Magic, come watch Grant Hill and the Detroit Pistons. Ten years ago, the NBA resisted doing that. It was just that Michael's force was so overwhelming. Basketball will never be an individual sport, but it's become a hybrid."

It was in Jordan's rookie year that Falk took his client shoe-shopping. "Instead of asking for offers I asked all the shoe companies to make a presentation to us and explain what they would do to market Michael," Falk recounts. An ailing sneaker company called Nike turned out to be the keenest suitor. "But still they refused to call it the Michael Jordan line," Falk says. "That's when I came up with the idea of calling the shoe Air Jordan, as a compromise between Michael Jordan and Nike." The result was then the largest basketball endorsement deal ever—worth about $2.5 million over five years, plus royalties. Falk insisted that the company spend at least a million dollars on promotion, and so guarantee his client that measure of commercial exposure. Nike insisted on an out clause if sales didn't take off. In fact, Air Jordan revenues reached $130 million by the end of the first year, and Nike happily spent several million dollars to promote the line. It was the most successful sneaker launch in history. The lesson wasn't lost on the national marketing executives at McDonald's and at Coca-Cola.

It is easy to lose sight of McDonald's and Coca-Cola as the cultural promontories they are, in the way that it is hard to take in the Empire State Building from its base. They are the planet's two most successful brands, as ubiquitous as the ground underfoot—or the buildings over-head—and sometimes as unnoticeable. In tandem, they elevated Jordan far beyond his peers, and not just through visibility alone. A recent study by four experimental psychologists published in the *Journal of Personality and Social Psychology* employs the term "spontaneous trait transference," but you might as well call it the Michael Jordan Effect. Over time, speakers are seen as themselves possessing the qualities that they describe in others.

The basic notion is hardly new: It's what underlies talk about basking in reflected glory, or the urge to kill the messenger. Even so, the strength of such "trait transference" is startling. For instance, in the recent study participants were shown a videotape of a man talking about an acquaintance who was cruel to animals. In follow-up surveys, they associated that specific trait with the communicator: He was viewed as cruel to animals. And the effect was equally strong when the participants were told what was going on—when they knew that the "interview" might have been scripted. Even when you eliminate rational warrant for the inference, people still make the association: Somehow we can't not. It is, the researchers conclude, a "relatively mindless" process, and one that may powerfully affect our impression even of those well-known to us.

Yet the literature on the effect of endorsements upon the perception of brands has notably ignored the effect of brands upon the perception of their endorsers. Redoubtable though Jordan is, you might wonder whether his singular and singularly American charisma doesn't derive in part from the venerable magic of history's most powerful consumer brands. Dismiss Coke as mere sugared water if you like, but, culturally speaking, it's a powerful concoction, and in ways that go beyond its core values of permanence ("Always Coca-Cola") and authenticity ("The Real Thing"). The Coca-Cola Company conducts regular consumer surveys to determine how the beverage scores on more than a dozen value attributes, which have included "young," "modern," "warm," and "friendly." The tracking polls are keyed to a compensatory strategy: When the scores in a particular value wane, advertisements are designed to bolster them. Yet over the six years of Jordan's association with the product (he was lured over to Gatorade in 1991) the more powerful trait transference surely went from brand to spokesperson—from the attributes to their communicator. Who seems more modern, warm, and friendly than Jordan? Who seems more enduring (Always Michael Jordan) and authentic (The Real Thing)? And the same mechanism applies to his early association with McDonald's. Consider those core attributes of being reliable, fast, wholesome, American, and family-minded. Did somebody say Michael Jordan?

Fame, not water, is the universal solvent. What to do with the fact that the voice and the face of American corporate capitalism belong to an African American—a very dark and very male one at that? Various critics have offered conjectures about the phenomenon, but it may be that David Falk sums it up best. "Celebrities aren't black," he tells me patiently, in the way one might make an observation about heat regulation in reptiles. "People don't look at Michael as being black. They accept that he's different because he's a celebrity. I'm not saying it to be derogatory. People who are exclusive and discriminatory don't look at those people as being black." Without ever playing the "raceless" card—without ever pretending to be anything other than what he was, a black kid from the South—Jordan has made race a nonissue. Talk about your fadeaway.

You can't assess the marketing of Michael without taking the measure of his own business savvy. Executives at Nike will tell you that Jordan has a knack for taking charge of any meeting at which he is present. He has clearly learned a lot from sorcerers like Falk—and Stern—but he is no longer an apprentice. To an unusual degree, he has helped shape his "creatives." Working with Tinker Hatfield, a senior designer at Nike, he has even been involved in styling his athletic footwear. All of which is to say that Jordan is, in a very 1990s way, both talent and suit. His partners know that he is sensitive to matters of dignity and does not care for every transaction to be commercial; but they also know that he can be wonderfully hard-core where matters of money are concerned. Indeed, the Falk relationship has lasted partly because Falk has been exquisitely attuned to this quality.

"For the first four or five years, Michael really kept me at arm's length," Falk says, "which only increases my admiration for him, because he shouldn't have trusted me." How, then, did Falk win Jordan's trust? By strategic sacrifices, he'll tell you, with the confidence of a chess master who knows when to forfeit a piece for a positional advantage. In 1988, Falk negotiated Jordan's second contract, which (though its eight-year duration ultimately proved a bane) was then the most lucrative ever in basketball. Afterward, Falk presented Jordan with a bill—the standard sports agent's fee, which is 4 percent of the client's salary. Falk recalls that Jordan wasn't pleased: "He said immediately, 'I think it's too high,' and he offered to pay roughly half of what I had proposed." Falk agreed, but then went even further: He told Jordan that he was going to reduce the agency's marketing fee—the percentage, usually around 20 percent, that it took on a player's marketing and endorsement deals—by a quarter. Falk recounts, "When he left, my partner said to me, 'He told you he was happy with the marketing—why on earth would you propose that?' I said, 'Because, as the market continues to escalate, one day he's gonna feel that it's too high, and I'd rather offer it to him voluntarily, as a gesture of good faith.' And from that day on we've never discussed fees again." This way, as Falk figured the angles, he himself benefited from "the goodwill of Michael's knowing that it was voluntary, as opposed to his putting a gun to your head one day and saying, 'I want to pay half.'" Agents—even one as brilliant, innovative, and aggressive as David Falk—are replaceable. A client like Michael Jordan is not.

Which is why, two years ago, when Jordan starred in *Space Jam,* Falk took a deep breath and made the same move. "I waived all my producing fees on the movie," he says, and you know that it must have felt like passing a kidney stone. "Since I was the executive producer of the movie, I got a very substantial fee. And I talked to different people who said, 'You're crazy. We have to explain to Michael that in Hollywood whether you got a dollar or ten million dollars to be executive producer of the movie wouldn't affect how much he made as an actor by one penny.' I said, 'I understand that, and you understand that, but I know he's not comfortable with it.' He just didn't feel it was appropriate for me to be involved on two or three different levels. He never asked me to do it. I went to him one day and just told him, 'I want you to know, I've earned x and I'm going to give it back to you.' And he was very appreciative of that. That's really what he wanted me to do."

This is the kind of thing you do when you value and protect your assets. Jordan got flak in the late eighties when, frustrated by the Bulls' poor performance in the playoffs, he took to calling his teammates "my supporting cast," but that's pretty much the way Falk sees things. He says, "You could almost have a lottery and take all the players in the league and say, 'OK, Michael, you need eleven players. Take any four centers, any four forwards, and any three guards.' And you'd have a pretty damn good team."

I start to protest. "But you wouldn't have the Bulls and their dynasty."

"I think that's overrated," Falk says breezily. "Truthfully. I think you take Michael away and I think they're a very average team." Spoken, we can agree, like a man who secured his client a thirty-odd-million-dollar contract for the current season. Nothing but net worth.

Not all Jordan's relationships involve commercial transactions, of course, and if he's been buoyed by his business ties he's been both protected and grounded by his personal ones. It's a significant fact about him that he has never surrounded himself with a gangsta-style posse—that his closest friend is a sixty-one-year-old black guy named Gus Lett, who used to work for him as a security consultant, and who somehow reminds him of a fellow who is no longer around, his father. Like James Jordan, Gus is an Air Force veteran and is almost exactly the age James would have been had he lived; he's also a man who worked long hours for many years, as an officer in the Chicago Police Department. When I finally met him, I was reminded of guys who used to hang out at my local black barbershop: this was the kind of fellow who knew how to drink bourbon and play bid whist at the same time, who taught his kids to do the right thing and call their elders "Ma'am" and "Sir." Dressed in jeans and a cap, Gus came across as both earthy and down-to-earth, well versed in sports but not obsessed with them, and quietly, vigilantly protective of Jordan. They became friends in 1985, when Jordan was limping around with a broken foot and Gus was working as a security guard at the Chicago Stadium. Gus used to help the young player with his bags as he negotiated the stairs, and somehow the two clicked. How close are Jordan and Gus? Jordan gave the man his championship rings.

Jordan became almost misty when he described the friendship. "Gus is very smart, very intelligent, but yet our rapport together is always joking and kidding," he told me. "And we can't do anything without hanging together. If it's going to the riverboat, he goes. I would never—I feel awkward telling him how much I love him, but yet . . . he knows."

For the first time, Jordan's speech was halting. "And it's reciprocal, I can feel it. It's so unique where honestly my best, best friend is sixty-some years old and we share so much now. I can see it's like my father has come back and is living through this guy." Jordan's gaze drifted over to the large photograph of his father, who was killed in the summer of 1993, the victim of a roadside robbery in North Carolina. "It's God's way of telling me that I've gotta make some mature decisions without the support system of a father," he has said of his father's death, and yet he has also sought to re-create such a support system. "I trust Gus," Jordan said softly. "I know he's watching out for me, no matter what."

It has been a blow to him that, just recently, Gus was found to have metastatic lung cancer, and has had to undergo chemotherapy. Over the past several weeks, Jordan has been paying him regular visits and has made sure that he receives the best possible treatment. "He's got my back," Jordan has always said of Gus. Those guys have each other's back.

"Michael's just a southern guy," Juanita Jordan, his wife of eight years, tells me. "The night before a big game in the playoffs, he'll sit down and write out a list of names of the people that he has to remember to give tickets to. I find it amazing that he still does that. And he's always welcoming people to the house. His friends—friends he's known since North Carolina—are always there hanging out." She sounds faintly exasperated on this score, and makes it clear that she has had to establish certain boundaries. She grew up on the South Side of Chicago, and her husband's country ways are still slightly foreign to her. "It used to be that they'd just show up. I'd open the door and say 'Yes?' 'Oh, Michael didn't tell you?' 'No, he didn't. What do you want?' And meanwhile the cab's pulling off." A tight smile: "So now they call."

Juanita, who is four years older than her husband, is a poised, attractive, light-skinned woman, who has grown accustomed to the glare of publicity, though not inured to it. She's had a stint writing a column for a Chicago gazette, and recently returned to school, taking courses in journalism at Northwestern University. A lot of her time these days is spent helping to set up the M & J Endowment Fund, which will support community endeavors like shelters for battered women. And a lot of her time is spent raising their three children: Jeffrey, who is nine; Marcus, who is seven; and Jasmine, who is five. They're a photogenic family, though for the most part Michael has sensibly protected them from the klieg lights. Even so, being married to fame—having a husband you can see more easily on the tube than in the flesh—has been a curious experience. "In the early days of our relationship, I almost felt I wasn't part of his life: I was watching this celebrity person, and it was really kind of surreal," she told me. "In the beginning, the children would also be mesmerized by his appearance on the television set, almost thinking, What's he doing in there? But now when one of Daddy's commercials comes on, they'll just say, 'Oh, there's Daddy again,' and go on about their business." Not that turning the TV off would make much difference; these kids live in a world festooned with their father's image.

Michael Jordan has, indeed, been called a human billboard, but he's acutely conscious of the fact that a billboard can be defaced. There are ironies here. Basketball is the most naked of team sports. Jordan has conjectured that he and other players tend to overdress off the court because they must wear so little on the court. Unlike other players, though, he never changes when reporters are patrolling the locker rooms. He will not risk being pictured—by word or image—in a state of undress; and surely it isn't much for even the world's most famous man to ask that his privates not be made public. There's a larger sense, too, in which Jordan doesn't wish to be caught undressed. He who lives by the image may also perish by it. In the fall of 1990, James Worthy, Jordan's old college teammate and a power forward with the Los Angeles Lakers, was arrested in Houston on charges of solicitation when two call girls he hired turned out to be undercover policewomen; the episode received widespread and undue attention, along with many predictable jests about double-teaming. Among the athletic elect, schadenfreude vies with an even stronger emotion: there but for the grace of God. (One of the oldest NBA jokes: "What's the toughest thing about going on the road?" "Not smiling when you kiss your wife goodbye.") Jordan has said that being caught in a scandal that would taint his image is one of the things he dreads most.

It's an anxiety that his corporate clientele undoubtedly share. David Aaker, who is the author of *Building Strong Brands*, and is a marketing professor at Berkeley, says, "There's a big advantage in having a Pillsbury Doughboy or a Betty Crocker, because at least you know they won't take drugs." Or accumulate large gambling debts to convicted felons, which proved to be Jordan's principal indiscretion. In the early nineties, checks of his amounting to more than a hundred thousand dollars turned up in the possession of some unsavory characters, apparently as a result of high-stakes golf and poker games. Falk told reporters that his client had got hustled; Jordan told them that he was "no Pete Rose"; and Jordan's father told them, reasonably, "The amounts of money to me and you would have been astronomical. But with the kind of money he's making it's peanuts." Then a onetime golf partner wrote a book—tackily titled *Michael & Me: Our Gambling Addiction . . . My Cry for Help!*—claiming that Jordan had lost more than a million dollars in bets to him. Jordan was known to be fiercely competitive; now he was known to be a man who would bet on anything.

Not good. But not that bad, either. The betting was confined to recreational pursuits, golf and poker, and, though the stakes were high, Jordan's father was right to point out that they weren't anything he couldn't handle. As a rule of thumb, an indiscretion is truly damaging only if it is discordant with your perceived character: Thus teen idols should be discouraged from cruising the men's rooms in public parks, and children's-television actors from getting off in adult movie theaters. In this case, though, the picture of Jordan as a man possessed to win—in any endeavor—wasn't inconsistent with his demonic presence driving the lane. Besides, the misdeeds were, in nature, nonvenal, nonsexual, and nonviolent. Most fans figured he was much more the better for being a little bad.

Jordan, you could even argue, is as much at risk from his corporate clients as they are from him. It must have been discomfiting when, in the summer of 1990, Jesse Jackson's Operation Push announced a boycott against Nike, charging that the company was taking from the black community without giving back to it. It must have been discomfiting when subsequent controversies arose over Nike's use of low-paid overseas labor. But Jordan has handled the situations with considerable skill, chastising neither the company nor its critics. To be sure, that nimbleness in sidestepping political controversy has itself come under attack. The football legend Jim Brown—speaking at President Clinton's town meeting on race and sports in April—was only the latest activist to complain that Jordan had failed to use his visibility for social or political causes. Falk says, "Michael is definitely apolitical," and he means it as a recommendation. Others say it as a rebuke.

But should athletes be required to serve as political spokesmen? Jesse Jackson, who likes to say that his role is to be the social conscience of the mighty ("Whether Michael or the president," he says, in a significant pairing), urges a sensible division of labor. "Why is it expected of a ballplayer or a boxer to be an astute sociopolitical analyst?" he asks. "That is not what they are really qualified to do. They move from city to city, and they're on the road six months a year, and they're not in the best position to be social interpreters. Michael has not succumbed to that temptation."

This could sound like a backhanded compliment, but I'm not sure Jackson means it that way. "You're saying he has sense enough to keep his mouth shut?"

"And that is a great contribution," Jackson replies smoothly. "Besides, the issue of trading with Indonesia without regard to human rights or child labor is fundamentally a matter that United States trade policy must address. It isn't right to shift the burden to him because he's a high-profile salesman."

Jordan has never sacrificed himself to a political cause in the way that Muhammad Ali did, but he isn't apolitical, either, in the way that Falk makes out. First, he's not afraid to admit some mildly partisan allegiances. ("I told Colin Powell I would be right next to him, supporting him.") But, more than that, he does have a strong social conscience, as was clear when I asked him about the predominance of blacks in sports. "To be honest, I think it's a curse," Jordan said. He was talking about the odds—the simple fact that to practice hoops instead of hitting the books is like spending food money on the lottery. "Doctors, lawyers, dentists will be practicing for thirty years, but our window of opportunity is, at the most, eight years," he went on. "That's a heck of a risk. And we're our own worst problem in terms of the marketing and projecting"—of burnishing the mystique of the black athlete as opposed to that of the black professional. Jordan has not occupied the crow's nest of popular culture so long as to have forgotten how powerful the perch is. Or how precarious.

Everyone on top lives with a morbid consciousness that fame—heat, stardom, sociocultural fit—is a waterwheel. The rule obtains in the political and the recreational realms alike: There is, as it were, a physiognomy of fortune, and sooner or later it alters. Robert Coover, in one of his early novellas, writes about a political fixer who, back when he was a congressman, had the sagacity to foresee his own electoral defeat against a "young tight-lipped challenger":

> You see, I am blessed—or damned, as you will—with puffy pink lips. They helped me to win my seat in the House of Representatives, just as later they helped me to lose it. My short stature, round belly, smooth pink scalp, anonymous name, and occasionally irascible temper no doubt contributed, but mainly it was the fat lips. By thrusting the lower one forward, I was able to project a marvelous complexion of self-righteous anger, a kind of holy Bible-belting zeal for judgment, which complemented nicely the central issue, so-called, of my winning campaign: an attack on my incumbent opponent's corruption. That wonderful pout did me little service, however, in defending myself against the same attacks two years later. Of course, there were many factors, many vectors, but the fat lips were decisive.

And there you have it. One day the star wakes up, and those projectile Gaultier breastplates aren't doing it anymore; the masses want a toothy, virginal, choir-girl Whitney Houston, not the platinum-haired, sexually adventurous material girl. Fandom starts out like a love affair: No detail about the object of desire is too trivial to be of interest, and tabloid reams are filled with personal minutiae. But in time there comes a phase when the object, although prized, is taken for granted; then a measure of boredom sets in; and then you agree to see other people.

So the real question, as Jordan correctly maintains, is how the Jordan mystique has lasted as long as it has. "Each and every year, I've been expecting it—the drop-off," Jordan says. "Just from human nature, from seeing someone's name in lights for so many years that everyone gets tired of hearing about that person. When you see something consistent all the time, you start to say, 'Well, wait, where's the change? Where is the next person? Where is the next phenomenon?' But it's not happening. And I don't really know why, or how long it's going to last."

In this respect, Jordan's core product—shoes—may be a useful augury. Nike, in the years since its original alliance with Jordan, has become the Microsoft of the sneaker, accounting for more than 40 percent of the 350 million pairs of sneakers that Americans bought last year. But now sneaker sales are in general starting to ebb. To Nike's distress, "brown shoes"—as non-sneakers are known in the trade—are gaining among its customers. In March, Nike announced that its 1998 earnings had declined by 70 percent, and that it had laid off sixteen hundred employees. Jordan's imminent retirement is likely to show up on the bottom line, too: This has been clear since he spent that sabbatical, courtesy of Jerry Reinsdorf, playing minor-league baseball. "We didn't sell enough baseball shoes to make up for what we lost in basketball shoes," Phil Knight, Nike's charismatic chairman and CEO, says dryly.

Part of Nike's problem may be the overfamiliarity of its distinctive, high-impact advertising. Jordan's sneaker spots have come in every imaginable cinematic style, but during most of the past decade the campaigns produced by the ad agency Wieden & Kennedy, under the creative director Jim Riswold, set the tone: the play of silvery chiaroscuro, the beautiful black-and-white camerawork, the edgy message and understated product sell. What Josef von Sternberg was to Marlene Dietrich or what Scorsese was to De Niro, Wieden & Kennedy has been to Jordan. Its ads depicted him as an object of allure, a mascot of urban manhood—supple, smooth, commanding, powerful, and hip. A stunning achievement, by any yardstick, but has it overtaken its sell-by date? Joanne DeLuca, a market researcher at Sputnik, has concluded that the deification of unreal athletes is losing its lustre, and that the "hard-edged 'win-at-all-costs' message" is beginning "to turn off younger consumers." More worrisome is the growing sense of backlash against the Air Jordan dynasty, against the hegemony of Nike generally, and even against what some people are cattily calling the swooshtika.

Has Jordan been overexposed? Phil Knight has made no secret of his concern that Jordan's value to Nike was attenuated by his other endorsements. Nike may own the "jumpman" logo—an icon of Jordan jumping toward an unseen basket—but it doesn't own Jordan's visage. His endorsements for other companies may have helped entrench the brand that is Michael Jordan but lessened the specialness of his association with Nike. "If you were teaching a course in marketing, that wouldn't be the way to do it," Knight told me, adding quickly, "But he has overcome all those mistakes by his greatness." It's possible to be less sanguine about this situation. The advertiser's main enemy, of course, is what the industry calls "clutter," which is to say other people's ads. You hear estimates that the average consumer encounters almost three thousand marketing messages a day. Not a few of those messages bear the countenance of Michael Jordan. A koan for Madison Avenue: What do you do when you are your own clutter?

Jordan's counselors grapple with these issues. After a few years of an endorsement spree, they halved the number of his corporate affiliations and increasingly emphasized long-term deals: Since 1989, Jordan hasn't made a deal shorter than ten years. In general, Falk has been imposing discipline upon his client's endorsement range, restricting his principal product associations to Nike, Quaker Oats, Rayovac, Sara Lee, Bijan (Michael Jordan Cologne was the top-selling new fragrance in its debut year), Wilson, CBS SportsLine, and WorldCom. Last year, Jordan's income was estimated to have been in excess of seventy million dollars.

Jordan's price tag not only reflects his extraordinary utility as an endorser; it may even contribute to it. There's a school of thought that says the cost of advertising must be considered part of the content of the advertising—that the key message of lots of ad campaigns is "Look how much we're spending on this ad campaign!" Marshall McLuhan didn't get it quite right: The medium isn't the message; the moola is the message. And the value of the celebrity endorsement? According to the economist Mark Hertzendorf, a big problem with ad campaigns is that consumers are unlikely to see all of an advertiser's commercials, and so might not be properly impressed by its lavishness—a lavishness that implies its expectation of strong sales, which, in turn, implies the excellence of its product. The solution is to pack more price information into every spot; and you can do that by featuring a celebrity endorsement, since viewers know that such endorsements cost big. ("For example, a consumer who views one commercial containing an endorsement by Jerry Seinfeld can immediately conclude that the firm is spending millions of dollars on advertising," Hertzendorf observes.) The fact that Jordan is the winner-take-all pitchman—the one whose services are known to be the priciest—means that, whatever the product is, he can be relied upon to send a message about a generous ad budget, and so about company confidence.

Falk has long had an intuitive grasp of the Hertzendorf effect—he knew it would be good for Gatorade to cough up eighteen million dollars for the privilege of being guzzled by the greatest—but his latest brainstorm is to generate "marketing synergies" among Jordan's client corporations. "We're trying to intermarry his companies," Falk tells me. "For instance, since his next-to-last deal was with the telephone company WorldCom, we're trying to get as many of his existing companies to pick up WorldCom for their long-distance carrier and business carrier as possible." So far, it's unclear that any of them have done so, corporations being an even harder sell than consumers.

Still, Falk gets points for innovation. He likes to speak of himself as an artist, and his clients as canvases. The paint is pretty much dry on the Jordan landscape. "Most of my work for Michael is finished," he says, sounding almost elegiac. "It's not like he's looking for a lot more deals."

Truth to tell, it's hard to stay entirely unmoved on the subject of Jordan's retirement. From a fan's perspective, that's because the game will have lost its greatest and most exciting player—a man who, at the advanced age of thirty-five, is the highest scorer in the NBA this season. From Falk's perspective, it's because—Joe Namath and those Noxzema commercials notwithstanding—the record concerning the commercial longevity of retired athletes is not altogether encouraging. All the same, Juanita Jordan tells me, "once he retires, the companies that he endorses products for are going to pick up a lot of his time—I think he really wants to sink his teeth into the Brand Jordan concept with Nike, and to follow through with the commitments he has made to the major companies he is endorsing." Hence Falk's mantra: "Being a basketball player has become his job, but it's not his image." And yet you might say that Jordan's job is his image, in that being Michael Jordan has become his principal line of work.

Which means that Jordan has become a prisoner of repute. His livelihood as an endorser amounts to a gilded captivity, because his currency is his character. And it is so very hard to be so very good. He has summed up his relationship with Charles Barkley, the trash-talking forward of the Houston Rockets, as "a sort of good-son, bad-son thing," where "Charles gets to say all the things I'd like to say." And, though Jordan isn't so close to the Bulls' own enfant terrible, Dennis Rodman—he's recently made it clear how much his patience has been taxed by him—he views Rodman's bad-as-I-wanna-be act with some wistfulness. We're talking about what happened to Dennis Rodman years ago, when, the story goes, he came home to find out that his wife was sleeping with Vinnie Johnson, then Rodman's teammate on the Detroit Pistons. "It flipped him out," Jordan says. "It changed him. It changed his whole persona, his personality toward his teammates." He's referring to Rodman's now trademark combination of introversion and flamboyance. I tend to be skeptical about the lore of formative moments, but what strikes me is how fraternal Jordan sounds. Again, there's a sort of division of labor, with Rodman's freakishness helping to secure Jordan's normality. Jordan says, "I think he's a good person at heart. Like most people, he's found a niche to make a living."

Like most people, but not like Jordan. His burdens come from being the very opposite of a niche player. For one thing, the work of exposure, of supporting a global brand, presents clear-cut logistical problems for maintaining something resembling a private life. Jordan figures that it's been a decade since he has been able to go outside without getting mobbed, and says that he "can't wait till it changes." The media frenzy has its own troughs and peaks. In the speculation-filled days before his official return to basketball in the spring of 1995, the paparazzi would do things like tape over the card reader on the players' parking lot, hoping that Jordan would have to get out of his car and expose himself to their cameras. Of necessity, Jordan has become adept at setting limits: "I've come to grips, saying, 'Leave me alone, this is my family time, this is my private time.' And there are a lot of assholes who don't understand that. I can really get harsh if I feel you're infringing way past the niceness that I try to show you." He speaks softly, but you can hear the steel.

There are various people who help protect him, and sometimes become part of his extended family. As we're winding things up at North LaSalle Street, Jordan tells me about George Koehler, his friend and driver: "When I first came to Chicago, thirteen years ago, I didn't know one soul, and the Bulls didn't pick me up. I'm getting off the plane, and I run into this guy. He has his own limousine company, and his passenger didn't show up. So he comes over to me and gives me a ride."

At some point during the account, George Koehler himself makes an appearance, and is affably assured by Jordan that he's been telling me lies about him. For both of them, in a manner that's typically American and male, the vocabulary of intimacy is insult.

"Did you charge him?" I ask Koehler.

"Yeah," Jordan puts in, "he overcharged me, I tell you."

"I didn't overcharge him." Koehler sulks.

"He ripped me off then," Jordan says, "and he's been ripping me off ever since."

"Actually, he gave me a huge tip," Koehler says, brightening at the memory. "I told him twenty-five bucks, he gave me fifty bucks and said, 'Keep the change.' "

"So I'm down here looking around and I'm scared as shit," Jordan says. "I don't know where the hell I'm going in a city that I've never been to. But he watched out for me."

"I'm paying for it now," George says.

"And he watches out for me now," Jordan says. Maybe it sounds a little earnest, so he adds, "By lying. Being a pain in the ass."

In *The Frenzy of Renown,* a classic study of fame and its history, Leo Braudy writes that seasoned spectators "look not for style so much as sincerity," and that, traditionally, it was "the sports stars who most significantly handled the problem of public exposure because at their best they represented an unself-conscious perfection of the body, displayed for the pleasure of their fans. Here was fame unsullied by the alloy of history, language, or any mediation but the body's own." Jordan has rewritten the rules. In one magical package, Michael Jordan is both Muhammad Ali and Mister Clean, Willie Mays and the Marlboro Man. But if America's powerbrands helped insure Jordan's status as an international symbol of America, Jordan—and the sense we have that he's ours—has become one of those things that constitute our identity as Americans, as citizens of the winner-take-all society. Trait transference isn't a one-stop affair. And the work of what we call globalization, and what the rest of the world knows as Americanization, is never done. Michael Jordan, putting on his game face, says, "My father told me, 'If you're going to die, son, don't die with no bullets in your gun.' And I live by that."

When I venture beyond the quiet of Jordan's suite and into his restaurant, I feel oddly reassured by the loud carnival of Jordan iconog-

raphy: huge posters, enormous murals, rows and rows of framed magazine covers, cascades of photographs—an empire of signs. The bar-
and-grill on the first floor is dominated by a twenty-foot-by-six-foot
video screen where customers can watch Jordan's greatest moments
over and over and over again. It's a spectacle of kitsch—and, yes, of
utter physical transcendence. Gazing for a spell at the highlights loop,
I feel somehow uplifted by the procession of fadeaways, jump shots,
dunks, fakeouts, double-pumps, alley-oops, layups. They also serve who
only stand and cheer.

1998

"Here's another one, men. Hang on!"

THE LONG RIDE

MICHAEL SPECTER

A couple of weeks ago, on a sweltering Saturday afternoon, I found myself in the passenger seat of a small Volkswagen, careering so rapidly around the hairpin turns of the French Alps that I could smell the tires burning. Johan Bruyneel, the suave, unflappable director of the United States Postal Service Pro Cycling Team, was behind the wheel. Driving at ninety kilometers an hour occupied half his attention. The rest was devoted to fiddling with a small television mounted in the dashboard, examining a set of complicated topographical maps, and talking into one of two radio transmitters in the car. The first connected Bruyneel to the team's support vehicle, laden with extra bicycles, water bottles, power bars, and other tools and equipment. The second fed into the earpieces of the eight U.S. Postal Service cyclists who were racing along the switchbacks ahead of us. The entire team could hear every word that Bruyneel said, but most of the time he was talking to just one man: Lance Armstrong.

We had been on the road for about three hours and Armstrong was a kilometer in front of us, pedaling so fast that it was hard to keep up. It was the sixth day of the Dauphiné Libéré, a weeklong race that is run in daily stages. Armstrong doesn't enter races like the Dauphiné to win (though often enough he does); he enters to test his legs in preparation for a greater goal—the Tour de France. Since 1998, when he returned to cycling after almost losing his life to testicular cancer, Armstrong has focused exclusively on dominating the 3,500-kilometer, near month-long Tour, which, in the world of cycling, matters more than all other races combined. This week, he begins a quest to become the fourth person in the hundred-year history of the Tour—the world's most grueling test of human endurance—to win four times in a row. (In 1995, the Spanish cyclist Miguel Indurain became the first to win five consecutively—a record that is clearly on Armstrong's mind.)

The cyclists had covered 108 kilometers, much of it over mountain passes still capped with snow, despite temperatures edging into the nineties. Now the peloton—the term is French for "platoon," and it de-

scribes the pack of riders who make up the main group in every race—
was about to start one of the most agonizing climbs in Europe, the pass
between Mont Blanc and Lake Geneva, which is known as the Col de
Joux Plane. In cycling, climbs are rated according to how long and steep
they are: The easiest is category four, the hardest category one. The
seventeen-hundred-meter Joux Plane has a special rating, known as
hors categorie, or beyond category; for nearly twelve kilometers, it rises
so sharply that it seems a man could get to the top only by helicopter.

"We start the Joux Plane with a lot of respect for this mountain,"
Bruyneel said quietly into his radio. "It is long, it is hard. Take it easy. If
people are breaking away, let them go. Do you hear me, Lance?"

"Yes, Johan," Armstrong replied flatly. "I remember the mountain."

With only a few days remaining in the 2000 Tour de France, Armstrong had what most observers agreed was an insurmountable lead
when he headed toward this pass. He was riding with his two main rivals of that year: Marco Pantani, the best-known Italian cyclist, and Jan
Ullrich, the twenty-eight-year-old German who won the Tour in 1997,
and who in the world of cycling plays the role of Joe Frazier to Armstrong's Ali. As they started to climb, Armstrong seemed invincible.
Halfway up, though, he slumped over his handlebars, looking as if he
had suffered a stroke, and Ullrich blew right by him.

"I bonked," Armstrong said later, using a cyclist's term for running
out of fuel. A professional cyclist consumes so much energy—up to ten
thousand calories during a two-hundred-kilometer mountain stage—
that, unless some of it is replaced, his body will run through all the
glycogen (the principal short-term supply of carbohydrates the body
uses for power) stored in his muscles. Armstrong hadn't eaten properly
that morning; then he found himself cut off from his *domestiques*—the
teammates who, among other things, are responsible for bringing him
supplies of food and water during the race. "That was the hardest day
of my life on a bike," Armstrong said later. He was lucky to finish the
day's stage, and even luckier to hold on and win the race.

"This isn't just a stage in a race for Lance," Bruyneel said now, as
Armstrong approached the bottom of the slope. "He needs to defeat
this mountain to feel ready for the Tour." This time, Bruyneel made
sure that the *domestiques* ferried water, carbohydrate drinks, and extra
power bars to Armstrong throughout the day. They periodically drifted
back to our car and performed a kind of high-speed docking maneuver

so that Bruyneel could thrust water bottles, five or six at a time, into their outstretched arms.

Last year, Armstrong won the Tour, for the third time in a row, by covering 3,462 kilometers at an average speed of more than forty kilometers an hour—the third-fastest time in the history of the event. In all, during those three weeks in July, Armstrong spent eighty-six hours, seventeen minutes, and twenty-eight seconds on the bike. "Lance almost killed himself training for the last Tour," Bruyneel told me. "This year, he is in even better shape. But the press still wants to talk about drugs."

It is, of course, hard to write about cycling and not discuss performance-enhancing drugs, because at times so many of the leading competitors seem to have used them. Strict testing measures have been in force since 1998, when the Tour was nearly canceled after an assistant for the Festina team was caught with hundreds of vials of erythropoietin, or EPO, a hormone that can increase the oxygen supply to the blood. But the changes have brought only limited success: just this May, Stefano Garzelli and Gilberto Simoni, two of Europe's leading cyclists, were forced to withdraw from the Giro d'Italia, Italy's most important race.

Because Armstrong is the best cyclist in the world, there is an assumption among some of those who follow the sport that he, too, must use drugs. Armstrong has never failed a drug test, however, and he may well be the most frequently examined athlete in the history of sports. Whenever he wins a day's stage, or finishes as one of the top cyclists in a longer race, he is required to provide a urine sample. Like other professionals, Armstrong is also tested randomly throughout the year. (The World Anti-Doping Agency, which regularly tests athletes, has even appeared at his home, in Austin, Texas, at dawn, to demand a urine sample.) Nobody questions Armstrong's excellence. And yet doubts remain: Is he really so gifted that, like Secretariat, he easily dominates even his most talented competitors?

"It's terribly unfair," Bruyneel told me as we drove through the mountains. "He is already winning, and is extremely fit. Still, people always ask that one question: How can he do this without drugs? I understand why people ask, because our sport has been tainted. But Lance has a different trick, and I have watched him do it now for four years: He just works harder than anyone else alive."

Lance Armstrong's heart is almost a third larger than that of an average man. During those rare moments when he is at rest, it beats about thirty-two times a minute—slowly enough so that a doctor who knew nothing about him would call a hospital as soon as he heard it. (When Armstrong is exerting himself, his heart rate can edge up above two hundred beats a minute.) Physically, he was a prodigy. Born in 1971, Armstrong was raised by his mother in Plano, a drab suburb of Dallas that he quickly came to despise. He never knew his father, and refers to him as "the DNA donor." He has written that "the main thing you need to know about my childhood is that I never had a real father, but I never sat around wishing for one, either. . . . I've never had a single conversation with my mother about him."

He was a willful child and didn't like to listen to advice. "I have loved him every minute of his life, but, God, there were times when it was a struggle," his mother, Linda, told me. She is a demure woman with the kind of big blond hair once favored by wives of astronauts. "He has always wanted to test the boundaries," she said. Armstrong admits that he was never an easy child. In his autobiography, *It's Not About the Bike*, which was written with the journalist Sally Jenkins, he said, "When I was a boy I invented a game called fireball, which entailed soaking a tennis ball in kerosene, lighting it on fire, and playing catch with it."

Armstrong was an outstanding young swimmer, and as an adolescent he began to enter triathlons. By 1987, when he was sixteen, he was also winning bicycle races. That year, he was invited to the Cooper Institute, in Dallas, which was one of the first centers to recognize the relationship between fitness and aerobic conditioning. Everyone uses oxygen to break down food into the components that provide energy; the more oxygen you are able to use, the more energy you will produce, and the faster you can run, ride, or swim. Armstrong was given a test called the VO2 Max, which is commonly used to assess an athlete's aerobic ability: It measures the maximum amount of oxygen the lungs can consume during exercise. His levels were the highest ever recorded at the clinic. (Currently, they are about eighty-five milliliters per kilogram of body weight; a healthy man might have a VO2 Max of forty.)

Chris Carmichael, who became his coach when Armstrong was still a teenager, told me that even then Armstrong was among the most remarkable athletes he had ever seen. Not only has his cardiovascular strength always been exceptional; his body seems specially constructed for cycling. His thigh bones are unusually long, for example, which permits him to apply just the right amount of torque to the pedals.

Although Armstrong was talented, he wasn't very disciplined. He acted as if he had nothing to learn. "I had never met him when I took over as his coach," Carmichael told me. "I called him up and we talked on the phone. He was kind of rude. Not kind of rude. He was completely rude. He was, like, 'So you are the new coach—what are you going to teach me?' He just thought he was King Shit. I would tell him to wait till the end of a race before making a break. He just couldn't do that. He would get out in front and set the pace. He would burn up the field, and when other riders came alive he would be done, spent." Still, Armstrong did well in one-day races, in which bursts of energy count as much as patience or tactical precision. In 1991, after several years of increasingly impressive performances, he became the U.S. amateur champion, and the next year he turned pro. In 1993, he became the youngest man ever to win a stage in the Tour de France; he won the World Road Championships the same year.

In 1996, Armstrong signed a contract with the French cycling team Cofidis, for a salary of more than two million dollars over two years. He had a beautiful new home in Austin, and a Porsche that he liked to drive fast. Then, in September, he became unusually weak and felt soreness in one of his testicles. Since soreness is a part of any cyclist's life, he didn't give it much thought. One night later that month, however, several days after his twenty-fifth birthday, he felt something metallic in his throat while he was talking on the phone. He put his friend on hold, and ran into the bathroom. "I coughed into the sink," he later wrote. "It splattered with blood. I coughed again, and spit up another stream of red. I couldn't believe the mass of blood and clotted matter had come from my own body."

Within a week, Armstrong had surgery to remove the cancerous testicle. By then, the disease had spread to his lungs, abdomen, and brain. He needed brain surgery and the most aggressive type of chemotherapy. "At that point, he had a minority chance of living another year," Craig Nichols, who was Armstrong's principal oncologist, told me. "We cure at most a third of the people in situations like that." A professor at Oregon Health Sciences University who specializes in testicular cancer, Nichols has remained a friend and is an adviser to the Lance

Armstrong Foundation, which supports cancer research. Nichols described Armstrong as the "most willful person I have ever met." And, he said, "he wasn't willing to die." Armstrong underwent four rounds of chemotherapy so powerful that the chemicals destroyed his musculature and caused permanent kidney damage; in the final treatments, the chemicals left burns on his skin from the inside out. Cofidis, convinced that Armstrong's career (and perhaps his life) was over, told his agent while he was still in the hospital that it wanted to reconsider the terms of his contract. That may have turned out to be the worst bet in the history of sports.

Armstrong did recover, but his first attempts to return to competition ended in exhaustion and depression. "In an odd way, having cancer was easier than recovery—at least in chemo I was doing something, instead of just waiting for it to come back," he wrote. In 1998, he decided to make a more serious effort to return to racing. Again, he couldn't stick with it. "The comeback was still amazingly risky," Carmichael told me. "There wasn't a doctor on this earth who could say that Lance Armstrong's lungs weren't fucked up, the cancer wasn't going to come back. Nobody said, 'You will be successful and, by the way, you will win the Tour.' He was afraid, so he just quit. I was shocked. He beats cancer. Goes to hell and back. Goes to Europe. Trains his ass off. Trained harder than ever. In the Ruta del Sol"—a five-day race held each year in Spain—"he was fourteenth. He had never done better, even before cancer, and all indications were that he was on the verge of the greatest comeback in sports, and he said, 'Hey, I'm quitting.' My coaching side just wanted to scream."

Carmichael and Bill Stapleton, Armstrong's close friend and agent, helped persuade him that this wasn't the way to end his career. "We said, 'You will look back on this and be disappointed—you are going out as a quitter,'" Carmichael told me. Armstrong agreed to prepare for one last race, in the United States. He, Carmichael, and a friend went to Boone, a small town in North Carolina where Armstrong liked to train. "Early April," Carmichael recalled. "The first day was nice. Then the weather turned ugly. I would follow behind in the car as they trained. One day, we were to finish at the top of Beech Mountain. It was a long ride, a hundred-plus miles, then the ride to the top. Something happened on that mountain. He just dropped his partner and he went for it. He was racing. It was weird. I was following behind him in the car. This cold rain was now a wet snow. And I rolled down the window and I was honking the horn and yelling, 'Go, Lance, go!' He was attacking and cranking away as though we were in the Tour. Nobody was around. No human being. Not even a cow. He got up to the top of that mountain and I said, 'OK, I'll load the bike on the car and we can go home.' He said, 'Give me my rain jacket—I'm riding back.' Another thirty miles. That was all he said. It was like throwing on a light switch."

Armstrong now says that cancer was the best thing that ever happened to him. Before becoming ill, he didn't care about strategy or tactics or teamwork—and nobody (no matter what his abilities) becomes a great cyclist without mastering those aspects of the sport. Despite Armstrong's brilliant early start in the 1993 Tour, for example, he didn't even finish the race; he dropped out when the teams entered the most difficult mountain phase, in the Alps. (He also failed to finish in 1994 and 1996.)

As Carmichael pointed out to me, Armstrong had always been gifted, but "genetically he is not alone. He is near the top but not at the top. I have seen people better than Lance that never go anywhere. Before Lance had cancer, we argued all the time. He never trained right. He just relied on his gift. He would do what you asked for two weeks, then flake off and do his own thing for a month or two. And then a big race would be coming up and he would call me up, all tense, telling me, 'God, I have got to start training, and you guys better start sending me some programs.' I would say, 'Lance, you don't just start preparing things four weeks before a race. This is a long process.' "

Cycling is, above all, a team sport, and the tactics involved are as complicated as those of baseball or basketball. "Ever try to explain the infield-fly rule to somebody?" Armstrong asked me when we were in Texas, where he lives when he is not racing or training in Europe. "You have to watch it to get it. As soon as you pay some attention to the tactics, cycling makes a lot of sense."

Riding through the French mountains with Bruyneel, a genial thirty-seven-year-old who has been with U.S. Postal since 1999, soon after Armstrong joined the team, I saw what he meant. (Armstrong's athletic advisers complement each other: Carmichael is the physical strategist, and Bruyneel the tactician.) "It looks like Victor is good today, so let's save him a bit longer for the Colombiere," Bruyneel radioed to Armstrong about halfway through the day's ride. "Sounds like a good idea," Armstrong replied. In other words, Victor Hugo Peña, a promising young Colombian climber on the team, seemed strong enough to lead Armstrong over one of the big peaks that the racers would encounter before the Col de Joux Plane. Riders like Hugo Peña "work" for Armstrong; they are not attempting to win the race themselves but, rather, focusing on preventing another team from defeating Armstrong. Their job is to patrol the peloton. If a competing star tries to escape from the pack in a breakaway, they must be ready to chase him down, in order to tire him out and make him less of a threat later in the race.

Until it is time to sprint, climb, or attempt a breakaway, there is usually at least one team rider positioned in front of his leader. Riding directly behind another man—which is called drafting—can save a skilled cyclist as much as 40 percent of his energy. Asker Jeukendrup, a physiologist who directs the Human Performance Laboratory at the University of Birmingham, has carried out extensive studies of the energy expended by cyclists when they race. Several years ago, Jeukendrup attached power meters to the bicycles of several Tour participants during critical stages. A power meter records a rider's heart rate, his pedal cadence, his speed, and, most important, the watts that he generates with every turn of the wheels. (Watts provide the most accurate measurement of the intensity of exercise; heart rates vary and so does speed. The amount of work needed to climb a hill remains the same no matter how fast you ride.)

Jeukendrup recorded the effort expended by a cyclist riding for six hours at forty kilometers an hour in the middle of the peloton, shielded from the wind. He compared this figure with the power needed to propel that same man riding alone. In the pack, the cyclist used an average of 98 watts—which would never tire a well-trained professional. On his own, however, the cyclist expended an average of 275 watts—nearly three times the power—to maintain the same speed. It is easy to see what this means: In any race, the guy out front is often suffering in his attempt to lead the peloton, while somebody like Armstrong, safely tucked into a cocoon of teammates, can cruise just a few yards behind the leader and be "pulled" at essentially the same speed, conserving energy for later.

The peloton can cover up to 250 kilometers a day without stopping, like a rolling army; there is a "feed zone" about halfway through each stage, where cyclists slow down enough to be draped with a cloth pouch, called a musette, which is filled with fruit, power bars, and other high-carbohydrate snacks. The team members take turns "working," or pulling, at the front to give each other a rest. (Even competitors, when they ride together, take turns out front, sharing the advantages of drafting.) In some ways, cycling retains an odd chivalry that is more readily associated with the trenches of the First World War. During last year's Tour, for instance, at a crucial moment in the Pyrenees, Jan Ullrich veered off the road and into a ditch; Armstrong waited for him to get back on his bike and catch up. Ullrich almost certainly would have done the same for him. When a leader needs to urinate, the whole pack slows down. It is an unspoken but very clear element of the etiquette of professional cycling that nobody is permitted to benefit by breaking away while an opponent urinates (or, worse yet, when part of the peloton is caught at a train crossing). Anyone who did would be unlikely to finish the race. After all, it takes little to knock a man off a bicycle, particularly at high speeds; this is called flicking, from the German *ficken*—which means "to fuck."

Apart from the Olympics and World Cup soccer, the Tour is the most popular sporting event in Europe. In France, July is a carnival, complete with thousands of cars, buses, motorcycles, and helicopters following the Tour, and daily television coverage. This year, at least fifteen million people—a quarter of the country's population—are expected to line the highways to watch the cyclists whiz by in a blurred instant. Every morning, kids mass outside the team buses, begging for autographs. If a spectator is lucky, someone in the peloton will toss a used water bottle his way; it is the cycling world's version of a foul ball.

The Tour de France is exactly what its name suggests: a tour of France. The race takes place over the course of three weeks, with a day or two of rest, and the course is altered slightly each year, so that it passes through different villages. Each day, there is a new stage; when all the stages have been completed, the man with the fastest cumulative time wins. (This year's Tour will be the shortest in its history; some people believe this is an attempt to reduce Armstrong's advantage.) As a commercial and logistical endeavor, the Tour could be compared to a presidential campaign or the Super Bowl. Its budget is in the tens of millions of dollars, and the winner receives close to four hundred thousand dollars. The money comes from location fees, paid by towns that host a stage, and from advertising revenues and broadcast licenses. The Tour is treated as if it were its own sovereign state within France: It has a police force and a traveling bank (the only one in the country open on Bastille Day). The entourage includes riders, mechanics, masseurs, managers, doctors, cooks, journalists, and race officials. Each team starts the race with nine riders (though it is common for as many as half to drop out), who usually work to further the goals of their leader, like Armstrong or Ullrich—who injured his knee earlier this year and will not compete.

Since individual excellence can get one only so far in a race of this magnitude, it is also crucial to have the right team, to provide organization, finances, and experience. U.S. Postal has all that; it is, in its way, pro cycling's Yankees—with climbing specialists, sprinters, and a powerful bench. This is why so many cyclists agree to work as *domestiques*, putting their success second to Armstrong's. "You work for a teammate who is older and more experienced," Victor Hugo Peña told me late one day between stages of the Dauphiné.

I was curious why a talented cyclist would agree to play such a role. "It is an apprenticeship—you have to learn the business," Hugo Peña said. "If you get respect, work well, and are good, you move up." Armstrong himself worked as a *domestique* when he was starting out. He told me that he finds the system reassuring. Bruyneel, who was a successful professional, and won two stages in the Tour, agreed. "What does a man gain from riding for himself and coming in fiftieth?" he said. "If you see your job as helping your team win, you will get more out of that than simply riding and losing. It's fun to be part of a winning team." And it is also profitable; even a journeyman cyclist can make a hundred thousand dollars a year. (This is nothing like what the winners make, of course; between his salary and the endorsements, Armstrong earned about fifteen million dollars last year.) Still, there comes a point when a talented cyclist no longer wants to occupy a supporting role and tries to establish himself as a potential leader. For several years, Armstrong's deputy on the U.S. Postal team was his friend Tyler Hamilton. This year, with Armstrong's encouragement, Hamilton began riding for a Danish competitor, CSC Tiscali, and, as one of its leaders, he placed second in the Giro d'Italia.

The physical demands on competitive cyclists are immense. One day, they will have to ride two hundred kilometers through the mountains; the next day there might be a long, flat sprint lasting seven hours. Because cyclists have such a low percentage of body fat, they are more susceptible to infections than other people. (At the beginning of the Tour, Armstrong's body fat is around 4 or 5 percent; this season, Shaquille O'Neal, the most powerful player in the NBA, boasted that his body-fat level was 16 percent.)

The Tour de France has been described as the equivalent of running twenty marathons in twenty days. During the 1980s and '90s, Wim H. M. Saris, a professor of nutrition at the University of Maastricht, conducted a study of human endurance by following participants in the Tour. "It is without any doubt the most demanding athletic event," he told me. "For one day, two days—sure, you may find something that expends more energy. But for three weeks? Never."

Looking at a wide range of physical activities, Saris and his colleagues measured the metabolic demands made on people engaged in each of them. "On average, the cyclists expend sixty-five hundred calories a day for three weeks, with peak days of ten thousand calories," he said. "If you are sedentary, you are burning perhaps twenty-five hundred calories a day. Active people might burn as many as thirty-five hundred." Saris compared the metabolic rates of professional cyclists while they were riding with those of a variety of animal species, and he created a kind of energy index—dividing daily expenditure of energy by resting metabolic rate. This figure turned out to range from one to seven. An active male rates about two on Saris's index and an average professional cyclist four and a half. Almost no species can survive with a number that is greater than five. For example, the effort made by birds foraging for food sometimes kills them, and they scored a little more than five. In fact, only four species are known to have higher rates on Saris's energy index than the professional cyclists in his study: a small Australian possum, a macaroni penguin, a large seabird called a gannet, and one species of marsupial mouse.

This spring, Armstrong, who doesn't relax much to begin with, was spending up to thirty-five hours a week on his bicycle. When I met him, in April, he had just flown to Austin from Europe, where he had been racing, for a forty-eight-hour "drop-in," in order to raise money for the Lance Armstrong Foundation. This required him to take the Concorde from Paris to New York, change planes, and, once he'd landed in Austin, drive to an afternoon photo shoot. Then he signed books, cycling jerseys, and posters for cancer survivors and sponsors of the foundation. After that, he went to a fund-raising dinner. A few hours later, the foundation's annual charity weekend, the Ride for the Roses, would officially begin, with an outdoor rock concert at the Austin Auditorium Shores arena. But Armstrong was feeling restless; he hadn't been on his bicycle for nearly a day. So he changed, and went for a thirty-five-mile spin. At eight-thirty that evening, he was standing backstage at the benefit concert, which featured Cake and the Stone Temple Pilots. I met up with him there; Armstrong, who is surprisingly slight, wore jeans, sandals, and a Nike golf cap. He didn't seem a bit tired.

Every ounce of fat, bone, and muscle on Armstrong's body is regularly inventoried, analyzed, and accounted for. I asked him if he felt it was necessary to endure the daily prodding and poking required to provide all this information, and to adhere so rigidly to his training schedules. "Depends whether you want to win," he replied. "I do. The Tour is a two-thousand-mile race, and people sometimes win by one minute. Or less. One minute in nearly a month of suffering isn't that much. So the people who win are the ones willing to suffer the most." Suffering is to cyclists what poll data are to politicians; they rely on it to tell them how well they are doing their job. Like many of his competitors in the peloton, Armstrong seems to love pain, and even to crave it.

"Cycling is so hard, the suffering is so intense, that it's absolutely cleansing," he wrote in his autobiography. "The pain is so deep and strong that a curtain descends over your brain. . . . Once, someone asked me what pleasure I took in riding for so long. 'Pleasure?' I said. 'I don't understand the question.' I didn't do it for pleasure. I did it for pain." Armstrong mentioned suffering (favorably) in each of my conversations with him. Even his weekend in Texas, which was ostensibly time off from the grinding spring training schedule, seemed designed to drive him to the brink of exhaustion; there were dozens of meetings with donors, cancer survivors, and friends. On Sunday, he led the foundation's annual ride with his friend Robin Williams, a surprisingly fit and aggressive cyclist. Williams and Armstrong rode at a fairly rapid pace for about two hours, at which point a car suddenly pulled up alongside them on the highway. Armstrong hopped off his bike, climbed in, and was driven to the airport to catch a plane for New York and then Paris. During his forty-eight-hour drop-in, the Lance Armstrong Foundation raised nearly three million dollars.

In Austin, Lance (other than Dubya, he is the only one-name Texan) has a more devoted following than Bush, Lyle Lovett, and the Texas Longhorns football team combined. One night during my weekend in Austin, I drove over to Chuy's, an informal Tex-Mex place that is one of Armstrong's favorite local restaurants. (It was famous locally even before a hardworking bartender carded President Bush's nineteen-year-old daughter Jenna.) Armstrong has a weakness for Chuy's burritos. I asked my waiter what he thought of Armstrong. "When he walks in here, you can feel the buzz coming right off him," he said. "When Lance shows up, people are delirious. They love the guy. His life is like an Alamo-level myth, and everybody loves a myth, particularly in Texas."

Armstrong tries to resist being described as a hero of any kind. "I want my kids to grow up and be normal," he told me, backstage at the concert, as he tentatively ate exactly two Dorito chips. He and his wife, Kristin, have three children: a son, Luke, who is two, and twin girls, Isabelle and Grace, born last year. "I want them to think their father worked hard for what he got, not that it was the result of some kind of magic," Armstrong said.

Three types of riders succeed in long stage races like the Tour de France: those who excel at climbing but are only adequate in time trials, in which a cyclist races alone against the clock; those who can win time trials but struggle in the mountains; and cyclists who are moderately good at both. Now there appears to be a fourth group: Armstrong. He has become the best climber in the world, although he wasn't much of one in his early years. And there is no cyclist better at time trials. He lost nearly twenty pounds when he was sick, but he is no less powerful and is therefore faster. Still, many people have wondered how, so soon after a nearly fatal illness, he managed to take such complete control of the sport.

"After the cancer, Lance got a second chance," Carmichael explained to me. "It was that simple. You get a second chance at something that you took for granted before and all of a sudden you see everything you could have lost. When he came back, he just went into a different zone. He works as if he is possessed. It's a little bit nutty, in fact, what he puts himself through so that he can win the Tour de France each year." As a young man, Carmichael was an Olympic cyclist himself, but he almost died in a freakish skiing accident, in 1986. He returned to competition, but something was gone. While he was trying to figure out what to do next, he took a job coaching the United States national team. He has now been training people for fifteen years. He works with many elite athletes in addition to Armstrong—runners, hockey players, even one Indy driver—and also with thousands who just want to ride faster every Sunday with their local club. He has a company, Carmichael Training Systems, based in Colorado Springs, that employs more than seventy-five coaches; his clients, including Armstrong, log on to the company website to find their latest training instructions.

Carmichael believes that rigorous training is what ultimately turns a talented athlete into a star. "Who hits more practice balls every day than any other golfer?" Carmichael asked. "Guess what? It's Tiger Woods. Well, Lance trains more than his competitors. He was the first to go out and actually ride the important Tour stages in advance. He doesn't just wake up in July and say, 'God, I hope I am ready for this race.' He knows he is ready, because he has whipped himself all year long."

Armstrong describes his bike as his office. "It's my job," he told me. "I love it, and I wouldn't ride if I didn't. But it's incredibly hard work, full of sacrifices. And you have to be able to go out there every single day." In the morning, he rises, eats, and gets on his bike; sometimes, before a particularly long day, he waits to eat again (in order to store up carbohydrates) before taking off. "We schedule his daily workouts to leave late in the morning, so that he can ride for six hours," Carmichael said. "He returns home about five or six o'clock, in time for a quick dinner—a protein-carb smoothie, a little pasta. Then it is time for bed."

During the cycling season, Armstrong calculates each watt he has burned on his bike and then uses a digital scale to weigh every morsel of food that passes his lips. This way, he knows exactly how many calories he needs to get through the day. When he is racing, his meals are gargantuan. (It took three men to lug the team's rations—boxes full of cereal, bread, yogurt, eggs, fruit, honey, chocolate spread, jam, peanut butter, and other snacks—into the hotel breakfast room during the Dauphiné.) On days when a race begins at noon or later, Armstrong will eat two heaping plates of pasta and perhaps a power bar three hours before the race, after having had a full breakfast.

When I visited Carmichael in Colorado Springs, he showed me Armstrong's training schedule for a few weeks this spring. On April 28, a Sunday, Armstrong competed in the Amstel Gold, a one-day annual World Cup race in Holland. He finished fourth, covering the 254-kilometer course (which included thirty-three climbs) in six hours, forty-nine minutes, and seventeen seconds. His average speed was 37.32 kph, the same as that of the winner, who beat him by about three feet. Carmichael scheduled a rest day and urged Armstrong to stay off his bicycle. "He almost never listens when I tell him to do that," Carmichael said. "But I tell him anyway." Tuesday was an easy day: a two-hour ride, maintaining an approximate heart rate of 135 beats a minute. The next day was more typical: five hours over rolling terrain, with a heart rate of about 155 beats a minute and an average effort of 320 watts. Friday was a slow ride for two hours. Then, on Saturday, Armstrong rode for four hours with two climbs, each lasting about half an hour, during which he kept a heart rate of 175 beats a minute with a power expenditure of about 400 watts. After that, Carmichael had him draft at a fast rate behind a motorcycle for two hours without a break. In addition, Armstrong always stretches for about an hour a day, and during the off-season he spends hours in the gym, improving his core strength. "Nobody else puts himself through this," Carmichael said. "Nobody would dare."

I have been riding a bicycle since I was a boy, and over the years, as the technology improved, I kept trading up, from heavy steel to aluminum, and then to titanium. Only once have I traveled more than a hundred miles in a day; I have never entered a race (or wanted to), and I don't ride particularly fast. Yet, like a lot of middle-aged cycling enthusiasts, I now have a bicycle that is far better than I am and I have become a fetishistic devotee of the sport. I have never quite permitted myself to attend bicycle camp or to take lessons from a bicycle mechanic (though I have considered both). But I have never seen Campagnolo gears, an

aerodynamically advanced set of wheels, or a complicated cycle computer that I didn't want to buy. My apartment is littered with catalogs
advertising "carbon titanium supercycles," and bicycling magazines
with stories about obscure pro races.

Every month or two, Carmichael tests Armstrong's capacity to generate power—or watts—and, when I told him that I rode a lot, he suggested that if he tested me in the same way I might have a better sense
of what these measures really meant.

Our plan was to cruise up into the mountains not far from Carmichael's office, in a converted grain barn in downtown Colorado
Springs. The wind was strong enough so that he asked if I wanted to reconsider. The answer was yes, of course, but that's not what I said. We
rode for about five miles through the thin air six thousand feet above sea
level. Carmichael chatted the whole time—about pedal motion, femur
length (the longer the better, since length improves leverage), gearing
choices, and the finer details of carbon-fiber technology. I gasped and
answered only when I had to. We rode into North Cheyenne Cañon
until, finally, it looked as if we had ridden as far as he could ask me to go.
Carmichael got off his bike. "Now the test begins," he said. He pointed
at the mountain slope—it wasn't as steep as some of the slopes in France,
but it looked unconquerable nonetheless—and said, "I want you to ride
as fast as you can up that road for ten minutes and then come back."

I was seriously winded within two minutes. My legs were burning
within five. I remember watching four men and women climbing a
steep rock face and rappelling down. They waved at me, but I was far
too light-headed to risk lifting an arm from the handlebars. Finally, I
couldn't take it anymore. (I managed to continue for eight minutes and
thirty-two seconds. Naïvely, I had asked Carmichael what I should do
when I reached the top. "You won't be seeing the top," he had said.) I
turned the bike around and met up with Carmichael, and we coasted
most of the way back to the office. Then we looked at my data: I had
generated an average of 200 watts on the test, and had climbed exactly
one mile. Carmichael told me that a decent pro cyclist would have put
out at least 400 watts, and that the stragglers at the end of the peloton
(known as the gruppetto) would clock in at perhaps 350. Armstrong—
in top Tour shape—would have come close to 500.

I stared at the graph of my performance, which Carmichael and his
colleagues had printed out for me. I had managed to generate 470 watts

for just ten seconds. That's about average for Armstrong over the course of a four-hour ride.

After that humbling experience, I went across town to see Edmund Burke, a former physiologist for the U.S. Olympic cycling team, who has written several books on training for cyclists (including one with Carmichael). "I think the genius of Chris is that he understands how much small gains matter," Burke said. "In fact, small gains are all you will ever see. People will say, 'You have shown only half a percent of improvement.' Well, half a percent is huge. I am not talking marketing or sales here. I am talking about elite athletic performance."

Carmichael takes nothing for granted and relies heavily on technology. (He noted with approval, for instance, that Greg LeMond won the Tour by just eight seconds, on the last day of the race, in 1989. He was the first cyclist in the Tour to use aerodynamically tapered handlebars for the final time trial. "It made all the difference," Carmichael said. "Technology might not win you the Tour. But why wouldn't you want to have the best chances possible?") Every few months, Armstrong trains in a wind tunnel, which allows Carmichael to measure his aerodynamic efficiency under a variety of conditions. He will push his seat back a centimeter or his stem up a few millimeters. (Each adjustment is a trade-off between power and speed; when you sit farther back, you can use more of your leg muscles, but you also expose more of your body to the resistance of the air.)

Carmichael takes the same radical approach to the physical limits of endurance. It had long been assumed, for example, that aerobic power doesn't vary greatly in adults. Carmichael refutes this emphatically. "Look at Lance," he said to me in his office one day. Over the past eight years, through specific programs aimed at building endurance and speed, Armstrong has increased this critical value—his aerobic power—by sixteen percent. That means he saves almost four minutes in a sixty-kilometer time trial.

In fact, Armstrong is superior to other athletes in two respects: He can rely on his aerobic powers longer, and his anaerobic abilities are unusually high as well. When muscles begin to work beyond their aerobic ability, they produce lactic acid, which eventually accumulates and causes a burning sensation well known to anyone who has ever run too far or too fast. Somehow, though, Armstrong produces less lactic acid than others do, and metabolizes it more effectively. "For whatever physiological reason—and science can't really explain it, because we don't know that much about what is occurring—the effect is clear," Carmichael said. "Lance goes on when others are done."

At the end of last year's Tour, the French sports newspaper *L'Équipe* ran an article with the headline SHOULD WE BELIEVE IN ARMSTRONG?, suggesting it was time to consider the possibility that, since Armstrong has never been found guilty of doping, he may indeed be innocent.

After I watched Armstrong train and spent time with his coaches, the only way I could be convinced that he uses illegal drugs would be to see him inject them. After all, the doubts about him have always been a function of his excellence. Greg LeMond, America's first Tour de France champion (he has also won three times), put it well, if somewhat uncharitably, after Armstrong won the 2001 Tour: "If Lance is clean, it is the greatest comeback in the history of sport. If he isn't, it would be the greatest fraud." It is impossible to prove a negative, and so Armstrong can do nothing to dispel the doubts. But his frustration is clear; in 2000, he made a television ad for Nike in which he said, "Everybody wants to know what I'm on. What am I on? I'm on my bike, busting my ass six hours a day. What are you on?"

If the French don't approve of Armstrong, it is not only—or even principally—because they suspect him of using drugs. They don't believe that he suffers enough. French intellectuals love the agony displayed on the roads each July in the same way that American writers love to wail over the fate of the Red Sox. Thirty years ago, before much was known about sports nutrition, riders would finish the race—if they could—having lost twenty pounds, their eyes vacant even in victory. Armstrong represents a new kind of athlete. He has been at the forefront of a technological renaissance that has made European cycling purists uncomfortable. Referring to the gulf that now exists between the race and the racers, the French philosopher Robert Redeker has written, "The athletic type represented by Lance Armstrong, unlike Fausto Coppi or Jean Robic"—two cycling heroes from a generation ago—"is coming closer to Lara Croft, the virtually fabricated cyberheroine. Cycling is becoming a video game; the onetime 'prisoners of the road' have become virtual human beings . . . Robocop on wheels, someone no fan can relate to or identify with."

"It's so funny to hear people talk that way about Lance," Craig Nichols, Armstrong's oncologist, told me. "The fact is that no cyclist can have seen more pain than he has. The hard work and the inconvenience of the Tour just can't scare him, because he has been through so much worse."

Despite Bruyneel's warning not to push himself on the treacherous slope of the Col de Joux Plane, Armstrong was spinning the pedals a hundred times a minute, faster than any other competitor. (This cadence is a technique that he, Carmichael, and Bruyneel have been working on for years.) With just two days to go, Armstrong was in the lead of the Dauphiné Libéré, and there was little doubt that he would go on to win the race. ("There are not so many guys left," Bruyneel said to me with a smile and a shrug. "If he feels good, you have to let him go.") It would have been understandable—maybe even smart—for Armstrong to take it slow just a few weeks before the Tour. Yet clearly he wasn't going to be satisfied unless he also took this stage.

"Good job, Lance!" Bruyneel cheered into the radio. "Go! Go! Go!" Armstrong picked up speed; he was dropping his opponents one by one. "Moreau is done, Lance, he is over!" Bruyneel shouted into the radio as Armstrong whizzed by Christophe Moreau, the lead rider for Crédit Agricole. "Go if you can. But, remember, the mountain is not your friend."

"Kivilev is dropped, Kivilev is dropped!" Bruyneel screamed, as Armstrong began to pedal faster. "Lance, get on Menchov's wheel. He is a great train to the top." Denis Menchov, of the Ibanesto.com team, is a fine climber. Bruyneel had hoped that Armstrong would glide in behind him and conserve energy on the way up. Instead, Armstrong blew past Menchov, and then overtook the last two men between him and the summit. He wove through the fans gathered at the top of the mountain.

Armstrong shifted into a higher gear to descend, and suddenly he was in trouble. His radio stopped working, his leg began to cramp, and Kivilev and Moreau were gaining on him. "Twenty-seven seconds," Bruyneel said. He was screaming. "Lance, they are gaining!" We could see the little ski resort of Morzine in the near distance. Chalets were built everywhere into the steep slopes of the mountain. The thickening wall of fans suggested that we must be near the end, but we were driving so fast that it was hard to tell.

Incredibly, Bruyneel drove right up beside Armstrong. He was in pain and was massaging his thigh while pedaling as fast as he could. "Six seconds!" Bruyneel shouted out the window at full speed. "Move!"

Armstrong barreled across the finish line, six seconds before his rivals. He got off his bike and hobbled directly into a tent that had been set up for drug testing. When he emerged, he came over to say hello. I congratulated him on winning the stage. "It's always fun to win," he said, smiling broadly. "But, man, I am in such agony."

2002

BORN SLIPPY

JOHN SEABROOK

A year ago, when Michelle Kwan launched herself into a triple-toe/triple-toe combination jump at the 1997 United States Figure Skating Championships, in Nashville, she was the favorite to win the next Olympic gold medal in ladies' figure skating. The gold is a prize estimated to be worth five to ten million dollars in product endorsements, and the skating world, embarrassed by the scandals of the 1993–94 season, was looking for a champion who would conduct herself with dignity. Kwan, then sixteen and the defending national and world champion, seemed like a gift from heaven. Not only was she exceptionally talented, combining athleticism and artistry like no other skater in history, but she was also an intelligent, attractive, and well-behaved girl from a strong Asian American family, apparently free of the brattiness of Nancy Kerrigan or the Anna Karenina–meets-the-train theatrics of Oksana Baiul. "Michelle is a *beautiful* skater," skating people would say of Kwan, with the same emphasis on the word *beautiful* that fashion people use to describe a certain model who radiates an ethereal loveliness that is greater than the sum of her parts. With her smooth features, bright eyes, and charmingly girlish smile, Kwan continues a tradition of lovely, levelheaded American girls, going back through Peggy Fleming, the 1968 ladies' champion, to the Radcliffe graduate Tenley Albright, who won the gold medal in 1956.

In Nashville, Kwan performed the first triple-jump combination perfectly, but slipped skating out of the second one, and, in a weird and utterly graceless loss of balance, she ended up in a *Christina's World*–like sprawl on the ice. "That was absolutely unnecessary and uncalled for!" the TV commentator and two-time Olympic champion Dick Button declared, his voice carrying a slightly schoolmarmish note of disapproval. Kwan got up, with ice shavings clinging to her skating dress, only to fall again, later in the program, which allowed Tara Lipinski to take the title away from her and to become, at fourteen, the youngest national champion ever. Afterward, the camera found Michelle gripping her face in shock. A month later, she stumbled in her short program at the World Championships, and Tara claimed that title, too, becoming the youngest world champion ever. Michelle was now the youngest ex–world champion ever.

Why did Michelle fall? Kwan's entourage was reluctant to answer that question. "I can't talk about that," her choreographer, Lori Nichol, told me. "My understanding is that it was a simple technical thing, but you'll have to talk to Frank." Frank Carroll, Kwan's coach, said, "I think Michelle began to feel she had something to lose, and, as much as I wanted to change that notion, it was very difficult, getting into her head. At sixteen, they have their own things going on in their minds." Michelle's older sister Karen, who is also a top competitive skater and is now a sophomore at Boston University, told me, "Last year, Michelle would sometimes break down and cry for no reason. Like, she'd miss one jump and then she'd cry. I think it was just overwhelming to her, what she had to go out and do."

The simplest explanation was that Michelle fell because she had grown up. Since 1993, when she arrived on the international stage at thirteen, a jumping phenom, she had gained thirty pounds and grown five inches. She now had breasts and hips, which is just about the worst thing that can happen to a skater, torquewise. "Once your body starts to develop, it's difficult to keep your jumps, because you start getting hips and become shapely," Dorothy Hamill, who won the gold in 1976, told me recently. "You can't remain compact." At the same time, all the doubt and uncertainty that are felt by any adolescent girl were visited on Michelle, and they showed in her skating. Fleming told me, "If you're feeling something, it will come out on the ice."

Many athletes fetishize confidence and mental toughness, but this is especially true in skating, where there is a semimystical element to "getting" and "losing" one's triple jumps—the axel, the lutz, the flip, the loop, the salchow, and the toe loop, in descending order of difficulty. Oksana Baiul, who had just turned sixteen when she won the gold medal, told me, "As you get older, you start gaining weight, and you have a lot of things inside of you—especially inside of your head. You start thinking differently, seeing things differently. When you're young, you're just thinking about skating."

The figure-skating world doesn't know quite what to think about the ever-younger girls who now dominate the sport. Skating is an inbred, hybrid culture that includes elements from the worlds of dance, sports, and theater, and combines a new media focus on individuals and personalities with the old media world of ice spectaculars. No one wants the freakish gymnastics element to creep into the sport. Yet the TV audiences love to see triple jumps, and girlish bodies are better than womanly ones at doing triples. So at the same time that the sport has become more athletic it has become more theatrical: Judges insist that the athletes have the "presentation" of mature women, and the girls comply by wearing lots of makeup and playing adult roles. But roleplaying alone can't convey the grownup self-awareness that informs the best skating. For a teenage girl, finding the balance between childhood fearlessness and adult vulnerability can be tougher than landing a triple axel.

Kwan began the current season skating well, but she reinjured a stress fracture in one toe in November and canceled the rest of her competitions. Her only head-to-head competition with Lipinski prior to the 1998 National Championships, taking place this week in Philadelphia, was at Skate America, which was held in October, in Detroit. On that occasion, I spent a wintry weekend shuttling between the Westin Hotel Renaissance Center, where the skaters were staying, and the Joe Louis Arena, where the competition was held.

On Friday, the Renaissance Center was filled with coaches, judges, agents, athletes, and United States Figure Skating Association officials. Surrounding the lobby was a labyrinth of hallways designed to take pedestrians past as many shops as possible, and the skating people were meandering through in an attempt to find the exit where the shuttle buses were to leave for the Joe Louis Arena. "Keep going past the Burger King, and when you see Winkelman's go right," one Skate America volunteer advised.

The skaters paraded through the lobby in DKNY warmup tops and skintight leggings that delineated the amazing "glutes"—gluteus muscles—in their backsides. The tremendous strength in their adductors—the muscles on the inside of your thighs that ache after your annual trip to the rink—made them walk both bowlegged and stiffkneed, as though they already had their skates on. Michelle was escorted by her mother, Estella, who was trundling a metal case that held Michelle's skates, and by her agent, Shep Goldberg, who also represents the gymnast Mary Lou Retton. Tara was accompanied by her agent, Mike Burg. Earlier, Tara had been seen tearing around the Renaissance Center with her friends (whom you can read about on Tara's website, www.taralipinski.com). She lives in nearby Bloomfield Hills and trains at the Detroit Skating Club, with Richard Callaghan, a well-known coach. Legions of eight-year-old girls were pursuing both skaters everywhere. Too young to have learned "Thrilled to meet you!" or other adult forms of flattery, the little girls just studied Tara and Michelle with hard dolls' eyes while waiting for their heroines to sign their autograph books. Michelle dotted the *i* in her name with a little heart.

Michelle and Tara seem prepared for ice-princesshood in ways that Nancy Kerrigan and Oksana Baiul did not. Both are named after mass-culture commodities—Michelle for the Beatles song, Tara for the plantation in *Gone with the Wind*—and both learned to skate in malls before they were seven. Both sets of parents got their daughters into elite training centers when they were very young, and made great sacrifices to raise the sixty thousand dollars that a top skater can chew up in annual expenses. The Lipinskis mortgaged their home; the Kwans sold theirs. And both families had the girls homeschooled with private tutors. Tara trained at the University of Delaware's Ice Skating Science Development Center. Michelle spent her formative years living with her mother in what is known as "the Debi Thomas tepee"—a cabin next to the Ice Castle International Training Center in Lake Arrowhead, situated high in the San Bernardino Mountains. (She and her parents now live in a bigger house nearby.)

Although Michelle is originally from Torrance, California, and Tara was born in Philadelphia, both actually grew up in Skatingland, a never-never land halfway between Mount Olympus and Las Vegas, and not far from Disney. Skatingland is a world of faux Bavarian chalets and snow-frosted peaks that have perfectly frozen skating ponds nestled among them. Kris Kringle is in residence there, and Belgian waffles are served three times a day. It occupies the same space in the cultural mind as *The Sound of Music,* Sonja Henie, and Sun Valley. It's the place that the mail-order catalogs like Coldwater Creek and Bridgehead come from. It smells strongly of scented candles and has an odd baroque sentimentality about it—the sentimentality of the movie *Ice Castles,* in which a young girl from the Iowa hinterland (the actress

Lynn-Holly Johnson) overcomes her lack of formal training and her gruff but sweet-hearted dad (the young Tom Skerritt) to triumph over the snooty rich skaters at the championships, but then is blinded in a freak skating accident and becomes a basket case who never leaves the house until, with the loving support of her boyfriend (Robby Benson), she returns to the ice and, still blind, skates triumphantly at the Midwest Regionals to the schmaltzy Marvin Hamlisch tune "Looking Through the Eyes of Love," sung by Melissa Manchester.

But, while seventy years of kitsch and nostalgia cling to figure skating, modern skaters also live in the Jerry Maguire world of big-time sports marketing. Both Tara and Michelle have the weird savvy that develops when you get an agent at thirteen, write your autobiography a couple of years later (each girl has recently published her memoirs), earn hundreds of thousands of dollars a year in the sixty-odd-city Campbell's Soups Champions on Ice Tour (despite the girls' so-called amateur status), and play Truth or Dare on the tour bus with the more sexually experienced skaters. They're like sixteen-year-olds going on thirty-eight. At the same time, both girls are under enormous pressure not to grow up, since growing up makes it harder to do the triple jumps, and, as a result, they have preserved oddly undeveloped, childlike parts of themselves. Both collect Beanie Babies, and Michelle still has her childhood stuffed animals. In interviews this year, Michelle has been saying, "I want to get the joy back into my skating," as though at seventeen she were already too old, things were already too messy, and she needed to return to a more carefree period of her life. Part of the job of a skating champion these days is to enact in symbolic form a larger cultural transaction: We make available to certain children the wealth and authority formerly enjoyed only by adults, and in return we ask that they not become actual adults. Their end of the bargain is to preserve our fantasy of gifted childhood forever.

When I caught up with Tara, she was flopped on a couch under the Westin Hotel escalators, her long blond hair spread out over its cushion, her jewelled fingers—two rings on the right hand, three on the left—resting on the back of its seat. Tara has a wide, shapely mouth, which is usually slightly open. At four feet ten and a half and eighty-two pounds, her body looks like a Vanna White doll. (Richard Callaghan, her coach, looks unnervingly like Pat Sajak.) "I put my arms around her and I go, 'Oh, gosh, it feels like my little boy,' " Peggy Fleming told me. "Those little, teeny shoulders and that little, teeny frame!" Kwan's coach, Frank Carroll, explained, "As a skater, your strength-size ratio is at its highest when you're a thirteen-year-old girl. With boys, that's not true. Their backs aren't strong enough yet at that age." He also told me, "Tara rotates like a bat out of hell."

Tara's advisers refer to her as the Boss. Her confidence is terrifying. "A lot of skaters love to skate, but when they're out there competing they're like 'Just get me out of this!' " she told me now, sucking on a squirt bottle that was half full of a pink sports drink. "But I love to compete. Even as much as you hate the nervousness when you're out there, when you look back it's the best part of it—competing."

Her agent has got Tara endorsement deals with Minute Maid orange juice and Campbell's soups, and has signed her up with DKNY to flog a line of kids' clothing and with Mattel to promote a new line of Barbie dolls on ice skates, which will be marketed around the time of the Olympics. Tara likes to warm up to "Barbie Girl," by the Danish group Aqua: "I'm a Barbie Girl/In a Barbie World/Life in plastic/It's fantastic!"

I asked Tara whether she had any fear of winning. She looked at me like this was a funny joke. "Nope. I don't think about it," she said.

"Do you ever doubt yourself?"

"Oh, I think every skater has doubts. You'll go out there, and doubt will come in, and that's when you have to fight against it, and not hold back. Sometimes when I do my triple lutz in my short program, it's like 'Oh, my gosh, it's coming.' That's when you just have to let go and do it, and I think that's the hardest part of competing—keeping yourself strong like that. You just have to let the doubt come in and let it roll back out and do your thing. It's hard. And sometimes if you're tired, and your legs aren't perfect that day, that's when the doubt will get you."

Some skaters say that the top international skating events are often decided at the practice sessions on the afternoon of the day they take place. The skaters do their routines with no pressure on them, and it's easy to tell who's got the jumps and who hasn't. Watching the girls practice gives the judges a good idea of who should win, and that will figure in the marks they give that night. Also, at practice the judges can mingle and meet the girls. In some ways, the campaign for the women's gold medal remains a charm contest. The competition itself is only the last of a long series of opportunities the skaters have had to show themselves as happy, beautiful, and ladylike for the judges.

At practice on Friday afternoon in the arena, the judges were sitting at their tables, chatting with some of the skaters who were seated behind them. The judges were, for the most part, older people with deep roots in the pre-athletic skating era; some had been volunteering for forty years. They are the ministers of Skatingland, whose authority as interpreters of beautiful skating is under siege from vulgar athleticism. Most amateur competitions are now largely a matter of counting the number of a skater's jumps and rotations rather than of assessing the skater's grace. Professional competitions are becoming the last refuge of "artistic merit." The skating establishment has also been slow to adopt the new boot-making technologies that have revolutionized roller-skating. Dorothy Hamill told me, "The boots are all hand-lasted and custom-made, and the blades are steel, so they weigh a lot. If Brian Boitano were wearing a lightweight plastic boot and a titanium blade, he'd be able to do five rotations in the air tomorrow."

Dick Button was holding court down below the platform where he would be seated with Peggy Fleming that night. The skating people in the stands talked about the height on the fourteen-year-old Russian Yevgeny Plushenko's triple axel: "And he does a Bielmann spin, the only man who does one!" And where was Nicole Bobek, the vixen, the current scarlet woman of U.S. skating, who has had to shoulder all the adult sexuality that Michelle and Tara have shrugged off? ("Nicole will eat you alive," I was told when I inquired about interviewing her.) Reporters from both the respectable and the tabloid media were combing the rows, searching for narratives to replace the Tonya Harding–Nancy Kerrigan mother lode of four years ago. The clean, cutting sound of blades on ice pleasantly filled the huge, empty arena, in which the Red Wings won the Stanley Cup last June.

Tara's physique was the hot topic of the practice. Her rivals, looking hopefully for some sign of development in the bust or hips, were disappointed, but she was definitely longer in the body than she had been last winter—two inches, by some estimates, though Mike Burg, her agent, said she had grown only an inch. I sat with Burg for a while, about twenty rows behind the judges. Nearby, Tara was stretching her glutes. Photographers honeybeed around her. The camera loves Tara for some of the same reasons that the camera loved JonBenet Ramsey. That particular combination of woman and child is something you don't see every day.

Tara and Michelle began working through their routines, gliding around three other skaters who were on the ice. It was amazing how none of them crashed into one another, but then near-misses are a good way of psyching out an opponent. Whether or not Surya Bonaly, from France, had intended to rattle the Japanese skater Midori Ito by doing a backflip near her in the 1992 Winter Olympics is the stuff of which skating lore is made.

Most of the people I saw at the practice thought Kwan was the better skater. "I think Michelle is much more of an artist than Tara is ready to be," Peggy Fleming said, "so, if it turns out that both are skating really, really well, Michelle has it, hands down." Dick Button told me, "Tara doesn't yet know how to command you to understand what she's doing." To me it seemed that the difference between Michelle and Tara was not the jumps but the awareness of what a jump means. With Michelle, there is a moment of thought before the jump and then a delicious afterthought—a look back at the jump—when it's over, whereas Tara flings herself into her jumps without those little bits of embroidery that connect the airborne to the earthbound. Her jumps lack the awareness of what they overcome.

But if the knowledge that one could fall was what made Michelle a more artistic skater than Tara, it also increased the chances that Michelle would fall. The consensus among the skating press was that Tara had the psychological advantage. Michelle knew she had to make no mistakes, because Tara certainly wouldn't make any, and the pressure this knowledge placed on Michelle would cause a slip—some sixteenth of an inch off on her triple-loop combination—and a slip was all it would take for Tara to win.

The short program, which was skated on Friday night, is the only thing that remains of the old world of school figures, of which there were sixty-nine in all—eights, threes, double threes, loops, brackets, done on all edges, skating forward and skating backward. Skaters called them "doing patch," because each skater made the figures on his or her own patch of clean ice. (The reason there were so many 4 A.M. days in a skater's life was that the skater had to get the cleanest ice.) School used to be all there was to figure skating until Sonja Henie brought dance to the sport, in the thirties. The remaining required elements in the short program are spins, footwork, and jumps, including a double axel and one triple-jump combination. Both the short and the long programs get two marks—a "technical" mark and a mark for "presentation," or artistic impression.

The girls came out in their new skating outfits—each girl has one for the short program, one for the long—which they will wear throughout the season. Michelle's was a backless burnt-orange-and-cream number with flutters around the skirt; Tara's was sequined around the shoulders, and was done in a style that Jere Longman, of the *Times,* described as conveying the message "I'm going to my First Communion and I intend to yodel." Both Michelle and Tara were heavily made up, and their hair was in elegantly coiffed buns on the top of their heads.

Michelle looked awful in the warmup. She fell on her triple-lutz/double-toe, and then, incredibly, she missed a routine double axel. Frank Carroll, her coach, was standing in the skaters' box, called the Kiss and Cry, on the edge of the rink. Wearing a dark-blue pinstriped suit, with a camel overcoat draped over one arm, he watched as his best hope for an Olympic gold in a long and distinguished career—it had reached silver with Linda Fratianne, in 1980—started falling apart. After missing the axel, Michelle just stood there, her hands on her hips, looking down. Then she left the ice.

"She's cracking," one of the reporters said.

But both girls skated error-free short programs. Artistically, Michelle looked better. Technically, Tara's program was more difficult than Michelle's: it had a triple flip in it, whereas Michelle's had only the triple lutz. Even so, eight of the nine judges marked Michelle ahead of Tara on technical merit. At the press conference afterward, Tara seemed a little annoyed. "My jumps actually felt stronger than they did at Worlds," she said, "but I guess the judges didn't think so." Mike Burg later elaborated on Tara's remarks, explaining that in his view the judges, who were very old-fashioned, were simply biased against Tara. Having tolerated athleticism for the sake of TV ratings, and unleashed these young triple-jumping demons, he said the judges were now trying to put a lid on it by marking the better athletes down. In other words, the judges were voting for Skatingland.

The ladies' "free skate," or long program, is by far the most popular activity in women's sports—the only sports event in which the women's version is more popular than the men's. (In 1994, the ladies' long program at Lillehammer ranked fourth on TV's all-time most-watched list.) These four minutes are as pure a dose of live performance as the media offer. For the athletes, they are also among the most pitiless and harrowing four minutes in sports. Although the long program is an endurance event—within a minute and a half the exercise becomes anaerobic—the skater has to continue to look as if she were enjoying herself. The smile at the end of the routine is of the utmost importance: Skaters practice many hours in front of the mirror to get it right. Sweat, which is celebrated by the new magazines for women's sports, is still not acceptable in figure skating. (Among the lingering images of the tawdry Tonya affair are the chalky white clumps of deodorant you saw whenever she lifted her arms.) "If you show you're sweating, you're not in shape," Peggy Fleming told me. "You're showing that you're weak." She added, "The process is designed to find any sign of weakness and apply pressure until it breaks."

In the morning on the day of the ladies' long program, I ran into Frank Carroll in the Renaissance Burger King. We talked about Michelle's short. Carroll observed that it was a relief that the program seemed to have been well received by the judges. "I just wish Michelle had a little more confidence," he said before biting into his Croissan'wich. "She is the best, after all."

That night, at the Joe Louis Arena, the crowd was dressier. Even the Zamboni driver had made an effort to spruce himself up. Peggy Fleming was wearing a startlingly low-cut black dress, her cleavage partly obscured by a chiffon modesty panel, which is very skating. Dick was in his usual blue blazer and conservative slacks. The flower girls—little girls who skate onto the ice and collect flowers and stuffed animals that fans have thrown to their idols—wore tartan skirts, white kneesocks, and blouses with Polish folk sleeves.

As the awful, blinding pressure began to build, partisans of both the Tara and the Michelle camps could be found prowling the great old halls outside the Joe Louis Arena. "At least, it's not me out there," Lori

Nichol, Michelle's choreographer, said. The concessions weren't doing much business: People seemed too nervous to eat. Only the eight-year-old-girl fans, practicing axels on the way to the ladies' room, seemed unfazed by the pressure.

Michelle's father, Danny, went by, and disappeared into the recesses of the hall. When Michelle skates, he settles somewhere in the rafters to watch. He doesn't want the camera to find him. Like Venus Williams's dad and Tiger Woods's dad, Danny is Michelle's sports superego. He retired early from his job at Pacific Bell, and this summer he sold a family-owned Chinese restaurant in Torrance, the Golden Pheasant. He now lives in Lake Arrowhead with Michelle, and keeps a close eye on her, giving her few chances to slip up.

"Have you ever made a huge mistake?" I once asked Michelle when we were having lunch with her mom and dad in Lake Arrowhead. "Done something really foolish?"

"I don't know," Michelle said, thinking. "I'm not really good at lying, so . . ." She looked across the table at her father and said, laughing, "Why do you have that smirk on your face?"

Danny said, "I'm thinking. I can't think of anything."

"How about boys?" I asked Michelle. "You have a boyfriend?"

Danny made a face, then smiled.

"Dad always laughs," Michelle said. "No, I don't. It's Lake Arrowhead."

"No suitable boys?"

Michelle giggled. "Not in skating."

Estella said, "She's still very young."

"Asian parents . . ." Michelle grumbled.

"I don't think it's Asian," Danny said, and leaned forward. "Let me try to go back to—"

"Lecture No. 1,859," Michelle put in.

"I never say you can't have a boyfriend. I don't. As I try to explain to her, you put three things together in life. What's No. 1 in priority for you? Your No. 1 priority is skating. And then you also have school. Then comes the fun part—like dating, or something else. So you put the three things together— She always complains I analyze too much, but I say put these three things together, you make the decision. Dating, can it wait? Yes, it can wait. Can education wait? Yes and no. Can skating wait? No, it can't wait. You have to do it now."

Michelle sighed. "I always look at my parents like they're so wise. But if they're so wise, how come they're not millionaires?"

"Because I'm a loser," Danny said. "I lose too much."

Michelle came out of the tunnel and stood by the rink, waiting to skate. She tugged on her dress, practiced some moves with her arms, and made little shaking movements with her legs, trying to stay loose. When it was time for her to take the ice, she relaxed her shoulders and stepped with her left skate first, an old habit. She assumed her pose in the center of the ice, looking down, and took a deep breath. The music began—"Lyra Angelica," by William Alwyn. First came the triple-lutz/double-toe-loop, right into the triple-toe-loop/double-toe-loop, which landed perfectly, right in front of the Thrifty Car Rental sign. Then the triple flip, then a double axel. Three triples down. The music changed, and Michelle took a charming little giddyap stride of happiness. Away, doubt and confusion. Hello, Mickey, President Clinton, David Letterman. A triple loop, then a triple salchow, and then the final jump, the triple lutz—perfect. Hello, America! She glided into her spiral sequence—the loveliest part of her program, in which she spreads her arms, leans out, and joyously offers up this beautiful thing she has just done for the audience to savor. She finished with a triple toe loop and a butterfly jump. And then the smile, which is the deal clincher. Michelle has the best smile in the business. It has a limpid quality, like the Little Mermaid's smile.

The crowd stood and applauded for several minutes. Cellophane-wrapped bouquets rained down on the ice; the flower girls delivered them to Michelle in Kiss and Cry. The marks were very good: all 5.8s for technical merit, and all 5.9s for presentation. A cameraman found Danny, and the Jumbotron over the scoreboard showed him slapping someone a high five.

"Representing the United States, Tara Lipinski . . ."

As Tara skated to the center of the ice, eight-year-old girls' voices calling out "Go, Tara!" echoed in the otherwise silent arena. Tara's music began, the soundtrack for the movie *The Rainbow*. She smoothly landed a double axel, then did a perfect triple flip. Now came her triple lutz. She kicked her right leg high, jumped, and—bang!—she hit the ice hard. A quick, shocked intake of crowd breath. Tara fell! Tara hadn't fallen since Germany in 1996. But there she was, sitting on her glutes, another fallen princess. She got up off the ice and skated the rest of the program cleanly, finishing second to Michelle.

Afterward, both girls faced the skating press, sitting side by side on a raised dais. Michelle spoke first. "I can say that I came out of my coma," she said. "I feel different this year. The joy is back." She smiled her thrilled-little-girl smile.

Tara sat there with her lips parted, a slightly haughty look on her face. When Michelle finished, she spoke curtly. "The mistake I made was not a big deal," she said, crossing her arms. "It was just a mistake." She paused, and looked over the heads of the press, perhaps catching a glimpse of her rapidly vanishing childhood, with its unself-conscious, ballerina-on-a-music-box rotations. You could hear in her voice a slight false note of confidence as she said, "I think I am still in a good spot."

1998

"Er—haven't you forgotten something?"

THE CHOSEN ONE

DAVID OWEN

On a hot Sunday afternoon last May, Tiger Woods conducted a golf exhibition in Oklahoma City. During the hour before he appeared, while a large crowd baked in the bleachers, a member of his entourage held a trivia contest, with T-shirts for prizes. One of the questions: In what year was Tiger Woods born? The first guess, by a very young fan, was 1925. That's off by half a century, but the error is understandable. Woods has accomplished so much as a golfer that it's easy to forget that he's only twenty-four. In a sport in which good players seldom peak before their thirties, and often remain competitive at the highest levels well into their forties, Woods is off to a mind-boggling start. Most recently, he won the British Open with a record-breaking score of nineteen under par. After that blowout, Ernie Els, a terrific young South African player and the winner of two United States Opens, said with a resigned smile, "We'll have to go to the drawing board again, and maybe make the holes bigger for us and a little smaller for him."

When Woods eventually appeared for his Oklahoma exhibition, his entrance was appropriately dramatic. A small convoy of golf carts bore down on the bleachers from the far end of the driving range, while martial-sounding rock music blasted from the public-address system. The exhibition was the final event in a two-day program sponsored by the Tiger Woods Foundation, a charitable organization whose goal is to inspire children—especially underprivileged children—and "to make golf look more like America," as Woods himself says. Forty-two cities had applied to be visited by Woods and his team in 2000, and Oklahoma City was the first of just four cities to be chosen. Among the reasons for its selection was the existence of this particular facility: a low-fee public golf course, with free lessons for children on weekends, situated in an unprepossessing neighborhood not far from Oklahoma City's unprepossessing downtown.

Before stepping up to the practice tee, Woods answered questions from the audience, whose members differed from golf's principal constituency in that many of them were neither middle-aged nor white. One of the first questions came from a junior-high-school-aged fan, who asked, "How do you maintain your personal life and your golf career at the same time?"

Woods, who was leaning on his pitching wedge, said, "That's a great question. When I'm off the golf course, I like to get away from everything, and I like to keep everything private, because I feel that I have a right to that." There was heavy applause from the crowd. "There are exceptions to that, where the press likes to make up a few stories here and there. But that's just the way it goes."

Many very famous people become very famous because, for some compelling and probably unwholesome reason, they crave the approval of the rest of us. That's why they put up with the media, among other things. Even the ones who vigorously defend their privacy seem to do so in a way that attracts an awful lot of publicity, suggesting that their aversion to celebrity is more complicated than they let on. With Woods, though, you get the feeling that his fame mostly gets in the way. We intrude on his golf when he's playing golf, and we intrude on his private life when he's not. He can be a dazzlingly emotional and telegenic performer, and he surely finds it thrilling to walk down fairways lined with thousands of deliriously happy admirers shouting his name, but he conveys the impression that he would play every bit as hard if the cameras and the microphones and the galleries simply disappeared.

That's an awe-inspiring character trait, but it's also a chilling one. Part of the fun of being a sports fan is harboring the delusion that great athletic achievements are in some sense collaborations between athletes and their rooting sections. Woods's accomplishments are so outsized that it's hard to conceive of them as belonging to anyone but himself. As Tom Watson said of him after the British Open, "He is something supernatural."

Before Woods turned thirteen, he had researched and memorized the main competitive accomplishments of Jack Nicklaus because he already intended to exceed them. Between the mid-1970s and a month or two ago, sportswriters viewed Nicklaus's remarkable career (which was crowned by eighteen victories in golf's four major championships) as the permanent benchmark of greatness in golf; the new consensus is that Woods is capable of breaking all of Nicklaus's records, unless he loses interest in the game or injures himself or decides to run for president instead. Nicklaus himself has always been one of Woods's most enthusiastic cheerleaders. In 1996, he said that Woods could ultimately win the Masters more times than he and Arnold Palmer had combined—more than ten times, in other words. That statement seemed like crazy hyperbole at the time; it doesn't any longer.

Here in Oklahoma, though, Woods wasn't focusing on the record book. Earlier in the day, he had worked one on one with twenty-five young local golfers, most of whom were members of ethnic minorities. He watched them swing, offered advice, teed up balls for them, and made them laugh. The kids all looked nervous while they awaited their turns, but most were smiling by the time he moved on. One of those golfers was Treas Nelson, a high school junior from Lawton, Oklahoma, who had just won the Class 5A Girls' State Championship; she is the first black golfer in Oklahoma to win a statewide high school title. After she finished her session with Woods, I violated a ban on over-the-rope media fraternization and asked her what Tiger had told her.

"He said I have the pizza-man syndrome," she told me. "I get my right hand too much like this." She lifted her right arm with the elbow bent, as though she were holding a pizza on a tray at shoulder height. "He said he has the same problem." She was beaming. Like almost all the kids who received individual instruction, she was wearing Nike shorts and a Nike shirt—goodies provided by Woods's biggest commercial sponsor. She had supplemented this uniform with a pair of Nike earrings. "I don't know if he noticed that," she said. But she hoped he had.

"I can relate to these kids," Woods said a little later that day. "I'm not too far from their age. If these kids saw Jack Nicklaus, I don't think they would have an appreciation for what he's done in the game or what he has to offer, just because of the fact that it's hard for a person of Nicklaus's age to relate to a kid. But I'm not too far removed from my teens. I can say 'Dude,' and that's cool—that's fine."

It's only because of Woods that most of these kids even know who Jack Nicklaus is. Woods spends almost as much time studying golf's history as he does making it, and he goes out of his way to share his knowledge of that history with the youngsters who idolize him. In answer to a question from the audience at his exhibition, he said, "When

I was young, I looked up to a lot of different players for a lot of different reasons. Obviously, Jack Nicklaus was the greatest of all time. Ben Hogan was the greatest driver there ever was. Seve Ballesteros probably had the best short game. Ben Crenshaw putted the best. So what I did was analyze every different player's game and try to pick the best out of each and every player and try to look up to that. I wasn't going to look up to just one person." For young golfers twenty years from now, however, looking up to the best player in each of the areas Woods mentioned may be no more complicated than looking up to Woods himself. He leads the tour in most of the several dozen statistical categories that tour officials keep track of, including career earnings. (His tournament winnings during the first seven months of 2000 alone exceeded Nicklaus's lifetime earnings.)

During Woods's exhibition, the younger members of the crowd weren't thinking about statistics. What they really wanted to see was a trick they had watched him perform in a hugely popular Nike television commercial: They wanted to see him bounce a golf ball on the face of his wedge while passing the club from hand to hand and between his legs and behind his back, and then hit the ball right out of the air as easily as if it were teed up on the ground. (That commercial arose by accident, when Woods, feeling bored between takes on a shoot for another Nike commercial, began amusing himself with a stunt he had taught himself as a kid, and the director, entranced, asked him if he could do it again.)

"I heard a rumor that this thing I did on TV was all computerized," Woods said, as he began bouncing the ball. "It's kind of a vicious rumor." He passed the club between his legs. "Now, I don't know where that rumor started, whether it was the public or the press, but they obviously hadn't seen me do this before." He bounced the ball up high. "And catch it like this." He stopped the ball, frozen, on the face of his club, let it sit there a moment, then began bouncing it again. "Or I can start out doing it left-handed, if you want me to." Bounce, bounce, bounce. "Or go back to the right." He bounced the ball up over his shoulder from behind, and caught it on the club face in front. "Now, I didn't put this one in the commercial, because it's the hardest one—it's when you hit the ball off the butt end of the club." He bounced the ball high again, twirled the club so that its shaft was perpendicular to the ground, bounced the ball straight up off the top of the rubber grip, twirled the club back to its former position, and resumed bouncing the ball on the face. "Let's see—it took me four takes to do the Nike spot. Let's see if I can do this out here." He bounced the ball high, took his regular grip on the club, planted his feet, and, just before the ball fell back to earth, smacked it more than a third of the way down the range.

A few hours before Woods's exhibition, I sat with the all-black congregation of the St. John Missionary Baptist Church (motto: "We Strive to Be 'The Best Church This Side of Judgement' ") while Tiger's father, Earl Woods, gave a guest sermon. His talk was preceded by hymns, prayers, and half a dozen full-immersion baptisms, which were conducted in a large tank that was visible through an opening in the wall above the altar. His subject was his only subject. "Tiger was not created to be a golfer," he said. "Tiger was made to be a good person, and that was first and foremost in our family." Earl is shorter and considerably wider than Tiger. He has a good preaching voice, which caught in his throat a couple of times, despite the fact that he had given essentially the same presentation dozens, if not hundreds, of times before. "Sometimes when I talk about my son, I get very emotional," he explained. "So bear with me."

Earl divides his life into two distinct phases, the first of which he now considers to have been a divinely directed training mission for the second. In the first phase, which began during the Great Depression, he grew up poor in eastern Kansas, lost both parents by the time he was thirteen, attended a mostly white high school, became the first black baseball player in what is today the Big Twelve, spent twenty years in the Army, served two widely separated tours of duty in Vietnam (the second as a Green Beret), and endured an increasingly loveless marriage for the sake of his three children, to whom he was a remote father at best. In the second phase, which began in the late sixties, he divorced his first wife, married a Thai receptionist named Kultida Punswad (whom he had met in Thailand during his second Southeast Asian tour), took up golf, and produced Tiger Woods—whose real first name is Eldrick, and whose nickname Earl had given first to a South Vietnamese lieutenant colonel named Vuong Dang Phong, who was his colleague, close friend, and protector during the war.

Earl was determined to be a better parent to the last of his four children than he had been to the first three, and after he retired from the Army, in 1974, he had more time to be attentive. His one significant distraction—other than his job, as a contract administrator and materials manager at McDonnell Douglas, in Huntington Beach, California—was golf, a game at which he had become remarkably proficient despite having taken it up just four years earlier, at the age of forty-two. He worked on his swing in the evenings, by hitting balls into a net in his garage, and he often placed his infant son in a high chair beside him so that the two of them could commune while he practiced. "It was a way of spending time together," he told me recently. The baby, far from being bored, was captivated by the motion. One momentous day, when Tiger was still young enough not to have mastered all the finer points of walking, he astonished his father by climbing down from his high chair, picking up a club, and executing a passable imitation of Earl's (quite good) golf swing. At that moment, his father realized he was the steward of an extraordinary talent.

Earl also began to believe that the birth of his son had been—as he told the St. John congregation—"the plan of the man upstairs." Looking back on his life, he detected a pattern of trials and tests and close escapes from tragedy, and he decided that God had been grooming him all along for something big. As the child grew, Earl was struck more and more by what he described in church that day as "the charismatic power that resides in my son Tiger"—a power that he had otherwise noticed only in Nelson Mandela.

Even to someone sitting in a church pew, this might sound sort of mystical and wacky—and yet the more you learn about Tiger Woods's preternatural relationship to the game of golf the easier it becomes to understand why terrestrial interpretations seem inadequate to Earl. When Tiger was still a toddler, Earl says, the child was able to identify the swing flaws of adult players. (" 'Look, Daddy,' Tiger would say, 'that man has a reverse pivot!' ") Tiger putted with Bob Hope on the *Mike Douglas Show* at the age of two, broke 50 for nine holes at the age of three, hit golf balls on *That's Incredible!* at the age of five, and received his first autograph request when he was still too young to have a signature. Before he had learned to count to ten, Earl says, Tiger could tell you, on any golf hole, where each member of a foursome stood in relation to par. While his grade school contemporaries drew pictures of racing cars and robots, Tiger sketched the trajectories of his irons. He came from behind to win the Junior World Championship, in San Diego, against an international field, when he was eight.

Tiger first beat his father in golf, by a single stroke, with a score of 71, when he was eleven. That same summer, he entered thirty-three junior tournaments, and won them all. ("That's when I peaked. It's been downhill since.") At fifteen, he became the youngest player ever to win the United States Junior Amateur Championship—and then the only player in history to win it three years in a row. At eighteen, he became the youngest player ever to win the United States Amateur Championship— and then the only player in history to win it three years in a row.

When Tiger first began to attract national attention, people often assumed that the real force behind his game must be the oldest one in modern sports: a pushy father with frustrated athletic aspirations and a powerful yearning for unearned income. In early 1998, the sportswriter John Feinstein published a short, mean-spirited book called *The First Coming,* in which he compared Earl to the manipulative father of the tennis prodigy Jennifer Capriati, who burned out on the women's tour at seventeen. (She has since returned.) But Feinstein was clearly wrong. It has gradually become apparent that Tiger's drive has always been internal, and that while Earl and Kultida may have been its facilitators they were not its authors. When Tiger was still very small, for example, he memorized his father's office telephone number so that he could call Earl each afternoon to ask if the two of them could practice at the golf course after work. Earl was a tireless (and innovative) practice companion and coach, but he believed that the initiative must always be taken by the boy.

Rather than pushing their son, the Woodses sometimes worried that his infatuation with golf was eclipsing other parts of his life. "In junior golf, I was all-out," Tiger said in Oklahoma. "My parents would say, 'You can't play, you're playing too much.' But I wanted to play every tournament, and play twice in one day." Earl repeatedly urged him, with little success, to try other sports. Kultida used golf as an incentive—for example, by forbidding her son to hit practice balls until he had finished his homework. ("My wife was the disciplinarian in the family," Earl told me, "and I was the friend.") Earl once fretted that Tiger was so focused on winning that he had ceased to enjoy himself on the golf course. Tiger replied curtly, "That's how I enjoy myself, by shooting low scores." After that, Earl kept his opinions to himself.

Although Earl and Kultida did not force Tiger to become a golfer, they both made enormous sacrifices to help him realize his ambition. Earl estimates that the family's annual travel expenses during Tiger's junior golf years amounted to as much as thirty thousand dollars, a sum Earl couldn't have covered without the help of a succession of home equity loans. Kultida was an infinitely patient chauffeur, rising long before dawn to drive Tiger to distant tournaments (and reminding him to bring his pillow so that he could go back to sleep in the car). Both parents believed that their son's needs must always come before their own, and they were determined that the only impediment to his success—in golf or in whatever other field he might choose to pursue—would be the level of his own desire.

Earl and Kultida's sacrifices took a toll on their marriage; they have lived apart for several years now, although they have not divorced. Their living arrangement inevitably comes to mind when Earl says, as he did in church in Oklahoma that day, "The family is the most important institution in the world." But Earl doesn't view his own domestic situation as conflicting with his beliefs. The family as Earl conceives it is mainly a relationship between parents and their children. He told me recently, "Tiger has a mother and a father who love him dearly, and who have always supported him and always will. He is the top priority in the family. There is no bitterness between his parents, and there is no animosity. The only thing is that we live in separate places. My wife likes a great, big-ass house, and I like a small house. That's all." Still awaiting Tiger is the challenge of raising a family of his own—an achievement, Earl says, from which Tiger must not allow himself to be distracted by his golf.

Tiger's obsession was obviously indulged by his parents, but the child wasn't spoiled. Almost from the beginning, he was made to take responsibility for his own aspirations. Starting when he was quite young, for example, he was put in charge of making the family's tournament-related travel arrangements, including hotel reservations. When he was asked what he intended to study in school, he would say that he hoped to major in accounting because he wanted to know how to keep track of the people who would one day keep track of his earnings. He went by himself to check out the colleges that had recruited him, and he went by himself when it was time to enroll at Stanford, the college he ultimately chose. (Tiger's best friends today include three former Stanford teammates: Notah Begay III, who is the first full-blooded American Indian to play on the PGA Tour; Casey Martin, who is physically disabled and won a court decision allowing him to use a motorized cart in PGA Tour events; and Jerry Chang, to whom Tiger quietly returned a favor by serving as his caddie during a thirty-six-hole qualifying tournament the week following his own victory in the U.S. Open.)

The real purpose of the Woods family's lifestyle, both parents have said, was not to turn Tiger into a professional golfer but to strengthen his character. "Golf prepares children for life," Earl told me recently, "because golf is a microcosm of life." According to Earl, the truly important lessons he imparted on the golf course had to do with things like honesty, etiquette, patience, and discipline—virtues for which golf provided handy talking points. (Golf is the only competitive sport, for example, in which the players call penalties on themselves.) Earl also stressed to Tiger that his athletic gift, if he continued to pursue it, would always entail outsized public obligations—not least because of his racial background. Tiger lived in a mostly white neighborhood in Cypress, California, and he attended mostly white schools, and he was sometimes harassed by bigoted bullies—one of whom tied him to a tree one day when he was in elementary school—but both his parents taught him to rise above such incidents and to understand that racism is evidence of a defect in the racist, not in the racist's victim. Kultida urged him to be remorseless in competition, but she also steeped him in the Buddhist tradition in which she herself had been raised.

It appears that Earl and Kultida provided their son with exactly what he turned out to need (competitive focus, immunity to intimidation, a cut-down one-iron) at every critical juncture in his development. But I sometimes wonder whether Tiger didn't in some sense "create" his parents as much as they "created" him. From the moment he climbed down from that high chair, he seems to have been phenomenally well equipped—temperamentally, emotionally, intellectually—to exploit the physical gift that he was born with. Is it outlandish to wonder whether part of his genius didn't lie in an ability to inspire his parents to conduct their lives in perfect harmony with his ambition?

I first saw Woods in person at the Augusta National Golf Club, in Augusta, Georgia, during the week of the 1997 Masters Tournament. He had turned pro just seven months earlier, after winning his third United States Amateur Championship, and he had dominated the tour almost from that moment. I was standing near Augusta National's first tee late one afternoon early in the week when he emerged from the clubhouse to play a practice round. I didn't see him at first, but I quickly guessed that he was near, because the crowd loitering between the clubhouse and the first tee suddenly convulsed. He was moving fast, and he was encircled by guards. "Tiger! Tiger! Tiger!" The ardor of those fans I can think to describe only as ferocious. Their supplications sounded almost angry. Woods's face, meanwhile, floated expressionless among the grimaces of his protectors.

The 1997 Masters provided Woods's formal introduction not only to many golf fans but also to some of the best golfers from outside the United States. In the third round, which he began with a three-stroke lead, Woods was paired with Colin Montgomerie, who had played well enough the day before to have shared the lead himself for a short time. He was now tied for second. Montgomerie, who is Scottish, was (and still is) the best player on the European PGA Tour, and he had been a star of the European Ryder Cup team. He had never won a tournament in the United States, but he had come close several times, and he was especially optimistic about his chances that week in Augusta.

Playing side by side with Woods, however, was a transforming experience for Montgomerie. He shot 74—a score that ordinarily wouldn't have been disastrous at that stage in a major tournament, except that Woods shot 65, and thereby increased his lead over the field to nine strokes, and his lead over Montgomerie to twelve. When their round was over, Montgomerie was taken to the press building for a postmortem, as the top players always are. He looked frazzled and discouraged as he stepped onto the stage, and he didn't wait for anyone to ask a question.

"All I have to say is one brief comment today," he began. "There is no chance. We're all human beings here, but there's no chance humanly possible that Tiger is going to lose this tournament. No way."

"What makes you say that?" a reporter asked.

Montgomerie looked at the reporter with palpable incredulity. "Have you just come in?" he said. "Or have you been away? Have you been on holiday or something?"

Montgomerie was clearly shaken by what he had witnessed at close quarters. In his encounter with Tiger Woods, he had crossed from the first stage to the second stage in the process described by Emily Dickinson as "First Chill—then Stupor—then the Letting Go." In the fourth and final round, he shot 81, a dismal score, which left him in a tie for thirtieth place. When he finished, he looked as though his body had been drained of blood.

Weekend golfers who attend professional tournaments for the first time are almost always struck by the breathtaking quality of the pros' shots, and they end up realizing sadly that professional golf and weekend golf, despite superficial similarities, are very different games. I had been to tournaments before the 1997 Masters, and I had even played golf with a couple of touring pros, so I had no remaining illusions about my own abilities. But some of Woods's golf shots during that tournament seemed almost as different from an average pro's shots as an average pro's shots would seem from mine. They belonged in a category of their own. David Feherty, a former tour player from Ireland, who now works mainly as a television commentator, told me recently, "I've played with just about everybody, and I think I can say now that Tiger has hit virtually every truly great shot I've ever seen. As we speak, he is deleting some of my greatest memories and replacing them with his. He simply does things other golfers can't do. He's like the Heineken in the commercial: He refreshes the parts other beers cannot reach."

Woods's swing is so powerful that it is difficult to capture on film. For many years, *Golf Digest* has published detailed photographic sequences that anatomize the swings of the game's best players—sequences that are descended in spirit from the studies of running athletes and galloping horses that were made in the late nineteenth century by the photographic pioneer Eadweard Muybridge. Since 1973, the magazine's photographers have shot their swing sequences with a high-speed camera called a Hulcher, which was originally developed, at the request of a government agency, to take stop-action photographs of missiles. The camera can shoot hundreds of high-quality images at a rate of sixty-five frames a second—plenty fast enough to break a golf swing into its constituent parts.

Woods performed for the Hulcher a few months after his Masters victory. The camera recorded fifteen driver swings from five different angles. When the prints came back from the lab, the magazine's editors discovered that only five frames among the hundreds taken during the shoot had captured Woods's swing at the approximate moment his club head came into contact with the ball—a problem they had never encountered before. "With other tour players, we almost always get a picture of impact with every swing," Roger Schiffman, the executive editor, told me. When Woods makes his normal swing, the head of his driver moves at about 120 miles an hour—a good fifteen miles an hour faster than the club head of a typical touring pro, and about thirty miles an hour faster than the club head of an average amateur. Between one Hulcher frame and the next, Woods's driver traveled through roughly 200 degrees of arc, which means that a ball sitting unthreatened on the tee in one frame would be long gone by the next.

That *Golf Digest* swing sequence was photographed two days before the start of the 1997 Western Open, which Woods went on to win. "When he saw the pictures later, he said, 'No wonder I won,'" Schiffman told me. "He said his swing looked almost perfect." It was quite a surprise, therefore, when Woods decided not long afterward that his game required a major overhaul. With the help of Butch Harmon, a former touring pro who has been Woods's teacher since he was seventeen, Woods spent more than a year taking apart his "almost perfect" swing and putting it back together.

In paying his dues and becoming the best, Woods has changed almost everything there is to change about golf. The conventional wisdom among sportswriters used to be that the PGA Tour had become so deep in talent that no modern player could hope to dominate it the way Palmer or Nicklaus or Watson did in the sixties and seventies and eighties, or the way Snead or Nelson or Hogan did in the thirties and forties and fifties. Now, though, Woods becomes the favorite in any tournament simply by signing up, and professional golfers all over the world have begun lifting heavier weights, eating healthier food, and going to bed earlier, in the hope of becoming good enough to be considered second best. "He's in their heads," the sportswriter Tom Callahan told me. Callahan recalled the corrective eye surgery that Woods had last year. "The first thing he said afterward was 'The hole looks bigger.' Now, if you're Davis Love, is that what you want to hear?" More than a few pros once viewed Woods as dangerously overhyped; nowadays, like most of the rest of his awestruck admirers, they tend to stop what they are doing and watch—perhaps thinking ahead to a day when they'll be able to brag to their grandchildren that they once got personally whomped by the "Chosen One" (as the tour player Mark Calcavecchia called him at the British Open).

Woods has also changed golf's public image, which has suffered for decades from the game's suburban association with saddle shoes, cigars, and miniature electric cars. Twelve-year-olds who used to dream only of becoming professional basketball players now sometimes decide that they might like to give the PGA Tour a try, too, at least in the off-season. Tubby middle-aged hackers now stand a little taller at cocktail parties, because Woods, miracle of miracles, has made golf seem kind of cool. Woods has even taken the most shameful aspect of the game's long history—its legacy as a decadent pastime for white people with too much time on their hands—and turned it inside out.

Between 1934 and 1961, the constitution of the Professional Golfers Association of America—the direct predecessor of the modern PGA Tour—explicitly limited that organization's membership to "Professional golfers of the Caucasian race." The Caucasian-only clause was not some esoteric historical artifact; the rule merely formalized a policy that had always been followed, and the PGA apparently bothered to put it on paper only after discovering that a light-skinned black man had managed to work as a club pro since 1928. The PGA methodically fought efforts by black players to overturn or circumvent the rule, and it didn't amend its constitution until it was forced to do so by the attorney general of California, who threatened to ban tour events in that state and to encourage other attorneys general to do the same. The pressure for change did not come from the white pros of that era; the vast majority of those men were happy with their world the way it was.

Less than nine months before Woods's birth, Lee Elder became the first black golfer to play in the Masters. Elder's appearance at Augusta has been celebrated ever since as an early milestone in the drearily slow enlightenment of white Americans, but it did not herald a new generation of black golfers. Like most of the few other black tour players of that time, Elder was a veteran of the old United Golfers Association, golf's equivalent of baseball's Negro leagues, and his athletic prime was mostly behind him. (He was already forty-one.) A black player named Calvin Peete, who was born in 1943 and took up golf too late to have been involved with the UGA, became one of the truly dominant players on the PGA Tour in the eighties, a decade during which he won more tournaments (eleven) than any player except Tom Kite. But Peete was virtually the end of the line; Woods is the only black member of the PGA Tour, and he is the first in a very long time. In the past fifteen years, only one African American golfer has won a PGA Tour card by way of the tour's qualifying "school" (actually, a notoriously arduous six-day tournament). That was a now forgotten player named Adrian Stills, who qualified in 1985. "We're a dying breed," Lee Elder told me last month.

Why did the black presence on tour shrink to the vanishing point between the midseventies and the midnineties, just when one would have expected the opposite? Pete McDaniel—who is the author of *Uneven Lies,* a cultural history of black golf in America, which will be published this fall—recently told me, "It was the golf cart. The rise of the motorized golf cart marked the beginning of the end of minority golf, especially among African Americans, because golf clubs that had carts didn't need caddies, and most of the black professional players had come from the caddie ranks." Golf carts, in addition to being a typically American response to the threat of mild physical exercise, eliminated what to golf clubs had been the unappealing necessity of maintaining on their premises large pools of mostly young, mostly disadvantaged workers. As carts displaced caddies, kids whose families were excluded from private clubs lost their principal avenue of access to the game.

Of course, a world in which a handful of black men managed to claw their way into mostly marginal professional careers as a result of having lugged the weekend baggage of wealthy whites was hardly a utopia. The real problem with golf in America, as far as race is concerned, is not that caddying declined as an occupation but that the game, over the course of more than a century, has only grudgingly made room for more than a privileged few. Given the inexorability of the cultural forces at work, it seems almost unbelievable that Tiger Woods emerged as a golfer at all, much less as a golfer who has a decent chance of one day being remembered as the greatest of all time. As Earl says, his son is the first "naturally born and bred black professional golfer"—the first whose initial exposure to the game did not come through the service entrance. For Woods simply to have earned a tour card and kept it for a couple of years would have made him a pioneer. Doing what he has actually done moves him into the category of myth.

Woods's own views about race are attractively complicated. He dislikes being referred to as "African American," because he regards that term as an insult to his mother—and so does his mother—who, after all, is Asian. Earl's ancestors were black, white, American Indian, and Asian, and Tiger once referred to his own ethnicity as "Caublinasian," a word he made up in an effort to suggest the diversity of his genealogy. He often seems inclined to concentrate on golf and let American race relations look after themselves, but he has invested a great deal of his increasingly scarce and valuable time in reaching out to disadvantaged children through his clinics.

Woods has been conducting clinics for young golfers since he was in high school, when he and Earl set up exhibitions in cities where Woods was playing in tournaments. The clinics ended when Woods was at Stanford, because the National Collegiate Athletic Association held that they were in violation of a rule concerning individual college athletes and public exhibitions. (Earl and Tiger had several running battles with the NCAA during Tiger's two years in college, and Earl says those battles contributed to Tiger's decision to turn pro shortly after the beginning of what would have been his junior year.) After Woods left the aegis of the NCAA, late in 1996, he and Earl established the Tiger Woods Foundation to continue their mission.

The foundation has been accused by some of creating unrealistic expectations among children who have limited opportunities for becoming even recreational golfers, and virtually no chance at all of becoming touring pros. ("You wonder if it's false hope," a skeptical sportswriter said to me recently.) What good does it do—the critics have asked—to introduce an inner-city kid to a game that, for all practical purposes, can't be played in an inner city? And, indeed, if the goal is to turn more members of ethnic minorities into golfers, a simpler approach might be to concentrate directly on transforming ghetto youngsters into middle-aged Republicans—the kind of people who seem to take up the game as a matter of course. There's a public-service commercial on television which shows a black child using a hammer to drive a tee into the pavement on a dark urban street, so that he can tee off in his neighborhood. Well, exactly.

Although it's true that playing on tour is an unreasonable ambition for almost everyone—the PGA Tour has only 125 fully exempt playing spots, and many of those are locked up by golfers whose careers will ultimately be measured in decades rather than in years—earning a different kind of living in the world of golf is within reach for many. Unlike most other spectator sports, golf is played by millions of nonprofessionals, whose needs are served by a large industry that comprises equipment manufacturers, clothing retailers, agronomists, golf-course maintenance workers, traveling salespeople, teaching professionals, scuba-diving golf-ball recyclers, and others—even journalists. Within that industry, there is now a widespread conviction that if golf is to grow significantly as an economic enterprise it needs to extend its reach far beyond white suburban males. Woods's foundation, in connection with its clinics and exhibitions, conducts seminars for children and parents in which such job opportunities are described and explained. Woods himself has estimated that as many as 5 percent of the children who pass through his foundation's programs will one day end up in jobs that are somehow connected with golf. That seems like a lot, but who knows?

Even for kids who have no interest in golf-related careers, the game as a pastime has virtues that its more grotesque attributes have often obscured. Golf has a work ethic (the driving range and the practice green), a dress code (no jeans or T-shirts), and a tradition of etiquette based on personal responsibility and consideration for others (replace your divots). Spectator behavior that is tolerated and even encouraged in other sports—the frantic waving of plastic-foam tubes in an effort to fluster free-throw shooters in basketball games, for example—would be considered grounds for arrest at golf tournaments, where fans are expected to keep even their shadows under control. Aspiring golfers who set out to be just like Tiger Woods may never make it to the tour, but they will inevitably end up learning something about what it takes to find and keep a job more demanding than that of filling orders at a drive-through window. "The first thing they learn is to play by the rules," Earl told me, "and we have a lot of knuckleheads in prison today who never learned to play by the rules."

White golfers also tend to underestimate the emotional impact that Woods's racial background has had on non-Caucasians. For upper-middle-class white fans, a big part of Woods's appeal is that he seems to negate racial issues altogether—he's just Tiger, the best golfer in the world. I've seen sixty-year-old white chief executive officers with their own personal jets who were as excited as a ten-year-old kid would be about having a chance to see Woods in person. Their excitement was genuine, and, to the extent that such a thing is possible, it was color-blind. When white golfers do think about Woods's racial background, it's often with a sense of relief: His dominance feels like an act of forgiveness, as though in a single spectacular career he could make up for the game's ugly past all by himself.

For many of the young players I saw in Oklahoma, though, Woods's appeal had everything to do with race: The color of his skin was the bridge they were crossing into the game. Dennis Burns, who works for the Tiger Woods Foundation and is one of a handful of black American golf professionals (the kind who give lessons and work at golf clubs rather than play on tour), told me, "Kids walk away from Tiger's clinics with a sense that here's a guy who looks like me and has done it. It's a feeling of confidence—and it doesn't just have to do with golf." Children generally admire great athletes for most of the same reasons they admire cartoon superheroes: The constraints of the adult-ruled world don't seem to apply. But, for teenagers who are outside America's cultural mainstream, Woods has meant incalculably more. He is the fearless conqueror of a world that has never wanted anything to do with them.

A lesson in fearlessness may be what professional golfers need as well. Woods has upended their universe. Ernie Els has finished second to him five times now, twice in major tournaments. Els is one of the very nicest people on any golf tour—and he has made nothing but generous, flabbergasted remarks about Woods—but surely it must have occurred to him that if Woods had spent four years at Stanford and then gone to graduate school, he himself might today be considered the best player in the world. He and the other young golfers who used to contend for that position, including Phil Mickelson and David Duval (who briefly supplanted Woods at the top of the world rankings around the time that Woods was making his big swing change), have to wonder if their moment in golf history passed before it arrived.

Superb athletes fascinate in part because they seem like proxies for ourselves in a metaphorical battle with the eternal: broken records are death-negating acts. Even Woods's most lopsided victories have been thrilling to watch, because his efforts have seemed so effortless—as though he had found a way to win the game that can't be won. But will we feel the same way five years from now if no player has stepped forward to challenge him? Nicklaus had the considerable advantage during his career of being chased and, not infrequently, elbowed aside by other great players, among them Arnold Palmer, Billy Casper, Gary Player, Lee Trevino, and Tom Watson. Woods's principal rival, so far, has been the record book. If that doesn't change, then those of us who can only watch—sports fans, television commentators, sports reporters—may someday come to view his triumphs with the same dispassion that he seems to feel toward us, until the passage of time erodes his powers and makes it all seem like a contest again.

2000

LEGEND OF A SPORT

ALVA JOHNSTON

Wilson Mizner had been devoted to prizefighting for many years before he became manager of the middleweight champion Stanley Ketchel in 1910. He gave convincing evidence of his love of the game in 1906 when, after marrying "the forty-million-dollar widow," Mrs. Charles T. Yerkes, he turned one wing of the Yerkes mansion, on Fifth Avenue, into a training camp for prizefighters. Mizner was proud of his big brown home, with its Italian garden and two fine art galleries. He was highly pleased at being the successor of the late Yerkes, who had constructed the Chicago "L" and part of the London Tube. In one moment of enthusiasm, he exclaimed, "I own everything that runs on wheels in Chicago," and in another he said, "I'm the only man who was ever accused of stealing a subway." It had taken Yerkes a lifetime of industry and rascality to build up his estate; Wilson sang himself into it in a few weeks. He had good looks and a wonderful line of conversation, but it was his singing of sad old ballads that made him irresistible to the widow.

Mizner was proud of his neighbors. He was close enough to the Astors to run over with a plate of soup in case of illness. Thomas Fortune Ryan lived next door. Andy Carnegie was a few blocks up the Avenue. Mizner was now as close to the Fricks and Garys, Vanderbilts, Goelets, and Whitneys as he had been in the Klondike to Diamond Tooth Gertie, the Scurvy Kid, Nellie the Pig, Two-Toothed Mike, Deep-Hole Johnson, and Jerkline Sam. Yerkes had fixed the house up very much to the taste of Wilson Mizner. He had spent several million dollars building the stately four-story edifice on the south corner of Fifth Avenue and Sixty-fourth Street. He had poured out additional millions on carving, painting, gilding, and inlaying the interior and had stocked it with art treasures selected with considerable judgment. Prizefighters have seldom worked off their surplus fat in more elegant surroundings.

Mizner said later that he had the shock and scare of his life when he was running his palace as a training camp. Waking late one morning with a hangover, he had walked to the great Roman pool of gold-

mounted green onyx that served him as a bathtub. He was halfway
down the marble stairs to the water when he was petrified by the sight
of the symbol of the Black Hand on a tapestry. After his marriage,
Mizner had received sacks of begging letters, which were followed by
sacks of threatening letters. He had scoffed at Black Hand letters, but
in 1906 no man could scoff at the dread emblem in his own bathroom.
The Black Hand was then a busy organization, and bombs and infernal
machines were popping all over town. Mizner's first thought was that
some of his battalion of servants must be Black Handers. Suddenly,
however, to his immense relief, the explanation occurred to him. On
the preceding day, one of the footmen had, with some misgivings, ush-
ered in a fighter named Kid Broad, and Mizner had told the Kid to take
a bath. As the Kid was cautiously tiptoeing into the water, he steadied
himself by putting his hand on the tapestry.

The mansion was a marvelous playhouse for Mizner and his sporting pals. Yerkes, who belonged to the old school of miscellaneous col-
lectors, had picked up a vast variety of antique hand bells, enameled
and jewelled with saints, heroes, and landscapes, and Mizner could ring
for his servants with any one of a hundred little instruments of exquisite workmanship. Yerkes had also been a collector of antique time-
pieces, and Mizner, a perpetual adolescent, lost his mind over the Clock
Room. The clocks were silent when he became master of the mansion,
and one of his first directions to his servants was to wind them all up
and to bring in experts to deal with the recalcitrant ones. Every hour on
the hour, the Clock Room was a pandemonium. A whole aviary of
stuffed birds began to whistle and sing. Muscular men in cast metal
stepped out of hidden doors and smote gongs with sledge hammers.
A full orchestra of tiny musicians swung out on a turntable, slowly
raised their bows, and then frantically sawed away at violin strings.
Nineteenth-century railroad clocks clanged and whistled as locomo-
tives emerged from one tunnel with a train of passenger coaches and
disappeared into another. Steamships came out screeching, paddled
under bridges, and cruised back into their cases. Peasants came forth
and called their cows with melodious horns. Clocks pealed, tolled, and
jingled, and rendered minuets from hidden music boxes. Roy L.
McCardell, writer and inventor of a thousand advertising slogans, was
a friend of Mizner's and a visitor at the mansion. He estimated the
number of clocks at two thousand. The cream of the fun for Mizner

was showing the room to friends with hangovers and seeing their nervous systems murdered when all the clocks let go at once. Mizner told
McCardell that his first serious domestic strife arose over the clock situation. He came home sober one morning, went to bed a little after
3 A.M., and was roused at four by the shrieking of a cuckoo clock in his
own room. He had ordered his servants to make every clock run, and
they had taken him literally. He got up, cursing, and found the clock,
high up on the wall and out of reach. He went to the Yerkes arsenal, on
the fourth floor, returned to his room, and went to bed again. When the
cuckoo screamed at 5 A.M., he lit the lights and gave it both barrels of
one of the Yerkes shotguns. That, according to McCardell, started the
bride wondering whether her new consort had the true Fifth Avenue
spirit.

Mizner's honeymoon was still producing dividends when Willus
Britt, one of the superior crazy men of San Francisco, arrived in New
York. Mizner loved him like a brother. They had been pals and accom-
plices for years in Nome and San Francisco. Willus, who preceded
Mizner in the dynasty of managers of Stanley Ketchel, was in 1906
managing his brother, Jimmy Britt, a great lightweight, who was scheduled to fight at the old Madison Square Garden with Terrible Terry
McGovern. Willus felt that the training camp in the Yerkes mansion
lacked facilities for roadwork, and he took his brother to Coney Island.
Mizner closed up his palatial gym and joined them there. This caused a
certain amount of domestic friction. Mrs. Yerkes had been horrified by
the publicity attending her marriage to Mizner, especially by the cartoons of Tom Powers and by reports that had reached her of the ribald
ballads on the Mizner-Yerkes nuptials that were sung at Hammer-
stein's by Jack Norworth. Just as the notoriety was simmering down, the
sporting pages broke out with accounts of Mizner's sparring with Sam
Berger, the learned and philosophical heavyweight of San Francisco.
Mizner was not a man to let a few millions stand between him and the
fun of hanging around a training camp, and he became the new Coney
Island sensation. He hired an infant prodigy called Groucho Marx to
sing to Jimmy Britt in order to cure him of homesickness, and he
helped Willus with the arrangements for the fight, which resulted in a
victory for Jimmy Britt before ten thousand people. After the fight, the
fighters were arrested on suspicion of fighting, but the case was
dropped for lack of evidence. Mizner went home and made up with his

lawfully wedded lady, but after several additional differences and recon-
ciliations he chucked the millions out the window forever, in the summer of 1906, by going to Goldfield, Nevada, to hang around the
training camps of Joe Gans and Battling Nelson.

Mizner was thirty-three when, in 1910, he became the manager of
Stanley Ketchel. At seventeen, he had managed a boxing black bear,
and in the sixteen intervening years he had managed fighters in Dawson City and Nome and picked up great fistic experience in San Francisco. Bat Masterson, onetime free-shooting Western marshal and later
sportswriter on the New York *Morning Telegraph,* has said that Mizner
attracted much favorable attention as a gentleman sparring partner.
Mizner, according to Bat, made such a showing against the great
heavyweight Tom Sharkey that he was implored by Sharkey's manager,
Tim McGrath, to turn professional, but Mizner was afraid of alienat-
ing his extremely respectable family. According to Bat, Mizner contemplated turning professional only once, and that was when a miner
named Jack Munroe was matched with Jeffries for the heavyweight
title. As Wilson made a practice of sampling the punches of all champions and contenders, he sparred with Munroe and found that he could
handle him like a sack of potatoes. Thereupon, Mizner confided to intimates that he was going to take a shot at the heavyweight crown himself if Jeffries had any trouble with the miner. But when Munroe
collapsed almost at sight of the champion, Mizner decided to cling to
his amateur standing. Mizner was, in fact, a rather silly amateur in most
matters. While he devoted much of his life to preying on suckers, he
was himself the prize sucker of the era. He let everybody else cash in on
his wit and brilliance. Short stories and theatrical dialogue were plun-
dered from his conversation; he threw more anecdotes and epigrams
into the public domain than any other man of his time. In similar fashion, he gave away his fistic science as an unpaid sparring partner and
lavished it on the public in street fights and saloon brawls. Jack Hines,
a globetrotter and the author of *Minstrel of the Yukon,* said he was present when Mizner took the revolvers out of the hands of two men who
were blazing away at each other in a Nome saloon, and said, "You kids
oughtn't to be allowed to play with these toys." One of the San Francisco weeklies commemorated a fracas at Spider Kelly's saloon in which

Mizner fought against enormous odds until he was finally subdued by three civilians, a policeman with a nightstick, and a bartender with a bung starter named Dearest, in honor of Little Lord Fauntleroy's mother.

Tim McGrath wrote a letter to Mark Kelly, Los Angeles sports and screen writer, describing a battle in which Mizner knocked out long-shoremen by platoons in a San Francisco barroom. Wilson, one of the leading dudes in town, wore a suit that was a declaration of war in a waterfront saloon. He started to sing "Sweet Alice, Ben Bolt," with which he had melted sourdough audiences in the Klondike and Alaska. There was a horse laugh. Mizner resented it, and in a moment everybody was punching. Mizner was, luckily, accompanied not only by McGrath but also by the savage middleweight Mysterious Billy Smith, so called because in his early days in the ring he kept disappearing and changing his name. He was famous for biting off a chunk of the ear of the Barbados Demon, Joe Walcott, and for biting a chunk off the index finger of his manager, who had taken the liberty of shaking it at him. McGrath wrote that in the end only one of the longshoremen was on his feet. Mizner was punching away at this man, and the man was paying no attention. Poor Mizner was in despair, believing he had lost his wallop, until Mysterious Billy Smith shouted, "Leave him alone, Wilson! I knocked him out five minutes ago!" Billy's punch had wedged the man between two pieces of furniture, so he couldn't fall.

Mizner was arrested several times in New York for rough-and-tumble fighting, twice becoming the hero of spectacular trials that resulted in acquittals. One complainant asserted that he thought Mizner had hit him with a pile driver; another penned a challenge to Mizner in blood. Wilson's physical condition deteriorated in his early thirties, but he was still able to throw one terrific punch. If his one punch landed, it would finish an average opponent; if it missed, Mizner was through. Old-time acquaintances of his say that when Mizner saw that war was inevitable, he would arrange for friends to interfere and stop the brawl after his one punch. In an interview in San Francisco, in his riper days, Mizner delivered a sermon against striking one's fellow man with one's fist. "If you do," he said, "he goes out to the washbasin and is soon almost as good as new. But you go to the emergency hospital with two awkward doctors trying to get your broken knuckles back in place. Then you are out for two months. Always hit a man with a bottle—

a ketchup bottle preferred, for when that breaks he thinks he's bleeding to death." Mizner was loyal to this principle in the latter part of his life. Once, a year or two before his death, when he was dining in a Los Angeles restaurant with Cecil Beaton, Irving Berlin, and Anita Loos, some people at another table started to heckle Berlin. Fat and decrepit though he was, Mizner went into action with bottles, glasses, and crockery, driving out not only the hecklers but the peaceful patrons of the restaurant. "How are you, Cecil?" Berlin asked after it was all over. "I am gray," said Beaton.

Mizner was introduced to Ketchel by Willus Britt in a hotel room in San Francisco, and Ketchel opened the conversation by cursing Mizner hysterically for throwing his hat on the bed—the worst kind of bad luck. After this poor start, Mizner and Ketchel got on wonderfully. They had much in common. Both of them were ordinarily brimming over with high spirits, and neither of them cared much about anything, although they were both rank sentimentalists, always ready to cry over a sad story or a sad song. The main difference between them was that Mizner was a sophisticated child of nature and Ketchel was an unsophisticated one. Ketchel had been a bouncer in the underworld of Butte, and Mizner had been an executive in the underworld of Nome, and each was tinged with the red-light philosophy of life. Ketchel had a thirst for knowledge, and Mizner had a passion for imparting it. Whenever he could get his clutches on an untaught intellect, he tried to inspire it with a love of literature by reciting poetry. Irving Berlin was the most eminent of Mizner's pupils. Catching Berlin just after his singing-waiter days, when his mind was still a blank sheet of paper as far as general culture was concerned, Mizner sought to create an appetite for literature in the young genius by reciting Kipling's "If" and Wallace Irwin's "Chinatown Ballads" to him. Ketchel delighted in hearing Mizner declaim verses and read O. Henry stories. The middleweight champ was stunned by Mizner's recitation of the Langdon Smith classic that starts "When you were a tadpole and I was a fish, In the Palaeozoic time" and follows the romance of two lovers from one geological age to another, until they wind up in Rector's. Ketchel had a thousand questions about the tadpole and the fish, and Mizner, a pedagogue at heart, took immense pleasure in wedging the whole theory of evolution into the fighter's untutored head. Ketchel became silent and thoughtful. He declined an invitation to see the town that night with Mizner and Britt. When they rolled in at 5 A.M., Ketchel was sitting up with his eyes glued on a bowl of goldfish. "That evolution is all the bunk!" he shouted angrily. "I've been watching those fish nine hours and they haven't changed a bit." Mizner had to talk fast; one thing Ketchel couldn't bear was to have anybody cross him. He was a creature of emotions, and he could be a lamb or a devil, according to which emotion happened to be stirred up.

One night, Mizner, Britt, and a famous newspaper artist took Ketchel to meet the chatelaine and maids of honor of one of New York's gaudiest establishments. They received a wild welcome. Corks popped, and eyes sparkled with love and larceny. Suddenly it was discovered that Ketchel was missing. There was a quick search, and he was found in the entrance hall weeping and wailing. On the wall was the picture titled "Lost in the Storm," showing a sheep in a blizzard. "Oh, the poor little thing!" Ketchel sobbed again and again. A few days later, he opened fire with a Colt .44 through the door of his bedroom at Woodlawn Inn and put a bullet through the leg of one of his best friends, Peter (Pete the Goat) Stone, a nightclub owner, who had persisted in knocking at the door to get him up for his roadwork. In the ring, Ketchel was handicapped at times by his humanity. He was loath to hurt any opponent he regarded as a nice fellow. Edward Dean Sullivan, author of *The Fabulous Wilson Mizner,* stated that Ketchel, in order to overcome the disadvantage of his good humor, would say to himself in the middle of a round, "That son of a bitch insulted your mother," and filial piety would then turn him into "an example of tumultuous ferocity"—to borrow Philadelphia Jack O'Brien's description of him.

Ketchel had emerged from obscurity on July 4, 1907, when he fought a twenty-round draw at Marysville, California, with Joe Thomas, claimant of the middleweight championship. In the next two years, Ketchel knocked out middleweights and heavyweights in great abundance. He was being managed by a San Francisco photographer named Joe Coffman, who was said to hypnotize him, keep him locked in a bedroom, and impound his clothes every night to prevent other managers from stealing him. In 1908, Willus Britt climbed up a fire escape and stole Ketchel in a bathrobe, according to W. O. McGeehan, the famous sports columnist. Britt was regarded as the smartest manager in the country. A few years earlier, he had been considered rattle-brained. He had once tried to borrow five hundred dollars from James W. Coffroth, the San Francisco sporting czar, for a business trip to New York. Noticing that he was dressed in evening trousers but no coat, Coffroth loaned him a hundred freshly minted pennies, which Willus took for five-dollar gold pieces. Overwhelming Coffroth with gratitude, Britt caught the next train east in his shirtsleeves, with his rouleau of one-cent pieces, and a few weeks later came home comparatively wealthy. Coffroth was greatly impressed, named a saloon the Willus in Britt's honor, and went into business with him. Willus was credited with inventing the Native Son decision, according to which any Californian, if alive at the end of a prizefight, was automatically victorious over any nonresident. After mopping up the Western territory with Ketchel, Britt decided to take him East. W. O. McGeehan, who was then living in San Francisco, called on Britt and Ketchel shortly before they left California and was surprised to find Ketchel wearing a Phi Beta Kappa key. Britt said that he had procured it at Abe Attell's pawnshop and that he intended to present Ketchel in New York as a young fellow fighting his way through college. Coffroth disapproved of the idea because Ketchel said "dese," "dem," and "dose." Britt said that New Yorkers would never know the difference, but Coffroth had the key stolen, and Britt decided to take Ketchel to New York as a cowboy in high-heeled boots, spurs, chaps, and a sombrero.

Mizner became involved in the management of Ketchel as an unpaid specialist on the political and graft setup in New York. Prizefighting was as illegal as cockfighting or bullfighting. The referees never named a winner, since the fighters were not supposed to seek victory but to cooperate like dancing partners. Any person who "instigated a contention" was liable to a five-hundred-dollar fine or a year in jail; the same penalties were incurred by persons who "published a challenge" or who "trained or assisted a fighter to train." Like streetwalking and gambling, however, prizefighting was generally tolerated upon the payment of protection money. In his ignorance of New York, Britt found himself paying protection to the wrong parasites, and he called Mizner in to teach him the difference between the responsible tapeworms and the frauds. Fights were at that time put on by "athletic clubs," which were organized the way speakeasies were later. Every new arrival was scrutinized by sentinels; anybody who looked like a reformer or stool pigeon was barred. There was no public sale of tickets. Only duly elected club members were admitted. The payment of two dollars at any saloon near the arena made any man a duly elected club member and provided him with a card calling for a good seat; one dollar made him a junior member, with a card entitling him to a bad seat. According to the late Bob Davis, every card was issued in the name of John Smith, in order to simplify the clerical work. Club meetings usually started with a speech bawling out members for being derelict in attendance at previous meetings and threatening drastic action under the bylaws.

In spite of the punctual payment of graft, fights were raided whenever the authorities were seized with a fit of law and order, and elaborate precautions were considered necessary to prove that the entertainment consisted strictly of amateur sparring exhibitions of, for, and by club members. The principal arenas were an old dance hall and an old stable, Madison Square Garden having become too ladylike for fistic programs. The legal niceties of boxing were like those of drinking in the prohibition era. Soft punches were innocent, like soft drinks under the Volstead Act. But a hard blow was like hard liquor and instantly transformed all present into criminals. The only thing that saved the boxing game in those dark days was club loyalty. It was impossible to find a clubman who had seen a violation of the law. On one occasion, a Headquarters detective tried to stop a fight in the stable. He was thrown down a twenty-foot hay chute. The incident was invisible to fifteen hundred clubmen, including about a hundred policemen, all honorary members. But at best the boxing situation was precarious. Newspapers joined the reformers in demanding the suppression of the sport. The New York *Globe* asserted that the so-called sparring matches were gory encounters, denoting a low state of civilization, and charged that "the brutalized spectators howl with delight at a knockout." A bill was offered in Congress making it a crime to mail a picture of a fighter and canceling the postal rights of newspapers that printed news of fights. It was dangerous for a pugilist to admit that he was a pugilist; it placed him outside the law and in danger of being "vagged," or jugged as a vagabond. Ketchel and Mizner were once arrested on a charge of speeding. When Ketchel appeared in court, he was asked his occupation. "Physical instructor," he said. In view of the general situation, Britt felt that he couldn't have too much unpaid advice. He wouldn't trust anybody but Californians, and Mizner became his chief adviser. Britt and Mizner called in Hype Igoe, a cartoonist and sportswriter of Native Son origin, as an additional consultant.

One of Britt's peculiarities was that although he constantly solicited advice, he seldom took it. After collecting the best opinions available, he would leave all important decisions to a pack of playing cards. He had studied under celebrated fortune-tellers, and he always carried in his pocket a deck of cards, which he used as an artificial brain. Whenever he had to make a decision, he would select a card and take a surreptitious look at it. If the card was lucky, he would say "Yes"; if unlucky, "No"; if dubious, "We'll cross that bridge when we come to it." One day, Mizner stole Britt's little god of fifty-two opinions and substituted a deck consisting entirely of queens of spades. Every time Britt peered into the future, the lady of disaster glared at him. He went all to pieces, spent a week in bed under a doctor's care, and thereafter meekly accepted the suggestions of Mizner and Igoe.

Ketchel's most spectacular fight in New York was his ten-round battle with Philadelphia Jack O'Brien. Nobody knows who won it. O'Brien, the light-heavyweight champion, was one of the cleverest fighters alive—a jigging, feinting, shuttling, sidestepping, jabbing artist. For seven rounds, he played Ketchel like a snare drum. But his style required incessant motion and, beginning to tire in the eighth round, he spent the rest of the fight trying to save himself. Ketchel landed one of his authentic knockout punches in the closing seconds of the last round. As the referee was counting "six," the gong sounded. O'Brien was unconscious for half an hour. Referees' decisions being forbidden by law, there was only the "newspaper decision," which was mixed, some writers declaring for Jack, since he had won the majority of rounds and was way ahead on points, while others maintained that no man could win a fight in a coma. Some weeks later, in Philadelphia, Ketchel knocked O'Brien out in three rounds. The contemporary accounts credit O'Brien with great gameness under a savage battering, but O'Brien told a different story to Leo McClatchy and other Washington correspondents nearly twenty years later, when he was in the capital in quest of publicity for Philadelphia Jack's Gymnasium for Business Men, in New York. The newspapers had revealed that President Coolidge was taking off weight by riding a mechanical horse, and O'Brien had memorized a speech to the president in which he offered to come to Washington three times a week and fight the president into condition in the White House basement—FREE. But when he was presented to the president, Jack turned pale, trembled, and couldn't say a word. He tried afterward to salvage a little publicity by telling the correspondents the nature of his mission, and he threw in the story of his life, including the statement that he had taken a dive in the third round of his second fight with Ketchel. Ketchel's backers, he said, were willing to pay for a quick knockout, believing that it would convince the public that Ketchel was a genuine White Hope, with a real chance of delivering the great Caucasian race from its bondage to Jack Johnson, the colored champion.

Nineteen hundred and nine was the big year of the White Hopes. The barrooms were the chief intellectual centers of the country at the time, and it was their despairing conviction that the long career of the fair-skinned peoples had ended with the defeat of Tommy Burns by Jack Johnson in 1908. The gymnasiums were full of clumsy giants training to save our pasty-faced civilization. Ketchel was the best bet of the disinherited albino, although he weighed only 155 pounds, while Johnson weighed over two hundred. This discrepancy was minimized by the use of crooked scales, which built Ketchel up to 170 and cut Johnson down to 195. The fight between Ketchel and Johnson was held in Colma, California, on October 16, 1909, and the high tide of Ketchel's career came in the twelfth round, when he knocked Johnson down. Low tide came an instant later, when Johnson knocked him out. The orthodox analysis of this contest was that Johnson had agreed to "carry" Ketchel, or handle him carefully, but that Ketchel attempted to double-cross him. According to Marty Forkins, manager of the late Bill Robinson, the only agreement was that the men were to fight gently for ten rounds in order to let the motion pictures run for a decent length, and that after ten rounds it was each man for himself. Tiv Krelling, a photographer at the fight, says that both the knockdown and the knockout were faked in order to give a box-office climax to the fight pictures. The greatest of living ring chroniclers, Dumb Dan Morgan—nicknamed Dumb by the cartoonist Tad Dorgan because he once talked seven and a half hours without pausing for punctuation—was told by Johnson that Ketchel hit him honestly and hurt him badly. Johnson said that he had a few seconds of intense meditation when he was sitting on the canvas; he felt that his situation was distinctly awkward and that the only course to pursue was to put all he had into one tremendous punch. This was a critical resolution for Johnson to take, since he was preeminently a defensive fighter. A great defensive fighter hates to turn loose his best wallop at an undamaged adversary; it spoils his defensive arrangements, for if the punch misses, he is likely to find himself a wide-open target for a counterpunch. But Johnson didn't miss. His final punch not only flattened Ketchel but knocked out his two upper front teeth, sensational relics that Willus carried in his vest pocket and displayed to spellbound crowds in San Francisco barrooms.

Willus Britt died shortly after the Johnson-Ketchel fight, and Mizner became the full-fledged manager of Ketchel. In his first few months under the Mizner banner, the middleweight champion added little to his reputation. Wurra Wurra McLaughlin, sporting editor of the New York *World,* wrote that Ketchel had ruined himself by "hitting the hop." Ketchel refused to leave a bar in Johnstown, Pennsylvania, to keep a contract to spar in the local opera house, and he was chased out of town by a posse. Mizner pledged the appearance of Ketchel at another exhibition there, but he couldn't find his fighter in time. He eventually located Ketchel lying in bed smoking opium with a blonde and a brunette. Mizner was later asked how he met this crisis. "What the hell could I do?" said Mizner. "I said, 'Move over.' "

Ketchel was a fighter who often took his training seriously, and, in spite of his wild life, he would at times work furiously at Woodlawn Inn, or at New Dorp, S. I., to get himself back into condition. His most famous fight under Mizner's management was a six-round, no-decision battle with Sam Langford, the Boston Tar Baby, in Philadelphia, on April 27, 1910. According to the accounts, it was a savage affair in which each man gave and received terrific punishment. The *Morning Telegraph* said that Ketchel looked like the loser at the end of the fifth round but that he earned a draw by pounding Langford ferociously in the sixth. The New York *Press* also called it a draw. The *Morning* and *Evening World* reported that Ketchel had won by a wide margin. His share of the receipts was nine thousand dollars, the largest sum he ever collected for a fight in the East. In retrospect, it was the Battle of the Legends. Ketchel and Langford are the twin Paul Bunyans of prizering folklore. As a whim, Ketchel is said to have knocked out six heavyweights in Butte one afternoon and, while half stupefied with opium, to have knocked out four heavyweights by mistake at a charity benefit in New York. Damon Runyon wrote, "It has been my observation that the memory of Ketchel prejudiced the judgment of everyone who was ever associated with him. They can never see any other fighter." There is an ever growing flood of reminiscences about Ketchel in the sporting pages and the gladiatorial magazines. Ketchel's ghost is the biggest contemporary ring figure, next to Joe Louis. Langford is not the swaggering demigod that Ketchel is, but the old-time experts generally rated him above Ketchel. Dumb Dan Morgan, for example, claims that no fighter, with the exception of Jeffries, could have held his own with Langford in an unfixed combat. Langford was short and weighed only 165 pounds, but he had long, powerful arms, and staggering statistics are presented as to the number of ribs he broke with his left to the body. Jack Johnson is said to have fled three continents to avoid risking his title against Langford. Veteran fight fans tell of one of Langford's exploits that parallels Babe Ruth's alleged feat of pointing his bat toward the center-field bleachers and then driving a ball to the spot indicated. Langford, they say, once fought a White Hope whose manager had proclaimed him to be the coming champion of the world. Skillfully maneuvering the White Hope along the ropes, Langford knocked him into the manager's lap, shouting, "Here comes your champion!" It is asserted that Langford, when he was old and almost totally blind, knocked men out by ear, getting the range of his opponent's jaw by calculations based on the sound of the opponent's feet shuffling on the canvas.

Many of the thirty-third-degree experts of 1910 refused to make the trip from New York to Philadelphia to see the Ketchel-Langford bout. They were convinced that Ketchel wouldn't enter the ring with Langford unless the fight was fixed. The newspapers said it was a glorious and evenly matched contest, but many of the experts were skeptical, and some of them are skeptical to this day. One of the Langford idolizers happened to be Mizner's lawyer. He asked his client for inside information. "Why, the fight was written like a play," said Mizner. "We had it surge to and fro like a melodrama. First, Ketchel in dire distress, then Langford, then Ketchel, and so on. It's the old, old plot." Mizner told his lawyer that he would have had Ketchel win the newspaper decision had he not feared an outcry from the Langford fans that might hurt the fight business, so he arranged to have Philadelphia newspaper opinion add up to a draw. Mizner stated further that, in order to make sure that the scenario was enacted as written, Langford was authoritatively informed that he would not receive a cent of his five-thousand-dollar share of the purse if he knocked Ketchel out.

Ketchel was matched to put on a similar six-act melodrama, ending in a draw, with Willie Lewis, a dashing middleweight. Both fighters gave their word of honor that they wouldn't try for a knockout. The day before the fight, Willie's manager went into a church and lit several candles before the statue of a saint—a common practice of pious fighters and managers. Dumb Dan Morgan, who accompanied Lewis's manager to the church, was aware of the gentlemen's agreement for a draw and was surprised to hear his companion utter a petition for a victory for Willie Lewis and then drop twenty-five cents in the contribution box. As the fight got under way, Ketchel began to swing with studied inaccuracy at his opponent. Willie, however, picked a nice opening, and hit Ketchel with all his power, and followed the blow up with a try for a knockout. Ketchel barely managed to weather the storm. At the end of the round, instead of sitting on his stool and being fussed over by his seconds, Ketchel stood up on it and fixed his eye on Willie with an eloquent and reproachful stare. In the second round, Willie kept running away, but Ketchel caught up with him and summarily knocked him out. "You are the smartest manager in the business," said Dumb Dan Morgan to Willie's manager. "You tried to get the world's middleweight championship for two bits." "I would've if that saint had stood up," replied Willie's manager.

In New York, on June 10, 1910, Ketchel fought his last fight, his opponent being Jim Smith, a mediocre heavyweight. Reporting the Ketchel-Smith fight, the *Morning Telegraph* said, "Wilson Mizner was on deck, of course, bossing the fight in the champion's corner. He was dressed as though for a party instead of a fight and did not soil his immaculate attire by swinging a towel or dashing water with a sponge." The *Telegraph* added that Mizner's face showed signs of anxiety under its icy gambler's mask. Ketchel failed to exhibit his old power. He nearly exhausted himself before he succeeded in dropping Smith in the fifth round. The general opinion of the fight critics was that Ketchel was no longer the old Michigan Assassin. Bat Masterson said that Ketchel had been ruined by dancing masters and tailors. He also remarked that with his own eyes he had seen Ketchel leading a grand march at Hot Springs, Arkansas, and that he had a wardrobe of beautiful clothes that would sap any fighter's vitality.

Ketchel was still deeply concerned over the destiny of the white race. Its last Hope was the former champion Jim Jeffries, who after six years of retirement was matched to fight Johnson in Reno on July 4, 1910. Ketchel and Mizner went to Reno late in June. They were realistic enough to see that Jeffries was in no condition to save the white race, and they were philosophers enough to bet their shirts on Johnson, but Ketchel brooded and brooded. Shortly before the fight, he came to Mizner with a statesmanlike project. Just before the bout, the attending celebrities would be introduced to the spectators and would shake hands with the fighters. Ketchel proposed that, instead of shaking hands with Jeffries, he clip him on the chin. One punch, he said, would knock him cold. This would save the honor of the unpigmented, since a Caucasian wallop would have finished the career of Jeffries. "But think of our dough!" said Mizner. "Look at the money we stand to win when Johnson beats him!" It took an hour's arguing to convince Ketchel that he ought to let the white race take care of itself.

In August 1910, Mizner arranged for Ketchel to fight Bill Lang, an Australian heavyweight, in New York. At the last minute, Mizner cancelled the match, saying that Ketchel had a boil and a sore foot. Charles I. Meegan charged on the front page of the *Telegraph* that the bout had been shelved because Hugh McIntosh, manager of Lang, refused to post a five-thousand-dollar guarantee that Lang wouldn't knock Ketchel out. Mizner treated the Meegan charges with haughty silence. He had his defenders among the insiders in the fight game. Most of them knew that Ketchel was on the downgrade when Mizner became his manager and that "knockout insurance" was necessary to prolong the colorful battler's career.

In September 1910, Ketchel went to a farm near Springfield, Missouri, to live the simple life for a while. A dispatch from Springfield to the New York *Sun* said that his doctor had told him that he could not last out the year at the pace he was traveling. Ketchel had been living at the Bartholdi Hotel in New York; the *Morning Telegraph* said that his bill for his last two weeks there had been $593—whirlwind spending at a time when highballs were ten cents apiece. Ketchel was only twenty-four and hoped to get back into fighting trim. By then Mizner's first successful play, *The Deep Purple,* had opened in Chicago and he had lost interest in the prize ring. According to Bat Masterson, Mizner planned a stage career for Ketchel and was working on a vaudeville monologue for him. Out in Missouri, the middleweight champion behaved like a model boy at first, but there was a woman on the farm. Dispatches bluntly described her as ugly, but she possessed the irresistible magic of propinquity. She was known as Goldie Hurtz, and one morning Mr. Hurtz, a farmhand, shot and killed Ketchel with a .22 rifle. It looked for a time as if Hurtz would be saved by the plea that he only did what any honest farmhand would do under the circumstances. But it turned out that the honest farmhand was really a dishonest barber named Walter Dipley, a city slicker hiding out from the Kansas City police. The unwritten-law defense collapsed when it was found that Mr. and Mrs. Hurtz had never been married. Tried as accomplices in the crime, they were both convicted and sent up for long terms.

1950

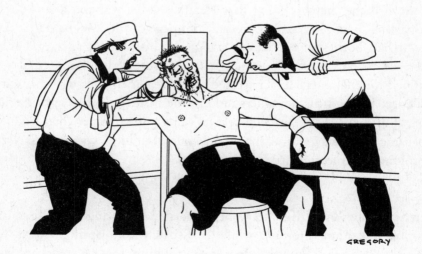

"Sure, he's pulverizing your face, but you're chipping away at his likability."

A MAN-CHILD IN LOTUSLAND

REBECCA MEAD

Shaquille O'Neal, the Los Angeles Lakers center, lives, during the basketball season, in a large cream-colored mansion at the end of a leafy cul-de-sac in Beverly Hills. The exterior of O'Neal's house is discreetly opulent, and it is not until you approach the double front doors that you notice, etched in the glass, two large Superman symbols. The first superhero that O'Neal ever felt an affinity with was the Incredible Hulk, because, as he told me recently, "he was big and green." The young O'Neal knew what it was to be a physical oddity; when he was five years old, his mother was obliged to carry her son's birth certificate with her around their hometown of Newark, New Jersey, to prove to bus drivers that he was not eight or nine. Somewhere around the age of seven, O'Neal switched over to Superman, and now, at the age of thirty, his allegiance is steady.

Today, O'Neal, who is seven feet one, has a Superman *S* tattooed on his left biceps, and when he slams the ball into the basket with a particularly incontrovertible defiance at the Staples Center, the Lakers' home court, the Superman theme is played over the loudspeakers. The Superman logo is engraved in the headlights of his silver Mercedes, one of about fifteen cars and trucks he owns. More than five hundred framed Superman comic-book covers hang on the wall of a corridor in his off-season house, in Orlando, where he also has a vintage Superman pinball machine. For a while, he had a Superman bedspread on his bed. O'Neal considers it lucky that he shares a first initial with Superman. "The only reason I call myself Superman is that it starts with *S*," he says. "If my name was Tim, I couldn't be Superman. It wouldn't look right."

One of O'Neal's grandmothers died recently, and at her funeral he contemplated the design of his own final resting place. "I started to think about what my mausoleum would look like, and I thought it should be all marble, with Superman logos everywhere," he told me. "There would be stadium seating, and only my family would have the key, and they would be able to go in there and sit down, like in a little apartment. My grave would be right there, and there would be a TV showing, like, an hour-long video of who I was."

O'Neal considers himself to have a dual nature. "Shaquille is corporate, nice-looking, soft-spoken, wears suits, and is very cordial to people, whereas Shaq is the dominant athlete who is the two-time champion," he told me. "They are the same person, but it's kind of like Clark Kent and Superman. During the day, I am Shaquille, and at night I am Shaq." O'Neal also has a nemesis, an evil twin, whom he calls Elliuqahs Laeno. "That's my name spelled backward," he said. "That's the person that I am not allowed to be because of my status. He does what a normal young rich guy would do—party, hang out, use bad language. He stays out all night, tries to practice the next day, isn't focused. That is him. He's dead, though. I killed him off."

We were talking in a back office at the Lakers' training facility, in El Segundo, a suburb of Los Angeles, after O'Neal had come off the court from an afternoon practice. His skin was tide-marked with drying sweat, and he sat with his legs spread wide, like those riders on the New York subway who laugh in the face of the one-man-one-seat convention. O'Neal, who weighs somewhere around 340 pounds, would need at least three seats, and perhaps four. His identification with Superman is based on his sense of himself as a crusading force for good—good being, for the moment, the continued success of the Los Angeles Lakers, who are currently in the NBA playoffs—but it is also grounded in a sense of physical supremacy.

O'Neal is one of the largest men alive. He wears size-22 basketball shoes, which are made for him by a company called Starter; they are all white and finished with a shiny gloss, reminiscent, in their sheen and size, of the hull of a luxury yacht. (When the Lakers' equipment manager, a rotund man in the mid-five-foot range named Rudy Garciduenas, carries the shoes into the locker room before a game, he cradles them in gentle arms, as if he were the nursemaid of Otus and Ephialtes, the twin giant sons of Poseidon.) O'Neal's cars must have their interiors ripped out and their seats moved back ten inches before he is able to drive them. (His most recent acquisition is a Ferrari Spider convertible, a birthday gift from his father that was, as he pointed out to reporters in the Lakers' locker room one night, bought with his own earnings. O'Neal's Spider has its top down permanently, since he's too big for the convertible to convert.) O'Neal's pants have an outside seam of four feet six and a half inches. He has never encountered a hotel-room showerhead that was high enough for him to stand under, an inconvenience for a man who spends months at a time on the road. When he speaks on a cellphone, he holds it in front of his mouth and talks into it as if it were a walkie-talkie, and then swivels it up to his ear to listen, as if the phone were a tiny planet making a quarter orbit around the sun of his enormous head.

O'Neal isn't the tallest player in the NBA—that's Shawn Bradley, of the Dallas Mavericks, who is seven feet six—and many teams have at least one seven-footer. But Shawn Bradley is seventy-odd pounds lighter than O'Neal, and when they are on the court together it looks as if Bradley would be well advised to abandon basketball and return to his former calling, as a Mormon missionary. O'Neal is daunting even to the most accomplished of seven-footers, like Dikembe Mutombo, of the Philadelphia 76ers, who is an inch taller than O'Neal but, at 265 pounds, a bantamweight by comparison. When the 76ers met the Lakers in last year's NBA Finals, Mutombo and O'Neal clashed repeatedly under the boards, with Mutombo bouncing off O'Neal's body—the hulking, barging shoulder, the prodigious posterior backing into implacable reverse.

Many centers move like articulated trucks on a highway filled with Mercedes SLs—they can't weave from lane to lane or make sharp turns or suddenly accelerate. But O'Neal's physical power is augmented by an unlikely agility: He is able to jump and loft his massive body above the rim, and his recovery when he hits the ground is such that should he miss the basket on the first try he can go up again, just as high and just as quickly, grab the ball, feint to fool the three defenders leaping around him, and hit his mark. On the official play-by-play reports that are given to reporters covering the game, O'Neal's performance is condensed into a code: "MISS O'Neal Lay-up/O'Neal REBOUND/MISS O'Neal Lay-up/O'Neal REBOUND/O'Neal Slam Dunk"—all happening within the space of seven seconds. O'Neal was the second-best scorer in the league this season, with 27.2 points per game, after Philadelphia's Allen Iverson, who scored an average of 31.4. And he has been the NBA Finals' Most Valuable Player for the past two years.

O'Neal's body isn't as cut as he'd like it to be, and friends say that what he really wants is a six-pack stomach, but he takes pride in his solid muscularity. At one point while we were talking, he rose from his chair, hoisted up his yellow No. 34 jersey, and invited me to pinch his fat. A brief investigation revealed that there wasn't any fat to pinch—though there was an acreage of belly, tattooed just above the navel with "LILWarrior"; and, glinting on the higher reaches of his torso, a gold bar piercing a nipple. "Sixteen percent body fat, baby," O'Neal said.

It is perhaps inevitable that O'Neal is routinely described as having a huge personality, although his personality is probably the most ordinary-sized thing about him. Even when he is silent in the presence of reporters, which he often is, or when his public comments are restricted to mumbles, his importance on the court means that his pronouncements are invested with extra significance. When O'Neal does talk to reporters, after a game, they swarm around him, pointing miniature tape recorders up over their heads, toward his mouth. His voice can be so low that you don't know what he's said until you bring the tape recorder back down to earth and play the tape.

O'Neal's on-court persona is ferocious, and his comments about his opponents are usually of the standard aggressive-athlete variety. "They ought to make those lazy-ass millionaires play some defense," he told me one day. O'Neal aspires to a career in law enforcement after he retires from basketball, and his profile as a player is that of a crushing, point-scoring bad cop, with no good cops in sight. "He likes to enforce things," Herb More, one of O'Neal's high school coaches, says. But his disposition is fundamentally sunny, and if his sense of humor runs to the excruciatingly broad—he derives great pleasure from picking up a defenseless member of the Lakers' staff, or a reporter, and manhandling him like a burly father with a squealing three-year-old—it is deeply felt.

These characteristics, along with his enthusiastic if less than triumphant excursions into the territories of rap music and movie acting, have made him a central figure in the popular culture. His affability is currently being harnessed to promote Burger King, Nestlé Crunch, and Swatch; and his endorsements have been estimated to earn him between eight and ten million dollars a year. He offers a combination of cartoonish playfulness and wholesome values. He has never taken drugs, unless you count a brief dalliance with creatine and androstenedione, the legal bodybuilding supplements. He never drinks in public, unless it's a soda he's endorsing. He is well-known for his rapport with children, and he does a lot of charity work with them. Every Christmas, he dresses up in a Santa suit and hands out gifts in an event known as Shaq-A-Claus, and he has granted twelve wishes through the Make-A-Wish Foundation over the past two years. He's not the kind of player you'd expect to see slapped with a paternity suit. (O'Neal has four children: two with his girlfriend of three years, Shaunie Nelson, one daughter from a previous relationship, and a son of Shaunie's whom O'Neal considers his own.) Nor is he likely to participate in any of those activities that advertisers most fear, and be charged with DUI, like Rod Strickland, who plays for the Miami Heat, or, like the former New Jersey Net Jayson Williams, have a chauffeur found shot to death in his bedroom.

O'Neal has had some misadventures in marketing, largely because he and his former agent Leonard Armato tried in the late nineties to sell Shaq as an independent brand, something that had never been done by a basketball player. They launched an online clothing-and-shoe company, Dunk.net, which never took off and went bust after the dot-com crash; another clothing line, called TWIsM.—"The world is mine," O'Neal's personal motto—was similarly unsuccessful. O'Neal and Armato parted ways last year, and O'Neal replaced him with Perry Rogers, a sports marketer who built his career on selling Andre Agassi; Mike Parris, O'Neal's uncle and a former cop, has become O'Neal's manager. "Shaq is a brand, and we are trying to match him up with companies that match his personality and caliber as an athlete," Parris explained to me. (This realignment has yet to be entirely accomplished—O'Neal has until recently been associated with a health-club company called ZNetix, whose founder was accused of bilking investors of millions of dollars.)

Apart from Michael Jordan, who has made more than $425 million from the likes of Nike and Gatorade during the course of his career, the only other player whose advertising deals rival O'Neal's is Kobe Bryant, his Lakers teammate. Unlike some Lakers before him, such as Kareem Abdul-Jabbar, O'Neal thoroughly enjoys being a celebrity. He considers it his duty to present a friendly face in public, even on occasions when he would prefer not to be badgered by autograph hunters, and he accepts the inevitability of being recognized. O'Neal was startled to discover, after being stranded on September 11 in Baton Rouge for sev-

eral days, that he was expected to show ID when boarding the charter
plane he'd hired. "I'm not prejudiced, but those pilots had better have
some ID," he told a friend.

O'Neal's public persona could not be more different from that of Jordan, who was the dominant force in basketball throughout most of the
late eighties and the nineties, and is still the world's best-known athlete. Jordan, like the style of basketball he perfected, was transcendent.
His athleticism resembled aeronautics, and he regularly evoked celestial
comparisons: Larry Bird once described him as "God disguised as
Michael Jordan." O'Neal, by contrast, is solidly earthbound. (On the
court, Kobe Bryant is Ariel to O'Neal's Caliban.) Michael Jordan was a
wise adult figure who invited aspiration: The elegant Nike commercials
that urged fans to Be Like Mike encouraged an identification with his
prowess, even as they celebrated his superlative capacities.

Being Like Shaq is demonstrably impossible, and more or less
unimaginable. Instead, O'Neal, with his taste for souped-up cars, and
his appetite for dumb jokes, and his tendency toward braggadocio,
looks like a regular American guy, albeit a drastically oversized one.
Shaq appears to want to Be Like Us.

The growth of professional basketball over the past twenty-odd years
from a relatively minor spectator sport to a mass-cultural phenomenon
is an example of the way in which all of American culture is increasingly geared to the tastes of teenage boys. Marketers hold that adolescent boys, with their swiftly changing appetites and their enormous
buying power, are the most difficult and most critical consumers to
reach. Basketball is a perfect game for teenagers: It's fast, it's energetic,
it requires little equipment, and it can be practiced in driveways and on
the playground without so much as an opponent; and it has been ap-
propriated by products that have nothing to do with sports—Coke,
milk—as an excellent way to reach that desired demographic. Teen
boys function, in turn, as cultural emissaries to the global population:
Nikes aren't cool all over the world because Vince Carter wears them
but because cool American teenagers wear them.

Basketball itself is marketed with teen tastes in mind. The theater of
a Lakers game has an adolescent-boy aesthetic: goofy and overheated.
There are the whirling spotlights when the players emerge from the

locker room, high-fiving; the snippets of roaring rap music and of the teen-boy anthem "We Will Rock You," by Queen; the absurd contests held between quarters, in which competitors do things like play musical chairs on a set of huge inflatable seats. Should all this hilarity be inadequate to the task of holding a young man's interest, there is always the Laker Girls. The prevalence of teen-boy tastes in American culture is something that suits Shaquille O'Neal, since those are also his tastes. There are, of course, certain adult dimensions to his life. He talks of marrying Shaunie—she wears a big diamond engagement ring—although he says he's not quite ready yet. And he speaks often of his responsibilities and the fact that he doesn't go clubbing the way he used to. "When I was by myself, the only people I had to take care of were my parents," he says. "But then I had my first child and I had to slow down; and now I've got four." But in many ways his lifestyle is a thirteen-year-old's fantasy existence. O'Neal has surrounded himself with cousins from Newark and old friends from high school, who share his interests in goofing off, breaking stuff, making noise, shooting guns, and driving a wide range of motorized vehicles, which include customized Harley-Davidsons and, on the lake at his house in Orlando, a fleet of Jet-Skis.

O'Neal has installed one of his high school buddies, Joe Cavallero, to look after the Orlando house, which also appears to mean wreaking measured destruction. "We have food fights, where Thomas, the chef, will come in from the grocery store with all these things, and Shaquille will break a whole watermelon over my head, and I'll hit him with a pudding cake," Cavallero told me. "Shaquille doesn't really have many books, but he has got a big video collection: the whole Little Rascals series, and every kung-fu thing you can think of, and sometimes we play-fight like that, too. And every night he'll get on his DJ deck and play for a couple of hours, and he'll turn that thing up as loud as it will go, and everything in his house is marble, so it echoes through the whole house. And Shaquille likes to wake me up with a pillow smash to the face. You know how you get to being sound asleep, and someone smashes you in the face with a pillow? It is so funny."

The house in Los Angeles is home not only to Shaunie and the children but to Thomas Gosney, Shaq's chef, factotum, and close friend, whose loyalty is such that he responds to questions about O'Neal in the first-person plural: When I asked Gosney whether O'Neal was ever going to get around to marrying Shaunie, he said, "I think we will, but I think we need to get out of the NBA first." In addition to feeding O'Neal lots of fruit and vegetables and preventing him from indulging his particular culinary vice of eating sandwiches late at night, Gosney provides round-the-clock companionship if necessary. "The night before that first championship that we won, O'Neal was up all night," Gosney said. "He was stressing out, and I knew he needed a release. He came in and found me and said, 'Are you sleeping?' So we got up, and we rode go-carts, and then we rode motorcycles. He needed to get up and do these things in the middle of the night." O'Neal depends on his friends not just for entertainment but for home management, and Gosney told me, "Before Shaunie came and lived with us, I would say that I was his wife, except for the sex. Shaquille has said to me, 'If you were a girl, I don't know what I would do.' "

O'Neal's size gives him a storybook quality that also exaggerates the childish aspect of his nature. In myth, giants are primordial creatures, who are often beloved for their lumbering doltishness. O'Neal is much sharper than the typical fairy-tale giant, but the simplicity of his tastes and of his manner of expression has currency in a popular culture where childishness is valued above adult sophistication. "Kids like me because they see themselves in me," he said. "I don't speak with a Harvard-type vocabulary. I only wear suits when I need to. I don't talk about stuff I haven't gone through. I am just me. They like rims; I like rims. They like rap music; I like rap music. They like platinum; I like platinum."

A few years ago, O'Neal took up hunting, and one of his favorite activities is disappearing for the day into a game preserve in Florida with a few friends and a few guns. He is a bit defensive about this hobby. "It's not like I'm just sneaking around and killing animals. I am a law-abiding citizen," he told me. "What I like about it, first, is looking at the animals, and then I like getting the big ones. You can be out there all day, walking around, looking at leaves, looking at grass, looking at footprints." Off the marble entrance hall of O'Neal's house in Beverly Hills, there is a carpeted room, filled with his hunting trophies: Mounted heads of antlered creatures cover the walls and, because the walls are filled, cover the floor, too, their noses pointing quirkily up at the high ceiling. There are a few animals that O'Neal bought already stuffed: a polar bear, and a taxidermic tableau of a lion attacking a zebra. The scent of the room is a pungent mixture of the chemical and the irredeemably organic, and the door is usually kept closed, like Bluebeard's bloody chamber.

A few days after O'Neal turned thirty, in March, he threw a party for himself at his house for a couple of hundred friends, family members, and business associates. An archway of red balloons had been set up at the foot of the driveway, which was covered with a red carpet upon which Superman logos were projected in spinning light. The red carpet led into a large tent behind the house, above the tennis court, which was decorated with long tubular balloons in red and yellow and blue, twisted together like something from a medical diagram of the lymphatic system.

Large Superman logos hung from the tent's ceiling, and on either side of a DJ deck were two telephone booths with Superman logos on them. There were buffet tables piled with food: steaming lobster tails and a pyramid of shrimp; a birthday cake featuring a cardboard image of O'Neal in full Superman attire, swooping up through a basketball hoop. Guests could help themselves to Häagen-Dazs from a refrigerated cart, and order drinks from bars sponsored by Red Bull and E&J cognac. A cigar company had set up a table arrayed with different kinds of cigars, each of them bearing a paper ring printed with the words "Happy 30th Shaq."

O'Neal, who had a cigar clamped in his mouth, wore a gray leather suit with a three-quarter-length jacket. (The suit required 150 square feet of leather, the skins of about eighteen lambs.) He greeted his guests—his Lakers teammate Rick Fox and Fox's wife, the actress Vanessa Williams; Ray Lewis, the Baltimore Ravens linebacker; the actor Tom Arnold, who lives across the street; the rap musicians Lord Tariq and Peter Gunz; and any number of Shaq service-industry members, including his masseur and the guy who installed the audio and video equipment in his house—with unflagging enthusiasm, hugging the men, bending down low to kiss the women's cheeks. Guests wandered in and out of the house, past the triangular swimming pool on the patio, in which a surfboard decorated with an image of O'Neal's Lakers jersey floated, and into the kitchen, which was filled with gifts that he'd received: sugar cookies, a big toy truck, a box from the Sharper Image.

On the walls of the marble hallway leading out of the kitchen, there was bad basketball art—a painting of tall figures leaping around a basket, and another of an athlete's back as he holds a basketball on his shoulders, Atlas-like. There were photographs of O'Neal's children, and a framed clipping from the *Star* bearing the headline CAUGHT! SHAQ DATING UP A STORM WITH HALLE BERRY.

The living room, which has a view of the San Fernando Valley, is flanked by two fish tanks made from curving glass. The tanks are filled with brightly colored exotic fish, swimming flickeringly, and at one point in the evening O'Neal, coming into the house, found a few guests standing mesmerized in front of the tanks. He went behind a staircase that led off the hallway, where, hidden from view, was a smaller tank, filled with goldfish. He scooped into the goldfish tank with a net and filled a glass with slippery orange bodies. Then he climbed up a stepladder that was set alongside one of the big tanks, lifted its lid, and dumped in the goldfish. The angel fish and clown fish and puffer fish went wild, darting to swallow the flailing goldfish whole. A ruthless-looking barracuda snapped one up, and then went for the rebound and snared another. O'Neal looked extremely satisfied with the whole scene. "I love the sport of hunting," he said.

The host spent most of the night bopping among a crowd of his friends in the middle of the dance floor, head and shoulders and most of a torso above everyone around him. Halfway through the evening, the music was turned down, and O'Neal was summoned to the stage, where he sat in a chair and, along with everyone else, watched a video tribute devoted to the greatness of Shaq. There was O'Neal playing basketball at Louisiana State University, a spindly version of himself, breaking the hoop from the backboard. There was home-video footage of him on a beach, and playing with his kids, and dancing—to one Dr. Dre tune, he dropped to his knees, kicked his legs in the air behind him, and humped the carpet. There were also innumerable shots of him mooning the camera. The final image was of O'Neal, shirtless and sweaty, at the turntables; he unzipped his pants, shifted them gradually down his ample hips, hoisted his underwear up above his waist, and finally turned around and dropped his pants to show the camera his glistening rear. After the show was over, O'Neal stood up, unzipped his fly, zipped it up again, and said, "I never knew I had such a good ass until I saw that film. Damn, I'm sexy."

The reason O'Neal dedicated himself to the pursuit of excellence in basketball, he says, was to impress girls. "I was always the class clown, and always wanted everybody to like me," he told me recently. "Everyone else had a girlfriend, and how come I couldn't have a girlfriend?" We were at the Mondrian Hotel, in Los Angeles, where he was being photographed by ESPN while perched on top of a six-foot-tall flowerpot, a design feature of the hotel's pool area. When we sat down at a table to talk, O'Neal smashed his head against the light fixture hanging overhead. "I had to learn around age fifteen to accept my size," he said. "My father told me, 'You are going to be someone. Just keep playing and you are going to be a football player, a basketball player, or even a baseball player.' Around the age of thirteen, I got my name in the papers for basketball and the girls started liking me, and ever since then it's been nothing but up."

O'Neal gets his height from his mother's side of the family. Lucille O'Neal Harrison is six feet two inches tall, and her grandfather, who was a farmer in Georgia, was about six-ten. O'Neal met his great-grandfather once before he died, and says he is one of the people from history he'd most like to know. The others are Walter Matthau, because of the movie *The Bad News Bears* ("He was a drunk coach who got a bunch of misfit kids together—black kids, Chinese kids, girls—and they played baseball and won the championship"), and Redd Foxx, "because I used to watch *Sanford and Son* all the time, and laughter is the best stress reliever."

He credits Phil Harrison, his stepfather, actually, with having given him the emotional impetus to succeed in basketball. (Harrison married O'Neal's mother when Shaq was two. His biological father is Joe Toney, who, in 1994, appeared in the *National Enquirer* claiming paternity and thereafter did the talk-show rounds. O'Neal's response was to write a rap song called "Biological Didn't Bother.") Harrison, who was a sergeant in the Army, was a disciplinarian, the kind of father who wouldn't let O'Neal keep trophies in the house for fear that he would become conceited. O'Neal still gives all his trophies to Harrison, and he tends to treat older men with the utmost respect.

O'Neal's earliest years were spent in Newark, but when he was in the sixth grade the family was transferred to an Army base in Wildflecken,

Germany. There O'Neal started to play basketball seriously, and though he was not a prodigious talent, he worked hard and was unfeasibly tall. As O'Neal recounts in his autobiography, *Shaq Talks Back*, he was scouted by Dale Brown, the coach of LSU, who had come to Germany to give a basketball clinic. Brown asked how long the six-foot-nine-inch O'Neal had been in the Army; O'Neal replied that he was just fourteen. By the middle of O'Neal's sophomore year in high school, when he was six-eleven, the family had moved back to the United States, to San Antonio, where he was on his school's basketball team. From San Antonio, O'Neal went to LSU, and after three years there he opted for the NBA draft and signed, in 1992, with the Orlando Magic for forty million dollars over seven years, which was then the most lucrative contract in NBA history. O'Neal spent four years in Orlando, long enough to earn a reputation as a weak playoff player and to endure an ugly falling-out with his teammate Penny Hardaway. And yet there was no doubt that he had the potential to be one of the most formidable centers to play the game since Abdul-Jabbar, and even Bill Russell and Wilt Chamberlain. In 1996, Jerry Buss, the owner of the Lakers, and his general manager, Jerry West, lured O'Neal to Los Angeles, at a salary of $120 million over seven years—the biggest contract in the game.

By that time, O'Neal had started to make rap records for Jive—for example, *Shaq Diesel*, which included songs with titles such as "Shoot Pass Slam" and "(I Know I Got) Skillz"—and had played a genie in the movie *Kazaam*, one of a handful of films in which he demonstrated the limitations of his acting ability. He had not, however, helped Orlando win an NBA championship, and critics suggested that his proximity to Hollywood would lead to similar results for the Lakers. But O'Neal's performing career failed to take off; and his game improved when, in 1999, Phil Jackson, the former coach of the Chicago Bulls, took over the job of coaching the Lakers. Under Jackson, O'Neal started to play more of a team game, passing to other players rather than bullying his way to the hoop. In 2000, the team won its first championship since 1988, the era of Magic Johnson and Abdul-Jabbar.

Jackson is well-known for applying the principles of Zen to the game of basketball, and O'Neal says that Jackson's methods meshed with his own strategies for victory. "I control my dreams," O'Neal told me. "So-called educated people call it meditation, but I don't. I call it 'dreamful attraction.' The mind controls everything, so you just close your eyes and see yourself dribbling, see yourself shooting." Contrary to some reports, O'Neal says that Jackson has not induced the team to practice yoga. "We tried Tai Chi one year, but the guys didn't like it, because, even though it was stretching, it would make us tight," he said. "Anyway, I don't stretch. I just play."

O'Neal is regularly described as the league's most dominant player: There is no other single player who can match him physically, and there is no defensive strategy that another team can devise that will decisively shut him down. Jerry West told me, "If you could construct a basketball player physically, Shaq would be the model. He has this great size and incredible strength, but on top of that he has unbelievable balance, incredible footwork, and a great sense of where he is on the court." Most dominant isn't synonymous with best, however; the players who usually win that accolade are smaller, faster men like Kobe Bryant or Jason Kidd of the New Jersey Nets. And O'Neal's weaknesses, for all his power, are transparently evident. His free-throw average has been only around 50 percent for most of his career.

His detractors say that he is dominant only because of his size. Whenever *Slam*, whose readers are the young fans upon whom the game depends, puts O'Neal on the cover, the editors receive letters complaining that Shaq is just big and fat and boring. O'Neal's weight is given in the official statistics about the team as an implausible 315 pounds. (People close to Shaq claim that he sometimes hits 350.) When, in mid-March, I asked O'Neal what he weighed, he told me 338 pounds, though he said it in the slightly hesitant tone of a kid asserting that he has done his homework. "I'm just a big-boned guy," he said. "Muscle weighs more than fat, and a big guy has big muscles. People look at me and see this big guy and they think it's fat. How can I be fat and out of shape and do what I do? You could put me up against any athlete in the world, you could put them on a computerized diet, and on a treadmill and all that, and I will bust their ass."

Being called the most dominant rather than the best is fine with O'Neal. "They've changed the game because of me; other organizations whine and cry because of me," he said. "Being the best is too easy for me." His free-throw failings are spurs to his ambition, he says. "If I played the game I play and shot eighty-eight percent from the line, it would take away from my mental focus, because I would know how good I was and I wouldn't work so hard." (In fact, O'Neal has been making about 65 percent of his free throws during the current playoffs.) "I'm not allowed to be as dominant as I want to be," he told me. "I would probably average fifty points a game, twenty rebounds, and the opponents would foul out in the first or second quarter." O'Neal suspects that his game is being reined in by the NBA referees. "I guess they have to keep it even so that the viewers won't get bored," he said. David Stern, the NBA commissioner, recently acknowledged to the *Los Angeles Daily News* that it is difficult to know when to call a foul on Shaq, and said, "We used to get the same calls on Kareem and every other big man that's been as great as Shaq is."

NBA viewing figures are well down since their peak of 6.6 million at the height of Jordan's career. Last year, an average of four million people watched the regular season games on NBC. But a game in which O'Neal plays can sometimes make for dull viewing. His strengths aren't as thrilling to watch as those of a player who flies and leaps, and the defenses used against him slow everything down so much that a viewer's attention can dwindle. The most notorious of these is the Hack-a-Shaq, in which opposing players make repeated fouls on O'Neal by throwing their arms around his waist, hoping to regain possession of the ball at little cost by sending him to the free-throw line. Phil Jackson agrees that O'Neal is expected to play by different rules from everyone else. "It's totally unfair, but the referees have to be," Jackson told me. "Everybody fouls Shaq all the time, because they know the referees can't call every foul that is created against him. There isn't a shot in which he's not fouled except maybe twice a game. There are guys hitting him on the way up, hitting him at the top, knocking him around." O'Neal says, "The beating that I take is like wrestling. It ain't even basketball sometimes. I'm the NBA's best WWF wrestler, and I'm the WWF's best NBA player."

O'Neal has a tattoo on his right arm that says "Against the Law," and, since he's famously supportive of the uniformed services, I asked him what he meant by it. "It's against the law to be this talented, this beautiful, this smart, this sexy," he said. "I don't mean penal-code law. I mean laws of nature."

Like a Hollywood movie or a mass-market paperback, every sports season needs a narrative of conflict and resolution, and in the 2000–01 season the story was the rivalry and animosity between O'Neal and Kobe
Bryant. The narrative is crafted by the Lakers' beat reporters, who attend around a hundred games a season—hanging out in the locker
rooms for their appointed forty-five minutes before the game—and
show up at countless closed practice sessions. The structure of team
coverage creates what a therapist would diagnose as a cycle of depen-
dency and resentment on the part of the reporters, who are a group of
mostly smallish men obliged to wait around grudgingly for a bunch of
mostly huge men to stoop and speak to them. The reporters exercise
their own power, of course, in making a drama out of the daily shifts in
locker-room mood, which in turn earns them the occasional enmity of
the players. O'Neal barely talks to the press for weeks at a time, or does
what he calls "SHAM-ming them"—giving them the Short Answer
Method. "They're yellow journalists," he said to me one day. "Don't
focus on whether Shaq is having problems with Phil, or whether Shaq
is liking Kobe or not, or what Rick and Vanessa are doing—if we're a
great team, say we're a great team. I think they get so bored with us
winning all the time, they focus on that other stuff."

But the Shaq-Kobe feud was genuine, and it provided excellent copy.
O'Neal and Bryant had never got along. Bryant, who came to the
league a polished eighteen-year-old from a wealthy family, seemed to
find O'Neal's antic goofiness distasteful; O'Neal thought Bryant was a
selfish player who was interested only in demonstrating his own virtu-
osity and was insufficiently deferential. O'Neal would say ominous
things like "If the big dog don't get fed, the house won't get guarded,"
after nights of what he saw as Kobe hogging the ball, and Kobe would
say to reporters, "Turn my game down? I need to turn it up." The whole
affair culminated, happily enough for the team and its chroniclers, in a
reconciliation sentimental enough for the most golden-hued of Hollywood dramas, with Bryant shucking off his natural aloofness both on
and off the court—he started to laugh at teammates' jokes on the bus
instead of listening to his Walkman—and with O'Neal referring to the
quicksilver Bryant as "my idol." (The saga forms the basis of a new
book, *Ain't No Tomorrow: Kobe, Shaq and the Making of a Lakers Dynasty*, by Elizabeth Kaye.) This season, Bryant and O'Neal have been
coexisting quite chummily. O'Neal took a few shots at Bryant while de-

livering an impromptu rap to the crowd at his birthday party, castigating him for not showing up ("Kobe, if you hear me, I'm talking about your ass," and so on), but the razzing seemed good-natured.

This season's master narrative has been Shaq vs. Shaq—O'Neal's battle with his own body and its ailments. Chronic pain in an arthritic toe and other injuries that have cropped up have been endlessly inquired after by the beat reporters. "We started out with the small toe on his left foot—that was getting to him early—and at some point in the season we all made the transition to the right big toe," Tim Brown, who covers the team for the *Los Angeles Times,* explained. The paper has been running headlines like LAKERS' BIG HOPES REST IN SHAQ'S BIG TOE, and reams of newsprint have been devoted to the orthotics that have been devised by O'Neal's podiatrist, Robert Mohr, to alleviate the strain on the big toe. Last week, the papers reported that not only had O'Neal cut his finger while playing against the San Antonio Spurs in the first game of the Western Conference semifinals but he had also required stitches to mend a cut sustained earlier that day at home while he was pretending to be Spider-Man.

This season, O'Neal has thought a lot about the toll the game is taking on his body. "I feel beat up," he told me a few days after his birthday. "I'm probably one of the only guys in history who has taken a pounding night in and night out." He was sitting on a massage bench after a practice session, and he rubbed his arms and slapped his biceps as if he were looking over a recalcitrant piece of machinery. "With the last two championships, afterward I just had to sit down for a week and do nothing, like this"—and he struck a catatonic pose, stiff-limbed and staring into space—"and let all the injuries go away. And then there's another week to do this"—he stretched his thick, muscled arms above his head, exposing the spacious geography of his armpits—"and then, by the time my shit is all gone, we've only got another week until training camp." He was worried, too, about the effects of the anti-inflammatory drugs he was taking. "They are the same drugs they say might have messed up Alonzo Mourning's kidneys," he said, referring to the Miami center who missed most of last season as a result of kidney disease.

Rick Fox, O'Neal's teammate, coming off the court after a practice in New Jersey a few weeks ago, said, "Shaq is dealing with injuries that he never thought he'd have to deal with. This is new to him. Even Superman had his kryptonite, but after ten years there are only so many hits of kryptonite you can take." One day, O'Neal told me, mournfully, "When I was Kobe's age, I could play a magnificent game and stay out all night, but now I am old, and my toe is killing me." O'Neal, whose contract expires in 2006, has started to say that he may have only two more years in the game, though in 1999 he told Slam that he thought he might be out by the time he reached thirty.

O'Neal will be under pressure to keep playing. Jerry West told me, "If I ever see him retire early, I'll kill him. You play until you can't play. This is a tough guy, and he can play through things that mortal people wouldn't want to." Sometimes O'Neal talks about himself this way, too. Toward the end of this year's regular season, he was out for two games, with a sprained wrist, causing the reporters to shift their focus from foot to arm. The Lakers lost both games, and just before the next game, in which O'Neal was to return, against Miami, I asked him whether he felt responsible for being hurt or whether he felt as if his body were betraying him as well as the team.

He rejected the premise of the question. "I don't get hurt—I get taken out," he said. "My wrist is hurting for a reason—it's not hurting because I fell on it. My stomach is hurting for a reason. My knee is hurting for a reason. I don't get hurt, baby, I get taken out. You can't hurt this"—and, with that, he flexed his left biceps, like a bodybuilder, and, with one huge fist, banged on his Superman tattoo. Then he went out and scored forty points against Miami, leading the Lakers to victory.

In other moods, though, O'Neal admits to his own mortality. "Everything hurts," he told me. "A pinch is a pinch. If you pinch an elephant, it will hurt him. Pain is pain, and pain doesn't care how big you are or how strong you are." One day, he said, "You know who my favorite basketball player is? People might be surprised when they hear this. It's Dave Bing." I said I didn't know who Dave Bing was. "I don't know who he is, either," said O'Neal. "Who did he play for? Detroit? He's retired now, and he owns a big steel factory in Detroit." Bing left the game in 1978, and subsequently became a Hall of Famer, and the winner, in 1984, of the National Minority Small Business Person of the Year and the National Minority Supplier of the Year awards.

O'Neal says he's starting to develop business interests that have nothing to do with basketball: He told me he'd bought a couple of car washes and strip malls, and had just signed a deal for some Burger King franchises. "Basketball is cool, but we can't do it forever. After basketball, Dave Bing is my guy," he said. "Those players who are smart enough save their money, so that after you stop playing you can keep it going—that is what I plan on doing, like the Kennedy money." I asked O'Neal whether he saw himself as Joe Kennedy, a patriarch establishing a dynasty. "No, I'm the one who passed away in a plane crash—what's his name?" he said. "The good-looking one. That's who I am: good-looking, educated."

On those few evenings and afternoons when O'Neal is not playing basketball or filming a commercial or visiting the children's ward of a hospital or otherwise engaging in the various duties of an NBA superstar, he is often in a classroom, studying penal-code law. O'Neal has always been fascinated by the police—both Mike Parris, his business manager, and Jerome Crawford, who serves as his bodyguard, are retired police officers—and some years ago O'Neal decided that he wanted to train as a cop himself, with the intention of pursuing a law enforcement career after he leaves basketball, along with developing his business interests. He is already an honorary deputy for the Orange County sheriff's office in Orlando, where he once surprised an international group of SWAT team officers who were performing a practice exercise of freeing a hostage from a bus by playing the hostage.

In Los Angeles, he is training to become an auxiliary member of the Port of Los Angeles Police, and he drives around with a senior officer, learning about how the law works. O'Neal frequently practices his law enforcement techniques on his teammates and the Lakers' staff: Mark Madsen, a six-foot-nine-inch, 236-pound twenty-six-year-old, who has become a close friend of O'Neal's since joining the Lakers, last season, told me, "He will come up to me and put me in all these police grips. He'll say, 'Which wrist did you have surgery on?' and then he'll do it on the other wrist. If I put up any sort of fight, I'm on the ground, quick."

O'Neal hasn't arrested anyone yet, but he does horse around by threatening to make citizen's arrests on Lakers employees, and regularly orders members of the team's support staff to stand against the wall with their legs spread. It's unlikely that he will ever be a beat cop, since what he really wants to do is be a chief of police or run for sheriff, either in Louisiana or in Orlando: "Sheriff is an elective position, and I don't just want to be a figurehead. And I don't want to win because I'm Shaq, but because I have the knowledge and understand what is going on." O'Neal generally avoids politics (though he recently went to a Nation of Islam meeting to hear Louis Farrakhan speak, and says that he is a friend of the Farrakhan family). He says that he wouldn't run for sheriff on either a Republican or a Democratic ticket, but as an Independent, "like Ross Perot." He told me, "Of course, I am not going to stop crime, make it zero percent, but I would try."

When O'Neal returns to Orlando this summer, with or without a third championship ring, there will be plenty to do. He may undergo surgery on his foot, which would put him out of action for six to eight weeks. "Without any surgery, nothing is going to change," Robert Mohr, the podiatrist, says. "For ordinary motion, you need about sixty degrees of pain-free movement in your toe. For jumping or running, you need close to ninety degrees. He has maybe twenty or thirty degrees. You imagine a three-hundred-and-fifty-pound body coming down on that joint."

Fortunately, if O'Neal is recovering from surgery he will have the solace of various home improvements that are under way in Orlando, where his house measures thirty-six thousand square feet, and faces four hundred yards of waterfront. He has already added an eight-thousand-square-foot gym and a regulation-size basketball court, and contractors have started on the other side of the house, adding a new swimming pool and another nine thousand square feet of living space, including seven new bedrooms (O'Neal already has a master bedroom with a circular bed measuring twenty feet across), a recreation room, a cigar room, a movie theater, and a private dance club with a state-of-the-art DJ booth.

Injuries permitting, O'Neal will also be able to engage in one of his favorite activities—going on the Skycoaster, an amusement park ride in Orlando, which combines the sensations of hang gliding, bungee jumping, and skydiving. Riders are strapped into harnesses and hoisted to the top of a hundred-foot tower, where they pull a release cord that puts them into a pendulum swing, above an expanse that is the size of a football field, at about sixty miles an hour. The sensation is as close to flying as anyone who is not Superman or Michael Jordan is likely to experience, and O'Neal is fanatical about it.

"It's like a roller coaster, and it is dangerous—if that cord breaks, you can die," O'Neal told me. "It's scary. It feels like you're actually flying. It's like you are falling from the top of a building, and someone grabs you and says, 'OK, I ain't going to let you die.' And then they swing you—whoosh. I go on it all the time." One evening, he flew for two hours, in his own, customized harness; and when other would-be Skycoasters asked for his autograph he offered instead to take them on a ride with him. So all evening astonished patrons stood in line to fly with Shaq, waiting for their chance to swoop through the air, the kind of thing that happens in dreams.

2002

PART THREE

PERSONAL BEST

"There's your problem."

"*I think you just missed something. The ball went up
in the air and somebody caught it and the crowd's yelling like mad.*"

DANGEROUS GAME

NICK PAUMGARTEN

In the ski-bum brain, the chance to ski with a magus like Andrew McLean is the equivalent of an invitation for a night on the town with Don Juan. The allure is great, but there's always a possibility that the excursion will not end well. McLean is a ski mountaineer; he climbs mountains and then skis down them. He is especially fond of skiing chutes—steep, narrow flumes of snow that plunge like elevator shafts through otherwise impassable terrain. Last fall, before he and I met, he'd sent me a copy of *The Chuting Gallery*, his self-published guide to the chutes in his home range, the Wasatch Mountains, which are just east of Salt Lake City. He had inscribed it: "I'm looking forward to skiing with you this winter. If you die skiing one of these, I promise it will be renamed in your honor!" I can't say that the prospect hadn't crossed my mind.

McLean has a bit of a history. One of the runs described in *The Chuting Gallery* is named Roman's, after McLean's friend Roman Latta, who, on an outing with him there in 1993, set off an avalanche in which he was buried and killed. Latta was the first of four men who have died while climbing or skiing with McLean. The most famous was Alex Lowe, who was considered by many to be the best mountaineer in the world; Lowe disappeared in a giant avalanche on Shishapangma, in Tibet, in 1999, when he and McLean and others were attempting to become the first Americans to ski a peak higher than eight thousand meters. In all, McLean has lost more than a dozen friends to the mountains—"lost to the mountains" being a locution favored by alpinists, as though skiing or climbing were a sacrificial rite, instead of a voluntary act.

My family has a bit of history, too. My father's father, Harald, was a devoted alpinist, as well as a ski racer and jumper who competed for Austria in the 1928 and 1932 Winter Olympics. After the 1932 Games, in Lake Placid, he stayed in America. He briefly held a job at a bank in New York (the story goes that on his lunch breaks he'd head out to Central Park, remove his suit, hang it on a tree, and go running in his underwear) before deciding that the office life was not for him. He moved to New England to teach skiing, which is how he met my grandmother, a Philadelphia society girl who was among the early wave of modish flatlanders to take up the sport under the tutelage of the Austrians. In the summers, my grandfather went on expeditions to the Fairweather Range, in Alaska. He lived in Philadelphia during the war, but afterward he began spending his winters in St. Anton, in Austria, in order to ski. He was killed in an avalanche there in 1952, when my father, the youngest of five children, was six. Twenty years later, one of my father's sisters died in an avalanche while skiing. She had two children, ages seven and three. Since then, there have been a few other incidents. My father was nearly killed in an avalanche while I was skiing with him, and between us we have witnessed a fair number of slides. There was also a disturbing encounter with a crevasse—a snow bridge gave way, and I fell in. I hung by my arms over a void until two guides pulled me out.

Friends and relatives treat this high incidence of snow trouble as evidence of a family curse, or plain idiocy. The weight of these opinions is such that every time I head out on a trip that involves the kind of skiing that can lead to trouble—glaciers, powder fields, steeps—a certain premonitory queasiness sneaks up on me. The anxiety that comes of tempting fate, especially in pursuit of such an indulgence, helps generate dreams of death by suffocation or falling. But in daylight disquiet gives way to delight, and I find myself doing things that may or may not be dangerous, half aware that at any second my situation, as well as that of my wife and children, could dramatically change. It's a fraught kind of bliss.

A year and a half ago, I read a story in the magazine *Skiing* titled "11

Excuses for NOT Skiing with Andrew McLean." One was "He'll dust you." Another was "Tragedy dogs him." Perhaps with that in mind, I found myself, within minutes of meeting McLean, telling him about my family, under the guise of trying to persuade him to take it easy on me. (A more direct approach had failed. "Don't know what you think you signed up for here, Nick. You're with the wrong guy.") He seemed to home in on the infatuation, rather than on its consequences. "Sounds like you've got skiing in the blood," he said. But later, when I passed along the additional piece of information that my great-aunt—my grandfather's sister—a world-champion racer and fervent mountain girl, had been crippled in the fifties by a runaway ski, he said, "Maybe I should be a little concerned about skiing with *you*."

McLean's approach to peril is to see humor in it. Certainly, close calls can be comic, and McLean can laugh, in the way of soldiers and crooks, over many of his near-misses. There was the time he cartwheeled down five hundred vertical feet of cliffs, only to land upright on his skis, unaccountably alive and intact, or the time a boulder fell and pulverized itself on a ledge just above his head. Although there isn't really anything funny about avalanches, his manner of survival, in a few of the half dozen or so that he has been caught in—clinging to the trunk of an aspen tree, high above the ground, or buried upside down, with his legs sticking straight out of the snow—can sound cartoonish. The only thing that spoils the Wile E. Coyote effect (he is forty-three years old, yet he has never so much as broken a bone while skiing) is that a number of his narrow escapes have coincided with the deaths of other people. This is something he doesn't much like to discuss.

In *The Chuting Gallery,* McLean inventories the hazards of his favorite routes with a cheek that, in the solemn and superstitious realm of mountain chronicles, borders on blasphemy. In some quarters, it is considered an irresponsible book, as appropriate as a guide to robbing banks. The northeast couloir of a peak called the Pfeifferhorn, McLean writes, is "more fun than running with scissors, sticking paperclips into electrical sockets or taping firecrackers to a cat's tail." Of Hellgate Couloir, a run that involves rappelling down two cliffs, he writes, "Short, stout, steep and scary. What more could you ask for?"

The Chuting Gallery begins with a disclaimer, from McLean's mother: "The fact that this is a 'guidebook' does not mean that you, the reader, should take it seriously. Obviously, no one in their right mind would ski this stuff—and you shouldn't either." By "this stuff," she means terrain that is challenging enough to fit under the standard definition of extreme skiing, first codified by the American steep-skiing pioneer Chris Landry: "If you fall, you die." McLean ascends quickly, sometimes with the aid of ropes, ice axes, and crampons. And he descends carefully. He is not a hot dog. What he's after is an elusive blend of anxiety and exhilaration—a level of difficulty that requires physical and analytical prowess, as well as self-discipline and imagination. He also wants to be first. It's the adventurer's injunction: Do it before anyone else does, or at least do it differently. His calling takes him to such remote places as Antarctica and the Himalayas. He goes on two big expeditions a year. This month, McLean and three friends are going to Alaska for four weeks in an effort to become the first people ever to ski the Archangel Ridge of Mount Foraker, a sister peak of Mount McKinley. It is a gruesome and isolated route, eleven thousand vertical feet—dark, cold, high, scary. It has been *climbed* only twice before. What's more, to reach Foraker the group will have to climb up and ski down another difficult peak, in order to avoid sixteen river crossings, not to mention bears.

There are, of course, many extreme skiers in the world, and many mountain climbers, and quite a few who combine the skills of both. The game has changed since my grandfather's day. The vogue is to refer to them as "adventure athletes." They star in films, have sponsorships, and market themselves aggressively, inspiring an ever-growing array of imitators who fan out into the hills and devour fresh terrain, like so many Scrubbing Bubbles. McLean, however, is a true shellback. He is as hungry for accomplishment as the rest, yet he has learned to balance the ragtag joys of wandering the mountains with the requirements of making a living at it. He'd be doing what he's doing even if nobody was watching. In some respects, he is not an extreme athlete at all but just a lucid and devoted rambler, with high standards and a low pulse—a descendant as much of Kit Carson as of Harry Houdini.

On my first morning in Utah, I met McLean in a parking lot at the base of Little Cottonwood Canyon, which cuts east into the Wasatch, about a half hour south of Salt Lake City. Little Cottonwood is home to the Snowbird and Alta ski areas and the gateway to a vast array of backcountry terrain. It is known for having the best powder snow in the world.

McLean has the trim and sinewy build of a Sherpa (he is five feet ten and weighs 145 pounds) and a rubbery, slightly hunched posture, but his bright blue eyes, bobblehead proportions, and anachronistic helmet of light brown hair give him an impish appearance. In warmer months, he likes to ride a unicycle on mountain trails. There is relish in his smile; he likes to say, in jest, "It isn't fun until someone gets hurt," and he enjoys watching lesser men attempt to keep up with him. He once wrote, "There is nothing finer in life than enjoying a chilled tin of congealed octopus while listening to the moans and groans of fellow human beings . . . as they struggle on a slick 45-degree track." The sado-stoicism is not bigheaded or bullying; it's how he conveys to his partners his own particular blend of enthusiasm and forbearance. It is a more garrulous version of the ethic you come across in the classic mountaineering tales of Chris Bonnington, in which the climbers, many of them former British military men, invariably respond to serious trouble—storms, avalanches, broken bones—by brewing up a pot of tea.

McLean was accompanied by Polly Samuels, his fiancée; they were to be married in two months. Samuels, thirty-five years old and a lawyer in the Utah attorney general's office, has red hair and an aspect of seriousness. She has become a formidable skier in her own right; last year, she was the North American women's champion in randonee racing—long slogs up and down mountains in touring gear. (Among the men, McLean usually finishes in the top three or four.) McLean drove. As he navigated the winding road up the canyon, he craned his neck and pointed out some favorite chutes, which coursed through the cliffs on either side like waterfalls. They were avalanche paths, basically, but if you have a taste for such things you begin to view all terrain in terms of what is plausible and you imagine leaving tracks everywhere—on distant peaks or a neighbor's snowy lawn—much as fishermen cannot regard a body of water without thinking of casting a line.

That morning, we took it easy: We started at the Alta ski area, where in order to gain altitude we took a chairlift, and to warm up we did two intermediate runs on machine-groomed snow. McLean, an advocate of leg power, doesn't often consent to such indignities. But after a couple of hours we ventured into more McLeanian terrain—Main Baldy

Chute, a long, regal cataract that, being avalanche-prone, is rarely open. It happened also to be the site of his conversion to chuting, fourteen years earlier. The run required a half-hour hike and several dozen compact turns on old chalky snow, the joy deriving, in part, from the sensation of simultaneously resisting and submitting to gravity. McLean's skiing style was tight and neat, but deliberately functional and in no obvious way vain. At the bottom, McLean called out, "Main Baldy—check!" as though he were planning to have me ski every chute in his book.

We went to the base of the mountain and retrieved more gear. We were using randonee equipment, which weighs less than standard alpine equipment and is designed for going uphill as well as down. For the ascent, the heel of the binding detaches from the ski, as with a cross-country or telemark ski, and you stick a climbing skin, which is a reusable adhesive strip with mohair or nylon on one side, to the base of each ski (people used to use real seal skins); the grain prevents you from sliding backward. To descend, you peel off the skins and lock down the heel. Each of us wore an avalanche beacon—a transceiver about the size of a Walkman, which sends out a signal in case of burial—and a pack that contained a probe and a shovel, for locating and digging out a buried companion.

We left Alta and hiked up a ridge for a half hour or so to a place called Wolverine Cirque, an amphitheater of chutes guarded by cornices. McLean dropped into one called the Scythe. He jumped up and down on a pillow of snow near the top, to see that it was stable, then hopped back and forth down the slope before skirting under an outcropping, in case the next skier, me, set off a slide. I did not. The snow was deep and a little windblown: not bad. After another pitch, the chute opened onto a bowl that looked like a place where you didn't want to hang around. It was where Roman Latta, among others over the years, had been buried. We crossed a basin, skinned up for forty-five minutes, then skied down to Alta.

Back at my desk five days later, I got an e-mail from McLean: "Utah had its first avalanche fatality the day after you left"—the first, that is, of the season. It had occurred at Wolverine. He sent a photograph of the accident site, with a diagram of our route and the victim's. They weren't far apart. "It turns out there was one other fatality, two other people missing, and one person who was buried and dug out." Also, he said, a place called the Meadow Chutes, where we had spent my last morning, going up and down, rapturously, during a snowstorm, had avalanched—"ripped out wall to wall"—right after we were there.

My aunt, whose name was Meta Burden, was skiing alone when she died. She had had an argument, so she did a rash thing. She skied into Cristy Gully, which in 1972 lay outside the area boundary at Aspen Mountain. Half a foot of new snow had fallen atop ten inches of two-day-old snow, and apparently there had been a great deal of avalanche activity in the area that morning. But she was a headstrong woman, confident in her abilities. She had lived in Aspen for four years, and was intermittently deranged by anger over the encroachment of more and more people into terrain that she liked to consider her own.

That evening, her husband reported her missing, and at half past six, ski patrollers began a search in the dark. They followed her tracks into Cristy Gully. There is an account of the search in *The Snowy Torrents,* a volume assembled by government avalanche forecasters, with evaluations of avalanche accidents in the United States. The rescuers, it says,

> probed and scuffed in the runout zone, and within 45 minutes they found one ski and one pole. Coleman lanterns were set up at the points where Burden's tracks ended and where the clues were found. . . . At 2230 hours, Burden was found on the first pass of the probe line 60 feet above her ski and pole. Efforts at resuscitation and heart massage were unsuccessful. Her body was buried in 3 feet of snow.

It appeared that she had died of suffocation. The report noted that she was an experienced skier, and concluded, "Burden knew the dangers involved and ignored them."

The novelist James Salter wrote about my aunt's death, some years ago, in an essay called "The Skiing Life." Like many men, he seems to have been somewhat smitten by her. He called her a "goddess." "There was a woman I knew who used to ski every day, all season long, whatever the weather, whatever the conditions," he wrote. "Later someone told me that she died on the very same day her father had, years before. I never bothered to confirm it, but I think it must be true; I think it was part of the pact." It was not true. The pact, though, I could understand.

Her father had died while skiing alone, too. The night before, he had remarked to his sister that he'd witnessed a lot of avalanches that afternoon and that he'd have to be careful. (His family was back home in Philadelphia; he had wanted Meta and her twin sister to cut school and spend the winter with him in Austria, but my grandmother had said no.) Still, the next afternoon, after a day out with a friend, my grandfather decided to take one last run by himself. An avalanche caught him in a gully between the Osthang and the old Kandahar downhill course; when rescuers found his body, they concluded, from the tranquil look on his face, that he had broken his neck.

This winter, I stumbled on a third account of my aunt's accident, a 1987 poem called "The Death of Meta Burden in an Avalanche," by Frederick Seidel. It is a difficult poem, as impenetrable as *The Snowy Torrents* is precise. "You are reborn flying to outski / The first avalanche each spring, / And buried alive." Seidel, who, it turns out, also met and admired my aunt, seems to imagine what it feels like to be entombed in snow: "I cannot see. / I will not wake though it's a dream. / I move my head from side to side. / I cannot move." Later, he writes, "Everything fits my body perfectly now that I'm about to disappear."

It is, not surprisingly, a grim way to go. If you trigger an avalanche, there are measures you can take to avoid burial, or at least to improve the odds of surviving. The first thing to do is attempt to ski out of it, although as the slab of snow breaks from the layer beneath it and begins to move, accelerating down the mountain face like a book sliding off a tilted table, it becomes impossible for a skier to generate enough speed or change direction. Within seconds, the slab degenerates into a whirlwind. The snow has astonishing power, and as it rips off your gear and throws you into a tumble you should thrash and swim, in order to stay near the surface. Any attempt to get one good last breath will likely result in a mouthful of snow. Snow crams into your ears and under your eyelids. You may be dashed into a tree or a rock, but the force of the snow alone can break your leg or neck. As the slide slows, you are supposed to cup your hands in front of your mouth to create a pocket of air. Your chances improve if you are head up and face up—and if some part of you is visible to others, if there are others—but this choice is not yours. As the snow comes to a stop, it is like cement. The weight of it can press your last breath out of you, like a python. Your little breathing pocket, if you have one, will soon become carbon dioxide or a block of ice. After five minutes, the odds of survival drop swiftly. You pray that someone digs you out.

Every year nearly two hundred people are caught in avalanches in the United States. On average, about thirty of them die. The fatality rate has risen steadily since 1991. An increasing percentage of the victims are snowmobilers, who engage in a practice called high-marking, competing to see who can cut a track highest on a steep slope. Still, with improvements in gear and a trend toward backcountry exploration, more and more skiers and snowboarders are venturing out into terrain where survival depends, to a certain degree, on luck.

"Nobody goes out to die," Jill Fredston, an avalanche specialist in Alaska, told me. "Everyone goes out in pursuit of life. We make a ton of mistakes, but we usually get away with them. Luck is negative reinforcement. And you have probability and complacency working against you."

Last winter, Mike Elggren, a forty-one-year-old friend of McLean's, was caught in a slide while backcountry skiing in British Columbia. He was skinning up a slope with ten friends and three guides. At one point, one of the guides decided that she didn't like where they were. She took two steps, and the whole slope jigsawed above them—a molten acre. Elggren was shoved forward and sucked downhill, head first. His skis pulled him deeper. "I looked up to see where I was, and the lights went out," Elggren told me. "I got crushed. The pressure was tremendous. As the snow stopped, it made a real squeaky sound." His hand was in front of his face, but he couldn't see it. His nose and mouth were choked with snow. He was indignant at first, incredulous that this should happen to him. "That gave way to utter panic. I was screaming. I remember not being embarrassed to be screaming like a little girl. I wanted to flail, but I was pinned." After a moment, he regained some composure. "My brain wouldn't allow me to have any hope, the situation was so dire. I was rebreathing my carbon dioxide. My diaphragm and lungs were crushed. And then I started going away. I made my peace with the world. I was sad for the people up top and for my family. I was thinking of my parents and my brother and sisters, and my dog. Then I just went away. It felt like fading into black velvet."

Elggren's friends, some of whom had been partially buried and had dug themselves out, picked up his beacon signal. They were extraordinarily efficient, taking turns digging, but he was buried head down, six feet deep. When they got to him, ten minutes had passed, and he wasn't breathing. It took twenty minutes to resuscitate him by mouth-to-mouth. He remembers coming to and wondering why everyone was making such a fuss. They built a sled out of their backpacks, and towed him a mile or so back to a hut, where a helicopter was waiting. Aside from ligament damage to both knees, he seems to be fine. He has gone backcountry skiing regularly this winter (although not with McLean: "Andrew's on a different plane. He's so damn badass"). After the accident, Elggren's mother pleaded with him to give up backcountry skiing, but, he said, "Luckily, she came around to a more rational point of view." A few weeks ago, he returned to British Columbia to repeat last year's trip—same guide, same friends, same hut.

One spring day, when I was eleven, my father and I were skiing off-piste (off the marked trails) in Verbier, Switzerland. The conditions were exquisite but dodgy—a half meter of fresh snow warming in the sun—and my father, realizing abruptly that we were in a place we shouldn't have been (always this belated moment of recognition), decided that we would traverse, one at a time, to more moderately pitched terrain. I stayed behind on a ridge, as he started across the top of a gully. Then the whole slope seemed to explode, and he disappeared. In those days, I had no experience with avalanches, only a dim sense that they killed Paumgartens, so I failed to keep an eye on him or to take any precautions of my own. Avalanche safety equipment wasn't widely used back then; anyway, we didn't have any. For several minutes, I assumed that he was gone (it seemed fitting that he would be) and sat crying in the snow until I heard him calling my name. I made it down in time to see a snow-splattered ghoul stumbling out of a vast field of debris. The avalanche had carried him a few hundred yards, and then, as it slowed, poured over a bump in the terrain, which caused him to pop up to the surface. The slide was a big one: he was lucky; we were lucky. He was beaten up but all right. When Meta's twin heard about the accident, she wrote him an angry letter. Except for my father, my mother—whose feelings about all this are rather complicated—and their two sons, the family had quit this kind of skiing. My uncle, for example, tends to ski in blue jeans and stick to marked trails. ("I like the groomed part, the avenues," he says.) But my father did not give it up, although he did resolve always to hire a guide if he was going to ski off-piste. In the years since, I have been more than happy to accompany him.

Skiing, McLean wrote me once, "is like some form of religious practice or martial arts discipline." Years of devotion lead to proficiency, which yields a sense of ease and a chance at transcendence. McLean started on the path at Alta; he was born in Salt Lake City. One of his earliest ski memories is of a man breaking his femur on the rope tow at the Alta Lodge. In his recollection, the bone ripped through the man's pant leg, but he was laughing, because he was drunk. McLean's father was an ophthalmologist and a devoted sailor, and the family spent several years trying to find a town where he could both practice medicine and get out on the water. Salt Lake was not the place. They moved around for a few years—Vermont, Connecticut, Florida, Haiti—and then settled in Seattle. McLean's mother taught skiing nearby, at Alpental, in the Cascades. McLean quickly progressed to a point where she had to make a deal with him: She'd buy him a season pass if he promised to ski one run with her a year. He tended to wait until the last day.

As a kid, McLean was an experimental prankster, a troublemaker of the promising kind. He owned a welding torch and used it both to build go-carts and to fill bread bags with oxyacetylene gas, which he and his younger brother would then place in mailboxes and blow up using fuses made of paper. "We eventually worked our way up to Hefty trash bags, which were deafening," he recalled. "Come to think of it, that might be a good idea for do-it-yourself backcountry avalanche bombs." (Explosives are commonly used at ski areas to set off controlled avalanches.)

He went to the Rhode Island School of Design, where he studied to become an industrial designer. His roommate there happened to be an avid rock climber from Oregon, who began teaching McLean how to climb. Rhode Island is not known for its mountains, but the two of them made the most of the available terrain. On one occasion, they were arrested for trespassing when the police found them dangling from a rope on an abandoned railroad bridge. On another occasion, campus police caught McLean on the roof of the museum ("It had this perfect chimney") and mistook his bag of climbing chalk for cocaine. While at RISD, he fashioned a device that he called the Talon, a three-pronged steel-plated climbing aid, which he eventually sold to Black Diamond, a climbing-equipment company. Six years later, after jobs designing medical equipment and boats, he was hired by Black Diamond, and he moved back to Salt Lake, where the company was based, and began designing technical gear—cams, carabiners, crampons, ice axes. Many of his inventions, including the Talon, are still widely used.

McLean left Black Diamond a few years ago in order to focus on skiing—a job does get in the way—but he still designs equipment for a number of companies on a freelance basis. When I visited him, he was working on avalanche safety products and ice climbing equipment; he was also helping a friend design giant dish antennas for the military. Then there's the money he gets from speeches and from writing for climbing and skiing magazines. Last year, he worked as an avalanche forecaster for the Forest Service but found the job constricting. His superiors disapproved of steep skiing, and he felt called upon to preach a gospel of caution that he did not wholeheartedly subscribe to. Now he pursues what he calls a "low-cost lifestyle." He said, "I haven't heard of any other professional ski mountaineers."

Black Diamond, in the early nineties, was a breeding ground for amateur ski mountaineers, foremost among them Alex Lowe. It was Lowe who introduced McLean to a mode of skiing that employed the tools and techniques of climbing, as European alpinists had been doing for decades. "More than anyone, he opened my eyes to what was possible on skis," McLean said. Their first outing together was to Main Baldy Chute, before Alta opened for the year. They started out at 5 A.M. and descended at dawn, in thigh-deep powder. When they were done, they were set upon by ski patrolmen on snowmobiles, who informed them that the patrol was bombing the chute that morning, to make it slide, and that Lowe and McLean were lucky not to have been blown to pieces by a Howitzer shell. McLean was hooked.

In a foreword to *The Chuting Gallery*, Lowe describes "a loose group of twisted individuals" who several days a week would convene in his kitchen at three in the morning and, to his wife's dismay ("Is this normal!!?"), head off to climb a chute or a peak, then ski down at sunrise and go to work, glowing with accomplishment and stinking of sweat. This regimen, which McLean still adheres to (minus the going-to-work part), was known as dawn patrol.

"You could always spot another chute or two in the distance that needed to be skied," McLean said. "I kept at it for a few years, thinking that I had almost ticked them all off, before realizing that there was no end to them. Some were bigger, steeper, or more classic than others, but there were hundreds of them in the Wasatch and then a few million more around the world."

"The skiing consumed us," Mark Holbrook, a former Black Diamond engineer, told me. "That maybe led to our divorces." (McLean's first marriage, to a graphic designer from Long Island whom he met at RISD, ended eight years ago.)

McLean would like, on his deathbed, to be able to look at a globe and know that he had been everywhere. "It's getting harder and harder to find big classic lines that haven't been skied," he said. "They're a precious commodity." The conquest game can get competitive. Exotic places—the Kamchatka peninsula or Ellesmere Island—catch on, and the athletes pour in. It is difficult to stay ahead of the Scrubbing Bubbles. Sometimes a team spends years planning an expedition to an obscure peak, only to find another team there upon arrival. When I was in Utah, McLean said that he and a nineteen-year-old acolyte named Dylan Freed had recently found a chute in the Wasatch that had never been skied. They had christened it Project Schnozzle. He revealed the location to no one, not even to Polly Samuels. "It takes four hours to get there, and it's only five hundred feet of vertical," he said. "You've got to really want it." Last month, McLean went and did it by himself. "The Schnozzle has fallen," he wrote me.

In 2002, McLean and a Black Diamond sales rep named Brad Barlage journeyed to Baffin Island, west of Greenland, on a hunch that there were chutes there. McLean had built giant kites, based on a Dutch modification of NASA technology (he'd come across some kiting Dutchmen in Antarctica). McLean and Barlage used the kites to sail across the frozen fjords—at speeds of up to forty miles an hour, on skis, towing gear-laden sleds. They discovered soaring chutes everywhere. McLean told me, "We ticked off nineteen first descents, of which ten were the best lines I've ever been in—three-thousand-to-five-thousand-foot screamers that came straight out of the frozen sea ice, surrounded by monstrous walls, stable creamy powder, wolf tracks, twenty-four hours of daylight, and surreal scenery." The skiing magazines took note, and the athletes poured into Baffin.

On a trip like that one, the salient requirements, besides being first and having fun, are imagination and ingenuity, as opposed purely to danger and death defiance. McLean has learned, he told me, that "fatalities are always a good way to ruin a trip." Holbrook said, "We've toned things down a little. That's a good thing for him, with the problems we've had in the past, with the deaths."

Clearly, the deaths have weighed on McLean. "You go to a funeral," he told me. "You know these people as ski buddies, and you see they have moms and dads and fiancées. It gives it all a human face." And it can give him pause. Thus the toning down. "I'm more conservative, in terms of risking big falls. No more cliff hucking"—skiing off cliffs. "I give avalanches a lot more leeway than I used to," he said. "On the other hand, each thing you ski tends to be a little bit harder. The ambitions keep getting bigger. Foraker may be as hard as anything I've ever done."

On my second morning in Utah, I met McLean in the Little Cottonwood parking lot. He had his pickup truck, on which he had rearranged the lettering of "Toyota" to read "Otto," in honor of his late Bernese mountain dog. He was accompanied by Dylan Freed. McLean had considered taking Freed on the Alaska trip to climb Mount Foraker, but Freed's uncle, Mark Twight, one of the world's top mountaineers, told McLean, "If anything happens to him and you survive, I'll hunt you down and kill you." ("This kind of raises the question as to why people would get their kids into skiing and the mountains in the first place if they really wanted them to be safe," McLean told me. "Darts might be a better activity.")

On the way up the canyon, we picked up another friend, Lorne Glick, an accomplished ski mountaineer. Glick lives in a sparsely furnished room (ice axes, topographical maps, banjo) inside a small hydroelectric plant just off the Little Cottonwood road. The generators outside the room roar day and night. For money, Glick occasionally drives a Sno-Cat at Alta or works as a guide, and recently, at the age of forty-one, he got a license to be a helicopter pilot.

Our plan was to hike up Mount Superior, a peak rising three thousand feet above Little Cottonwood Canyon, and ski down the south face, which, viewed from Alta and Snowbird, seemed to be a sheer white wall, studded with cliffs. On earlier trips, I had occasionally seen tracks etched on it and been half glad that they weren't mine. "With slides that cover the road 10–20' deep, Superior should be treated with the utmost respect," McLean writes in *The Chuting Gallery*. "Because of the road below, keep in mind that you are endangering others by attempting to ski it in less than ideal conditions." On this particular day, conditions were close to ideal—four inches or so of fresh snow atop a firm, older layer. I decided not to worry about endangering others.

The trail began at Alta, behind the Our Lady of the Snows chapel, an avalanche-proof box of reinforced concrete and plate glass that was built in 1993, ten years after the original chapel, made of wood, was destroyed by a slide. McLean handed me a pair of Whippet Self-Arrest poles, which he designed. They are regular ski poles with a steel ice-axe blade fixed to each handle. You appear to be skiing with two stubby handsaws. In the event of a fall on a steep slope, you jab the blades into the snow to stop yourself from sliding. The climb was gradual at first, but it took just three minutes for me to fall well behind. The track was slick. My technique was poor. The air was thin. I huffed my way uphill, doing my best to look around and remind myself that there was no place I'd rather be. The panorama was dazzling in the morning light, like the inside of a diamond; unbroken fields of snow stretched in all directions.

After an hour or so, I rejoined the others at Cardiff Pass, and we started up Superior. Here the skinning got more technical: A winding trail through the trees requiring awkward maneuvers. Again, I lagged; after a while, McLean skied back down to check on me—humbling enough, though he seemed glad for the exercise. After another hour, it was time to remove the skis, strap them to our packs, and start climbing up a narrow ridge leading to the summit. The trail was variable; stretches of thigh-deep drifted snow gave way to wind-cleared rock. Occasionally, there was climbing to do, on all fours; the Whippet blades helped me gain purchase. On my left, there were cliffs, and, on the right, snow-loaded chutes. In places, it was clear that a fall to either side would be highly problematic. The wind had kicked up, and through breaks in a cloud that seemed to have come out of nowhere I got vertiginous glimpses of the valley floor.

McLean, by this point, was waiting for me at the top of each pitch, to make sure that I was all right and to take some delight in the extent to which I wasn't. "You're still smiling," he'd say, to my grimace. After one stretch, when I crawled up onto a narrow shelf and collapsed at his feet, he said, "Nick, does your wife know you're doing this?"

And then we were on top, the slope below us dropping off into a foggy void. Freed and Glick were long gone. They had decided to ski the north side, which looked bright, powdery, and benign. We bundled up, drank water, ate chocolate, and prepared for the ski down. "There's more snow up here than I thought," McLean said. "I think we'll do the chute on the left. Wait up here until I call up to you." He dropped in, traversing back and forth a few times to test the snow—ski cutting, it's called—and then making a series of blocky turns, his wide stance and cautious pace indicating to me that this was no place to make a mistake. And then he disappeared.

I waited awhile in the wind but couldn't hear a thing. Bits of cloud blew past. Rock, cornice, cloud. Probability, complacency, luck. I decided not to wait any longer. I hopped into the wind-whipped snow on the upper face, then chopped my way into a steep, icy trough, intermittently jump-turning and side-slipping, chunks of snow and ice clattering around me like broken glass. When I found McLean, he was hiding behind a rock, a big grin on his face. "Isn't this great?" he said. It was. The pitch eased, and we were making turn after turn in powder. After a while, McLean stopped and pointed up at a steep east-facing shaft. "That's Suicide," he said. He wondered whether I had enough left for one more. The answer, that morning, was no.

Dawn patrol: I met McLean and Brad Barlage in the parking lot at 5 A.M. the following day. We drove up to the White Pine trailhead, donned headlamps, and started skinning up through the woods, a damp malevolent wind howling in the aspen trees. McLean had mercifully assented to a compromise: Instead of going all the way up to White Pine, we'd climb for an hour to Pink Pine. The name suggested achievability. We reached the top before first light. Snow had started to fall, spinning in the beams of our headlamps. We skied a run in the trees in darkness—a curious experience. Not feeling right, I continued down alone, while they went up for more.

That evening, I had dinner with McLean and Samuels. They live at the top of a rise in a modest development outside Park City, on the east slope of the Wasatch, giving them a view through fir trees of the Uinta

Mountains. The house is compact but spacious—three stories. McLean poured two glasses of Scotch and showed me around. The ground floor is dominated by his workshop. It contains twenty-three pairs of skis, as well as climbing skins, boots, bicycles, unicycles, and various heavy mechanical saws and drills. In a closet, neatly arranged, were twenty ice axes and an assortment of helmets and backpacks. Shovels, carabiners, headlamps. Next to the workshop is a sewing room, where he assembles his giant kites. Upstairs, he has an office full of maps and adventure books. He reads a lot; on expeditions, when the weather goes bad, he said, "you end up tearing paperbacks into chapters and passing them around to be read out of order."

When Samuels returned home from work, I remarked upon the neatness of the place. "Did you expect him to be living in some cave?" she asked. She and McLean met in the Little Cottonwood parking lot, when he made a comment about a bumper sticker on her car for a ski-mountaineering mecca in France called La Grave. She loves skiing and understands that he does, too, and so she tolerates the long absences, as well as the risks, though when he talks about them—when, for example, he enumerated some of the obstacles on Mount Foraker—she laid a hand on his leg, as if to keep him near.

For dinner, McLean made cheese fondue. As he cooked, he talked about some of his avalanche encounters over the years. He told the one about being out on avalanche patrol for the Forest Service, early in the season, and getting caught in a slow slide on a seemingly harmless pitch that buried him head down, so that he couldn't move or breathe. There were incidents in which he was buried up to the waist or thrown up against a tree. "I'm having second thoughts about skiing, suddenly," McLean said, laying the fondue pot on the table.

"I've never heard these stories," Samuels said.

"You haven't?"

"I guess I never asked."

The more you learn about snow, the clearer it becomes that skiing—in the backcountry, on glaciers, in deep snow, on extreme steeps—is more dangerous than most people who regularly do it acknowledge. The capriciousness of the snow is hard to figure. And, whether it's because of hubris or probability, the victims tend to be those who know their way around the mountains, or believe they do.

"Many people think that the way they do it is safe but that the way others do it isn't," McLean told me. "The only truly safe way of doing it is to stop doing it, which I don't want to do." McLean is not superstitious; he doesn't believe that this frank assessment inoculates him against trouble. But it does enable him to evaluate the risks more soberly. For all his seeming recklessness, he is a compulsive planner and a meticulous performer—a mountain scientist. He admits to having "nighttime fears" and "trip anxiety," but in the end such sensations manifest themselves in preparation and a fixation on gear. (Carabiners "are all about semi-intangible subtleties.") And, where acumen comes up short, he resorts, as most mountain men do, to a kind of fatalism. "I often torment myself with a theoretical question," he said. "What if you knew how and when you were going to die? If it was an avalanche or falling to your death, then you'd have to keep skiing, as you've already seen the end. If it was in your sleep at a ripe old age, then you'd have to keep skiing as well, since you'd know you were safe. The end result is the same: Keep making turns." He does have his limits: A few years ago, he took up parapenting—jumping off mountains with a parachute—and decided it was too dangerous.

What suits McLean may not suit others. "People get in trouble trying to be their hero," Bruce Tremper, the director of the Forest Service's avalanche center in Utah, told me. "People got hurt or killed trying to be Alex Lowe. Andrew McLean has taken over that mantle. A lot of people are trying to be Andrew McLean now, and they're getting hurt or killed, because they don't have his talent or experience. Life gives us cheap lessons sometimes."

McLean and Samuels's wedding was held in February at Our Lady of the Snows and presided over by Lou Dawson, a pioneer of North American ski mountaineering and a longtime mentor to McLean. He had managed to get an ordination over the Internet for the occasion. (Dawson, it turns out, knew my aunt Meta, and he himself barely survived a big avalanche behind Aspen Highlands, in 1982.) Many congregants were wearing touring boots and ski clothes. One friend had skinned over from Big Cottonwood Canyon with a tuxedo rolled in his pack. The skiers, bright-eyed, shaggy, ruddy, and lean, stood out among the many guests who had come from New York. They made me think of my grandfather and his fellow-*Skilehrers,* surrounded by Ivy League boys and debutantes. Samuels was brought up in Manhattan; she went to Brearley and Penn; her father, a prominent tax attorney, served as an assistant treasury secretary in the Clinton administration, and her mother is a residential real estate broker. Eager to partake of the mountain life, Samuels moved out to Salt Lake City in 2000 and insinuated herself into the area's clique of elite outdoorsmen and women by undertaking feats of courage and endurance. (In a toast at the wedding, one of these women said, "We think you have earned the right to marry the icon of the Wasatch.") Also present was Polly's older brother, Colin, who has himself become an avid backcountry skier and climber. He lives in La Grave. Two years ago, his fiancée was killed when she fell down a slope in Norway into a frozen hole. "Polly's parents don't understand it," McLean said. "Colin has moved to one of the centers of alpinism, and Polly is marrying an alpine geek. They're probably not thrilled by it."

McLean and Samuels left the church under an arch of ski poles held aloft by their guests, then put on boots and skis so that they could ski a celebratory run in wedding attire. They took a chairlift, his morning coat and her wedding dress apparently triggering another exemption to the leg-power rule. Afterward, they joined the reception, at a big hotel at Snowbird. The mountain men were scattered about, stooping to stay clear of the potted palms. Bob Athey, the saltiest of them all, sat by the door in his ski gear. He had a rusty beard and a grand frizz of hair, and he smelled of tobacco and sweat. From the way people lined up to talk to him, it was clear that he had not been observed indoors in some time. ("Bob, I haven't seen you since we scattered Alan's ashes," one woman said.) Athey told me, "I figure I got another twenty years of this, before I die in an avalanche."

McLean sidled up. The morning coat looked big on him, as though he were a boy in a man's suit. He had a fixed smile that thinly disguised a groom's simmering embarrassment. "So, Bob, how was the skiing today?"

"It was great."

"Where did you go?"

Athey mentioned some backcountry spots.

"How was the snow?"

"Crusty."

McLean nodded and looked thoughtful for a moment, before his father-in-law came by to suggest that he start herding the guests in to dinner. After dinner and a short slate of toasts ("And that's how my brother ended up in the position he's in now, with . . . no job!"), it was time for "Hava Nagila." Samuels and McLean were hoisted up and borne onto the dance floor. This being Utah, a good portion of the people holding the bride and groom aloft did not have a great deal of experience with this particular number, and it was hard not to notice, as the tempo sped up and McLean, lurching to and fro, gripped the sides of his chair, that the expression on his face contained an unfamiliar ingredient that you might call worry.

Twenty-four hours after the wedding, I talked to McLean on the phone. I was at Alta, he was at home. (The honeymoon, a trip with friends to a backcountry lodge in British Columbia, would come a few weeks later.) McLean invited me to accompany him and his new brother-in-law on an outing the next morning to the Y Couloir, a three-thousand-foot chute that you walk up in your boots, with crampons and an ice axe. (*The Chuting Gallery*: "You will be exposed to avalanche hazards 100 per cent of the time and getting caught in even a minor slide here could be fatal.") I recalled that earlier in the winter McLean had told me that the only expeditions he has ever regretted were the ones he pulled out of: "Whenever I get invited on a trip, I remember a fortune cookie that said 'Practice saying yes.'" To the Y Couloir invitation, however, I said something about not having the gear and having a plane to catch. McLean told me he had gear for me, and that we'd make it down by noon. "Come on, Nick. You'll love it!" I hung up and talked it over with my wife, with whom I was supposed to ski the following day. The consensus was that the answer should be no. I called McLean back. I told him that it was snowing at Alta, and he remarked that, if more than four or five inches accumulated, the Y Couloir would be too dangerous to ski. Later that evening, I stepped outside and noted, with more than the usual elation, that six inches had fallen. And it was still dumping. I called McLean and gave him my report; the Y Couloir would have to wait.

The next day was a powder day. At Alta, the Scrubbing Bubbles were out in force, devouring the new snow in less than an hour. Riding up the chairlift, I looked back hungrily across the canyon, at the vast untracked south face of Superior, and then followed the ridgeline east, until I saw a lone figure ascending a pristine snowfield. The skin track looked steep, the pace brisk. Ten minutes later, I saw the figure, a tiny speck, reach a peak called Flagstaff. My cellphone rang, and it was McLean, calling from the top to gloat. "Are you lonely?" I asked him.

"It is really good, Nick," he said. "And I have it all to myself." After a moment, he dropped off the backside, out of sight.

2005

THE RUNNING NOVELIST

HARUKI MURAKAMI

Translated, from the Japanese, by Philip Gabriel.

Along time has passed since I started running on an everyday basis. Specifically, it was the fall of 1982. I was thirty-three then.

Not long before that, I was the owner of a small jazz club in Tokyo, near Sendagaya Station. Soon after leaving college—I'd been so busy with side jobs that I was actually a few credits short of graduating and was still officially a student—I had opened a little club near the south entrance of Kokubunji Station. The club had stayed there for about three years; then, when the building it was in closed for renovations, I moved it to a new location, closer to the center of Tokyo. The new venue wasn't big—we had a grand piano and just barely enough space to squeeze in a quintet. During the day, it was a café; at night, it was a bar. We served decent food, too, and, on weekends, featured live performances. This kind of club was still quite rare in Tokyo back then, so we gained a steady clientele and the place did all right financially.

Most of my friends had predicted that the club would fail. They figured that an establishment that was run as a kind of hobby couldn't succeed, and that someone like me—I was pretty naïve and, they suspected, didn't have the slightest aptitude for business—wouldn't be able to make a go of it. Well, their predictions were totally off. To tell the truth, I didn't think that I had much aptitude for business, either. I just figured that since failure was not an option, I had to give it everything I had. My strength has always been the fact that I work hard and can handle a lot physically. I'm more of a workhorse than a racehorse. I grew up in a white-collar household, so I didn't know much about entrepreneurship, but fortunately my wife's family ran a business and her natural intuition was a great help.

The work itself was hard. I was at the club from morning till night and I left there exhausted. I had all kinds of painful experiences and plenty of disappointments. But, after a while, I began to make enough of a profit to hire other people, and I was finally able to take a breather. To get started, I'd borrowed as much money as I could from every bank that would lend to me, and by now I'd paid a lot of it back. Things were settling down. Up to that point, it had been a question of sheer survival, and I hadn't had time to think about anything else. Now I felt as though I'd reached the top of a steep staircase and emerged into an open space. I was confident that I'd be able to handle any new problems that might crop up. I took a deep breath, glanced back at the stairs I'd just climbed, then slowly gazed around me and began to contemplate the next stage of my life. I was about to turn thirty. I was reaching the age at which I wouldn't be considered young anymore. And, pretty much out of the blue, it occurred to me to write a novel.

I can pinpoint the exact moment when it happened. It was at 1:30 P.M., April 1, 1978. I was at Jingu Stadium, alone in the outfield, watching a baseball game. Jingu Stadium was within walking distance of my apartment at the time, and I was a fairly devoted Yakult Swallows fan. It was a beautiful spring day, cloudless, with a warm breeze blowing. There were no benches in the outfield seating area back then, just a grassy slope. I was lying on the grass, sipping a cold beer, gazing up occasionally at the sky, and enjoying the game. As usual, the stadium wasn't very crowded. It was the season opener, and the Swallows were taking on the Hiroshima Carp. Takeshi Yasuda was pitching for the Swallows. He was a short, stocky pitcher with a wicked curveball. He easily retired the side in the top of the first inning. The lead-off batter for the Swallows was Dave Hilton, a young American player who was new to the team. Hilton got a hit down the left-field line. The crack of bat meeting ball echoed through the stadium. Hilton easily rounded first and pulled up to second. And it was at just that moment that a thought struck me: You know what? I could try writing a novel. I still remember the wide-open sky, the feel of the new grass, the satisfying crack of the bat. Something flew down from the sky at that instant, and, whatever it was, I accepted it.

I didn't have any ambition to be a "novelist." I just had the strong desire to write a novel. I had no concrete image of what I wanted to write about—just the conviction that I could come up with something that I'd find convincing. When I thought about sitting down at my desk at home and starting to write, I realized that I didn't even own a decent fountain pen. So I went to the Kinokuniya store in Shinjuku and bought a sheaf of manuscript paper and a five-dollar Sailor pen. A small capital investment on my part.

By that fall, I'd finished a two-hundred-page handwritten work. I had no idea what to do with it, so I just let the momentum carry me and submitted it to the literary magazine *Gunzo*'s new-writers' contest. I shipped it off without making a copy, so it seems I didn't much care if it wasn't selected and vanished forever. I was more interested in having finished the book than in whether or not it would ever see the light of day.

That year, the Yakult Swallows, the perennial underdog, won the pennant and went on to defeat the Hankyu Braves in the Japan Series. I was really excited by this, and I attended several games at Korakuen Stadium. (Nobody had actually imagined that the Swallows would win, so their home venue, Jingu Stadium, had already been taken over by college baseball.) It was a particularly gorgeous autumn. The sky was clear and the ginkgo trees in front of the Meiji Memorial Gallery were more golden than I'd ever seen them. This was the last fall of my twenties.

By the following spring, when I got a phone call from an editor at *Gunzo* telling me that my novel had made the prize's short list, I'd completely forgotten having entered the contest. I'd been so busy with other things. But the novel went on to win the prize and was published that summer under the title *Hear the Wind Sing*. It was well received, and, without really knowing what was going on, I suddenly found myself labeled a new, up-and-coming writer. I was surprised, but the people who knew me were even more surprised.

After this, while still running the jazz club, I produced a medium-length second novel, *Pinball, 1973*. I also wrote a few short stories and translated some by F. Scott Fitzgerald. Both *Hear the Wind Sing* and *Pinball, 1973* were nominated for the prestigious Akutagawa Prize, but in the end neither won. I didn't care one way or the other. If I had won the prize, I'd have been taken up by interviews and writing assignments, and I was afraid that this would interfere with my duties at the club.

For three years I ran my jazz club—keeping the accounts, checking the inventory, scheduling my staff, standing behind the counter mixing cocktails and cooking, closing up in the wee hours of the morning, and only then being able to write, at home, at the kitchen table, until I got sleepy. I felt as if I were living two people's lives. And, gradually, I found myself wanting to write a more substantial kind of novel. I had enjoyed the process of writing my first two books, but there were parts of both that I wasn't pleased with. I was able to write only in spurts, snatching bits of time—a half hour here, an hour there—and, because I was always tired and felt as if I were competing against the clock, I was never able to concentrate very well. With this scattered kind of approach I was able to write a few interesting, fresh things, but the result was far from complex or profound. I felt as if I'd been given this wonderful opportunity to be a novelist, and I had a natural desire to take that opportunity as far as I possibly could. So, after giving it a lot of thought, I decided to close the business and focus solely on writing. At this point, my income from the jazz club was significantly more than my income as a novelist, a reality to which I resigned myself.

Most of my friends were adamantly against my decision, or at least had doubts about it. "Your business is doing fine now," they said. "Why not just let someone else run it while you write your novels?" But I couldn't follow their advice. I'm the kind of person who has to commit totally to whatever I do. If, having committed, I failed, I could accept that. But I knew that if I did things halfheartedly and they didn't work out I'd always have regrets.

So, despite everyone's objections, I sold the club and, a little embarrassedly, hung out my sign as a novelist. "I'd just like to be free to write for two years," I explained to my wife. "If it doesn't work out, we can always open up another bar somewhere. I'm still young and we'll have time to start over." This was in 1981 and we still had a considerable amount of debt, but I figured I'd just do my best and see what happened.

So I settled down to write my novel and, that fall, traveled to Hokkaido for a week to research it. By the following April, I'd completed *A Wild Sheep Chase*. This novel was much longer than the previous two, larger in scope and more story-driven. By the time I'd finished writing it, I had a good feeling that I'd created my own style. Now I could actually picture myself making a living as a novelist.

The editors at *Gunzo* were looking for something more mainstream, and they didn't much care for *A Wild Sheep Chase*. Readers, though, seemed to love the new book, and that was what made me happiest. This was the real starting point for me as a novelist.

Once I had decided to become a professional writer, another problem arose: the question of how to keep physically fit. Running the club had required constant physical labor, but once I was sitting at a desk writing all day I started putting on the pounds. I was also smoking too much—sixty cigarettes a day. My fingers were yellow, and my body reeked of smoke. This couldn't be good for me, I decided. If I wanted to have a long life as a novelist, I needed to find a way to stay in shape.

As a form of exercise, running has a lot of advantages. First of all, you don't need someone to help you with it; nor do you need any special equipment. You don't have to go to any particular place to do it. As long as you have a pair of running shoes and a good road you can run to your heart's content.

After I closed the bar, I resolved to change my lifestyle entirely, and my wife and I moved out to Narashino, in the Chiba prefecture. The area was pretty rural back then, and there were no decent sports facilities around. But there was a Self-Defense Force base nearby, and the roads were well maintained. There was also a training area in the neighborhood near Nihon University, and if I went there early in the morning, when nobody else was around, I could use the track. So I didn't have to think too much about what activity to choose. I just took up running.

Not long after that, I also quit smoking. It wasn't easy to do, but I couldn't really run and keep on smoking. My desire to run was a great help in overcoming the withdrawal symptoms. Quitting smoking was also like a symbolic gesture of farewell to the life I used to lead.

At school I had never much cared for gym class or Sports Day, since these involved activities that were forced on me from above. But whenever I was able to do something I liked to do, when I wanted to do it, and the way I wanted to do it, I'd give it everything I had. Since I wasn't that athletic or coordinated, I wasn't good at the kind of sports where things are decided in a flash. Long-distance running suits my personality better, which may explain why I was able to incorporate it so smoothly into my daily life. I can say the same thing about me and studying. For my entire education, from elementary school through college, I was never interested in things that I was forced to study. As a result, although my grades weren't the kind you have to hide from people, I don't recall ever being praised for a good performance or a good grade, or being the best in anything. I began to enjoy studying only after I had made it through the educational system and become a so-called member of society. If something interested me, and I could study it at my own pace, I was reasonably efficient at acquiring knowledge.

The best thing about becoming a professional writer was that I could go to bed early and get up early. When I was running the club, I often didn't get to sleep until nearly dawn. The club closed at twelve, but then I had to clean up, go over the receipts, sit and talk, and have a drink to relax. Do all that and, before you know it, it's 3 A.M. and sunrise is just around the corner. Often I'd still be sitting at my kitchen table, writing, as it started to get light outside. Naturally, by the time I woke up for the day, the sun was already high in the sky.

Once I began my life as a novelist, my wife and I decided that we'd go to bed soon after it got dark and wake up with the sun. To our minds, this was a more natural, respectable way to live. We also decided that from then on we'd try to see only the people we wanted to see, and, as much as possible, get by without seeing those we didn't. We felt that, for a time at least, we could allow ourselves this modest indulgence.

In my new, simple, regular life, I got up before 5 A.M. and went to bed before 10 P.M. Different people are at their best at different times of day, but I'm definitely a morning person. That's when I can focus. Afterward, I work out or do errands that don't take much concentration. At the end of the day, I relax, read, or listen to music. Thanks to this pattern, I've been able to work efficiently now for twenty-seven years. It's a pattern, though, that doesn't allow for much of a night life, and sometimes this makes relationships with other people problematic. People are offended when you repeatedly turn down their invitations. But, at that point, I felt that the indispensable relationship I should build in my life was not with a specific person but with an unspecified number of readers. My readers would welcome whatever lifestyle I chose, as long as I made sure that each new work was an improvement over the last. And shouldn't that be my duty—and my top priority—as a novelist? I don't see my readers' faces, so in a sense my relationship with them is a conceptual one, but I've consistently considered it the most important thing in my life.

In other words, you can't please everybody.

Even when I ran the club, I understood this. A lot of customers came to the club. If one out of ten enjoyed the place and decided to come again, that was enough. If one out of ten was a repeat customer, then the business would survive. To put it another way, it didn't matter if nine out of ten people didn't like the club. Realizing this lifted a weight off my shoulders. Still, I had to make sure that the one person who did like the place really liked it. In order to do that, I had to make my philosophy absolutely clear, and patiently maintain that philosophy no matter what. This is what I learned from running a business.

After *A Wild Sheep Chase,* I continued to write with the same attitude that I'd developed as a business owner. And with each work my readership—the one-in-ten repeaters—increased. Those readers, most of whom were young, would wait patiently for my next book to appear, then buy it and read it as soon as it hit the bookstores. This was for me the ideal, or at least a very comfortable, situation. I went on writing the kinds of things I wanted to write, exactly the way I wanted to write them, and, if that allowed me to make a living, then I couldn't ask for more. When my novel *Norwegian Wood* unexpectedly sold more than two million copies, things had to shift a little, but that was quite a bit later, in 1987.

When I first started running, I couldn't run long distances. I could run for only about twenty or thirty minutes. Even that left me panting, my heart pounding, my legs shaky. I hadn't really exercised for a long time. At first, I was also a little embarrassed to have people in the neighborhood see me running. But, as I continued to run, my body began to accept the fact that it was running, and I gradually increased my endurance. I acquired a runner's form, my breathing became more regular, and my pulse settled down. The main thing was not the speed or the distance so much as running every day, without fail.

So, like eating, sleeping, housework, and writing, running was incorporated into my daily routine. As it became a natural habit, I felt less embarrassed about it. I went to a sports store and purchased some running gear and some decent shoes. I bought a stopwatch, too, and read a book on running.

Looking back now, I think the most fortunate thing is that I was born with a strong, healthy body. This has made it possible for me to run on a daily basis for more than a quarter century now, competing in a number of races along the way. I've never been injured, never been hurt, and haven't once been sick. I'm not a great runner, but I'm a strong runner. That's one of the very few gifts I can be proud of.

The year 1983 rolled around and I participated in my first road race. It wasn't very long—a 5K—but for the first time I had a number pinned to my shirt and waited in a large group of other runners to hear an official shout, "On your mark, get set, go!" Afterward, I thought, Hey, that wasn't so bad! That May, I did a fifteen-kilometer race around Lake Yamanaka, and, in June, wanting to test how far I could go, I did laps around the Imperial Palace, in Tokyo. I went around seven times, for a total of 22.4 miles, at a fairly decent pace, and my legs didn't hurt at all. Maybe I could actually run a marathon, I concluded. Later, I found out the hard way that the toughest part of a marathon comes after twenty-two miles. (I have now competed in twenty-six marathons.)

When I look at photographs of me that were taken back in the mid-eighties, it's obvious that I didn't yet have a runner's physique. I hadn't run enough, hadn't built up the requisite muscles; my arms were too thin, my legs too skinny. I'm impressed that I could run a marathon at all with a body like that. (Now, after years of running, my musculature has changed completely.) But even then I could feel physical changes happening every day, which made me really happy. I felt that, even though I was past thirty, I and my body still had some possibilities left. The more I ran, the more my potential was revealed.

Along with this, my diet started to change as well. I began to eat mostly vegetables, with fish as my main source of protein. I had never liked meat much anyway, and this aversion now became even more pronounced. I cut back on rice and alcohol and began using only natural ingredients. Sweets weren't a problem, since I had never much cared for them.

When I think about it, having the kind of body that easily puts on weight is perhaps a blessing in disguise. In other words, if I don't want to gain weight I have to work out hard every day, watch what I eat, and cut down on indulgences. People who naturally keep the weight off don't need to exercise or watch their diet. Which is why, in many cases, their physical strength deteriorates as they age. Those of us who have a tendency to gain weight should consider ourselves lucky that the red light is so clearly visible. Of course, it's not always easy to see things this way.

I think this viewpoint applies as well to the job of the novelist. Writers who are blessed with inborn talent can write easily, no matter what they do—or don't do. Like water from a natural spring, the sentences just well up, and with little or no effort these writers can complete a work. Unfortunately, I don't fall into that category. I have to pound away at a rock with a chisel and dig out a deep hole before I can locate the source of my creativity. Every time I begin a new novel, I have to dredge out another hole. But, as I've sustained this kind of life over many years, I've become quite efficient, both technically and physically, at opening those holes in the rock and locating new water veins. As soon as I notice one source drying up, I move on to another. If people who rely on a natural spring of talent suddenly find they've exhausted their source, they're in trouble.

In other words, let's face it: Life is basically unfair. But, even in a situation that's unfair, I think it's possible to seek out a kind of fairness.

When I tell people that I run every day, some are quite impressed. "You must have a lot of willpower," they tell me. Of course, it's nice to be praised like this—a lot better than being disparaged. But I don't think it's merely willpower that makes one able to do something. The world isn't that simple. To tell the truth, I don't even think there's much correlation between my running every day and whether or not I have willpower. I think that I've been able to run for more than twenty-five years for one reason: It suits me. Or, at least, I don't find it all that painful. Human beings naturally continue doing things they like, and they don't continue doing what they don't like.

That's why I've never recommended running to others. If someone has an interest in long-distance running, he'll start running on his own. If he's not interested in it, no amount of persuasion will make any difference. Marathon running is not a sport for everyone, just as being a novelist isn't a job for everyone. Nobody ever recommended or even suggested that I be a novelist—in fact, some tried to stop me. I simply had the idea to be one, and that's what I did. People become runners because they're meant to.

No matter how much long-distance running might suit me, of course there are days when I feel lethargic and don't want to do it. On days like that, I try to come up with all kinds of plausible excuses not to run. Once, I interviewed the Olympic runner Toshihiko Seko, just after he had retired from running. I asked him, "Does a runner at your level ever feel like you'd rather not run today?" He stared at me and then, in a voice that made it abundantly clear how stupid he thought the question was, replied, "Of course. All the time!"

Now that I look back on it, I can see what a dumb question it was. I guess that even back then I knew how dumb it was, but I wanted to hear the answer directly from someone of Seko's caliber. I wanted to know whether, although we were worlds apart in terms of strength and motivation, we felt the same way when we laced up our running shoes in the morning. Seko's reply came as a great relief. In the final analysis, we're all the same, I thought.

Now, whenever I feel like I don't want to run, I always ask myself the same thing: You're able to make a living as a novelist, working at home, setting your own hours. You don't have to commute on a packed train or sit through boring meetings. Don't you realize how fortunate you are? Compared with that, running an hour around the neighborhood is nothing, right? Then I lace up my running shoes and set off without hesitating. (I say this knowing full well that there are people who'd pick riding a crowded train and attending meetings over running every day.)

At any rate, this is how I started running. Thirty-three—that's how old I was then. Still young enough, though no longer a young man. The age that Jesus Christ died. The age that F. Scott Fitzgerald started to go downhill. It's an age that may be a kind of crossroads in life. It was the age when I began my life as a runner, and it was my belated, but real, starting point as a novelist.

2008

BACK TO THE BASEMENT

NANCY FRANKLIN

I loved the house I grew up in, a big mock-Tudor, built in the twenties, with stained-glass windows and an old-time solidity, but I was afraid of the basement. It had two rooms where, for all eighteen years that my parents owned the house, I thought I might die. One was a storage room, with a raw rock outcropping that extended back farther than the light in the room allowed you to see. I thought that the black space above the rock went on more or less forever, and I was always expecting a man to emerge from it and kill me. The other was the small, hot room where the furnace was; there was a blood-red switchplate with a printed warning on it telling you not to turn the switch off, and, hanging next to the furnace, a large glass container full of red liquid, whose function I never knew. I was sure that if I touched it or the light switch the house would explode. And then, if I didn't actually die, I would be in a lot of trouble. Beyond those two rooms, down a hallway and two steps, there was what we called the playroom. There wasn't much in there— nothing good that might get ruined, and not much to play with, either—but there was a Ping-Pong table, which for me was, if not quite a reason for being, at least a reason for risking a trip to the basement. In this room, I was the killer.

My father had made the Ping-Pong table himself: It consisted of two pieces of plywood hinged in the middle and stained dark green, with a white painted center line, laid over a brown wool blanket on an old dining room table from the Philippines, where my parents had lived when they were first married. It was the only piece of furniture in the room, except for an ugly blue couch in a corner, which sometimes had to be pulled scrapingly across the linoleum floor in order for you to get at an inevitably errant Ping-Pong ball. At some point, we got a pool table, adding another obstacle under or around which you had to go to fetch the ball.

I had one friend who liked to play almost as much as I did, but mainly I played with my father, starting when I was about six. He was a very good tennis player, and a very good Ping-Pong player, and he didn't tone down his game for me. I really wanted to beat him, and I knew that one day I would. Because I was good, too. I was really good. I had excellent hand-eye coordination and timing—I knew when and how to put spin on the ball, dump a short ball just over the net, or put it away with a slam. I loved everything about the game: the rhythmic pock-pock, pock-pock of the ball hitting the table and racquet again and again, the hummy all-over pleasure I got when I hit a ball well, the back-and-forth conversational aspect of it. I was always in the mood to play. Dick Miles, a ten-time United States champion in the 1940s, '50s, and '60s, wrote in one of his instructional books, "Table tennis is, for me, one of those world-blotting-out activities, the ultimate escape." It was a little like that for me, too. I was completely at home with a racquet in my hand; I played without any tentativeness or self-consciousness, which made the game different from everything else in my life. My father, who had a military bent and was not a big proponent of self-assertion in his children, nevertheless allowed me my insistence on my own existence when it came to Ping-Pong—my killer instinct, my agonized howls after missing a big shot—and he would laugh appreciatively when I went all-out and hit a winning slam. He had his little jokes, which became my little jokes. If either of us had the other person at zero and the other person got a point, we'd say, "There goes my love game," as if we'd been sure we had a shutout going. Each time we finished playing, my father would pretend to be a boxing announcer and declare himself "the winner and still champeen!" And for quite a few years, until I was twelve or thirteen, and good enough to beat him at the game he'd taught me, he was.

After I left home and went to college, I stopped playing, except once or twice a year at my parents'. They'd sold our house, in a suburb of New York City, and bought a place in Massachusetts. The green plywood, the wool blanket, and the dining room table are set up there now, in an uninviting storage room that has an off-putting number of places for a ball to hide after a missed shot. I always beat my father when we play these days, but perhaps I should add that he is now eighty-two. Once, after I moved to New York, in 1979, I played in the Ping-Pong parlor on Broadway and Ninety-sixth Street, which was owned by the legendary player Marty Reisman. It was just a few blocks from my apartment, but the place closed a year later, to make way for a never-to-be-legendary high-rise. Not playing much Ping-Pong for all those years cemented my belief that I was a good player—not to mention the fact that I'd gone out on a high note, having won my high school championship in my senior year. I only had to beat two people to do it, but still.

Here's the thing, though: I really wasn't very good. I was . . . OK . . . sort of. Other amateur athletes dream of being better than they are, but a peculiar trait of basement Ping-Pong players is that they think they're better than they are. They're not. The expert and the amateur "play different games," Dick Miles writes in *The Game of Table Tennis*. "The expert plays table tennis as a sport; the basement player is, for the most part, piddling at ping pong." In his book *The Money Player*, Reisman, a three-time U.S. singles champion and the winner of some twenty national and international titles, tells of a middle-aged man who challenged him one day when he was a young, topflight player. Reisman beat him 21–0 three games in a row, but the man didn't get the message. " 'With a little practice,' he said, 'I think I could beat you.' " People who play baseball, soccer, golf, tennis, basketball, or football have plenty of opportunities to get an idea of the size and nature of the gap that separates them from the pros. But Ping-Pong isn't televised much in this country, and most of the spectators at tournaments are other tournament players. Also, the modest scale of the game—a nine-by-five table, a six-inch-high net, a little plastic ball, and a wooden racquet that is barely bigger than a hand span—makes it look so easy. And then there is the name, which is hard to take seriously. *Ping-Pong* was coined a little more than a century ago by an English sporting goods firm, which sold the American rights to the name to Parker Brothers in 1901, during a craze for the game that lasted about four years. When the game became popular again, in the 1920s, other manufacturers had to use the generic term *table tennis,* and that is the term the professionals use; the governing body for the sport in this country is called U.S.A. Table Tennis. But the name *Ping-Pong* persists.

Kids—even kids who eventually become champions—discover and take to Ping-Pong by accident. Dick Miles, who had asked for a pool table for his eleventh birthday, was given a "tea-table table-tennis" set instead. Marty Reisman began playing at eleven, because his older brother did. Ruth Aarons, who in 1936, at the age of seventeen, became the only American player ever to win a world singles championship, discovered the game at fourteen in a hotel basement. (For some of this table-tennis lore, I have relied on the invaluable writings of Tim Boggan, the sport's premier historian.) Even these players didn't realize what they were up against until they happened upon a club where top players gathered. Miles and Reisman became world-class players by going to a club known as Lawrence's, on Broadway between Fifty-fourth and Fifty-fifth streets, where the great players of the day congregated. City players have an advantage in this respect: they didn't grow up with Ping-Pong tables in their basement and take the game for granted; they had to make a journey of discovery for themselves. At one time, there were a handful of active world-class players who were born and brought up in New York City. (Four of them are still living here: Reisman and Miles, and Sol Schiff and Lou Pagliaro, who were two of the greats of the thirties and forties.) Even though table tennis is the No. 2 sport in the world, after soccer, it is all but invisible in this country. (There are no "Ping-Pong moms" whose vote anyone is trying to get.) A brief flurry of interest in the game in 1971, at the time of "Ping-Pong diplomacy," when an American delegation of players was invited to China, was just that. None of the sport's players have ever been household names, and the only journey that most Americans make when it comes to Ping-Pong is to their basement, to a table that is generally coated with dust and marked with sticky rings where the kids put their sodas while they're playing air hockey.

During the years when I didn't play much, I still thought of Ping-Pong as something I played, not as something I used to play, and I kept waiting for a table to fall into my life. I was flabbergasted when my company moved, four years ago, into a brand-new building that had amenities like a multimillion-dollar cafeteria and lights that go out while you're working unless you flail your arms around (internal, psychic flailing won't do it) but didn't have even one Ping-Pong table. Similarly, what helped me endure a year and a half of noise and dust while a new Jewish community center was being built down the street from my apartment was the thought that at least they'd have a Ping-Pong table there. But they didn't! (So much for the would-be Reismans, Schiffs, Mileses, and Aaronses of the future.) Ping-Pong didn't come knocking at my door again until a little more than a year ago. That's when I first got a true idea of my place in the Ping-Pong pantheon—or, to be more accurate, my distance from the Ping-Pong pantheon, which is something like the distance from Earth to Alpha Centauri.

In December 2001, the editor and writer Harold Evans invited me along to a publication party for a new book about Ping-Pong, by Jerome Charyn, called *Sizzling Chops & Devilish Spins*. Harry was known to be a good player and a fan—he competed in the 1948 English Open, and he had edited a 1959 book by the English player Ken Stanley called *Table Tennis: A New Approach*. The party was held at a table-tennis club I hadn't known about, on Broadway between Ninety-ninth and a Hundredth streets, called the Manhattan Table Tennis Club. Founded in 1999 by a Polish-born businessman named Jerry Wartski, who plays there regularly, it is the only Ping-Pong club in Manhattan, which years ago used to have half a dozen such places on the stretch of Broadway between midtown and Ninety-sixth Street alone. It's a third-floor hole in the wall, dingy and welcoming in a pre-gentrification sort of way, and its windows have been painted over to keep the light, and the world, out. (It is managed by Atanda Musa, a former Nigerian champion, who is the best African player in the history of the game.) At the party, Harry was to play some games with Marty Reisman, whom I'd never met or seen play, though his photograph was a fixture in the Chinese restaurants in the neighborhood. The two men, both in their seventies (Reisman turned seventy-three this month), went at it with a skill and an intensity that were delightful to see. Reisman was dazzling. He wore a panama hat, as he always does, and he didn't break a sweat. Sure, he missed some shots—everybody does—but the core of his game was still there: the devastating fast forehand, which had been his signature shot, and which had helped make him, at one point, one of the top five players in the world, and his chess-master-like ability to control the game. (Reisman's accuracy is such that with his deadly forehand he can—famously—snap in two a cigarette standing on end on the far side of the table.)

Harry arranged to play with Marty on a regular basis, and I got in on the act, too. Reisman had been given playing privileges at a sports club in midtown for a few months, and, during that time, I was lucky enough to be coached by him once or twice a week. I was several decades out of practice, but after I'd hit the ball back and forth just a few times Reisman could see that rustiness wasn't really the problem. I had been doing everything wrong my whole life: I had basically been playing tennis on a smaller scale. I held the racquet too low on the handle, and I tended to hit with too much of a sideways spin. (Proper strokes in table tennis combine an up-and-down motion with forward motion; these motions, and the angle of the racquet face as it comes into contact with the ball, determine its speed and spin.) I also didn't move unless I had to—when you're young, you think that a shot you can reach for and get without moving is, by definition, a good shot. So I had to learn—and constantly try to remember—to stay on the balls of my feet and be ready to move, and then actually move, and then get ready for the next shot.

Because I still had a vestigial feel for the sport, and because Reisman is a terrific teacher, I made rapid progress on a couple of aspects of my game. I had lost some things—I used to have a decent backhand slam, and I remember being good at hitting down the line on both sides of the table when my opponent (Dad) was expecting a cross-court shot— but I quickly gained a couple of shots I had never had, such as a backhand chop, which is a defensive shot with backspin, and a forehand drive. With these tools, I could surely have won my high school championship a year sooner, instead of losing to Elaine Lang.

By playing with Reisman, I had, in addition to getting a far greater teacher than I deserved, walked into a fifty-year-old argument. Reisman plays with the kind of racquet called a hardbat, whose covering is a thin layer of pimpled rubber. This used to be the standard racquet for pros and basement players alike, though pros had access to higher-quality equipment than you'd find in a sporting-goods store or at Sears—better-balanced racquets, better rubber. It's what I had always used, too, and I stuck with it because that's the way I am; I still have my forty-year-old paddles, even though the rubber on them is now so hard that they're unusable. I had noticed over the years that I'd stopped seeing this kind of paddle at people's houses and in stores, and that it had been replaced by racquets with a smooth rubber covering and no pimples. I didn't like the new racquets, mainly because I couldn't feel the ball as well when I hit it, and I missed the sound of the ball's resonant smack against the racquet. The new racquets, instead of saying *pock* when they hit the ball, gave off a muted, indefinite *pah*—the difference was comparable to the difference between the sound of a manual typewriter and the sound of a computer keyboard.

This new kind of rubber—it will always seem new to me, though it has been in use since the early fifties—completely changed the game of table tennis, and it has been Reisman's bête noir since it was first introduced. Reisman, the winner of the English Open in 1949—then the most prestigious title next to that of world champion—was poised to win the world championship a few years later, in 1952. It was, he thought, his year. But, in an early round, he faced an unknown Japanese player named Hiroji Satoh, whose racquet was covered with this strange new rubber—three-quarters of an inch of foam—which no one had ever seen. Reisman writes in *The Money Player*, "Outfielders in baseball often can judge the flight of a ball from the crack it makes as it comes off the bat. So too can table tennis players judge the velocity of a ball by the noise it makes when it is struck by the opponent's racket. . . . But against Satoh there was no sound." Because of the catapult-like quality of his equipment, Satoh, who wasn't even one of the best players on the Japanese team, was able to use Reisman's own attacking-style game against him. Reisman's shots "sank into the foam rubber of Satoh's racket and were flung back at me with amazing force. . . . I was throwing lethal punches and hitting myself in the face." Reisman had shown up with a bow and arrow, and his opponent came armed with an automatic rifle—and it won him the world title.

Americans were slow to switch to the new paddle, called a sponge racquet, and their world stature, which was already on the way down by the early fifties, suffered further because of it. The new surface took over everywhere, and eventually it became standard here, too. Reisman's beef with the sponge game is not merely that it robbed him of a world championship, though that would be reason enough to hate it— he believes that it is a lesser game, and that it rewards lesser players. Where the game once had drama, it now had mere excitement—a generalized, impersonal excitement that extinguished the game's formerly inherent gladiatorial sense of struggle, its me-against-you-ness. Now it was my racquet against your racquet. (Reisman won the U.S. Open in 1960 with a sponge racquet, but playing with it gave him no satisfaction; he put it down and never played with it again.) There are still people who play with the hardbat, but it is a niche game, which had all but disappeared from serious competition until a sidebar tournament was instated in the National Championships, six years ago.

The National Championships are held at the Las Vegas Convention Center, and it is an indicator of the sport's marginality and semi-geekiness that the four-day tournament takes place just a few days before Christmas, when so-called normal people are busy at home with real life—holiday preparations, families, parties, shopping, seasonal affective disorder. I didn't see any publicity for the tournament around town, even at the hotel where the players—some seven hundred of them—were staying, and at the tournament itself it was hard to figure out who was playing when and where in the huge hall, which held ninety tables. The USATT has something of a basement-player mentality: When I asked the tournament director for a printout of the day's matches, he told me that the file was in his computer at home. And the association's slogan—"Putting a New Spin on an Old Favorite!"—sounds like something your all-too-helpful aunt cooked up.

This was an interesting year to go to the Nationals, because it was the first time that an important new rule, instituted by the International Table Tennis Federation, the sport's ultimate governing body, was in effect. Players were now forbidden to block their opponents' view of their serve and thereby prevent them from judging the degree and direction of spin. The ITTF had made a couple of other big changes in recent years, in an effort to make the sport more spectator-friendly. The game was now played to eleven points, not twenty-one, and each player served just twice, instead of five times, in a row. The ball, which had been thirty-eight millimeters in diameter for decades, had been enlarged to forty. The idea was that the eleven-point game would keep matches moving apace; at the same time, the bigger ball would slow down individual points, and be easier to see on television; and the service rule would eliminate the deception that had caused tournament play to follow a monotonous pattern: confusing serve, confused return, slam. The new rules have had mixed results. Players try to appear to be adhering to the service rule while coming as close to flouting it as they possibly can. The ball is easier to see, although, from all reports, its meliorative effects have been negligible. (I find it floaty and elusive, like a balloon in the wind.) The eleven-point game, however, has unquestionably sapped the sport of something essential. Games have a beginning and an end, but no middle—there's no wiggle room for players, and no dramatic traction for spectators.

The ITTF has never set any meaningful standards for racquet cov-

erings; a player can have two completely different surfaces on his racquet, of different thicknesses and different rubber. While the hard rubber that Reisman uses can last for years, sponge rubber has to be
replaced every few months, if not more frequently. There are hundreds
of types of rubber, and hundreds of blades—the wooden racquet, without the rubber—to choose from. And then there is the added wrinkle
of "speed glue," which has become almost a fetish among players. Top
players remove the rubber from their racquet and reglue it each time
they play. The glue—don't ask me how—makes the ball carom off the
racquet with even more speed and spin. The manufacturers of all this
stuff—and rubbers and blades are not cheap—pretty much rule the
sport; they are virtually the only advertisers in the USATT's magazine,
and one of them sponsored the Nationals. (I don't know how hard the
USATT tries to get other corporate sponsorship of its activities.
George Brathwaite, a USATT vice president—and a many-titled
player, who has long been involved in trying to raise the sport's profile—told me he'd heard that Bill Gates had regularly attended the
table-tennis events at the Sydney Olympics. Yet the association hadn't
thought about approaching Gates to help develop the sport or to sponsor tournaments. The championship purse at the Nationals was pathetic: two thousand dollars for the men's singles winner, and—did
somebody say "sexism"?—fifteen hundred dollars for the women's. By
the way, I have read that there are tables—tables, plural—at Microsoft.)

Still, it was possible to put aside these concerns about the sport and
get good and drunk on table tennis at the Nationals. Matches were
being played as far as the eye could see, and even farther than that, and
there were competitors of every shape and size and age and level. One
of the first matches I happened to notice was between a plump Chinese
boy and an old bald white guy. There was a competition for players in
wheelchairs, and a competition for disabled ambulatory players. (To
play in the Nationals, you have to be an American citizen. Most of the
players and the spectators—who were largely the family members and
coaches of the players—were either of Asian birth or of Asian parentage. Four of the top six seeds in the women's singles competition were
born in China, and the future of the sport appears to reside in young
Asian Americans, who have table-tennis culture in their blood; the four
teenage girls featured as "top youth players" in the tournament program
were named Jackie Lee, Whitney Ping, Michelle Do, and Katherine

Wu.) You could get close to the play, and sometimes, when the ball was mis-hit and came your way over the thigh-high barriers surrounding each playing area, you'd get to throw it back to the players, which was totally cool. One of the funny things about table tennis is that, no matter how big you get, you still have to chase after the ball. There are no ball boys or girls kneeling in wait. (Steve Berger, a teacher and a player I met in Las Vegas, told me that players don't mind; the interval gives them a chance to think about their next shot.) There is one big difference between basement and elite players, though. They may both say "Come on!" out loud to themselves after a missed shot, but being a tournament player means never having to say "Sorry!" or "Whoops!"

When I first laid eyes on Marty Reisman in Vegas, he was zooming through the convention center (Marty walks faster than most people run), in his panama hat and a bright orange sports jacket, on his way to a match. Reisman, who marches to his own drummer and likes to talk about his march and his drummer at length, introduced me to various people, all of whom had fun commenting on Marty in front of him. "He's a legend," one USATT official said. "You're talking to a very questionable character here," another said. Lily Yip, a two-time Olympian and a dynamic force in organized table tennis (and the mother of two top-ranked teenagers), said to me, with a smile directed at Reisman, "Everything he says is not true." At one point, I saw a ten-year-old staring at Reisman's hardbat—he had obviously never seen such a thing before—and I suggested to Marty that he hit with him a little. Reisman, who, like all the top players of his generation, played mostly money matches, as a way both to practice and to make some dough, said to the boy, "Do you want to play for money?"

Some of the playing at the Nationals was spectacular, some of it was extremely good, and some of it was moving: Thelma (Tybie) Sommer was playing in the over-seventy women's singles—her game wasn't what it had been when she won the world championship mixed doubles with Dick Miles, in 1948, of course, but there she was, playing.

One of the reasons I had gone to the Nationals was to meet Dick Miles, who, at the age of seventy-seven, was being honored by the USATT for lifetime achievement. Miles, who is generally considered the greatest American player of the twentieth century, was, if not the anti-Reisman, then the non-Reisman of table tennis. He was Björn Borg to Reisman's Jimmy Connors—a no-nonsense, self-contained player. The two men, who have known each other for sixty years, since the days at Lawrence's, are physically and sartorially poles apart as well: Reisman is a lanky, balletic six-footer, given to wearing attention-getting—what my father would call "zooty"—clothes, and Miles is a compact five feet seven, who, the day I met him, was wearing light brown corduroys and an oatmeal-colored wool sweater over a plaid flannel shirt.

At the end of the hardbat finals, between Lily Yip and Steve Berger, I introduced myself to Miles and asked him whether he thought the hardbat game was superior to sponge. He likes both—he switched to sponge in the early sixties—but he said that a problem with the sponge game, from the point of view of spectatorship, is that the speed of the game is such that the unsophisticated viewer can't see that the winner of a point has actually earned it, with the spin he put on the ball. "In tennis, you can see it," he said. "In table tennis, it looks like an error."

Miles told me that as a young man he had wanted to be a writer. (He once took a job at *The New Yorker*, as what was then called an office boy, but quit after five days.) Both he and Reisman are, in fact, writers; Miles covered table tennis and wrote features for *Sports Illustrated* and has written an unpublished novel, and Reisman recently finished a second autobiography. Miles was known for carrying around a copy of *Ulysses*; Reisman called me the other morning ("Did I wake you up?" he said. "Yes," I said, and he kept talking for forty-five minutes) and recited a John Donne poem. But what Miles really wanted to talk about was a young man named Jake Carter, whom he had coached a little, and who was here at the Nationals.

One Saturday afternoon just over a year ago, Miles had gone to play at the Manhattan club but couldn't get a table—a birthday party was in session. "I said to the guy who runs it, 'Look, do you mind if I give the kids some pointers?' Jake's mother and father were there, and they said to me, 'Dick, do you ever give lessons?' I said, 'No, I don't want to.' They asked again, so I named a price that was so high I thought they'd say no—a hundred dollars an hour—and they said yes. I gave him three lessons and then went to Hawaii." (Miles spends four months of the year in Hawaii.) "He has talent, so I gave him to Steve Berger." (Berger, who also plays jazz guitar with Bob Dorough at Iridium every Sunday, played table tennis at Reisman's when he was a teenager, in the seventies, and became a protégé of Miles's when he was about twenty. He is one of the few people who have close ties to both players—in the table-tennis world, that's a little like being the patient of both Freud and Jung.)

I talked to Jake, a slender twelve-year-old with brown hair and a dusting of freckles on his nose, who was polite and friendly, despite having just lost a tough match during which the spectators—the large, unsportsmanlike family of his opponent—had been loud and distracting, and he had hurt his ankle. Jake told me that he was in the sixth grade at the Dalton School, in Manhattan, and that his interest in table tennis had started the summer before last, when his family got a table for their country house. "Then I found this place on a Hundredth and Broadway, so I had my eleventh-birthday party there." What did his friends think of his enthusiasm for the sport? "It's mixed," he said. "There are some people who think it's cool, and some people who think it's kind of dumb, like 'Ping-Pong? Why would anybody want to play Ping-Pong?'"

While I was in Las Vegas, I did a terrible thing: I bought a sponge racquet. I had to—I didn't have a usable hardbat of my own anymore, and the racquet that Reisman had promised to have made for me hadn't materialized after almost a year. I had to have something to play with, and I also knew that, if I was going to play with the general run of humanity, I would need this kind of racquet. I was with Marty, though—I didn't approve of sponge, so I bought a cheap, ready-made racquet, and deliberately avoided learning anything about particular rubbers, sponge thickness, blades, and speed glue (and also thereby avoided spending a hundred dollars more than the nineteen I did spend). I went back to New York, and asked Jake Carter to give me a lesson. Jake did his best, but perhaps he was a little shy about instructing someone thirty-four years his senior, and it didn't help that I was using my new sponge racquet for the first time. He tried to show me how to make a forehand loop drive—the essential shot of the sponge game—but I couldn't quite do it; my racquet wanted to go forward more than it wanted to go up. So we just played some games. He spotted me six points, and beat me. (We played to eleven points.) Then he spotted me eight points, and beat me again. I beat him once, but that's because he couldn't play his usual game against me. Steve Berger told me that

Jake's strongest suit was letting an opponent open an attack: "He'll allow you to do that and then he'll hit it right at you. We call it a kishke shot. You aim it at their elbow." But I couldn't get a rhythm going, and my hitting was unpredictable. ("Whoops!" "Sorry!")

A week or so later, I got a lesson from Berger, and that went much better. Steve had been at the club the night I played with Jake, and, when Jake was playing with someone else, I'd heard Steve yelling at him to keep his head down, and I'd thought his approach was unnecessarily harsh. Once I realized, when Steve was showing me the starting position for the forehand loop drive, that he'd been talking about the racquet head and not Jake's own head, I revised my opinion of his approach, and I revised it even further when he told me that I was a natural. Still, I found the sponge racquet hard to get used to. Berger had taken off the rubber that my racquet came with, which was of mediocre quality, and replaced it with top-notch rubber; it was disconcertingly lively, and I didn't feel the connection with the racquet that I had when I played with a hardbat. Hitting the ball didn't give me that "Aaaahhh" feeling; instead I got a "Whoa! Hey, what the—" feeling. But I did all right, for a beginner. At least, Steve said so.

A couple of weeks ago, I played with Marty for the first time since the spring. His new favorite place to play is the basement of Harry Evans's apartment building; last summer, Harry got the building's board to agree to let him put a table down there. There is, of course, a couch for balls to get lost under (there must be something about this in the USATT rule book: "a couch, preferably inconveniently placed, must be present at all times during play"), but the conditions—the lighting, the amount of space around the table, the *pock-pock* acoustics, the distance from the inhabited area of the building, so that no one can hear you shout "Nooooo!" when you miss a shot that you should have made—are excellent. Marty spots Harry between ten and thirteen points when they play. (The hardbat game is still played to twenty-one points.) Several times, Harry was up 20–15, and Marty said, "It's another deuce game, Harry," meaning that he was going to get the next five points. And then he did. And then he'd win the game. Harry didn't talk during points, but Marty did—during a rally, he'd look ahead to what he thought Harry was going to do and he'd say, "Forget it, Harry."

The racquet Marty had promised me still wasn't ready, so he let me use one of his—an old, classic paddle made by Bernard Hock. Though it was clear that, once again, I was out of practice, it was a pleasure to hold a hardbat in my hand for the first time in months. I was home. My backhand chop started coming back, and I hit a couple of good forehands. When Harry suggested that Marty and I play a game— something we had never done—I told him to play his normal game, as if he were playing for real. He said OK, and spotted me eighteen points. He won the first game almost as soon as it started, and I realized that he had never unleashed even a tenth of his arsenal on me. The second game was close, but I won—Marty made two shots that went long and missed the table, and then he hit a fairly hard forehand of mine into the net. I turned to Harry, who was sitting on the couch, watching, and said, "Let the record show: I beat Marty Reisman." I have a feeling, though, that Marty hit my shot into the net on purpose. In fact, I'm quite sure of it. I didn't win the game—he let me win it. But, if he'll keep spotting me eighteen points, I think that, with a little practice, I can beat him.

2003

PLAYING DOC'S GAMES

WILLIAM FINNEGAN

It was a shining February afternoon. The tide was low, and Ocean Beach, a four-mile-long north-south strip that accounts for nearly all of San Francisco's seafront and is normally narrow and deserted, was wide and full of people. I stutter-stepped down the bank at the foot of Sloat Boulevard, surfboard in hand, and hurried across the sand. Off to my left, two young black men in 49ers warmup jackets were silently putting a pair of miniature remote-control dune buggies through their paces; they wove and whirled and fishtailed in the sand. Off to my right, a group of white people were beating the hell out of pillows with yellow plastic clubs. As I passed, I could hear screaming and cursing: "Bitch! Bitch!" "Get out of this house!" Some people were weeping. They were also kicking the pillows around on the sand. A chubby man in his forties was pounding a sheet of paper laid on a pillow. When it flew off, he chased it down, bellowing, "Get back on there, you bitch!" Near the water's edge, I found another middle-aged man, gazing out to sea, his yellow club at his feet, a beatific expression on his face. He eyed my board as I knelt to strap on an ankle leash. I asked about the pillow beaters, and he said they were engaged in something called the Pacific Process. Thirteen weeks, three thousand dollars. This exercise, he said, was called Bitching at Mom. I noticed he was wearing work gloves. Hey, no use getting blisters while beating the bejeezus out of Mom.

It was the third day of a solid west swell. Winter is the prime season for surfing Ocean Beach—it's when the biggest waves and the cleanest conditions (little or no wind, orderly sandbars) coincide—but this joyful conjunction usually falls apart in early February, so each good day now was gravy. Conditions this afternoon were superb: six-foot waves, not a breath of wind. Unfortunately, the prolonged season had brought out unprecedented crowds, and half the surfers in Northern California seemed to be on hand. Ocean Beach didn't normally suffer from the overpopulation that spoils most California surf spots. There were only a few dozen local surfers, and visitors were rare. My theory was that surfers from nearby towns and cities didn't want to know about Ocean

Beach, because, while it sometimes got great waves, it was just as often ferociously intimidating. But crowds of sixty or more had become common in the last couple of weeks. It was as if a whole layer of the regional surf population had decided that, with the major winter swells probably over and conditions still improbably clean, Ocean Beach could be safely raided. I understood this selective bravado, because I felt it, too, along with an immense relief at having survived another winter—this was my third—of surfing Ocean Beach. Still, I resented the horde whose spidery silhouettes I could barely see, gliding and thrashing in the glare beyond the shore break, as I prepared to paddle out.

The water was atrociously cold. I could feel it tracing the seams in my wetsuit as I danced through the shallows; my hands throbbed when I started paddling. The first wall of sandy, grumbling white water felt like a barrel of gritty ice cubes poured down my back. I gasped, and kept churning toward what looked like a channel—a passage where fewer waves broke. At this tide, the waves near shore had little power, and I made steady progress. But I still had to cross the inside sandbar—a shallow ridge about halfway between the shore and the outermost surf—where unridable waves broke with pulverizing force. The first wave I saw break on the bar as I approached looked as if a string of land mines had exploded inside it. Sunlight splintered in long shards behind a curtain of falling water, then blew through the wall like a million grains of glass. An instant later, there was nothing but angry foam. I could see no channel. My progress stopped. For a couple of minutes, the waves and I quietly banged heads. Then came a lull: no waves. I sprint-paddled straight at the bar. A thick, glistening wave made a delayed appearance, but I got to the bar before it did, and hurled myself with an involuntary cry through its harmless, shiny, icy crest.

Beyond the inside bar, in the deepwater trough that separated it from the outside bar, scores of people came suddenly into view. They were scattered for two hundred yards in each direction: sitting in clumps far outside, scrambling for waves, scratching to get back out. Two or three were actually on their feet, riding waves. All had passed the snarling mastiff of the inside bar—the price of admission to this green-gold world of glassy low-tide peaks. The channels through the outside bar looked wide and easy to read. I angled north, toward a field of open water. Slightly farther north, a surfer I didn't recognize, riding a needle-nosed pale blue board, caught a good-sized wave. He fought to keep his balance as the wave, which was about twice his height, jacked and began to pitch. He didn't fall, but he lost speed in the struggle to keep his feet, and his first turn, now deep in the wave's shadow, was weak. If the wave hadn't hit a patch of deep water, and paused for a beat, he would have been buried by the first section. He managed to steer around it, though, and then pull into the next section and set a high line across a long green wall. By the time he passed me, he was in full command, perhaps one turn from the end of an excellent ride. But his face, I saw in the moment he shot past, was twisted with anguish, and with something that looked like rage.

Riding a serious wave is for an accomplished surfer what playing, say, Chopin's Polonaise in F-Sharp Minor might be for an accomplished pianist. Intense technical concentration is essential, but many less self-less emotions also crowd around. Even in unchallenging waves, the faces of surfers as they ride become terrible masks of fear, frustration, anger. The most revealing moment is the pullout, the end of a ride, which usually provokes a mixed grimace of relief, distress, elation, and dissatisfaction. The assumption, common among nonsurfers, that riding waves is a slaphappy, lighthearted business—fun in the sun—is for the most part mistaken. The face of the stranger on the pale blue board had reminded me, in fact, of nothing so much as the weeping, contorted faces of the pillow beaters on the beach.

I slipped between the big, shifting peaks of the outside bar and arrived at the takeoff area, known as the lineup. I half knew a few of the people I could see there, but the crowd seemed amorphous, unfocused—there were no conversations in progress. Everyone seemed intent on the waves, on himself. I caught my breath, chose a lineup marker—a school bus parked in the Sloat lot—and went to work. It was important, especially in a strange crowd, to make a good showing on one's first waves, for they established one's place in the pecking order. Blowing a takeoff or failing to catch a catchable wave usually sent one to the end of the queue for waves; this was an improvised but fierce arrangement, and in an aggressive crowd where waves were scarce one could easily be stuck there for the duration. I moved to a spot about fifteen yards inside a group of four or five surfers—a risky position, vulnerable to a big set, or series of waves, breaking farther out, but I was fit after a winter of paddling, and had the advantage of knowing the bars off this part of Ocean Beach. And, as it happened, the next wave to come through held up nicely, shrugging off the efforts of two guys farther out to catch it, and handing me a swift, swooping, surefooted first ride.

Paddling back out, I burned to tell somebody about the wave—about the great crack the lip had made as it split the surface behind me, about the mottled amber upper hollows of the inside wall. But there was no one to tell. A surf crowd is a delicate social unit. Everyone out there is starring in his own movie, and permission is required before you inflict your exploits on anyone else. Vocal instant replays and noisy exultation are not unknown, but they're subject to a strict code of collective ego control. Young kids sometimes misunderstand this part of the surfing social contract, and brag and browbeat each other in the water, but they generally cool it when older surfers are in earshot. The usual crowd at Ocean Beach was older than most—in fact, I couldn't remember ever seeing a teenager out on a big day—and the unwritten limits on garrulity among strangers there were correspondingly firm. Those who exceeded them were shunned. Those who consistently exceeded them were hated, for they failed to respect the powerfully self-enclosed quality of what other surfers, especially the less garrulous, were doing out there—the emotions that many of them were surfing through.

Two black grebes popped out of the foam beside me, their spindly necks like feathered periscopes, their big, surprised eyes staring. I murmured, "Did you see my wave?"

I headed for an empty peak slightly north of the school bus. I caught two quick waves there, and half a dozen people saw fit to join me. The jockeying for waves got, for Ocean Beach, fairly bad. Nobody spoke. Each dreamer stayed deep in his own dream—hustling, feinting, gliding, windmilling into every possible wave. Then a cleanup set rolled through, breaking fifty yards outside the bar we were surfing. Huge walls of white water swatted all of us off our boards, pushing a few unlucky souls clear across the inside bar. The group that reconvened a few minutes later was smaller, and now had something to talk about. "My leash leg just got six inches longer." "Those waves looked like December." We settled into a rough rotation. Waves were given and taken, and givers were sometimes even thanked. After noteworthy rides, compliments were muttered. The chances of this swell's lasting another day were discussed in general session. A burly Asian from Marin County was pessimistic—"It's a three-day west. We get 'em every year." He repeated his prediction, then said it again for those who might have missed it. The little group at the school bus peak, while it would never be known for its repartee, had achieved some rude coherence. A delicate fabric of shared enterprise had settled over all of us out there, and I found that my resentment of the non-locals had faded. The tide, which was now rising, was unanimously blamed for a lengthy lull. The sun, nearing the horizon, ignited a fiery Z of sea-facing windows along a road that switchbacked up a distant San Francisco hillside.

Then a familiar howl and raucous laugh rose from the inside bar. Heads turned. "Doc," someone said, unnecessarily. It was Dr. Mark Renneker, on his rounds. Doc Hazard, as he was sometimes called, was the one San Francisco surfer whom nonlocals were likely to know. His fame derived mainly from his exploits in giant Ocean Beach surf, but he was hard to miss in waves of any size. He was paddling alongside somebody I didn't know, regaling him with the plot of a horror movie: "So the head starts running around by itself, biting people to death." Before they reached the lineup, Mark interrupted himself, swerved, sprint-paddled north, wheeled, and picked off a wave that had somehow slipped past the rest of us. Ten minutes later, I saw him steaming in my direction again. There was, it struck me, a gawkiness about Mark; today, for instance, he was wearing an absurd-looking short-billed neoprene hood, with his beard jutting over the chin strap and his ponytail flopping out the back. But when Mark was on a surfboard his gawkiness was completely obscured by the power and precision of his movements. He paddled like a Grand Prix racer, always poised for agile cornering and breathtaking accelerations. Mark was six feet four but rode boards as short as six feet—a sign of rare strength and confidence. I watched him bearing down on me. When he was still ten yards away, he made a face and yelled, "This is a zoo!" I wondered what the people around us made of that observation. "Let's go surf Santiago," he said. Mark didn't recognize the unwritten limits on garrulity in the water. He tore up the surfing social contract and blew his great, sunburned nose on the tatters. And he was too big, too witty, and far too fearless for anyone to object. Feeling compromised, I reluctantly abandoned my spot in the rotation at the school bus peak and set off with Mark for the peaks breaking near the base of Santiago Street, half a mile north. " 'A three-day west'!" Mark snorted. "Who are these guys? It's going to be bigger tomorrow. All the indicators say so." An amateur meteorologist, Mark diligently monitored weather and buoy reports from the North

Pacific, and he was usually right about what the surf would do. He was wrong about Santiago, though. The bars, we saw as we approached, were plainly sloppier than those we had left behind at Sloat. There was nobody surfing anywhere nearby. That was why Mark wanted to surf there, of course.

It was an old disagreement between us. Mark believed that crowds were stupid. "People are sheep," he liked to say. And he often claimed to know more than the crowd did about where and when to surf. He would head down the beach to some unlikely-looking spot and stubbornly stay there, riding marginal, inconsistent waves, rather than grub it out with the masses. I had spent a lifetime paddling hopefully off toward uncrowded peaks myself, dreaming that they were about to start working better than the popular break, and sometimes—rarely, briefly—they actually seemed to do so. But I had a rueful faith in the basic good judgment of the herd. Crowds collected where the waves were best. This attitude drove Mark nuts. And Ocean Beach, with its great uncrowded winter waves, did in fact bend the universal Malthusian surf equation. Freezing water and abject fear and ungodly punishment were helpful that way.

A block or so before we reached Santiago, I took off, over Mark's objections, on a midsized wave, a detour that I quickly regretted: The set behind my wave gave me a thorough drubbing, almost driving me over the inside bar. By the time I got back outside, the sun was setting, I was shivering, and Mark was a hundred yards farther north. I decided not to follow him. I would see him later; there was going to be a slide show at his apartment that evening. Now shivering badly, I started looking for a last wave. But the peaks along here were shifty, and I kept misjudging their speed and steepness. I nearly got sucked over backward by a vicious, ledging wave, then had to scramble to avoid a monstrous set.

The twilight deepened. The spray lifting off the wave tops still had a crimson sunset tinge, but the waves themselves were now just big, featureless blue-black walls. They were getting more and more difficult to judge. There were no longer any other surfers in sight. I was ready to try to paddle in—an ignominious maneuver. And, when a lull came, that's what I did, digging hard, struggling to keep my board pointed shoreward through the crosscurrents of the outside bar, using a campfire on the beach as a visual fix, and glancing back over my shoulder every five or six strokes.

I was about halfway to shore, coming up on the inside bar, when a set appeared outside. I was safely in deep water, and there was no sense trying to cross the inside bar during a set, so I turned and sat up to wait. Against the still bright sky, at the top of a massive wave off to the south and far, far outside, a lithe silhouette leaped to its feet, then plunged into darkness. I strained to see what happened next, but the wave disappeared behind others, nearer by. My stomach had done a flutter kick at the sight of someone dropping into such a wave at dusk, and as I bobbed over the swells gathering themselves for the assault on the inside bar I kept peering toward where he had vanished, watching for a riderless board washing in. That wave had looked like a leash breaker. Finally, less than forty yards away, a dim figure appeared, speeding across a ragged inside wall. Whoever it was had not only made the drop but was still on his feet, and flying. As the wave hit deep water, he leaned into a huge, elegant carving cutback. The cutback told me who it was. Bill Bergerson, known around Ocean Beach as Peewee, was the only local surfer who could turn like that. He made one more turn, driving to within a few yards of me, and pulled out. His expression, I saw, was bland. He nodded at me but said nothing. I felt tongue-tied. I was relieved, though, by the thought of having company for the passage across the inside bar, which was now detonating continuously. But Peewee had other plans. He turned and, without a word, started paddling back out to sea.

Surfing is not a spectator sport. There is an international contest circuit, and a handful of surfers earn a living from competition, but most of the professionals actually make ends meet by endorsing products—surfboards, wetsuits, or the output of one of the many companies in the surf apparel industry. Contest surfing is seldom exciting to watch: The ocean cannot be relied on to provide memorable waves on an organizer's schedule, and few of the world's great surf spots happen to be natural amphitheaters.

One of the few times I've seen nonsurfers get their money's worth was on a minor Indonesian island about a hundred miles west of Sumatra, in 1979. Half a dozen of us, Australians and Americans, had found our way to a fishing village on the southwest shore of the island. Photographs of the wave that breaks near the village would later be

splashed across the surf magazines, putting the spot on the world surfing map, but at that time it was known only to a small, malaria-ridden
band. Two Swiss travelers—hearty types in hiking boots, who had
come to the island to look at Stone Age fortifications—turned up in
the village one day, and decided that it might be interesting to join us
in the surf. They came out on borrowed big-wave boards and, following instructions, took up positions in a deepwater channel near the edge
of the reef. The waves happened to be magnificent that day: big, powerful, flawless. The rides were long, fast, and extremely intense, and
most of them ended in the channel right where the Swiss travelers
bobbed like a pair of buoys, slowly turning orange in the equatorial sun.
We would come screaming through the final, jacking section and skit-
tering onto the wind-brushed flat, steering around them as we coasted
out of the waves, too pumped up to reply when they applauded
solemnly and said things like "Marvelous! How I admire you!" I wanted
to try to explain to them that they were witnessing the culmination of
years of hard search and sacrifice. But they clearly thought they were
just watching a bit of sport. They weren't even afraid of the waves. Two
of the surfers there that afternoon had boards they had dragged thousands of miles—across oceans, through Asian cities and jungles—
destroyed, snapped in half by the waves, but the Swiss observers just
splashed blithely back toward the channel whenever we warned them
they were drifting too close.

My girlfriend, Caroline, watched surfing for years, with no particular interest, until one day in Santa Cruz. We were standing on the cliffs
at a popular break called Steamer Lane. As surfers rode past the point
where we stood, we could see the waves from the side and then from
the back. For a few seconds, we saw an elevated version of what the
surfers themselves saw, and Caroline's idea of surfing was transformed
on the spot. Before, she said, waves to her had been two-dimensional
objects, sheer and onrushing, standing up against the sky. Suddenly, she
could see that they were in fact pyramids, with steep sides, thickness,
broad, sloping backs, and an incredibly complex three-dimensional
construction, which changed, collapsing and rising and collapsing, very
quickly. It was nearly enough, she said, to make watching surfing interesting.

It was also nearly enough, she said, to make the desire to surf com-
prehensible. Caroline had never understood why, after surfers spent

hours studying the waves from shore, they often announced their intention of going out by saying things like "Let's get it over with." But
then she wasn't there in Ventura, on a cold afternoon in 1964, when my
father ordered me back into the water after a dismal session during
which I had caught no waves. I was eleven years old, just learning to
surf, still too small to get my arm around my battered, beloved old
board. Three waves, Dad said, and we could go. My feet were bloody—
it was a rocky shore, and this was before the invention of ankle
leashes—and I was probably crying, and I wanted desperately to get
warm and go home. But he had the car keys, not to mention the keys
to manhood, and I bitterly paddled back out and caught my three
waves, riding them in on my knees. My father has always claimed that
I would never have learned to surf if it had not been for that episode.
All I know is that over the next few years I lost all interest in other
sports—especially team sports. By high school, when the other boys
were doing or dying for the school, their parents cheering in the stands,
my friends and I were skulking in Mexico, camping on lonely beaches
and bluffs, looking for waves.

The only audience that matters to most surfers is other surfers, for
they alone can truly appreciate what they are seeing. They have been
through the special ordeal of learning to surf, and know what a good
performance involves. Also, they share the obsession. Sunday surfers—
people for whom surfing is a hobby, who keep their surfboards in the
closet next to their skis and tennis racquets—undoubtedly exist. But
every Sunday surfer who can stand up on his board was, at some stage,
obsessed, for nothing less can get one through the hundreds of difficult,
discouraging hours it takes to gain basic skills. And retaining those
skills requires constant practice; in other words, competence presumes
obsession. It also takes exceptional physical fitness. James Michener
once reported, in a book called *Sports in America*, that the demands
made on the muscles, lungs, and heart by surfing were roughly the same
as those made by paddleball and slightly less than those made by badminton. Michener must have meant by *surfing* only the act of riding a
wave, because if paddling out and catching waves are included—and it
would be hard to surf without catching a wave—the level of fitness required for surfing is more like what might be needed for a combination
of long-distance rowing, white-water kayaking, and ballet. Brian Lowdon, an Australian exercise physiologist, has published studies showing

that surfers have a faster return to baseline pulse and respiratory rate after exertion than even Olympic pentathletes. (Lowdon's studies fail to mention badminton players.)

Not all surfers are robust young males; plenty of females and graying diehards surf, some of them well. Still, it's not really a sport that the entire family—unless the family is a marine version of the Flying Wallendas—can enjoy. Hence the insular codes and cryptic slang of surfers, and the relegation of all nonsurfers to alien status—"inlanders," "chalk people." Much of the tribe's language isn't even language. If you listen closely to surfers in the water, you are likely to hear little intelligible speech. Mainly, you'll hear a strange, primitive chorus of whoops, war cries, karate shouts. The first time Caroline and I looked at waves together was months after we met, and she was appalled to hear me start jabbering in a language that she didn't know I knew. "It wasn't just the vocabulary, all those words I had never heard you use—*gnarly* and *suck-out* and *funkdog*," she said, once she had recovered. "It was the sounds—the grunts and roars and horrible snarls."

Grunts and roars and horrible snarls filled the air in Mark's apartment. Slides from the past couple of winters at Ocean Beach were being shown, and most of the surfers featured in the slides were on hand, so the audience was agitated. "That can't be you, Edwin. You hide under the bed when it gets that big!" Mark convened these gatherings quasi-annually, provided most of the slides, and emceed. "This was the best day last winter," he said, projecting a shot of huge, immaculate Sloat that elicited a deep general groan. "But I don't have any more pictures of it. I paddled out after taking this one, and stayed out all day." Mark's voice actually had the nasal, waterlogged quality it got after a long session. And, in fact, he had already told me that he'd come in from the surf—its steady thunder from across the Great Highway, the coast road where Mark lives, was supplying the bass line for this evening's entertainment—only an hour before. "The moon rose just as it got really dark," he said. "I went back to Sloat, and surfed there for another hour. All those kooks were gone. It was just Peewee and me. It was great." I found this scene hard to picture. It wasn't that I didn't believe Mark—his hair was still wet. I just couldn't imagine how anyone could surf by moonlight in waves as big and powerful as the ones that had been breaking at Sloat at dusk. "Sure," Mark said. "Peewee and I do it once every winter."

Peewee was there at Mark's that night. Most of the surfers I knew by name in San Francisco were. Because the surf in and around the city is so formidable, few people learn to surf there—perhaps half of the city's surfers come from elsewhere. These migrants, who tend to be middle class, remain distinct in some ways from the homegrown surfers, who tend to be working class, but the fifteen or twenty men at Mark's that evening came from both groups. Ages ranged from the late teens to the midforties. With only three years' seniority, I was probably the most recent arrival in San Francisco. Peewee, who was about the same age as Mark and I—early thirties—and who worked as a carpenter, was a lifelong local. Mark, who grew up in Los Angeles, was still regarded by some natives as a newcomer, but in fact he had been around for more than ten years—he had gone to medical school at the University of California at San Francisco—and during that time had probably logged more hours in the water at Ocean Beach than any three other people combined. He had also become a central figure in local surf society. At least, no one else, from what I had seen, ever put together evenings such as this—and Mark did it with almost no visible effort.

"San Francisco is what I imagine surfing in Southern California was like in the fifties," Mark once told me. "Great waves, not too many people, lots of eccentrics, and everybody pretty much knowing everybody else." After the surf craze of the 1960s, Southern California surfing became a mob scene, with a cast of hundreds of thousands. An Ocean Beach denizen known as Sloat Bill had recently moved back to San Francisco after a stint in San Diego, declaring, "Surfing down there was like driving on the freeway. Totally anonymous." Sloat Bill, who qualified in my book as an eccentric, was a commodities trader from Texas via Harvard. He got his nickname when, following one of his divorces, he moved into his car and lived for a month in the Sloat parking lot, vowing not to leave until he had mastered the harsh art of surfing Sloat. There was room for argument about whether he had achieved that aim, but certainly he had made more money, after tapping market quotations into a computer plugged into his car's cigarette lighter, than any of the rest of us ever did while sitting in the Sloat parking lot. Sloat Bill wasn't at Mark's that night, but Mark showed several slides of him anyway—taking gruesome spills. A slide of me surfing Ocean Beach the previous winter drew a couple of hoots but no insults—I hadn't been around long enough for that. Mark said he had two new sequences he wanted to show, and then he would turn the projector over to others.

The first sequence illustrated a recent expedition to a remote point break near Cape Mendocino, far up in Northern California. Mark and another San Francisco surfer, a gardener named Rob, had traveled the last ten miles to the surf on dune bikes, racing at low tide along what looked like an extraordinarily rugged wilderness coast. They had camped on the beach for three days. The surf looked very cold and scary, and nobody watching the slides volunteered for a return trip that Mark was planning. On the way home, he said, they had been forced to travel at night, because that was the only time the tide got low enough. There had been a lot of rain while they were camping, so the streams crossing the beach had become major obstacles, especially in the dark. Rob had inadvertently sailed off the bank of one stream and crashed, bending the forks on his bike and soaking the sparkplugs. The tide had started rising while they were trying to get the bike going again. Bob Wise, who owns and operates the only surf shop in San Francisco, had heard enough. He had changed his mind, he said. "Doc, please take me with you next time."

The second sequence showed another North Coast exploit: Mark pioneering a fearsome surf spot known as Saunders Reef, in Mendocino County. Local surfers had been watching Saunders break for years, but no one had ever tried to surf it until, earlier that winter, Mark persuaded two big-wave riders from the area to paddle out with him. The wave broke at least half a mile from shore, on a shallow rock reef, and featured what was plainly a horrendous drop, along with some troublesome kelp. Mark's slides, taken by an accomplice with a telephoto lens from a mountainside, showed him cautiously riding deep-green walls two or three times his height. The trickiest part, he said, had actually come not in the water but in a nearby town that evening. People at the local hangout had been alarmed to hear that he'd surfed Saunders, and suspicious, he said, until they learned that he had done it in the company of two locals.

It was surprising to hear Mark mention local sensitivities. They were a real issue—I once saw a clipping from a Mendocino newspaper in which a local columnist described Mark as "a legendary super surfer from the Bay Area," adding, perhaps sarcastically, "I'm sorry I didn't stick around for his autograph"—but I usually thought of Mark as impervious to such matters. Of course, it was also a little tricky showing these slides to this audience; it required a delicate touch, even a measure of self-deprecation. Mark might disregard the finer points of the surfing social contract among strangers in the water, but Ocean Beach was home; here the strong drink of his personality needed sweetening. Earlier in the evening, when Mark, who suffers from asthma, complained that he was having trouble breathing, as he often does in February, an Ocean Beach homeboy known as Beeper Dave had muttered, "Now you know how us mortals feel."

A parade of photographers with their slide carousels followed Mark. There were water shots, some of them good, taken at a couple of the gentler San Francisco breaks. There were many blurry shots of giant Ocean Beach. Each time an especially frightening wave appeared on the wall, the youngest member of the audience, a teenager named Aaron Plank, snarled, "That's disgusting." Aaron, who was easily the most talented young surfer in San Francisco, was not yet a big-wave rider. Some old-timers showed slides from the seventies, featuring surfers I'd never heard of. "Gone to Kauai," I was told. "Gone to Western Australia, last we heard."

Finally, Peewee was prevailed upon to show a handful of slides from a recent trip to Hawaii. Taken at Sunset Beach, one of the best big-wave spots in the world, Peewee's pictures, which were of poor quality, showed some friends windsurfing on a small, blown-out day. "Unbelievable," somebody muttered. "Windsurfing." Peewee, who was probably the best pure surfer San Francisco had ever produced—and one of the few people from the city who were actually capable of surfing big Sunset Beach—said little. But he seemed amused by the crowd's disappointment.

As the slide party ended, I stuck around to help Mark clean up— and, watching the crowd drift off down the stairs, I suddenly recalled something that Kim Bodkin, the wife of a local big-wave surfer named Tim Bodkin, had said to me a few days before. I was clearly a charter member, she had said mock-innocently, of what she called "the Doc squad." The remark had mortified me. It meant that I was seen as one of Mark's acolytes. He did have acolytes—guys who wandered into his psychic gravitational field and found themselves orbiting around his fixed, surf-centered ideas about how to live. And it was true that since the day I moved to San Francisco, Mark had made himself my surf coach, health director, and general adviser, urging me on what he called "the surfer's path." And I had largely followed his lead—"played Doc's games," as Edwin Salem, another protégé, put it—letting his exuberance carry me along, letting him be the engine that powered my surfing life. But the fact was that I felt deeply ambivalent about surfing. I had been doing it for more than twenty years, yet I had long been reluctant to think of it as part of my real life as an adult. On balance, I seemed to spend as much energy these days resisting Mark's exhortations as I did actually surfing. So it was dispiriting to hear that I came off as an eager follower. Mark was like the guru character in every Hollywood attempt at a surfing movie—the Kahuna. The last thing I wanted was a walk-on part as one of the slack-jawed chorus.

Really, it shouldn't have mattered. Surfing wasn't supposed to be about one's standing in a company—about caste. In fact, I had spent years slogging through tropical backwaters in search of empty surf, looking for the purest possible encounter with the remotest possible waves. Still, some dogged essence of common vanity, of grubby society, had followed me everywhere. It was a paradox at the heart of my surfing: a desire to be alone with waves fused to an equal desire to be watched, to perform. The old Hawaiians, who institutionalized the spiritual side of surfing, had no illusions about its locker room aspects: they loved to gamble on organized competitions. Of course, they were not, from all accounts, prey to self-conscious conflicts about their place in the world, or to a Western-style dichotomy between Society and Nature.

They didn't have to cope with photography, either. The passion of virtually all surfers for photographs of themselves in the act of surfing approaches fetishism. To say that waves and the rides they provide are inherently fleeting events, and that surfers naturally therefore want mementos, barely begins to explain the mania for photographs. For a start, pictures are rarely about what a ride felt like; they are about what a ride looked like to others. Mark understood the surf-photo mania. He not only put on these slide shows, and had pictures of himself surfing tacked up all over the walls of his apartment; he also delighted in presenting friends with pictures of themselves surfing. I'd seen these photographs hanging in the homes of their subjects, framed like religious icons. I have one here—of me—as I write. Mark likes to say that surfing "is essentially a religious practice." What I've always had trouble deciding is just who or what is being worshipped.

On the wall by my desk in New York a photograph hangs: me half crouched inside a slate-gray barrel off Noriega Street, Ocean Beach. Mark gave Caroline the photograph; she had it framed for my birthday. It's a great shot, but it frustrates me to look at it, because the photographer fired an instant too soon. Just after the moment recorded by the camera, I disappeared into the wave. That's the shot I covet: the wave alone, with the knowledge that I am in there, drawing a high line behind the thick, pouring, silver-beaded curtain. That invisible passage, not this moment of anticipation, was the heart of the ride. But pictures are not about what a ride felt like; they are about what it looked like to others. This picture shows a dark sea; my memory of that wave is drenched with silver light. That's because I was looking south while I navigated its depths, and as I slipped through its brilliant almond eye back into the world.

1992

LAST OF THE METROZOIDS

ADAM GOPNIK

In the spring of 2003, the American art historian Kirk Varnedoe accepted the title of head coach of a football team called the Giant Metrozoids, which practiced then every week in Central Park. It was a busy time for him. He had just become a member of the Institute for Advanced Study, in Princeton, after thirteen years as the chief curator of painting and sculpture at the Museum of Modern Art in New York, and he was preparing the Mellon lectures for the National Gallery of Art in Washington—a series of six lectures on abstract art that he was supposed to deliver that spring. He was also dying, with a metastasis in his lung of a colon cancer that had been discovered in 1996, and, at Memorial Sloan-Kettering Cancer Center, in New York, he was running through all the possible varieties of chemotherapy, none of which did much good, at least not for very long.

The Giant Metrozoids were not, on the face of it, much of a challenge for him. They began with a group of eight-year-olds in my son Luke's second-grade class. Football had replaced Yu-Gi-Oh cards and the sinister water yo-yo (poisonous) as a preoccupation and a craze. The boys had become wrapped up in the Tampa Bay Buccaneers' march to victory in the Super Bowl that winter, and they had made up their minds to be football players. They wanted a team—"a real team that practices and has T-shirts and knows plays and everything"—that could play flag football, against an as yet unknown opponent, and I set about trying to organize it. (The name was a compromise: some of the boys had wanted to be called the Giants, while cool opinion had landed on the Freakazoids; *Metrozoids* was arrived at by some diplomatic back-formation with *Metropolitan*.)

Once I had the T-shirts, white and blue, we needed a coach, and Kirk, Luke's godfather, was the only choice; during one of his chemotherapy sessions, I suggested, a little tentatively, that he might try it. He had been a defensive-backfield coach at Williams College for a year after graduation, before he went to Stanford to do art history, and I knew that he had thought of taking up coaching as a full-time profession, only to decide, as he said once, "If you're going to spend your life coaching football, you have to be smart enough to do it well and dumb enough to think it matters." But he said yes, eagerly. He gave me instructions on what he would need, and made a date with the boys.

On the first Friday afternoon, I took the red cones he had asked for and arranged them carefully on our chosen field, at the corner of Fifth Avenue and Seventy-ninth Street. I looked over my shoulder at the pseudo-Renaissance mansion that houses NYU's Institute of Fine Arts, right across the street. We had met there, twenty-three years earlier, his first year at the Institute of Fine Arts, and mine, too. He had arrived from Stanford and Paris and Columbia, a young scholar, just thirty-four, who had made his reputation by cleaning up one of the messier stalls in the art-historical stable, the question of the authentic Rodin drawings. Then he had helped revive some unfairly forgotten reputations, particularly that of the misunderstood "academic" Impressionist Gustave Caillebotte.

But, as with Lawrence Taylor's first season with the Giants, though we knew he was supposed to be good, nobody was this good. He would come into the lecture room, in turtleneck and sports jacket, professor-wear, and, staring at his shoes, and without any preliminaries, wait for the lights to dim, demand, "First slide, please," and, pacing back and forth, look up at the image, no text in his hand but a list of slides. "Last time, we left off looking at Cézanne in the eighties, when the conversation between his code, registered in the deliberately crippled, dot-dot-dash, telegraphic repetition of brushstrokes, and his construction, built up in the blocky, stage-set recessional spaces, set out like flats on a theatre," he would begin, improvising, spitballing, seeing meaning in everything. A Judd box was as alive for him as a Rodin bronze, and his natural mode was to talk in terms of tension rather than harmony. What was weird about the pictures was exactly what there was to prize about them, and, his style implied, all the nettled and querulous critics who tried to homogenize the pictures into a single story undervalued them, because, in a sense, they undervalued life, which was never going to be harmonized, either.

It was football that made us friends. In that first fall, he had me typed as a clever guy, and his attitude was that in the professions of the mind clever guys finish nowhere at all. Then, that spring, we organized a touch-football game at the institute, and although I am the most flat-footed, least gifted touch-football player in the whole history of the world, I somehow managed to play in it. A bunch of us persuaded our young professor to come out and join in one Sunday. The game was meant to be a gentle, co-ed touch game. But Kirk altered it by his presence. He was slamming so many bodies and dominating so much that a wary, alarmed circle of caution formed around him.

Finally, I insisted to John Wilson, the Texan Renaissance scholar in the huddle, that if he faked a short pass, and everybody made a lot of noise—"I got it!" "There it is!," and so on—Kirk would react instantly and run toward the sound, and I could sneak behind him for the touchdown.

Well, the play worked, and, perhaps recognizing that it was an entirely verbal construction, he spotted its author and came right over, narrow-eyed and almost angry. "Smart play," he said shortly, with the unspoken words "Smart-ass play" resonating in the leaves above our heads. But then he shook his fist happily, a sign meaning OK, nice one. He turned away. He sees right through me, I thought; he knows exactly what I'm up to. I began working harder, and we became friends.

A quarter century later, he was coming to the same field from the hospital. He was a handsome man, in a big-screen way, with the deep-set eyes and boyish smile and even the lumpy, interesting complexion of a Harrison Ford or a Robert Redford. The bull-like constitution that had kept him alive for seven years, as the doctors poured drugs into him like Drano into a clogged sink, might have explained why the chemo, which thinned and balded almost everyone else, had somehow made him gain weight and grow hair, so, though he was a little stocky now, and a little gray, his step was solid and his eyes were rimmed with oddly long Egyptian lashes.

The boys came running from school, excited to have been wearing their Metrozoid T-shirts all day, waiting for practice: Eric and Derek and Ken, good athletes, determined and knowing and nodding brief, been-there-before nods as they chucked the ball around; Jacob and Charlie and Garrett talking a little too quickly and uncertainly about how many downs you had and how many yards you had to go; Will and Luke and Matthew very verbal, evangelizing for a game, please, can't we, like, have a game with another team, right away, we're ready; and Gabriel just eager for a chance to get the ball and roll joyfully in the mud. I was curious to see what Kirk would do with them. He was, first and foremost, a teacher, and his lectures still resonated in the halls of the institute. But how would he teach these eight-year-olds to play football? Orate at them? Motivate them? Dazzle them with plays and schemes?

"OK," he said, very gently, as the boys gathered around him in an attentive, slightly wary circle. "Let's break it down. First thing is how you stand. Everybody get down in a three-point stance." .

The boys dropped to their haunches confidently.

Kirk frowned. He walked up and down the line, shoving each one lightly on a shoulder or a knee, and showing how a three-point stance could be a weak or strong tripod, a launching pad or a stopping place, one that let you push off strongly or one that held you back. At last, he got everybody's stance correct. "OK, let's run," he said. "Just run the length of the field, from these cones to those cones, and then turn back. Last guy does fifteen pushups." Luke stumbled and was the last guy, and Kirk had him do fifteen pushups. The point was made: No favorites.

Right around then, a young park worker came up in one of those officious little green carts the park people ride around in. "I'm sorry," he said, "you can't play here. It's ruled off for games."

I was ready to get mad—I mean, hey, who was making these rules? We had been playing touch football here for years—when Kirk stepped in.

"We-ell," Kirk said, and the southern accent he brought with him from his youth in Savannah was suddenly more intense, an airplane captain's accent. "Well, uh, we got ten young men here eager to play football. Where can we take them to play?"

To my surprise, the park worker was there for the enlisting. "Let me see—I'll come back," he said. We went on with the drills, and ten minutes later the guy scooted up again in his cart.

"I think I've found just the place," he said. "If you go off there, right over the road, and take the left fork, you'll find this field that's hidden there behind the parking lot." He added, almost confidentially, "It's just opposite the toilets near the Ramble, but it's flat and large, and I think it's perfect."

"Much obliged," Kirk said, and he gestured to the boys, a big arm-sweeping gesture, and led them off in search of the promised field. They followed him like Israelites. We walked across the road, took the left, and went down a hill, and there it was—a little glade that I had never seen before, flat and fringed by tall trees, offering shade to the waiting moms and dads. It had a slightly derelict look—I could imagine that in a livelier era this field might have been a Francis Bacon mural, men struggling in the grass—but today it was perfect.

"Gentlemen," Kirk said clearly to the boys as they straggled on, looking around a little dubiously at the tufts of grass and the facing bathrooms. "Welcome to Metrozoid Field. This is the place we have been looking for." He set out the red cones again around the fringes.

"OK, let's scrimmage," he ordered. He divided the guys in half with a firm, cutting gesture, and they began an intense, slightly nervous touch-football game. Kirk watched them, smiling and silent.

"Shouldn't we teach them a play?" I suggested.

"No," he said. "They're off to a good start. Running and standing is a good start."

The scrimmage ended, and the winning team began to hurrah and high-five.

"Hey," he said, stepping forward, and for the first time I heard his classroom voice, his full-out voice, a combination of southern drawl and acquired New England sharpness.

"No celebrations," he said, arriving at the middle of the field. "This is a scrimmage. It's just the first step. We're all one team. We are the Giant Metrozoids." He said the ridiculous name as though it were Fighting Irish, or Rambling Wrecks, an old and hallowed name in the American pigskin tradition. The kids stopped, subdued and puzzled. "Hands together," he said, and stretched his out, and solemnly the boys laid their hands on his, one after another. "One, two, three, together!" and all the hands sprang up. He had replaced a ritual of celebration with one of solidarity—and the boys sensed that solidarity was somehow at once more solemn and more fun than any passing victory could be.

He had, I realized on the way home, accomplished a lot of things. He had taught them how to stand and how to kneel—not just how to do these things but that there was a right way to do these things. He had taught them that playing was a form of learning—that a scrimmage was a step somewhere on the way toward a goal. And he had taught them that they were the Giant Metrozoids. It was actually a lot for one hour.

When I say that I began working harder, I can barely begin to explain what his idea of working hard meant: It was Bear Bryant's idea of hard work circa 1955, it was General Patton's idea of being driven, only more military. It was coupled with a complete openness and equality, a vulnerability to his students' criticisms so great that it was almost alarming. He was working that hard, and was as eager to have you spot his weights as he was to spot yours. In what now seems like the halcyon days of 1984, a Saturday morning in winter would begin with a phone call and a voice booming, breaking right through the diaphanous protection of the answering machine, "Hey, folks, it's Kirk. I got up early to walk the pooch and I think I got some progress made on this here problem. What say we meet at eleven and trade papers?" I would curse, get out of bed, get to work, and be ready three hours later, with a new draft of whatever the hell I was supposed to be working on. We would meet at the little island that separates SoHo, where we lived, and Tribeca, where he and his wife, the artist Elyn Zimmerman, had their loft, and, standing there, he would turn the pages, and I would turn the pages, and he would show me all the ways in which I had missed the boat. Above all, he would insist, break it down: Who were the artists? What were the pictures? Give me the dates. Compile lists, make them inclusive, walk through it. You break it down in order to build it back up. What does it mean, why does it matter, for this artist, for art history, for the development of human consciousness? I would go back to work and the phone would ring again at three. "Hey, folks, it's Kirk. What do you say we meet and go over this new draft I've done and then maybe get some dinner?" And we would meet, and all four—or six or eight or ten—people would come together around him, and have dinner, and drink a good bottle of white wine and a good bottle of red wine and finally, exhausted, I would get to bed.

And then the phone would ring again. "Hey, folks, it's Kirk. I got to walk the pooch one last time, and I was just thinking that I may finally have sorted out the locomotive from the caboose in this thing. What do you say . . ." And I would put a coat on over my pajamas and go out one last time, in the whipping cold of midnight, and he would open the envelope right there and start reading, signaling to me to do the same, while his black Chow raced around, and we would try one more time to clarify exactly why Picasso looked at African art or why Gauguin went to Tahiti, while a generation walked by us in Astor Place haircuts and long vintage coats on their way to the Odeon.

He gave football all the credit. He had discovered himself playing football, first at his prep school, St. Andrew's in Delaware, as an over-weight and, by all reports, unimpressive adolescent, and then at Williams, where, improbably, he became a starting defensive end. The appeal of football wasn't that it "built character"—he knew just how cruddy a character a football player could have. It was that it allowed you to make a self. You were one kind of person with one kind of body and one set of possibilities, and then you worked at it and you were an-other. This model was so simple and so powerful that you could apply it to anything. It was ordinary magic: You worked harder than the next guy, and you were better than the next guy. It put your fate in your own hands.

I had always loved football, too, and we watched it together on Sat-urday afternoons and Monday nights for years. We saw a lot of good games, but we missed the big one. In 1984, we went up to New En-gland to celebrate Thanksgiving, and we were supposed to watch what promised to be the greatest college football game of all time, Boston College–Miami, Doug Flutie vs. Bernie Kosar. But our wives wanted to do something else—go look at things at a Shaker fair, I think—and we came home to find that we'd skipped the greatest college football game of all time, which Flutie had won by a Hail Mary, a long, desper-ation heave, on the last play of the game. We stared at each other in disbelief—we missed that?—and for the next twenty years "Boston College–Miami" was code between us for something you really, really wanted to do but couldn't, because your wife wanted to do something else. "You want to try and grab a burger at six?" "Uh—Boston Col-lege–Miami." It was code between us also for the ironies of life, our great, overlooked game, the one that got away.

"I think I'm going to make the motivational speech," I said to Luke as we walked over to Metrozoid Field the next Friday. I had been working on the motivational speech for several days. I didn't see a role for myself on the Metrozoids as a leader, and I thought I might make a contribu-tion as the Tommy Lasorda type, raising everyone's spirits and bleeding Metrozoid blue.

"OK," he said, relenting for the moment. "Tell it to me again."

"We're here to separate the men from the boys," I said, stopping at the Miner's Gate entrance to the Park, at Seventy-ninth Street, and trying to growl like Gary Busey as the Bear, "and then we're going to separate the warriors from the men." I paused to let this sink in. "And then we're going to separate the heroes from the warriors—and then we're going to separate the legends from the heroes. And then, at last, we're going to separate the gods from the legends. So, if you're not ready to be a football god, you don't want to be a Metrozoid." Long pause. "Now, won't that make the guys motivated?"

He reflected. "I don't know if they'll be motivated. They'll certainly be nauseated. Nobody wants to be motivated to play football, Dad. They want to play football."

Kirk ran another minimalist practice on this second week, and he missed the next because he was too sick from the chemo. I ran the session, and I thought, ambitiously, that it would be good to try a play at last, so I set about teaching them a simple stop-and-go. I got them to line up and run short, stop, and then go long. They ran it one by one, but none of them could get the timing quite right, and the boy who was supposed to be quarterbacking the thing couldn't get the right zip on the ball. Everyone was more annoyed than motivated, so I stopped after ten minutes, and sent them back to scrimmaging. They were restless for their coach.

It wasn't any surprise that he missed a practice; the surprise was that he made as many as he did. The chemo he was getting was so caustic that it had to be infused gradually, over sessions lasting three or four hours. Years of chemotherapy had left the veins in his arms so collapsed that sometimes it took half an hour for a nurse just to find an entry. He would grimace while being poked at with the needle, and then go on talking. He had the chemotherapy at one of the midtown extensions of the hospital, where the walls were earnestly decorated with Impressionist posters, Manet and Monet and Renoir—the art that he had taught a generation to relish for its spring-coiled internal contradictions and tensions there as something soothing for dying patients to look at.

He would talk, for hours. Sometimes he talked about the Metrozoids, and sometimes about Dylan or Elvis, but mostly he tried to talk through the Mellon lectures he was to give in Washington. He was, he said, going to speak without a text, just with a slide list. This was partly a bravura performer's desire to do one last bravura performance. It was also because he had come to believe that in art history, description was all the theory you needed; if you could describe what was there, and what it meant (to the painter, to his time, to you), you didn't need a deeper supporting theory. Art wasn't meaningful because, after you looked at it, someone explained it; art explained itself by being there to look at.

He thought that modern art was a part of modern life: not a reaction against it, or a subversion of it, but set within its values and contradictions, as surely as Renaissance art was set in its time. His book on the origins of modernism, *A Fine Disregard,* used an analogy from the history of rugby to illuminate the moment of artistic innovation: During a soccer game at the Rugby School, in England, an unknown young man named William Webb Ellis picked up the ball and ran with it, and a new game came into being. A lot of people thought that Kirk was celebrating a Romantic view of invention. But his was a liberal, not a Romantic, view of art. It began with an individual and extended to a community. What fascinated him was the circumstances that let someone act creatively and other people applaud instead of blowing the whistle.

That was what he loved to talk about when he talked about Elvis. He revered the moment when, in 1954, Elvis walked into a studio and played with Scotty and Bill and Sam, and everything suddenly came together. Had any of the elements been absent, as they easily might have been, as they usually are—had the guitarist Scotty Moore been less adaptable, the producer Sam Phillips less patient—then Elvis would have crooned his songs, no one would have cared, and nothing would have happened. The readiness was all. These moments were his faith, his stations: Picasso and Braque in their studios cutting the headlines right out of the newspapers and pasting them on the pictures to make collage, Richard Serra (first among Kirk's contemporary heroes) throwing hot lead in a studio corner and finding art in its rococo patterns.

Toward the end of one chemotherapy session, as he worried his way through his themes, a young man wearing the usual wool cap on his head came around the usually inviolable barrier of drapery that separated one "suite" from the next.

"You are professor?" he asked shyly, with a Russian accent, and Kirk shook his head.

"No, you are professor. I know. We have treatment at same time, every week. Same three hours," and he gestured toward his cap, with a short, we're-in-this-together smile. "I used to bring book, but now I just listen to you."

That Sunday of the first Mellon lecture, Kirk walked to the lectern after an introduction. The room was sold out, and the overflow had been sent to another lecture room. "Can I have the lights down, please," he said, and I saw that he had kept his word: He had no text, no notes, just a list of slides. He began to show and describe objects from sixties American minimalism—plywood boxes and laid-out bricks and striped paintings. He didn't offer a "theory," or a historical point. He tried, instead, to explain that a landscape that looked simple—there had been Abstract Expressionist splashes, and then there were all these boxes—was actually extraordinarily complex: There was a big difference between the boxes of Donald Judd, elegizing New York Canal Street culture, and the gleaming, body-shop boxes of the West Coast minimalists, glorifying California car culture.

"The less there is to look at," he said, pacing, as he always did, "the more important it is that we look at it closely and carefully. Small differences make all the difference. So, for example, the next time somebody tries to sell you on the mechanical exactitude of Frank Stella's stripes, think again about the beautiful, delicate breathing space in these stripes, the incredible feathered edge of the touch of the picture, which has everything to do with its kind of espresso-grounds, Beat Generation blackness that gives the picture its particular relationship to its epoch and time."

So he walked people through it. There were the bright, Matissean stripes of Ellsworth Kelly, made from the traced shapes of Parisian shadows, and those dark, espresso-bar simplicities of Stella. There was the tradition of the Bauhaus diaspora, all those German refugee artists who had been forced to go to South America, and who had proselytized for a kind of utopian, geometric abstraction—which had then appeared in New York just as New York artists were using geometric forms to indicate a cool-guy stoical distaste for utopian aspirations, creating a comedy of misunderstanding and crossbreeding. An art that had seemed like a group of quadratic equations set by a joyless teacher had been revealed as a sequence of inventions thought up by people. Where there seemed to be things, there were stories. The audience, at the end of the hour, was riveted. Someone was breaking it down, and then was going to build it back up. You didn't want to miss it.

"OK, we're going to learn a play," he said, the next Friday at Metrozoid practice.

The boys were standing on Metrozoid Field in their Metrozoid shirts in a semicircle around him. He showed them the play he had in mind, tracing it in the dirt with a stick: The quarterback takes the ball from the center and laterals to the halfback, who looks for one of three downfield receivers, who go in overlapping paths down the right side-line—one long, one medium, one short. The boys clapped hands and ran to the center of the field, terrier-quick and terrier-eager.

"No, no. Don't run. Just walk through it the first few times."

The boys then ostentatiously walked through the play, clowning around a bit, as though in slow motion. He laughed at that. But he had them do it anyway, five or six times, at a walk.

"Now let's just amble through it, same thing." The play took on a courtly quality, like a seventeenth-century dance. The boys did it at that pace, again and again: hike and pitch and look and throw.

"Now let's just run easy." The boys trotted through their pattern, and Garrett, the chosen quarterback, kept overthrowing the ball. Gently but firmly, Kirk changed the running back with the quarterback, Ken for Garrett, so that Garrett had the honor of being official quarterback but wouldn't have to throw, and then had them trot through it again. Ken threw hard, and the ball was caught.

After twenty minutes, Kirk clapped his hands. "Full speed. Every-body run." The boys got in their stances, and took off—really zoomed. The ball came nervously back, the quarterback tossed it to the halfback, he turned and threw it to the short receiver.

"Great!" At top eight-year-old speed, the ball had been thrown for a completion. The Metrozoids had mastered a play.

"Now let's do it again," Kirk said. I heard him whisper to Matthew, the short receiver, as he lined up, "Fall down!" They started the play, Garrett to Ken. Matthew fell down. Ken's eyes showed a moment of panic, but then he looked up, and saw the next boy, the middle receiver, Luke, waiting right in line, and he threw there. Complete.

"Nice read," Kirk said, clapping his hands. "Nice read, nice throw, nice catch. Well-executed play."

The boys beamed at each other.

"You break it down, and then you build it back up," Kirk said as they met at the center of the field to do the pile of hands. "The hardest play you learn is just steps put together."

By the fourth and fifth weeks of the Mellons, the scene at the National Gallery was almost absurd. People were lining up at nine in the morning for the two-o'clock lecture; I met a woman who had driven down from Maine to be there. The overflow room had to be supplied with its own overflow room, and the museum finally printed a slightly short-tempered handout. ("But what if I need to use the restroom while standing in line?" "If you need to use the restroom while in line, ask your neighbor to save your place.")

The fifth lecture would, he thought, be the toughest to put over. He found it easy to make an audience feel the variety, the humanity, of abstract art, even an art as refined and obstinate as the art of Judd or the young Frank Stella. But it was harder to make people accept, and relish, that art's perversity, and harder still to make them see that its perversity was exactly the humanism it offered. In the lecture hall, he explained that, as E. H. Gombrich had shown half a century ago in his Mellon lectures, representational artists were always making forms and then matching them—taking inherited stereotypes and "correcting" them in the light of new things seen. Leonardo, for instance, had inherited the heraldic image of a horse, and he had bent it and reshaped it until it looked like an actual animal. Abstract artists were always making forms and then trying to unmatch them, to make sure that their art didn't look like things in the world. Sooner or later, though, they always did, and this meant that, alongside abstraction, there was a kind of sardonic running commentary, which jumped on it anytime that it did look like some banal familiar thing.

Pop art was the most obvious source and form of this mockery: Roy Lichtenstein made fun of the abstract Op artist Victor Vasarely for making pictures that looked like the bottom of a sneaker, and Andy Warhol thumbed his nose at Barnett Newman for making pictures that looked like matchbook covers, and so on. But this counter-tradition wasn't mere jeering. It was generative, too: It forced and inspired new art. It kept abstraction from wallowing complacently in a vague mystical humanism. In the parody and satire of abstraction, its apparent negation, lay its renewal.

This process, Kirk explained, easily visible in the dialogue of minimalism and Pop, was just as vital, if less obvious, in the relationship between Jackson Pollock and Cy Twombly, two of his heroes. Twombly's squiggles and scribbles were not dutifully inspired by but actually parodied Pollock's method: "Everything that Twombly achieves he achieves by the ironic distancing of himself from Pollock. Everything that is liquid is turned dry. Everything that is light is turned dark. Everything that is simple and spontaneous and athletic is turned obsessive, repetitive, self-conscious in Twombly. By this kind of negation, he rerealizes, on a completely different scale and completely different terms, the exact immediacy of energy conveyed to canvas that Pollock has." Negation and parody were forms of influence as powerful as any solemn "transmission" of received icons. Doubt led to argument; argument made art.

That Friday, out on Metrozoid Field, Kirk divided the boys into two teams. "A team runs the play and B team defends," he said.

"But they'll know what we're gonna do," someone on the A team complained.

"That's OK. Most of the time, the other team knows what you're gonna do. That's called your tendency. The key is to do it anyway."

"But if they know—"

"Just run the play. Most of the time, the other team knows. The hard part is doing it right even when you know exactly what's coming."

The offense boys ran their one play, the flea-flicker, and the defense boys ran around trying to stop it. Standing on the sidelines, I was amazed to see how hard it was to stop the play even if you did know it was coming. The boys on defense ran around, nettled, converging on the wrong receiver and waving their hands blindly at the ball. The boys on offense looked a little smug.

He called them together. "You know what they're going to do. Why can't you stop it?"

The boys on the B team, slightly out of breath, shrugged.

"You can't stop it because they know what they're going to do but you don't know what you're going to do against it. One team has a plan and the other team doesn't. One team knows what it's doing, and the other team knows what they're doing but it doesn't know what it's doing. Now let's figure out what you're going to do."

He went to work. Who's the fastest kid they have? OK, let's put the fastest kid we have on him. Or, better, what if each guy takes a part of the field and just stays there and knocks the ball down if it comes near him? Don't move now; just stay there and knock it down. They tried both ways—man-to-man and zone—and found that both ways worked. The play lost its luster. The boys on the B team now seemed smug, and the boys on the A team lost.

"Maybe you need another wrinkle," he said to the A team. "Let's work on it."

Watching him on Metrozoid Field, you could see what made him a great teacher on bigger questions for bigger kids. Football was a set of steps, art a set of actions. The mysterious, baffling things—modern art, the zone defense—weren't so mysterious or baffling if you broke them down. By the end of the spring practice, the eight-year-olds were instinctively rotating out of man-to-man into a zone and the offense audibling out of a spread formation into a halfback option, just as the grownups in Washington were suddenly seeing the differences and similarities between Pollock's drips and Twombly's scrawls.

One particularly bright kid, Jacob, was scared of the ball, the onrushing object and the thousand intricate adjustments you had to make to catch it. He would throw his arms out and look away, instead of bringing his hands together. Kirk worked with him. He stood nearby and threw him the ball, underhanded, and then got him to do one thing right. When he caught it, Kirk wasn't too encouraging; when he dropped one he wasn't too hard. He did not make him think it was easy. He did not make him think that he had done it when he hadn't. He made him think that he could do it if he chose.

It is said sometimes that the great teachers and mentors, the rabbis and gurus, achieve their ends by inducting the disciple into a kind of secret circle of knowledge and belief, make of their charisma a kind of gift. The more I think about it, though, the more I suspect that the best teachers—and, for that matter, the truly long-term winning coaches, the Walshes and Woodens and Weavers—do something else. They don't mystify the work and offer themselves as a model of rabbinical authority, a practice that nearly always lapses into a history of acolytes and excommunications. The real teachers and coaches may offer a charismatic model—they probably have to—but then they insist that all the magic they have to offer is a commitment to repetition and perseverance. The great oracles may enthrall, but the really great teachers demystify. They make particle physics into a series of diagrams that anyone can follow, football into a series of steps that anyone can master, and art into a series of slides that anyone can see. A guru gives us himself and then his system; a teacher gives us his subject, and then ourselves.

If this story was the made-for-television movie that every story about early death threatens to become, we would have arranged one fiery game between the Giant Metrozoids and another team, a bigger, faster, slightly evil team, and the Metrozoids would win it for their coach. It didn't happen like that. Not that the Metrozoids didn't want a game. As their self-confidence increased, they kept urging us to find some other team of eight-year-olds that they could test themselves against. I was all for it, but Kirk, I sensed, was not. Whenever the boys raised the possibility, he would say, diffidently, "Let's wait till the fall," knowing, of course, that the fall, his fall, would never come.

I understood the hold he had on the Metrozoids. But when I thought about his hesitation I started to understand the hold that the Metrozoids had on him. I had once said something fatuous to him about enjoying tonight's sunset, whatever tomorrow would bring, and he had replied that when you know you are dying you cannot simply "live in the moment." You loved a fine sunset because it slipped so easily into a history, yours and the world's; part of the pleasure lay in knowing that it was one in a stream of sunsets you had loved, each good, some better, one or two perfect, moving forward in an open series. Once you knew that this one could be the last, it filled you with a sense of dread; what was the point of collecting paintings in a museum you knew was doomed to burn down?

But there were pleasures in life that were meaningful in themselves, that did not depend on their place in an ongoing story, now interrupted. These pleasures were not "aesthetic" thrills—not the hang gliding you had never done or the trip to Maui you had never taken—but things that existed outside the passage of time, things that were beyond comparison, or, rather, beside comparison, off to one side of it. He loved the Metrozoid practices, I came to see, because for him they weren't really practicing. The game would never come, and the game didn't matter. What mattered was doing it.

At the last practice of the school year, the boys ran their plays and scrimmaged, and the familiar forms of football, of protection and pass routes and coverages, were all there, almost magically emerging from the chaos of eight-year-olds in motion. At the end, the boys came running up to him, and he stood in place, and low-fived each one of them. "See you in September," the kids cried, and Kirk let the small hands slap his broad one, and smiled. "We'll work again in the fall," he said, and I knew he meant that someone would.

That Sunday, he did something that surprised me. It was the last lecture of the Mellons, and he talked about death. Until then, I had never heard him mention it in public. He had dealt with it by refusing to describe it—from Kirk the ultimate insult. Now, in this last lecture, he turned on the audience and quoted a line from a favorite movie, *Blade Runner,* in which the android leader says, "Time to die," and at the very end he showed them one of his favorite works, a Richard Serra *Torqued Ellipse,* and he showed them how the work itself, in the physical experiences it offered—inside and outside, safe and precarious, cold and warm—made all the case that needed to be made for the complexity, the emotional urgency, of abstract art. Then he began to talk about his faith. "But what kind of faith?" he asked. "Not a faith in absolutes. Not a religious kind of faith. A faith only in possibility, a faith not that we will know something, finally, but a faith in not knowing, a faith in our ignorance, a faith in our being confounded and dumbfounded, as something fertile with possible meaning and growth. . . . Because it can be done, it will be done. And now I am done." The applause, when it came, was stadium applause, and it went on a long time.

By July, the doctors had passed him right out of even the compassionate trials, and were into the world of guesses and radiation. "It's a Hail Mary," he said of a new radiation therapy that they were proposing. "But, who knows, maybe I'll get the Doug Flutie of radiologists." Then a slight ache in his back that he thought was a disk he'd hurt water-skiing turned out to be a large tumor in his spine, and the end came quickly.

His wife, Elyn, had to be out of the city, and I spent the last Saturday afternoon of his life with him. In the old way, I went into his office to work on something I was writing. Kirk went to see what was on television. He had, I noticed, a team photograph of the Metrozoids at their last practice propped up on the coffee table. By then, he could hardly walk, and his breath came hard.

But he called out, "Yo. You got to come here."

"What?"

"You won't believe this. Boston College–Miami."

Damned if it wasn't. ESPN Classics had a "Hail Mary" Saturday, all the great games decided on the last play, and now, twenty years late, they were showing the game from beginning to end: the whole game, with the old graphics and the announcer's promos, exactly as it had first been shown.

So we finally got to watch the game. And it was 1984 again, and the game was still thrilling, even though you knew what the outcome would be, and how it would happen. Kirk's brother, Sam, came around, and he watched, too, the three of us just enjoying a good game, until at last here we were, at that famous, miraculous, final Hail Mary, Doug Flutie dropping back and rolling out, to heave the ball desperately downfield.

"Look at that!" Kirk cried, and the ball was still in midair out of view, up above the television screen.

"What?" I asked, as the ball made its arc and fell into the hands of Gerard Phelan and the announcers went wild.

"That's no Hail Mary. Watch it again and you'll see. That's a coverage breakdown." The old defensive-backfield coach spoke evenly, as, twenty years before, the crowd jumped and screamed. "Safety steps up too soon because he doesn't think Flutie can make that throw on the run. What he doesn't see is that Flutie has time to square around and get his feet set on the rollout, which adds fifteen yards to his range. Safety steps up too soon, Phelan runs a standard post route, and that's it. That safety sees Flutie get his feet set, makes the right read, and there's no completion." Turning to us, he said, "That is no Hail Mary, friends. That's no miracle. That is just the play you make. That is one gentleman making the right read and running the right pattern and the other gentleman making the wrong read." And for one moment he looked as happy as I had ever known him: one more piece of the world's mysteries demystified without being debunked, a thing legendary and hallowed broken down into the real pattern of human initiative and human weakness and human action that had made it happen. We had been waiting twenty years to see a miracle, and what we saw—what he saw, once again, and showed us—was one more work of art, a pattern made by people out of the possibilities the moment offered to a ready mind. It was no Hail Mary, friends; it was a play you made.

He turned to me and Sam, and, still elated by the revelation of what had really happened all those years ago, we began to talk about Ralph Emerson and Richard Serra. And then Kirk said, heavily, "There is nothing in the world I would rather be doing than taking part in this conversation. But I have to lie down." He died four days afterward, late at night, having spent the day talking about Hitchcock films and eighteenth-century hospital architecture.

Luke and Elyn and I went up to the football field at Williams last fall and, with some other friends, spread his ashes in the end zone, under the goalposts. At his memorial, at the Metropolitan Museum of Art, Renée Fleming sang and the violinist Arnold Steinhardt played and the art world of New York turned out and listened and recalled him. I think a lot of them must have been puzzled, in the slide show that Elyn had prepared to begin the evening, and which recapitulated his career, from Savannah to Princeton, to see toward the end a separate section gravely titled "The Giant Metrozoids," with the big figure surrounded by small boys. But I'm sure he would have been glad to see them there. The Metrozoids are getting back in business again, with an inadequate coach. I've thought about finally making the motivational speech, but I don't think I need to. The Metrozoids don't need to learn how to separate the men from the heroes. They know.

2004

THE *SANDY FRAZIER* DREAM TEAM

IAN FRAZIER

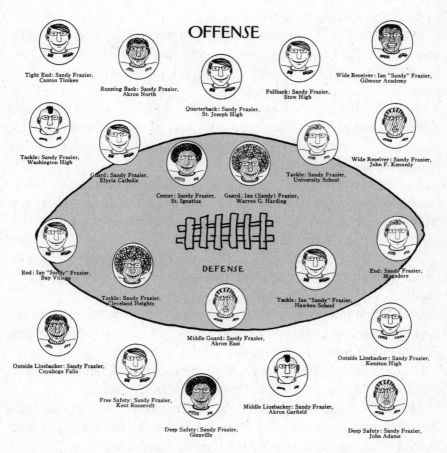

OFFENSE

Tight End: Sandy Frazier, Canton Timken

Running Back: Sandy Frazier, Akron North

Quarterback: Sandy Frazier, St. Joseph High

Fullback: Sandy Frazier, Stow High

Wide Receiver: Ian "Sandy" Frazier, Gilmour Academy

Tackle: Sandy Frazier, Washington High

Guard: Sandy Frazier, Elyria Catholic

Center: Sandy Frazier, St. Ignatius

Guard: Ian (Sandy) Frazier, Warren G. Harding

Tackle: Sandy Frazier, University School

Wide Receiver: Sandy Frazier, John F. Kennedy

End: Ian "Sandy" Frazier, Bay Village

Tackle: Sandy Frazier, Cleveland Heights

DEFENSE

Tackle: Ian "Sandy" Frazier, Hawken School

End: Sandy Frazier, Mogadore

Middle Guard: Sandy Frazier, Akron East

Outside Linebacker: Sandy Frazier, Cuyahoga Falls

Free Safety: Sandy Frazier, Kent Roosevelt

Middle Linebacker: Sandy Frazier, Akron Garfield

Outside Linebacker: Sandy Frazier, Kenston High

Deep Safety: Sandy Frazier, Glenville

Deep Safety: Sandy Frazier, John Adams

Quarterback: 6′4″, 185-lb. senior Sandy Frazier led St. Joe's Vikings to their second straight all-city championship, amassing 1,593 yards in the air with an 87 percent completion ratio. Set state mark for rushing by a quarterback with 830 yards for the season.

Fullback: Stow junior Sandy Frazier (6′5″, 217 lbs.) broke all rushing records set at Stow in 1962 by star alum Larry Csonka. Frazier is tremendously quick for a big man.

Running Back: Suspended early in the season for disciplinary reasons, Akron North's Sandy Frazier came back in the final three games to beat

Hoban, Buchtel, and Firestone with his spectacular catches and kickoff returns. He runs the hundred in 9.4, an excellent time for a man his size.

Wide Receiver: Sandy Frazier of John F. Kennedy caught 45 passes for touchdowns this season. Team captain in his sophomore year, he will make the Fighting Eagles squad of 17 returning lettermen a power in the '78 city championships.

Wide Receiver: The Lancers cruised to the Greater Cleveland Private School title behind the receiving and open-field blocking of 6'5", 195-lb. junior end Ian "Sandy" Frazier. For a man of his size, he possesses outstanding quickness and agility.

Tight End: Canton Timken relied on their big junior tight end Sandy Frazier for his blocking on traps and sweeps, as well as for his pass-catching abilities. His quickness is amazing, considering his height and weight (6'7", 223 lbs.).

Tackle: Massillon's Washington High has produced more pro tackles than any other high school in the country, and 6'8", 260-lb. junior Sandy Frazier is well on his way to joining that list. He moves with great agility for a tackle that large.

Tackle: University School's four-year letterman and team captain Sandy Frazier displays surprising quickness, despite his 6'2", 230-lb. frame.

Guard: Ian (Sandy) Frazier of Warren G. Harding really made the Panthers' ground game roll. The 6'3", 215-lb. senior is an excellent pulling guard, with his 9.8 speed.

Guard: Elyria Catholic senior Sandy Frazier, at 6'4" and 240 lbs., is a lineman who can do it all. He has great mobility for a big man.

Center: St. Ignatius sophomore Sandy Frazier, at 5'11", 212 lbs., was the dependable keystone of the Maize and Blue offense this year, which ranked third in total yardage in the state prep totals.

DEFENSE

Deep Safety: John Adams coach Paul Feldermacher calls 5'9", 165-lb. junior defensive back Sandy Frazier "Pound for pound the best player I have ever coached." He wins the Dream-Team Headhunter Award for most tackles this season.

Deep Safety: 5'11", 175-lb. senior Sandy Frazier of Glenville won the East Cleveland Thanksgiving Turkey Day Game with his 85-yard runback of an interception in the final seconds.

Free Safety: A player skilled at reading defenses who also loves to hit people, Kent Roosevelt junior Sandy Frazier was the headache of running backs throughout the greater Akron area, with his 6′7″, 210-lb. build coupled with his excellent speed.

Outside Linebacker: Sandy Frazier of Cuyahoga Falls, a 6′3″, 210-lb. junior, led the Suburban League in tackles per game. He is as fast and nimble as a man half his size.

Outside Linebacker: Kenston High's junior defender Sandy Frazier (6′4″, 215 lbs.) played with reckless abandon in the Class AA Divisional Championship, blocking three punts. Even though he is huge, he is also swift.

Middle Linebacker: A narrow choice in the Dream Team voting over Walsh Jesuit's outstanding MLB Sandy Frazier, Akron Garfield senior captain Sandy Frazier won out because even though he clocks a speedy 4.2 in the 40-yard dash, he is still extremely large (6′2″, 210 lbs.).

End: Bay Village High senior DE Ian "Sandy" Frazier, at 6′6″, 231 lbs., has the catlike quickness that makes him a really tough defender, when you consider how big he is.

End: Mogadore owes most of its 6-3 won-lost record to sophomore defensive end Sandy Frazier, who intimidated blockers with his agility, which was outstanding when operating in concert with his 6′5″, 223-lb. body.

Tackle: Ian "Sandy" Frazier of Hawken School is a player who you would think would move slow off the ball when you realized that he weighs in at 6′8″, 240 lbs., but that was not the case, as many prep-league opponents can attest.

Tackle: Cleveland Heights junior standout Sandy Frazier (6′3″, 219 lbs.) made game-saving tackles three times in goal-line stands when the Heights Tigers shut out the mighty Blue Bombers of Cleveland East. He is very large, in addition to being very fast.

Middle Guard: Akron East junior Sandy Frazier was the mainstay of East's defense, which allowed only 24 points all season. For a man of his quickness and agility, he possesses tremendous size.

1977

PART FOUR

A DEEPER GAME

"Would you mind picking me up, Bill? Agnes is using the car after all."

BR'ER RABBIT BALL

RING LARDNER

In spite of the fact that some of my friends in the baseball industry are kind enough to send me passes every spring, my average attendance at ball parks for the last three seasons has been two times per season (aside from World's Series) and I probably wouldn't have gone that often but for the alleged necessity of getting my innumerable grandchildren out in the fresh air once in a while. During the games, I answer what questions they ask me to the best of my knowledge and belief, but most of the afternoon I devote to a handy pocket edition of one of Edgar Wallace's sex stories because the events on the field make me yearn for a bottle of Mothersill's Remedy.

Manufacturers of what they are using for a ball, and high officials of the big leagues, claim that the sphere contains the same ingredients, mixed in the same way, as in days of old. Those who believe them should visit their neighborhood psychiatrist at the earliest possible moment.

When I was chasing around the circuit as chronicler of the important deeds of Cubs or White Sox, it was my custom and that of my colleagues to start making up our box scores along about the seventh inning in cases where one club was leading its opponent by ten runs. Nowadays the baseball reporters don't dare try to guess the answer even if there are two out in the last half of the ninth inning and the score is 21 to 14.

I have always been a fellow who liked to see efficiency rewarded. If a pitcher pitched a swell game, I wanted him to win it. So it kind of sickens me to watch a typical pastime of today in which a good pitcher, after an hour and fifty minutes of deserved mastery of his opponents, can suddenly be made to look like a bum by four or five great sluggers who couldn't have held a job as bat boy on the Niles High School scrubs.

Let us say that the Cubs have a series in Brooklyn. They get over there at eleven in the morning so they can find the park by the time the game begins. The game develops into a pitchers' battle between Charlie Root, Bud Teachout, Guy Bush, and Pat Malone for the Cubs and Dazzy Vance, Jim Elliott, and Adolfo Luque for the Robins. The last half of the ninth inning arrives with the score 12 to 8 in Chicago's favor—practically a no-hit game in these days. Somebody tries to strike out, but Malone hits his bat and the ball travels lightly along the ground toward third base. Woody English courageously gets in front of it and has two fingers broken. This is a superficial injury for an infielder of the present, so Woody stays in the game. The Brooklyn man is safe at first. The next Brooklyn man, left-handed and a born perpendicular swatsman, takes a toehold and crashes a pop fly toward Charlie Grimm. The pellet goes over the right-field fence like a shot and breaks a window in a synagogue four blocks away.

Manager McCarthy removes Malone and substitutes Blake, hoping the latter will give a few bases on balls and slow up the scoring. But Blake gives only two bases on balls and then loses control. He pitches one over the plate and the batsman, another left-hander who, with the old ball, would have been considered too feeble to hit fungoes on one of these here miniature golf courses, pops it over the fence to the beach at Far Rockaway, where it just misses a young married couple called Rosenwald. The victory is Brooklyn's and the official scorer puts the names of a lot of pitchers, including Rucker and Grimes, into a hat and the first name drawn out gets the credit.

I mean it kind of upsets me to see good pitchers shot to pieces by boys who, in my time, would have been ushers. It gnaws at my vitals to see a club with three regular outfielders who are smacked on top of the head by every fly ball that miraculously stays inside the park—who ought to pay their way in, but who draw large salaries and are known as stars because of the lofty heights to which they can hoist a leather-covered sphere stuffed with dynamite.

Those who are cognizant of my great age ask me sometimes what Larry Lajoie would do in this "game." Well, he wouldn't do anything after one day. Larry wasn't a fly-ball hitter. When he got a hold of one, it usually hit the fence on the first bounce, traveling about five feet three inches above the ground most of the way and removing the ears of all infielders who didn't throw themselves flat on their stomachs the instant they saw him swing. They wouldn't have time to duck this ball, and after the battle there would be a meeting of earless infielders, threatening a general walkout if that big French gunman were allowed in the park again, even with a toothpick in his hand.

But without consulting my archives I can recall a dozen left-handed batsmen who hit fly balls or high line drives and who hit them so far that opposing right and center fielders moved back and rested their spinal columns against the fence when it was these guys' turn to bat.

I need mention only four of this bunch—two from each league—to give my contemporaries a talking point when their grandchildren boast of the prowess of the O'Douls, Kleins, and Hermans of today. The four I will select offhand are Elmer Flick and Sam Crawford of the American League and Harry Lumley and Frank Schulte of the National.

In the year 1911 (I think it was) Mr. Schulte led the National League in homers with a total of twenty-one. Such a number would be disgraceful in these days, when a pitcher gets almost that many. Just the same, I am willing to make a bet, which never can be decided, that Frank, with the present ball in play, would just about treble that total and finish so close to the Babe himself that it would take until December to count the ballots. I have frequently seen, in the dim, dead past, the figures of Fielder Jones and Eddie Hahn backing up against the haywire when Flick or Crawford came to bat, and on one occasion, when we traveled east on the same train as the Detroit club, I overheard a bit of repartee between Jones and Samuel. That afternoon Jones had caught three fly balls off Sam without moving more than a yard out of his position, which was a comfortable one, with the fence for a back rest.

"Why," said Sam grumblingly, "were you playing pretty near out of the park for me?"

"Why," said Jones, "do you always hit to the same place?"

Right-fielders were constantly robbing Lumley and Flick of two-base hits or worse by lolling against the bleacher wall—and it must be remembered that in those ancient times bleachers were far enough from the playing field so that the first- and third-base coachers couldn't sit in them.

Speaking of Mr. Lumley (if you've heard this before, don't stop me), we (the Cubs) came east one season and we had a pitcher named Edward Reulbach, who was great when he had control and terrible when he lacked it. On this trip he lacked it to such an extent that Manager Chance ordered him to pay forenoon visits to each hostile battlefield and pitch to the rival batsmen in their practice. The latter had no objection—it just meant somebody to hit against without wearing out one of their own men.

Well, we got to Brooklyn and after a certain game the same idea entered the minds of Mr. Schulte, Mr. Lumley, and your reporter, namely: that we should see the Borough by night. The next morning, Lumley had to report for practice and, so far as he was concerned, the visibility was very bad. Reulbach struck him out three times on low curve balls inside.

"I have got Lumley's weakness!" said Ed to Chance that afternoon.

"All right," said the manager. "When they come to Chicago, you can try it against him."

Brooklyn eventually came to Chicago and Reulbach pitched Lumley a low curve ball on the inside. Lumley had enjoyed a good night's sleep, and if it had been a 1930 vintage ball, it would have landed in Des Moines, Iowa. As it was, it cleared the fence by ten feet and Schulte, playing right field and watching its flight, shouted: "There goes Lumley's weakness!"

Well, the other day a great ballplayer whom I won't name (he holds the home-run record and gets eighty thousand dollars a year) told a friend of mine in confidence (so you must keep this under your hat) that there are at least fifteen outfielders now playing regular positions in his own league who would not have been allowed bench-room the year he broke in. Myself, I just can't stomach it, but Brooklyn recently played to one hundred and ten thousand people in four games at Chicago, so I don't believe we'll ever get even light wines and beer.

1930

"This is our beginners' slope."

THE GREENS OF IRELAND

HERBERT WARREN WIND

When most people think of sport in Ireland, the first things that come to mind are the wonderful horses raised in the Curragh and the national exuberance for horse racing, and, after that, the excellent salmon fishing in the southwest and the Irish fondness for two native games that are played practically nowhere else—Gaelic football, which is a combination of soccer and Rugby, and hurling, which is a combination of field hockey and a special Celtic brand of karate. Since scarcely anyone associates the Irish with golf, it almost invariably comes as a surprise to the sports-minded to learn that the island is one of the great golfing lands—and, indeed, has more authentic golf courses per inhabitant than any other country in the world except Scotland, the cradle of the game. Where golf is concerned, it should be noted, Ireland is divided by no political boundary line; the Golfing Union of Ireland governs the game both in the Republic of Ireland, or Eire, and in Northern Ireland, which is, of course, a part of the United Kingdom. At the present time, there are 228 golf courses in the two countries, and since the combined population is around 4,300,000, this works out to one course for every nineteen thousand inhabitants. In the United States, despite the proliferation of new courses in recent years, the ratio is one for every twenty thousand people, and in Japan, to name another notoriously golf-struck nation, it is one for every 175,000. In Ireland, the courses are not only numerous but of an exceptionally high quality. Most well-traveled golf experts, if asked to select the twelve finest courses in the world, would surely include at least one in Ireland, and some might include as many as three.

Like the famous courses in Scotland, the best ones in Ireland are situated on the duny linksland deposited centuries ago by the retreating ocean. While the thought of Irish linksland (as opposed to meadowland) may be startling, it really shouldn't be, because the coastal stretches of Scotland and Ireland are remarkably similar. (Less than fourteen miles of water separates Torr Head, in Northern Ireland, from the Mull of Kintyre, in Scotland.) In the last twenty-five years, the Irish have taken to their splendid seaside links and to their satisfactory, if less testing, inland courses with a tremendous rush. Whereas there were only twenty-five thousand golfers on the island at the close of the Second World War, there are three times that number today. All the clubs are filled to the brim with members, and an estimated ten thousand applicants are at present on various waiting lists, ready to spring forward whenever a vacancy occurs. In the meantime, since Ireland has no municipal courses, this frustrated horde of potential golfers has been hacking away on the more than a hundred pitch-and-putt courses that have popped up all over the countryside in response to the demand for golf facilities, however abbreviated. In short, unlikely as it may seem when one recalls the historic Hibernian predilection for strenuous pastimes, golf has now become Ireland's most popular participant sport.

One of the primary reasons the game has found such high favor among the Irish is its inexpensiveness. Portmarnock, which is just outside Dublin, is generally accepted as the island's premier golf club, but its members are required to pay an entrance fee that amounts to only $125. Annual dues come to approximately that same mild figure. Moreover, the dues at the average Irish golf club are a good deal lower than the dues at Portmarnock, which reflects the comparatively high cost of everything in and around the Republic's capital city. For instance, at the Lahinch Golf Club, in County Clare—a first-rate course where the South of Ireland Amateur Championship is held each year—the annual dues are thirty dollars and there is no entrance fee at all, at all. Such modest rates are possible because the cost of maintaining a course is extremely low and, concomitantly, the revenue from the club bar can be depended on to be quite robust. In any event, nearly every Irishman who wants to play golf can afford to, and its addicts therefore constitute an almost complete cross-section of the Irish socioeconomic strata. Another fundamental reason for the Irish golfing boom is that the game is beautifully suited to the native temperament and character. A County Sligo man once explained it to me this way: "If a golfer so chooses, he can groove a tight little swing and plod around hitting safe little shots down the fairway. But that isn't how the typical Irish golfer approaches the game. He sees in golf a heaven-sent opportunity to perform spectacular deeds—bash his drives farther than mortal man has ever done before, or come slashing out of a briar patch with a phenomenal recovery shot that prostrates his opponent. It's a solo game, golf, so it's perfect for a people like us, who admire feats of individual bravery and derring-do. There they are, within the reach of the most ordinary man."

It follows, I think, that the considerable success that Irish golfers have enjoyed in international tournaments over the past twenty-five years has had more than a little to do with the huge advances the game has made there. Until 1946, no Irish golfer had ever won an important international amateur or professional championship, but that year James Bruen, a prodigious hitter from Cork, broke through in the British Amateur. Three years later, Max McCready, an Irishman living in England, won the same championship, and in 1953 it went to Joe Carr, a young golfer from Dublin, whose father had been a steward at Portmarnock. A model athlete, as cheery in defeat as in victory, Carr took the British Amateur twice again, in 1958 and 1960, and more recently, in recognition of his exceptional record and his personal substance, he has been accorded the honor—unprecedented for an Irishman—of being named captain of the British Eisenhower Trophy team and the British Walker Cup team. (Technically, these teams represent both Great Britain and Ireland.) Irish professionals also made their mark during this period. In 1947, Fred Daly, from Portrush, in Northern Ireland, won the British Open and also the first of three titles in the British Match Play Championship. In the early fifties, when Daly's star began to fade, two professionals from the Republic—Harry Bradshaw and Christy O'Connor—took over, scoring notable victories on the British tournament circuit and winning places on British Ryder Cup teams. Though neither Bradshaw nor O'Connor managed to capture the British Open, together they brought off perhaps the most glorious of all Irish golfing triumphs when, in 1958, they won the World Cup (then known as the Canada Cup), in Mexico City, defeating a field of more than thirty two-man teams, which included the top players from the United States, Australia, England, Scotland, South Africa, and the other traditional strongholds of the game. The news of Bradshaw and O'Connor's exploit was celebrated with champagne parties and informal parades down the streets of Dublin, and when the two heroes arrived home they were wined and dined for weeks. The World Cup match is held in a different country each year, and its sponsors, appreciating the frenetic pride that the Irish, golfers and nongolfers alike, took in their compatriots' victory, scheduled the event for Portmarnock in 1960.

It was the 1960 World Cup match that clearly marked the coming of age of Irish golf. During the four days of play, sixty thousand keyed-up spectators—a record attendance for the competition—converged on Portmarnock to troop after such illustrious champions as Sam Snead, Arnold Palmer, Peter Thomson, Bobby Locke, and Gary Player, and to root for the home team of O'Connor and Norman Drew, who was substituting for the ailing Bradshaw. O'Connor and Drew eventually finished fourth—a commendable performance. Perhaps it was a good thing that they came no closer to winning, for late in the afternoon of the final round, when all that remained to be decided was whether Snead could overtake Flory van Donck, of Belgium, in their battle for the individual prize, the excited gallery broke through the restraining ropes, the better to watch Snead's progress, and roared down the last two fairways like a tidal wave, sweeping over hillocks and through bunkers. As one who was caught in the wild foam, I have often wondered what it would have been like if the Irish team had come to the final holes that afternoon with a chance to win, and a shudder goes through my bones.

In all, I have made three visits to Ireland. When I went there first, in the autumn of 1958, I played Portmarnock with Joe Carr. The virtues of Portmarnock's handsomely varied holes are so obvious that I would probably have grasped them under any circumstances, but this opportunity to observe the superb shots Carr was required to produce in order to stay even with par made it plain as day why Bernard Darwin, the matchless English golf writer, had called the course "one of the few unquestionably great golf links of the world." I came to know the layout much better two years later, when I attended the World Cup match there, and my fondness for it deepened, familiarity breeding anything but contempt in the case of a first-class golf course. At that time, though, I had no chance to inspect the other Irish links that I had heard such enthusiastic reports about over the years, and, accordingly, I undertook to do this on my latest trip. I was able to persuade an old friend, Paul MacWeeney, to arrange for a brief holiday—he writes about golf and Rugby for the *Irish Times* and acts as the paper's sports editor—so that we could make the expedition together. I was sure that Paul MacWeeney, a pleasant, well-organized man in his middle fifties, with, for a Dubliner, a most untheatrical nature, would be the ideal cicerone, for he had long been the country's leading golf writer and there was nothing about—and no one in—Irish golf he didn't know. Unfortunately, the plans we worked out in an exchange of letters fell through. A few days before I was scheduled to fly to Ireland, I learned from MacWeeney that one of the key members of the *Times'* sports staff had become ill, and that, as a result, he would not be able to get away from his desk after all. "You'll have an excellent trip and an enjoyable one," he assured me when we met early in the afternoon of my arrival in Dublin. "You'll have no trouble. I've phoned the people at the different clubs. Everything's fixed up. I've arranged for you to do your jaunt in two loops. First, you do a loop up north. They expect you at Newcastle County Down tomorrow and at Portrush the day after tomorrow, Wednesday. On Thursday, you return to Dublin. We'll have dinner that night and I'll brief you on the southwestern loop. That's all set up, too—Lahinch on Friday, Killarney on Saturday, Ballybunion on Sunday, and back to Dublin on Monday." MacWeeney handed me some papers relating to an automobile he had hired for me from Ryan Self-Drive, Ltd., and, along with these, a neatly written list of the secretaries and captains of the different clubs, the phone numbers of the clubs, and my estimated time of arrival at each of them. "You could string your trip out longer," MacWeeney continued, with a smile that was both sanguine and cautionary, "but I'd advise against it. The hospitality at our golf clubs can be pretty formidable. About three years ago, I spent a fortnight myself gathering material for a series of pieces on fifteen or sixteen courses in the west and the south. When I got back to Dublin— *limped* back to Dublin would be more accurate—it took me three weeks to recover, for a fact. You're wisest not to string it out."

Later that day, MacWeeney drove me out to Portmarnock, after we had taken a quick look at Phoenix Park, an enormous tract on the western rim of the city. The park has a special significance for golfers, because it was there that golf was first played in Ireland, and MacWeeney wanted to point out the site of that first course—long vanished—which a homesick Scottish regiment had built around 1850. This was the course that during the height of "the troubles" of 1887 Arthur Balfour, then chief secretary for Ireland, insisted on playing—accompanied, necessarily, by a bodyguard of detectives. In those days, it was a rare thing for a public figure to be so smitten with golf, and though Balfour's conspicuous love of the game did nothing to heal the centuries-old breach between Ireland and England, it gave golf a colossal boost. (At that date, incidentally, there were seventy-three golf courses in Scotland, fifty-seven in England, two in Wales, and six in Ireland—most of these in the north.) Two years after this, the members of the golf club in Phoenix Park closed that course and moved first to Sutton, on Dublin Bay, and then, in 1892, to a lovely strip of bayside land at Dollymount, three and a half miles north of the city, where their club, the Royal Dublin, still stands. We drove past it on our way to Portmarnock, which lies some six miles farther to the north, athwart a tiny peninsula shaped like Florida. Portmarnock was "discovered" in 1893 by W. C. Pickeman and George Ross, two Dublin golfers, who had a feeling that the land would be perfect for the growing game. At this time, the peninsula, the home of small farmers and fishermen, was a virtually sealed-off community, with its own brick plant and its own distillery. The land that was not farmed was a wild tangle of bracken and dunes, and there the Portmarnock Golf Club was established in 1894. Soon afterward, the little community on the peninsula began to disappear, for the club, as it acquired more and more property, chopped the bracken back and pushed its fairways to the edges of the water.

To reach the course in those early days, the golfers crossed Portmarnock Inlet, which is about half a mile wide, by boat or, at low tide, by horse and carriage. Today, a paved road leads around the northern end of the inlet to the clubhouse, a low white stucco building with an orange slate roof, which was erected in 1905 and has been remodeled periodically over the years. Except for the presence of the clubhouse, a visiting golfer's first sight of the heaving green land across the inlet cannot be much different today from what it was for Portmarnock's pioneers—and there are few invitations in golf as beckoning. The course, as you would expect, has been completely altered since 1894, but, happily, none of the improvements have introduced a note of artificiality. The chief credit for this belongs to H. M. (Guppy) Cairnes, an outstanding Portmarnock golfer, who between 1900 and 1930 took it upon himself to lengthen and revise the original holes to suit the changing game, and who succeeded so well that only minor revisions have since been necessary. Far more talented than most amateur architects, Cairnes laid out his holes so that they ran to all the points of the compass, and he routed his fairways adroitly through the sand hills so that there would be a minimum of blind shots. He installed new bunkers, which looked hardly less natural than the ones nature had provided, and though he placed several of his new greens at sites where the land rose or tilted sharply, he saw to it that a well-played approach shot would seldom be penalized by a freak bounce. When experienced golfers speak about Portmarnock, they invariably mention its "fairness." Of the classic British links, only Muirfield, perhaps, is as free from caprice, and Muirfield, on the south shore of the Firth of Forth, occupies far less rugged terrain. From the back tees, Portmarnock today measures 7,093 yards and has a par of 71. It has yielded several 64s, but old hands at Portmarnock insist that the most inspired round ever played over it was a 74 by George Duncan on the final day of the 1927 Irish Open. A furious gale was sweeping over the links, and Duncan's 74 enabled him to make up seventeen strokes on the third-round leader, who brought in a 91; nearly all the other scores were in the 90s. The story has it that Duncan played his historic round swathed from neck to toe in brown wrapping paper, to keep out the biting wind.

At present, Portmarnock has around four hundred regular members and, counting the "five-day members" (who cannot play on the weekends), "country members" (who must reside seventy-five miles or more from the club), junior members, and overseas members, a total membership of about 750. It is the most truly national of the Irish clubs, for it serves golfers from all over the island, and particularly from the Republic, as a second club, much the way the Royal and Ancient Golf Club of St. Andrews serves as a second club for British golfers. Portmarnock, because it is comfortably close to Dublin, also draws an extraordinarily high number of foreign golfers—more than fifteen thousand last year. The sagacious tourist usually manages to work in a lesson with Harry Bradshaw, the Portmarnock professional. Bradshaw, who has apparently never talked economics with Snead, sometimes charges less than a pound, but never more, for a forty-five-minute lesson. His fee for an eighteen-hole playing lesson is a pound. There is no better bargain in golf.

On the evening MacWeeney and I called in, Bradshaw joined us in the bar, where we were talking with Rex Buck, the secretary. Bradshaw looks nothing at all like the standard modern golf professional. Now well into his fifties, he has the paunchy build and the round, florid face

of an old-time baseball umpire. In his peak competitive years, he was
not noticeably leaner, and the sight of him padding down the fairways
with the flat-footed gait of a country mailman astounded American
galleries when he appeared here in the 1955 Ryder Cup match. They
were also startled by his casual manner of play. Disdaining the refine-
ments of the overlapping grip, he simply grabbed the club in his
gnarled hands and, after a quick squint at the flag, rocked himself into
a wide, pivotless, slappy swing, which somehow or other sent the ball
flying dead on target. No golfer of his class has ever played more
swiftly, and it was typical of him that when, as a young man, he first
came to national attention by shooting two 60s at the Delgany Golf
Club, in County Wicklow, he completed each round in under two
hours. Bradshaw, who was the pro at Delgany, has been at Portmarnock
for more than twenty years now and has become a permanent part of
the scenery. During our chat with him that evening, he poured forth a
stream of amusing stories and observations, but I can reconstruct only
one. It was prompted by a remark of mine to the effect that the first
hole at Portmarnock must be one of the toughest starting holes in golf,
what with the waters of the inlet lapping close along the right-hand
edge of the fairway. "Ah, that it is," Bradshaw agreed. "We get a lot of
American visitors here who come into my shop and purchase a package
of three new balls before they go out. They get on the first tee, and—
wouldn't you know it?—they slice all three balls into the water. Then
they have to come back to the shop and buy three more balls. I believe
this is what you people in the States call merchandising."

Ireland—north and south together—is a rather small place, about the
size of the state of Maine. Traveling around it by car, however, takes
appreciably longer than a visitor expects it to, even in times of peace,
which then prevailed. The roads are in fairly good shape, but as a rule
they are only two lanes wide and offer few straightaway stretches, so if
you get stuck behind a line of lorries your progress can be pretty poky.
In any event, it took me over three and a half hours to do the hundred
miles between Dublin and Newcastle—a seaside town, thirty miles
below Belfast, that was once a fishing village and is now a popular holiday center. The trip was enlivened a bit by the grimness of the customs
officials on both sides of the border, which the Dublin–Belfast road

crosses halfway between the towns of Dundalk and Newry. As the Republic of Ireland man was checking my car-rental documents, I handed him one additional paper that the Ryan auto people had given me. "No, that's not for us," he said matter-of-factly. He then added, with a touch of asperity, "That's for Her Majesty up the road." Moments later, when I presented the documents to his Northern Ireland counterpart, I said, "Good morning"—standard procedure in the greeting-conscious Republic. The man said, "Take them to the second door," indicating the small customs house, and I knew then that I was in a slightly different country.

North of the border, both the towns and the rural stretches seemed a shade more ordered, and in its general appearance, as MacWeeney had said it would, Ulster reminded me of Scotland. The area around Newcastle, though, is quite distinctive. The Mountains of Mourne, a chain of gentle green hills, slope down to the Irish Sea—or, to be more specific, to Dundrum Bay. They have been celebrated in song, and for good reason. Indeed, I wonder whether the links at Newcastle County Down, for all their golfing worth, would have attracted as many championships as they have if it weren't for the lovely backdrop of mountains.

Although Newcastle County Down is what most people call the course—to set it apart from courses at sundry other Newcastles—its correct name is the Royal County Down Golf Club. It has been a royal club since 1908, when King Edward VII agreed to become its patron, but it was founded eighteen years earlier. The moving spirits were a group of Belfast men who liked the idea of playing weekend golf on real seaside terrain, which Newcastle offered. Old Tom Morris, the revered St. Andrews professional and one of the most sought-after golf architects of that period, laid out the original nine holes and outlined his suggestions for a second nine, which were built the following year. The club records show that Morris was to receive a fee "not to exceed four pounds," so, regardless of how much farther money went in those days, it is to be hoped that he had the presence of mind to turn in at least a skeletal expense account. County Down's original eighteen holes, like most layouts of that vintage, were soon modified by local hands—at every club there is always a member or two, be he credit manager or poet, who would rather be a golf architect than anything else in the world—and by 1897 the revised course extended to 5,490 yards. Just a few years later, however, the modern, more resilient, rubber-cored golf ball replaced the old solid-gutta-percha ball, and longer holes were needed to accommodate it. Here County Down was extremely fortunate, for George Combe, the member who supervised the necessary changes, possessed uncommon golf knowledge; the holes he devised were not only long and stiff but marvelously interesting. In the mid-1920s, the club was fortunate again, for C. S. Harden was appointed course curator, as the post was called. Harden, who went on to become chairman of the Joint Advisory Council of the British Golf Unions, stayed on at County Down for six years, during which he superintended many sensible alterations and brought the condition of the turf and the course in general to an exceptionally high level. Both Combe and Harden, like Cairnes of Portmarnock, had the intelligence to leave the physiognomy of the links essentially as it was. As a result, the fascination of County Down lies in its pristine naturalness. Much wilder in its overall character than Portmarnock, it is a froth of spectacular sand hills rising thirty or forty feet above the narrow, winding fairways. Once a golfer enters this wonderland, he is entirely cut off from the outside world, and as the moody grandeur of the links envelops him further he is transported back many decades in time, to the era of Old Tom Morris.

One gets used to everything, so it's unlikely that the members of County Down find the course the heady experience that the first-time visitor does. At present, the club has 440 regular and associated members—a figure that does not include either the members of the Mourne Golf Club, established at County Down in 1947 for the workingmen of the town of Newcastle, or the members of the Royal County Down Ladies' Golf Club, a separate organization, which pays an annual fee for the use of the links. On weekends, when the Mourne golfers and the ladies are not permitted to play the championship course, they get their rounds in on a second eighteen-hole course that County Down operates; this is a much shorter, quieter layout, farther inland. The Mourne Golf Club maintains a small clubhouse not far from the main one. The ladies maintain another, and they can almost always be found there, for a regulation that was propounded by the members of County Down in 1894, when the ladies formed their offshoot, still prohibits a woman from entering the main clubhouse unless she is accompanied by a man. To Americans, so long accustomed to country clubs where the

women are not only on equal footing with the men but usually in roaring command, this setup seems an anachronism, but it is fairly standard
both in the British Isles and on the Continent. There, with few exceptions, the golf club remains primarily, if not exclusively, a male sanctu-
ary. Most of the time, too, the clubhouse is a much more modest edifice
than the adaptations of Mount Vernon or Chenonceaux at which the
devotees of American country club life forgather. For example, County
Down's original clubhouse, which is still in use, is a gaunt Victorian
structure that seems infinitely older than its seventy-five years. A sizable addition has recently been finished, and this is an excellent thing.
I am thinking particularly of the old locker room, which, like many
such rooms in Britain, is a dark and fusty cavern, in whose depths I
wouldn't have been surprised to come upon Old Tom Morris changing
out of his hobnailed golf shoes.

The club secretary, Arthur Jones, made my visit a most comfortable
one. In the years before the Second World War, the secretaries at most
of the leading golf clubs in the United Kingdom were retired military
men—fussy old boys who, in spirit, had never left the plains of Luck-
now. Some of them are still around, but nowadays they are decidedly in
the minority. Arthur Jones is typical of the hospitable, relaxed new
breed, although he has a military background. A Gloucestershire man
who was a squadron leader in the Royal Air Force during the Second
World War, Jones got his first taste of golf administration during the
occupation of Germany, when he was assigned to run the RAF golf
club at Brüggen. He liked the work, and, upon his retirement from the
service, in 1957, became the secretary at County Down. Before I went
out onto the course to bring it to its knees, Jones and I met in the club
bar. (It was early afternoon, and the bar was deserted; in fact, the only
interruption was provided by an area representative of the Guinness
Company, straight from Central Casting, who came in to check with
the bartender on how the new stout-dispensing machine was behav-
ing.) Jones became as nearly rhapsodic as a calm man can when he
talked about the course: the rambunctiousness of the terrain, the fine-
ness of the fairway turf, the trueness of the greens. "I'm afraid, though,
that you won't find County Down at its best," he went on. "We've gone
three straight weeks without a real rain, and we've had to let the grass
grow up a bit to keep the greens and fairways from burning out. Too
much sun doesn't agree with our grass: it's fescue and *Poa annua* on the

greens, *Poa annua* on the fairways. Some fairways have been burned almost bare in spots, but, oddly enough, the older members seem to like
that. They can remember when the course was nothing but sand covered by a thin layer of turf, and that's how they think a golf course
should be—hard as a bone and fast as lightning. Five more sunny, rain-
less days like this and we *will* be back to a primeval links." Jones handed
me a scorecard and suggested that since it was such a warm, breezeless
day, I might find the course more of a challenge if I played the extreme
back tee on the second and ninth holes. He had noted on the scorecard
that, with that added yardage, County Down, par 72, would measure
6,952 yards.

I soon discovered that there were a few things Jones had neglected to
tell me about the course. To begin with, the fairways are the tightest I
have ever seen—only thirty yards wide on the average and at many
points less than twenty. Moreover, the rough that edges them graduates
within the space of a couple of yards from nice, normal, civilized rough
into a dense growth of heather and bracken. On top of this, on several
holes the golfer must fly his tee shot over a distant rough-bearded sand
hill to reach the start of the fairway. Faced with just such a carry from
the back tee on the second hole (where I foolishly took Jones's tip and
passed up the regular tee), I hit the ball so far off line to the right that it
almost kicked onto the sandy bathing beach along Dundrum Bay. On
the third hole, I hit an even worse push-slice, which may or may not
have made the beach—we never did find the ball. While my caddie and
I were searching for it, my gaze traveled to the beach and then to the
girls lolling on the sand in their Presbyterian bikinis, and I longed to be
lolling sensibly on the sand myself instead of fighting a golf course that
was patently going to be more than I could handle. Errors of the kind I
had been making usually result when one attempts to steer his shots,
rather than swinging freely, but, confronted by one stringbean fairway
after another and a succession of very small greens, I found it quite impossible to stop trying to steer them. Consequently, my recollection of
the first nine holes is blurred, the individual ones all mixed up together
in my mind like a stew. Somewhere on that first nine, I can remember,
there is an especially dramatic green tucked close to an open-faced sand
hill, which towers fifty feet above it; somewhere else, on a long par 4,
the second shot must be rifled through a narrow passageway between
two massive hummocks; and somewhere else the correct line off the tee

on a dogleg par 4 is over a long ridge of gorse studded with bunkers. I managed to play the second nine more creditably, and so was able to appreciate somewhat better the masterly way the linksland's natural features had been incorporated into the strategic design of the holes—which, when you come right down to it, is what golf architecture is all about. On the final holes, as the long Irish evening came on, rabbits began to appear in great numbers, and the sight of them munching in the rough was strangely soothing.

When I finished my round, I met Jones in the bar. How had I found County Down? My answers came fast. It was the most difficult test of driving I had ever encountered. It was, in fact, the sternest examination in golf I had ever taken. Since it was well beyond my abilities on a comparatively bland day, I could not imagine how even an expert player could cope with it in a ripping wind. "Whenever any of my American friends thinks he's playing terrific golf, I'd love to fly him straight to this course," I concluded. "He'd soon find out just how good he was!"

"Yes, it's a fine test," Jones said with an easy, consular smile. "I personally think it's the best course I've ever seen. Granted, I could be prejudiced. We get lots of suggestions, however. People are always coming to me and pointing out that if we did x or y it would improve this hole or that hole tremendously. I tend to discount these suggestions. I think that the men who came before us at the club did an awfully good job, and I respect them for it. I think the course is right just as it is."

I followed the secretary over to a table, where he had a date to play cards with two members, also retired military men—a dapper little colonel in his late seventies and a heavyset captain a few years the colonel's senior. I didn't recognize the game, so I declined their invitation to join in. In a break between hands, the old captain asked me what I thought of the fourteenth hole, a 216-yard par 3 that is a waste of sand almost all the way to the green area, where the land falls off quickly toward a small pond on the left, and a stout bunker protects the high, right-hand side of the green. I replied that I thought it a first-rate hole. After all, I had escaped with a 4 there.

"Know what one visitor told me?" the old captain said, laughing heartily. "He said the hole was fit only for the natives."

This drew long corroborative chuckles and a poke in the ribs from his friend the colonel. A minute or two later, when the colonel had calmed down, he said to the secretary, "Arthur, I have a suggestion to make."

"Here it comes," Jones said to me with a wink.

"The fourteenth hole is too damned far from the bar," the colonel went on. "You should do something about that."

This in turn broke the old captain up completely.

Jones had thoughtfully asked me to stay on for dinner, but a few hands later I decided that it was time to head for the local hotel, where he had booked a room for me. I retired at ten. Trudging for miles through bracken, gorse, and heather makes a man weary.

This early-to-bed proved to be a wise move, for the next day—the day when I visited the Royal Portrush Golf Club—was a long one. It began with a three-hour drive to the north coast along a route that, bypassing Belfast, ran through Ballynahinch, Ballymena, and Ballymoney. (*Bally* is the Gaelic word for town.) It was another sunny day, and all along the road portly women in bright-colored sweaters were out walking their dogs. Portrush, like Newcastle, is an old fishing village that has burgeoned into a holiday resort. The links have had a great deal to do with its growth, but for the hardy there is also good ocean bathing, and only seven miles to the east, just offshore, is one of the country's outstanding tourist attractions—the Giant's Causeway, a fantastic procession of basalt pillars. The links are about a mile outside town in the direction of the Causeway, with the sea behind them and the clubhouse in front, off the shore road. The clubhouse is an ungraceful white stucco building with the blank stare of a roadhouse, and the secretary, Tom Beveridge, told me that it had been a minor resort hotel before the club acquired it, in 1946. Beveridge, a businessman from Banffshire, in Scotland, who had only recently taken the post at Portrush, showed me around the clubhouse. Its interior far exceeded my expectations. For example, the locker room, a new addition, proved to be an airy place with commodious wooden lockers, and the washroom and the shower room, faced with yellow and blue tiles, have a bright, Stateside gleam. But what struck me most about the clubhouse was its animated atmosphere. Though this was a weekday, the dining room and the bar were jammed, and there was an appealing low-key cordiality among the members, as if they knew one another well. Portrush is a large club, however, with a total membership of over a thousand, counting the members of a separate club for ladies and of one other affiliate, the Rathmore Golf Club, which, like the Mourne Golf Club, at Newcastle, serves the local residents who cannot afford to join the main club. (In the old days, the Rathmore men and the Mourne men would have been called artisan golfers, but that term is considered to be in poor taste nowadays, and it is customary to refer to them as town golfers and to their club as the town club.)

Portrush's championship course, which I played in the afternoon, is something like the clubhouse in that there is a lot more to it than first meets the eye. The opening hole is a good par 4 and the second a good par 5, but there is nothing special about them. A short uphill walk takes you to the third tee, and from that high ground a wide vista opens. To the east you can see the Giant's Causeway; to the north, a group of rocky islets, the Skerries; in the far distance, past the Skerries but easily visible on a clear day, two of the inner Hebrides—Jura and Islay. If you are a golfer, however, the most impressive part of the view is the vast extent of the links themselves, which constitute the largest single tract of golfable duneland in the world—480 undulating acres dominated by three ridges of high sand hills, each parallel to the sea. The land between the ridge nearest the water and the second ridge is a sheltered, swaybacked valley about a quarter of a mile wide. Stretching between the second and third ridges is a higher plateau. Nongolfers who scanned this treeless acreage before it was converted into fairways and greens may well have found it grim and perhaps forbidding, but it is the kind of land that stirs a man with a golfer's eye, and it quite overwhelmed Harry Colt, the celebrated English golf architect, when the club brought him in, shortly before the First World War, to look things over. At that time, Portrush's original eighteen holes, completed in 1889 on a flattish strip on the inland side of the third ridge of sand hills, had been only cautiously extended toward the sea here and there. What excited Colt was, of course, the enormous possibilities of the still unused duneland. In reporting to the club officials that there was room enough and more to lay out thirty-six fine holes, he estimated that designing and constructing them would cost about seventeen thousand dollars. (This is about what it costs today to build one good golf hole in the United States.) This proposal was turned down as more than Portrush could afford, whereupon Colt, dismayed at the thought of losing the chance to work with that wonderful terrain, found a way to pare down his figure by several thousand dollars: He volunteered to supervise the construction personally, without pay, if the club would arrange to put him up during this period and to take care of his basic expenses. This was agreeable to the board of governors, and Colt, whose many credits include the Worplesdon and Swinley Forest courses in England, and the New Course at St. Andrews, plus an assist on Pine Valley in New Jersey, got down to work on what many golf critics consider his chef-d'œuvre. He began by routing the opening holes of a championship-length course over the high ground beyond the second ridge of dunes, then swung the course down to the edge of the shore, looped it inland and then out to the shore again, and, finally, brought it back to the high ground. This is the Dunluce course, named after Dunluce Castle, a nearby medieval ruin that overlooks the sea. In the valley between the first and second ridges, Colt built the Valley course. Only 6,207 yards long from the regular tee but extendible to 6,641 yards, the Valley is less exacting than the Dunluce, which measures 6,809 yards, but there is a lot of golf on it. It has marvelous turf, which dries out quickly, and this, combined with its protected position, makes it a particular favorite in winter, when the wet winds prowl in off the ocean. As for the Dunluce, or championship, course, its supreme merit is that golfers of all degrees of skill can play it with equal pleasure; like the Augusta National, it puts the expert on his mettle but does not crush the average player. The fairways have a generous width, and although the holes are separated from one another by dense tangles of gorse, bracken, and wild dwarf rosebushes, the rough directly adjoining the fairways is humane. Besides, there are only thirty-eight bunkers on the course, counting the double bunkers as singles. In my case, which I think might be quite typical, I hit a couple of wayward shots on the opening holes but was given a chance to recover adequately both times. This had the effect of bolstering my confidence—a pretty shaky thing after my assault on County Down—and in no time I was playing "my game," which means that I was hitting the ball far better than I normally do. This enabled me to see the subtler side of Colt's handiwork, for the better you are playing, the more Portrush asks you to do. On the first nine, for example, there are two beautifully designed dogleg par 4s on which length off the tee can be a substantial asset, but only if it is controlled length. Similarly, the hazards in the green area tend to be quiescent except when a golfer attempts to play a too ambitious approach to the pin itself instead of settling for the center of the green.

Since the artist, even in golf, frequently goes unappreciated, I found it heartwarming to learn that when Colt unveiled his championship course the club members instantly realized what a superb job he had done. In the British Isles, it is a common practice to give each hole a name as well as a number, and the sixth at Portrush, a 196-yard par 3 that invites a nicely cut-up 4-wood shot or a long iron, was named Harry Colt's, in honor of the architect. Farther along, there is another memorable short hole, the 211-yard fourteenth. Here the fairway swings off to the left, and the direct line to the pin is over a steep-sided gully of rough that starts just beyond the tee and runs lengthwise almost to the green; a shot that catches the top edge of the downslope usually tumbles all the way to the bottom of the gully, thirty feet below the level of the green. This hole is called Calamity Corner, and more often than not the members use the name rather than the number in referring to it. In our country, some clubs have gone through the motions of bestowing names on individual holes, but if any of them have really caught on I can't remember them. The trouble is that the names we give our holes are, with few exceptions, either unimaginative or irrelevant. On an American course, Calamity Corner would probably have emerged as Trouble Spot, Ravine, Grand Canyon, or, say, plain Ernest R. Hall, after a wealthy member who once sprained his ankle on the hole when disembarking from his golf cart.

To enjoy a course, a golfer must play it relatively well, for him, and while the acceptable golf I managed to produce was undoubtedly the principal reason I thought so highly of Portrush, a contributing factor should be mentioned: I couldn't have played in a more pleasant foursome. I was paired with a young university-educated plumber in a four-ball match against a left-hander whose company painted the center stripe down highways and a middle-aged building contractor, a former captain of the club. It is one of the charms of the game that even when you are in a foreign land you can become quickly and honestly at home with your fellow golfers, and by the end of our round I felt that I had known my Irish companions for years. The man who had arranged the foursome was the captain of the club—Robin Wray, a lawyer of about fifty, whose office is in the neighboring town of Coleraine. At golf clubs in the British Isles and on the Continent, two men carry the load: the secretary, who is a paid employee, and the captain, a member who has displayed a sincere and active interest in the club's welfare. The secretary handles the administrative chores and maintains liaison with the head steward, the professional, and the greenkeeper to see to it that their provinces are in good order. He also works closely with the captain, whose chief concerns are the club's tournaments and other matters relating to the smooth operation of the golf activities, such as the condition of the course. The captain serves for either one or two years. At the end of his term, he is generally a somewhat poorer man, for it is a definite honor to be appointed or elected to the office, and it carries a few social burdens, among them entertaining the members (at his own expense) at the annual Captain's Dinner, picking up unreached-for bar checks with genial alacrity, and donating the prizes for the club's biggest annual competition—the Captain's Day tournament. For some reason, seven or eight years ago a number of exceptionally well-heeled captains of Irish golf clubs began to engage in a private competition to see who could put up the most lavish Captain's Prize. Finally, after one grandee had announced that his members would be shooting for a brand-new giant-screen television set, the Golfing Union decided that things had gone too far, and stipulated that thenceforward no Captain's Prize could exceed $150 in value. The Portrush members I talked with felt that Wray had struck just the right balance the previous year by putting up a set of matched luggage as first prize. A polished, convivial man, Wray had come over from Coleraine at noon to meet me and see me through lunch and the inevitable rounds of drinks that preceded it. A business appointment prevented his playing golf that afternoon, but when our foursome got in he was waiting to take me in hand again. Because the local hotels turned out to be filled up, he was kind enough to invite me to spend the night at his home. Our evening was a full one: more whiskey at the club, of course; home for a restorative stroll through Mrs. Wray's gardens, which featured an astonishing variety of roses and the biggest pansies I have ever seen; dinner at a restaurant on the shore road, and, subsequently, a stop at the Rathmore clubhouse, filled with friendly young men from the town who welcomed the captain warmly; then back to the Wrays' for a long discussion of British and American golf, for Wray has twice visited our country and knows our golfing mores well. It was past two when we called it a day. As I headed for my room, Mrs. Wray, carrying coals to Newcastle (County Down), handed me a bedside book, Patrick Campbell's *How to Become a Scratch Golfer,* and pointed out one chapter she felt was "super." Why I read it at that hour I do not know, but I did, and it *was* super.

After listening to my report on how the trip had gone, MacWeeney handed me a slip of paper with the names and telephone numbers of the men I should get in touch with at Lahinch, Killarney, and Bally-bunion, on my second loop, which I would be starting the next morning; with his invariable tidiness, he had phoned them that afternoon to make certain that everything was in order. Then we just talked golf. Somewhere in our conversation, I remarked that the courses I had visited had far surpassed my considerable expectations. "They *are* good," MacWeeney said. "We haven't thrown away what nature provided. And we've been sufficiently intelligent to call in the best golf architects. Old Tom Morris not only did Newcastle County Down but the original layout at Lahinch. H. S. Colt did Portrush and County Sligo; Alister MacKenzie, the modern remodeling of Lahinch; Sir Guy Campbell, Killarney; Tom Simpson, some of the revisions at Ballybunion. When you stop and think of it, at one time or another we've lured over just about all the top English and Scottish architects. For example, take the course at Mullingar. James Braid did the course there, and it's an exceedingly good one. It has a wonderful plan: No hole is more than four hundred yards from the clubhouse." MacWeeney paused a moment and smiled to himself. "I was just thinking of the story of how Braid laid out Mullingar. The old boy must have been close to seventy at that time— back in the nineteen-thirties. He was the professional then, as he was throughout his later years, at Walton Heath, outside London. He did his architecture on the side. He was very Scottish, you know, and he hated to throw away time or money just as much then as he had when he was a young man and winning those five British Opens. In the case of Mullingar, you could sympathize with him for not wanting to dawdle around—his fee was some ridiculously small amount like twenty-five pounds. Anyway, he left Walton Heath one afternoon and caught the Dublin night boat at Holyhead. He was met at the dock the next morning by the committee from Mullingar, and they whisked him by auto to the club property, two hours away. 'Gentlemen,' he told the committee, 'I would prefer to be left alone while I do my work. I will let you know when it's finished.' And with that he began to walk over the property, looking for natural green sites, and so on. Four hours later, when he had the whole eighteen staked out, he called in the committee, showed them what he had done, and issued a few instructions for the construction superintendent. Then he shook everyone's hand, motored back to Dublin, and caught the night boat for Holyhead. The next afternoon, he was back in his shop at Walton Heath.

"There's a sort of companion story about Mullingar," MacWeeney continued, with a fresh smile. "Some three years after the course was opened, a foursome of fairly good golfers was playing one of the par threes—the second hole, I think, a tough one-shotter about a hundred and ninety yards long. None of the four managed to put his tee shot on the green, and this led to some loud grumbles about how unfair the hole was, because the green wouldn't hold a well-hit shot. At this, an old gentleman who had been sitting unnoticed on a bench by the tee, taking it all in—Braid, of course, over on an inspection trip—asked one of the golfers to lend him a two-iron and a few golf balls. Without removing his jacket, he hit four lovely shots, all of them on the green within twenty feet of the flag. 'Gentlemen, I don't see anything wrong with this hole,' he said. 'I think it plays verra well.' "

We talked until nearly three. When MacWeeney left, he cautioned me once again about Irish hospitality. "If you don't watch them, the people here will keep you up all hours," he said. "They simply hate to go to bed."

1971

OBRIAN

"I'm __thinking__!"

Tennis as a Metaphor for the Tri-State Area

TENNIS PERSONALITIES

MARTIN AMIS

I have a problem with—I am uncomfortable with—the word *person-ality* and its plural, as in "Modern tennis lacks personalities" and "Tennis needs a new star who is a genuine personality." But if, from now on, I can put "personality" between quotation marks, and use it as an exact synonym of a seven-letter duosyllable starting with *a* and end-ing with *e* (and also featuring, in order of appearance, an *ss*, an *h*, an *o*, and an *l*), why, then, *personality* and I are going to get along just fine.

How come it is always the old "personalities" who lead complaints about the supposed scarcity of young "personalities"? Because it takes a "personality" to know a "personality"? No. Because it takes a "personal-ity" to like a "personality."

Ilie Nastase was a serious "personality"—probably the most complete "personality" the game has ever boasted. In his memoir, *Days of Grace*, Arthur Ashe, while acknowledging that Nastase was an "unforgettable personality," also recalls that Ilie called him "Negroni" to his face and, once, "nigger" behind his back. Ilie, of course, was known as a "clown" and a "showman"; i.e., as an embarrassing narcissist. Earlier this year, his tireless "antics" earned him a dismissal and a suspension as Romania's Davis Cup captain ("audible obscenities and constant abuse and intimidation"). Ilie is forty-seven. But true "personalities" merely scoff at the passage of time. They just become even bigger "personalities."

Jimmy Connors: another total "personality." Imagine the sepsis of helpless loathing he must have inspired in his opponents during his "great runs" at the U.S. Open. There's Jimmy (what a "personality"), orchestrating mass sex with the Grandstand Court. It's great for the mild-mannered Swede or Swiss up at the other end: He double-faults, and New York goes wild. Jimmy was such an out-and-out "personality" that he managed to get into a legal dispute with the president of his own fan club. Remember how he used to wedge his racket between his legs with the handle protuding and mime the act of masturbation when a call went against him? That's a "personality."

Twenty-odd years ago, I encountered Connors and Nastase at some PR nightmare in a Park Lane hotel. Someone asked these two bronzed and seersuckered "personalities" what they had been doing with themselves in London. "Screwing each other," Nastase said, and collapsed in Connors's arms. I was reminded of this incident when, last fall, I saw an account of a whistle-stop tour undertaken by John McEnroe and Andre Agassi. Questioned about their relationship, Agassi described it as "completely sexual." Does such raillery inevitably come about when self-love runs up against mutual admiration? Or is it part of a bonding ritual between "personalities" of the same peer group?

By turning my TV up dangerously loud, I once heard McEnroe mutter to a linesman (and this wasn't a Grand Slam event but one of those German greed fests where the first prize is something like a gold helicopter), "Get your fucking head out of your fucking [personality]." Arthur Ashe also reveals that McEnroe once called a middle-aged black linesman "boy." With McEnroe gone, it falls to Agassi to shoulder the flagstaff of the "personalities"—Agassi, the Vegas traffic light, the "Zen master" (B. Streisand) who used to smash forty rackets a year. And I don't think he has the stomach for it, funnily enough. Nastase, Connors, McEnroe, and Agassi are "personalities" of descending magnitude and stamina. McEnroe, at heart, was more tremulous than vicious; and Agassi shows telltale signs of generosity—even of sportsmanship.

There is a "demand" for "personalities," because that's the kind of age we're living in. Laver, Rosewall, Ashe: These were dynamic and exemplary figures; they didn't need "personality" because they had character. Interestingly, too, there have never been any "personalities" in the women's game. What does this tell us? That being a "personality" is men's work? Or that it's boys' work?

We do want our champions to be vivid. How about Pete Sampras, then—so often found wanting in the "personality" department? According to the computer, Sampras is almost twice as good as anyone else in the sport. What form would his "personality" take? Strutting, fist-clenching, loin-thrusting? All great tennis players are vivid, if great tennis is what you're interested in (rather than something more tawdrily generalized). The hare-eyed Medvedev, the snake-eyed Courier, the droll and fiery Ivanisevic, the innocent Bruguera, the Wagnerian (and Machiavellian) Becker, the fanatical Michael Chang. These players demonstrate that it is perfectly possible to have, or to contain, a personality—without being an asshole.

1994

"We beat the spread!"

PROJECT KNUCKLEBALL

BEN MCGRATH

As season-ending home runs go, Aaron Boone's eleventh-inning shot for the Yankees against the Red Sox last October looks pretty unimpressive in retrospect. Watch the video replay once more: A paunchy, goateed pitcher, his cap pulled down low, begins to wind up for what appears to be a practice pitch—hasn't a batter stepped in already?—and releases the ball from a contorted claw's grip, right pinkie finger extended, with a prim, abbreviated follow-through, the right foot landing in quick succession after the left, as though in a limp. The miles-per-hour indicator flashes "69" at the top of the screen as the ball floats, then hangs. If you didn't know better, you might not believe that the Boston pitcher—he's quietly walking off the field now, as Yankee Stadium erupts with joy—intended to get Boone out, or that he had any business being on the mound in a postseason Game Seven in the first place, much less during extra innings. In fact, though, Tim Wakefield, the pitcher in question, had beaten the Yankees more often than any pitcher all season by doing much the same thing. Sixty-nine mph is routine for a sophomore in high school; it is on the fast side for a Wakefield delivery.

The Yankees and the Red Sox are engaged in what is often called an arms race. This past off-season, the two teams, already possessing stratospheric payrolls, went about adding more firepower to their rosters. The Sox, most notably, added a couple of hard-throwing All-Star pitchers (New York allowed fewer runs last season), while the Yanks added a couple of All-Star sluggers (Boston scored more). In Fort Myers, on the first Sunday in March, the Yankees arrived at City of Palms Park (Florida's Fenway) to play the Red Sox in a meaningless early spring-training game that was nonetheless billed by various players and writers as "Game Eight"—the continuation of last fall's epic series, which seemed merely to have paused for the winter. Before the game, several fans paraded around the grandstand carrying signs taunting Alex Rodriguez, New York's studly new third baseman (he'd recently posed with his wife for *Sports Illustrated*'s swimsuit issue), and

alluding to the simmering steroids controversy (the Yankees' new right
fielder, Gary Sheffield, was among those called to testify before a grand
jury). Obscured by all the commotion was the fact that, in this cold-war
buildup, the weakest arm may still make all the difference.

Two miles down the road, at about the same time, a twenty-four-
year-old former art student named Charlie Zink was throwing from a
practice mound at the Red Sox' sprawling Player Development Complex, while the rest of the hundred or so minor-leaguers in the Boston
organization, spread out over five diamonds, took batting practice and
shagged fly balls. Zink was twelve when he first saw Wakefield—then
a rookie with the Pittsburgh Pirates—pitching in the National League
playoffs, in 1992. Now, although he is capable of throwing standard-
issue jock heat, Zink was trying to mimic the Wakefield delivery as well
as he could, right down to the apparent lack of exertion and the junior-
varsity speed. From a side view, there was nothing at all remarkable
about Zink's pitches, except that occasionally the catcher didn't catch
them. In those instances, the coach who was standing behind the
mound tended to exclaim, "That is outstanding!" Zink, who went un-
drafted as a fastball pitcher, is, at the Red Sox' urging, reinventing himself as a rare specialist: a knuckleballer. With Wakefield, one of only
two knuckleball pitchers currently on a major-league roster, and now
Zink, the Red Sox are cornering the market on low-grade weaponry.
Project Knuckleball is only just beginning its second year, but, according to Baseball Prospectus, a leading baseball-analysis website, Zink is
already the Red Sox' top-rated prospect.

The knuckleball—also known as the knuckler, the fingernail ball, the
fingertip ball, the flutterball, the floater, the dancer, the bug, the butterfly ball, the moth, the bubble, the ghostball, the horseshoe, the dry spit-
ter, and, curiously, the spinner—has been around, in one form or
another, for nearly as long as professional baseball itself, though for
much of that time it has been regarded with suspicion. Spinning is precisely what it does not do. In fact, a lack of spin is about the only identifying characteristic of the pitch. There is no right way to hold a
knuckleball when throwing it (seams, no seams; two fingers, three), and
no predictable flight pattern once it leaves the hand. "Butterflies aren't
bullets," the longtime knuckleballer Charlie Hough once said. "You

can't aim 'em—you just let 'em go." The pitch shakes, shimmies, wobbles, drops—it *knuckles,* as they say. Which is doubly confusing, because the term *knuckleball* is itself a kind of misnomer, a holdover from the pitch's largely forgotten infancy.

Depending on how you look at it, the first knuckleball was probably thrown in the late nineteenth century, by a bricklayer named Toad Ramsey, or shortly after the turn of the century, by the famous junkball ace Eddie Cicotte. Ramsey, who pitched for Louisville in the old American Association, severed a tendon in his left middle finger (that was his pitching hand), and thereafter adopted a peculiar grip, in which he curled his middle fingertip on the top of the ball, exposing the knuckle. His newfangled pitch probably more closely resembled what is now known as a knuckle curve—a pitch that, despite the name, bears little in-flight resemblance to Wakefield's floater. (The knuckle curve, thrown today by the Yankees' Mike Mussina, is released with topspin, or overspin, and so does not even belong in the flutterball's extended low-spin family.)

Cicotte, for his part, discovered early in his career that by pressing the knuckles of his middle and index fingers against the ball's surface, and steadying the ball with his thumb, he could produce a spinless pitch, which would behave erratically and set batters on edge. In 1908, pitching with the Red Sox, he took the nickname Knuckles—by which point others had already begun to figure out that the same flitting effect could be achieved, and with greater control, by simply clamping down on the rawhide with one's fingernails. The actual use of the knuckles in pushing the ball plateward has essentially been out of style for ninety years.

All told, there have been about seventy pitchers who have entrusted their livelihoods, at one point or another, to the vagaries of the knuckleball (by the count of baseball writer Rob Neyer). Some have preferred to throw a faster, harder-breaking version of the pitch, which arrives in the 70–75-mph range, exhibiting only minor turbulence en route to a crash landing. Others have favored a more arcing, directionally indecisive floater—the Pittsburgh Pirates slugger Willie Stargell called it "a butterfly with hiccups"—which takes care to obey interstate speed limits. Neither enterprise is a growth industry. In the past fifty years, the fluttering ranks have dwindled to just a few per generation.

Once comfortably ensconced in the flourishing community of oddball pitches—spitball, palm ball, shine ball, eephus—the knuckleball has fallen victim, in recent decades, to a prejudice against deception and a fear of the unknown. If a kid throwing 95 mph has a bad outing, scouts chalk it up to growing pains; at least he can *bring it*. If a knuckleballer flounders, it is proof, somehow, that the craft itself—just *look* at it—is unreliable.

"Catchers hate it," Jim Bouton, the author of *Ball Four: My Life and Hard Times Throwing the Knuckleball in the Big Leagues*, said recently. "Nobody likes to warm up with you. Coaches don't respect it. You can pitch seven good innings with a knuckleball, and as soon as you walk a guy they go, 'See, there's that damn knuckleball.'"

The pitch is minimally taxing from a physical standpoint, and thus affords its practitioners the ability to pitch in virtually any situation, on any day. Knuckleball pitchers seldom need to ice their arms after working. They lift weights only sparingly, and almost never get injured. The knuckleball favors old age—or at least doesn't discourage it—and forgives weakness. These are considerable advantages, yet the pitch is, for the same reasons, taken as an affront to the entrenched jock ethic of blood, sweat, and tears.

"Baseball science isn't rocket science," Robert K. Adair, a professor emeritus at Yale and the author of *The Physics of Baseball*, says. "It's a lot harder." To understand how a knuckleball works, it helps to have a basic familiarity with Bernoulli's principle, the Magnus effect, and the Prandtl boundary-layer theory, for a start. This much is easy: The stitches on a baseball interrupt the flow of air around the leather surface. Then it gets complicated. The air meeting the ball speeds up as it's disturbed, to compensate for the initial holdup. This increased airspeed causes the pressure (on the side of the interrupting, forwardmost stitch) to drop. The ball follows the lower pressure.

That's the short story, at least. Wake, drag, aerodynamic regime changes in midflight: All these and more come into play. When the knuckleball is dancing with particular verve and inspiration, as Wakefield's did (pre-Boone) against the Yankees last fall, batters and their fans tend to argue, only half in jest, that it is unfair—unhittable, even. ("You're better off trying to hit Wakefield when you're in a drunken stupor," the Yankees first baseman Jason Giambi said recently.) This may in fact literally be the case. "A knuckleball can change so close to the batter that he cannot physiologically adjust to it, so in some sense it's impossible to hit a breaking knuckleball," Adair says. "I mean, you can close your eyes and swing, and you *might* hit it. . . ."

Grumpy catchers may well have a point, too: Maybe all those passed balls are not their fault. "The fastest possible voluntary reaction time of a person is about a hundred and fifty milliseconds," Adair says. "And during that time the ball can change its direction so much that you can't catch it." Adair's conclusion: "When Tim Wakefield is on, it's pretty tough—tough to hit, tough to catch."

And when he's off? "All you need to know is that if you put any kind of a spin on it at all it'll travel about four hundred and seventy-five feet in the opposite direction," Bouton likes to say.

Tim Wakefield was not supposed to be a major-league pitcher. He was a standout high-school ballplayer in Melbourne, Florida, where he still lives. Like most good young players, he pitched some, but mainly he played first base. He was a power hitter. In college, at nearby Florida Tech, Wakefield broke the school home run record, and in 1988, his senior year, he was drafted by the Pirates. He reported that summer to Watertown, New York, where the Pirates had a Class A minor-league affiliate, and promptly set about proving to the club that selecting him had been a mistake: He hit .189 and struck out more than once every three times at bat.

Woody Huyke, one of Pittsburgh's developmental coaches, saved Wakefield's career. He saw Tim playing catch one day in the spring of 1989, during warmups, when many players goof around with sideline knuckleballs. (Like card tricks, everybody's got one.) Tim's ball was visibly of a different order from any garden-variety stunt pitch. "I thought, Jesus Christ," Huyke recalled recently. "I didn't say anything, I just played dumb. And then two days later we had an organizational meeting, because, you know, he was on the bubble as an infielder. I said, 'Before you let him go, I'd like to see him on the mound, 'cause he's got a good knuckleball.' So they kept him around. They told him, 'Either you pitch or go home.' "

Wakefield, as a boy, had learned about the knuckleball the hard way—by trying to catch it. ("You don't catch the knuckleball," Yankees manager Joe Torre, himself a former catcher, has said. "You defend against it.") His father, at the end of their backyard throwing sessions, would invariably end up pitching him butterflies. "Dad comes home from work, and I'm, you know, 'Let's go play catch,' " Wakefield told me. "He was tired, and he wanted to go inside. So the knuckleball was his way of trying to tire *me* out, 'cause I didn't want to have to catch it— it'd go by me and I'd have to go pick it up. It was kind of a subtle way of Dad saying, 'Time to go, let's quit.' "

At the time of Huyke's intervention, there were just two knuckle-ballers in the bigs—Charlie Hough, who was then forty-one and pitching for the Texas Rangers, and Tom Candiotti, thirty-one and with the Cleveland Indians—and no promising apprentices. "We are, unjustly, in the twilight of an era," one premature eulogy, by the former Rangers consultant Craig Wright, read. "We may be witnessing the last days of one of baseball's most baffling, most charming, and most effective pitches."

Reluctantly, Wakefield took to the mound—and within a few short years, as if by some kind of extended practical joke, there he was on national television in 1992, the rookie ace, in young Charlie Zink's living room, winning two games in the playoffs. Then, just as suddenly, he lost it. Flutterballs are exceedingly difficult to control, and the ability to land pitches anywhere near the strike zone with consistency is what separates a true knuckleballer from a Sunday-afternoon showoff. Wakefield walked twenty-eight batters over a three-game stretch in April 1993. He spent half of that season, and all of the next, in the minors, trying to regain his confidence; he lost twenty games and won just eight. In the spring of 1995, two years after he had been the Opening Day starter, the Pirates handed him his pink slip.

It seems fitting that a pitch as fickle as the knuckleball would produce a career filled (in the early going, at least) with herky-jerky ups and downs, but it would be a mistake to think that this volatility reflects the person. Wakefield is a quiet, studious-seeming man, who does everything—from walking to playing the guitar to singing harmony— with visible deliberation. (One of his favorite songs is "Take It Easy," by the Eagles.) He likes to call himself the "blue-collarite" on the pitching staff, a label that is reinforced by his friendship with various country musicians. Last winter, he made a guest appearance on the reality show *Average Joe.*

"It's not a macho-type thing," Wakefield said recently, about his un-likely livelihood. "I had to come up with a way to get outs, and that's the bottom line as a pitcher. It doesn't matter if you roll it underhand, as long as you get outs." He works hard, still, at practicing his fastball and curveball, each of which he throws between 5 and 10 percent of the time, to preserve at least some element of surprise. "I've hit eighty on the radar gun maybe half a dozen times," he said, cracking a restrained smile. "That's a huge accomplishment for me. I get high fives when I get to the dugout."

Wakefield was picked up for cheap by the Red Sox shortly after the Pirates cut him loose, and the accidental pitcher is now, improbably, starting his tenth season in Boston, which makes him the longest-serving member of the club. In the history of the Red Sox franchise, only three pitchers have appeared in more games or struck out more batters. Wakefield is thirty-seven, an age that spells retirement planning for ordinary players, and he is just entering his prime.

"I plan on pitching as long as I can, as long as I'm having fun," Wakefield told me earlier this year. He said that last season was the most fun he'd ever had in his baseball life. "I kind of look at it now as something special. It's an art. It's something that may be a lost art here, soon, if somebody else doesn't come up and start throwing it again."

Knuckleball pitchers are not just a rare but also a close-knit breed—the Fraternal Order of Knuckleheads, bound by their shared experiences of alienation and finger cramps. "We always root for each other across the miles," Bouton says. "We all understand we're a little weird."

Barry Meister, Wakefield's agent, also represents Steve Sparks, the other knuckleballer currently pitching in the majors. (Sparks, who is thirty-eight, has enjoyed less success than Wakefield, shuttling from team to team. He began this season as the fifth starter, and spot reliever, for the Arizona Diamondbacks.) "It's like some strange disease—they all hang out together," Meister told me, before the start of spring training. "I called Sparks last week and he said, 'Hey, I'm out in California, staying at Charlie Hough's house, playing golf.'"

The uniform No. 49, worn by Wakefield, and previously by Hough and Candiotti, serves as an unofficial pledge pin, honoring Hoyt Wilhelm, the most famous midcentury knuckleballer, whose career reflects many of the perks and humiliations of the tribe. Wilhelm was a few months shy of his thirtieth birthday when he was finally called upon to throw his first big-league pitch, for the New York Giants, in 1952. Over the course of twenty years, serving reliably as both a starter and a reliever, he was released four times, sold twice, traded four times, and offered up once to the expansion draft. Yet when he retired, just a week before his fiftieth birthday, he'd managed to pitch in more games than any player in history, and he was later inducted into the Hall of Fame.

Now that Wilhelm is gone (he died in 2002), the undisputed Grand Poobah is Phil Niekro, or Knucksie, as he is known among his brethren (though not to his brother Joe, another knuckler; together they amassed 539 wins, the most of any sibling pair in baseball). Knucksie won 208 games—of his career 318—after turning thirty-five. He is now sixty-five, and the resident prankster of the crew, an amateur magician always eager to impress with his sleight of hand.

Over the years, despite their scarcity, the knuckleball bunch have produced more than their fair share of bizarre and noteworthy feats. The last pitcher to start both games of a doubleheader, Wilbur Wood, was a knuckleballer. (That was for the White Sox, against the Yankees, in 1973. He lost both games.) And who can forget Eddie Rommel, a bug-tosser for the Philadelphia A's? On July 10, 1932, having already pitched on each of the previous two days, the thirty-four-year-old Rommel threw batting practice, took a breather for the first inning, and then came out of the bullpen, in the bottom of the second, to pitch for what turned out to be seventeen straight innings over four hours, along the way yielding twenty-nine hits and fourteen runs. (He won, 18–17. It was the last win of his career.)

Baseball manicures are a popular topic of conversation when any two or three from the gang get together. Knucksie once recommended that Sparks scuff his nails on concrete before pitching, to achieve the ideal gripping texture—a strategy that backfired when Sparks shattered one of his nails in the process. Others have tried laminating their nails with horse-hoof solution as a sort of reinforcement. "I did all sorts of things," Bouton told me. "I even tried filing saw teeth in my fingers to sort of get, like, an alligator grip on the ball, but the little points would break off—and they weren't too popular in bed, either."

The weather—artificial or real—comes up frequently, too. Most knucklers agree that wind in the face is good (anything to add resistance and turbulence), while wind blowing from behind spells doom. Heat and humidity are welcome, unless you're pitching in a dome; for whatever reason, the consensus seems to be that central air-conditioning can work wonders. Boston's Doug Mirabelli, who catches Wakefield exclusively (knucklers often get their own personal back-stops), has observed that the SkyDome in Toronto causes an extra hic-cup per pitch. And in the Astrodome in the seventies, conspiracy theorists will swear, the temperature was always suspiciously cool—the AC set to full blast—on days when Joe Niekro was starting for the home team.

All that's missing is an actual frat house, a fact that hasn't been lost on Bouton. "I just hope that one day there may be a home for aged knuckleball pitchers to go to," he said. "You know, like polka meetings, the Friars Club. That'd be nice. You could spend your final days rock-ing on a porch talking about some of the great games, laughing at all the broken bones that you've created for catchers, broken backs for bat-ters trying to swing and swat it."

Charlie Zink, the Red Sox' knuckler-in-training, had two main ambi-tions as he entered his late teens, neither of which was to be a pro base-ball player. He thought he might like to join the PGA Tour—golf suited his laid-back demeanor—or else get involved with law enforce-ment. "My parents were both wardens at Folsom State Prison, and I was thinking of doing something like that," he said this spring. "But then art school came along."

Art school was the Savannah College of Art and Design, known to its students as SCAD. Zink had been attending junior college in Sacra-mento, and playing on the baseball team there, but he found the atmo-sphere too competitive. "I was kind of burned out on baseball," he said. "I just wanted a change of scenery. I was looking for something easier at the time, and SCAD seemed like a good fit."

SCAD had a baseball team—a perfectly uncompetitive Division III team—whose coach, strangely, was Luis Tiant, the 1970s Red Sox star famous for his pretzel-twist pitching motion. Tiant took a liking to Zink, who seemed game to try anything—even turning his back on home plate during his windup, as Tiant himself had done. Though Zink graduated with roughly twice as many losses as wins on his record, Tiant got him a spring tryout with the Red Sox in 2002. Zink at least had a strong arm—he could throw 94 mph—and, well, he had a distinctive pitching motion; it was worth a shot.

Zink's reincarnation story, set in the summer of 2002, is similar to

Wakefield's, only more vivid. "I was just getting ready to throw one day, messing around like everyone else does, and our trainer asked me to throw a knuckleball," he told me. The trainer was not wearing a mask, and Zink's pitch—inspired by that long-ago glimpse of Wakefield as a rookie on national TV—danced its way squarely into his eye socket. "Our pitching coördinator was there to see it," Zink went on. "He told me to throw it a few more times, and I hit a few more guys in the chest."

If the black eye sealed Zink's conversion from Tiant protégé to Wakefield disciple, he didn't realize it at the time. He even went home to California for the winter and hit the gym ("All off-season, I was just lifting my butt off"), hoping to increase his arm strength and velocity for the following year. When he showed up in camp last spring, the Red Sox had new plans for him, and an increase in velocity was not among them. Wakefield told him, in a private knuckling tutorial, that in those infrequent instances when he'd be throwing fastballs, he ought to throw them slower than he was capable of—he ought to throw them from a half-assed knuckleball windup, that is, not a Tiant Twist—so as not to tip the batter off.

"The only thing I don't like about it is I still think of myself as an athlete," Zink, who has broad shoulders and an effortless grace that disintegrates when he throws his knuckler, told me. "And most people don't think of knuckleballers as athletes, which kind of makes me upset." A little early success goes a long way toward erasing such concerns. Late last summer, Zink was promoted from Class A Sarasota to Class AA Portland, where he twice carried no-hitters into the eighth inning. "My first double-A game, I was pitching in Binghamton against the Mets," he said. "And the second hitter I faced pulled a rib-cage muscle from swinging so hard. He had to get taken out of the game. I mean, that was one of the funniest things I've seen." Zink has even started having dreams about the knuckleball—about different grips and release points, and the inimitable flight patterns they can produce.

It takes a certain kind of seven-year-old—possessed of an extraordinary sense of his own limitations, or else an unimaginative fantasy life—to watch a professional baseball game and immediately identify with the oldest, slowest person on the field, the guy who, if not for the uniform, could plausibly pass for a math teacher. Sean Flaherty, of Englewood, Florida, was that kid. In April 1993, the expansion Florida Marlins played their first-ever game, and Sean's dad pulled him out of first grade to watch at a local sports bar. The Marlins' starting pitcher that day was the leather-faced forty-five-year-old Charlie Hough, still hanging on after all those years, throwing ghostballs in slo-mo.

"Sean was just mesmerized," Mike Flaherty, his father, remembers. "From that point on, he grew his nails out, and we played catch every day. I had bruises all over my body."

Sean Flaherty is now a senior in high school, and possibly the only full-fledged knuckleballer pitching for any secondary school, anywhere. (Like Wakefield, he throws knucklers at least 85 percent of the time.) He is five feet ten and not an obvious athlete—his aspect is that of a firefly chaser—but next year, against all odds, he will be suiting up for the University of Miami, a Division I powerhouse. Sean is also hoping to become the first of his breed ever to be selected in the amateur draft, next month. (And also, presumably, the first pitcher ever drafted who cannot hit eighty on a radar gun. His knuckleball ranges from 45 to 68 mph, and his fastball tops out in the seventies.)

The day of Tim Wakefield's first appearance this spring, Sean's team, the Lemon Bay Manta Rays, had a game of their own in Fort Myers, against the local Riverdale Raiders. Sean arrived at the field late, wearing a tuxedo. He plays tuba in the Florida West Coast Youth Symphony and was coming straight from a performance.

"Sean's journey has been unique," Mike Flaherty said, sitting in the bleachers. "He's a pioneer—he really is." During the regular season, Mike said, he and Sean catch all of Wakefield's starts on satellite TV at the same sports bar where the journey began. Last year, they also made regular trips to Sarasota and befriended Charlie Zink. (Sean, who has been throwing the knuckleball for much longer, offered Zink some pointers.) It was the fourth inning, and Lemon Bay was down, 10–3, by the time Sean took the mound. Riverdale, as it happened, was coached by the former Red Sox left fielder Mike Greenwell. (His son Bo is a freshman first baseman.) Greenwell, who said he'd hit knuckleballs quite well during his playing days, imparted what wisdom he could to his players: "Swing under it—the ball will always drop. Try to lift it." (This undoubtedly beats the famous hitting coach Charlie Lau's advice: "There are two theories on hitting the knuckleball. Unfortunately, nei-

ther of them works.") Sean warmed up to the song "Eye of the Tiger,"
played on someone's boom box, and then floated his bubbles: three innings, four strikeouts, one run allowed.

After the game (Riverdale won, 11–5), I joined Sean on the field for
a crash course in knuckleball catching. When I'd told Dave Clark, an
amateur flutterball fanatic who sent me his "Knucklebook" manuscript,
that I planned to play catch with a serious knuckleballer, he said I
should make sure to wear a cup. "Wear a mask, too," he added. "And
stand behind the backstop." I had neither a cup nor a mask, nor an
oversized softball mitt (which is what big-league knuckleball catchers
traditionally use), but I took my chances, and tried to remember the advice that Doug Mirabelli had given me earlier in the day: Let it travel
as far as possible; don't reach out to meet it, or you're asking for trouble.
The first pitch did a little jig about midway, and then darted down and
to my right. I got some glove on the ball, but not enough to squeeze it.
On two occasions, the ball swerved particularly late—I'd like to believe
these were instances such as Professor Adair described, where it is
physiologically impossible to react—and struck my unprotected throwing hand.

"How's it moving?" Sean called out at one point, to my surprise.
Then I recalled something Wakefield had told me. "I can't really see it,"
he'd said. "They say it shakes a lot—it goes back and forth. The only
thing I can see is the break down or the break to the left or to the right."
For the full visual effect, catcher is where it's at.

"We call that one the spinner," Sean said at another moment, after
the ball he'd just thrown forged a path almost like that of a roller coaster
turning over. The "spinner" is what Hoyt Wilhelm used to call his
corkscrew knuckler, perhaps because the pitch itself—not the ball—
appears to spin around an invisible axis. Accomplished knuckleballers
manage to throw it once in a while, usually by accident—it seems to require a lone, slow rotation of the ball while in orbit. It is, in a sense, the
profession's prize elixir—"If you could bottle one up, that'd be the one
you want to keep," Steve Sparks says—and catching it is a slightly
nerve-racking and dizzying experience. Not just for a novice, either:
Mirabelli warned me that the corkscrew "kind of hypnotizes you."

The first pitch of this season's ongoing Yankees–Red Sox showdown was thrown by—who else?—Tim Wakefield: a lazily arriving called strike. Boston won the game, 6–2, and the Yankees' three heaviest hitters, Alex Rodriguez, Gary Sheffield, and Jason Giambi, failed to register a hit. Notwithstanding the Game Seven relief appearance, with its Boone misfire (home run balls remain his Achilles' heel; no Sox pitcher has allowed more dingers in his Boston career), Wakefield has now beaten the Yankees in four consecutive starts, holding New York's batters to a pathetic .163 average.

"I don't want to see that thing again," Giambi told reporters afterward, and later quipped, "They should pitch him every day against us."

Wakefield didn't lose his first game until the beginning of May, when he was outdueled on ESPN by an unheralded Texas Rangers pitcher named R. A. Dickey, who lacks an ulnar collateral ligament in his right elbow. Dickey, seemingly an unwitting descendant of Toad Ramsey, throws a specialty knuckle-gripped pitch that he calls "the Thing," which Boston's general manager, Theo Epstein, described to me as "one-third knuckleball, one-third breaking ball, one-third split-finger."

More than once, while I was in Fort Myers, I heard a rumor that the Yankees' owner, George Steinbrenner, fed up with watching his high-priced stars flail helplessly at Wakefield's flittering moths, had ordered his legions to produce a knuckleballer of their own.

In the meantime, the Red Sox are slowly approaching the day when Giambi's suggestion might not be so far-fetched. As of this writing, Zink is leading Portland in innings pitched, and in the last week of April the Sox signed the left-handed pitcher Joe Rogers from the discard heap—forgettable news, if not for the fact that Epstein had told me that the club planned to convert him immediately to the Zink regimen. Rogers, who is twenty-three, was relieved of his fastball-throwing duties with the St. Louis Cardinals organization at the end of spring training, and he has now been assigned to Boston's Sarasota affiliate, where, throwing mostly knuckleballs, he allowed just one earned run in his first seven innings of work. "We're trying to remind ourselves that there are lots of ways to get guys out," Epstein said.

2004

GAME PLAN

DON DeLILLO

O f the game itself, a spectacle of high-shouldered men panting in the grass, I remember little or nothing. We played well that night or didn't play well; we won or lost. What I do recall are the names of plays and of players. Our opponent was West Centrex Biotechnical Institute. They were bigger than we were, a bit faster, possibly better trained, but as far as I could tell our plays had the better names.

At the kickoff, the receiving team dropped back and found its ground, holding a moment. Under the tumbling ball, the other team charged, verbs running into mammoth nouns, small wars commencing here and there, exultation and first blood, a helmet bouncing brightly on the phosphorescent grass, the breathless impact of two destructive masses, quite pretty to watch.

We huddled at the thirty-one.

"Blue turk right," Hobbs said. "Double-slot, re-T chuck-and-go, gap-angle wide, near-in belly toss, counter-sag, middle-sift W, zero snag delay."

"You forgot the snap number," Onan Moley said.

"How about three?" Ed Jessup said.

"How about two?" I said.

"Two it is," Hobbs said.

Six plays later, we left the huddle with a sharp handclap and trotted up to the Centrex twenty, eager to move off the ball, sensing a faint anxiety on the other side of the line.

"How to hit!" George Dole shouted out to us from the bench. "Way to pop, way to go, way to move! How to sting them, big Jerry! Huh huh huh huh! How to play this game!"

We scored, and Bing Jackmin kicked the extra point. I went over to the sideline and got down on one knee, the chin strap of my helmet undone—material for a prize-winning sports photo. Commotion everywhere. Offensive Backfield Coach Oscar Veech was shouting into my left ear.

"On the 32-break I want you to catapult out of there. I want you to really bulldoze. I want to see you cascade into the secondary."

"Tremendous imagery," I said.

"But be sure you protect that ball."

"Right."

"Get fetal, get fetal."

"Fetal!" I shouted back.

Our defense rolled into a gut 4-3 with variable off-picks. Down at the end of the bench, Raymond Toon seemed to be talking into his right fist. I got up and went over there. When he saw me coming, he covered the fist with his other hand.

"What are you doing, Toonie?" I asked.

"Nothing."

"I know what you're doing."

"Broadcasting the game," he admitted.

Their quarterback, Artie Telcon, moved them on the ground past midfield. At the sideline, I listened to one of our backfield coaches lecturing Garland Hobbs: "Employ the aerial game to implement the running game whereby you force their defense to respect the run, which is what they won't do if they can anticipate pass and read pass and if our frequency, say on second and long, indicates pass. If they send their linebackers, you've been trained and briefed and you know how to counter this. You counter this by audibilizing. You've got your screen, your flare, your quick slant-in. Audibilize. Audibilize. Audibilize."

They tried a long field goal, wide, and we went out. Hobbs hit Ron Steeples for good yardage. Steeples was knocked cold on the play, and the ref called a time-out to get him off. Chuck Deering came running in to replace him, tripping and falling as he reached the huddle. His left ankle appeared to be broken, and the ref called time again to get him off.

When we rehuddled Hobbs said, "Stem left, L and R hitch and cross, F weak switch to strong. On hut."

"What?" Flanders said.

"On hut."

"No, the other thing. F something."

"F weak switch to strong."

"What kind of pattern is that?"

"Are you kidding? Are you serious?"

"What a bunch of turf-eaters." Co-Captain Moody Kimbrough said.

"When did they put that pattern in, Hobbsie?"

"Tuesday or Wednesday. Where were you?"

"It must have been Wednesday," Flanders said. "I was at the dentist Wednesday."

"Nobody told you about the weak switch to strong?"

"I don't think so, Hobbsie."

"Look, run out ten yards, put some moves on your man, and then wait for further instructions."

"I'm co-captain to a bunch of turf-eaters," Kimbrough said.

"On hut. Break."

Centrex sent their linebackers. Hobbs left the pocket and I had Mallon, their psychotic middle linebacker, by the jersey. He tripped and I released, moving into a passing plane for Hobbs. He saw me but threw low. I didn't bother diving for it. One of the coaches, Vern Feck, screamed into our chests as we came off. "What in the hell is going on here? What are you feebs doing out there? What in the goddam goat-smelling hell is the name of the game you people are playing?"

Head Coach said nothing.

Lenny Wells came off in pain—groin damage or hamstring. Telcon spotted a man absolutely alone in the end zone and hit him easily, and I looked around for my helmet.

"Our uniforms are green and white," Bing Jackmin said as we watched them kick off. "The field itself is green and white—grass and chalk markings. We melt into our environment. We are doubled in the primitive mirror."

Centrex called time because they had only seven men on the field. We assembled near our own forty-five while they got straightened out. Ed Jessup, our tight end, was bleeding from his mouth.

"That ass-belly 62 got his fist in," he said.

"You'd better go off," I said.

"I'm gonna hang in."

"A tough area to bandage, Ed. Looks like it's just under the skin-bridge running to the upper gum."

"I get that 62. I get that meatman," he said.

"Let's ching those nancies," Flanders said.

"Maybe if you rinsed with warm water, Eddie."

Their left tackle was an immense and very geometric piece of work, about six-seven and two-seventy—an oblong monument to intimidation. It was the responsibility of our right guard, Cecil Rector, to contain this man. Offensive Line Coach Tweego had Cecil Rector by the pads as I crossed the sideline.

"I want you to fire out, boy," Tweego said. "You're not blowing them out. You're not popping. You're not putting any hurt on those people."

I sat on the bench next to Billy Mast as Telcon riddled our secondary with seam patterns. Billy was wearing his helmet. I leaned toward him and spoke in a monotonous intonation.

"Uh, this is Maxcom, Robomat."

Billy Mast looked at me.

"Robomat, this is Maxcom. Do you read?"

"Uh, Roger, Maxcom," he said.

"You're looking real good, Robomat. Is that affirm?"

"Uh, Roger. We're looking real good."

"What is your thermal passive mode control?"

"Vector five and locking."

"Uh, what is your inertial thrust correction on fourth and long?"

"We read circularize and non-adjust."

"That is affirm, Robomat. You are looking real super on the inset retro deployment thing. We read three one niner five niner. Twelve seconds to adapter vent circuit cutoff."

"Affirmative, Maxcom. Three one niner five niner. Twelve seconds to vent cut. There is God. We have just seen God. He is all around us."

"Uh, Roger, Robomat. Suggest braking burn and midcourse tracking profile. Blue and holding."

Hobbs faked a trigger pitch to Taft Robinson and handed to me, a variation off the KC draw. I was leveled by Mallon. He came down on top of me, chuffing like a train. In the huddle, Hobbs called the same play. For some reason, it seemed a very beautiful thing to do. More than the thoughtful gesture of a teammate—a near-philosophic statement. Hobbs received the snapback, Roy Yellin pulled, and there I was with the football, the pigskin, running to daylight, to starlight, and getting hit again by Mike Mallon, by No. 55, by five five. A lyrical moment, the sum of something doubled.

Three firecrackers went off in the stands. The crowd responded with prolonged applause. I flared to the left, taking Mallon with me. Taft Robinson held for a two-count and then swung over the middle. Hobbs threw high under pressure. Third and four, or maybe fourth and three. The gun sounded and we headed for the tunnel.

Here before our cubicles we sit quietly, content to suck the sweet flesh out of quartered oranges. We are preoccupied with conserving ourselves for the second half and do not make work by gesturing to each other, or taking more than the minimum number of steps from here to there. A park bench has somehow found its way into the dressing area.

From nearby, I hear Sam Trammel's voice: "Crackback. Crackback."

I get to my feet and take six steps to the water fountain. Cecil Rector stands against the wall. Tweego has him by the shoulder pads once again.

"Contain, contain, contain that man," Tweego says. "Rape him. Ray-yape that sumbitch. Do not let that sumbitch infringe."

Slowly I swing my arms over my head. I see Jerry Fallon and approach him. He is standing in front of his cubicle, hands at his sides, headgear on the floor between his feet.

"Jerry boy, big Jerry," I say.

"Huh huh huh," he mutters.

George Owen, a line coach, stands on a chair. His gaze moves slowly across the room, then back again. He holds his clenched fists against the sides of his head. Slowly his knees begin to bend. "Footbawl!" he shouts. "This is footbawl. You throw it, you ketch it, you kick it. Footbawl! Footbawl! Footbawl!"

Bing Jackmin squib-kicked down the middle. Andy Chudko hit the ballcarrier at full force and skidded on his knees over the fallen player's body. I watched Head Coach assume his stance at the midfield stripe. Dennis Smee, our middle linebacker, shouted down at the front four: "Tango-2. Reset red. Choke off that sweep!"

Garland Hobbs opened with a burn-7 hitch to his flanker off the fake picket. I moved into my frozen-insect pose, ready to pass-block. Their big tackle shed Cecil Rector and came dog-paddling in. I jammed my helmet into his chest and brought it up fast, striking his chin. He kept coming, kept mauling me, finally driving me down and putting an elbow into my neck. I couldn't think of anything to say.

Hobbs looked toward the head coach for guidance on a tough third-down call. Head Coach said nothing. His arms remained folded, his right foot tamping the grass. This was his power, to deny us the words we needed. He was the maker of plays, the namegiver. We were his chalk-scrawls. Something like that.

Hobbs said, "Zone set, triple tex, delta-3 series, jumbo trap delay, cable blocking, double-D to right, shallow hinge reverse."

The crowd was up and screaming—a massive, sustained, but somehow vacuous roar. I slowed to a walk and watched Taft Robinson glide into the end zone. Touchdown. He executed a dainty little curl to the left and casually dropped the football. Moody Kimbrough lifted him up. Spurgeon Cole stood beneath the goalposts, repeating them, arms raised in the shape of a crossbar and uprights, his fists clenched.

Jessup to No. 62: "Suckmouth. Nipplenose. Bluefinger."

I walked down to the end of the bench. Raymond Toon was all alone, still broadcasting into his right fist.

"There it goes, end over end, a high spiral. The deep man avoids—or evades would be better. Down he goes, woof. First and ten at the twenty-six or thirty-one. Here they come and Andy Chudko, in now for Butler, goes in high, No. 61, Andy Chudko—Fumble! Fumble!—six feet even, about two-twenty-five, doubles at center on offense. Chudko, majoring in airport-commissary management, plays a guitar to relax, no other hobbies, fumbles after the whistle. College football—a pleasant and colorful way to spend an autumn afternoon."

"It's nighttime, Toonie," I said.

"There he goes—five, six, seven, eight, nine, ten, eleven yards, power sweep, *twelve* yards, from our vantage point here at the Orange Bowl in sun-drenched Miami, Florida. John Billy Small combined to bring him down. John Billy, as they break the huddle—what a story behind this boy, a message of hope and inspiration to all those likewise afflicted, and now look at him literally slicing through those big ballcarriers! Flag, flag, flag—a flag down. All the color and excitement here. Oh, he's got it with a yard to spare off a good block by 53 or 63. Three Rivers Stadium in Pittsburgh or Cincinnati. Perfect weather for football. He's a good one, that Telcon. Multitalented. Woof! Plenty of hitting down there. I'm sure glad I'm up here. D.C. Stadium in the heart of the nation's capital. Crisp blue skies. A new wrinkle in that offense, or is it a broken play? Time-out on the field with the score all locked up at something-something. And now back to our studios for this message."

I watched Lloyd Philpot, Jr., come toward the bench. His jersey wasn't tucked into his pants. Tape was hanging from his left wrist and hand. He squatted down next to me on the sideline.

"I didn't infringe," he said sadly. "The coaches wanted optimum in-fringement. They insisted on that all week in practice. But I didn't do the job. I didn't infringe."

Centrex was running sweeps. I went over and sat with Garland Hobbs. Somebody in the stands behind us, way up high, was blowing into some kind of air horn. It sent a prehistoric cry across the night.

"String-in left, modified crossbow, quickside brake and swing, flow-and-go, dummy stitch, on two, on two," Hobbs said.

"You're always giving us on two, on two," Roy Yellin said. "All freak-ing night—'on two, on two.' What about four for a change? 'On four'?"

"Four it is," Hobbs said.

More firecrackers went off in the stands, and newspapers blew across the line of scrimmage. I ran a desultory curl pattern over the middle, putting moves on everybody I passed, including teammates. The sta-dium was emptying out. I returned to the huddle. We went to the line and set. The left side of our line was offside. The gun sounded, and we walked off the field and went through the tunnel into the locker room.

Onan Moley is already naked as we walk in. We sit before our cubicles and pound our cleated shoes on the stone floor ten times. One of the school's oldest traditions. The coaches gather at one end of the room. Onan's right arm is in a cast and he stands against a wall absently wav-ing his left hand to keep a fly away from his face. There are blades of grass stuck to the dried blood on his cheekbone. Next to me, Garland Hobbs takes a long red box from the bottom of his cubicle. The label on it reads: "All-American Quarterback. A Mendelsohn-Topping Sports Motivation Concept." Hobbs opens the box and puts it on the bench between us. He arranges twenty-two figurines on a tiny gridiron and then spins a dial. His team moves smartly downfield. Before it gets to be my turn to spin, the coaches call for quiet, clapping their hands and whistling. Head Coach is standing before a blackboard at the front of the room. His arms are crossed over his chest and he holds his base-ball cap in his right hand. We are all waiting. He looks at his watch and then nods to Rolf Hauptführer, his defensive backfield coach.

Hauptführer faces us, assuming a stance of sorts. "Be ready," he says.

We sit waiting, immobile in our soaked equipment, until Hauptführer begins to read our names from the team roster, pausing after each one to give us time to chant an answer.

1971

THE ART OF FAILURE

MALCOLM GLADWELL

There was a moment, in the third and deciding set of the 1993 Wimbledon final, when Jana Novotna seemed invincible. She was leading 4–1 and serving at 40–30, meaning that she was one point from winning the game, and just five points from the most coveted championship in tennis. She had just hit a backhand to her opponent, Steffi Graf, that skimmed the net and landed so abruptly on the far side of the court that Graf could only watch, in flat-footed frustration. The stands at Center Court were packed. The Duke and Duchess of Kent were in their customary place in the royal box. Novotna was in white, poised and confident, her blond hair held back with a headband—and then something happened. She served the ball straight into the net. She stopped and steadied herself for the second serve—the toss, the arch of the back—but this time it was worse. Her swing seemed halfhearted, all arm and no legs and torso. Double fault. On the next point, she was slow to react to a high shot by Graf, and badly missed on a forehand volley. At game point, she hit an overhead straight into the net. Instead of 5–1, it was now 4–2. Graf to serve: an easy victory, 4–3. Novotna to serve. She wasn't tossing the ball high enough. Her head was down. Her movements had slowed markedly. She double-faulted once, twice, three times. Pulled wide by a Graf forehand, Novotna inexplicably hit a low, flat shot directly at Graf, instead of a high crosscourt forehand that would have given her time to get back into position: 4–4. Did she suddenly realize how terrifyingly close she was to victory? Did she remember that she had never won a major tournament before? Did she look across the net and see Steffi Graf—Steffi Graf!—the greatest player of her generation?

On the baseline, awaiting Graf's serve, Novotna was now visibly agitated, rocking back and forth, jumping up and down. She talked to herself under her breath. Her eyes darted around the court. Graf took the game at love; Novotna, moving as if in slow motion, did not win a single point: 5–4, Graf. On the sidelines, Novotna wiped her racquet and her face with a towel, and then each finger individually. It was her turn to serve. She missed a routine volley wide, shook her head, talked to herself. She missed her first serve, made the second, then, in the resulting rally, mis-hit a backhand so badly that it sailed off her racquet as if launched into flight. Novotna was unrecognizable, not an elite tennis player but a beginner again. She was crumbling under pressure, but exactly why was as baffling to her as it was to all those looking on. Isn't pressure supposed to bring out the best in us? We try harder. We concentrate harder. We get a boost of adrenaline. We care more about how well we perform. So what was happening to her?

At championship point, Novotna hit a low, cautious, and shallow lob to Graf. Graf answered with an unreturnable overhead smash, and, mercifully, it was over. Stunned, Novotna moved to the net. Graf kissed her twice. At the awards ceremony, the Duchess of Kent handed Novotna the runner-up's trophy, a small silver plate, and whispered something in her ear, and what Novotna had done finally caught up with her. There she was, sweaty and exhausted, looming over the delicate white-haired Duchess in her pearl necklace. The Duchess reached up and pulled her head down onto her shoulder, and Novotna started to sob.

Human beings sometimes falter under pressure. Pilots crash and divers drown. Under the glare of competition, basketball players cannot find the basket and golfers cannot find the pin. When that happens, we say variously that people have "panicked" or, to use the sports colloquialism, "choked." But what do those words mean? Both are pejoratives. To choke or panic is considered to be as bad as to quit. But are all forms of failure equal? And what do the forms in which we fail say about who we are and how we think? We live in an age obsessed with success, with documenting the myriad ways by which talented people overcome challenges and obstacles. There is as much to be learned, though, from documenting the myriad ways in which talented people sometimes fail.

Choking sounds like a vague and all-encompassing term, yet it describes a very specific kind of failure. For example, psychologists often use a primitive video game to test motor skills. They'll sit you in front of a computer with a screen that shows four boxes in a row, and a keyboard that has four corresponding buttons in a row. One at a time, *x*'s start to appear in the boxes on the screen, and you are told that every time this happens you are to push the key corresponding to the box. According to Daniel Willingham, a psychologist at the University of Virginia, if you're told ahead of time about the pattern in which those *x*'s will appear, your reaction time in hitting the right key will improve dramatically. You'll play the game very carefully for a few rounds, until you've learned the sequence, and then you'll get faster and faster. Willingham calls this "explicit learning." But suppose you're not told that the *x*'s appear in a regular sequence, and even after playing the game for a while you're not aware that there is a pattern. You'll still get faster: You'll learn the sequence unconsciously. Willingham calls that "implicit learning"—learning that takes place outside of awareness. These two learning systems are quite separate, based in different parts of the brain. Willingham says that when you are first taught something—say, how to hit a backhand or an overhead forehand—you think it through in a very deliberate, mechanical manner. But as you get better the implicit system takes over: You start to hit a backhand fluidly, without thinking. The basal ganglia, where implicit learning partially resides, are concerned with force and timing, and when that system kicks in you begin to develop touch and accuracy, the ability to hit a drop shot or place a serve at a hundred miles per hour. "This is something that is going to happen gradually," Willingham says. "You hit several thousand forehands, after a while you may still be attending to it. But not very much. In the end, you don't really notice what your hand is doing at all."

Under conditions of stress, however, the explicit system sometimes takes over. That's what it means to choke. When Jana Novotna faltered at Wimbledon, it was because she began thinking about her shots again. She lost her fluidity, her touch. She double-faulted on her serves and mis-hit her overheads, the shots that demand the greatest sensitivity in force and timing. She seemed like a different person—playing with the slow, cautious deliberation of a beginner—because, in a sense, she was a beginner again: She was relying on a learning system that she hadn't used to hit serves and overhead forehands and volleys since she was first taught tennis, as a child. The same thing has happened to Chuck Knoblauch, the New York Yankees' second baseman, who inexplicably has had trouble throwing the ball to first base. Under the stress of playing in front of forty thousand fans at Yankee Stadium, Knoblauch finds himself reverting to explicit mode, throwing like a Little Leaguer again.

Panic is something else altogether. Consider the following account of a scuba-diving accident, recounted to me by Ephimia Morphew, a human-factors specialist at NASA: "It was an open-water certification dive, Monterey Bay, California, about ten years ago. I was nineteen. I'd been diving for two weeks. This was my first time in the open ocean without the instructor. Just my buddy and I. We had to go about forty feet down, to the bottom of the ocean, and do an exercise where we took our regulators out of our mouth, picked up a spare one that we had on our vest, and practiced breathing out of the spare. My buddy did hers. Then it was my turn. I removed my regulator. I lifted up my secondary regulator. I put it in my mouth, exhaled, to clear the lines, and then I inhaled, and, to my surprise, it was water. I inhaled water. Then the hose that connected that mouthpiece to my tank, my air source, came unlatched and air from the hose came exploding into my face.

"Right away, my hand reached out for my partner's air supply, as if I was going to rip it out. It was without thought. It was a physiological response. My eyes are seeing my hand do something irresponsible. I'm fighting with myself. Don't do it. Then I searched my mind for what I could do. And nothing came to mind. All I could remember was one thing: If you can't take care of yourself, let your buddy take care of you. I let my hand fall back to my side, and I just stood there."

This is a textbook example of panic. In that moment, Morphew stopped thinking. She forgot that she had another source of air, one that worked perfectly well and that, moments before, she had taken out of her mouth. She forgot that her partner had a working air supply as well, which could easily be shared, and she forgot that grabbing her partner's regulator would imperil both of them. All she had was her most basic instinct: Get air. Stress wipes out short-term memory. People with lots of experience tend not to panic, because when the stress suppresses their short-term memory they still have some residue of experience to draw on. But what did a novice like Morphew have? *I searched my mind for what I could do. And nothing came to mind.*

Panic also causes what psychologists call perceptual narrowing. In one study, from the early seventies, a group of subjects were asked to perform a visual acuity task while undergoing what they thought was a sixty-foot dive in a pressure chamber. At the same time, they were asked to push a button whenever they saw a small light flash on and off in their peripheral vision. The subjects in the pressure chamber had much higher heart rates than the control group, indicating that they were under stress. That stress didn't affect their accuracy at the visual-acuity task, but they were only half as good as the control group at picking up the peripheral light. "You tend to focus or obsess on one thing," Morphew says. "There's a famous airplane example, where the landing light went off, and the pilots had no way of knowing if the landing gear was down. The pilots were so focused on that light that no one noticed the autopilot had been disengaged, and they crashed the plane." Morphew reached for her buddy's air supply because it was the only air supply she could see.

Panic, in this sense, is the opposite of choking. Choking is about thinking too much. Panic is about thinking too little. Choking is about loss of instinct. Panic is reversion to instinct. They may look the same, but they are worlds apart.

Why does this distinction matter? In some instances, it doesn't much. If you lose a close tennis match, it's of little moment whether you choked or panicked; either way, you lost. But there are clearly cases when how failure happens is central to understanding why failure happens.

Take the plane crash in which John F. Kennedy, Jr., was killed last summer. The details of the flight are well-known. On a Friday evening last July, Kennedy took off with his wife and sister-in-law for Martha's Vineyard. The night was hazy, and Kennedy flew along the Connecticut coastline, using the trail of lights below him as a guide. At Westerly, Rhode Island, he left the shoreline, heading straight out over Rhode Island Sound, and at that point, apparently disoriented by the darkness and haze, he began a series of curious maneuvers: He banked his plane to the right, farther out into the ocean, and then to the left. He climbed and descended. He sped up and slowed down. Just a few miles from his destination, Kennedy lost control of the plane, and it crashed into the ocean.

Kennedy's mistake, in technical terms, was that he failed to keep his wings level. That was critical, because when a plane banks to one side it begins to turn and its wings lose some of their vertical lift. Left unchecked, this process accelerates. The angle of the bank increases, the turn gets sharper and sharper, and the plane starts to dive toward the ground in an ever-narrowing corkscrew. Pilots call this the graveyard spiral. And why didn't Kennedy stop the dive? Because, in times of low visibility and high stress, keeping your wings level—indeed, even knowing whether you are in a graveyard spiral—turns out to be surprisingly difficult. Kennedy failed under pressure.

Had Kennedy been flying during the day or with a clear moon, he would have been fine. If you are the pilot, looking straight ahead from the cockpit, the angle of your wings will be obvious from the straight line of the horizon in front of you. But when it's dark outside, the horizon disappears. There is no external measure of the plane's bank. On the ground, we know whether we are level even when it's dark, because of the motion-sensing mechanisms in the inner ear. In a spiral dive, though, the effect of the plane's G-force on the inner ear means that the pilot feels perfectly level even if his plane is not. Similarly, when you are in a jetliner that is banking at 30 degrees after takeoff, the book on your neighbor's lap does not slide into your lap, nor will a pen on the floor roll toward the "down" side of the plane. The physics of flying is such that an airplane in the midst of a turn always feels perfectly level to someone inside the cabin.

This is a difficult notion, and to understand it I went flying with William Langewiesche, the author of a superb book on flying, *Inside the Sky*. We met at San Jose Airport, in the jet center where the Silicon Valley billionaires keep their private planes. Langewiesche is a rugged man in his forties, deeply tanned, and handsome in the way that pilots (at least since the movie *The Right Stuff*) are supposed to be. We took off at dusk, heading out toward Monterey Bay, until we had left the lights of the coast behind and night had erased the horizon. Langewiesche let the plane bank gently to the left. He took his hands off the stick. The sky told me nothing now, so I concentrated on the instruments. The nose of the plane was dropping. The gyroscope told me that we were banking, first fifteen, then thirty, then forty-five degrees. "We're in a spiral dive," Langewiesche said calmly. Our airspeed was steadily accelerating, from a hundred and eighty to a hundred and ninety to two hundred knots. The needle on the altimeter was moving down. The plane was dropping like a stone, at three thousand feet per minute. I could hear, faintly, a slight increase in the hum of the engine, and the wind noise as we picked up speed. But if Langewiesche and I had been talking I would have caught none of that. Had the cabin been unpressurized, my ears might have popped, particularly as we went into the steep part of the dive. But beyond that? Nothing at all. In a spiral dive, the G-load—the force of inertia—is normal. As Langewiesche puts it, the plane likes to spiral-dive. The total time elapsed since we started diving was no more than six or seven seconds. Suddenly, Langewiesche straightened the wings and pulled back on the stick to get the nose of the plane up, breaking out of the dive. Only now did I feel the full force of the G-load, pushing me back in my seat. "You feel no G-load in a bank," Langewiesche said. "There's nothing more confusing for the uninitiated."

I asked Langewiesche how much longer we could have fallen. "Within five seconds, we would have exceeded the limits of the airplane," he replied, by which he meant that the force of trying to pull out of the dive would have broken the plane into pieces. I looked away from the instruments and asked Langewiesche to spiral-dive again, this time without telling me. I sat and waited. I was about to tell Langewiesche that he could start diving anytime, when, suddenly, I was thrown back in my chair. "We just lost a thousand feet," he said.

This inability to sense, experientially, what your plane is doing is what makes night flying so stressful. And this was the stress that Kennedy must have felt when he turned out across the water at Westerly, leaving the guiding lights of the Connecticut coastline behind him. A pilot who flew into Nantucket that night told the National Transportation Safety Board that when he descended over Martha's Vineyard he looked down and there was "nothing to see. There was no horizon and no light. . . . I thought the island might [have] suffered a power failure." Kennedy was now blind, in every sense, and he must have known the danger he was in. He had very little experience in flying strictly by instruments. Most of the time when he had flown up to the Vineyard the horizon or lights had still been visible. That strange, final sequence of maneuvers was Kennedy's frantic search for a clearing in the haze. He was trying to pick up the lights of Martha's Vineyard, to restore the lost horizon. Between the lines of the NTSB report on the crash, you can almost feel his desperation:

> About 2138 the target began a right turn in a southerly direction. About 30 seconds later, the target stopped its descent at 2200 feet and began a climb that lasted another 30 seconds.

During this period of time, the target stopped the turn, and the airspeed decreased to about 153 KIAS. About 2139, the target leveled off at 2500 feet and flew in a southeasterly direction. About 50 seconds later, the target entered a left turn and climbed to 2600 feet. As the target continued in the left turn, it began a descent that reached a rate of about 900 fpm.

But was he choking or panicking? Here the distinction between those two states is critical. Had he choked, he would have reverted to the mode of explicit learning. His movements in the cockpit would have become markedly slower and less fluid. He would have gone back to the mechanical, self-conscious application of the lessons he had first received as a pilot—and that might have been a good thing. Kennedy needed to think, to concentrate on his instruments, to break away from the instinctive flying that served him when he had a visible horizon.

But instead, from all appearances, he panicked. At the moment when he needed to remember the lessons he had been taught about instrument flying, his mind—like Morphew's when she was underwater—must have gone blank. Instead of reviewing the instruments, he seems to have been focused on one question: Where are the lights of Martha's Vineyard? His gyroscope and his other instruments may well have become as invisible as the peripheral lights in the underwater-panic experiments. He had fallen back on his instincts—on the way the plane felt—and in the dark, of course, instinct can tell you nothing. The NTSB report says that the last time the Piper's wings were level was seven seconds past 9:40, and the plane hit the water at about 9:41, so the critical period here was less than sixty seconds. At twenty-five seconds past the minute, the plane was tilted at an angle greater than 45 degrees. Inside the cockpit it would have felt normal. At some point, Kennedy must have heard the rising wind outside, or the roar of the engine as it picked up speed. Again, relying on instinct, he might have pulled back on the stick, trying to raise the nose of the plane. But pulling back on the stick without first leveling the wings only makes the spiral tighter and the problem worse. It's also possible that Kennedy did nothing at all, and that he was frozen at the controls, still frantically searching for the lights of the Vineyard, when his plane hit the water. Sometimes pilots don't even try to make it out of a spiral dive. Langewiesche calls that "one G all the way down."

What happened to Kennedy that night illustrates a second major difference between panicking and choking. Panicking is conventional failure, of the sort we tacitly understand. Kennedy panicked because he didn't know enough about instrument flying. If he'd had another year in the air, he might not have panicked, and that fits with what we believe—that performance ought to improve with experience, and that pressure is an obstacle that the diligent can overcome. But choking makes little intuitive sense. Novotna's problem wasn't lack of diligence; she was as superbly conditioned and schooled as anyone on the tennis tour. And what did experience do for her? In 1995, in the third round of the French Open, Novotna choked even more spectacularly than she had against Graf, losing to Chanda Rubin after surrendering a 5–0 lead in the third set. There seems little doubt that part of the reason for her collapse against Rubin was her collapse against Graf—that the second failure built on the first, making it possible for her to be up 5–0 in the third set and yet entertain the thought *I can still lose.* If panicking is conventional failure, choking is paradoxical failure.

Claude Steele, a psychologist at Stanford University, and his colleagues have done a number of experiments in recent years looking at how certain groups perform under pressure, and their findings go to the heart of what is so strange about choking. Steele and Joshua Aronson found that when they gave a group of Stanford undergraduates a standardized test and told them that it was a measure of their intellectual ability, the white students did much better than their black counterparts. But when the same test was presented simply as an abstract laboratory tool, with no relevance to ability, the scores of blacks and whites were virtually identical. Steele and Aronson attribute this disparity to what they call "stereotype threat": When black students are put into a situation where they are directly confronted with a stereotype about their group—in this case, one having to do with intelligence—the resulting pressure causes their performance to suffer.

Steele and others have found stereotype threat at work in any situation where groups are depicted in negative ways. Give a group of qualified women a math test and tell them it will measure their quantitative ability and they'll do much worse than equally skilled men will; present the same test simply as a research tool and they'll do just as well as the men. Or consider a handful of experiments conducted by one of Steele's former graduate students, Julio Garcia, a professor at Tufts University. Garcia gathered together a group of white, athletic students and had a white instructor lead them through a series of physical tests: to jump as high as they could, to do a standing broad jump, and to see how many pushups they could do in twenty seconds. The instructor then asked them to do the tests a second time, and, as you'd expect, Garcia found that the students did a little better on each of the tasks the second time around. Then Garcia ran a second group of students through the tests, this time replacing the instructor between the first and second trials with an African American. Now the white students ceased to improve on their vertical leaps. He did the experiment again, only this time he replaced the white instructor with a black instructor who was much taller and heavier than the previous black instructor. In this trial, the white students actually jumped less high than they had the first time around. Their performance on the pushups, though, was unchanged in each of the conditions. There is no stereotype, after all, that suggests that whites can't do as many pushups as blacks. The task that was affected was the vertical leap, because of what our culture says: *White men can't jump*.

It doesn't come as news, of course, that black students aren't as good at test-taking as white students, or that white students aren't as good at jumping as black students. The problem is that we've always assumed that this kind of failure under pressure is panic. What is it we tell underperforming athletes and students? The same thing we tell novice pilots or scuba divers: to work harder, to buckle down, to take the tests of their ability more seriously. But Steele says that when you look at the way black or female students perform under stereotype threat you don't see the wild guessing of a panicked test taker. "What you tend to see is carefulness and second-guessing," he explains. "When you go and interview them, you have the sense that when they are in the stereotype-threat condition they say to themselves, 'Look, I'm going to be careful here. I'm not going to mess things up.' Then, after having decided to take that strategy, they calm down and go through the test. But that's not the way to succeed on a standardized test. The more you do that, the more you will get away from the intuitions that help you, the quick processing. They think they did well, and they are trying to do well. But they are not." This is choking, not panicking. Garcia's athletes and

Steele's students are like Novotna, not Kennedy. They failed because they were good at what they did: only those who care about how well they perform ever feel the pressure of stereotype threat. The usual prescription for failure—to work harder and take the test more seriously—would only make their problems worse.

That is a hard lesson to grasp, but harder still is the fact that choking requires us to concern ourselves less with the performer and more with the situation in which the performance occurs. Novotna herself could do nothing to prevent her collapse against Graf. The only thing that could have saved her is if—at that critical moment in the third set—the television cameras had been turned off, the Duke and Duchess had gone home, and the spectators had been told to wait outside. In sports, of course, you can't do that. Choking is a central part of the drama of athletic competition, because the spectators have to be there—and the ability to overcome the pressure of the spectators is part of what it means to be a champion. But the same ruthless inflexibility need not govern the rest of our lives. We have to learn that sometimes a poor performance reflects not the innate ability of the performer but the complexion of the audience; and that sometimes a poor test score is the sign not of a poor student but of a good one.

Through the first three rounds of the 1996 Masters golf tournament, Greg Norman held a seemingly insurmountable lead over his nearest rival, the Englishman Nick Faldo. He was the best player in the world. His nickname was the Shark. He didn't saunter down the fairways; he stalked the course, blond and broad-shouldered, his caddy behind him, struggling to keep up. But then came the ninth hole on the tournament's final day. Norman was paired with Faldo, and the two hit their first shots well. They were now facing the green. In front of the pin, there was a steep slope, so that any ball hit short would come rolling back down the hill into oblivion. Faldo shot first, and the ball landed safely long, well past the cup.

Norman was next. He stood over the ball. "The one thing you guard against here is short," the announcer said, stating the obvious. Norman swung and then froze, his club in midair, following the ball in flight. It was short. Norman watched, stone-faced, as the ball rolled thirty yards back down the hill, and with that error something inside of him broke.

At the tenth hole, he hooked the ball to the left, hit his third shot well past the cup, and missed a makable putt. At eleven, Norman had a three-and-a-half-foot putt for par—the kind he had been making all week. He shook out his hands and legs before grasping the club, trying to relax. He missed: his third straight bogey. At twelve, Norman hit the ball straight into the water. At thirteen, he hit it into a patch of pine needles. At sixteen, his movements were so mechanical and out of synch that, when he swung, his hips spun out ahead of his body and the ball sailed into another pond. At that, he took his club and made a frustrated scythelike motion through the grass, because what had been obvious for twenty minutes was now official: He had fumbled away the chance of a lifetime.

Faldo had begun the day six strokes behind Norman. By the time the two started their slow walk to the eighteenth hole, through the throng of spectators, Faldo had a four-stroke lead. But he took those final steps quietly, giving only the smallest of nods, keeping his head low. He understood what had happened on the greens and fairways that day. And he was bound by the particular etiquette of choking, the understanding that what he had earned was something less than a victory and what Norman had suffered was something less than a defeat.

When it was all over, Faldo wrapped his arms around Norman. "I don't know what to say—I just want to give you a hug," he whispered, and then he said the only thing you can say to a choker: "I feel horrible about what happened. I'm so sorry." With that, the two men began to cry.

2000

PART FIVE

OUT OF LEFT FIELD

"I love you. We all love you. Now throw some strikes."

"Help! I've changed my mind!"

SWIMMING WITH SHARKS

CHARLES SPRAWSON

Some say the bravest of swims was Ted Erikson's in 1967, when he survived the thirty miles from the Farallon Islands to the Golden Gate Bridge, San Francisco, a trek that took him through waters in which there are more shark attacks than anywhere else in the world. But Lynne Cox's attempt on the Bering Strait was without doubt the most remarkable.

At 9:30 A.M. on August 7, 1987, Cox, a thirty-year-old marathon swimmer, jumped feet first from a rock on the shore of Little Diomede island into the frigid Arctic Ocean and set out for Big Diomede, nearly two and a half miles away. The Diomedes, tiny volcanic islands, situated between Alaska and Siberia, that rise abruptly from the ocean floor, are the peaks of a submarine ridge that once connected the two continents. The international date line bisects the channel between them and forms the boundary line between the United States and Russia. These territorial waters, which are strictly guarded, had not been open to boats since 1948, and had never been swum.

Cox's father had come up with the idea of swimming between the Diomedes back in 1976, when American-Soviet relations were at a low ebb, to show just how close the superpowers were. It had taken Lynne Cox eleven years of negotiation, at the highest government levels, before the Bering Strait swim was authorized, and final permission from the Soviets had been granted only the day before. During those years,

Cox had been training and, with the help of medical tests, preparing her body for water temperatures that would kill most human beings within thirty minutes.

Cox had been advised by the Naval Arctic Research Laboratory to expect a strong northerly flow of water through the channel, causing eddies and currents of up to three miles per hour, along with winds that could vary abruptly from periods of calm to gale force. Although the islands were only 2.4 miles apart, Cox would be forced by the currents to swim at least twice as far. The water temperature in the Strait, which freezes over during the long winter months, would vary from thirty-four degrees Fahrenheit to forty-four. She was warned about the presence of walruses and sharks, particularly the fifteen-foot Great Pacific shark, though it wasn't known if Great Pacifics in the Strait would attack humans. Yet Cox refused artificial aid: She would not use a shark cage, or wear a wetsuit, or even coat her body in lanolin grease. Her only form of protection was her swimsuit.

She had arranged to be accompanied by two umiaks—walrus-skin canoes—belonging to the Inuits who lived on Little Diomede in a settlement of shacks clinging to a cliff face. The local mayor, a cynic who wore a baseball cap that said "Patrick was a saint but I ain't," had insisted on five thousand dollars as a fee for the boats, believing that this was a chance to make money for the desolate community, whose livelihood came from seal hunting and selling scrimshaw on the mainland. Cox, who had borrowed money from her parents to get to Little Diomede and was living on bagels and peanut butter for breakfast, lunch, and dinner, eventually bargained him down to five hundred dollars. Two Soviet naval vessels were due to meet her at the boundary.

When Cox entered the Arctic Ocean, the water temperature was, at forty-four degrees, comparable to a glass of iced water; if she had dived in head first, the sudden impact could have stopped her heart beating. Once she was in the sea, she said later, she concentrated on making her body move, to avoid focusing on the pain she felt. A dense fog had descended, which calmed the surface of the water but also made it impossible for her to see her destination. The umiaks started leaking immediately and had to be bailed out with empty Coca-Cola cans. One boat contained five journalists and the other three doctors, including Bill Keatinge, an erudite Englishman from London University, whose particular field of research was the effect of cold on the human body.

At the beginning of the year, Cox had got in touch with Keatinge and asked if there was a medical system that could register her temperature during the swim: It was essential that her inner body temperature never drop below ninety-three degrees. Keatinge recommended a thermosensitive capsule containing a tiny transmitter which had been devised for astronauts. She swallowed the capsule before the swim, and every twenty minutes while she was in the ocean she rolled on to her back and one of the doctors pointed a radio receiver at her stomach in order to register a digital reading. As a further precaution, a rectal thermometer on a lead was inserted into her body and the wire coiled into her swimsuit. If the capsule did not work, a reading could be taken from the thermometer.

The doctors were in a continuous state of apprehension, but Cox remained calmer than the seals in the Arctic Ocean; several rose to the surface to gaze quizzically at this intruder. Every so often, the boats got lost in the fog as Cox sprinted ahead, and she was forced to shout back through the mist to make sure that she was swimming in the right direction. She crossed the boundary after an hour and a half; then one of the journalists thought he could hear an engine, and suddenly the bow of a ship emerged through the fog. The Russians invited the two umiaks to follow them. As they crossed the date line, a journalist called out "It's tomorrow!" and everyone cheered.

Fifty yards from shore, the fog cleared, and the cliffs of Big Diomede loomed above Cox. The closest point of land was a rock directly ahead of her, but a welcoming committee was waiting to receive her half a mile away on a snowbank. Cox knew that a deep trough developed where the island sloped down to the ocean floor, through which a sudden current, with thirty-eight-degree water, raced north into the Chukchi Sea. The ocean here was like a washing machine, with cold water churned up from below and driven out into the Arctic waste. To go that extra half mile would mean swimming against the current. "You should land now," the doctors said, but she refused. The object of her swim was, in her words, "to reach out to the Soviets." She explained later, "Touching a rock rather than someone's hand would have meant so much less. I had to keep on reaching, going." She swam close to the rock to avoid the strongest part of the current, then turned south. Finally, after two hours and six minutes in the water, she struggled up the ice on the beach and felt the warmth of two Russian hands hoisting her.

She was engulfed in blankets and presented with a bouquet of flowers and a pair of sealskin slippers. Surprisingly, her inner temperature had remained constant for much of the swim, but after she'd had a brief interview with Soviet television and walked seventy-five yards to a recovery tent, her temperature dropped to ninety-four—borderline hypothermia. She was slurring her words and having difficulty walking. When she slumped to the ground in the recovery tent, a Soviet woman wrapped herself around Cox in order to keep her warm. The Russians and the Americans then celebrated Cox's achievement with a tea party, prepared by a chef in a white uniform. Tables had been set out on the beach and covered with white cloths, and samovars were placed on top.

At the end of that year, Mikhail Gorbachev flew to Washington to sign the INF treaty, which would reduce the number of nuclear missiles. At an official dinner given by President Reagan in his honor, Gorbachev cited Cox's swim as a symbol of the thawing relations between the two countries. "It took one brave American by the name of Lynne Cox just two hours to swim from one of our countries to the other. We saw on television how sincerely amiable was the meeting between our people and Americans when she stepped on to the Soviet shore. She proved by her courage how closely to each other our peoples live." Reagan was mystified by this tribute. The national security adviser had to call the State Department to find out whom Gorbachev was referring to.

Today, at the age of forty-two, Lynne Cox lives with her parents in Los Alamitos, a few miles from the great beaches that line the California coast below Los Angeles. Los Alamitos is a quiet suburb distinguished by a good fish restaurant and avenues of palm and cottonwood trees. When Cox is not preparing for her swims, she writes articles and short stories, gives lectures to business executives, and coaches swimmers. (One current student is an opera singer who, like Frank Sinatra, feels that swimming might improve her singing.)

A large harbor scene painted by Cox's mother hangs in her room. On top of a bookcase are the sealskin slippers; its shelves are crammed with copies of *National Geographic*. There are no trophies to impress the visitor—they were discarded or donated to a local museum years ago. The Coxes' home is an unremarkable, well-ordered place, but from the confines of that domesticity Cox plans her forays to some of the most desolate and far-flung places in the world, often venturing into seas and lakes where no one has swum before.

Lord Byron was one of the first to swim through dark waters and over great depths, and he did so at a time when the submarine world was still relatively unknown. He crossed the Hellespont, from what is now European Turkey to what is now Asian Turkey, on May 3, 1810, in emulation of Leander's legendary swims to his lover, Hero. The distance is little more than a mile, but the current made it so arduous that Byron doubted "whether Leander's conjugal powers must not have been exhausted in his passage to Paradise." He later wrote of his crossing, "I plume myself on this achievement more than I could possibly do any kind of glory, political, poetical, or rhetorical."

The greatest swim in the history of marathon swimming, however, was Captain Matthew Webb's conquest of the English Channel, in 1875, and the most sensational was the American Gertrude Ederle's triumph there in 1926, when she became the first woman to swim across—using the crawl all the way—and beat the existing record by two hours. On her return to New York, she was greeted by sirens, flowers showering down from planes, and a ticker-tape parade; the enthusiasm for her welcome equaled that for Charles Lindbergh the following year. Captain Webb drowned in 1883 while attempting to swim the rapids below Niagara Falls, in a suicidal bid for "money and imperishable fame." A crowd of ten thousand watched Webb disappear beneath the waves after he cracked open his head on a series of submerged rocks that surrounded a whirlpool where the river bends.

Webb's death was unfortunate, but his financial enterprise and his flair for self-promotion would have appealed to William Wrigley, Jr., the chewing-gum millionaire. In 1927, Wrigley instituted the first professional swimming race in the world: Competitors would swim from Catalina Island, twenty miles off the coast of Southern California, to the mainland for a first prize of twenty-five thousand dollars. He had just bought the island as a commercial proposition, and, impressed by Ederle's reception in New York the previous year, concocted the pageant to solve the problem of a lack of tourists in California during the winter months. Some fifteen thousand spectators watched the winner swim home at three in the morning, illuminated by the searchlights of yachts. Wrigley's venture was so successful that he inaugurated an annual twenty-one-mile race on Lake Ontario for a prize of thirty thousand dollars. Other businessmen followed his example, in bays and lakes all over America, and further afield—in Yugoslavia, South America, Australia, Mexico, Italy, England, and Egypt. Like modern golfers or tennis players on tour, the same group of swimmers would assemble in various parts of the world to compete for large amounts of money.

Marathon swimmers are a different breed from short-distance swimmers. Compared with the long, lithe, and adolescent figures you see in the Olympics, marathon swimmers appear in photographs to be built like bisons rather than like cheetahs, with gnarled faces and stubborn expressions, their pendulous breasts and stomachs drooping down to stubby legs. (Only the Dane Greta Andersen has excelled in both forms of competition. After winning the gold medal in the hundred-meter freestyle in the Olympic Games in 1948, she won the English Channel race twice and became one of the greatest open-water swimmers in the world.)

These swimmers need a tenacity and a stocky build to withstand the impact of waves and tides, the sudden nausea inflicted by oil slicks and bilge, the prolonged effects of salt water, which causes the lips and tongue to swell and reduces the face to something resembling fungus. So intense and concentrated are the conditions that marathon swimmers become prey to delusions and neuroses that are often beyond the experiences of other athletes. The huge distances that the swimmers cover, sometimes up to sixty miles, can bring on hallucinations. In 1961, in the first back-to-back swim of the English Channel, the Argentine Tony Abertondo imagined posts and dogs obstructing his path over the last two miles. During the same swim four years later, Ted Erikson saw his pilot boat suddenly fade into a black smear and then turn into a rosebush, at which point he found that there were roses growing all around him. In May 1975, Ben Haggard, a New York policeman, attempted to swim from Florida to Nassau, across the so-called Bermuda Triangle, using a shark cage. As night fell, floodlights from the boats accompanying him revealed sharks circling his cage. Haggard recalled feeling the presence of a hostile force. "I had this feeling that something wanted me to come out through the door," he said afterward. "I knew what would happen, with the sharks outside, but the urge was irresistible. I swam over and grabbed the trapdoor. I was shaking, but I held on to it. I kept saying to myself: I am not going to let it take me out of the cage, whatever it is."

Swimming, particularly long-distance swimming, appeals to the solitary and the eccentric. An informal survey of fourteen champion long-distance swimmers concluded that only two of them were swimming under no particular stress, while the others were all reacting to severe emotional tension. No one knows, for example, why Britt Sullivan, a hard-drinking former Wave from Nebraska, decided to swim the Atlantic Ocean in 1964. She lost touch with her escort boat off Fire Island, twenty miles from her starting point, and was never seen again.

Lynne Cox appears to be devoid of neuroses and delusions, yet no doubt the long hours she has spent submerged in water have made her in some ways remote. Her endeavors seem to defy the limits of human possibility: She was the first swimmer to cross the Strait of Magellan, among the most treacherous stretches of water in the world; she has swum through Lake Baikal, one of the deepest, longest, and coldest lakes in the world. She follows a solitary course: The impulse behind her swims has been hers, as are the organization and negotiation. She is no longer registered with the United States Swimming Association, because races don't interest her, nor does prize money. The purpose of her swims is not to promote rivalry but to create harmony.

For Cox, swimming is an "emotional and spiritual necessity," a phrase used by George Mallory, the mountaineer, to describe his own compulsion to dive into any lake or river that he came upon. Cox is drawn to the challenge of a confrontation with nature—a struggle perhaps familiar to mountain climbers. "It involves a lot of planning, training, and physical obstacles," she says of marathon swimming. "In a pool, you know there's a finish, because there are two walls. In a marathon swim or a mountain climb, you are never sure. There is a much higher risk involved. Basically, you can die." If there is one image, now that all sports are so commercial and technologically sophisticated, that grips the imagination as much as Mallory, dressed like a gamekeeper and glimpsed through a brief break in the clouds, "going strong for the top," it is that of Lynne Cox, virtually naked, forcing her way through the waves of the Bering Strait.

I first met Lynne Cox by the Pacific, earlier this summer, among the palms of the Hotel Laguna. The hotel, built in 1888, was once dedicated to glamour, but now it is the haunt of earnest couples who seem intent on closing deals and analyzing "relationships." Cox, with her

generous smile, lilting voice, and long black hair, appeared to be everything they were not. Like the two plain syllables of her name, Cox was
simple and direct. I had been drawn originally to American swimmers
by their names, redolent of romance and dash—Donna deVarona,
Casey Converse, Chet Jastremski, Zac Zorn—but Cox was in a different category.

We changed and went to swim. The outline of Catalina showed
through the haze in the distance. There had been a storm the night before; waves hammered the shore and threw me onto a rock. Cox
laughed and shouted that at the start of her swim around the Cape of
Good Hope, in 1978, she had had to dive through waves four times as
high. At five feet six inches and 180 pounds, she is not particularly tall
or lean; in fact, her body is between 30 and 35 percent fat. (Most
women's bodies are between 18 and 25 percent.) What makes her body
remarkable, according to doctors who have tested her, is an "even" covering of fat that acts like a wetsuit; the porpoise bulk of her build forms
a protective surface that keeps the temperature of her inner body normal in extreme conditions. Most of her power seems to derive from her
mermaid hips. She doesn't have the orangutan arms and shoulders of a
shorter-distance swimmer, but as we swam I noticed that she kept up a
rhythmic, consistent stroke, zigzagging her hand viciously underwater,
where it counts. She seemed to melt into the water. (To achieve a similar effect, East German swimmers were rumored to inject gas into
their colons.) Her skin looked so smooth that I asked her if she went
through the ritual of shaving before a swim, like Olympic swimmers,
but she told me that long-distance swimmers preserve body hair for
greater insulation.

A harmless jellyfish floated by, which reminded her of the worst jellyfish she had encountered, in warm waters off Sweden. They were
"red, yellow, and transparent—the size of a garbage-can lid—with long
tentacles that slammed into my face and burned my body," she said.
"Every stroke was tentative and I could never relax—I would swim
onto the back of one before realizing I was in the middle of it."

As we swam, Cox spoke of her childhood in New Hampshire, and
summer holidays her family spent in Maine, on a lake called Snow
Pond, where she swam all day and often at night, too, when she was
"sticky with sweat." She described her sense of relief on entering the
black water, recalling "the smell of pine accentuated at night, the

moonlight that turned the edge of the shore to silver." Frogs and snakes and sandfish snatched at her body. Swimming among white and yellow water lilies, she would dive down through the clear water to follow the long stems that attached the flowers to the sandy bottom. A mile out, in the middle of the lake, there was an island that she always wanted to swim to. Years later, she went back to the lake. "I swam around to the original smooth, sloping stone from which I entered the lake as a child," she told me. "I slid off it again and swam out to the island, across a surface disfigured by Jet-Skis and motorboats." At the end of each summer, she hated returning to the local public pool. She loathed the routine and the regimentation, the innumerable laps spent staring at a black line on the bottom of the pool.

In 1969, when she was twelve, her father, a radiologist, moved the family from the East Coast to California. His experience in the Medical Corps on Iwo Jima during the war had turned him into an idealist, and he determined to bring up his four children in a healthy climate and make them all into good swimmers, believing that swimming extended the body more safely than any other sport. In California, Cox started training with a swimming coach, Don Gambril, who was also the coach of the Olympic team. He noticed that she picked up the pace only after a mile, and so had no prospects as an Olympic swimmer, and he encouraged her instead to join a group of young swimmers who were training for the open sea. "Suddenly I felt released from a cage. I was actually going somewhere, not merely back and forth," Cox recalls. "I felt exhilarated by the challenge of swimming against the current and into the waves." When the group swam from Catalina Island to the mainland, Cox was so far ahead of the other swimmers that she had to tread water while they caught up. She was then fourteen.

She returned to Catalina in 1974 to break the record. She started at night, when conditions are usually most favorable. "The whole atmosphere seems somehow refined," she says, "and you feel you are really swimming on the upper inches of the ocean." But on this occasion fog descended five miles offshore. Cox became separated from her escort boat. "I felt the sea welling up around me and huge shapes brush up against my body," she recalls. "Within half an hour, I became hysterical." The boat found her shortly afterward, and she gave up the attempt.

When we finished our swim, we lay on the sand and watched the body of a dead seal drifting about in the shallows; its head had been snapped off by a shark. Although Cox swims often in shark-infested seas, she refuses to use a cage, believing that it divorces a swimmer from the elements and creates currents and conditions of its own, sometimes causing a drag that can help a swimmer along. She says that this is "unfair—like climbing Everest on an escalator." On two attempts made by marathon swimmers to cross from Cuba to Florida which I followed, cages were used. One swimmer was able to relax motionless for hours while being towed along; the other took a ten-minute break every two miles to stand on the bars while he prayed and consulted his psychiatrist.

The first time Cox swam from Catalina Island, she was warned that fear reduces energy. In order to avoid thinking of sharks, she concentrated on her hands moving through the water and the phosphorescent bubbles trailing off her fingertips. She has always managed to divert her mind from what may lurk below the surface. She was forced to confront reality once, however, when a frogman who was protecting her as she swam around the Cape of Good Hope shot a shark that had emerged from the kelp, its jaws wide open, and was making straight for her. She was almost home, but had to sprint the final four hundred yards—a cloud of blood was attracting other sharks.

Sometimes, Cox admitted to me, reflections of clouds could assume sinister shapes in the water and affect her imagination. I asked her how she felt when she studied navigational charts and discovered, as the light blue on the map gradually turned to dark, the depths over which she would be swimming. I wanted to know what went through her mind as she peered down through goggles into two or three miles of water. Anything can rise out of that shadowy line ten or fifteen feet below a swimmer, where the shafts of sunlight fade into blackness. At this point, her insouciance momentarily faltered and she seemed almost to shudder; then she quickly told me to stop my questions.

The English Channel is the ultimate goal of any long-distance swimmer. Cox first became aware of it at the age of nine, even though she had no idea where it was. She was swimming in an outdoor pool in New Hampshire when "there was a sudden hailstorm and strong winds sent waves racing across the surface of the pool," she recalls.

"Everyone was ordered to get out and practice calisthenics indoors. Only I remained, and I exulted in the conditions." When she finally did emerge, a woman at the pool predicted that one day Cox would swim the Channel.

In 1972, when she was fifteen, she felt ready for an attempt. Her coach, however, thought her too inexperienced. At this critical moment, she met a Coptic Egyptian living in California called Fahmy Attallah, who describes himself as a "clinical humanist psychologist." He had attempted the Channel on five occasions, between 1939 and 1950, and had failed every time. In 1950, he missed by a mere three hundred feet: He had raised his arms to shield his eyes from the sun as he gazed in disbelief at the nearby shore. The pilot presumed he had given up and bent down to pull him out of the sea. Fahmy was disqualified. (His various attempts made headline news in Cairo, and influenced a great period of Egyptian swimming which followed the Second World War and culminated with Abo-Heif, a suave and brave Old Etonian, and one of the world's strongest swimmers.)

Fahmy inspired Cox to achieve what he hadn't. He described Dover and Folkestone, and told her where to train and how to find a pilot. Her training was much more intense than his had ever been—to increase her speed, she adopted methods used by Olympic swimmers—but he emphasized the discipline required to swim in cold water.

In the summer, Cox traveled to England with her mother. Throughout her swim, she felt that she had the record within her grasp, but two miles off Cape Gris-Nez she was forced sidewise, and a gap of five miles opened up between her and the shore. The currents a mile or so off the peninsula are terribly strong, and she had heard numerous stories of swimmers who got within a mile of the French coast and just couldn't get ashore. They got pulled back into the middle of the Channel, or were swept up toward Calais, or simply gave up.

She spotted a rocky promontory and decided to sprint for that, even though her pilot said that the rocks looked too dangerous and advised her to go for the beach. Her decision was crucial: She made it to the rocks, and her time of nine hours and fifty-seven minutes broke the men's record by thirty minutes and the women's by almost four hours. Telegrams of congratulations followed from all over the world, a few including offers of marriage. Some months later, her record was broken. Cox went back the following year to break the new record: She wanted to prove that her first swim hadn't been a fluke. Stronger currents forced her to swim three miles farther, through rougher seas, and still she broke the record by ten minutes.

On her return to America, Fahmy encouraged her to look for further challenges. She was invited to Cairo to compete in an annual twenty-mile race through the Nile. Fahmy assured her that it would be clean, but years away from Egypt had blunted his memory of local conditions. Cox struggled through fifteen miles of sewage, rats, and dead dogs before she was forced to retire. Fahmy also persuaded her to reattempt the Catalina record after she lost her nerve.

Now aged ninety, the diminutive, dignified Fahmy lives across the road from the Pacific in a Long Beach apartment whose sliding doors open on to a pool. He still swims daily. The author of the recent *Beauty of Being: Psychological Tips for Holistic Wellness,* he has continued to act as a mentor to Cox over the years. "More than anything," she told me, "he taught me to experience the spirituality of water: how we feel embraced and freed and connected to something much larger than ourselves when we are swimming through it."

Whenever I met Cox after our first swim, I noticed that she always veered toward a table by a fountain or a pool. When it rains, she told me, she opens her windows wide, and when it rains hard she drives down to the ocean to swim. To the amazement of her neighbors, she washes her car in her swimsuit in the rain. One night while we were talking, she looked up at the stars and exclaimed how excited she was by the thought of the frozen lakes of Europa.

In 1975, Cox flew to New Zealand for an attempt on the sixteen-mile Cook Strait, between the country's North and South Island. This would prove to be one of her most arduous swims. Caught on a massive swell caused by conflicting currents, she found herself farther from the finish after five hours than when she started, but the sight of dolphins spinning and leaping renewed her spirits. The whole of New Zealand seemed to be following the swim. "The escort turned up the radio so that I could hear messages of public support," she recalls. "A cross-channel ferry diverted its course and spectators lined the sides to cheer. Airlines altered their flight paths to fly low over the Strait. When I was halfway across, the prime minister called to say that the New Zealand people were behind me." After she touched the rocks at South Island, church bells were rung throughout the country to celebrate.

That swim was the turning point of her career. She felt that she had affected and somehow even inspired a whole nation. For the first time, she became aware of the transcendent power of the solo swimmer. Breaking records no longer interested her: From now on, her swims would be used as vehicles for a more personal goal. She believed that the lone swimmer among the waves, pitting her courage against great odds, could become a symbolic figure. "My goal is not just to be a great swimmer," she told me. "I think people identify with the athletic struggle, and I am trying to use sports to help bring people together." The ancient Greeks felt the same way—wars between city-states were put off during the Olympic games, as if people believed that, through the spirit and example of athletic contest, individual differences might somehow be sublimated and reconciled.

"Lynne was always interested in impossible things done in history by individual people," her history teacher at Los Alamitos High School recalls. And there is something of Joan of Arc about Cox—the enthusiasm and the innocence, the nerve, the vulnerability, the self-belief, the courage to go to people at the highest official levels and make them sympathetic to her cause.

Preparations for a swim are often more torturous than the swim itself, but it is in the course of these negotiations, she believes, that differences between countries are somehow made to look trivial. A year after she swam the Bering Strait, she traveled to Lake Baikal. She arrived in Russia to find herself a celebrity. Thousands of people lined the shore, throwing long-stemmed roses as she passed, crying out, in English, "Welcome, Lynne Cox, welcome, U.S.A.!" A cape on the lake was named after her, next to Cape Tolstoy.

Cox continued to search out political challenges. In June 1990, she swam down the River Spree between East and West Berlin, escorted by East German guards in boats, who could negotiate the various mines and razors they had placed below the surface. Later that year, aware of border disputes between Argentina and Chile, she flew down to the Beagle Channel. Her aim was to somehow break the deadlock by involving the two navies in her swim, across seven miles of fierce currents. At first, the Argentinians and the Chileans refused to cooperate with each other, but ultimately Cox prevailed, and both countries provided escort boats. Afterward, she was told by the American ambassador to Chile that her swim had set a precedent. A year later, representatives of Argentina and Chile met on an oil rig in the Straits of Magellan to settle the disputes. And in 1994, while Jordan was mediating the peace process between Palestinians and Israelis, Cox swam across the Gulf of Aqaba, a narrow slip of water at the Red Sea's northern tip, which is bordered by Israel, Egypt, and Jordan. The talks, which were taking place at a nearby hotel, stopped while the politicians walked to the edge of the sea to witness the end of the swim.

It is difficult to know if her "political" swims have affected the course of history, but as she described them I was often reminded of the hero of John Cheever's short story "The Swimmer," who swims home one summer day across the pools of his neighbors. I began to visualize his swims as a microcosm of hers. He moves from pool to pool, just as she travels from sea to sea, and his influence is that of some mythical figure at first awakening in those around him a sense of something missing in their lives, a certain generosity and vitality of spirit. He imagines his swims as a romantic voyage into unknown waters, a form of knightly quest. He believes himself "a pilgrim, an explorer, a man with a destiny." As he erupts onto his neighbors' lawns and plunges unbidden into their pools, their reaction is one of puzzled amazement.

Cox's life has been a form of knightly quest, and her spirit has remained essentially romantic—she has swum in the classical Mediterranean, between the pillars of Hercules, across the three-mile Strait of Messina, guarded in legend by Scylla and Charybdis. She has swum in the Orient, through the ancient bridges of Kunming Lake, below the old summer palace of the emperor of China. She is drawn, she says, to dangerous places that intimidate ships, and to straits like Cook and Magellan, because they are named after sea captains who opened up a new world.

We had a final swim off Malibu, the day before I left California. Once again, we were the only people in the water. Cox warned me to avoid possible stingrays on the sand in the shallows, and never to wear a yellow bathing suit, because it is the color most attractive to sharks— "Yummy yellow they call it." She had just returned from Fiji and talked about the forty-to-fifty-foot sharks that locals had claimed to spot off the reefs there. She knew which species of shark twisted over to bite, and which didn't. I continued to wonder how, with all her acute awareness of the threat of the submarine world, she felt free to swim far out beyond the horizon. Then I thought of a passage in the autobiography of Annette Kellerman, the great Australian swimmer at the beginning of the century, that might well refer to Lynne Cox: "I learn much from people in the way they meet the unknown of life, and water is a great test. If they've come to it bravely they've gone far along the best way. I am sure no adventurer nor discoverer ever lived who could not swim. Swimming cultivates imagination; the man with the most is he who can swim his solitary course night or day and forget a black earth full of people that push. This love of the unknown is the greatest of all the joys which swimming has for me."

1999

"By the time I develop a true understanding of sand, I'll probably be forced into some sort of organized sports."

THE NATIONAL PASTIME

JOHN CHEEVER

To be an American and unable to play baseball is comparable to being a Polynesian and unable to swim. It's an impossible situation. This will be apparent to everyone, and it was to me, a country boy brought up on a farm—or, to be precise, in a country house—just outside the village of St. Botolph's, in Massachusetts. The place is called West Farm. My ancestors had lived in that village and in that house since the seventeenth century, and they had distinguished themselves as sailors and athletes. Leander, my father (his brothers were named Orpheus and Hamlet), had played shortstop for the St. Botolph's Hose Company. Although the hose-company games sometimes figured in his recollections, his memories were usually of a different order. He was nearly sixty when I was born, and he could remember the last days of St. Botolph's as a port. My grandfather had been a ship's master, and when I was a boy, our house was partly furnished with things that he had brought back from Ceylon and China. The maritime past that my father glimpsed had been glorious, full of gold and silver, full of Samoan beauties and tests of courage. Then—so he told me—boxwood had grown in our garden, and the paths had been covered once a year with pebbles that were brought from a cove near West Travertine where the stones were as round and white as pearls. In the rear wing of our house, there was a peculiar, very clean smell that was supposed to have been left there by my grandfather's Chinese servants. My father liked to recall this period of splendor, but he liked even better to recall his success as a partner in the gold-bead factory that had been built in St. Botolph's when its maritime prosperity was ended. He had gone to work as an office boy, and his rise had been brilliant and swift. He had business acumen, and he was convivial. He took an intense pleasure in having the factory whistle blown. He had it blown for all our birthdays and for his wedding anniversary, and when my mother had guests for lunch, the whistle usually blew as the ladies sat down.

In the twenties, the gold-bead factory was mortgaged and converted to the manufacture of table silver, and presently my father and his partner were ruined. My father felt that he was an old man who had spent all his energy and all his money on things that were unredeemable and vulgar, and he was inconsolable. He went away, and my mother called my two sisters and me to her room and told us that she was afraid he had killed himself. He had left a note hinting at this, and he had taken a pistol with him. I was nine years old then, and my sisters were fourteen and fifteen. Suicide may have been my father's intention, but he returned a few days later and began to support the family by selling the valuables that had come to him from the shipmaster. I had decided to become a professional baseball player. I had bought a Louisville Slugger, a ball, and a first baseman's mitt. I asked my father to play catch with me one Sunday afternoon, but he refused. My mother must have overheard this conversation, because she called him to her room, where they quarrelled. In a little while, he came out to the garden and asked me to throw the ball to him. What happened then was ridiculous and ugly. I threw the ball clumsily once or twice and missed the catches he threw to me. Then I turned my head to see something—a boat on the river. He threw the ball, and it got me in the nape of the neck and stretched me out unconscious in my grandfather's ruined garden. When I came to, my nose was bleeding and my mouth was full of blood. I felt that I was being drowned. My father was standing over me. "Don't tell your mother about this," he said. When I sat up and he saw that I was all right, he went down through the garden toward the barn and the river.

My mother called me to her room that night after supper. She had become an invalid and she seldom left her bed. All the furniture in her room was white, and the rugs were white, and there was a picture of "Jesus the Shepherd" on the wall beside her bed. The room was getting dark, I remember, and I felt, from the tone of her voice, that we were approaching a kind of emotional darkness I had noticed before in our family affairs. "You must try to understand your father," she said, putting down her Bible and reaching for my hand. "He is old. He is spoiled." Then, although I don't think he was in the house, she lowered her voice to a whisper, so that we could not be overheard. "You see, some years ago his cousin Lucy Hartshorn left him a great deal of money, in trust. She was a meddlesome old lady. I guess you don't remember her. She was an antivivisectionist, and wanted to abolish the celebration of Christmas. She liked to order your father around, and she felt the family was petering out. We had Grace and Vikery then, and she left your father the money on condition that he not have any more children. He was very upset when he found out that I was *enceinte*. I wouldn't want you to know what went on. He had planned a luxurious old age—he wanted to raise pigeons and have a sailboat—and I think he sometimes sees in you the difference between what he had planned and what he has been reduced to. You'll have to try and understand." Her words made almost no impression on me at the time. I remember counting the larches outside her window while she talked to me, and looking beyond them to the faded lettering on the wall of the barn—BOSTON STORE: ROCK BOTTOM PRICES—and to some pines ringed with darkness beyond the barn. The little that I knew of our family history was made up of revokable trusts, purloined wills, and dark human secrets, and since I had never seen Lucy Hartshorn, this new secret seemed to have no more to do with me than the others did.

The school I went to was an old frame building in the village, and every morning I walked two miles upriver to get there. Two of the spinster teachers were cousins of mine, and the man who taught manual training and coached athletics was the son of our garbage collector. My parents had helped him through normal school. The New England spring was in force, and one fine morning we left the gymnasium for the ball field. The instructor was carrying some baseball equipment, and as soon as I saw it, the sweet, salty taste of blood came into my mouth. My heart began to pound, my legs felt weak, and while I thought, from these symptoms, that I must be sick, I knew instinctively how to cure myself. On the way to the field, we passed an old field house that stood on some concrete posts, concealed by a scrim of rotten lattice. I began to walk slowly, and when the rest of the class had passed the field house, I got down on my hands and knees and crawled through a broken place in the lattice and underneath the building. There was hardly room for me to lie there between the dirt and the sills that were covered with cobwebs. Someone had stuffed an old sneaker and a rusted watering can under the building, confident that they would never be seen again. I could hear from the field the voices of my friends choosing sides, and I felt the horror of having expelled myself from the light of a fine day, but I also felt, lying in the dirt, that the taste of blood was beginning to leave my mouth, that my heart was beginning to regulate its beating, and that the strength was returning to my legs. I lay in the dirt until the game ended and I could see, through the lattice, the players returning to school.

I felt that the fault was Leander's, and that if I could bring myself to approach him again, when he was in a better humor, he would respond humanely. The feeling that I could not assume my responsibilities as a baseball player without some help from him was deep, as if parental love and baseball were both national pastimes. One afternoon, I got my ball and mitt and went into the library, where he was taking books down from the shelves and tying them up in bundles of ten, to be taken into Boston and sold. He had been a handsome man, I think. I had heard my relations speak of how he had aged, and so I suppose that his looks had begun to deteriorate. He would have been taken for a Yankee anywhere, and he seemed to feel that his alliance to the sea was by blood as well as tradition. When he went into an oyster bar and found people who were patently not American-born eating oysters, he would be stirred. He ate quantities of fish, swam daily in the salt river, and washed himself each morning with a sea sponge, so he always smelled faintly of brine and iodine, as if he had only recently come dripping out of the Atlantic. The brilliant blue of his eyes had not faded, and the boyish character of his face—its lightness and ovalness—was intact. He had not understood the economic fragility of his world, his wife's invalidism seemed to be a manifest rebuke for the confusion of his affairs, and his mind must have been thronged with feelings of being unwanted and also feelings of guilt. The books he was preparing to sell were his father's and his grandfather's; he would rail about this later, feeling that if histrionics would not redeem him, they would at least recapture for a minute his sense of identity and pride. If I had looked closely, I might have seen a face harried with anxiety and the weaknesses of old age, but I expected him, for my sake, to regain his youth and to appear like the paternal images I had seen on calendars and in magazine advertisements.

"Will you please play catch with me, Poppa?" I asked.

"How can you ask me to play baseball when I will be dead in another month!" he said. He sighed and then said, "I won't live through the summer. Your mother has been complaining all morning. She has nothing to say to me unless she has a complaint to make. She's complaining now of pains in her feet. She can't leave her bed because of the pains in her feet. She's trying to make me more unhappy than I already am, but I have some facts to fall back on. Here, let me show you." He took down one of the many volumes in which he had recorded his life, and searched through the pages until he found what he wanted. "Your mother wore custom-made shoes from 1904 until 1908, when Mr. Schults died. He made her six, twelve, fourteen— He made her seventeen pairs of shoes in four years. Then she began buying her shoes at Nettleton's." He wet his finger and turned a page. "She never paid less than twelve dollars a pair there, and in 1908 she bought four pairs of shoes and two pairs of canvas pumps. In 1910, she bought four pairs of shoes at Nettleton's and a pair of evening slippers at Stetson's. She said the slippers pinched her feet, but we couldn't take them back because she'd worn them. In 1911, she bought three pairs of shoes at Stetson's and two at Nettleton's. In 1912, she had Henderson make her a pair of walking shoes. They cost eighteen dollars. She paid twenty-four dollars for a pair of gold pumps at Stetson's. In 1913, she bought another pair of canvas pumps, two pairs of suede shoes, golf shoes, and some beaded shoes." He looked to me for some confirmation of the unreasonableness of my mother's illness, but I hung my head and went out of the library.

The next time the class went out for baseball, I hid in a building closer to the school, where rakes and rollers and other grounds equipment were stored. This place also was dark, but there was room to stand and move and enjoy an illusion of freedom, although the light of day and the voices on the field from which I was hidden seemed like the lights and the sounds of life. I had been there only a few minutes when I heard someone approach and open the door. I had thought it would be the old grounds keeper, but it was a classmate of mine, who recognized, a second after he saw me, what I was doing, and seemed—since he was doing the same thing—delighted to have a conspirator. I disliked him and his friends, but I couldn't have disliked him more than I disliked the symptoms of my own panic, for I didn't leave the building. After this, I had to hide not only from the ball game but from my classmate. He continued to hide in the tool shed and I hid near the playing field, in some woods behind the backstop, and chewed pieces of grass until the period ended.

That fall, I went out for football, and I had always liked winter sports, but in the spring, when the garbage man's son took the balls and bats out of the chest near the door of the gymnasium, the taste of blood in my mouth, the beating of my heart, and the weakness in my legs were keener than ever, and I found myself stuffed in the dirt under the track house again, with the old tennis sneaker and the watering can, horrified that I should have chosen or should have been made to lie in this filth when I could be walking freely over a green field. As the season progressed, I began to find new hiding places and to invent new ailments that would excuse me from having to play baseball, and the feeling that Leander had the cure to my cowardice returned, although I could not bring myself to approach him again. He still seemed to preserve, well on the dark side of his mind, some hard feelings about my being responsible for the revocation of Lucy Hartshorn's trust. Several times when I went to a movie or a dance, he locked the house up so tight that I couldn't find any way to get in, and had to sleep in the barn. Once, I returned in the daytime and found the house locked. I heard him moving inside and I rang the bell. He opened the door long enough to say, "Whatever it is you're selling, I don't want any." Then he slammed the door in my face. A minute later, he opened the door again. "I'm sorry, Eben," he said. "I didn't realize it was you."

My mother died when I was in my third year of high school. When I graduated the following year, Leander claimed to be too infirm to come to the ceremony, and when I looked down from the platform into a gathering where there were no near relatives of mine, it occurred to me—without pleasure or guilt—that I had probably not been up to bat more than three times.

My Cousin Juliana put up the money to send me to college, and I entered college feeling that my troubles with Leander and baseball were over. Both my sisters had married by then, and gone to live in the West, and I dutifully spent part of my Christmas holiday at West Farm and planned to spend all my Easter vacation there. On the morning that college closed for the spring recess, I drove with my two roommates over to Mount Holyoke, where we picked up three girls. We were planning to have a picnic somewhere along the river. When we stopped for lunch, one of my roommates went around to the back of the car and got out his camera to take a picture of the girls. Glancing into the luggage compartment, I noticed a baseball and a bat. Everyone was around in front of the car. I couldn't be seen. The ground was loose, and with my hands I dug a hole nearly a foot deep. Then I dropped the baseball into this hole and buried it.

It was late when we got into Boston, and I took the last train down to St. Botolph's. I had written Leander that I was coming, in the hope that he would not lock the house up, but when I reached there, after midnight, all the doors and windows were secured. I didn't feel like spending the night in the barn, and I broke a windowpane in the dining room and climbed in. I could hear Leander moving around upstairs, and because I felt irritated, I didn't call out to him. A few seconds later, there was an explosion in the room. Somebody had shot off a pistol and I thought I had been killed. I got to a switch and turned on the lights and saw, with a wild, crazy uprush of joy, that I was alive and unharmed. Then I saw Leander standing in the doorway with the pistol in his hand. He dropped it to the floor and, stumbling toward me, laid his head on my shoulder and wept. "Oh, Eben! Eben! Eben!" he sobbed. "I thought it was a prowler! I heard someone trying to get in! I heard the breaking glass. Forgive me, forgive me."

I remember that he was wearing a fez, and some kind of ragged and outrageous robe over his shoulders. He had, up until that year, always dressed with great simplicity and care, feeling that a sensible regard for appearances facilitated human relationships. He had always put on a dark coat for dinner, and he would never consider as acquaintances or as business associates men with grease in their hair, men with curls, men who wore pointed shoes or diamond cuff links or who put pheasant feathers in their colored hats. Age seemed to have revised these principles, and during the Easter holidays he appeared in many brilliant costumes, many of them the robes and surplices of a fraternal order that had been disbanded in the twenties. Once when I stepped into the bathroom, I found him before the full-length mirror in the ostrich-plumed hat, the cross-ribbon heavy with orders, and the ornate sword of a Poor Knight of Christ and the Temple and a Guardian of the Gates of Gaza. He often quoted from Shakespeare.

The first job I got after leaving college was at Chatfield Academy. The school was in New Hampshire—in the mountains—and I went north in the fall. I liked teaching, and the place itself seemed oddly detached and peaceful. Chimes rang at the quarter hour, the buildings were old or copied old forms, the leaves fell past the classroom windows for a month, the nights smelled of smoke, and, leaving my classroom one evening in December, I found the air full of a swift, dry snow. The school was conservative, and at its helm was old Dr. Wareham. Robust on the playing field, tearful in chapel, bull-necked and vigorous in spite of his advanced age, he was that kind of monolithic father image that used to be thought a necessity for the education of youth. After the Easter recess, I signed a contract for the following year and arranged to teach summer school. In April, I got a notice that faculty participation in the annual meeting of the board of trustees was mandatory. I asked a man at supper one night what this meant.

"Well, they come up on Friday," my colleague said, "and Wareham gives them a dinner. Then they have their annual meeting. We have demonstration classes on Saturday and they snoop around, but they're mostly intelligent and they don't make trouble. Then Saturday noon, the old troll barbecues a side of beef and we have lunch with them. After this, there's a ball game between the trustees and the faculty members. The new members are always expected to play, and you'd better be good. The old troll feels that men get to know one another best on the playing field, and he doesn't miss a trick. We had a frail art teacher here a couple of years ago who claimed to have a headache, but Wareham got him out of bed and made him play third base. He made three errors and Wareham fired him. Then, after that, there's a cocktail party at Wareham's house, with good sour-mash bourbon for the brass and sherry for the rest of us. Then they go home."

The old taste of blood came into my mouth. My appetite for the meat and potatoes I had heaped onto my plate was gone. I nevertheless gorged myself, for I seemed to have been put into a position where my only recourse was to overlook my feelings or to conceal them where this was not possible. I knew by then that a thorough inspection of the history of the problem would not alter the facts, and that the best I could bring to the situation was a kind of hollow good cheer. I told myself that the game was inconsequential, and presently I seemed to feel this. There was some gossip the next day about Dr. Wareham's seriousness about the game. The piano teacher—a tall man named Bacon—had refused to play, and somebody said that he would be fired. But I was occupied with my classwork and I nearly forgot about the annual meeting until, leaving my classroom on a Friday afternoon, I saw a large car driven by a chauffeur go around the quadrangle and stop at Dr. Wareham's house. The trustees were beginning to arrive.

After supper, I corrected papers until about eleven, when I went to bed. Something woke me at three in the morning, and I went to the open window and I looked out at the night for signs of rain before I realized that this was an old habit of childhood. Rain had meant that I would be free, for a day, of hiding under the field house or in the woods behind the backstop. And now, still half asleep, I turned my ear to the window, listening with the purest anxiety, colored by a kind of pleading, for the stir of rain beginning or the heavier sound of a settled storm. A single drop of water would have sounded like music. I knew from which quarter the rain wind might rise; I knew how cumbrously the wind would blow, how it would smell of wetness, how the storm, as it came west through the village, would make a distant roar, how the first drops would sound on the elm trees in the yard and the shrubs against the wall, how the rain would drum in the grass, how it would swell, how it would wet the kindling at the barbecue pit and disintegrate the paper bags that contained the charcoal, how it would confine the trustees to Dr. Wareham's house and prevail on one or two of them to leave before the cocktail party, and how it would first fill in the slight indentation around second base and then spread slowly toward first and third, until the whole field was flooded. . . . But I saw only a starry and a windless night. I got back into bed and, settling for the best I had—a kind of hollow good cheer—fell asleep.

The morning was the best kind of spring weather; even I saw this. The demonstration classes satisfied everyone, and at noon we went over to the barbecue pit to have our lunch with the trustees. The food seemed to stick in my throat, but this may have been the fault of the barbecue itself, because the meat was raw and the cooking arrangements were a disappointment all around. I was still eating my dessert when the Doctor gave the rallying cry "Into your uniforms, men!" I put down my plate and started for the field house, with the arm of a French instructor thrown warmly over my shoulder and in a cheerful, friendly crowd that seemed blamelessly on their way to recapturing, or at least to reenacting, the secure pleasures of youth. But since the hour they returned to was one that I had never possessed, I felt the falseness of my position. I was handed a uniform—a gesture that seemed unalterably to be one of parting. But it was the too large shoes, wrapped with friction tape, that, when I bent over to lace them, gave me the worst spasm of despair. I picked a glove out of a box near the door and jogged out to the field.

The bleachers were full of students and faculty wives, and Dr. Wareham was walking up and down, leading them in singing to the band. The faculty members were first up, facing a formidable concentration of power and wealth in the field. The first batter got a line drive that was missed by the bank president on first and was good for a double. The second man up struck out, but the third man up reached first, and the industrialist who was pitching walked the fourth batter. I gave a yank to my cap and stepped up to the plate, working my mouth and swallowing to clean it, if I could, of the salty taste of blood. I kept my eye on the ball, and when the first pitch seemed to be coming straight over the plate, I chopped at it with all my might. I heard the crack, I felt the vibration up my forearm, and, telling myself that a baseball diamond, like most things, must operate on a clockwise principle, I sprinted for third and knocked down the runner who was coming in to score. I knocked him flat, and, bending over to see if he was all right, I heard Dr. Wareham roaring at me, "Get off the field! Get out of my sight!"

I walked back to the field house alone. The soberness of my feeling seemed almost to verge on romantic love—it seemed to make the air I walked through heavy—as if I were sick at heart for some gorgeous raven-haired woman who had been separated from me by a convulsion of nature. I took off my uniform and stood for a long time in the shower. Then I dressed and walked back across the quadrangle, where I could hear, from the open windows of the music building, Bacon playing the Chopin preludes. The music—swept with rains, with ruins, with unrequited and autumnal loves, with here and there a passage of the purest narcissism—seemed to outrage my senses, and I wanted to stop my ears. It took me an hour or so to pack, and when I carried my bags downstairs, I could still hear the cheering from the field. I drove into the village and had the tank filled with gas. At the edge of town, I wondered what direction to take, and then I turned south, for the farm.

It was six or seven when I got to St. Botolph's, and I took the precaution of calling Leander before I drove out to the house. "Hello, hello, hello!" the old man shouted. "You must have the wrong number. Oh,

hello, Eben . . ." When I got to the house, I left my bags in the hall and
went upstairs. Leander was in his room. "Welcome home, Eben," he
said. "I was reading a little Shakespeare to the cat."

When I sat down, the arm of my chair crashed to the floor, and I let
it lie there. On his thick white hair Leander still wore his fez. For clothing, he had drawn from his store of old-fashioned bathing suits one
with a striped skirt. It must have been stolen, since there were some nu-
merals stenciled on the back. He had decided some time before that the
most comfortable shoes he had were some old riding boots, and he was
wearing these. Pictures of lost sailboats, lost cottages, dead friends, and
dogs gazed down at him from the wall. He had tied a length of string
between the four wooden pineapples of his high poster bed and had
hung his wash there to dry. The cat and his copy of Shakespeare were
on his lap. "What are your plans?" he asked.

"I've been fired," I said. "I thought I'd leave some clothes here. I think
I'll go for a swim now."

"Have you any clothes I can wear?"

"You're welcome to anything I have. The bags are downstairs."

"I still swim every day," Leander said. "Every day, that is, until the
first of October. Last year I went swimming through the fifteenth—the
fifteenth or the sixteenth. If you'll wait a minute, I'll make sure." He got
up from his chair, and, stooping a little, so the tassel of his fez hung over
his brow, he walked to his journal. After consulting it, he said, "I went
swimming on the fifteenth last year. I went swimming on the twenty-
fifth the year before that. Of course, that was nothing to what I could
do when I was younger. I went swimming on the fourth of December,
the eighth of January, the second of March. I went swimming on
Christmas Day, New Year's Day, the twelfth of January, and the tenth
of February . . ."

After I left him to go out to the river, he went downstairs to where
my bags were. An old pair of riding pants took his eye. He managed to
get his legs well into them before he realized that they were too small.
He tried to remove the pants and couldn't, because his legs had begun
to swell. And when he tried to stand, the pants knifed him in the ten-
dons at the back of his knees and brought him to the floor. Halfway out
in the river, I could hear him roaring for help, and I swam back to shore
and ran up to the house and found him moving slowly and painfully
toward the kitchen, where he hoped to find a knife and cut himself free.

I cut the riding breeches off him, and we drank some whiskey together, but I left in the morning for New York.

It was a good thing that I did leave, because I got a job the day I reached the city, and sailed three days later for Basra, to work for an oil company. I took the long voyage out on one of the company ships; it was five weeks after leaving New York that we stopped at Aden and another four days before we docked at Basra. It was hot. The flat volcanic ruins trembled in the heat, and the car that took me across the city to the oil-company settlement traveled through a maze of foul-smelling streets. The dormitory where I was to be quartered was like an army barracks, and when I reached it, in midafternoon, there was no one there but some Arabs, who helped me with my bags and told me the other men would be in after four, when the offices closed. When the men I shared the barracks with came in, they seemed pleased to see anyone newly arrived from the States, and they were full of practical information about how to make a life in Basra. "We practice baseball two or three nights a week," one of them said, "and then on Sundays we play Shell or Standard Oil. We only have eleven men on the squad now, so if you could play outfield? We call ourselves the Infidels . . ."

It was not until long after my return from Basra, long after my marriage, that Leander died, one summer afternoon, sitting in the rose garden, with a copy of *Primitive Sexual Mores* on his lap. The housekeeper found him there, and the local undertaker sent me a wire in New York. I did not feel any grief when I got the news. Alice and I had three children by then, and my life would not in any way be affected by Leander's death. I telephoned my sisters, in Denver, but neither of them felt that they could come East. The next day, I drove to St. Botolph's, and found that the undertaker had made all the arrangements. The services were to be at two. Three old cousins came out from Boston, to my surprise, and we were the only mourners. It was the kind of weather that we used to call haying weather when I lived in the valley. The fields of timothy and sweet grass had been cut, the cemetery smelled of cut hay, and while the minister was praying, I heard the sound of distant thunder and saw the daylight dim, the way the lights dim in a farmhouse during a storm. After the ceremony, I returned to the house, feeling that there would be a lot there to occupy me, but it turned out that there was not much to do. It had begun to rain. I wandered through the rooms to see if there was anything left in them. I found some whiskey. The bird cages, the three-legged tables, and the cracked soup tureens must have been refused by the junkman. I thought that there must be a will, and I went reluctantly—disconsolately, at any rate—up to Leander's room and sat uneasily in his chair. His papers were copious and bizarre, and it took me nearly two hours to find the will. He left the house and the land to my older sister. To my other sister he left the jewelry, but this was immaterial, since all the jewelry had been sold. I was mentioned. "To my changeling son, Eben," he wrote, "the author of all my misfortunes, I leave my copy of Shakespeare, a hacking cough . . ." The list was long and wicked, and although he had written it ten years earlier and although I had buried him that afternoon, I couldn't help feeling, for a minute, that the piece of paper was evidence of my own defeat. It was dark then, and it was still raining. The whiskey bottle was empty and the unshaded electric light was baneful. The old house, which had always seemed to have an extensive life of its own, was creaking and stirring under the slender weight of the storm. The feeling that in burying Leander I had resolved a sad story seemed farcical, and if my reaction to his will was evidence, the old fool had pierced the rites and ceremonies of death. I thought desperately of my family in New York, and of the rooms where my return was waited with anxiety and love, but I had never been able to build any kind of bridge from Leander's world to the worlds where I lived, and I failed now in my efforts to remember New York. I went downstairs to telephone my wife, but the telephone was dead, and for all I knew it might have been disconnected years ago. I packed my bag, turned out the lights, threw the house key into the river, and started home.

In the years that followed, I thought now and then about Leander and the farm, and although I had resolved to break with these memories, they both continued to enjoy the perfect freedom of my dreams; the bare halls of the house, the massive granite stoop, the rain dripping from the wooden gutters, and the mass of weeds in the garden often surrounded me while I slept. My participation in baseball continued to be painful. I drove a ball through my mother-in-law's parlor window— and the rest of the family, who were intimidated, didn't understand why I should feel so happy—but it was not enough to lay Leander's ghost, and I still didn't like old men with white hair to be at the helm of the ships I traveled on. Some years later—my oldest son was nine—I took all five boys uptown to Yankee Stadium to see their first game. It was one of the hottest days of the year. I bought my sons food, eyeshades, pennants, score cards, pencils, and souvenir pins, and I took the youngest two to the bathroom several times. Mantle was up in the sixth, with a count of three and two. He fouled three balls into the netting above the backstop and fouled the fourth straight toward where we were sitting—a little high. It was coming like a shot, but I made the catch—one-handed, barehanded—and although I thought the impact had broken some bones in my hand, the pain was followed swiftly by a sense of perfect joy. The old man and the old house seemed at last to fall from the company and the places of my dreams, and I smelled the timothy and the sweet grass again, and saw a gravedigger hidden behind a marble angel, and the smoky, the grainy light of a thunderstorm, when the clearness of the green world—the emblazoned fields—reminds us briefly of a great freedom of body and mind. Then the boys began to argue for possession of the ball, and I gave it to the oldest one, hoping that I wouldn't have any more use for it. It would have troubled Leander to think that he would be buried in any place as distant from West Farm as Yankee Stadium, but that is where his bones were laid to rest.

1953

SNO

CALVIN TRILLIN

Walking from the Oval Track to the Endurance Track at the Fifth Annual Paul Bunyan Snowmobile Derby, I happened on a man in a parka who was trying to peddle a Chevroletful of canvas snowmobile covers. Since I judged the temperature to be four or five degrees short of the temperature necessary to sustain human life, it was possible that his constant patter was only an attempt to keep his mouth from freezing shut, but, all in all, he struck me as an aggressive salesman—a man quick with persuasive explanations of why it would be pound foolish not to invest twenty-five dollars to protect a thousand-dollar machine. He was experiencing unrelieved failure. It suddenly occurred to me that I had stumbled across what may have been the only example of unsuccessful merchandising in the short, awesomely profitable history of snowmobiling. I immediately took the salesman in hand. "You should be wearing a snowmobile suit!" I shouted to him. It was necessary to shout, because the way a lot of snowmobilers enjoy a derby most is to bring their own machines on trailers and spend most of the day buzzing around the grounds, stopping at the track occasionally to watch the contestants in the two-and-a-half-hour Grand Prix race zip by. "Nobody at a snowmobile derby is going to pay any attention to anybody who isn't wearing a snowmobile suit," I explained. I spoke from some experience, being dressed at the time in a sheepskin coat that I had considered quite fashionable until I realized that everyone at the derby assumed I was there to replace the hot-dog supply at the refreshment tent or repair the loudspeaker system. A snowmobile suit is ordinarily a one-piece coverall of quilted material—the kind of thing an airplane mechanic might wear if he happened to work at a very cold airport. Like mechanics, a lot of snowmobile owners wear patches identifying the make of machine they tinker with, but the color of a snowmobile suit alone is usually enough to indicate whether the wearer drives an Arctic Cat or a Polaris or a Scorpion. The snowmobile industry is color-keyed. The owner of a Ski-Doo—a black-and-yellow machine that has the largest share of the market—ordinarily wears a suit that is black with yellow piping, plus black snowmobile boots with Ski-

Doo patches on them. A snowmobiler who is particularly fashion-conscious—most often a female snowmobiler—may wear under the Ski-Doo suit yellow wool tights and a yellow sweater with black piping. The inner clothing can be used as what is known as an après-snowmobile outfit, making the wearer a merchandiser's dream—brand identification almost down to the skin.

The cover salesman happened to have a red deer-hunting outfit in his car that we decided might pass for a snowmobile suit, although the patch sewn on it said "National Rifle Association" instead of "Sno-Pony" or "Ski-Daddler" or "Sno*Jet." When I couldn't find him later in the afternoon, I assumed that my marketing advice had enabled him to sell all his covers and go home to watch some game on television—the way he had wanted to spend his Saturday afternoon in the first place. I wanted to tell him about meeting a couple wearing black-and-white snowmobile suits with patches that said "Snow Goer." When I asked if they knew why whoever had named their make was the only person in the field who felt it necessary to spell out *snow* to the very end, they told me that Snow Goer was not a machine but a magazine—a publication that happened to consider it good business to have its own snowmobile suits. I did find the salesman again at the end of the day, and he reported, with restrained gratitude, that he had sold three covers. Brainerd, Minnesota, like all the other places that call themselves the Snowmobile Capital of the World, is a small town, and the salesman thought his problem might be that not many people in a small town walk around on a Saturday with twenty-five dollars extra in their pockets. That was not the problem. "Get a proper patch!" I shouted. It was obvious that all he needed was a patch on his hunting suit saying something like "Sno-Cougar Covers." I didn't see him Sunday, but if he followed my instructions he is now a very rich snowmobile-cover salesman.

None of the people representing snowmobile manufacturers at the derby seemed in need of my marketing advice. They all had snowmobile suits on, all bepatched with their brand names, and the fact that a state like Minnesota, which ten years ago had no snowmobiles, now has a hundred thousand seemed to be an indication that the snowmobile industry had been getting good advice from somewhere. Also, I couldn't think of any promotional possibilities in a snowmobile derby that they hadn't exhausted. Although the Brainerd derby is considered only a middle-sized event on the snowmobile-racing circuit, several of the manufacturers had brought their factory racing teams, the results of certain races having too great an impact on sales to be left to amateurs. "People are kind of silly about racing," the representative of one manufacturer told me. "They know that the machines that race are not the same ones they get in the showroom, and very few people actually buy snowmobiles to race them anyway. But they don't like the thought of being left behind on the trail. They want a machine just a little faster than their neighbor's. Not much; just a little." Johnson Motors, which makes a snowmobile called a Skee-Horse, sponsored a Skeeburger Fest on Friday night at the Brainerd Armory, where the Exchange Club served the skeeburgers and Miss Brainerd welcomed everyone to town ("Have a good time, eat a whole bunch, and have a ball"). On Saturday, a few hundred snowmobilers went on a Snowmobile Moonlight Cruise—driving their machines twelve miles to a cookout and back, with guides, mechanics, trailmarkings, hot dogs, and souvenir patches furnished by Evinrude, the producer of the Evinrude Skeeter. A couple of the companies that make snowmobile oil offered extra prize money for drivers who won races while displaying the company decals, and another oil company towed its banner above the derby grounds by plane Saturday afternoon and furnished placemats and matches for the Awards Banquet at the Elks Lodge that night. The local race officials, sanctioned by the United States Snowmobile Association, wore bright-orange snowmobile suits with a patch that said "Miller High Life Snowmobiler."

At a Friday-evening parade through the streets of Brainerd, and during the day at the derby, the public-relations man from the largest distributor of Ski-Doos hauled behind his snowmobile a yellow sleigh that held Miss Minnesota, accompanied, for good measure, by Miss North Dakota—both of whom would alight occasionally to hand out Ski-Doo "Think Snow" buttons or Ski-Doo safety booklets. Miss Minnesota is retained for such duties through the Miss Minnesota Pageant at a straight hundred dollars a day (with special rates for appearances under two hours), and both she and Miss North Dakota appear at snowmobile functions exclusively for Ski-Doo—leaving Arctic Cat, a Minnesota company, to make do with Miss Wisconsin and Miss Michigan. At the Skeeburger Fest, the Johnson representative, in a friendly mood, asked Miss Minnesota if it would be in violation of her contract for him to pin one of his limited-supply "LOVE is a Johnson

Skee-Horse" buttons on her. She thought about it a moment, smiled pleasantly, and said it would be. The Awards Banquet guests included not only the Misses Minnesota and North Dakota but also Miss Brainerd, Miss Little Falls, Miss Park Rapids, and the Princess of Silver Bay—almost all of them with tiny crowns perched on their heads. But the star was Miss Minnesota. She is known in the state for having won the talent competition at the Miss America Pageant, playing the flute, and before the banquet ended the master of ceremonies announced, "She's going to perform her talent for us tonight." Having dressed for the banquet in a gown that was totally without brand identification, Miss Minnesota first reminded those present that she and Miss North Dakota were sponsored by Ski-Doo, although they both hoped everybody had a good time, no matter what kind of machine he drove. Then she played the flute. At a hundred a day, Miss Minnesota is considered a bargain.

Brainerd is about 120 miles north of Minneapolis and St. Paul, in what the snowmobile industry usually refers to as the Snowbelt—an area where the billboards are as likely to advertise Arctic Cats as Fords (on the Arctic Cats, imitation leopard-skin seat covers are standard rather than optional), where sporting-goods stores sell snowmobile racing stripes made of contact paper, and where some small towns average more than one snowmobile per family. In Brainerd, which has nearby lakes that make it a summer recreation center, the word snowmobile enthusiasts often use to describe what life was like in winter before snowmobiles came along is *hibernation*. Anyone who listens to a few snowmobilers talk about how dismal existence was in the old days begins to find it amazing that they managed to survive until someone discovered that a revolving belt and skis and a one-cylinder motor will propel a small vehicle over the snow at thirty or forty miles an hour. "I grew up around here," the employee of a snowmobile distributor told me as we sat in a roadhouse one dark, cold night. "And in the winter the only sound was the Grain Belt beer sign creaking in the wind." I shivered.

To businessmen, an area of hibernating people amounts to a block of dormant consumers just waiting for the right product to bring them to life. In the Snowbelt, no testimony of a snowmobiler on how glorious it is to have something to do all winter is quite as rhapsodic as the testimony of a banker on how glorious it is to have something to give loans on all winter. Snowmobiling has been marketed not as a sport but as a culture—a way to turn the former hibernation period into a time of what snowmobile marketers often refer to as Family Fun. Once winter is considered fun, the rest follows automatically. People in the Snowbelt enjoy being outdoors in groups, and now they can enjoy being outdoors in groups all winter merely by purchasing snowmobiles, snowmobile clothing, snowmobile trailers, snowmobile oil, and a drink called Snowshoe Grog. They like competitive sports, so there are snowmobile derbies every weekend. People who like to hunt can get to the hunting grounds in a snowmobile. People who like to drink can go from roadhouse to roadhouse in a snowmobile. The only adjustment necessary is to the cold, and snowmobilers are militantly oblivious of the cold. They like to talk about how explorers have proved snowmobile suits to be warm in temperatures as low as thirty or forty below zero, and they often stand outside when they could just as easily stand inside—the way little boys with new boots go out of their way to splash through puddles.

Snowmobile manufacturers are quite aware that their customers are, for the most part, small-town people—people who might like to go on outings pulling their kids behind them in a sled attachment, people who are more likely to be the townies of summer resorts than the owners of summer houses, people who, in the words of one snowmobile promotion man, "might feel uncomfortable in a ski resort."

"You might call them the Silent Majority," a spokesman for the industry told me at the derby, as we stood chatting just outside a heated tent.

"About the noise . . ." I replied, raising my voice enough to be heard over the sound of two passing Ski-Doos.

"It's terrible," he said. "Awful. Our worst problem."

Like the manufacturers of anything else, manufacturers of snowmobiles are organized to protect their interests—the International Snowmobile Industry Association has an executive secretary in Washington, the same man who serves as executive secretary of the American Golf Car Manufacturers Association, the Power Saw Manufacturers Association, and the Outdoor Power Equipment Institute—but even a trade association could never hope to persuade anybody that snowmobiles are anything but noisy. People in the industry admit that six or eight snowmobiles cutting through a backyard in the middle of the night can bring a homeowner leaping from his bed in the belief that, somehow, an anti-aircraft battery has just opened fire from his bedroom. They also admit—as they increase the power of some models to the point of being able to travel sixty miles an hour—that snowmobiles can be dangerous. On the theory that excesses could eventually result in a nasty backlash against Family Fun, the ISIA representative who makes the rounds of the Snowbelt legislatures acknowledges the need for legislation to prevent people from riding snowmobiles on highways or hunting from snowmobiles or using snowmobiles in populated areas late at night. He says his goal is "regulatory encouragement."

What nobody connected with snowmobiles will acknowledge is that the peaceful woods are being violated by snowmobiling—an idea they associate with people from big cities who know nothing about snowmobiles or woods. It is true that there is an automatic disdain for snowmobiles among the people I have always thought of as Abercrombie & Fitch Conservationists—sailing enthusiasts who complain about the noise the riffraff make with their outboards, people who build tasteful hundred-thousand-dollar houses on the unspoiled parts of the California coast and then talk about preserving the natural beauty of the area against the ugliness of tacky beach cottages. There are also serious conservationists who believe that, for a number of reasons, inaccessible woods ought to remain inaccessible, but their arguments have no effect on serious snowmobilers, who like to think that they are outdoorsmen and conservationists themselves. One snowmobiler I was talking with dismissed the idea that the noise of the machines frightens animals by saying that a snowmobile makes less noise in the woods than a chain saw. When I said that the comparison might not be the most felicitous to use with conservationists, he informed me that a chain saw attracts deer faster than a salt lick. Listening to a snowmobiler talk about the joy of riding through the woods at night, with the snow on the jack pines glistening in the moonlight, I found it hard to keep in mind that the scene would have to include the smell of gas fumes and the noise of an indoor go-cart race.

"I wouldn't have one of the things," a Brainerd citizen told me during a derby social hour at the Elks Lodge. "They just amount to a way of getting from one bar to the next, and I can get to a bar without a snowmobile." It is true that some people in Brainerd use the snowmobile as a kind of pub-crawl vehicle—the pubs in this case being the restaurants and bars on the nearby lake shores. But going to a bar with a group of snowmobilers—and snowmobilers seem to go to bars only in groups— is not at all the same as arriving in a car. One of the promotion men at the derby told me that, in his view, the success of snowmobiling is due partly to the secret yen middle-class people in places like upper Minnesota have for the life of motorcycle gangs. But a snowmobile group entering a Minnesota roadhouse also carries the mystique of the Western—the Cartwrights riding into town and coming into the bar together, part of a good, strong outdoor group. In a bar, snowmobilers usually keep their snowmobile suits on—just getting out of the top half and letting it hang over their belts behind them as they talk about the bumpiness of the trail on the way over or about the relative virtues of a Polaris and an Arctic Cat.

The Saturday night of the Paul Bunyan Derby, I was in a roadhouse near the race track. Its parking lot seemed to have as many snowmobiles as cars. A few couples from Fargo, North Dakota, were there— people who had driven over in their cars for the derby, pulling their snowmobiles behind them on trailers—and there were a lot of local people making the usual Saturday-night rounds in their snowmobiles. The place was jammed. A snowmobile promotion man I was with was talking about his company's spending a couple of hundred thousand dollars a year in racing, and about color-keying clothes to snowmobiles, and about putting out instructions to people on how to form snowmobile clubs. "Sometimes I think it's all a childish game," he said. "And sometimes I think we've rejuvenated these people." A lot of the snowmobilers were gathered around a piano bar. They were singing along with the piano player, and going over to the dance floor to jitterbug to the faster numbers, and drinking a lot of Grain Belt beer.

1970

MUSHER

SUSAN ORLEAN

These are the questions that Susan Butcher, Alaskan dog musher and two-time winner (and record holder) of the eleven-hundred-mile Iditarod Trail Sled Dog Race, is asked most often: How cold does it get in Alaska? How cold is it in Alaska *right now*? Is your house cold? What does caribou taste like? What's your dog's name? Susan's first four answers are: Very, very cold. Not too bad. Doesn't feel that way to me. Really good.

The last question has approximately 150 answers, because Susan has approximately 150 Alaskan Husky sled dogs, who live outside her log cabin in the Alaskan bush. Such a large number of animals strikes many people as unusual, and even unmanageable, so sometimes, instead of "What's your dog's name?" she is asked if she actually bothers to name all her dogs.

The people who ask that are not fellow mushers—dog-sled drivers—but, rather, the kind of people (including us) who came to the Plaza hotel last week to see Susan receive the Women's Sports Foundation's Professional Sportswoman of the Year Award, and who find the circumstances of Susan's life nearly unimaginable: the dozens of dogs, the rigors of sled racing, the near-isolation. (For much of the year, the only human being she sees is her husband, David Monson.) Susan, who told us she much prefers two days on a dog sled to two days in the Plaza, has accrued so much fame as a musher that she is used to being a curiosity, and she is gracious enough to answer even the most elementary dog-mushing, Alaska, or life-in-the-bush question with only a trace of exasperation. "Of course I name all the dogs," she explained. "I name some after places and some after people. Then, for a while, I'll have themes, like the names of book characters. One of my studs is Crackers, so another theme is to name his puppies after cracker brands. Another stud is Granite, and a lot of his puppies have rock names. I know every dog by name. I know every dog's parents. I know every dog's grandparents. I know which one has a cold, and which one didn't eat well last night, and I know each one's personality and where he likes to be scratched. You have to understand, this is all I care about, and this is all I think about. I don't understand anything else, and I don't care about anything else. I'm with the dogs twelve or sixteen hours a day, seven days a week. They're my friends and my family and my livelihood."

As she was talking, Susan kept glancing at her dog Fortuna, whom she had brought with her from Alaska to donate to the Women's Sports Foundation for a benefit auction. Fortuna is six years old and raced in the 1984 Iditarod, but now, according to Susan, she wants to be a pet. To us she didn't seem to like being in New York any more than Susan did, but she looked happier once she'd discovered the nice sled dog living in the Plaza Baroque Room's mirrored columns. "She misses her friends," Susan told us. "She thinks she's finally found another dog." She leaned over. "Hey, For*tuna*, good girl," she cooed. "*Good* girl!"

Susan is thirty-two and has a long black braid and very pale blue eyes. For a normal day of mushing, she wears polypropylene underwear, layers of Thinsulate and GoreTex outer garments, a beaver hat, a wolverine muff, wolfskin gloves, and sealskin mukluks. For the press conference, she wore jeans and a cotton T-shirt that said PURINA PRO-PLAN, which is a type of dog food put out by one of her sponsors. For the foundation's evening black-tie cocktail party, she said, she was going to wear a long gingham skirt, a black satin shirt, and an ivory miniature-dog-sled-and-team necklace. "I do own long skirts—I need them for the Iditarod awards banquet in Nome, for one thing," she explained, and then said, "Oh, *shoot*! I wish I'd brought my qiviut dress." She was wearing that dress—qiviut is the underwool of the musk ox— last March when she received first prize for the 1987 race, and also the year before when she picked up the trophy for the 1986 Iditarod. That was the race in which she set the world record (eleven days fifteen hours and six minutes), and it made up for the previous year, when a rogue moose attacked her team, killing three of her dogs and forcing her to drop out. "No one was going to beat me in 1986," she told us. "I was really determined."

Susan said that her first dog, Cabee, was a Labrador mix, and her second dog was an Alaskan Husky, and all her dogs since have been Huskies. She first mushed dogs in Massachusetts, where she was born, and she kept at it when she moved to Colorado and shared a house with a woman who had fifty Huskies. By the age of nineteen, she was sure enough of herself to know that she wanted to live in the wilderness with a lot of dogs, and that there was nowhere in the Lower Forty-eight that would satisfy her. "At first, I wanted to build wooden boats," she went on. "I really loved carpentry, and I wanted to sail around the world, because at the time I thought the ocean was the only place I could go to get away from people. But then I tried to figure out what I'd do with twenty or thirty dogs on a small boat." When she moved to Alaska, in 1975, she lived in a "fly-in"—an area accessible only by plane. Then her work as a dog breeder, trainer, and racer made living near a road necessary, so she and her husband (they were married in 1985) and the dogs moved to a slightly less remote spot, 150 miles north of Fairbanks and twenty-five miles from the closest village (Manley, pop. 62). She still hunts moose for food, but now there's a gravel road to her cabin. "Where we're living is very downtown to me," she said. "We chose it because it's good for mushing. There are very strong winds and it's stormy, and that's good, because it's the kind of weather you get during races. I just don't like city living. We do have a radio, and David likes to listen to it, but I don't. He likes to read newspapers. I like to burn them for firewood."

Someone passed out auction brochures—Fortuna was listed under the heading LUXURIOUS FUN—and then a man who was wearing a World Boxing Hall of Fame tie clip and belt buckle, and who had the cauliflower ears of a boxer, grabbed Susan by the elbow and said, "Are you the girl that did that thing on the dog sled?"

She nodded, and said, "Eleven days on a sled in the Alaskan wilderness."

The man turned to someone walking past and exclaimed, "I couldn't do the thing she did! I can go into the ring and get bashed up, but I couldn't do that thing she did!"

1987

HOME AND AWAY

PETER HESSLER

Little Fatty kept leaving it short. Twice he dropped the basketball on
the way up, and the third time, when Yao Ming finally lifted him
above the rim, he held the ball too low. His name was Sun Haoxuan; he
was four years old, weighed fifty-nine pounds, and had been selected by
an advertising firm that had recently scouted Beijing kindergartens for
a fat boy with round cheeks and big dark eyes. There was a substantial
talent pool. In Chinese cities, rising standards of living have combined
with the planned-birth policy in a way that recalls the law of conservation of mass: There are fewer children, but often there is more child. It's
common for adults to refer to these kids as Xiao Pangzi—Little Fatty.
"Get Little Fatty ready!" the director shouted whenever he needed Sun
Haoxuan. "Move Little Fatty back two steps!"

We were at the Beijing Film Studios, where Yao Ming, the starting
center for the Houston Rockets, was shooting a television commercial
for China Unicom, a telecommunications company. The script was
simple: fat child meets seven-foot-six-inch basketball player; basketball
player lifts fat child; fat child dunks. What had not been factored in was
Little Fatty's behavior. He squirmed away at every opportunity; sometimes he pointed directly at Yao Ming and announced, with an air of
sudden revelation, "Yao Ming!" For half an hour, the adults in the studio—cameramen, assistants, tech guys—had been silently aiming ill
wishes his way, and maybe that was why, on the fourth take, Yao stumbled and accidentally rammed Little Fatty's nose against the rim. The
sounds came in quick succession: a soft thud, a dropped ball—bounce,
bounce, bounce-bounce—and then the child began to wail.

The boy's mother rushed over, and Yao Ming stood helplessly, shoulders slumped. Somebody wiped Little Fatty's face—no blood, no foul.
On the next take, he finally dunked the ball, and there was a thin round
of applause. Yao wandered over to the edge of the set, where I was
standing, and said, in English, "Weight training."

After a sensational rookie season in the National Basketball Association, Yao, who is twenty-three, had returned to China in early May

with one clear objective: to lead the national team to the title in the Asian Basketball Championship, which serves as the regional qualifier for the 2004 Olympics. Usually, China dominates Asian basketball, but this year, because of political problems, Wang Zhizhi, the country's second-best player, had not come back from America. Yao Ming had become involved in a high-profile lawsuit, which was interpreted by the Chinese press as a clash between the rights of the individual and the authority of the state. Increasingly, Yao's world was divided: There was the sanctity of the sport and, off court, a whirlwind of distractions, ranging from the burdensome to the bizarre. When I had last visited him, in July, he was staying with the Chinese team in Qinhuangdao, a seaside town that was hosting an exhibition game against a squad from the United States Basketball Academy. Yao didn't play—he had just received eight stitches in the eyebrow after a teammate elbowed him in practice. Before the game, a China Unicom representative with a digital recorder coached Yao through a series of phrases that would be sold as alarm messages to mobile-phone subscribers. "Wake up, lazy insect!" Yao said obediently, and then his bandaged brow dipped when the woman asked him to repeat it ("More emphasis!").

That evening, the Chinese nearly threw the game away—in the final quarter, they couldn't handle a full-court press from the ragtag American team. "I think the center needs to come to half-court against the press," Yao told me afterward, in his hotel room. Liu Wei, the Chinese point guard and Yao's best friend, was sprawled on one bed. Yao sat on the other bed, which had been crudely extended: The head consisted of a wooden cabinet covered with blankets. We spoke in English; he talked about the NBA off-season news that he had culled from the Internet. He had not spoken to any of his Houston teammates since returning to China. "Did you hear about Rodman?" Yao said. "He might come back. I can't believe the Lakers got Payton and Malone. I can't believe they only spent six million. If Kobe is OK, it's like a Dream Team." The names sounded foreign and far away—Mark Cuban, Shaq, Kirilenko. "AK-47," Yao said, using the sports-talk nickname for Andrei Kirilenko, a Russian forward on the Utah Jazz. Yao smiled like a kid at the sound of the phrase. "AK-47," he said again.

Yao Ming weighed ten pounds at birth. His mother, Fang Fengdi, is over six-two; his father, Yao Zhiyuan, is six-ten. Both were centers: He played for the Shanghai city team, and she was on China's national team. Chinese sports couples aren't uncommon—Yao Ming is dating Ye Li, a six-two forward on the women's national team. When Yao was growing up, the apartment directly overhead was home to the Sha family; the parents had both been point guards for Shanghai teams. "My mother and father were introduced by the basketball organization," Sha Yifeng, a childhood friend of Yao Ming, told me. "In the old days, that's how they took care of your life."

Today, Yao's parents are in their early fifties, trim and black-haired, and they carry themselves with the physical dignity of athletes. But they speak about basketball with detachment. Neither played the game as a child; sports were a low priority for China in the 1960s, particularly during the early years of the Cultural Revolution. Later, officials began to restore the national sports system, scouting for height to fill out the basketball rosters. Yao Zhiyuan began to play at the age of nineteen. Fang Fengdi was discovered at sixteen. "To be honest, I didn't much like it," she told me, when I met them both in Shanghai. "I wanted to be a dancer or an actress." By 1970, she was traveling to games around the world with the national team. "I didn't think of it as something I did or didn't want to do," she said. "I thought of it as a responsibility. It was a job."

In China, competitive sport is a foreign import. Traditional physical activities like wushu and qigong are as much aesthetic and spiritual as they are athletic. Chinese historians say that modern sport began after the 1839–42 Opium War. In the following decades, as foreign traders and missionaries established themselves in treaty ports, their schools and charitable institutions introduced Western competitive sports. American missionaries brought basketball to China at the end of the nineteenth century.

During the early 1900s, as the Chinese struggled to overcome foreign occupation, they began to see sports as a symbolic way to avenge the injustices of the past century. The goal was to beat the foreigner at his own game. After the Communists came to power, in 1949, they established a state-funded sports-training system modeled on the Soviet Union's. Promising young athletes were recruited for special "sports schools."

When Yao Ming entered the third grade, he was five-seven, and Shanghai's Xuhui District Sports School selected him for its after-school basketball program. Recently, I visited Yao's first coach, Li Zhangming, who, like a traditional Chinese educator, spoke of Yao in completely unsentimental terms ("He didn't much like basketball. He was tall, but slow and uncoordinated"). After our conversation, I wandered around the basketball courts of Shanghai's No. 54 Middle School, where the Xuhui Sports School holds some of its practices. I watched a group of young girls performing basketball drills, then introduced myself to the coach, a tall woman named Tao Yanping.

"I was a teammate of Yao's mother," Tao said. "I went to their wedding. I remember giving them towels and thermoses—things you gave newlyweds back then. See that girl there?" She pointed out a red-faced child, the tallest on the court. "Her mother was also my teammate. That girl is in the third grade. Her mother is 1.83 meters tall, and she made the national team."

I asked Tao how she recruited. "We go to the schools and look at the children's height, and then we check their parents' height," she said.

The two-hour practice consisted mostly of ballhandling drills. Tao was attentive, shouting commands at her charges ("Little Swallow, you're traveling! Who taught you to do that?"). At the end of the practice, tall parents materialized at courtside. Zhang Jianrong, a woman who was nearly six feet tall, told me that basketball was just a healthy activity for her daughter; the girl's studies were more important. Like the other parents, Zhang was a basketball mom in a country that selects its basketball moms by height.

The method of early recruitment is a product of China's inability to provide every public school with coaches and sports facilities. The system has proved effective in low-participation, routine-based sports like gymnastics and diving, but when it comes to basketball it may be China's greatest weakness. In America, where community leagues and school coaches are plentiful, athletes emerge from an enormous pyramid of participants. Some, like Allen Iverson, rise to the top with remarkable passion and creativity—but if a recruiter had shown up at the Iverson home when Allen was in the third grade, he would have found no father and a short mother who had given birth at the age of fifteen. It's significant that China has yet to produce a great male guard—the position requires skill and intensity rather than height. All three Chinese players in the NBA are centers, and two are second-generation centers. The Chinese national team is notorious for choking in key games, partly because the ballhandling is inconsistent. Players rarely appear to enjoy themselves, and their character has not been formed by true competition; even as free-market reforms have changed many Chinese industries, the sports world is a throwback to socialism, with its careful planning and career stability. Once, when I asked Yao Ming how many Chinese would be in the NBA in a decade, he said only three or four.

Throughout Yao Ming's childhood, his parents emphasized that basketball was a hobby, not a career. "When I was small, I always wanted to be famous," Yao told me. "I thought I'd be a scientist or maybe a political figure. It didn't matter, as long as I was famous." In sixth grade, he grew taller than his mother. He surpassed his father's height in ninth grade. By then, he was already under contract to the Shanghai Sharks youth team. When he was seventeen, and seven-two, Yao Ming joined the Chinese national team. Relatives told me that it wasn't until then that his parents resigned themselves to his career as a professional athlete.

Once, I asked Fang Fengdi if there had been a moment when she first sensed that basketball inspired Yao Ming. It was the only time she really smiled when discussing the sport, and I sensed that she was talking about herself as much as about her son. She said, "The Harlem Globetrotters came to Shanghai when he was in elementary school. Tickets were really hard to get—I was able to find only two. I remember thinking, Americans are good at enjoying themselves! Those players took a normal sport and turned it into something else—a performance. Afterward, I could tell that it made a deep impression on Yao Ming."

The first male player to make the jump from mainland China to top-level American basketball was Ma Jian, a forward who played at the University of Utah for two years in the 1990s. Ma noticed that during Utah's pregame meetings, an assistant coach sometimes wrote a *W* or a *B* on the chalkboard next to an opposing player's name. "The white players were shooters," Ma explained to me, when we met recently in Beijing. "If he put a *B* there, we knew they were athletes." Ma never saw a *C* on the board. In 1995, Ma tried out for the Los Angeles Clippers. "The first time I stepped onto the team plane in the preseason, I saw the blacks sitting on one side and the whites on the other. I looked at myself—should I go on the brothers' side or the whites' side?"

Last year, after the Rockets selected Yao Ming with the first pick in the NBA draft, it was less than a week before somebody in the league made a remark that could be construed as racist. During a television interview, Shaquille O'Neal, the NBA's dominant center, announced, "Tell Yao Ming, 'Ching chong yang wah ah so.'" O'Neal's joke went largely unnoticed at the time, but it was resurrected in January of this year, when a columnist for *Asian Week* attacked O'Neal for it.

The column sparked a media frenzy shortly before Shaq and Yao's first on-court meeting. But Yao immediately defused the controversy. "There are a lot of difficulties in the two different cultures understanding each other," he said. "Chinese is hard to learn. I had trouble with it when I was little." The NBA released a statement pointing out that the league included players from thirty-four countries. By game time, the issue was all but dead. The Rockets won by four points, in overtime; O'Neal outplayed Yao, but Yao had a spectacular start and held his own. Afterward, O'Neal told the press, "Yao Ming is my brother. The Asian people are my brothers."

In February, I spent most of the month following Yao's games, and people repeatedly brought up the O'Neal incident. None of the black fans I talked to had anything bad to say about Yao—many believed he brought something fresh to American sports. "It's not like normal, where people say, well, he's a black athlete, so he moves like this, or he's a white athlete, so he shoots like that," Darice Hooper, a physical therapist who was attending the All-Star Game, in Atlanta, told me.

Juaquin Hawkins, one of Yao's teammates on the Rockets, agreed. "It's not just people thinking, I'm rooting for him because he's African American, or I'm rooting for him because he's white," he told me. Hawkins was familiar with the outsider's role. A native of Lynwood, California, he had failed to make the NBA in 1997, and the following year he wound up playing professionally in Chongqing, deep in the Chinese interior. I had lived in the same region, and Hawkins laughed when I mentioned the basketball slang there. If a player shoots an air ball, the fans shout "yangwei"; in the Sichuan dialect, it means "impotent." To encourage the home team, they chant "xiongqi" ("erection").

There are few foreigners in Chongqing, and even fewer blacks. I asked Hawkins how he had coped with being so different. "I always felt like I was representing my heritage," he said. "Lynwood is next to Compton. There's a lot of negative things said about that area, and that's something I take with me wherever I go. But I had a good childhood. I was raised by my mother. I try to represent that."

An uncle had introduced Hawkins to basketball as a child; he never met his father. "All I know is his first name, and the fact that he didn't want to deal with having a family," Hawkins said. He met his wife through basketball—both had played at Lynwood High School, and then at Long Beach State. In addition to Chongqing, Hawkins had played professional basketball in Taiwan, Japan, and the Philippines. He had toured with the Harlem Globetrotters ("That was actually real beneficial"). In the summer of 2002, he tried one last time to make the NBA, attending the Rockets' camp, where he established himself as a defensive specialist and beat out two other unsigned players for a roster spot. At twenty-nine, he was the oldest rookie in the league to make an opening-day lineup. When Hawkins learned that he was on the team, he telephoned his mother and wept.

Successful athletes are inevitably displaced—if you're good, you leave home—and something is always lost in transition. Much of what Hawkins carried onto the court would have been invisible to Chongqing fans, who know nothing about Compton or American single-parent families. In Chongqing, Hawkins was simply an excellent player who looked completely different from everybody else in the city. When I lived in a nearby town, it was common for crowds of twenty or more to gather and gawk at me on the street. A local night club once hired an African dancer, knowing that his freakishness would draw customers.

Yao Ming had an excellent rookie season, and there were clear signs that eventually he'd develop into a dominant center. But the Rockets ran only about thirty plays a game to him; initially, his American fame resulted from his height and his off-court persona. He handled attention with remarkable humor and grace. He also appealed to the national missionary instinct: If Americans had failed to convert the Chinese to God and democracy, at least we were turning them into

NBA fans. The American media portrayed Yao as a nonthreatening figure—a gentle giant.

But he entered another world whenever he dealt with the Chinese press. After a difficult defeat in Los Angeles, where Yao had fouled out for the first time in his NBA career, a Chinese reporter asked what it had been like to be dunked on by Kobe Bryant. Yao said evenly, "Please don't ask me about an incident in which I have no face." At an All-Star Game press conference, Yao showed up wearing an old Chinese national team sweatshirt, and a Chinese reporter asked why. "It's comfortable, that's all," Yao said. Another reporter asked, "If you could say one sentence to all of the young Chinese players back home, what would you say?" Yao's sentence: "I don't believe that I can say very much with one sentence."

Even as they idolized him, few people in China seemed to realize how different Yao was from the typical Chinese athlete. When he played, the joy was apparent on his face. He hit free throws in the clutch, and the Rockets learned to run plays to him at the end of close games. Often, he subtly deflected the patriotic questions of the Chinese media, as if sensing that such concerns were too heavy to bear on the court.

The Chinese motivation for sport is so specific and limited—the nationalism, the sports schools—that it rarely survives a transplant overseas. Athletics has meant little to most Chinese American communities, including the one in Houston, which has grown rapidly in the past decade. The city has an estimated fifty thousand Chinese, as well as large numbers of ethnic Chinese from Vietnam. Houston's Chinese tend to be highly educated, with an average annual household income of more than fifty thousand dollars—higher than the city's average.

The largest Asian district in Houston is along Bellaire Boulevard—a six-mile strip-mall Chinatown. In February, I spent two afternoons driving along Bellaire, where some of the signs reminded me that locals were adjusting to a new culture (All Stars Defensive Driving); others reflected success (Charles Schwab, in Chinese characters); and some were distinctly Chinese (a lot of beauty parlors—the Chinese are meticulous about their hair).

But I couldn't find anything having to do with basketball. Though everybody loved Yao Ming, people told me that the children in the community didn't play sports much; they were too busy studying. I searched for hours before finding a single sporting-goods store—Sports Net International, in a mall called Dynasty Plaza—and they stocked gear only for racquet sports. "The Chinese are not so interested in basketball, because of their size," David Chang, the owner, told me. "But if you're interested in Yao Ming you should talk to the people at Anna Beauty Design. They cut his hair."

Upstairs at the hair salon, a Taiwanese woman sat behind the receptionist's desk. I asked if Yao Ming got his hair cut there.

"No," she said. "Yao Ming does not get his hair cut here."

I tried again. "Does somebody from Anna's go to Yao Ming's home to cut his hair?"

"That's something I can't answer," she said coyly. A moment later, the manager walked in. "This guy's a reporter," she told him. "He wants to know if we cut Yao Ming's hair."

The manager shot me a dirty look. "Don't tell him we do that," he said.

The receptionist added, exactly five seconds too late, "He speaks Chinese."

All told, I tracked down three defensive-driving schools, six banks, and fourteen beauty salons—but no *lanqiu*. In Houston's Chinatown, it was easier to find Yao Ming's barber than a basketball.

At the end of February, the Rockets embarked on a critical East Coast road trip. Their final game was against the Washington Wizards; both teams were fighting to make the playoffs in their respective conferences, and Yao Ming was in the running to be named Rookie of the Year. This would be the final meeting between Yao Ming and Michael Jordan, who was retiring in order to return to his position as president of the Wizards.

The night before the Washington game, the Chinese Embassy hosted a special reception for Yao. Chinese food and Yanjing beer were served—the Beijing-based brewery had signed a Rockets sponsorship after Yao Ming was drafted. The Embassy's meeting room filled quickly: diplomats and émigrés, Sinophiles and market analysts. Scraps of conversation floated in the air.

"Yanjing paid six million dollars. Their distributor is Harbrew."

"Who gives a sixty-year distribution contract? But you know, from the Chinese point of view, it's a stream of production. They don't understand the concept of branding."

"He's been in China fifteen years as a value-added player."

"Actually, I'm with the White House press office."

"You know, Anheuser-Busch owns twenty-seven percent of Tsing-tao."

"There he is! Did you get a picture?"

"Imagine being that tall!"

A round of applause followed Yao into the room. Lan Lijun, the minister of the embassy, gave a short speech. He mentioned Ping-Pong diplomacy and "the unique role sports have played in bringing our countries together." In closing, he said, "We have full confidence that China and the United States will work together to continue to improve our bilateral relations."

Yao, in a gray suit, stooped to reach the microphone. Behind him, a display case held a ceramic horse from the Tang dynasty. Red lanterns hung from the ceiling. Yao spoke for less than a minute, and he didn't say anything about Sino-American relations. "Seeing all these lanterns reminds me of home," he said softly, in Chinese. "When I was growing up, my impression of the Chinese Embassy was like a fantasy, something you see on television and in the movies."

There was a rush for autographs, and staff members hustled Yao into a back room. In the corner, a pretty Eurasian girl in a red dress was crying. Her parents said that Yao had walked past without signing her invitation. "He's her favorite player," the mother told me, adding that the girl had been adopted from Uzbekistan. A staff member took her invitation, promising to get an autograph.

Yao was at the embassy for nearly two hours. After he left, people stood around in groups, chatting and drinking Yanjing. We had reached the Sino-American witching hour—the Chinese guests, always prompt, were gone, but the Americans lingered, in the way that Americans do. I found myself standing next to Chen Xiaogong, the defense attaché. Chen was glassy-eyed; he kept touching his watch. "I'm surprised so many Americans know Yao Ming," he said.

The next night, Kha Vo sings Francis Scott Key and Michael Jordan comes out hot. Four baskets in the first quarter: turnaround, jump shot, jump shot, turnaround. Ten days earlier, Jordan celebrated his fortieth birthday, and since then he's been averaging nearly thirty points a game. Yao works against Brendan Haywood, the Wizards' seven-foot center. Haywood looks short tonight. Six points for Yao in the first quarter; Rockets down by nine. Sold-out arena: twenty-thousand-plus. Lots of Asians—red flags in the upper levels.

Second quarter: Rudy Tomjanovich, the Rockets' coach, plays a hunch and goes with Juaquin Hawkins, who rarely sees action. Hawkins nails a twenty-footer, then a three-pointer. He draws a charge and steals a pass. Hawkins looks hungry, as if he'd just escaped from Chongqing: He hasn't scored in nine days. Moochie Norris runs the point for the Rockets. Moochie has cornrows, a barrel chest, and four Chinese characters tattooed on his left wrist: *huan de huan shi*. ("Never satisfied," he told me, when I asked him what it meant, and then I crossed to the other side of the locker room and asked Yao. "It actually doesn't have a very good meaning," he said. "Basically, you'll do whatever it takes to protect yourself.") Yao doesn't score in the second quarter. Jordan has eighteen. Rockets down by twenty. Halftime show: Chinese lion dance, followed by an announcement about Black History Month.

Houston sleepwalks through the third. At one point, they trail by twenty-four. In the final quarter, Maurice Taylor, a Rockets forward, starts to hit jumpers. With six minutes to go, Houston down by fourteen, Tomjanovich brings in Yao, and the game turns. Hawkins sinks a three, then knocks the ball loose from Tyronn Lue. The two players collide, and Lue falls, writhing in pain. Separated shoulder, cut eye: good night, Tyronn. Four straight baskets by the Rockets. In the final three minutes, Yao steps to the free-throw line four times, and nails everything. Haywood fouls out. Overtime.

Hawkins guards Jordan, and they trade baskets to start the extra period. Yao makes a baby hook to give the Rockets the lead. The Wizards feed Jordan every time down the court, and now, after playing for forty-five minutes, he suddenly finds new life. Turnaround jumper over Hawkins. Next possession: Jordan crossover dribble to his left; Hawkins freezes—dunk. Next possession: Jordan hard drive; Hawkins falls, no call—jumper. Next possession: Jordan drives; Hawkins lags, Yao goes for the block—goaltending. Jordan scores ten in overtime and finishes with thirty-five points and eleven rebounds. Yao has sixteen and eleven; Hawkins scores ten. In the final seconds, with the Rockets down by two, Yao gets a defensive rebound and, instead of calling a time-out, throws the outlet pass. Bad shot. Rockets lose.

After the game, in the Rockets' locker room, Hawkins sat alone on a bench. "It was frustrating," he told me, shaking his head. "He's the greatest player ever."

Yao sat in front of his locker, a towel wrapped around his waist; the Chinese media pressed close. He told them that he should have called the time-out.

In the Wizards' locker room, I joined a group of reporters waiting for Jordan. After the other players had left, he appeared behind a lectern, dressed in a gray pin-striped suit. Somebody asked if the Wizards would make the playoffs. "I've never had a doubt that we would," Jordan said.

Another reporter asked about the overtime period. Jordan talked about Hawkins: "I was going against a young kid who didn't really know how to play, and he tried a couple of flops."

Somebody asked about Yao. "You can sit here and talk about how good he eventually could be," Jordan said. "But at some point he's going to have to showcase what everybody expects."

Jordan spoke with an athlete's bluntness; on the court, it didn't matter where the players had come from or where they were going. For fifty-three minutes, the competition was more important than everything that surrounded it. But, like so many games, this one receded into the essence of statistics—the meaningless points, the pointless minutes. In the end, neither the Wizards nor the Rockets made the playoffs. Michael Jordan never again collected thirty points and ten rebounds in a game, and in May, after retiring, he was forced out of the Wizards organization. Less than three weeks after the Washington game, Rudy Tomjanovich was diagnosed with bladder cancer, and he stepped down as coach. Yao Ming did not win Rookie of the Year. And this season Juaquin Hawkins, after failing to make an NBA team, rejoined the Harlem Globetrotters.

Although it is difficult for a Chinese athlete to come to America, it may be even harder for him to return home. The most troubled transition has been that of Wang Zhizhi, a seven-one center, who emerged in the late nineties, when the Communist Party was restructuring many of its sports bureaus into for-profit entities. The Chinese Basketball Association hoped to become self-sufficient, through corporate sponsorships and income from its professional league, known as the CBA. In this climate, the CBA has become a strange beast: Its sponsors include private companies, state-owned enterprises, and the People's Liberation Army, which runs a team called the Bayi Rockets. Wang Zhizhi played for Bayi, and in 1999 the Dallas Mavericks selected him in the second round of the NBA draft. For nearly two years, Dallas courted Wang's bosses, trying to convince them to let the player go. Wang was officially a regimental commander in the PLA.

In the spring of 2001, Dallas and Bayi finally came to an agreement, and Wang became the first Chinese to play in the NBA. He was twenty-three years old. In the off-season, Wang returned home, as promised, representing both the national team and Bayi. But after Wang's second NBA season, in which he averaged about five points a game, he requested permission to delay his return to China so that he could play in the NBA's summer league. He promised to join the national team in time for the World Championships, in August.

The Chinese national team is notorious for its grueling practice schedule—twice a day, six days a week. Fear shapes the routine; coaches know that they will be blamed if the squad loses, so they log countless hours and resist innovation. Before games, the Chinese men's team warms up by conducting the same rudimentary ballhandling drills that I watched the third-grade girls perform in Shanghai.

In the summer of 2002, Chinese authorities refused Wang's request and ordered him to return, but he stayed in the United States anyway. Dallas did not offer him a contract, reportedly in part because they did not want to ruin the good relationship that they had developed with the Chinese. In October, Wang signed a three-year, six-million-dollar contract with the Los Angeles Clippers. Since then, Clippers games have been banned from Chinese television (NBA broadcasts often draw as many as fourteen million viewers in China). The ban has turned Wang into a marketing liability—one NBA general manager told me that teams are wary of signing him in the future.

Wang, whose military passport has expired, reportedly received a green card last season. Over the summer, he tried to negotiate a return to China, asking for a new civilian passport and a guarantee that he could come back to the NBA after the Asian Championship. The chain of communication had grown so complicated that Wang relied heavily on a Chinese sportswriter named Su Qun to contact PLA leaders and basketball officials. "I know that as a journalist I should stay out of this," Su, who writes for Beijing's *Titan Sports Daily*, told me. "But I happen to be close to Wang. We have to save him, like saving Private Ryan."

Wang, who declined my request for an interview, did not return to China. I spoke about him with Li Yuanwei, the secretary-general of the Chinese Basketball Association. "Wang has placed too much emphasis on his personal welfare," Li said. "I assured him that there is no risk. The PLA also assured him. But he doesn't believe us, and he keeps demanding conditions that are not necessary. It's very sad."

Wang's problems formed a troubling backdrop to Yao Ming's move to the NBA last year. Yao promised to fulfill his national-team commitments during the off-season, and he reportedly will pay the CBA 5 to 8 percent of his NBA salary for his entire career. He also will pay the Shanghai Sharks, his CBA team, a buyout that is estimated to be between eight million and fifteen million dollars, depending on his endorsements and the length of his career. Yao's four-year contract with the Rockets is worth $17.8 million, and already his endorsement income is higher than his salary.

But even Yao's sponsorship potential has been threatened by the irregularities of China's sports industry. In May, Coca-Cola issued a special can in Shanghai decorated with the images of three national-team players, including that of Yao, who already had a contract with Pepsi. The basketball association had sold Yao's image to Coca-Cola without his permission, taking advantage of an obscure sports commission regulation that grants the state the right to all "intangible assets" of a national-team player. The regulation appeared to be in direct conflict with Chinese civil law. Yao filed suit against Coca-Cola in Shanghai, demanding a public apology and one yuan—about twelve cents. The Chinese press interpreted the lawsuit as a direct challenge to the nation's traditional control of athletes.

When I spoke with Li Yuanwei, of the basketball association, he emphasized that Coca-Cola was an important source of funding, and he hoped that the company and Yao would reach an agreement out of court. Li told me that Americans have difficulty understanding the du-

ties of an athlete in China, where the state provides support from childhood. I asked if the same logic could be applied to a public school student who attends Peking University, starts a business, and becomes a
millionaire. "It's not the same," Li said. "Being an athlete is a kind of
mission. They have an enormous impact on the ideas of the common
people and children. That's their responsibility."

Before I traveled to Harbin, in northeastern China, to attend the
Asian Championship, I talked with Yang Lixin, a law professor at People's University in Beijing. Yang was preparing a seminar on the Coca-
Cola case. "Contact with American society probably gave Yao some
new ideas," Yang told me. "It's like Deng Xiaoping said—some people
will get wealthy first. Development isn't equal, and in a sense rights also
aren't equal. Of course, they are equal under law, but one person might
demand his rights while another does not. It's a choice. In this sense,
Yao Ming is a pioneer."

Displaced people have always wandered to Harbin. During the twentieth century, they came and went: White Russians, Japanese militants,
the Soviet Army. Even today, much of the architecture is Russian.
Harbin's symbol is the former St. Sofia Church: gold crosses, green
onion domes, yellow halos around white saints. The city has one of the
last Stalin Parks in China.

At the end of September, sixteen teams arrived for the Asian Championship; the winner would qualify for the Olympics. The squads came
from shadowy lands. Most of the Kazakhstan players were in fact Russians whose families had stayed after the collapse of the Soviet Union.
The Malaysian team had a peninsular range: ethnic Chinese, Indians,
Malays. Qatar's team included athletes from Africa and Canada—
opponents grumbled that they had loosened the definition of a Qatari.
The Syrian coach was a black man from Missouri; the Qatar coach was
a white man from Louisiana. Iran's coach was a Serb who told me that
his playing career had been cut short; he pulled up his sleeve to reveal a
cruel scar ("Not long after that, I started coaching").

Except for the Chinese team, everybody stayed at the Singapore
Hotel. Tall people in sweatsuits lounged in the lobby. The South Korean team included Ha Seung-Jin, an eighteen-year-old who is seven-
three, weighs 316 pounds, and has basketball bloodlines—his father

was once a center for the Korean national team. People expect Ha to be a first-round NBA draft pick next year. The league has never included a Korean. "I want to be a Korean Yao Ming," he told me, through an interpreter (who added that the young player's nickname is Ha-quille O'Neal). Ha was eager to play Yao; everybody expected China and South Korea to meet in the final. Last year, in the Asian Games, South Korea had upset the Chinese. Ha hoped to get Yao into foul trouble. "Yao Ming likes to spin to his right," Ha said. "I'll establish position there and draw the foul."

The other seven-three player in the tournament was an Iranian named Jaber Rouzbahani Darrehsari. Darrehsari had played for only three years, since being discovered in the city of Isfahan, where his father sells fruit and vegetables in a market. Darrehsari's wingspan is more than eight feet. Once, when he was leaving the court after a game, I asked him to touch the rim of the basket. He hopped ever so lightly, and then stood still: fingers curled around the metal, the balls of both feet planted firmly on the hardwood. He was seventeen years old. He had dark, long-lashed eyes, and he hadn't yet started shaving—it was as if a child's head had been attached to an elongated body with dangling arms. In Iran's first two games, Darrehsari played only a few minutes; smaller opponents shoved him mercilessly. He looked terrified on the court. Sitting on the bench, he almost never smiled.

The Chinese team stayed at the Garden Hamlet Hotel, a walled compound reserved for central-government leaders. All summer, Yao had been unable to appear in public without attracting a mob. In August, the Chinese media reported that a medical exam had revealed that Yao had high blood pressure. His agents said the condition was temporary, and a message from Yao appeared on his official website: "I have been exhausted because of the poor security at the National Team games . . . too many public appearances and commitments by the Chinese National Team, and incessant fan disturbances at the team hotel."

A few hours before China played Iran, one of Yao's agents told me that I could meet with his client. Yao is represented by an entity known as Team Yao, which consists of three Americans, two Chinese, and one Chinese American. Half the team had come to Harbin—Erik Zhang, Yao's distant cousin and the team leader; John Huizinga, a deputy dean at the University of Chicago Graduate School of Business, where Zhang is a student; and Bill A. Duffy, who heads BDA Sports Management. They were accompanied by Ric Bucher, a senior writer for *ESPN the Magazine,* who had signed on to write the official Yao biography. A day earlier, Yao had agreed to a multiyear endorsement contract with Reebok. A source close to the negotiations told me that the deal, which is heavy with incentives, could be worth well over a hundred million dollars—potentially the largest shoe contract ever given to an athlete.

A guard let us into the compound; we walked through rows of willows, past well-kept lawns decorated with concrete deer. It was raining hard. In Yao's room, there was little sign that the shoe contract had changed his life. The shades were drawn; discarded clothes were everywhere. Liu Wei, the point guard, lay in a tangle of sheets. The only difference from the day I'd seen Yao at his hotel room in Qinhuangdao was that this time they had put the wooden cabinet at the foot of his bed.

The night before, after China had defeated the Taiwanese team by sixty points, Yao had sprained his left ankle while boarding the team bus. Now Duffy, a former player in his forties, was examining him. The ankle was slightly swollen. He told Yao to ice it immediately after that night's game. Yao answered that there was no ice at the arena.

Duffy looked up at him, incredulous. "They don't have ice?" The games were being held in a converted skating rink in a sports complex less than two hundred miles from the Siberian border.

"No ice," Yao said again, and then he spoke in Chinese to Zhang: "I've been getting acupuncture."

After a few minutes, Team Yao left the room. Yao and I chatted about the tournament, and then I mentioned that his first coach had told me that Yao didn't like basketball as a child. "That's true," Yao said. "I didn't really like it until I was eighteen or nineteen."

I asked Yao about his first trip to the United States, in 1998, when Nike had organized a summer of training and basketball camps for him. "Before then, I was always playing with people who were two or three years older than me," he said. "They were always more developed, and I didn't think that I was any good. But in America I finally played against people my own age, and I realized that I was actually very good. That gave me a lot of confidence."

He talked about how difficult it had been when he first moved to Houston ("Everything about the environment was strange"), and I asked him about the differences between sport in China and in America.

"In China, the goal has always been to glorify the country," Yao said. "I'm not opposed to that. But I personally don't believe that that should be the entire purpose of athletics. I also have personal reasons for playing. We shouldn't entirely get rid of the nationalism, but I do think that the meaning of sport needs to change. I want people in China to know that part of why I play basketball is simply personal. In the eyes of Americans, if I fail then I fail. It's just me. But for the Chinese if I fail then that means that thousands of other people fail along with me. They feel as if I'm representing them."

I asked about the pressure. "It's like a sword," he said. "You can hold it with the blade out or with the blade pointing toward yourself." Then I mentioned Wang Zhizhi's situation.

"There's an aspect of it that I shouldn't talk about," Yao said slowly. "It's best if I simply speak about basketball. If Wang were here, it would be good for me. I just know that if he played I wouldn't feel as if so much of the pressure was falling onto one person."

I asked about the Coca-Cola lawsuit. "I always put the nation's benefit first and my own personal benefit second," Yao said. "But I won't simply forget my own interests. In this instance, I think that the lawsuit is good for my interests, and it's also good for other athletes. If this sort of situation comes up in the future for another athlete, I don't want people to say, 'Well, Yao Ming didn't sue, so why should you?'"

No pregame national anthems at the Asian Championship. Before tonight's game, the loudspeaker plays an instrumental version of the theme from *Titanic*. The Iranians look nervous. Sold-out arena: four-thousand-plus. The stands are full of Thundersticks—they are, after all, manufactured in China—but nobody seems to know how to use them. The lack of noise feels like intense concentration. The spectators cheer both sides—enthusiastically when the Chinese score, politely for an Iranian basket.

The coach plays a hunch and starts Darrehsari. On every possession, the Iranians avoid Yao's lane, swinging the ball along the perimeter: Eslamieh to Bahrami to Mashhady. Mashhady to Bahrami to Eslamieh. Yao does not score for nearly six minutes. At last, he brushes Darrehsari aside, grabs an offensive rebound, and dunks with both hands. Tie game. Next possession: China leads. Next possession: bigger lead. Eslamieh to Bahrami to Mashhady. Somebody throws it to Darrehsari, fifteen feet out. Yao doesn't bother to challenge. The shot develops as a chain reaction across the entire length of Darrehsari's frame: knees bend, waist drops, elbows buckle, long hands snap—swish. Running back down the floor, he tries to fight back a smile. A few possessions later, he fouls Yao hard. Darrehsari is all elbows and knees, but for the first time in the tournament he looks like he wants to be on the court. The coach plays him the entire half. He scores four and leads Iran with four rebounds. After the halftime buzzer, his teammates clap him on the back.

Yao plays half the game: fifteen points, ten rebounds. He looks bored. China wins by twenty-four. Later, Yao tells me diplomatically that Darrehsari has potential. "It depends on environment," Yao says. "Coaching, teammates, training." For the rest of the tournament, Darrehsari does not play half as many minutes. The day after the China game, he beams and tells me, "It was an honor to play against Yao Ming."

Before the final, China Unicom unveiled its new commercial at a press conference attended by more than a hundred Chinese journalists. Scenes flashed across a big screen: the ball, the boy, the giant, the dunk. Little Fatty looked adorable. Li Weichong, China Unicom's marketing director, gave a speech. "In America, people talk about the Ming dynasty," he said. "What does this mean? Now that Michael Jordan has retired, the NBA needs another great player. Our Yao Ming could be the one." The press conference ended with the theme from *Titanic*.

South Korea and China played for the title on National Day—the fifty-fourth anniversary of the founding of Communist China. Ha Seung-Jin, the eighteen-year-old, came out inspired: after false-starting the jump ball, he immediately collected four points, two rebounds, one block, and a huge two-handed dunk. He also committed four fouls in less than four minutes. For the rest of the game, Ha sat on the bench, dejected.

The Chinese starting point guard fouled out in the third quarter, and then the backcourt began to collapse. The Korean guards tightened the press, forcing turnovers and hitting threes: Bang, Yang, Moon. Bang three, Bang three, layup—and with five minutes left China's lead had dwindled to one point.

On every possession, Yao came to half-court, using his height and hands to break the press. At one point, he dove for a loose ball—all seven feet six inches. With the lead back at five and less than two minutes left, Yao grabbed an offensive rebound and dunked it. Thirty points, fifteen rebounds, six assists, five blocks. After the buzzer, when the two teams met at half-court, Yao Ming shook Ha Seung-Jin's hand, touched his shoulder, and said, "See you in the NBA."

The next morning, Yao caught the first flight out of Harbin. He sat in the front row of first class, wearing headphones. First the Indian team filed past, in dark wool blazers, and then the Filipinos, in tricolor sweatsuits. The Iranians were the last team to board, Darrehsari's head scraping the ceiling. Each player nodded and smiled as he walked past Yao. During the flight, many Chinese passengers came forward to have their tickets autographed. In three days, Yao would leave for America. Later that month, he would accept an apology from Coca-Cola and settle the lawsuit out of court.

I sat in the row behind Yao, beside a chubby man in his forties named Zhang Guojun, who had flown to Harbin to watch the game. He'd bought his ticket from a scalper for nearly two hundred dollars. Zhang was proud of his money—he showed me his cellphone, which used China Unicom services and had a built-in digital camera. Zhang told me that he constructed roads in Inner Mongolia. He sketched a map on the headrest: "This is Russia. This is Outer Mongolia. This is Inner Mongolia. And this"—he pointed to nowhere—"is where I'm from."

We talked about basketball. "Yao is important in our hearts," Zhang said solemnly. "He went to America, and he returned." Halfway through the flight, the man held up his cellphone, aimed carefully, and photographed the back of Yao Ming's head.

2003

NO OBSTACLES

ALEC WILKINSON

Parkour, a made-up word, cousin to the French *parcours*, which means "route," is a quasi commando system of leaps, vaults, rolls, and landings designed to help a person avoid or surmount whatever lies in his path—a vocabulary, that is, to be employed in finding one's way among obstacles. Parkour goes over walls, not around them; it takes the stair rail, not the stairs. Spread mainly by videos on the Internet, it has been embraced in Europe and the United States by thrill seekers and martial-arts adepts, who regard it as part extreme sport—its founder would like to see it included in the Olympics—and part grueling meditative pursuit. Movies like its daredevil qualities. A bracing parkour chase begins *Casino Royale*, the recent James Bond movie. It includes jumps from the boom of one tower crane to that of another, but parkour's customary obstacles are walls, stairwells, fences, railings, and gaps between roofs—it is an urban rather than a pastoral pursuit. The movements are performed at a dead run. The more efficient and fluid the path they define, and the more difficult and harrowing the terrain they cross, the more elegant the performance is considered by the discipline's practitioners.

Parkour was created in Lisses, a medium prosperous suburb of Paris, in the early 1990s, by a reserved and restless teenage boy named David Belle. His father, Raymond, who died in 1999, was an acrobat and a hero fireman. In 1969, he appeared in newspaper photographs hanging from a cable attached to a helicopter above Notre Dame. The night before, someone had hung a Vietcong flag on the cathedral's tower. Raymond was lowered like a spider on a thread, and he grabbed the flag. David Belle is now thirty-three. He has an older brother, Jeff, who is also a fireman; they have the same father but different mothers. (A third brother died a few years ago, of an overdose.) David was raised by his mother's father. On the few occasions when he tried to live with Raymond, their temperaments clashed. David's grandfather told him stories about Raymond that revolved around his exploits—"Spider-Man stories and Tarzan stories," David says—and left him wishing to emulate him. He wanted to be Spider-Man when he grew up.

The parkour scene in *Casino Royale* is performed by a childhood friend of Belle's named Sébastien Foucan, who has developed a parallel pursuit to parkour, called freerunning. Belle appears in two kinds of films, movies that show him performing parkour for its own sake, and movies and commercials in which he appears as an actor performing parkour. All of the films have the kind of vaudeville improbability of a video game. He leaps gaps between rooftops that it doesn't seem possible to cross. Or he jumps from a rooftop to one that is so much lower that he gets smaller and smaller, descending like a spike about to be driven into the ground. If parkour has a shrine, it is the climbing wall in Lisses, called the Dame du Lac, where Belle played as a teenager. The wall is about seventy-five feet high, and the films I like best show him fearlessly racing up and down it as if it had stairs. All are so steeped in risk that there are none I can watch without anxiety.

A young man who practices parkour is called a *traceur*; a woman is a *traceuse*. A *traceur*, Jeff Belle says, is someone "who traces David's footsteps, the way David traced our father's." Enthusiasts also say that a *traceur* is someone who goes fast. The video of Belle that *traceurs* seem to find most compelling, judging from how often they mention it, is one in which he crashes into a cement wall. I have found it on YouTube, using "David Belle fall" as the search term. Belle is attempting to leap over a double-wide ramp that leads to an underground parking garage. The ramp is enclosed by cinder-block walls, about three feet high. Belle arrives at a run from the left. He lowers his hands but they appear to miss the first wall entirely; he seems to be looking at where he means to land. Incredibly, while aloft, he turns, so that his shoulder, not his head, strikes the opposite wall. Ten feet beneath him, at the bottom of the ramp, a cameraman is lying on his back in order to shoot from below. Belle manages not to land on him. His first gesture is to see if the cameraman is all right. Then he begins walking briskly up the ramp. Toward the top, he turns and can be seen to be grinning.

Parkour has no explicit glossary, but *traceurs* typically describe the fundamental maneuvers as the cat leap, the precision jump, the roll, and the wall run. There is also the tic-tac, in which a nearly horizontal *traceur* takes at least one step and sometimes several steps along a wall and launches himself from it; and the underbar, in which a *traceur* dives feet first through a gap between fence rails, like a letter going through a slot, then grabs the upper rail as his shoulders pass under it. In addition, there are several vaults, including the lazy vault, the reverse vault, the turn vault, the speed vault, the dash vault, and the kong or monkey vault, in which a *traceur* runs straight at a wall or a railing, plants his hands on top, and brings his feet through his hands. All these moves link to one another, so that a *traceur* might say that he went cat to cat, or that he tic-taced a wall or konged it, then did a roll and a wall leap. The intention is to become so adept that the movements recede in one's awareness and can be performed without reflection. Jazz musicians occasionally say that a novice needs to learn all about his instrument, then he needs to learn all about music, then he needs to forget everything and learn how to play, which is a paradigm that also fits parkour, especially because both activities at their most proficient are improvised. A jazz musician wants to be comfortable in any key. Similarly, a *traceur* wants to be sufficiently fluent so that he can cross any terrain in flight without compromise.

Parkour's most prominent disciple in America is Mark Toorock, who lives in Washington, D.C., and runs a website called American Parkour. Toorock is thirty-six. In 2002, a brokerage firm where he worked as a computer technician sent him to London. "Some guys in my office were talking about this 'nutter' who was jumping across rooftops in an ad on TV—David Belle," Toorock says. "I started looking for him on the Internet, and I found a French forum where he was mentioned. Back then, there weren't any parkour sites. I made an attempt to speak to the people in the forum, but they were less than interested in talking to anyone who spoke English, and they weren't polite about it. I found out later that they didn't really want parkour spread. It was theirs, or so they felt. It's a very narrowly defined discipline, and they didn't want it misunderstood."

A few weeks later, Toorock discovered a British website called Urban Freeflow, which had just started up. Toorock arranged to meet some of the people involved in a park, and they went around climbing walls and jumping over benches. After two years, Toorock was transferred back to the United States and ended up in Washington, where he began his website.

Toorock is a little old for parkour. He says that he concentrates on "stuff close to the ground, on speed and efficiency." At his apartment, he showed me a photograph of a parkour artifact—a sign posted in a park in Bethesda, Maryland, that reads "No skateboards, bicycles, rollerblades, parkour type exercises or similar activities." "The only one in the world," he said. "So far as we know."

In 2005, Toorock organized a team of American *traceurs*—ten men and two women, who call themselves the Tribe—and when I asked him who among them was the most adept he said Ryan Ford, who is a sophomore at the University of Colorado at Boulder. Ford is five feet nine, and he weighs 145 pounds. His face is round, and his eyes are slightly slanted. He has Sioux and Navajo blood, and bristly dark brown hair. Everyone in the Tribe has a nickname. Ford's is Demon, but, being earnest and unassuming, he's not very comfortable with it. He lives in an apartment in a rambling house with two roommates. We sat in the living room. Ford said that he discovered parkour on the Internet toward the end of his junior year in high school, in Golden, Colorado. He wanted to learn how to run up to a wall, plant his foot on it, and do a backflip. Looking for instructions, he found images of David Belle, among others. In the fall, he quit the football team, on which he was a wide receiver, to pursue parkour.

"I was always climbing rocks and trees, so parkour was already kind of in me," he said. "Pretty much everyone you talk to will tell you that parkour was always part of them." His parents were unhappy with it, though. "To them, it just looked like I was jumping off stuff recklessly for no reason," he said. "But I kept saying, 'It's not pointless, there's a whole philosophy to it.' "

I asked how he had learned.

"A key factor in parkour is gradualism," he said. "You can't find the highest thing to jump from in order to practice your rolls. You get down on the ground first and practice your rolls, then maybe you find something three feet high to launch yourself from. When you can do something correctly a hundred times out of a hundred, you increase your task. Maybe. If you feel confident. People wonder how David Belle can leap between buildings and fall thirty feet. He started low and built up the difficulty."

It was a warm day, and the windows were open. We heard a dog bark, and a woman tell it to stop. "Parkour is about repetition and practice," Ford went on. "To say that no one in the U.S. has reached David Belle's level doesn't mean that there aren't extremely skilled people doing parkour; it means that he's trained for years, and no one here has. When I see a skilled *traceur,* I admire the dedication and the mental strength. There are some people who just have superior physical ability, but there are no secret techniques in parkour. A lot of the things *traceurs* do aren't necessarily impressive physically, anyway. From a *traceur's* point of view, the task is often mental. Some people can master fear. Other people might have more determination and, in the end, accomplish more things. I see myself fueled more by determination than by the ease of putting fear in the back of my mind. I overthink, and I don't have the craziness some people do, but I have the determination."

"How often do you practice?"

"I try to do something every day," he said. Then he frowned. "One thing we say is we do parkour, but a lot of the time we aren't; we're practicing for parkour. True parkour is hardly ever done. If I'm practicing a vault and I turn around and do it again, that's not parkour, because it's continuing a circle—it's not making a path. The videos on the Internet are spliced together, so that's not really parkour, either.

"My fantasy is to be walking late at night on the street in New York City and have some guys try to rob me, and I use parkour to get away from them, but I've never had to use parkour, so in a way I could say I've never really done parkour. I practice parkour not because I think I'm going to have to use it but because I see it as making me stronger physically and mentally, just the way people don't go into martial arts because they plan to fight someone—they keep fit or get discipline. Everyone's different, but the philosophy of parkour that drives me is that progression of ability, being better than I was the day before. There's a quote by Bruce Lee that's my motto: 'There are no limits. There are plateaus, but you must not stay there, you must go beyond them. A man must constantly exceed his level.' If you're not better than you were the day before, then what are you doing—what's the point?"

The next morning, I drove to Denver with Ford; his girlfriend, Kathryn Keller, who is brown-haired and petite and was a gymnast in high school but had to give it up when she hurt her back; and a tall, skinny high school boy with freckles and a turban named Sat, whose full name is Sat Santokh Khalsa. Sat's American mother and father had converted to Sikhism, and when Sat was nine they sent him to a Sikh boarding school in India, called Miri Piri Academy. He had gone there for six years—he was now fifteen—and had just started Boulder High

School. When he came home from India at the end of the school year, a friend had shown him a parkour video, and then he found Mark Toorock's website.

We drove downtown, to a small park called Skyline Park, outside a Westin hotel. Ford had invited several other *traceurs* to join us, and when we arrived one of them, a Russian named Nikita, was sitting beside a fountain that had been drained. Nikita was twenty. He had shaved his blond hair, and he had a small face, avid eyes, thin lips, and a sharp nose. He was six feet two and weighed 160 pounds. He looked like a big spider. He said that he was from Belarus. "I grew up in a village," he said. "It was just five houses." In New York, where his father now lived, he had trained for two years to be an ultimate fighter. "We paid money to a manager to arrange the fights, and he left," he said. "After that, my trainer went into the movies." He shrugged off a backpack. "Two more days, and it will be one month I have done parkour."

The fountain in Skyline Park is a collection of reddish-brown concrete forms, squares and rectangles, stacked like children's blocks. It is about twenty feet tall. "We call this the Cat Fountain," Ford said, "because there's a lot of cat leaps here." There is a fountain in a park nearby, designed by the same architect, which is called Precision Fountain, Ford said, "because it has a lot of precision jumps." The Cat Fountain was set into the plaza, so that from the pavement to the blocks there was a gap several feet wide and a few feet deep, which would be filled by water in warmer weather. Making a run toward the gap, Sat made a cat leap to one of the blocks. He was so slight that it seemed as if he had been lifted into the air by a wire. Once he had grabbed the block, his feet slid against it as he pulled himself up. "The slips are part of the technique," Ford said. "It's controlled. When you first start, you rely more on the equipment to hold you in place, your sneakers, then you learn to use your strength."

Warming up, Nikita twisted from side to side, like a screw. Ford did a handstand but had difficulty maintaining it. "My handstands are not so good," he said. "I fall over, since I got hurt."

"What happened?"

"Separated my shoulder," he said.

"Where'd you do that?"

Ford walked about ten paces. "Right here," he said. "Kong vault over this eight-foot gap. I should have landed in that flower bed, but I clipped a foot and fell into the gap and hit the wall. At first, I thought

I broke my collarbone. I also cut my head. I drove home using one arm."

Keller said, "He left a message on my answering machine: 'I got hurt pretty bad, so just call me back.'"

While we stood looking at the wall and the flower bed, another *traceur,* a high school boy named Dan Mancini, came walking across the plaza. He was tall and thin, with brown hair, and wore a T-shirt and jeans. Ford clasped his hands above his head and stretched, then said, "Shall we hit some stuff on the fountain?" When Ford talks about people naturally gifted for parkour, one of the people he means is Nikita. We watched him pace off a ten-foot gap from the border to the fountain, then approach it at a run. The first time, he landed short of the wall, and the second time he cleared the gap but couldn't hold on to the wall and dropped to the bottom of the fountain.

"I did that once," Ford said. "Never again."

Nikita said that he wanted to try one more time.

"You should," Ford said. "I'll film it."

"You shouldn't tell me," Nikita said.

Ford got a video camera from his knapsack. He stood on a block beside the one Nikita was attempting to surmount and filmed Nikita as he came rushing forward, leaped into the air, and struck the block feet first, like a hawk, then grabbed the edge and pulled himself to the top. He stood on top of the block, jiggling his hands, and said, "Scary vault."

They grew tired of the fountain shortly and began hoisting themselves onto a railing a few feet above the ground and walking along it on all fours: a maneuver called a cat balance or a cat walk. The railing framed three sides of a rectangle. The longest section was about thirty feet. "Cat walking is very tiring," Ford said. "Your legs start to burn." Nikita went up one side of the railing and made the turn and passed us. "Your legs burning yet?" Ford asked. Nikita shook his head. He turned the second corner. "Now burning," he said.

After Nikita got off the railing, he paced out a cat leap from the plaza, over a gap of about eight feet, to a block in the fountain.

"The last guy who did that hit his face," Ford said.

"Bit through his lip," one of the others said.

Nikita soared over the gap and held on to the block, and the others shook their heads. Ford said, "You guys want to move? I got another cat leap for you."

We crossed the street to a ramp that led to an underground garage. The boys leaned over the walls on either side of the ramp and looked down soberly. At the deep end, the drop to the pavement was about fifteen feet, and the distance across about twelve.

"This is the smallest parking garage ramp in Denver," one of them said.

"Yeah, we scouted it," another said.

"Those French guys do it at the deepest part."

"Yeah, but in France the cars are smaller, so it's as deep but not as wide."

They walked to the head of the ramp in a little pack. A few of them climbed up on the wall around the ramp and made tentative standing jumps to the pavement, landing at the far wall and grabbing the edge of it with their fingers, but no one wanted to try it for real. Embedded in the wall were pieces of gravel, making it rough to the touch. Nikita stood on a rail several inches above the wall, wobbling, as if on a branch. Through a window of the hotel, about ten floors up, a man watched him. Nikita bent his knees, thrust his arms forward, and leaped, his path making a little arc in the air. His fingers grasped the wall, but he landed hard and banged his shin. He lifted his pants leg to see if he'd cut himself. Then he said, "Let's get out of here," and everyone followed him across the street. His hands were scraped and bleeding. On a Velcro strap around his chest he had a zippered wallet from which he took some tape and wrapped his fingers.

After crossing several streets, we came to an apartment building and a concrete parking garage that was four floors tall. Between the levels, running nearly the length of each wall, were broad openings like slits. Each was about a foot tall. Using them, the boys began climbing. One said, "Is this, like, the Asian place where the lady yelled at us to get out?"

A door at the top of a flight of stairs in the apartment building opened and a small, black-haired woman stepped out. "What are you doing climbing here?" she yelled. "Are you supposed to be up there? Get off. The stairs are for going up and down." She glared at them, and one by one they sheepishly climbed down. We took the stairs to the roof, which was connected to a walkway leading to a row of stores, all of them closed—it was Sunday. By one of the stores were two sulky girls and a boy dressed in black clothes.

"Are you guys some kind of youth group?" one of the girls asked.

"No, this is just us using the buildings to keep fit," someone said.

"Oh, I understand," the girl said. "That's cool."

"She does *not* understand," Kathryn said.

"Oh, my God," the other girl said. "It's like *Spider-Man*."

I turned and saw Nikita climbing a drain pipe to the roof of one of the stores. While I was writing "Spider-Man" in my notebook, his shadow as he leaped from one roof to another passed over the page.

Jeff Belle has an office in Paris, where he handles fire department business. To speak with him, I brought a translator, Susan Chace, an American novelist who lives in Paris. Belle, who is forty-five, is small and wiry. He has a round face, a sharp chin, dark eyes, and black, cropped hair with flecks of gray. He was wearing a fireman's uniform, a dark blue garment like a jumpsuit. The legs ended just above the tops of his black combat boots. Over the uniform, he wore a long coat that had POMPIER DE PARIS written on the back. We met at his office, then he took us to an empty, low-ceilinged room with a bar and an espresso machine and some tables stacked on top of each other. On the wall were photographs of firefighters.

Jeff said that David was a restless boy. "He was always exercising in front of the TV," he said. "He still takes whatever's next to him, maybe a big book, and starts lifting it. He can't sit still. He lives with it." The brothers did not see much of each other until David, at fourteen, moved to Lisses to live with his mother. Then Jeff, who was already a fireman, began to look after him. He would show him how to climb ropes and perform gymnastic maneuvers, and David would go off and do it his own way. Now and then, David would go to the climbing wall in Lisses with his father and show him things he had taught himself, and Raymond, thinking that he was being encouraging, would say, "I could do that when I was nine."

Through Jeff, David was exposed to the methods of Georges Hébert, a French sports theorist, whose motto was "Be strong to be useful." Hébert believed that modern conveniences such as elevators were debilitating. He thought that Africans he had met while traveling were healthier and stronger than Europeans, and that the proportions of the bodies he saw in Greek and Roman statues were ideal. The philosophies and the exercises he developed, which are part of a French fireman's training, were also meant to cultivate courage and discipline. Inspired by Hébert, a Swiss architect developed an obstacle course called a parcours. "David took Hébert's ideas and said, 'I will adapt it to what I need,'" Jeff said. "Instead of stopping at a reasonable point, he just kept going."

David was briefly a fireman recruit, until he hurt his wrist. While he was recuperating, he started thinking things over and saw that the life of a fireman had too many rules, and not enough action, and he decided to join the Marines, but he didn't find the same values among them, the "traditional values." He left the Marines and went to India, where he stayed for six months. When he came back to Paris, he was twenty-four, and he didn't know what to do with himself.

"He came to see me at my house," Jeff said, "and he told me he didn't know where his life was going. He was only interested in parkour. You could be a super policeman or a firefighter using it, but you can't earn your living, because there's no championship. I said, 'Maybe if we film what you're doing.'"

It was 1997, and Jeff was involved in planning an annual ceremony in which recruits perform firefighting drills. He decided that David should put on a show. He told him to get a group together, so that he wouldn't look insignificant by himself. David collected two of his cousins and some other kids from the neighborhood, including Sébastien Foucan, with whom he ran around doing parkour. Jeff choreographed a routine for them. They dressed as ninjas and called themselves the Yamakasi. "It means 'strong spirit' in the language of Zaire," Jeff said, "but it sounded Asian." During the show, David climbed a tower and did a handstand at the top. He also scaled a fireman's ladder and did a backflip from it. After the demonstration, David began getting invitations to perform.

Jeff is proud of David, but worries about him. "This was a kid who refused any kind of system, who just wanted to live his life," he says. "If he's surrounded by the right people, he can do what he wants. Ordinary life really upsets him, though, because this world the rest of us live in is not where he finds his pleasure. He's easily disturbed by ordinary things. But he's also asking, 'Why am I doing this parkour?' All his family who did this physical stuff were doing it for a reason, but he's asking, 'Why am I doing this, what does it mean?'" Jeff added, "He's simple in his purposes. He doesn't like talking very much. He's someone who is looking for his way." I asked what sort of routines David observed in his training. Jeff shook his head. "He's still eating Big Macs and drinking Coke," Jeff said. "He likes chicken sandwiches. He trains when it comes to him. He's usually sleeping in the morning. He's really a night guy."

We arranged to meet with David the following day, in Lisses, where he was staying with his mother. When David is in France, he lives either with her or with Jeff. "He doesn't really have a lot of money," Jeff said, "although people think that he does." He added that David was very easy to live with. "We don't know about the inside of his head, but outside he's very neat. His room is always in perfect shape."

The next day, I took a taxi with Susan Chace to Lisses, about half an hour south of Paris. When we were under way, the driver asked why we were going there. Chace said, "To see David Belle." The driver nodded. Chace asked if he knew who Belle was, and the driver said, "Of course. *Il est unique.*" We left the highway and, following Jeff's directions, went around a rotary and came to a collection of low, flat-roofed, two-story buildings, like shoeboxes, painted light brown. We stopped in front of Belle's building. Chace knocked, the door opened, and the driver said, "That's him!" Belle had his chin tucked slightly, like a man looking out from under the brim of a hat. He had dark hair cut short like a pelt and a thin, asymmetrical face, with a sharp chin and a hook nose. He was wearing a red fleece top and jeans. As I paid the driver, Jeff Belle drove up behind us. We went into the apartment. The kitchen was by the door, and there was a living room beyond it with a circular stairway leading up. In the living room was David's girlfriend, Dorine Sane. David had his fleece top zipped to his chin—he had a sore throat—and he seemed subdued. He had just come back from three weeks in the Czech Republic, where he was making *Babylon AD*, which stars Vin Diesel, and is based on a French science-fiction novel. David plays the head of an Internet gang that does parkour, and he choreographed scenes for ten actors.

Jeff and David spoke for a few moments, and then Chace said that David was going to rest, while Jeff took us to the Dam du Lac. Outside, we crossed a parking lot, then took an asphalt path through a park. Several hundred yards off, the Dam du Lac rose up against the side of a small lake. It was the color of sandstone and had the shape of an arch. "David was afraid of it in the beginning," Jeff said. "Now he walks on it like it was solid ground." The *lac* turned out to be made of concrete. As we walked along the edge, ducks paddled away from us. For some time now, a fence has enclosed the wall, but it was easy to climb around it. The wall was slightly concave, and the top was intersected by a horizontal slab, which had roughly the dimensions of a king-size mattress and was curled up at one edge. Here and there on the face of the wall were footholds and handholds in the form of slots the size of bricks. On one side was a rectangular box, open at one end, like a cave, which is called the cabana. Below, sticking straight out from the wall and about fifteen feet tall, was a form in the shape, more or less, of a hammer. Jeff said that the first maneuver David had done was a backflip from the cabana to the hammer. About twenty feet from the ground was a sign saying ESCALADE INTERDITE. On it were signatures. "The kids climb up and sign their names," Jeff said. "David also went barefoot on it." He pointed at the top. "And at night sometimes he slept up there."

For a few minutes, my mind screened images of David in videos I had seen—running up and down the wall, doing a hair-raising handstand at the top—then we began walking back toward the apartment. We passed a low building with picture windows—a nursery school— and Jeff said that when David and his friends were young "they jumped over the bushes beside it to the roof. That was their first trick." While we were looking at a stairwell that appears as a prop in videos for a series of David's cat leaps, Jeff's cellphone rang, and it was David saying he was ready to talk.

When we got back to the apartment, David sat on a couch with Dorine, and I sat next to them. Jeff made coffee. For the most part, David sat quite still, like a machine at rest. The only part of him in motion was his right hand, which moved from Dorine's hand, to her knee, to her lap, and so on. I asked how he knew whether a movement was too dangerous. "It's just intuitive," he said, shrugging. "My body just knows if I can do something or not. It's sort of an animal thing. In athletics, they have rules—you have to take your distance and stop and jump, everything has a procedure—but I never did it that way. I don't take a risk, though, that I know I can't do. I like life too much."

He said that parkour hadn't changed much, since he started it, but his intention had become more specific. "When I was younger, I was playing, the way kids play at parkour, but now I ask the question 'Is this going to be useful for me to get to the other side?' The movement is simple. I don't do anything special, because I want to get to the other side. What I'm interested in for parkour is the utilitarian thing of getting to the other end, whether as a task or a challenge, but in film they like a little entertainment, so I do that, too, but it's not what I'm interested in.

"You always have to get through the first obstacle that says, 'I can't do it,' whether in your mind or for real, and be able to adapt to anything that's put in your path. It's a method for learning how to move in the world. For finding the liberty men used to have."

I asked David why he had gone to India, and he said that he had friends there.

"How did you pass the time?"

"I just kept training," he said. "I was training in the trees." Jeff handed me a scrapbook with a photograph of David leaping from the limb of one tree to another. He was stretched flat out, horizontal to the ground, like Superman.

"I was at a waterfall one day," David went on, "and there were huge trees all around, and in the trees were monkeys. There were fences and barriers around them, so they couldn't get out, but I went around the barriers and played with the monkeys. After that, I watched them all the time, learning how they climbed. All the techniques in parkour are from watching the monkeys."

He then showed us, on a computer, a documentary called *Warriors of the Monkey God*. It was about a tribe of monkeys who live on the rooftops of Jodhpur. The people regard the monkeys as holy. We watched them leaping from rooftop to rooftop and through the trees. The scene that made David smile was one in which numbers of them leaped onto, then off, a piece of corrugated tin that was loosely attached as a roof to some stakes. Their landings made the tin shake. Some of the monkeys were leaping from the ground, turning on their sides in the air, landing on the stakes and shoving off from them—a tic-tac.

Watching the movie, which was about forty-five minutes long, took only about fifteen minutes, because David kept advancing it to scenes of the monkeys in flight, looking exactly like *traceurs*. When it was finished, he said that after coming home he had just continued perfecting what he had learned from the monkeys. He had plans, he said, to make a movie with them.

I asked about the fall on the Internet, the one that the American *traceurs* always talk about. David gave a little smile. "I was a bit tired," he said. "It was the end of the day. I was just doing stuff with a bunch of kids. I fall all the time—I fall like the monkeys—but it never shows up on film, because they just want the spectacular stuff."

I thought of Nikita with his bleeding hands and said, "You never wear gloves?"

He said that he wanted to be able to feel the surfaces he was grabbing. He held his palms out for me to feel, and they were as hard and slick as linoleum.

I told him that I had been to see people do parkour in Colorado, and that they had imagined themselves as preparing to use it for an escape, and he said, "That's good. If you're really thinking about how to defend yourself, how to be useful, then that's a very different mind-set from just doing things to look good."

Last fall, David said, he had discussions with Sam Raimi, the director of *Spider-Man,* about playing the role of Spider-Man's double, but he decided he wasn't interested. "That was a childhood dream, to be in a Spider-Man costume," he said. "Now I'd rather appear on a poster with my own name, not as a character, saying, 'This is me performing.' " He was planning to tour the world doing parkour, he said. A French film company partly owned by the director Luc Besson paid his expenses to perform last winter in Madagascar, and David had also given exhibitions in Italy, Germany, and Portugal.

He yawned and rubbed his throat, and I took it as a sign that he was at the end of his interest in talking. I thanked him and stood up. We shook hands. He seemed to think for a moment, then he said, "I'm still learning. I'm not sure of anything yet, I'm just trying to be as complete as I can."

I nodded.

"What I do is not really something that can be explained," he said. "It can just be practiced." Then he went to call us a taxi.

2007

A STUD'S LIFE

KEVIN CONLEY

My first contact with the world's No. 1 stud at his place of business—that would be Storm Cat, at the stallion complex on W. T. Young's Overbrook Farm, in Lexington, Kentucky—came over the phone. "There's his holler now," Dr. Joe Yocum, the farm vet, said calmly, from his office in the breeding shed, above a noise that sounded like the fury of hell. "He just jumped on her. I'll look out my window here and tell you when he's finished. . . . Yup." The doctor chuckled. "He wouldn't be real popular with the women."

The Kentucky Derby is often called the most exciting two minutes in sports; Storm Cat is probably its most expensive thirty seconds. His stud fee for the 2000 season hit $300,000, nearly double that of his closest rival. It could easily have gone higher. A final pair of contracts offered at auction last November, before the farm shut his book for the season, brought in $415,000 and $430,000, respectively. Based on a conservative estimate of seventy guaranteed-live-foal contracts, Storm Cat will earn $21 million this year. If he played in the NBA, that figure would make him the league's third-highest-paid player. As a stud, no one's even close.

Why would anyone pay that much for Storm Cat's services? Last year, Storm Cat's offspring earned more than $12 million at the track, almost $4 million more than anyone else's. Furthermore, several Storm Cat colts who have recently launched their own stud careers—Storm Boot, Hennessy, Forest Wildcat—have begun siring stakes winners and high-priced yearlings, justifying hefty hikes in their stud fees. In other words, just thirty seconds with Storm Cat gives you a chance of landing your own franchise Thoroughbred.

If he were any other breed—miniature, trotter, quarter horse, Standardbred, Lipizzan, Arabian, American warmblood—Storm Cat could just jump on a padded phantom breeding mount (like a pommel horse, but "natural, mare-like," and equipped with a "side opening and quick release valve") and his half of the bargain could be frozen and shipped Priority Overnight to any mare in the world. But Storm Cat will never suffer this indignity, because the Jockey Club, the official registry of Thoroughbred racing, forbids artificial insemination. Only registered horses can race on the Thoroughbred circuit, and the Jockey Club registers only horses conceived by what is delicately termed "natural cover." Storm Cat's job—and the most profitable sector of a high-stakes industry—is safe.

Success at the track is merely a first step toward such profits. Take Cigar, who won sixteen races in a row and retired to stud in 1997, after earning a record $9.9 million. Not one of the eighty mares booked for his first and only season became pregnant, but his owners were lucky: Italy's Assicurazioni Generali made good on Cigar's $25 million infertility insurance policy. Far more common than infertility is mediocrity, and no policy covers the champion horse who fails to produce a winner. As Tom Wade, the groom to the 1977 Triple Crown winner, Seattle Slew, said, "Just because a horse wins a million dollars, that don't make him no stud."

For a stallion, the eagerness of a teenager is considered the mark of a professional—breeders call it "great libido." Although Storm Cat's libido is spoken of mostly in economic terms, from time to time something else creeps in: awe, fear, relief. Breeding horses is dangerous—last March, Class Secret, a twelve-year-old son of Secretariat, the 1973 Triple Crown winner, had to be euthanized after a mare he was mounting broke his leg—so dawdling is not appreciated. It's risky for the people involved, too. One stallion manager told me that sildenafil citrate—Viagra—had been tested on horses and rejected, largely because nobody who works in the breeding shed wants to fool around with a rearing half-ton, hormonally enraged animal trying to set a personal endurance record.

With a horse like Storm Cat, however, the worrying doesn't stop at the breeding shed. He's only seventeen years old, comfortably mid-career for a stud (Mr. Prospector, the sire of this year's Derby winner, Fusaichi Pegasus, was twenty-nine when he died last year). But even innocent conversations about him—what he likes to eat (bluegrass, oats, and sweet feed), where he sleeps (in a hilltop barn, near his winter paddock), what he does for fun (lies down in a big sandpile and rolls around)—tend to veer into elaborately imagined premonitions of his death and the state-of-the-art precautions taken to guard against it. One of his sandpiles, for example, is bounded by an unusual stretch of solid wood, because somebody worried that he might roll a foreleg under the standard fencing and break a bone as he tried to stand up. And if you want to meet the farm's entire staff in the next forty seconds? Just light a cigarette near Storm Cat's stall.

On a sunny morning in May, halfway through the four-and-a-half-month breeding season, the sire looks vigorous. In his official photographs, Storm Cat can come across as smug and bullnecked and a little thick in the waist, but the camera must add a few pounds, because in person, prancing in his paddock, he has the hauteur and the low body fat of an underwear model. He's a dark bay, but when he moves in the sunlight you can pick up flashes of a honey-gold color that comes from the chestnut horses on his mother's side—Terlingua, Storm Cat's dam (his mother), and his grandsire, Secretariat. He has white spats on his left legs, also from Terlingua, which give him a light-footed, high-stepping look, even when he's just pacing over the grass.

"I like his weight now," Wes Lanter, who manages the ten stallions at Overbrook Farm, says. "Twelve hundred and sixty pounds. I think that's a real good weight for him." Lanter runs the operations in the breeding shed with the nimbleness of a linebacker coach, but everywhere else he moves with hound-dog-like deliberateness. To introduce me to the planet's most valuable piece of horseflesh, for example, he folds his arms and says, "There he is." At first, Storm Cat just rips at the grass, pretending he doesn't see us, but after a while he edges over to the fence to investigate. He has a smoldering dark patch between his eyes with a white diamond on it, and a sharp crescent moon way over near his left nostril, a curious marking that makes him look moody and dangerously attractive. He ducks his head behind a board on the fence and gives me the once-over—more eye contact than his mares usually get—and I raise my hand to the little white line that runs down his muzzle. "Stand back," Lanter says, since stallions bite. "He can fool you." As soon as I touch him, Storm Cat ends the interview and walks away.

Suddenly, he lights out for the end of his paddock. Through a break in the trees, he looks over the creek, past the horses nearer the breeding shed—it's standard practice to place stallions with libidos lower than Storm Cat's closer to the parade of action, a cheap sort of stimulant that cuts down on the time spent waiting for arousal—and roars convincingly. "A mare has arrived," Lanter says. "Not yours, Stormy." Un-deterred, Storm Cat paces back and forth beside the fence—he has worn a path there—and roars again. Lanter seems pleased, in a proud and wistful prom-chaperone way. "He's looking for dates," he says.

Storm Cat has 714 children at last count, but he has seen only three: Mountain Cat, who was recently shipped off to Turkey, and two fellow studs on the roster at Overbrook Farm—Tactical Cat, a pretty gray horse (whose dam was Terre Haute), and Tabasco Cat, the winner of the Preakness and the Belmont in 1994 (whose dam was Barbicue Sauce). They often pass each other on the way to or from the breeding shed and he cuts them every time—no nicker, no friendly whinny. Apart from a few pointed, work-related roars, Storm Cat is laconic, even for a horse. But it's a menacing, eloquent sort of silence: it's on purpose.

Menace, apparently, is a job requirement for stallions. The senior managers at Overbrook, who generally live in picturesque houses tucked into the farm's manicured hills, like to expound upon the equine instinct for violence. They'll tell you how, in the wild, a lone stallion would command a roving harem-cum-nursery of broodmares and foals, until some other horse, probably one of his own sons, decided to bite, kick, and break his legs for it. Add to these instincts a few centuries of breeding specifically for aggressiveness—a trait Storm Cat is prized for and seems to be able to pass on to his foals—and you have the poten-tial for some very volatile relationships.

That's the theory. In practice, Storm Cat—apart from his twice-daily acts of sexual congress with the fastest, wealthiest, and most at-tractive available partners in the world, seven days a week throughout the breeding season—lives like a monk. He eats mostly grass, sleeps on straw, drinks only water. He has no visits with the other stallions. His one diversion is running away from his groom, which he is doing less of lately, because his current groom is kind but strict. He wears only a leather halter. He does not race, he does not train for racing, he does not even exercise. He has given all that up.

Regularly, en route to the breeding shed, he steps on a scale. If the number seems high, he cuts back on the sweet feed that is his sole in-dulgence. His weight is monitored minutely. When he dropped a few

pounds in February, at the beginning of the breeding season, he was
rushed to the Hagyard Davidson and McGee Veterinary Clinic, in
Lexington. "It wasn't much—enterocolitis," Doc Yocum said. "With
any other horse, we probably wouldn't have bothered." He traced its
onset to a few instances when Storm Cat arrived at the breeding shed
wringing wet before he even started: "My theory is he was just so
worked up to get back at the mares."

Storm Cat's stall—where he goes as infrequently as possible, to get
his coat brushed, say, or to sleep during inclement weather—is out-
wardly unremarkable: a foot and a half of straw in a whitewashed
cinder-block room with two wooden doors. (Even here, value creates
value: Storm Cat's muck is carted off and resold to the Campbell's
Soup Company, which uses it as the breeding ground for the mush-
rooms in its mushroom soup.) But while he sleeps, a box nestled in the
ridge of his barn projects an infrared beam that looks for obscurity—
smoke. An ultraviolet device picks up flickers of light in the hydrocar-
bon range—flame. A third mechanism compares ambient temperature
against its rate of rise—heat. These three devices monitoring the separate elements of fire are tied into the forty-second alarm system and
into a sprinkler system, fed by massive pipes capable of delivering six
inches of standing water to the stall in seconds. Fire is a problem because barns are drafty by design and straw is extremely flammable, but
Ben Giles, who guides the building projects at the farm, compares
Overbrook's safeguards favorably with fire detection measures in museums. "We don't have the luxury of being able to cut a barn up into small
spaces to confine or suppress a fire, because a horse needs air. In that
sense, the museums have it a little easier," Giles says. "Plus, their van
Goghs are worth a whole lot less than Storm Cat."

It took a long time for people to see that Storm Cat was a lucky horse.
As a yearling, he was smallish, long-haired, potbellied, with the kind of
turned-out knees that got him booted out of Kentucky's best auction.
Twice at the track, he lost races that he should have won, once because
he shouldered an inferior horse in the final stretch out of sheer cussed-
ness, and later because his mind wandered when he was too far in front
at the Breeders' Cup, a race that would have established him as the
leading contender for two-year-old horse of the year. He missed all his

Triple Crown races as a three-year-old because he was recovering from knee surgery, and when he tried to come back, late in the year, he trained on dirt that had turned greasy after a hard rain, and was never the same. When he retired from racing, in 1988, people quickly forgot about him. His stud fee dropped from thirty thousand to twenty-five to twenty, and he couldn't fill his book of mares.

Then his first crop of colts and fillies hit the track. Suddenly, people started remembering what a brilliant, blazingly fast runner he'd been, how he took a competitive streak that bordered on the criminal and used it to overcome his natural unsoundness. By the time his second and third crops hit, people knew that Storm Cats could run. They could run at two years old, or three, or four; colts or fillies, they could run long or short, turf or dirt, in Europe, Japan, or America. By 1994, when Tabasco Cat took the last two jewels of the Triple Crown, it was clear that Storm Cat had a calling.

The mares arrive for their appointments by horse van and walk over a gravel loading dock into the receiving barn—a sort of greenroom for mares in estrus. When a mare enters, somebody pushes a button, a window opens, and Cooperstown, an Overbrook teaser stallion, sticks his head in to try his luck, nuzzling her flank and nosing her haunches. If she kicks, he's the one she kicks at, not Storm Cat. ("If they don't make it at the track, they end up being teasers," Doc Yocum says. "So it's a little incentive deal.") In the past twenty years, veterinarians have grown very precise in pinpointing ovulation (an increase in accuracy that has allowed stallions to double their workload—and farms to double their profits—since fewer and fewer mares require follow-up visits), but final verification is still left to the teaser stallion. If there are any doubts about her receptivity after Cooperstown's initial interview, he is forced to try a jump himself—wearing a leather butcher's apron to ensure that the dry run goes unconsummated. Usually, though, she's willing, the window shuts for Coop, and the mare is led into a padded chute to be washed for the breeding shed.

Just before Storm Cat's mare is ready, his groom, Filemon Martinez, a quiet man with a Clark Gable mustache, walks the sire of sires across a covered bridge over Hickman Creek to the stallion barn. From the doorway of the barn, where Storm Cat and Martinez wait like actors in the wings, you can hear the business of breeding: "Easy, boss," and "Go, buddy," and, if it's a stallion with problems in the Valentino department, the pacesetting shouts of "Hyup! Hyup! Hyup!" Most do just fine in the breeding shed, although farm policy seems to be anywhere that works. At least one stallion, Cape Town, prefers to perform al fresco, on the grass, with all the usual team in attendance, plus one guy giving helpful pushes from the rear.

By the time Storm Cat enters the shed, the video camera is rolling (for lawsuits and insurance) and the mare—Rootentootenwooten, in this case—is standing with her head against the wall, wearing padded booties on both hind feet. Storm Cat neighs or hollers or roars—whatever it is, it's frightening and long and full of the inevitable, like the squeal of tires that you know will end in shattering glass. Then he measures himself and rears while the team rushes around him. There are two schools of natural cover: pasture breeding, where horses are let loose in a paddock together, and hand breeding, where a squad of breeding-shed professionals choreograph the proceedings for safety and speed. Overbrook prefers the latter, as practically all large-scale breeding operations do, and their version of it takes at least five people: two to soothe and distract the mare, one to steady the stallion, a tail man, and the stallion manager. When Storm Cat rears, the tail man lifts up the mare's tail, and Wes Lanter, wearing a latex glove, pilots Storm Cat to the place he probably would have found on his own, but not as quickly.

All the majesty of the act is in the roaring, apparently—count to fifteen and it's over. Somebody says "Good cover" with a mixture of appreciation and relief, and Storm Cat, still draped across Rooten-tootenwooten's back, fits the curl of his neck to hers and allows himself a moment of unstallionlike tenderness before he backs off and puts his feet on the ground again. The stallion manager pulls down a handheld shower nozzle, of the sort you find in French bathtubs, to wash Storm Cat off. Then the groom leads the sire away, through the stallion barn, down the hill, and back into the shadows of the covered bridge. Lanter pulls off his latex glove and says, "He's what everybody hopes happens to them when they retire."

2000

"No, I found my ball. I'm looking for the golf course."

ABOUT THE TYPE

This book was set in Adobe Caslon. William Caslon released his first typefaces in 1722. His types were based on seventeenth-century Dutch old style designs, which were then used extensively in England. Because of their incredible practicality Caslon's designs met with instant success. Caslon's types became popular throughout Europe and the American colonies; printer Benjamin Franklin hardly used any other typeface. The first printings of the American Declaration of Independence and the Constitution were set in Caslon. For her Caslon revival, designer Carol Twombly studied specimen pages printed by William Caslon between 1734 and 1770. Ideally suited for text, Adobe Caslon is right for magazines, journals, book publishing, and corporate communications.